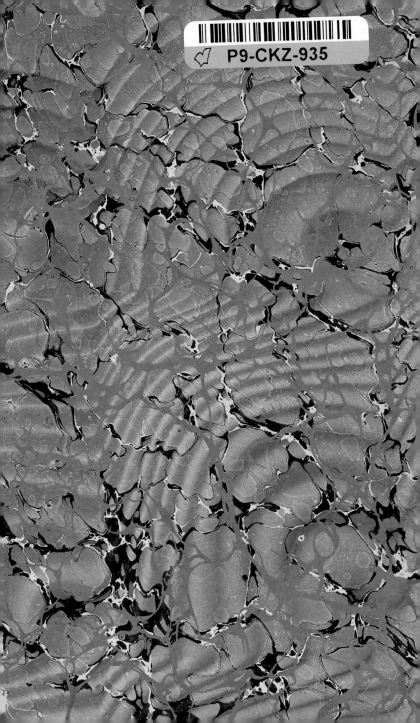

THE
POETICAL WORKS
OF
GEOFFREY CHAUCER

TO WHICH ARE APPENDED

POEMS ATTRIBUTED TO CHAUCER

EDITED BY

ARTHUR GILMAN, M. A.

"O Master, pardon me, if yet in vain
Thou art my Master, and I fail to bring
Before men's eyes the image of the thing
My heart is filled with."
WILLIAM MORRIS.

IN THREE VOLUMES
VOL. I.

BOSTON
HOUGHTON, MIFFLIN AND COMPANY
The Riverside Press, Cambridge

ADVERTISEMENT.

AT the time that the present collection of the works of the British Poets was issued in Boston, there was, in the opinion of the American Editor, no text of Chaucer's poems available for use that was worthy of the poet's name, or of the standard of excellence and purity established for the series.

The deficiency has at last to a great extent been supplied through the labors of scholars connected with the Chaucer Society, of London, established by Mr. Frederick J. Furnivall, and directed by him for a series of years with a persistent and self-sacrificing generosity seldom equaled.

This learned body has made available for the use of editors a large number of manuscripts of the different poems and prose works, and notably six entire texts of the Canterbury Tales.

In the present edition advantage has been taken of these important labors, which include investigations into the sources of Chaucer's stories, the meaning of his words, and the chronology of his poems. The arrangement devised by members of the Chaucer Society is in this edition adopted for the first time.

The text of the manuscript owned by Lord Ellesmere is now considered better than any other known, and much superior to those within the reach of editors before the Chaucer Society was originated. It forms the body of the text now presented to lovers of the great poet.

The labors of an editor who publishes a text of an author whose works appeared before the invention of printing differ in important points from those of one who prepares an edition of any publication that was put into type during its writer's lifetime. The poems of our poet, for example, cannot be printed for any but special students in exactly the form in which they exist in the manuscripts, and editors have differed essentially in the rules that they have followed in their work. Some, like John Urry, have made multitudinous arbitrary emendations and additions, while others have followed the manuscripts with more or less precision. The following are among the reasons for this diversity.

I. The manuscripts are not punctuated. It is apparent that every editor is obliged to follow the modern rules in this respect.

II. The manuscripts abound in contractions, which must of necessity be extended. A stroke over a vowel signified that it was followed by *m* or *n*. A stroke over *n* meant that it stood for *ne, nne, un,* or *n.* A curl over *n* or *s* signified *er;* over *p* it stood for *re.* A small, undotted *i* above the line meant *ri.* There were signs for *ra, ur, par, pro, es, is, us, com, con,* and other combinations of letters, though the signs did not always stand for the same combination.

III. The use of capital letters was variable, and, judged by modern standards, incorrect.

IV. The alphabet differed in some respects from that now used, there being in Old English two signs, now obsolete, for *th,* and another that represented the sound of *y, g, gh,* and sometimes *z.* In process of time one of the signs for *th* fell into desuetude ; and the sign which looked like a modern *g,* and stood for *y g, gh,* and *z,* was modified in its form until it resembled *z.* The manuscripts are not uniform in the use of these signs ; and in the absence of any rule or custom on the part of the ancient scribes, it only confuses the general reader if their irregular example is followed. There is no gain in printing *ayeyn* in one place and *ageyn* in another; nor are *yaf, yeue, yiue, yate*, any better forms than *gaf, geve, give, gate*, especially when we know that *ageyn* is allied to the Old English *ongean*, and the German *gegen*, and that *g* is the original consonant in the other words. Y was a distinct letter.

In cases where this sign has the guttural sound editors are obliged to use *gh*, or *h* (as *thurgh, thurh*), and when it stands for *z* that letter is used (as marchauntz).

V. The use of *u* and *v* was not in accordance with that of the present time. The former sign had both the modern sounds.

VI. The letter *j* was almost unknown, its place being supplied by the capital *I*.

In the use of *u* and *j*, the customs of editors have been various. In the texts edited for the Clarendon Press, Mr. Skeat prints *loue, Iugement, deuoir, yeueth, haue;* and Dr. Morris, *ιoue, jugement, devoir, yeveth, have,* — putting the *y* in *yeveth* in italics, to indicate that the manuscript had the sign that represents the sounds of *y, g, gh*, and *z*. (In like manner Dr. Morris prints hei*g*her, nou*g*ht, eyg*h*en, for it would be misleading to use *y* in these and similar words, even if it were italicized.)

The use of *i* for *j*, and *u* for *v*, was not discontinued until the present century, and yet the texts of Shakespeare and the Bible are printed in accordance with present usage. The same is true of the poems of Spenser, in the series to which the present volume belongs.

There is a positive loss when povre — Italian *povero*, French *pauvre* — is printed in an old author "poure," and poverte — *poverta*, *pauvreté* — is printed "pouerte." This is true also when iape, ioye, iade, iuge, take the places of *jape*, *joye*, *jade*, *juge*. On the contrary, the poet suffers no detriment when these words are presented with the letters which make the impression upon nineteenth-century readers that the other ones made upon readers accustomed to them in the fourteenth century.

VII. It is sometimes almost impossible to decide whether a letter is a *u* or an *n* in the manuscripts, a fact that accounts for the two forms Cambyuskan and Cambynscan in various editions of the Squire's Tale. Tyrwhitt printed the word Cambuscan, but Thynne (A. D. 1599) had given it Cambiuscan, which is equivalent to Cambyuskan, the reading of the best manuscript now known.

VIII. If a manuscript written by the poet, or under his direction, could be found, or even one produced during his lifetime, no question regarding spelling could well be raised. In the absence of such an authority, the aim should be to print the poet's words in an orthography as nearly as possible according with that which the author probably adopted. In times anterior to the invention of printing, there was no regularity in the spelling of words. The greatest variations abounded, the same word being often spelled differently on the same page, or in the same line. The Old English word *seah* is written *sauh, saugh, seigh, sigh, segh, sihe, sauhe, sawh, sagh, sy, sie, sey, say, seygh*, all of which mean *saw*. This is but a sample of the habits of the scribes; and we have also *moche, mokel, muchel, mochel, myche, mychel, michel*, and many like irregularities. In general, it may be said that Old English orthography was intended to be phonetic. It was not until several centuries had passed over Chaucer's grave that the rigid and arbitrary conventionalities of the modern dictionary obtained their controlling power. Any conces sion to modern precision would misrepresent the orthography of Chaucer, and none is at

tempted in the present work. The Editor's
rule has been to follow in this respect the usage
of the scribe, who had the advantage of living
at least four centuries nearer the time of the
author that he represents.

Care has been taken in collating the manuscripts, though it has been considered best not
to burden the volume with the various read-
ings

A comparison of texts that were not available by Tyrwhitt — to make but a single reference to former editors — has shown both the
wisdom and the accuracy of the scholarship
that he displayed, while it has enabled the
present Editor to perfect many lines without
offering his own emendations.

Mr. Tyrwhitt makes a note to line 759, to
say that he has ventured to lengthen the word
"amonges" to fulfill the requirements of the
metre, and quotes authorities for his action,
when in fact he unconsciously adopts the reading of the best manuscript.

Mr. Tyrwhitt amends line 3811 by introduc-
ing the word "al" before "aboute," a change
which the Ellesmere manuscript shows that the
metre does not demand.

Line 4711 has heretofore appeared hope-

essly corrupted. Mr. Tyrwhitt printed it, " Or
Ilion brent, or Thebes the citee," acknowledg-
ing that he could make little sense of it. A
collation of the Six Texts of the Chaucer Society seems to make it clear that the reading
adopted in the present text is the proper one.

At line 5818 Mr. Tyrwhitt gave " kalender "
instead of "chilyndre," a word that the late
investigations show is the one used by Chaucer.

The word *stoupen*, bent, given by Tyrwhitt, at
line 8433, it is now shown should be *stape*, advanced. The same verb occurs in line 13,850,
though it was formerly printed *stopen*.

Again, at line 11,256, Mr. Tyrwhitt intro-
duces an extra syllable, though it is not
needed.

The reader who is curious regarding Tyrwhitt's judicious treatment of the text will be
interested to compare with the present text
certain instances in which he made emendations. He will find that the latest investigations sustain that editor to a remarkable extent. In the first volume of the Aldine Chaucer Mr. Skeat quotes (page 174) ten lines which
Tyrwhitt emended, namely, lines 1510, 1516
1535, 1654, 1734, 1973, 2103, 2493, 2928, and

2996. Of these changes eight are supported by the Ellesmere text, and the remaining two are shown to have been unnecessary. These are lines used to prove that Chaucer intentionally made the first foot in some cases consist of a single syllable, a proposition that has been denied. Mr. Lowell's emphatic denial, made in "My Study Windows" (page 266), is supported by these lines.[1]

It might be further proved that the new manuscripts clear up many dark passages, and that the examination of the originals of the tales have also been of great service in the same direction.

While the text has been thus scrupulously dealt with, the rubrics found in the manuscripts have also been printed, so far as practicable, though, as they do not constitute an integral portion of the poems, they have in some cases been disregarded, or new ones, more in keeping with the true meaning of the text, have been introduced. In this way a distinction has been made between the prologues and preambles of the Canterbury Tales and the conversational links by which the continuity of the

---

[1] Mr. Ellis had already shown (*E. E. Pronunciation*, p. 333) that line 1734 was probably corrupt and could not fall into the category of lines deficient in the first foot.

narrative is sustained, and it is believed the reader is brought more completely into sympathy with the action of the poem.

Another aid to the reader will be found in the head-lines. On the left-hand page is the title of the current tale, or poem, while the subject of the folio is indicated at the top of the right-hand page, often by a quotation of the poet's words.

The lines of the Canterbury Tales are, for convenient reference, numbered from beginning to end, and the numberings of Tyrwhitt's edition are given in parentheses every fiftieth line, and also at places where lines are omitted from that edition, or from the present one. The prose story of Melibeus and the Parson's sermon are included in the numbering, every tenth break marked in the Six-Text edition being indicated. The elaborate system of the Six-Text edition, in which the lines are numbered by "Groups," in order to keep before the mind the fact that the poem is incomplete, has advantages for use in that place, but is less convenient than the one here adopted. The numbering of Mr. Tyrwhitt was consecutive but did not include the prose, to which exact reference has heretofore been difficult. The

Index in the present edition will facilitate reference to subjects and names.

The explanations usually relegated to a Glossary, or to a body of final Notes, will be found at the foot of the pages, and the reader will be saved the trouble of searching for a word in a long list, of holding in his hand two volumes at once, of weighing the conflicting definitions often placed opposite the same word, or of identifying a particular part of speech.

Unqualified thanks are due from the Editor, and from all who are interested in our first great English poet, to those scholars already referred to, who have given the Chaucer Society its high position, and in its publications, as well as in their own, have accomplished so much in the way of making the reading of Chaucer an intelligent pleasure. They have in effect added a new poet to the honorable list of English makers, for they have made him accessible and lucid to many readers who had been repelled by his unwonted appearance.

Professor Francis J. Child, of Harvard University, by his lectures on Chaucer, by his Observations on the Language of Chaucer and Gower published in the Memoirs of the American Academy, and by his efforts in behalf of

the Chaucer Society, has largely increased the
interest in our poet in America. Among the
other scholars who should be mentioned in
this connection are Professor Corson, of Cor-
nell University, who published an edition of
the "Legend of Good Women" before the
English society had been organized ; and Professor Lounsbury, of Yale College, who has
carefully edited a text of the "Parlement of
Foules."

In England, besides Mr. Furnivall, who has
edited all of the Chaucer Society's publications, there are the Rev. W. W. Skeat, of Cambridge, who has published, in the series of the
Clarendon Press, two volumes containing a text
of several of the Canterbury Tales with elaborate and scholarly notes, besides what he has
done elsewhere ; and the Rev. Richard Morris,
LL. D., of London, who has carefully edited
the General Prologue and two of the Canterbury Tales, for the Clarendon Press. Many
German scholars have made material additions
to the mass of Chaucerian information, their
writings bearing the marks of the erudition for
which the students of that nation are noted.

In the work of discriminating between the
true productions of Chaucer and those that

had for centuries been attributed to him, the
chief credit is due to Mr. Henry Bradshaw,
Fellow of King's College, and Librarian of the
University of Cambridge.   Independent researches, made by Professor Bernhard ten
Brink, of the University of Strassburg, had,
however, resulted in conclusions that did not
materially vary from those of Mr. Bradshaw.   A
full account of these researches may be found
in an article published in " Macmillan's Magazine " for March, 1873, entitled " Recent Work
at Chaucer."

TABLE OF CONTENTS.

VOL. I.   *b*

THE TIMES AND THE POET.

I.

THE Age of Beginnings, which gave to English letters a writer whose transcendent genius surpassed the conceptions of all previous intellectual toilers, and still holds rank second to that of the "myriad-minded" dramatist before whom every European writer bows as to a master, is worthy to be studied for its historic interest, because in it are found the springs of subsequent progress. The sun of spiritual and intellectual enfranchisement was beginning to appear above the horizon, and the darkness of the previous ages was slowly fading before its powerful rays. Every people seemed to be preparing for a step forward which should usher in an unexperienced life, brilliant by contrast with all previous eras, and already made radiant by the workings of an imagination not yet delivered from the bondage of superstition.

In Italy the great Poet of the Unseen had but lately gone behind the veil,[1] and Petrarch and Boccaccio were inditing verses that were to make them ever remembered. Among the English the credulous Mandeville was pursuing those voyages of discovery by which he is now known ; the author of " The Last Age "[2] was predicting the end of all things ; the Parson of Lutterworth was preparing his version of the Bible,[3] and bringing on a religious reformation ; the Dreamer on the Malvern Hills[4] was giving poetic voice to the moanings of the miserable laboring classes ; while the king was fighting his fruitless wars in France, the Black Prince was winning his spurs and honorably wearing them ; the nobles were indulging in the pomp and circumstance of jousts and tourneys ; and the Poet of the Gentles was standing by, eagerly noticing every step in the gay dance, or mingling in those scenes of court life and courtiers' work which it was soon to be his .o satirize and send down to the ages in immortal verse. It is with the fourteenth century that we have to do. In its twenty-first year

---

[1] Dante died in the autumn of 1321.

[2] This gloomy production was long attributed to Wiclif.

[3] Wiclif's version was finished at about the same time that the General Prologue of the Canterbury Tales was written.

[4] *The Vision concerning Piers the Plowman* was issued and is-sued, in three versions, from 1362 to 1399.

the exiled Dante died broken-hearted at Ravenna, leaving, as the fruit of his years of distress, an immortal epic and a never-dying fame that his native Florence eagerly sought to grasp and preserve. A score of years later the Easter sun gilded the laurel crown that an admiring king and populace solemnly placed upon the brow of the mourning lover of Laura, as he stood in the Capitol at the imperial city. The same fourteenth century witnessed in Italy a revival of classical learning under the reformed Boccaccio, who became a public interpreter of Dante, as he already had been the first to make known anew the faithfulness of a Troilus, the fickleness of a Cressida, and the unfailing obedience of a Griselda, all of which characters were to be transplanted into our literature by the poet of the Canterbury Pilgrimage, who, indeed, re-illumined the torch of his poetic fervor at the altars of Italian genius.

In England the fourteenth century saw the culmination of that spirit of chivalry which in its dry records on the pages of a Froissart is still capable of filling the imagination with pictures of brilliant tournaments and stately royal progresses, and in the poet's verse embalms forever the graces of fair women and the gentle

deeds of strong men, who in a rude age bat-
tled for virtue and honor. The long reign of
the third Edward saw all this magnificence and
kindliness, but as it wore on it witnessed a
change. Terrible plagues wasted the people ;
the Hundred Years' War made great taxes
necessary, and these pressed heavily upon the
hard-working and poorly paid laborers on the
land ; the king who had won cities in France
lost them also ; his chivalrous son went before
him to the grave, and there arose a young
ruler whose accession caused the Malvern
Dreamer to add to his popular vision the
Scriptural malediction, —

"Woe to thee, O land, when thy king is a child,
For I herde my sire seyne, is sevene yere ypassed,
There the catte is a kitoun, the court is ful elyng" (sad).

The times were bad when the traveled
Mandeville returned, and he exclaimed, "In
our time it may be spoken more truly than of
old, that virtue is gone, the Church is under
foot, the clergy is in error, the Devil reigneth,
and Simony beareth sway." The same view
of the state of affairs was taken by the author
of "The Vision of Piers the Plowman." If
the conjecture is to be believed, it was just as
the candle of King Edward was burning in its

socket that the gay and courtly Chaucer turned to the example of the last of the ancients, translated the "Consolations of Philosophy," and snatched from its picture of the bliss of the Former Age this wail over the misery of the present : —

> " Alas, alas, now may men wepe and crye,
> For in our days is nought but covetyse,
> Doubleness, tresoun, and envye,
> Poyson, manslawtyr, murder in sondry wyse."

Both in Italy and in England a period of barrenness ensued, marked in one country by the refinements of knowledge, and in the other by the quibbles and sophisms of an ignorance that aped wisdom. The French of Stratford atte Bow in Chaucer's time was neither English nor French, but twenty years later even University learning had grown so contemptible that " Oxford Latin " became a proverbial expression signifying an unmeaning jargon. The sciences were unknown, of course, though the heavens were methodically set off into twelve parts, called "houses," or "mansions," and medicine was practiced with confidence, but on superstitious and empiric principles, which had not been changed since the Emperor Nero's physician compounded the confection called, from him, *Theriaca Andromachi*, composed of the dried flesh of vipers and scores of other equally valuable ingredients. We find in Chaucer many allusions to the heavenly "houses" and to the influence of the signs upon the nature and welfare of men, as well as to the "treacle" which was esteemed an antidote to all bodily disease.

In the fourteenth century the three classes of society were always clashing. The House of Commons, representing the middle class, was continually impinging upon the prerogatives of the Crown and the ancient aristocracy, causing the great charters to be repeatedly confirmed and grievances to be diminished. On the other hand, the laboring class, comprising the majority of the population, was demanding the enactment of laws like the "Statute of Laborers," of 1350, and those aimed at the improvement of the administration of justice and the establishment of trial by jury.

The progress of Freedom lies often through revolution; and the reign of Richard II. presents a constant succession of social upheavals which ended during the last year of the century in the "renunciation" of the crown and the elevation of Henry Bolingbroke, Duke of Lancaster, to the throne as King Henry IV.

The rebellion of 1381 was one of the signs of the times. It resulted from a tax of the previous year, and began with the murder of the royal collector (a man of the Commons who represented the aristocracy above him) by Wat the Tyler (a man of the laboring order), and it did not end until all Essex and Kent and Suffolk and Norfolk had been involved in the wildest confusion, their palaces sacked, their towns besieged, their prisons destroyed, their hospitals burned, and their aristocracy massacred in large numbers. The end came, and it was followed by the legal execution of hundreds of those who had vainly risen to gain the freedom which, since the hour when the yeomen of England won the victory of Cressy, it had been the dream of their children one day to secure. Thus ended the reign of Richard II., in the overthrow of a tyrant by the agreement of the three classes of society, having generally different interests, but now united for the maintenance of freedom. It is not ours to inquire minutely into the measures by which one sovereign was placed at the mercy of his ambitious successor, nor to ask how far society was benefited by the change that was thus brought about. Our simple purpose is to note that there was a change which put upon the throne a grandson of Edward III., and son of John of Gaunt, the friend of the poet Chaucer.

As we close our historical survey there reach our ears hoarse murmurs of discontent from the Marches of Wales, where the "irregular and wild Glendower" is doing such deeds

> " As may not be,
> Without much shame, re-told or spoken of ; "

and from the North comes "more uneven and unwelcome news," for Harry Percy and the Earl of Northumberland are leading their forces to victory on the field of Holmedon ; and we close the book as the *Te Deum* of the Archbishop of Canterbury sounds above the popular clamor, while he goes forth to meet the procession bearing the heads of King Richard's personal attendants, over whose destruction he chants his barbarous exultations.

II.

With comparative ease the panorama of public events can be made vivid, even after centuries have spread their mists over the scenes but the case is quite otherwise when we essay to penetrate further and bring out the inner life of the fourteenth century.

It was a time of chivalry and magnificence at the beginning; but before it ended feudalism was decaying and tottering to its fall. In the reign of Edward III. the hierarchy was at the height of its grandeur: cathedrals were going up in Lincoln and Wells and Peterborough and Salisbury; churches were supplied everywhere; William of Wykeham was doing his great work at Winchester; the church at Westminster received extensive additions; and friars and other churchmen greatly increased in power. It was at about 1380,[1] however, that John Wiclif inaugurated his reforming work, and after that his tracts, and the poor preachers who carried them, circulated through the length and breadth of the land; the people saw that the Church was grasping, and that those who should be the promoters of purity and humility were often as corrupt and as proud as they appear on the pages of Piers the Plowman and of Chaucer. The doctrines of Wiclif became popular, and the Lollards, his followers, grew rapidly in numbers. The

[1] This date is not established beyond doubt. See Professor Lecher's *Life of Wiclif*.

masses had been dormant under the preaching of the parish priests, but they awoke at the call of the " poor parson of a town."

If there was spiritual corruption under the magnificence of the hierarchy, there was no less truly personal uncleanness beneath the liveries of the servants, the robes of the squires, and the glittering costumes of the higher orders. Conveniences were few, and soap appears to have been used for washing clothes only, though the garments of the poorer classes were seldom submitted to the process. Mr. Furnivall gives an interesting quotation that speaks volumes of the state of affairs before the introduction of India-rubber " atomizers," when it had not yet become popular to apply soap to the person. It is to the effect that when Cardinal Wolsey went to Westminster Hall, he had a custom of "holding in his hand a very fair orange, whereof the meat or substance within was taken out, and filled up again with the part of a sponge, wherein was vinegar and other confections against the pestilent airs ; the which he most commonly smelt unto, passing among the press, or else when he was pestered with many suitors." The use of perfumes to coun teract the effects of a want of personal neat

ness seems to be a relic of such times as this.
A vivid illustration is found in the picture
drawn by Hotspur, when describing the certain
lord, "perfumed like a milliner," who so irri-
tated him on the field of Holmedon. The passage is too long for quotation.[1] The rich were
by no means neat, and the poor were dirty indeed.   Erasmus ascribed the plague and other
diseases in England to the uncleanness of the
ways, and the almost inconceivable foulness of
the houses, in which much refuse might easily
accumulate beneath the rushes that served in
place of carpets.   In the household of Henry
VIII., in the next century, even, there was dis-
graceful filth, such as we can scarcely imagine
without the official records.[2] People had small
stocks of linen and of other garments.; many
worked and slept in the same clothes, if, indeed,
they were not completely denuded at night.

Classes were distinguished by their apparel
more than by manners or bearing ; and sump-
tuary laws strictly regulated many things which
we feel are beyond the domain of state inter-

[1] See 1 *King Henry IV.*, act i., sc. 3, l. 29.   Cf. also *Much Ado*,
act i., sc. 3, l. 52, and the notes on the word "perfumer," by Rolfe
and by the editor of the "Howard" Shakespeare.

[2] For the above, and many other interesting illustrations of mediæval life, see *Early English Meals and Manners*, edited by Mr.
F. J Furnivall, for the Early English Text Society.

ference. During the reign of Edward III. there grew up a remarkable degree of luxury and display among the lower orders, which was restrained by a law, passed in 1363, to put down "the outragious and excessive apparel of divers people against their estate and degree, to the great destruction and impoverishment of all the land."

The ordinary diet of the people was not of the best, nor is it probable that it was well cooked. Much salted meat was used, for the markets were uncertain and poor. The houses were inconvenient, often they had no chimneys or glazed windows, and there was no provision for the privacy that is so helpful to good manners and morals. Men and women lived much apart from each other, and the church encouraged the tendency in this direction. There was less conventional or constructional morality, and many acts now private were then of necessity open and public. This fact led to there being less "refinement" of thought and behavior, and it explains much that we find recorded concerning the doings of men and women of the period.

Not having attractive houses, the people loved the open air, the fields, the flowers, the groves; and they there engaged in that gay and spontaneous dancing that is healthy; there they practiced archery, went a-Maying and hawking; there they told stories, and baited their bulls and their bears; there they had the tournaments and jousts of the formality of which all their literature tells us so much. There, too, they settled questions of right or wrong, truth or falsehood, by the ordeal of battle, in the manner proposed by Mowbray and Bolingbroke, in Shakespeare's " King Richard II."

Chaucer, though the poet of the "gentles," as distinguished from the low-born masses whom the author of "Piers Plowman" describes, gives us no pictures in life higher than that of the Knight. From other sources it is plain that the comforts and conveniences of life were many of them unknown to royalty. Queen Elizabeth was the first sovereign to use a fork, and hers was a poor one, compared with those now found on the tables of farmers and artisans in Australia and on American prairies.

There was a great deal of romance, much lofty talk about ridiculous refinements in love, and long arguments in the courts of Cupid, but there were few comforts and not many of those

delicate social and personal luxuries which **five**
centuries have since developed.

III.

There is little doubt that if Chaucer had had
the opportunity to read the sketches of his life
which have been written with minuteness dur·
ing the past three hundred years he would
have warned readers against them. He lived
at an age when the importance of the individual was not appreciated so highly by historians
as it has since been. In the fourteenth century history was chronicles of the doings of
monarchs, generals, and armies, — of the dis-
ruptive, not the conservative, elements of society. It is not surprising that materials for a
life of Chaucer have been scarce, nor that diligent students have gathered up every fragment and have woven and re-woven them into
"lives" which may have borne some resemblance to that which men imagined their hero
to have lived, but were in reality crowded with
incidents and marked by characteristics that
Chaucer would not have recognized. Some
of these have been founded upon passages in
his writings supposed to be autobiographic in
their nature, and others upon compositions

wrongly attributed to him, which, of course, are of no value whatever. Few as are the records of Chaucer's life, we have more facts regarding him than are to be positively asserted of Shakespeare, though this is owing, not to his having been the greatest poet of his age, but to his official connection with the court.

The year of Chaucer's birth is now supposed to be 1340, and, if the conjecture be correct, he came into the world at the turn in the tide of British affairs, when the naval victory off Sluys had begun to revive English hearts, made heavy by King Edward's unsuccessful march into France, and out of it, the previous year. He was the son of John Chaucer, citizen and vintner of London, who lived on Thames Street, and his mother was probably named Agnes. His grandfather was Richard Chaucer, likewise citizen and vintner of London, and it is highly probable that the poet himself was born and bred in the city which has since given the world Spenser, Ben Jonson, and Milton, and which became the place where the genius of Shakespeare was developed and made the inheritance of the world.

For twenty years success crowned the efforts of British arms, and the praise of military glory

was on every courtly tongue. It is evident
that at this time young Chaucer was storing
his mind and adding to the wealth of his imagination, but in what way he acquired the
complete education that his attainments in
science and general literature prove him to
have had, it is impossible to say, for until re-
cently, nothing whatever has been known of
his earlier years. His father's calling did not
stand in the way of his progress, — in fact it
probably brought him into contact with many
phases of life that he was destined afterwards
to portray, and besides, we know that Sir
Henry Picard, the Lord Mayor of London,
was also a vintner, and Chaucer began to appear in court circles too early for us to suppose
that he was held back by anything. We are
to think of him hearing as a child of the new
and dreadful instruments of destructive war-
fare which at Cressy first vomited fire and shot
against a devoted enemy. Ten years later his
young blood was thrilled by the stories that
reached England from the field of Poictiers,
and we are at liberty to suppose that amid
such scenes of magnificence and pageantry as
that he had witnessed in May, 1358, when the
Black Prince rode through London with his

prisoner, King John of France, he was infatu-
ated with a longing to go with his elders to the
field of glory, — to that France whose lais
and romaunts were already familiar to his
young imagination.

If there was not another Geoffrey Chaucer
then living, it was the future poet who entered
the service of Prince Lionel, third son of Edward III., apparently as page, in 1357. It is
more than probable that he was present at the
great Feast of St. George, given by the king
to the king of France, the queen of Scotland,
the king of Cyprus, and other royal persons
who were in England in 1358, as well as at
other famous joustings and pageants of the
time. It is certain, however, and we have the
poet's own word for it, that his military experience began in 1359, when he joined Edward
III.'s army late in the year, as it went to in-
vade France. This expedition was inconse-
quent and was brought to an end by the Great
Peace, which famine and fatigue forced the
king to effect at Bretigny the next year. During this campaign Chaucer was made prisoner,
but he was ransomed March 1, 1360, before
the peace, the king himself contributing sixteen
pounds towards that end.

At this time France was suffering from the
Jacquerie horrors too awful to be detailed, and
contending factions were fast dragging the
nation to anarchy, but England was enjoying
a period of prosperity. What our poet was
doing cannot be stated, for no record tells us
anything of his movements for seven years
after his ransom from captivity. It seems
probable that during this period he began his
career of authorship, and it is a noteworthy
coincidence that it was in the year 1362 that
the English language was ordered to be used
in English courts, for the reason that French
had become "much unknown." French had
come into use when the triumphing Normans
wrested the throne from its Saxon possessor,
and it went out when the French sovereign
was a captive in England, and it seemed as if
Edward might succeed in enforcing his claim
to the throne of France. The hour had arrived
for the fusion of the discordant elements of
English speech into a flexible, forcible, and
elegant medium for the transmission of the
creations of genius ; and the man who was to do
the work was waiting for the moment to arrive
when he might show himself to the people and
give a reason why he had been saved from

death in "the imminent, deadly breach," and ransomed from languishing in a French dungeon.

In 1367 the name of the poet appears again in the records as that of one of the valets of the king's household, "a position," says Sir Harris Nicolas, "always filled by gentlemen," and, on the 20th of June of that year, he was granted an annual salary of twenty marks for life, or until he should be otherwise provided for. He received this pension at various dates in 1367, 1368, 1369, 1370, 1371, and 1372, when he was assigned more important duties. To this period is referred his marriage to Philippa, one of the ladies in attendance on the queen, and Sir Harris Nicolas, the poet's careful biographer, says that there is scarcely a doubt that she was the eldest daughter of Sir Payne Roet, and sister of Katherine, widow of Sir Hugh Swinford, who subsequently became wife of John of Gaunt, Duke of Lancaster. The assertion rests, however, upon proof that we cannot accept as final until it has been proved that the Thomas Chaucer who used the Roet arms was actually a son of the poet. There are reasons also for thinking it improbable that Chaucer was related to John of

Gaunt in this way.[1] This is also the date assigned to Chaucer's "hopeless love," a mal-
ady attributed to him very lately on account of
the following lines in the "Dethe of Blaunche
the Duchesse:" —

> "Trewly, as I gesse,
> I hold it be a sickenes
> That I have suffred this eight yeere,
> And yet my boote is never the nere;
> For there is phisicien but one
> That may me heale; but that is done.
> Passe we over untill efte;
> That will not be, mote nedes be lefte."

It is not, however, always safe to read bi-
ography in a poet's verse. We do not know
from other sources that Chaucer actually suffered the pains he here describes, and if he
did, the distressing anguish caused by one lady
was pretty soon removed by the fair Philippa,
if her marriage occurred at this time.[2]

We have now arrived at a new and most interesting period in Chaucer's life, during which
he was charged with important public business
in foreign parts, which gave him opportunities

[1] This subject is discussed at length by Sir Harris Nicolas in his
Life of Chaucer. See the Aldine edition of Chaucer (1869), pages
44-50.
[2] For an interesting discussion of this point, see the *Atlantic
Monthly* for November, 1877, article, "Fictitious Lives of Chaucer:
and for May, 1878, Letter from Mr. F. J. Furnivall.

for culture, added to his knowledge of human nature, made him acquainted with men and letters on the Continent, and opened more fully to him the wealth of Italian and perhaps of classical literature. We may suppose that he was well acquainted with the style and works of French writers, and that now he widened his knowledge until it embraced all European literature. For ten years, from 1370 to 1380, he was much of the time engaged in the king's service abroad. His first mission took him away from England during the summer of 1370. In 1372 he was sent with two others to treat with the duke, citizens, and merchants of Genoa, for the establishment of commercial relations between their city and England. We know but little of the mission, further than this, that the poet was absent less than a year went to Florence as well as Genoa, and was paid ninety-two pounds for his expenses on the journey.

The chief interest that attaches to this visit of Chaucer to Italy arises from the following words in the conversation between the Host and the Clerk, on the Canterbury pilgrimage, before the story of Patient Griselda was told : —

> " I wol yow telle a tale which that I
> Lerned at Padwe of a worthy clerk,
> As preved by his wordes and his werk ;
> He is now deed and nayled in his cheste,
> I prey to God so geve his soule reste !
> Fraunceys Petrak, the lauriat poete,
> Highte this clerk whos rethorike sweete
> Enlumyned al Ytaille of poetrie."

It is natural and probable that an interview
should have taken place between the rising
poet of England and the aged Petrarch, then
near the end of his life, who was at the time at
Arqua, two miles from Padua, but actual proof
of it is still wanting, after the most careful
search.

It is evident that Chaucer's commission on
this occasion was performed to his sovereign's
satisfaction, for he was made the recipient of
several royal grants. In April, 1374, probably
on the occasion of the celebration of the Feast
of St. George at Windsor, a pitcher of wine
was assigned him to be received daily in the
port of London from the hands of the king's
butler. In May the Corporation of London
gave him a lease for life of the dwelling above
the gate at Aldgate, with the rooms built over
and the cellar beneath ; and in June he was
appointed Comptroller of the customs and sub

sidies of wools, skins, and tanned hides, in the port of London, with the usual fees; it being expressly stipulated that he was to write the rolls with his own hands, be continually present, and perform the duties personally, and not by deputy, as a poet might well like to perform them.[1]

The first mention of Chaucer's wife occurs in connection with a pension of ten pounds, given her for life by John of Gaunt, before August, 1372, in consideration of the good service which Geoffrey and Philippa had rendered to the duke, his wife, and the queen his mother. It is possible that this is the same Philippa Chaucer who had been in waiting on Queen Philippa in 1366, and was then granted a pension of ten marks yearly for life, for she apparently received it subsequently by the hand of her husband, Geoffrey Chaucer. She may

---

[1] In his Prologue to *The Earthly Paradise*, William Morris thus poetically refers to this period in our poet's life: —

"Dream of London small and white and clean,
The clear Thames bordered by its gardens green;
Think, that below the bridge the green lapping waves
Smite some few keels that bear Levantine staves,
Cut from the yew wood on the burnt-up hill,
And pointed jars that Greek hands toiled to fill,
And treasured scanty spice from some far sea,
Florence gold cloth, and Ypres napery,
And cloth of Bruges, and hogsheads of Guienne;
While nigh the thronged wharf Geoffrey Chaucer's pen
Moves over bills of lading, — 'mid such times
Shall dwell the hollow puppets of my rhymes."

however, have been a relative, whom the poet married, say in 1374. Chaucer had now been an Esquire for some years.

His income was now constantly increasing. In 1375 it was augmented by his appointment as custodian of the estate of a minor, Edward Staplegate, of Kent, from which he had received one hundred and four pounds two years later; and by a grant of the custody of certain lands belonging to another minor, also in Kent. In July, 1376, he received seventy-one pounds, four shillings, and six pence, for wool, forfeited for non-payment of duties.

The same year he was sent on some secret service with Sir John Burley, and early in the next year he was employed on a similar service in Flanders with Sir Thomas Percy, afterwards Earl of Worcester; and in the spring of 1377 he was again absent from the country in the performance of confidential duties. It is probable that he was not in England in June, when King Edward died, for his wages for the last commission were not paid until August 30th of that year.

Under the new sovereign Chaucer was still favored, and in January, 1378, he appears to have been associated with the Earl of Hunting

don and others in a mission to France, to negotiate for a marriage between Richard II.
and a daughter of the French king. At least,
he was paid for going to France that year with
that object. In the following March, Chaucer
was sent to Lombardy with Sir Edward Berke-
ley, to treat with Bernardo Visconti, lord of Mi-
lan ("of Melan, grete Barnabo Viscounte"[1]).
Before leaving England on this occasion, he
appointed John Gower to be one of his repre-
sentatives in court, in case any legal business
should need attention during his absence. It
is presumed that this was the poet of the name,
and if that be so, the circumstance indicates
an intimate friendship between Gower and his
greater contemporary, which is also supported
by the fact that Chaucer dedicated his "Troylus and Cryseyde" to Gower; and that, in his
"Confessio Amantis," Gower inserted verses
complimentary to Chaucer. It is hardly worth
while to discuss the duration of this friendship,
which, it seems probable, lasted until death
closed it, though Tyrwhitt thought it was broken
off earlier.

Returning from Italy in the early part of
1379, Chaucer received moneys on account of

[1] See *Canterbury Tales*, l. 8011

his old grants, and of a new one lately made
by Richard II., in February, May, and December, though he may have been abroad again
during a portion of the time, for the payment
in May was not made to him in person. Other
sums were paid to him in July and November,
1380, and March, 1381, the last being twenty-
two pounds, on account of his mission to
France in 1377. In May, 1382, he was given
the additional office of Comptroller of Petty
Customs in the port of London, with permis-
sion to perform the duties by a deputy, a permanent officer of this kind being allowed him
in February, 1385. He was thus placed in easy
circumstances, and had ample leisure to en-
gage in the occupation which has made him
known ; and thus ends the second period in
his life.

In 1386 Chaucer was elected one of the
knights of the shire for Kent, to sit in the par-
liament holden at Westminster from October
1st to November 1st, of that year. Its proceed-
ings were all directed against the ministers of
the party at the head of which was John of
Gaunt, Chaucer's patron, at the time absent
from the country, asserting his claim to the
crown of Castile, the Duke of Gloucester being

at the head of the government. It is needless for us to go into details of public affairs at this juncture, and, indeed, the most painstaking historians find themselves unable to ravel the confused threads involved in the family quarrels with which England was now cursed.

We know that by the end of 1386 Chaucer had lost both of his public offices, and had been plunged from affluence into poverty. It is probable that his wife died at about the same time, for her name is not mentioned on the records after June, 1387. To this period belong certain supposititious events in the poet's life that have been founded upon passages in the "Testament of Love," a composition that was long ascribed to him, such as his having taken part in disputes between the court and citizens of London regarding the election of John of Northampton to the mayoralty in 1382, Chaucer's attempted arrest and his flight to Zealand, his return in 1386, his imprisonment in the Tower, and subsequent release on the petition of Good Queen Anne, all of which are contradicted by the official records. The reason for the loss of his offices is easily surmised, when we consider the relation of the parties, and recollect that Chaucer's patron was absent from England; and that a commission, probably inimical to him, was appointed in November, 1386, to investigate alleged abuses, which began its duties by examining the revenue accounts. However, it is not absolutely necessary that a reason be found for any of the acts done at a period when right and law were at the mercy of jealousy and power.

During this period of Chaucer's retirement, on the 10th of August, 1388, there occurred on the Scottish border the famous battle of Otterbourne, commemorated in the ballad beginning —

> " Yt felle abowght the Lamasse tyde,
>   When husbonds wynn ther haye,
>   The dowghtye Dowglasse bowynd hym to ryde
>   In Ynglond to take a praye."

If the old song of the Percy and Douglas moved the heart of a polished Sidney as with a trumpet, though " evill apparrelled in the dust and cob-webbes of that uncivill age," how must the heart of a poet like Chaucer have been stirred when the posts, breathless with the haste of the journey, pressed into London with the fresh news of the meeting of the Douglas and Percy, of the dash and death of the one and the capture of the other ! He could pict ure to himself as we cannot the meeting of the leaders as at a tourney, the personal encounter, the charge of the Douglas with the battle-axe, the loss of the Percy pennon, and all the exciting incidents of the rush of battle, which appear quite dimmed by the mists of the ages, as we read of them on the chronicler's record or in the poet's verses.

A great change came over public affairs in the spring of 1389, when the young king asserted himself, and appointed new ministers, one of whom was the Earl of Derby (son of John of Gaunt), afterwards King Henry IV. Chaucer appears to have been immediately remembered, and (before the Duke of Lancaster, who was in Guienne, could return to England) was placed in the valuable office of Clerk of the King's Works at the Palace of Westminster, the Tower of London, and in various manors, lodges, and so forth, with a salary of two shillings a day, and, probably, other emoluments. The next year he was commanded to procure men and materials for the repair of St. George's Chapel, Windsor. On the 3d of September, 1390, Chaucer was waylaid by certain notorious highwaymen, at a place called "Foule Ok," Westminster, and despoiled of twenty pounds of the king's money, besides his horse and other personal property. He appealed to be forgiven the repayment of the money, and it was the discovery of that fact that led to the finding of extensive records concerning the trial of the robbers, which were published by the Chaucer Society in 1875.

It is an interesting fact that the Clerk of the King's Works caused the erection of scaffolds in Smithfield, in May, 1390, from which King Richard and Good Queen Anne witnessed the jousts that took place at about the time that Richard was declared to have come of age. Thus closes the third period of Chaucer's life.

The good fortune that came to Chaucer with the restoration of the Lancastrians to power was of short duration, for we find him deprived of all his offices again in the autumn of 1391, and dependent for support upon his annuity of ten pounds from John of Gaunt, and his allowance of forty shillings for the robes, as the king's squire. In 1394 he was somewhat relieved by a grant from the king of twenty pounds a year for life, but he was still condemned to comparative poverty, and to much suffering, which continued until the end of the reign. It is supposed that it was under these

depressing circumstances that he sent to King
Richard the ballad beginning —

> "Somtyme this world was so stedfast and stable
> That mannes word was holde obligacioun;
>   And now it is so fals and diseyvable
> That word and worke, as in conclusioun,
> Been nothyng oon; for turned up-so-downe
> Is alle this worlde thurgh mede and wylfulnesse,
> That al is loste for lack of stedfastnesse.'

Passing over the record of Chaucer's finan-
cial affairs, that point to a galling lack of those
coins which, in his despairing verses to his
empty purse, he describes as being "of colour
lyke the sunne bryghte," we arrive at the year
1399, made memorable by the accession of
Henry Bolingbroke, and by the return of prosperity to our poet. In September of that year
he sent to the new king the poetical intimation
of his pecuniary needs that has just been referred to. It is a plaint characteristic of the
aged and naïve poet, in which he says to his
purse, —

> "I am so sory that now ye been lyghte!"

He concluded with these words :—

> "Now, purse, that been to me my lyves lyghte,
>   And saviour (as doun in this worlde here),
> Oute of this toune help me thurgh youre myghte

Syn that you wol not ben my tresorere,
For I am shave as nigh as is a frere ;
   But I pray unto youre courtesye,
Beth hevy ageyne, or elles moote I dye ! ''

From this unique petition there seems to have resulted an additional pension of forty marks a year, on the strength of which Chaucer took a lease of a house in the garden of St. Mary's Chapel, Westminster, for fifty-three years, at an annual rent of two pounds, thirteen shillings, and four pence, the lease to be void on the poet's death.

The records show that he was not out of debt yet, but we have the cheerful assurance that he was settled in peace and comfort, and in the enjoyment of the smiles of his sovereign. Here he is supposed to have finished his Parson's Tale, and here, in the autumn of the year 1400, he is said to have taken a farewell of the earthly scenes which he had done so much to make permanent for after generations.

Chaucer's wife preceded him to the grave ; his son Lewis, to whom he addressed his treatise on the Astrolabe, in 1391, appears to have died young; and there is no evidence that any other children survived the poet, whose line may therefore be considered extinct.

The best means of gaining a knowledge of Chaucer's character and personal appearance is to read his writings, and this is in fact the only way now open to us. In his "Life Records of Chaucer," Part II., published by the Chaucer Society in 1876, Mr. Furnivall quotes two descriptions of the poet in his old age, written in the sixteenth century. One, which is rather too completely a work of the imagination, exhibits "wittie Chaucer," sitting "in a chaire of gold covered with roses, writing prose and risme, accompanied by the spirites of many kinges, knyghtes, and faire ladies, whom he pleasantly besprinkled with the sweete water of the welle consecrated unto the muses." The other is more matter of fact, though probably incorrect in its details.

> "His stature was not very tall ;
> Leane he was ; and his legs were small,
> Hos'd within a stock of red ;
> A button'd bonnet on his head,
> From under which did hang, I weene,
> Silver haires both bright and sheene.
> His beard was white, trimmed round ;
> His countenance blithe and merry found.
> A sleevelesse jacket, large and wide,
> With many pleights and skirtes side,
> Of water chamlet did he weare
> A whittell by his belt he beare

His shooes were corned broad before ;
His inckhorne at his side he wore,
And in his hand he bore a booke :
Thus did the auntient Poet looke."

From this we turn to the Canterbury Tales and find, in the conversation introductory to the Ryme of Sir Thopas, the following lines : —

"Oure Hoost japen tho bigan,
And thanne at erst he looked up-on me,
And seyde thus : 'What man artow ?' quod he ;
'Thou lookest as thou woldest fynde an hare,
For evere up-on the ground I se thee stare.
Approche neer, and looke up murily.
Now war you, sires, and lat this man have place ;
He in the waast is shape as wel as I ;
This were a popet in an arm tenbrace,
For any womman smal and fair of face.
He semeth elvyssh by his contenaunce,
For un-to no wight dooth he daliaunce.'"

The impression conveyed by this description is that the poet was somewhat corpulent, with a small and intelligent face, and a meditative look, and that he was reserved before strangers. No testimony except his works is needed to prove that he was a severe student, and we can readily believe that the traits which he assigns himself in the " House of Fame " were in reality his own. There we are informed tha

he was no meddler in the affairs of his neigh-
bors, and that when he had finished his daily
labors at the customs office, instead of taking
rest, or searching for news, he went to his
house to sit like a hermit over a new book,
dumb as a stone, till his eyes were dazed,
though he was no enemy to the pleasures of
the table.

In estimating the genius of Chaucer it has
been too much the mode to consider him as
simply the poet of the Canterbury pilgrimage,
and to delineate him as ever tripping through
flowery meads, or, if resting, luxuriating in the
shade of some flower-embosomed arbor, always
enjoying holiday and singing with the thought-
lessness of his own nightingales. A careful
study of his life and of all that he wrote shows
him to have been a far different character.
Joyous he was, and full of lightsomeness, and
he often overflowed with wit and humor and
good-fellowship, but these traits are by no
means inconsistent with the earnestness and
other more serious characteristics which mark
and distinguish the typical Englishman, — are
they not rather essential to it?

Chaucer's was a well-balanced nature. His
acquirements and accomplishments were multi-

form.   He was, first of all, a gentleman and in sympathy with all that belonged to the best life of the upper classes in England in his day. He was a courtier, thoroughly educated in every department of court service, from the humble duties of page to the weighty responsibilities and delicate offices of the foreign ambassador.   He was a man of affairs, able to negotiate at Genoa for the extension of British trade, or to look out for violators of the revenue laws in the busy city of London.   His practical knowledge enabled him to superintend the king's works when that service involved repairing the palace of Westminster, or simply building a scaffolding from which a royal party might view the jousts.   He could negotiate with a foreign power for peace, or urge his sovereign's claim to the hand of a French princess ; he was equally at home in an interview with a Petrarch, or in studying an innkeeper from whom he might draw the jolly host of the Tabard.   The most tedious dissertations on penance did not daunt him when he wished to prepare a sermon with which his poor Parson should close the series of the Pilgrims' tales.   He could dwell day after day upon the discussions of a Boethius in search of

the consolations of Philosophy; and he evidently spared no pains to make himself familiar with the words and doctrines of the Vul-
gate Bible. He knew all the intricacies of the
arts of the astrologers, physicians, alchemists,
and guileful men of religion, and he estimated
each at its true value. He knew the literature
of Rome, of Italy, and of France, and had read
much of it in the original languages; above
all, he knew the English people, their language
and books, — knew just how to paint their peculiar traits and life, and how to fuse the com-
posite elements of their speech into one language which should thenceforth be accepted as
the national tongue.

Chaucer's life was one of hard work, and it
was his thoroughness that enabled him to pro-
duce so much that is permanent. His literary
and public life were kept almost entirely distinct, and it is but glimpses of his own doings
and of the more private affairs about him that
we find in his writings. He suffers not his
pen to dwell upon the subjects which the author of Piers the Plowman so diligently elabo-
rated, — the sufferings of the people, "progress," "reform," are utterly ignored by him;
nor does he permit himself to treat of the stir-

ring events of his day, events some of which must have appealed to every sympathy of his nature.

As he records it for us, Chaucer's life is that of a purely literary man. We find him first dominated by the gay literature of France; then, filled with draughts from Italian founts, he writes his Rime of Sir Thopas, in which he ridicules the love-longing knights of whom Don Quixote was to be the last; and, as time matures his genius, the French gayety and Italian grace are fused, and united with the English pathos, sarcasm, and humor, in the Canterbury Tales. Age finds him suffering in patience, employing his mind by writing subdued tales and by teaching his little Lewis the mysteries of the Astrolabe, until, at the end, he is rewarded for all his toil by gaining a quiet home in which to die.

IV.

The consideration of an author's productions should, without doubt, be pursued in the chronological order, and much labor has been expended in the effort to discover with certainty at what time Chaucer composed his various works. This effort has been more thoroughly made by the scholars associated with the Chaucer Society, since its establishment, in 1866, than ever before, and in the society's publications is presented a tentative chronological arrangement of all the productions of Chaucer's pen, the grounds for which, though not considered conclusive, are there given in full.

Another important labor of the same body of scholars has been the separation of those works that can be considered authentic from those wrongly attributed to the poet, or printed among his works. In the present edition those poems of doubtful authenticity which it has been deemed best to insert are placed in a body after the others. The arrangement of the Canterbury Tales adopted by Mr. Furnivall in the publications of the Chaucer Society, which adds much to their interest, is here for the first time followed. It must not be considered, however, that either the chronological order of the poet's works, or the arrangement of his Canterbury Tales, has yet been satisfactorily determined.

Though Chaucer was preëminently a poet, one third of the total product of his pen is prose. Beside the Parson's Tale and the story of Melibeus, — which, singularly enough, he put into his own mouth, when his turn came among the pilgrims, — he translated the whole of the "Consolations of Philosophy," written by the Roman statesman Ancius Manlius Severinus Boethius in his imprisonment, in the sixth century. This remarkable work was wonderfully popular all through the Middle Ages, and it is not surprising that its striking style should have made a lasting impression upon Chaucer, who echoes its thoughts in many places. In an eloquent passage in the seventh volume of his " Decline and Fall of the Roman Empire," Gibbon says that the genius of Boethius survived to diffuse a ray of knowledge over the darkest ages of the Latin world ; and Hallam, in the first chapter of his "Literature of Europe," says : "In elevation of sentiment equal to any of the philosophers, and mingling a Christian sanctity with their lessons, he speaks from his prison in the swan-like tones of dying eloquence." Among the passages in which Chaucer shows his indebtedness to Boethius 's a noteworthy discussion of Predestination and Free-Will, in the fourth book of " Troylus and Cryseyde," beginning, —

" Syn God seth everythynge, oute of doutance,
    And hem desponeth thurgh his ordinance."

The theme was a favorite with the Schoolmen and with Chaucer, his story of Melibeus being an adaptation of another work on the consolations of Philosophy.

Twenty-four titles comprise the whole of Chaucer's authentic works. Three are assigned to the period during which he was under the French influence.

I. *The A B C, A Prayer to the Virgin.* This is a poem of twenty-three eight-line stanzas, each of which begins with a different letter of the alphabet. It is translated from a French poem written by a Cistercian monk, Guillaume de Deguilleville, about thirty years previous to Chaucer's use of it. The version is quite free.[1]

II. *A Complainte of the Deathe of Pitie.* A poem of seventeen stanzas of seven lines each.

III. *The Dethe of Blaunche the Duchesse.* A poem of thirteen hundred and thirty-four lines. It is assigned to the year 1369, and is generally supposed to refer to the mourning of John of Gaunt for his first wife, Blanche, the mother of Henry IV.

[1] There are many examples of poems in which each verse begins with a different letter of the alphabet, both in Hebrew and in Greek. Psalm cxlv. is a case in point in Hebrew, and the Virgins' Song, composed by Methodius, Bishop of Olympas, who died in the year 311, in Greek. The latter has been translated into English verse by the Reverend Allen W. Chatfield, in a volume published by Rivingtons, London

Eight titles are assigned to the second period of Chaucer's life, during which he was under the Italian influence, but nine of the Canterbury Tales are also supposed to be the product of the period.

IV. *The Parlement of Foules*. A poem of six hundred and ninety-four lines, showing considerable growth of the poetic faculty, and the beginning of the love of nature and of the humor which were to be more marked in the poet's future work. There are indications also of an acquaintance with Dante and Boccaccio, a number of the lines being adapted from the "Inferno" and the "Teseide."

V. *The Compleynt of Mars*. A poem of two hundred and ninety-eight lines, distributed into twenty-two seven-line stanzas and sixteen stanzas of nine lines.

VI. *The Compleynte of Faire Anelyda ana False Arcyte*. An apparently unfinished poem of three hundred and sixty lines, reminding one at its beginning of the Knight's tale of Palamon and Arcite. Chaucer acknowledges himself under obligations for the story to P. Papinius Statius, who wrote in the first century a poem embodying the legends regarding the expedition of the Seven against Thebes, as well as to a now forgotten writer, whom he calls Corinne.

VII. *De Consolatione Philosophiæ.* This is the translation from Boethius, already mentioned. In describing it Gibbon says that it is "a golden volume not unworthy the leisure of Plato or Tully, but which claims incomparable merit from the barbarism of the times and situation of the author. The celestial guide [Philosophy] whom he had so long invoked at Rome and Athens [1] now condescended to illumine his dungeon, to revive his courage, and to pour into his wounds her salutary balm. She taught him to compare his long prosperity and his recent distress, and to conceive new hopes from the inconstancy of fortune. Reason had informed him of the precarious condition of her gifts; experience had satisfied him of their real value; he had enjoyed them without guilt, he might resign them without a sigh and calmly disdain the impotent malice of his enemies, who had left him happiness since they had left him virtue. From the earth Boethius ascended to heaven in search of the supreme good; explored the metaphysical labyrinth of chance

---

[1] It is probable, however that Boethius did not study at Athens as it was formerly supposed that he did.

and destiny, of prescience and free-will, of time and eternity; and generously attempted to reconcile the perfect attributes of the Deity with the apparent disorder of his moral and physical government."

VIII. *The Former Age*. A poem of sixty-four lines, based upon a passage in the second book of the work just mentioned.

IX. *Troylus and Cryseyde*. A poem of eight thousand two hundred and fifty-three lines, distributed into five books. It relates the story of the love of the hero and heroine, so familiar to the readers of Shakespeare, but it differs from the tragedy by being confined to that subject. It is based upon the "Filostrato" of Boccaccio, of which, according to Mr. William M. Rossetti, two thousand seven hundred and thirty lines are condensed by Chaucer into two thousand five hundred and eighty-three, the remainder being original, or supplied from other sources. Professor Ten Brink says that Chaucer took his definition of a tragedy from one of Dante's minor works, and wrote his poem after rules laid down by him in another, and that the poem shows indebtedness also to the "Inferno" and "Purgatorio." His heroine is a finer character or his pages than either Boccaccio or Shakespeare exhibit her. Mr. Rossetti says that we have to thank Chaucer for "presenting English readers with [*sic*] one of the most delightful of English or possible poems — an entire and perfect chrysolite." He adds that it is "peculiarly memorable and unfailingly fascinating, as combining in itself at once the very topmost blossom and crown of the chivalric passion and gallantry, and the exquisite first-fruits of that humorous study of character in which our national writers have so especially excelled. This is the quality which culminated so superbly in Shakespeare."

X. *Chaucer's Words to Adam, his Scrivener.* A stanza of seven lines, in which the poet complains of his scrivener's carelessness.

XI. *The House of Fame.* A poetic allegory of two thousand one hundred and seventy lines, showing the uncertainty of fame. It contains passages indicating a familiarity with Dante and the classics. Professor Ten Brink says that the general plot is imitated from the "Divina Commedia," and that special passages were suggested by the "Inferno," "Paradiso," and "Purgatorio," respectively. The description of the house of rumors, with its telephonic communication with all regions, is an amplification of a passage from Ovid's "Metamorphoses." There are also references to Boethius and the Bible.

Five titles are ascribed to the next period, during which Chaucer became thoroughly English in his literary character, and conceived, or began to put into shape, his Canterbury Tales, — the most vivid delineations of English life in our literature. The General Prologue and ten of the tales are thought to have been written at this period.

XII. *The Legende of Goode Women.* A poem of two thousand seven hundred and twenty lines, comprising a prologue and nine "legends," derived from Ovid, Virgil, Livy, and other authors. The prologue is characteristic, exhibiting all of Chaucer's love of spring and flowers, and the other portions are not wanting in picturesqueness and force. The reason for recording the virtues of these "good" women is stated in the prologue to be that the poet had offended the god of Love by the "heresy" in his translation of the "Romaunt of the Rose," and in "Troylus and Cryseyde."

XIII. *The Canterbury Tales.* A poem of seventeen thousand three hundred and eighty five lines (with which are incorporated two prose pieces) comprising twenty-four tales told by twenty-three pilgrims representing the different classes of society, who are made by the fiction of the poet to meet at the Tabard Inn, Southwark, all bound for the shrine of Thomas à Becket at Canterbury.

The poem explains itself. It was composed in parts, from time to time, during all of Chaucer's literary life. At about 1388, the intention appears to have been formed of arranging the tales in the order in which they might have been told on a horseback ride occupying three or four days. Then the General Prologue was written — an unrivaled production — and some of the tales were put in order, being joined together by brief conversational links, and in other ways. The work was never completed. The stories were not all written, and those which were finished were not all linked together, provision being made for the extension of the series.

The Prologue tells us that there were " wel nine and twenty " pilgrims, or as we might say, " some nine and twenty," a statement that agrees with the list given, which in fact includes thirty   The Host and the Poet

with the Canon and his Yeoman, who overtook
the party, raise the total to thirty-four.

In this group the different social classes are
represented in the following proportion. There
were three women; nine persons who may be
said to belong to the Church; four who stand
for the learned professions outside of the
Church; two, the Knight and his Squire, who
still supported the customs of chivalry; four-
teen are from the world of workers; and two,
the Franklin and Plowman, are the exponents
of country living. The characters are carefully
selected, the workers being in the majority, as
they should be in a well ordered society; the
churchmen coming next, as they actually did;
and the women being few, — the ladies none,
— as a mixed company of the sort would be
congenial only to a blatant Wife of Bath, or en-
durable to a Prioress or a Nun, who might consider it an opportunity for good works.

It is impossible to decide at what date the
particular tales were written, but in a general
way they have been assigned by Mr. Furnivall
to Chaucer's early life, middle age, and maturer
years, as follows : —

Eight tales of a pathetic nature, treating of
love in various phases, are attributed to the
first period : —

1. The Second Nun's story of St. Cecilia.

2. The Prioress's story of the Christian child killed by the Jews.

3. The Man of Law's story of Pious Custance.

4. The Clerk's tale of Patient Griselda.

5. The Doctor of Physic's story of Virginius and Virginia.

6. The Knight's tale of Palamon and Arcite.

7. The Squire's tale of Cambuscan.

8. The Franklin's tale of the removal of rocks by magic.

In middle life Chaucer is supposed to have composed his twelve humorous tales : —

1. The Nun's Priest's tale of the Cock and the Fox.

2. The Miller's tale of Nicholas and Absolon.

3. The Reeve's tale of Symkin the Miller.

4. The Cook's unfinished story of Perkin Revellour.

5. The Merchant's story of the Pavian knight, January, and his wife, May.

6. The Wife of Bath's fairy tale.

7. The Shipman's story of the duped merchant.

8. The Manciple's story of the Crow.

9. The Friar's tale of the Summoner.

10. The Summoner's story of the Friar Lim-
itor.

11. The Pardoner's tale of the Rioters.

12. The Canon's Yeoman's story of the Al-
chemist.

To the poet's latest years four tales are assigned : —

1. His own incomplete Rime of Sir Thopas.

2. His story of Melibeus.

3. The Monk's examples of fallen great
ones.[1]

4. The Parson's sermon on Penitence.

This very interesting arrangement gives a
probable indication of the progress of the
author's genius, but it is not to be supposed
that he intended the stories to be read in such
an order.   He designed that they should come
before the reader as he imagined them to have
been heard by the pilgrims on the journey.
Forty-six miles were to be passed over.   The
tales were evidently all told on the way to
Canterbury, three days and a half or four days
being occupied by the journey.

---

[1] Professor Child, Mr. Skeat, and others do not agree with Mr
Furnivall that the Monk's tale was written late.   For a discussion
of this point, see the Introduction to the volume in the series of the
Clarendon Press containing Mr. Skeat's text of the tales of the Prioress, the Monk, and others.

In the General Prologue we become acquainted with each of the interesting group of
pilgrims, and learn that when they started on
their way, the morning after the meeting at
the Tabard, the Knight drew the shortest cut,
and in accordance with the "forward," or
agreement, began the story of Palamon and
Arcite, the outline of which is taken from Boccaccio's " Teseide."

When the Knight had finished he was warm-
ly congratulated by the "gentles," and all the
party agreed that the story was a noble one.
The Miller was then called upon, though he
was drunken and unsteady, and he related a
licentious tale, for which Chaucer apologizes,
saying that he must report the words of the
pilgrims, be they better or worse, and that
those who do not like it may find on other
leaves stories of "gentilesse" (gentility) and
even of morality and holiness. The origin of
the story has not been discovered. It shows
plainly the growing disrespect felt and exhib-
ited towards churchmen.

There were different opinions among the
pilgrims upon this story, but for the most part
they laughed at it. Oswald, the Reve, did not
laugh, however, for it was not complimentary

to carpenters, and he was a carpenter. He
"quoke" with ire and said that he would be
even with the drunken Miller. As the party
arrived at Depford the Reve began his tale of
the "begiled" miller, which was of no higher
moral tone than the one that had just been
told. It was a favorite story in the Middle
Ages, and had been used by Boccaccio.

The Cook laughed heartily at the _dénoû-
ment,_ and asked leave to tell a "litel jape"
that happened in his town once. The Host
acceded, but in doing so made a remark that
provoked the Cook to threaten to tell a tale of
a host at a future time, to make himself even
with Harry Bailly. He then began to tell
about Perkin the Revellour, but his story is
abruptly ended on these pages with an impa-
tient remark by Chaucer, who seems to have
suddenly arrived at the conclusion that he had
allowed the tales of license to go far enough.

With this the first day's ride ended, leaving
the pilgrims at Dartford, fifteen miles from the
Tabard.

The next morning, the 18th of May, the
Host called upon the Man of Law for his tale,
and a little conversation ensued, in the course
of which Chaucer gave an outline of his plan

for the "Legende of Goode Women,"— a plan
that he never fully carried out. He intended
to write it year by year, as he composed the
Canterbury Tales. The Man of Law related
the very interesting story of the sufferings and
reward of pious Constance, which had been
told by Gower, and by others long before his
day.

With a fashionable oath, the Host then
called upon the Parson for a tale, but that
worthy exclaimed, "What eyleth the man so
synfully to swere?" This led the company
to suspect that the Parson was a Lollard, and
he did not deny an insinuation to that effect. Hereupon the Shipman declared that no
preaching was wanted, that they all believed
the gospel and wished no "cockle" sown
among them, and, finally, that *he* would wake
up the company with a tale, not of philosophy,
nor of physic, nor of law. He gave them a
story of much grossness, but considerable humor, which had also been included in the
"Decamerone."

At its close the burly Host expressed his de-
cided approval of it, and asked the Prioress to
favor the company with a tale. She assented,
and related the story of the child slain by Jews

'n Asia. It was a marvelous legend, but its only effect upon the Host was to cause him to " jape " more, and he immediately made a demand upon Chaucer for a tale of mirth, " some deynte " thing, and the poet responded by beginning the Rime ot Sir Thopas, in which he burlesqued the usages of chivalry. It was one of those stories which, having no natural end, might go on forever, and the Host stopped it with much impatience, in the midst of the second " fit," and asked for something in prose. He was even willing to take " doctrine," and Chaucer gave it to him with emphasis in the tale of Melibeus, which is little more than a translation of the philosophical work of Albertano of Brescia, entitled " Consolatione et Consilii." [1]

The Host was satisfied, and said that he would have given a barrel of ale to have had his shrew of a wife hear of the patience of Melibeus's wife, dame Prudence. He then made some bantering remarks to the worthy Monk and asked for his story, at the same time indicating the progress of the pilgrims by say-

---

[1] The work of Albertano, edited by Thor Sunby, of Copenhagen, was published by the Chaucer Society, in 1873. In that edition the Biblical and classical allusions and references are very carefully traced to their sources.

ing that they had nearly reached Rochester.
The tale which followed was a series of verses
on the fall of great men, similar to the work of
Boccaccio, "De Casibus Virorum Illustrium."
Before it had reached a natural end the Host
exclaimed that he could endure it no longer,
but would like to hear something about hunting. The Monk replied with dignity that he
was not in the humor for that, whereupon the
Nun's Priest was asked to make his contribu-
tion to the enjoyment of the company. His
tale was the old story of the Cock and the Fox,
but it was adorned by Chaucer's humorous
genius.

Here the second day ended, at Rochester,
thirty miles from London.

The tales of the third day opened with the
story of Virginia, told by the Doctor of Physic.
It is in the "Romaunt of the Rose" and in
Gower's "Confessio Amantis," but seems rather
to have been taken by Chaucer directly from
Livy. It excited the wrath of the Host ex-
ceedingly, and he cursed the false Appius, but
finally became calm enough to ask the Pardoner for the next story That charlatan said
that he must take a drink and a bite of cake
first the "gentles" of the party showing their

opinion of the class to which he belonged by demanding that he should give them no rib-aldry. While he was drinking he explained his mode of selling relics, and showed the hypocrite that he was. He then told a story of certain rioters, ostentatiously making it a warning against gluttony and dice, after which he closed by offering his relics for sale.

The Wife of Bath followed with a long dissertation on wedlock, illustrated by her own experience. It caused the Friar to laugh, which brought about a vituperative colloquy between him and the Summoner, which the Host interrupted, and demanded the Wife's tale. She willingly gave a characteristic story of the times of King Arthur, intended to illustrate her view that what women want most and ought to have is their own will. It contains quotations from Dante and the "Romaunt of the Rose." In its essentials the story had been told by Gower.

At this point a storm that had been long brewing broke out between the Summoner and the Friar, and each told a story aimed at the other. After a remark about the difficulty of the theme treated by the Wife, and after deprecating doctrinal stories, the Friar concluded with an offer to tell his tale, which should be about a summoner, of whom all knew no good could be said. To this the Summoner replied that he was ready for the worst, and would give as good as was sent.

The Friar's story was about a summoner who was carried off by the arch fiend. It made the member of the party at whom it was aimed more angry than he expected to be, but he asked only to be allowed to tell his tale about the friar, which he proceeded to do. After this the pilgrims seem to have halted for dinner, at Sittingbourne, forty miles from London.

After dinner, if the above supposition is correct, the Host abruptly called for a tale from the Clerk of Oxenford, who gave the story of the extravagant patience of Griselda, which was older than Boccaccio, who had recounted it. Chaucer followed a Latin version. In a few stanzas which he added, he indulged in a sly thrust at Griselda, and referred to the storied beast of mediæval times, called "Chichevache," [1] who fed upon patient wives, of whom

---

[1] The word Chichevache seems to contain a reference to the lean kine of Pharaoh, and is a corruption of the French *chicheface*, one whose meanness is impressed on his face. (*Chiche*, stingy; *face*, face; *vache*, cow.)

he found so small a supply as to be usually half starved.

The tale of Griselda led the Merchant to bemoan his matrimonial infelicity, upon hearing which the Host demanded a story founded upon his experience, but he declined to probe his own sore further, and gave an account of the troubles of January and May, of which a version had long been extant in Latin. It led to a few words by the Host *à-propos* of bad wives, a topic upon which experience made him fluent, after which the stories ceased for the day, the party resting at Ospring, forty-six miles from London.

The next morning the Host called out the Squire, who gave the tale, a fruit of Oriental fancy, by which Milton characterizes Chaucer's genius, full of picturesque descriptions and gorgeous imagery. Mr. Skeat says that the materials for the story came from the "Arabian Nights' Entertainments" and the travels of Marco Polo.[1] Notwithstanding that the story is, as Milton says, but "half told," and ends in the midst of a sentence, the Frank

---

[1] The reader of the Squire's Tale who does not refer to the admirable remarks of Mr. Skeat, in his introduction to his edition of it published by the Clarendon Press, will be the loser. All that Mr Skeat has written bears the marks of his acute and exact scholarship

in proceeded and told how carefully he snubbed his son when he played with dice and went into low society, in order to train him in "gentilesse." "A straw for your gentilesse!" exclaimed the Host, "tell on thy tale withouten wordes mo!" With an apology for his want of polish, the Franklin told a story that he said he had derived from an ancient Breton lay. It was the fiction of the magical removal of rocks from the Armorican coast, which had been used by Boccaccio in his "Decamerone" and "Filicopo." In the midst of its low morality occurs the line so highly praised by Mr. Lowell, —

"Trouthe is the hyeste thyng that man may kepe."[1]

The Second Nun's tale of St. Cecilia followed, but the words of connection, if ever written, have been lost. It is a translation from the "Legenda Aurea," a work written before 1300, and had evidently been prepared by Chaucer as a complete work, and long after incorporated into the Canterbury Tales. The party was then overtaken, at Boughton-under-Blean, by a Canon and his Yeoman. The former was a schemer, whose tricks his servant so circumstantially exposed that he in

Line 16,255. See *My Study Windows*, page 231

continently left in shame. The Yeoman's tale,
which was then told, proved to be a vigorous
satire of the alchemists, in the form of an ac
count of the deception practiced by a false
canon, not the one who had just fled.

At this point an altercation ensued between
the Cook and the Manciple, in the course of
which the former was thrown from his horse.
He was, by dint of much tugging, reseated,
after which the Manciple gave an amusing
version of Ovid's story of the Crow. Chaucer
seems to have forgotten that the Cook had
told a tale on the first morning, — or perhaps
he did not count it, as it was unfinished, —
and asked him for another, but the man had
drunk too much to be able to do anything but
quarrel.

It was four o'clock in the afternoon when
the Manciple concluded, upon which the Host
made a second demand upon the Parson, and
was successful in getting a sermon. It was
long enough to dismay those who had feared
lest the good man should prove a Wiclifite
who would sow tares in their orthodox hearts.[1]
It may well have been sundown before the
dreaded "predication" was finished. It was

[1] For a discussion of the question of the theological sympathies of
the Parson, see *Chaucer a Wiclifit*, by M. H. Simon, of Schmal-
kaiden, Hesse-Carsel, published by the Chaucer Society

evidently intended to complete the work, but it is equally plain that all the stories were not written that were to have gone before it.

It is followed by a prayer or retraction, in which Chaucer asks his readers to pray God to have mercy on him for his sins in general, and especially for the "worldly vanities" in his books, some of which he mentions by name; and he prays himself that he may be blessed in this life and saved "at the day of doom." The authenticity of this has been much dis cussed, but there appears to be no conclusive reason for rejecting it. It may well express the poet's feelings as he closed his life in the garden of St. Mary's, and if it does not, it still remains an eminently orthodox appendage to his writings, and must have been accepted as such by his first readers, who would never have thought of questioning its authenticity. Indeed, doubt was almost unknown in the four-teenth century.[1]

XIV. *Good Counsel of Chaucer.* A poem of twenty-eight lines in praise of truth.

[1] In all of the above remarks upon the Canterbury Tales, it has been thought best not to criticise the arrangement of them, nor their dis-tribution through the four days, because no better scheme has yet been worked out, and this one, thought not in all respects satisfactory has a certain consistency; besides, the entire fabric is an incomplete fable, though a wonderfully life-like and brilliant one.

XV. *Prayer to the Virgin*. A religious poem of one hundred and forty lines, which, it is suggested, may have been composed for Queen Anne of Bohemia.

XVI. *A Proverb*. Eight lines teaching that avarice overreaches itself.

Eight titles are assigned to the fourth period in the poet's life, in addition to five of the Canterbury Tales.

XVII. *A Treatise on the Astrolabe*. This is entitled *Tractatus de Conclusionibus Astrolabii*, or Bred and Mylk for Children. It is a prose description of the instrument and its use, addressed to the poet's son, Louis.

XVIII. *The Compleynt of Venus*. A poem of eighty-two lines, which is usually printed with the " Compleynt of Mars."

XIX. *Lines to Scogan*. A poem of forty-nine lines addressed to Henry Scogan, a courtier noted for his wit, who is mentioned by Shallow, in " 2 King Henry IV.," iii. 2, as having had his head broken.

XX. *Lines to Bukton*. Thirty-two lines on the subject of marriage, in which the Wife of Bath is referred to.

XXI. *Gentilnesse*. A ballad of twenty-one

lines, in which Christ is exalted as " the first fader and finder of gentilness," an idea that is enlarged upon by the Wife of Bath.

XXII. *A Ballad sent to King Richard.* Twenty-eight lines bewailing the decline of Steadfastness and lauding Truth.

XXIII. *Visage sanz Peinture.* A ballad of seventy-eight lines. It seems to be a translation from the French, and is a complaint of the fickleness of Fortune. It may have been used as a petition for office.

XXIV. *Compleynte to his Purse.* A poem of twenty-six lines addressed to King Henry IV., in view of the author's poverty.

Attention has already been called to one of the most important results of the establishment of the Chaucer Society, — the separation of the poet's authentic works from those which have been wrongly attributed to him. All editions of Chaucer contain some compositions that are acknowledged to be spurious. The edition of John Urry, for instance, published in 1721, comprises more than two spurious titles for every one that is authentic, and it is a curious fact that a number of them are assigned to other writers in the volume itself. The prose

" Testament of Love " is one of the productions
that editors have most persistently retained, on
account of the supposed biographical incidents
that it contains, though the best critics at the
present refuse to believe that it can possibly be
one of the poet's writings. A perusal of it
would seem to be all that is necessary to lead
every one to accept this conclusion.

Two spurious tales are often printed among
those of the Canterbury Pilgrims, — one being
assigned to the Plowman and the other to the
Cook, or, more appropriately, to the Yeoman.
The latter is a pleasant story, and is interesting
because it was possibly in the mind of Shakespeare when he wrote " As you Like It."   It is
the story of "Gamelyn."

Another poem usually included with Chaucer's is " The Complaint of a Lover's Life,"
which Mr. Skeat says " is now known, on manuscript authority, to be Lydgate's ; and the
critic who knows Lydgate's style will not dis-
pute this."   For various reasons ten of this
class of poems are grouped at the end of this
edition.

I. *The Romaunt of the Rose.*   This is a poem
of seven thousand nine hundred and sixty-
eight lines, translated from a French composi

tion by Guillaume de Lorris and Jean de Meun, one of whom continued the work of the other after an interval of some thirty years, in the thirteenth century. Two thirds of the original are omitted in the English version that we have, which is from a manuscript of the fifteenth century. Its interest to us consists in the fact that Chaucer made a translation of the original, though the version now extant is by another hand.

II. *The Court of Love.* A poem of one thousand four hundred and forty-lines, written at about 1500, the original manuscript being in the library of Trinity College, Cambridge. It is spoken of by its author as a little treatise addressed to his lady, and he gives in it an account of his experience at the court of Venus. It ends with an allegorical paraphrase of the morning service for Trinity Sunday, sung by a choir of birds in honor of the god of Love.

III. *The Flower and the Leaf.* A poem of five hundred and ninety-five lines, written probably at about 1450, in the allegorical form, either by a woman, or in the person of one.

IV. *The Cuckow and the Nightingale.* A poem of three hundred and seventeen lines in the same style of composition as the one just

mentioned, embodying the sentiments and su
perstitions connected with birds and flowers.

V. *A Goodly Ballad.* Sixty-four lines ad
dressed to a lady apparently named Margaret.

VI. *A Praise of Women.* A poem of one
hundred and seventy-five lines.

VII. *Chaucer's Dream.* An allegorical poem
of two thousand two hundred and thirty-five
lines, first published in 1598. It appears to be
intended merely as an imitation of the style
and language of Chaucer.

VIII. *A Virelay.* A lyric of forty lines.

IX. *Chaucer's Prophecy.* Thirteen lines of
doleful foreboding, ending with a prayer.

X. *Go forth King.* Sixteen lines of moral
advice to various classes, from the king down-
ward.

V.

The genius of Chaucer was an exceptional
development of our literature in the fourteenth
century, and there is but one author among
those who have risen since whose productions
are commanding enough to make us wish to
modify the words of Sir Philip Sidney, " I
know not whether to marvel more, either that
he in that misty age could see so clearly, or

that we in this clear age walk so stumblingly after him."

Chaucer furnishes one of the rare instances In which the contemporary verdict agrees with that pronounced in subsequent times. He was immediately appreciated and honored, at home as well as abroad, as the poet of his country. The prosy Gower saw his own position in the ranks of authorship made less prominent as young Chaucer stepped above him, and he welcomed his rival to the greater honors, singing in his "Confessio Amantis," that even in his youth Chaucer had filled all the land with the fame of his songs and ditties.

From over the Channel, too, the poet Eustache Deschamps sent verses in which he lauded Chaucer as a Socrates in philosophy, a Seneca in morals, an Ovid for grace, and in conduct an angel, — as one who by his noble style, sweet melody, and graceful imagery had already made Britain illustrious and strewn its language with flowers. Eustache was probably thirty or forty years older than Chaucer, and lauded him as the great translator, apparently for his version of the "Romaunt of the Rose," which naturally commended him to a Frenchman.

John Lydgate, the mechanical poet of Bury, was a younger man and took a more comprehensive view of Chaucer's works; probably he was more familiar with them. He did not forget his prose, and made special mention of his translation of Boethius and his treatise on the Astrolabe, describing the latter as "full noble and of gret prise." Lydgate says that Chaucer was the

"Floure of poetes throughout all Bretaine,"

gives him credit for a lofty moral purpose, and finally says, —

"Sith he of Engl'sh of making was the best,
Pray unto God to geve his soule good rest."

Thomas Occleve, a little older than Lydgate, is, if possible, still more unstinted in his praise, and in his book, "De Regimine Principis,' bewails Chaucer's death in stanzas of which the following lines will give some idea : —

"O Dethe ! thou didest not harme singulere
In slaughtre of hym, but alle this londe it smerteth ;
But natheles yet hast thou no powere
His name to slee ; his hye vertu asterteth
Unslayne fro the."

The list of Chaucer's eulogists might be

extended indefinitely, but his fame and position in the world of letters are too well established to make anything more of the kind necessary.   His name shone bright when Spenser took him for his master, and intervening
time had made it only the more natural that
in our very day William Morris should do the
same.   The hearty words of this last-mentioned
poet deserve quotation.   He says, in the "Life
and Death of Jason," book xvii. : —

"Would that I
Had but some portion of that mastery
That from the rose-hung lanes of woody Kent
Through these five hundred years such songs has sent
To us, who, meshed within this smoky net
Of unrejoicing labor, love them yet.
And thou, O Master, — yea, my Master still,
Whatever feet have scaled Parnassus' hill,
Since, like thy measures, clear and sweet and strong,
Thames' stream scarce fettered bore the bream along
Unto the bastioned bridge, its only chain, —
O Master, pardon me, if yet in vain
Thou art my Master, and I fail to bring
Before men's eyes the image of the thing
My heart is filled with : thou whose dreamy eyes
Beheld the flush to Cressid's cheeks arise,
As Troilus rode up the praising street,
As clearly as they saw thy townsmen meet
Those who in vineyards of Poictou withstood
The glittering horror of the steel-topped wood."

As we look at Chaucer now in the light of his works, we find it difficult to think of him as a man whose career closed centuries ago, for his pages are fresh with the perfume of flowers, and his pictures glow with a life and animation as real as that which we see around us all the time. He had the heart of a man, which he poured out in human sympathy. We cannot make him an antique in his scholarship, nor in his mental action. He is " our learned Chaucer," no less than he was Milton's. His words, at first sight, appear ancient, but when we come to understand his way of using them they lead us so gayly tripping through his lines, and are so limpid and simple, both in prose and in verse, that we wonder why men have not always since followed his literary example. He is wise and skillful as an artist, but he is the simplest and most artless of story-tellers. He is picturesque and dramatic in his manner of putting his men and women before us. He is genial, hearty, and sincere, always following artistic and moral truth. He is the poet of love and good-will, and cares not to treat of war and hate. If he tells the story of Troylus and Cryseyde, he confines his attention to their love, never letting the seductive possibil ities of the theme draw him into descriptions of the warriors and the strife which Shakespeare handled with such surpassing mastery.

He was a man, and therefore had the humors of a man; but he was himself most completely when the sunshine illumined his path and gave him liberty to indulge to the fullest his love of wit and kindly satire, or burlesque. It is pretty safe to conclude, as some one has said, that in his soberer passages he is following the lead of "myn olde auctor," of "Stace," or "Boece," or "Daunt;" and it is equally sure that in his passages of humor he is following no man's style, but only permitting his own nature to play with his theme, or indulging in the sly and subtle strokes which no "auctor," be he old or new, could have imagined, but Dan Geoffrey only.

It is usual to say that our poet was never melancholy or drooping, and it is true enough if he is considered merely as the author of the Canterbury Tales. It must not be forgotten, however, that it was the same Chaucer whom we have heard mourning for the loss of the bliss of the former age, and moaning as he contemplated the lack of steadfastness in his own time. It is true that he could not restrain his naïve humor even when he was bitterly complaining of the emptiness of his purse, but he was none the less "sory" for his lack of the yellow coins that his necessities humbled him to beg. It was he who cried out in view of the insufficiency of worldly happiness, —

"Here is none home, — her nys but wildernesse ; "

and it was he who bewailed the death of Pity, and said, —

"Thus for youre dethe I may wel wepe and pleyne
    With herte sore, al ful of busy peyne."

Chaucer could rebuke pretty sharply, and threaten as vigorously as a sterner man when his poor scrivener, Adam, made errors in his work.

We have remarked that Chaucer's prose was neither inconsiderable in amount nor inferior in style. It exhibits few of the traits most commonly attributed to him as an author, and is the work of a translator, who, however, felt free to enlarge, compress, or alter his original in accordance with his object or his taste.

Chaucer's treatment of the ecclesiastics accords in most respects with the fashion of the day, as seen especially in the " Vision of Piers the Plowman " and the works of Wiclif, though he paints in glowing colors the virtues of the Parson, and enlivens the whole subject with his hearty mirth. The Wife of Bath speaks with exquisite irony of

> "The grete charite and preyeres
> Of lymytours and other holy freres,"

who are the only incubuses in the land, and the "holy" men are in many passages made the butts of "japes" which a coarse social sentiment only would permit the recital of.

For woman Chaucer has many harsh or slighting words, such as his age called for, — such as every age demanded until man's help-mate had become free from some of her disabilities and been given a fair share in the production and criticism of literature, — but he compensated for the rudeness, in some measure at least, by making dame Prudence, in his tale on the pilgrimage, stand rather above her sweet-named husband, as his worthy adviser, as well as by his formal apology in the "Legende of Goode Women." If the latter was a perfunctory performance, it can hardly be supposed that anything but a hearty faith prompted the eulogy of matrimonial bliss in the Merchant's Tale. The sympathetic tears must have trickled down his cheeks as he traced the lines describing the pitiful resignation of Griselda when she laid on her lap the little child she was about to lose,

> "And lulled it, and after gan it blisse."

It was no anchorite and no trifling humorist who wrote the tender passage setting forth the life of pious Custance, and depicted her parting from her babe : —

> "Hir litel child lay wepyng in hir arm,
> And knelynge, pitously to hym she seyde,
> 'Pees, litel sone, I wol do thee noon harm!'
> With that hir kerchef of hir heed she breyde,
> And over hise litel eyen she it leyde,
> And in hir arm she lulleth it ful faste,
> And in-to hevene hire eyen up she caste."

It was no stickler for conventionalities who made righteousness the standard of " gentleness " (nobility) and anticipated Thomas Dekker in pointing to Jesus Christ as

> "The first true gentleman who ever breathed."

Chaucer's character is best studied in his works, but the student must have an acquaintance with his times and with the active share that the poet took in the national movements. When all is considered, Chaucer will be found a well-rounded man, respectful to his fellows and reverential to his God, child-like in his simplicity, and manful in his championship of the Truth.

CAMBRIDGE, *May,* 1879.

ON READING CHAUCER.

MANY readers unfamiliar with Early English find themselves repelled from Chaucer by the difficulties they see in the ancient construction and orthography, who would be able to derive pleasure from his works if they had a few easy rules to guide them. If the poems be modernized the charm is lost, as any one learns when he masters the subject, and no thorough student of Chaucer whom we have known has been willing either to reduce his orthography to uniformity, or to write his poems over in the fashion of to-day.

It is true that Dryden thought it necessary to "translate" Chaucer into what he called the refined English of his time, though he confessed that "something must be lost in all transfusion, that is, in all translations." He considered Chaucer a "rough diamond" which needed to be polished before it would shine, — that it was necessary to add to the "dignity" of Chaucer's productions by omitting

some of his "trivialities" and redundancies.
Dryden had been translating Ovid, and considered that he was doing the same sort of work
when he gave a seventeenth-century form to a
poet who wrote in the fourteenth century. Let
us see how he succeeded. Take ten lines from
the Knight's Tale in his recension and com
pare them with Chaucer. Dryden gives us, —

> "In days of old there lived, of mighty fame,
> A valiant Prince, and Theseus was his name ;
> A chief, who more in feats of arms excelled,
> The rising nor the setting sun beheld.
> Of Athens he was lord ; much land he won,
> And added foreign countries to his crown.
> In Scythia with the warrior Queen he strove,
> Whom first by force he conquered, then by love ;
> He brought in triumph back the beauteous dame,
> With whom her sister, fair Emilia, came."

We turn to Chaucer and read, —

> "Whilom, as oldè stories tellen us,
> Ther was a duc that hightè Theseus ;
> Of Atthenes he was lord and governour,
> And in his tymè swich a conquerour,
> That gretter was ther noon under the sonne
> Ful many a richè contree hadde he wonne ;
> That with his wysdom and his chivalrie
> He conquered al the regne of Femenye.
> That whilom was ycleped Scithia ;
> And weddedè the queene Ypolita,

And broghte hire hoom with hym in his contree
With muchel glorie and greet solempnytee,
And eek hir fairè suster Emelye."

The first may be good verse, it may be en-
tertaining, but it is evidently not Chaucer.
The flavor, the "bouquet" of the old writer
has fled. It does not appear that any great
knowledge of Old English is needed to understand the second extract. The only word over
which the ordinary reader would probably hesi-
tate is " Femenye," and a little thought makes
it clear that " al the regne of Femenye " means
all the kingdom, or realm, of the Amazons, or
feminine warriors, of which Hippolita was sovereign.

The following suggestions are mainly condensed from the writings of Professor Child, of
Harvard University, and Mr. Alexander J. Ellis,
of England.[1]

I. It must be remembered that Chaucer
wrote before the days of printed books, that he
addressed the ear rather than the eye, and that
the scribes whose manuscripts have come down
to us indulged in much orthographic variety.
The poems were read to others by persons able

[1] See *Memoirs of the American Academy*, vols. vii., ix.; and
Early English Pronunciation, pt. i., pp. 241–416. The latter was
published by the Early English Text Society in 1867

to recite them in the proper rhythm, and who had probably greater intellectual attainments than their auditors. A word that appears strange to the eye is often very clear to the ear if an attempt be made to pronounce it, and this is especially true if the reader understand the sounds of the vowels in the fourteenth century.

II. Letters are often reversed in order, or changed, as in *meve, preve, chese, brest, brid, crull, thurgh,* for move, prove, choose, burst, bird, curl, through.

III. The definite article is often contracted by the omission of the vowel, and joined to a word following that begins with a vowel, as *theffect, thencrese, thencens, thenchauntementz, thentre,* for the effect, tne increase, the incense, the enchantments, the entrance.

IV. *Y* stands for the prefix *ge* (as in German) ; *y-clept, y-haten,* for named, called.

V. *Ch* is used where *k* is now written, as in *seche, wirch, thenche, yliche, schenche,* for seek, work, think, like, skink.

VI. *K* is used where *ch* now occurs, as *biseke* for beseech.

VII. *W* is used where we now write *y,* or *i* as *dawes, faw, i-slaw,* for days, fain, slain.

VIII. *D* sometimes stands for *th*, and *vice versa*, as *fader, moder, weder, whider, gader, rother*, for father, mother, weather, whither, gather, rudder.

IX. *Ne* negative is often joined to the following word, as *I not, I nam, I nas, I nold*, for I know not, I am not, I was not, I would not.

X. Two negatives are often used, as in very Early English, as "*I nam no divinistre*," I am no diviner.

XI. *To* and *for* are used as intensive prefixes, as *to-break, for-spent, for-lorn*, to break to pieces, completely used up, entirely lost.

XII. *Gesse* means to think, as in New England.

XIII. *Do* means to cause, as *do to deye, don wrought*, cause to die, caused to be made.

XIV. *Eth* marks the imperative mode, as *listeneth*, listen.

XV. The order of words is often inverted, as *al that a man belongeth unto*, all that belongeth unto a man.

XVI. Many words are apparently contractions, as *ferne, halwe, bet, ferre*, foreign, saint (hallowed), better, farther.

XVII. *En*, often contracted into *e*, marks

the infinitive mode, as *tellen, speken, speke*, for tell, speak.

XVIII. *Toon, tother, atone, atwynne*, mean the one, the other, reconcile, separate.

XIX. German and French words often ex plain those of Chaucer, as *wone*, dwell (German, *wohnen*), *maugre*, in spite of (French, *mal-gré*), *verray*, true (French, *vrai*), *purchas*, any-thing acquired (French, *pourchasser*).

XX. Many contracted forms are allowed, and in many cases a foreign pronunciation is given to words, as *wostow, farforthly, somdel, parde, were*, which mean knowest thou, as far forth (far forth like), some deal, *par dieux* (by the gods), who were. *Glorie* (see line 870),[1] and *contrarie* (see line 17,877), are sometimes pronounced like the French *gloire* and *con-traire*. See also *constable*, line 5216. *Con-trarie* is rhymed with *debonaire* in "Troylus and Cryseyde," i. 212, 214. *Coverchief* is pro-nounced in two syllables at line 272 of the "Parlement of Foules" (where, in fact, it was so written by the scribe, who omitted the let-ters *er*), making it resemble our kerchief, or the French *couvrechef*. The words *nevere* and *levere* are examples of the same contraction

---

[1] The references, when not otherwise indicated, are to lines of the *Canterbury Tales*

the letters *er* being often omitted by the scribes and by the reader, as in lines 16,298, 16,307, and many others. This practice was not uniform. In line 732 the scribe contracts *evere*, and in line 734 he writes *never* in full, but without the final *e*. The syllable *er* is omitted by the scribe in the following cases, in the Ellesmere MS.: pe*r*turben, line 906, pe*r*petuelly, line 1176, Pe*r*otheus, line 1205, me*r*cy, line 1757, prove*r*be, line 3391, pe*r*son, line 3977, ce*r*tein, line 4666. *Benedicite* is sometimes pronounced ben'cité, as at lines 5592, 6396, 17,028, while at other times it is uttered in full, as at line 1785.

XXI. A large proportion of the words in Chaucer that appear difficult are found more fully explained in the dictionaries of Worcester and Webster than in the ordinary editions of the poet's works.

In pronouncing Chaucer it is necessary to remember that spelling was in some respects more nearly phonetic than it now is, and that syllables now unpronounced were formerly heard. The final *e* was, for example, pronounced in many cases, and in verse it often perfects the metre and adds to the musical effect.

Mr. Skeat classes the final *e's* as (1) Essen
tial, (2) Grammatical, and (3) Superfluous.

The Essential final *e* represents an Old Eng·
lish or Latin termination, as *stede* (O. E. *steda*)
diademe (Latin, *diadema*).

The Grammatical final *e* represents a dative
or a genitive case, an adjectival, a verbal, or
an adverbial form.

The Superfluous final *e* is added by license
for the metre, as in line 7960, where *queene*
represents the O. E. *cwen*, or in line 15,109,
where *betwixe* is the O. E. *betweox*. This
license was also used, in O. E. at least, in the
cases of *cwen* and *betweox*, quoted by Mr. Skeat.
Cwene is found in the " Ancren Riwle ; " *betwixe*
in Layamon, a century before Chaucer ; *cwena*
was used by Alfred the Great in the ninth
century, and *cwene* by the writer of the Chron-
icle, in the eleventh century.

Mr. Skeat's views concerning the final *e* are
essentially those of Tyrwhitt, Child, Ellis, and
Morris. Professor Child has published an
elaborate inquiry into its use in the paper
contributed to the " Memoirs of the American
Academy," already mentioned, the principal
portions of which are incorporated in the ex
tensive work, above referred to, on Early Eng-

lish Pronunciation, by A. J. Ellis, published by the Early English Text and Chaucer Societies.

Exception was taken to the views of Mr. Skeat by the late Professor Joseph Payne, of the Philological Society, whose hypothesis is presented in an essay published by the Chaucer Society in 1874. Mr. Payne held that "when Chaucer wrote the Canterbury Tales, the final *e* had become little more than a modal orthographic note of spelling, scarcely, if at all, recognized in common parlance, while at the same time the use of it as an element of rhythmical composition was freely admitted. It was therefore adopted at the will of the poet, wherever thought necessary, in the middle of his verse (except at the sectional pause, where as a rule it was silent), but not at the end, where it was unnecessary."

There is little difficulty with regard to the consonants, though the following hints will be of service.

C is hard before *a*, *o*, *u*, and consonants, as *cow*, *clerk ;* soft before *e*, *i*, and *y*, as *cell*, *city ;* and never *sh*, as in *vicious*, which should be pronounced vi-si-us.

Ch is always hard, as in *cheese*, and is some‑ times sounded like *k*, in words from the Greek, as *christen*.

S final was frequently sharp, as in *hiss*. It was never sounded like *sh*, or *zh*, as in *vision*, which was pronounced in three syllables.

Tion, sion, cion, were pronounced *sĭ-on*.

U consonant is equivalent to *v*, though the use of *u* and *v* is irregular in the MSS., and is not followed in the present text.

Y consonant has the sound of *y* in *yet*, but *y* vowel was usually sounded like *i* in *pin*.

The chief vowel sounds are the following : —

A long is equivalent to *a* in *father*, *alms*. The sound of *a* in *same* did not arise till two centuries after Chaucer.

A short is like no sound now heard in re‑ ceived English. It is the continental short *a* heard in the French *chat*.

Aa is equivalent to *a* long, above.

Ai is equivalent to *ah'ee*. The sound in *wait* is modern.

Au, aw, are equivalent to *ah'oo* (not as in Paul).

Ay is equivalent to *ah'ee*, as *ai* above.

E long is equivalent to *ai* in *pair*, *e* in *there*

E short is equivalent to *e* in *met*.

Ea is equivalent to *ea* in *break.* The sound in *seal* is modern.

Ee is equivalent to *e* in *there.*

Ei, ey, are equivalent to *ah¹ee,* as in *aye* now.

Eo is equivalent to *e* in *there;* not as in *people.*

Es final is generally pronounced.

• *Eu, ew,* are equivalent to *ui,* or the German *ü,* or the French long *u.*

Ge final, or before *a* or *o* in French words, is equivalent to *j.* Sometimes the *e* of *ge* final was omitted.

I long is equivalent to *ee* in *meek,* nearly. The present sound of *i* in *sine* was never given to that letter, but was represented by *y.*[1]

I short is equivalent to *i* in *pit.*

---

[1] In an essay published by the Chaucer Society in 1878, entitled *"Here"* and *"There" in Chaucer,* by R. F. Weymouth, Doctor of Literature, the conclusions of Mr. Ellis regarding the sounds of *e, i, ei,* and *ai* are excepted to at considerable length. Mr. Weymouth argues (1) that "'here' and the words that rhyme with it were probably sounded in Chaucer's time with the same vowel as in the present day;" (2) "that *i* in Chaucer's time was diphthongal, or approaching the sound that symbol still represents in" *mine, drive;* (3) that *ai* and *ei* were equivalent to *ey* in *they, ay* in *day.* Mr. Weymouth considers that the words rhyming with "here" and "there" in Chaucer fall into two classes, which rhyme among themselves only, the exceptions (out of the twelve hundred and forty-six cases in Chaucer) being eighty-nine, or a little over seven per cent., — less than the percentage of imperfect rhymes in Cowper, Byron, Keats, Scott, Morris, and other modern poets. The words that he finds most frequently rhyming with "here" are *dere, deer, manere, manere, bachiler, bokeler, neer, fere* (companion), *appere, peer, compeer, spere* (sphere), *frere emispere, lere.* Among those rhyming with "there" are *were, bear, forbear, here* (her), *spere* (spear), *swere, fere* (fear), *ere* (ear), *where.*

Ie is equivalent to *e* in *there*. The sound **in** *sieve* is modern.

O long is equivalent to *oa* in *boar*. *Oo* had the same value.

O short is equivalent to *o* in *got*, nearly.

Oi is equivalent to *oo'ee*, as in *wooing*, nearly.

Ou had three sounds : —

1. *Oo* in *boot* was the most common, as in *schoures, flour, pourchase, south, ploughman*, pronounced *shoo'ress, floor, poorchass, sooth, ploochman*. In the last example *ch* stands for the sound of *ch* in the Scotch *loch*, and the German *licht*.

2. *U* in *pull, put*. This is not very common, but is found in *boucleer*, of which the last syllable is sounded like *ere* in *there*.

3. *Ou* in *soul, ow* in *snow*. This is found in words having *aw*, or *ow* in very Early English. *Yknow, though*, i-kno-oo, tho-oo-ch.

Ow has the sounds of *ou* just mentioned.

U long is equivalent to the German *ü* and occurs in French words only. The *u* in *tune* comes near it.

U short is equivalent to *u* in *bull*, never *u* in *but*.

W vowel is equivalent to *u*, or *oo*, as *wde, herberwe*, oodë, herberoo.

In compiling these brief directions the effort
has been to make them as simple and comprehensive as possible. In reading Chaucer it
should be remembered that even the writers of
the present day cannot all be understood fully
without a dictionary.   Many of the words used
by Emerson, Browning, or Ruskin are not completely comprehended by the ordinary reader at
first sight. When Mr. Lowell writes of the
"secular leisures of Methuselah," it is probable that all do not immediately understand
him to use the word "secular" in its primary
sense ; and when Mr. Longfellow entitled his
lines to Tennyson "Wapentake," not a few
were surprised to find the word in their dictionaries.   It is by no means strange if we meet
many words that we do not fully understand in
a poet who lived half a millennium ago.   The
real wonder is that we can read Chaucer as
readily as we can.   He is much more easily
read than is the "Vision concerning Piers the
Plowman," of the same date.

ASTROLOGICAL TERMS AND DI-VISIONS OF TIME.

An acquaintance with the terms of astrology and with the nomenclature of divisions of time in use in the fourteenth century is a help to the understanding of many passages in Chaucer. Much light has been thrown on these subjects by the Rev. Mr. Skeat, in his edition of Chaucer's treatise on the Astrolabe, and by Mr. Furnivall in his "Trial Forewords to Chaucer's Minor Poems," from which the following remarks have been compiled.

The astrologers seemed to derive from Aristotle the notion that the heavenly bodies were ensouled, and that a power flowed out from them to affect human beings. The translators expression "sweet influences of Pleiades" (Job xxxviii. 31) is a relic of this belief. Upon the relative positions of the planets were founded predictions and rules for action.

Houses, Mansions, Lords. — The celestial

sphere was divided into twelve equal portions by six circles which passed through the north and south points of the horizon. Two of the circles were the meridian and the horizon. The portions were called Houses or Mansions. Each House is assigned to one of the heavenly bodies, which is called its Lord.

Exaltation. — The Exaltation of a planet is that degree of a sign in which it has its greatest power.

Dejection. — The Dejection of a planet is the sign opposite its Exaltation.

Combust. — A planet is said to be combust when it is so near the sun as to have its own light extinguished. "Troylus and Cryseyde," iii. 717.

Fall. — The Fall of a planet is the sign opposite its Mansion.

1. Aries is the mansion of Mars, and the exaltation of the Sun.

2. Taurus is the mansion of Venus, and the exaltation of the Moon.

3. Gemini is the mansion of Mercury, and the exaltation of the Dragon's Head.

4. Cancer is the mansion of the Moon, and the exaltation of Jupiter.

5. Leo is the mansion of the Sun, and the exaltation of none.

6. Virgo is the mansion of Mercury, and the exaltation of Mercury.

7. Libra is the mansion of Venus, and the exaltation of Saturn.

8. Scorpio is the mansion of Mars, and the exaltation of none.

9. Sagittarius is the mansion of Jupiter, and the exaltation of the Dragon's Tail.

10. Capricorn is the mansion of Saturn, and the exaltation of Mars.

11. Aquarius is the mansion of Saturn, and the exaltation of none.

12. Pisces is the mansion of Jupiter, and the exaltation of Venus.

This arrangement is that of Mr. Skeat (compiled from Raphael's "Manual of Astrology," London, 1828); but Mr. Brae, another editor of Chaucer's "Astrolabe," dissents from it.

The Houses have also the following names: I. The House of Life; II. Of Riches; III. Of Brothers; IV. Of Parents; V. Of Children; VI. Of Health; VII. Of Marriage; VIII. Of Death; IX. Of Religion; X. Of Dignities; XI. Of Friends; XII. Of Enemies.

Powers of the Houses. — Each of the Houses has a different Power, the first, the House o

Life, the Mansion of Mars, the Exaltation of the Sun, being the greatest.

Aspects. — There were five Aspects, or angular distances between planets, with individual qualities : —

1. Conjunction, indifferent.
2. Sextile, benignant.
3. Quartile, malignant.
4. Trine, benignant or propitious.
5. Opposition, malignant or adverse.

Angles. — Four of the Houses were called Angles. Aries was called the Angle of the East, Capricorn of the South, Libra of the West, and Cancer of the North. Next in "power" of the Houses came the Succedents, Taurus, Aquarius, Leo. The last are the Cadents, Gemini, Pisces, Sagittarius, Scorpio, Virgo. The "Angle meridional," or southern Angle (line 15,039), the tenth House, corresponded, at the equinox, with the time from ten o'clock to noon.

Spheres. — The spheres were the spaces in which the celestial bodies were supposed to move. The first was that of the Moon, the second that of Mercury, the third that of Venus, the fourth that of the Sun, the fifth that of Mars, the sixth that of Jupiter, the seventh that of Saturn, the eighth that of the fixed stars, the ninth the *Primum Mobile*, which has a very rapid motion and produces the alternations of day and night. This was the system of Ptolemy, Dante, and Milton. See "Parlement of Foules," line 59; "Troylus and Cryseyde," v. 1823.

Nativity. — A representation of the position of the heavenly bodies at the moment of one's birth.

The Seven Planets were Saturn, Jupiter, Mars, the Sun, Venus, Mercury, and the Moon.

Seven metals belonged to the seven planets, namely: Saturn, lead; Mars, iron; the Sun, gold; Venus, copper; Mercury, quicksilver; the Moon, silver. (Cf. lines 17,222–17,229.) Quicksilver is still mercury; nitrate of silver is lunar caustic; the sun has golden beams; Mars suggests iron or strength; the dull, slow motion of Saturn, lead; and Venus and copper (Latin, *cuprum*) are connected with Cyprus.

Qualities of the Planets. — Saturn was *cold* Saturn and Mars, *dangerous;* Jupiter, Venus, and the Moon, *temperate* and *benignant;* the Sun and Mercury, *variable.*

Triplicity was a combination of three signs

in the form of a triangle, each being one hundred and twenty degrees.

Classes of the Signs. — I. Movable : Aries,
Cancer, Libra, Capricorn.   II. Fixed : Taurus,
Leo, Scorpio, Aquarius.   III. Common : Gem-
ini, Virgo, Sagittarius, Pisces.   IV. Diurnal or
Masculine : Aries, Gemini, Leo, Libra, Sagitta-
rius, Aquarius.   V. Nocturnal or Feminine :
Taurus, Cancer, Virgo, Scorpio, Capricorn,
Pisces.   VI. Northern or Sinister (left-hand,
because the observer looked toward the east,
or ascendent) : Aries, Taurus, Gemini, Cancer,
Leo, Virgo.   VII. Southern or Dexter (right-
hand) : Libra, Scorpio, Sagittarius, Capricorn,
Aquarius, Pisces.   VIII. Western, Right, Sov-
ereign, or Direct : Cancer, Leo, Virgo, Libra,
Scorpio, Sagittarius.   IX. Eastern, Obedient,
Tortuous, or Oblique : Capricorn, Aquarius,
Pisces, Aries, Taurus, Gemini.

Divisions of the Signs. — Equal divisions of
signs were called Faces, of which there were
three.   Unequal divisions were called Terms.

Collect Years, in the Alphonsine Astronom-
ical Tables, are certain sums of years with the
motions of the heavenly bodies correspond-
ing to them, as 20, 40, 60, arranged in tables.
Cf. line 16,051.

Expanse Years are the single years with the answering motions of the heavenly bodies, beginning at one, and continuing to the smallest collect sum.

Radix or Root. — Any certain time taken at pleasure as a basis for computation.

Argument. — An arc by which an unknown and dependent arc is sought, or the angle on which a tabulated quantity depends.

Kalends. — The first day of the month, according to the Roman calendar, therefore the beginning of anything. See " Troylus and Cryseyde," ii. 7.

Nones. — The fifth day of the Roman months, excepting March, May, July, and October, when it was the seventh.

Ides. — The ides, according to the Roman calendar, fell on the 13th of the months, excepting March, May, July, and October, in which it fell on the 15th. See line 14,823.

The Platonic Year. — In the space of twenty-six thousand years the stars and constellations were considered to make an entire revolution about a centre. The *Annus Magnus* of the Egyptians was thirty thousand, and of the Arabians forty-nine thousand years. It is referred to in the " Parlement of Foules," line 67

Day Natural. — Twenty-four hours.

Day Artificial. — From sunrise to sunset.

The Hours of the artificial day and night were assigned to the Seven Planets in the order in which they stand above. This will explain lines 2217, 2367, the hour of Venus, in the first case, being Monday two hours before sunrise, and that of Mars, in the second, being the fourth after sunrise. The third hour is called "inequal" in line 2271 because, the day being artificial, the divisions varied at different seasons of the year. It will be noticed that it was the hour of Luna the Moon, or Diana.

Prime is a word applied with some looseness, but meaning the end of the first quarter of the day, or about nine o'clock. We meet the expressions *high prime, prime large, passed prime, half prime, half-way prime, not fully prime.* See lines 2189, 3554, 3906, 5700, 5818, 6437, 9736, 11,518, 14,193, 15,136, and others.

Underne is applied to the same hour as *prime*, and to a meal taken in the forenoon.

Undermele was the time after dinner, that meal being taken at prime or underne.

Compline. — The last of the hours in the Breviary, said just before retiring. (Lat. *completorium*, Fr. *complie*.) See lines 4171, 18,629.

Astrolabe. — An instrument used in making a variety of observations and calculations with reference to the zodiac and the heavenly bodies. Chaucer compiled a treatise upon its use, which he addressed to his son Louis, in 1391. See line 3209.

Chilyndre. — A rude and inaccurate instrument for measuring time, called also the traveler's dial. It consisted of a cylindrical piece of wood pierced by a central perpendicular bore (through which a cord passed upon which it hung), having a movable, rotary lid, and marked with tables and spaces adapted to its use. See line 5818. It was fairly accurate during the summer months.

The following lines [1] are some of those explained by the above definitions : —

> The yonge sonne
> 8 Hath in the Ram his halfe cours yronne.

In April, as the Astrolabe shows, the sun runs a half-course in Aries and a half-course in Taurus, and the expression in the text means that it was past the 11th of April. The sun

[1] Mr. Skeat, in his edition of Chaucer's *Astrolabe*, published by the Chaucer Society in 1872, gives full elucidation of most of these passages, and deserves all the credit.

was "yonge" because it had passed through but one sign since its course began, at the vernal equinox.

1087 Som wikke aspect or disposicioun
       Of Saturne, by sum constellacioun.
1328 But I moot been in prisoun thurgh Saturne.
2453 "My deere doghter Venus," quod Saturne,
       "My cours, that hath so wyde for to turne."
2469 My lookyng is the fader of pestilence.

The influence of Saturn was cold and dangerous, and he was called a wicked or unfortunate planet.

1462   In May,
       The thridde nyght.
1536 Right so kan geery Venus over-caste
       The hertes of hir folk, right as hir day
       Is gereful.
1850 And this day fifty wykes, — fer ne ner.
 621 Right as his happy day was, sothe to seyne.[1]

Palamon broke out of prison on Friday, May 4th, before one A. M., and the duel was fought the next day, presided over by wicked Saturn, which caused the duelists to be unfortunate. The tournament was fixed for one year afterwards, that is, Sunday, May 5th. The tenth hour inequal of Sunday night, being the second

---

[1] *Troylus and Cryseyde*, ii. 621

before sunrise of Monday, was dedicated to
Venus, to whose temple Palamon accordingly
went. The third hour subsequent to this, being the first after sunrise on Monday, was ded
icated to Luna, or Diana, to whose temple Em-
ily went. The third hour after this, being the
fourth after sunrise, was dedicated to Mars, to
whose temple Arcite went. All Monday was
devoted to jousts and dances, and on Tuesday,
the day of Mars, the tournament took place.
"Mars hath his wille," line 2669. May 5th
occurred on Sunday in 1387, and it was the
opinion of Sir Harris Nicolas that the Canterbury Tales were written after 1386. The
last quotation shows the use of "his day" as
applied to a man. It was the happy day of
Troylus.

1559 Allas, thou felle Mars ! allas, Juno !
2021 Noght was forgeten by the infortune of Marte.
2035 By manasynge of Mars, right by figure.

Mars being a wicked planet, it was inauspi-
cious or threatening if in the ascendent or
in the horoscope, which is the degree of the
zodiac seen upon the eastern horizon at the
time of observation.

2037 As is depeynted in the sterres above.
4616 For in the sterres, clerer than is glas.
14,306 The hevene stood, that tyme fortunaat.

These references are explained above.

2059 And after was she maad the loode-sterre.

The misconception involved in this line is
mentioned in the notes.

2217 And in hir houre he walketh forth a paas.
2271 The thridde houre in-equal that Palamon.
2367 The nexte houre of Mars folwynge this.

These references to the hours of the planets
are explained above.

3193 And koude a certeyn of conclusiouns.
3208 His Almageste, and bookes grete and smale,
His astrelabie, longynge for his art,
His augrym stones, layen faire a part.

In these things and in the conclusions of the
horoscope Chaucer declares his disbelief at
line 3454, and in his work on the Astrolabe.

3516 A Monday next, at quarter nyght,
Shal falle a reyn.

That is, at the sixteenth hour since Monday
began, which was the hour of Saturn, the unpropitious.

4427 He wiste it was the eightetethe day.
4436 It was ten at the clokke, he gan conclude.

The calculations of Mr. Skeat and others prove
that Chaucer wrote "eightetethe" here, and not
another date as some editors have supposed,
and add weight to Mr. Furnivall's opinion that
(the pilgrimage having begun on the 16th of
April) the tale of the Man of Law began the
second day's series of tales.

4717 O firste moevyng, crueel firmament,
 With thy diurnal sweigh that crowdest ay,
 And hurlest al from Est til Occident,
 That naturelly wolde holde another way.

The *primum mobile* was the ninth sphere, in-
cluding all the others and giving motion to
them from east to west, contrary to that of the
fixed stars, which, according to Ptolemy, moved
slowly the other way.   Dante likewise makes
the *primum mobile* the ninth sphere, in which
is the Divine Mind alone.   "Paradiso," xxvii.
110 ; xxviii. 70.

4724 Infortunat ascendent tortuous.

The tortuous or crooked signs were from Capricorn to Gemini ; Pisces, and Aries, the house
ot Mars, being the most tortuous.   The Moon

was likewise far from its best position at the time referred to.

4734 Of viage is ther noon eleccioun. . . .
    Noght whan a roote is of a burthe yknowe ?

That is, may not persons able to employ astrologers, or "philosophres," choose the time for their journeys, when the radix of a birth is known ?

    And also blisful Venus, wel arayed,
    Sat in hire seventhe hous of hevene tho,
        Disposed wel, and with aspectes payed
    To helpen sely Troylus of his wo ;
    And soth to seyn, she nas nat al a fo
        To Troylus, in his nativitee ;
        God woot that wele the sonner spedde he.[1]

8467 By nature he knew eche ascencioun.

Compare, also, lines 8799–8802, 8805–8811. Mr. Skeat says that the cock crew every hour (fifteen degrees making an hour). It was May 3d, March was complete, and thirty-two days more had passed. Calculations prove that "prime" at this date was nine A. M., though, as has been said, the term was used loosely.

10,655 Myn ascendent was Taur and Mars ther-inne.
: c,661 Yet have I Martes mark up-on my face.

Taurus, the mansion of Venus, was in the as

---

[1] *Troylus and Cryseyde*, ii. 680–686.

cendent at the time of the birth of the Wife of
Bath.   See the "Compleynt of Mars."

10,745   Mercurie is desolat
       In Pisces, wher Venus is exaltat;
       And Venus falleth ther Mercurie is reysed.

The exaltation of Venus is in Pisces, which is
the dejection of Mercury, and the exaltation of
Mercury is in Virgo, which is the dejection of
Venus, the signs being exactly opposite.

14,221 The moone, that at noon was thilke day
        That Januarie hathe wedded fresshe May
        In two of Tawr, was into Cancre glyden!

Mr. Tyrwhitt changed two to ten because he
thought it impossible that the moon should
move from the second degree of Taurus to the
first of Cancer in four days.   Subsequent cal-
culators decide, however, that Chaucer was
correct.

14,468   Er that dayes eighte
        Were passed er the monthe of Juyn bifille.
14,558 He was that tyme in Geminis, as I gesse,
        But litel fro his declynacioun
        Of Cancer, Jovis exaltacioun.

The sun enters Cancer about June 12th, and
the fact shows that Juyn and not Juyl should
be the reading in the first passage.   The sun

attains its maximum northern declination on
entering Cancer, at the summer solstice, in
June, not July. Cancer is the exaltation of
Jupiter and the dejection of Mars.

14,823   The last Idus of March after the yeer.
          Phebus, the sonne, ful joly was and cleer,
          For he was neigh his exaltacioun
          In Martes face, and in his mansioun
          In Aries, the colerik hoote signe.

The "last Idus" is the very day of the ides,
the 15th of March, at which time the sun,
having entered Aries on the 12th, was in the
fourth degree of that sign, which was the exaltation of the sun. The expression "neigh his
exaltacioun" is appropriate because the nine-
teenth degree of any sign in particular was the
one in which the exaltation was supposed to
occur.

15,039   Phebus hath laft the angle meridional,
          And yet ascendynge was the beest roial,
          The gentil Leon, with his Aldrian.

Having left the southern angle and entered the
"succedent" Leo, the sun showed that it was
past noon.

15,048   Now dauncen lusty Venus children deere,
          For in the Fyssh hir lady sat ful hye,
          And looketh on hem with a freendly eye.

The children of pleasure danced joyfully because their lady Venus was in her exaltation,
in Pisces.

15,161 As rody and bright as dooth the yonge sonne
    That in the Ram is foure degrees up ronne.

On March 16th the sun was in the fourth degree, which proves Tyrwhitt correct, and those
manuscripts which read "ten" wrong.

15,682 And this was in the sixte morwe of May.
15,809 That gevest after thy declinacioun,
    To ech of hem his tyme and his sesoun,
    As thyn herberwe chaungeth lowe or heighe.
15,833 That now next at this opposicioun,
    Which in the signe shal be of the Leoun.

The 6th of May is marked by the twenty-third
degree of Taurus. "After" means according
to, the sun's position or resting-place changing
from day to day, and vegetation changing
with it. A "spring-flood" or high tide might
be expected if the sun and moon could remain in opposition, and the moon would be
full under the circumstances indicated. See
line 15,845.

15,905 Which book spak muchel of the operaciouns
    Touchynge the eighte and twenty mansiouns
    That longen to the moone, and swich folye.

The Arabs count twenty-eight stations of the moon, having "influences." Twelve are temperate mansions, six dry, and ten moist.

16,021 Phebus wox old, and hewed lyk latoun,
   That in his hoote declynacioun
   Shoon as the burned gold, with stremes brighte ;
   But now in Capricorn adoun he lighte,
   Where as he shoon ful pale.

The sun was in the winter solstice, at its lowest altitude, having entered Capricorn on the 13th of December.

16,049 Hise tables Tolletanes forth he brought
   Ful wel corrected. . . .
16,056 And by his eighte speere in his wirkyng
   He knew ful wel how fer Alnath was shove
   Fro the heed of thilke fixe Aries above,
   That in the nynte speere considered is. . . .

In this passage the Harleian manuscript gives "thre" instead of "eighte," and "fourthe" instead of "nynte," which made bad sense and imperfect scansion. Tyrwhitt was correct in each case. The reference is to the exact amount of the precession of the equinoxes ascertained by measurements of the true equinoctial point and the nearest convenient bright star, Alnath, a star of the first magnitude, being taken for the purpose.

18,245 The sonne fro the south lyne was descended
    So lowe that he ne nas nat to my sighte
    Degrees nyne-and-twenty as in highte ;
    Foure of the clokke it was tho, as I gesse,
    For ellevene foot, or litel moore or lesse,
    My shadwe was at thilke tyme, as there
    Of swiche feet as my lengthe parted were
    In sixe feet equal of proporcioun.
    Ther-with the moones exaltacioun,
    I meene *Libra*, alwey gan ascende.

This passage shows that " four " was the hour, and not " ten," as some manuscripts have it, for at four in the afternoon of April 20th, the sun was twenty-nine degrees above the western horizon, and caused Chaucer's shadow to be in the proportion of eleven to six. In this case again Tyrwhitt was correct.

The expression " I meene Libra " is similar to " I mene Venus " (line 2216), but Libra is the exaltation of Saturn ; though the first " face " of Libra was the face of the Moon, and we may well agree with Mr. Skeat that the poet here made a slip in the use of the arbitrary terms of astrology.

    When Phebus dothe his bryghte bemes sprede,
    Ryght in the white Bool it so bytydde
    As I shal synge, — on Mayes day the thridde.[1]

The sun is in Taurus at the beginning of May.

---

[1] *Troylus and Crvseyde*, ii. 54.

BIBLICAL REFERENCES.

———◆———

THE great number of Chaucer's allusions
to and quotations from the Bible, and their
familiarity, makes it inexpedient to indicate
them. Living at the time when Wiclif,
through his writings and his poor preachers,
was making the people everywhere acquainted
with the words and doctrines of the Bible, a
complete version of which he gave them in
their own tongue before Chaucer had reached
his prime, and when, as has been said, every
third man in the street was a Lollard, it would
have been strange if the great poet had not
derived the largest share of his allusions and
illustrations from the revered book of the people.

Chaucer was familiar with the Scriptures
from Genesis to Revelation, and made hundreds of references to the ancient historical
books, to the poetry of Job, David, and Solomon, to the Apocryphal books, to the Gospels
of the four Evangelists, to the Epistles of St.
Paul, and to the apocalyptic vision of the Seer

of Patmos. He did this, too, not with the con-
strained and exact style of one who prepared
himself for the occasion, but with the freedom
of a man who was acquainted with the subject
and who believed his readers to be possessed
of the same general knowledge.

THE CANTERBURY TALES

THE GENERAL PROLOGUE.

Here bygynneth the Book of the tales of Caunter-
bury.

WHAN that Aprille with hise shoures soote
The droghte of March hath perced to the roote,
And bathed every veyne in swich[1] licour
Of which vertu engendred is the flour;
Whan Zephirus eek with his swete breeth
Inspired hath in every holt and heeth
The tendre croppes, and the yonge sonne
Hath in the Ram[2] his halfe cours yronne,
And smale foweles maken melodye
That slepen al the nyght with open eye, — 10
So priketh hem Nature in hir corages,[3] —
Thanne longen folk to goon on pilgrimages
And palmeres for to seken straunge strondes
To ferne halwes, kowthe[4] in sondry londes;
And specially, from every shires ende
Of Engelond, to Caunturbury they wende

[1] Such. [2] The sign of the Ram. [3] Their hearts. [4] Ancient
saints, known

The hooly blisful martir [1] for to seke
That hem hath holpen whan that they were
    seeke.

  Bifil that in that seson on a day,
In Southwerk at the Tabard as I lay,   20
Redy to wenden on my pilgrymage
To Caunterbury with ful devout corage,
At nyght were come in-to that hostelrye
Wel [2] nyne-and-twenty in a compaignye,
Of sondry folk, by aventure y-falle
In felaweshipe, and pilgrimes were they alle,
That toward Caunterbury wolden ryde.
The chambres and the stables weren wyde
And wel we weren esed atte [3] beste.
And shortly whan the sonne was to-reste,   30
So hadde I spoken with hem everychon [4]
That I was of hir felaweshipe anon,
And made forward [5] erly for to ryse
To take oure wey, ther [6] as I yow devyse.
  But nathelees, whil I have tyme and space,
Er that I ferther in this tale pace,[7]
Me thynketh it acordaunt to resoun
To telle yow al the condicioun
Of ech of hem, so as it semed me,
And whiche they weren and of what degree 40
And eek in what array that they were inne ;
And at a Knyght than wol I first bigynne.

---

    [1] Thomas à Becket. [2] Full. Cf. l. 15, 159. [3] Accommodated at
the. [4] Each one. [5] Promise. [6] Where. [7] Pass.

A KNYGHT ther was and that a worthy man,
That fro the tyme that he first bigan
To riden out, he loved chivalrie,
Trouthe and honour, fredom and curteisie.
Ful worthy was he in his lordes werre,
And therto hadde he riden no man ferre,[1]
As wel in cristendom as in hethenesse,
And evere honoured for his worthynesse.   50
At Alisaundre[2] he was whan it was wonne ;
Ful ofte tyme he hadde the bord bigonne[3]
Aboven alle nacions in Pruce.[4]
In Lettow[5] hadde he reysed[6] and in Ruce,[7] —
No cristen man so ofte of his degree.
In Gernade,[8] at the seege eek hadde he be
Of Algezir, and riden in Belmarye.[9]
At Lyeys[10] was he, and at Satalye,[11]
Whan they were wonne ; and in the Grete See
At many a noble armee hadde he be.   60
    At mortal batailles hadde he been fiftene,
And foughten for oure feith at Tramyssene[9]
In lystes thries, and ay slayn his foo.
This ilke worthy knyght hadde been also
Somtyme with the lord of Palatye[12]
Agayn another hethen in Turkye ;
And everemoore he hadde a sovereyn prys.[13]
And though that he were worthy, he was wys,
And of his port as meeke as is a mayde.

[1] Further. [2] Alexandria. Cf. l. 8004. [3] Taken the lead. [4] Prussia. [5] Lithuania. [6] Made inroad. [7] Russia. [8] Granada. [9] African kingdom. Belmarye is, perhaps, Palmyra. [10] In Armenia. [11] Attalia [12] In Anatolia [13] Praise, renown.

He nevere yet no vileynye [1] ne sayde   70
In al his lyf un-to no maner wight.
He was a verray parfit, gentil knyght.
   But for to tellen yow of his array,
His hors was goode but he was nat gay,
Of fustian he wered a gypoun [2]
Al bismotered with his habergeoun, [3]
For he was late ycome from his viage, [4]
And wente for to doon his pilgrymage.

   With hym ther was his sone, a yong SQUIER,
A lovyere and a lusty bacheler,   80
With lokkes crulle [5] as they were leyd in presse.
Of twenty yeer of age he was, I gesse.
Of his stature he was of evene lengthe, [6]
And wonderly delyvere [7] and of greet strengthe,
And he hadde been somtyme in chyvachie, [8]
In Flaundres, in Artoys and Pycardie,
And born hym weel, as of so litel space,
In hope to stonden in his lady grace.
Embrouded [9] was he, as it were a meede
Al ful of fresshe floures whyte and reede ;   90
Syngynge he was or floytynge, [10] al the day ;
He was as fressh as is the monthe of May.
Short was his gowne, with sleves longe and
          wyde.
Wel koude he sitte on hors and faire ryde ;
He koude songes make and wel endite,

---

[1] Nothing unbecoming. [2] Short cassock. [3] Hauberk. [4] Travels [5] Curled. [6] Average height. [7] Agile [8] Active training on raids for knighthood. [9] Embroidered. [10] Playing on the flute.

Juste and eek daunce and weel purtreye and
    write.
So hoote he lovede that by nyghtertale [1]
He slepte namoore than dooth a nyghtyngale ;
Curteis he was, lowely and servysable,
And carf biforn his fader at the table.   100

   A YEMAN [2] hadde he and servantz namo
At that tyme, for hym liste ride soo ;
And he was clad in cote and hood of grene.
A sheef of pecok arwes [3] bright and kene
Under his belt he bar ful thriftily.
Wel koude he dresse his takel yemanly ;
His arwes drouped noght with fetheres lowe,
And in his hand he baar a myghty bowe ;
A not-heed [4] hadde he with a broun visage ;
Of woodecraft wel koude [5] he al the usage ; 110
Up-on his arm he baar a gay bracer, [6]
And by his syde a swerd and a bokeler,
And on that oother syde a gay daggere
Harneised wel and sharpe as point of spere ;
A Cristophere [7] on his brest of silver sheene ;
An horn he bar, the bawdryk was of grene.
A forster [8] was he, soothly as I gesse.

   Ther was also a Nonne, a PRIORESSE,
That of hir smylyng was ful symple and coy ;
Hire gretteste ooth was but by seint Loy, [9] 120

---

[1] Night. [2] Yeoman. [3] Arrows. [4] Round head. [5] Knew.
Arm armor. [7] Image of St. Christopher. [8] Forester. [9] St
Louis, probably

And she was cleped madame Eglentyne.
Ful weel she soonge the service dyvyne,
Entuned in hir nose ful semeely,
And Frenssh she spak ful faire and fetisly[1]
After the scole of Stratford-atte-Bowe,[2]
For Frenssh of Parys was to hire unknowe.
At mete wel ytaught was she with alle,
She leet no morsel from hir lippes falle,
Ne wette hir fyngres in hir sauce depe.
Wel koude she carie a morsel and wel kepe, 13o
That no drope ne fille up-on hire breste ;
In curteisie was set ful muchel hir leste.
Hire over-lippe wyped she so clene,
That in hir coppe ther was no ferthyng[3] sene
Of grece, whan she dronken hadde hir draughte.
Ful semely after hir mete she raughte,
And sikerly[4] she was of greet desport,
And ful plesaunt and amyable of port,
And peyned hire to countrefete cheere[5]
Of Court, and to been estatlich of manere, 14o
And to ben holden digne[6] of reverence ;
But for to speken of hire conscience,
She was so charitable and so pitous
She wolde wepe if that she saugh a mous
Kaught in a trappe, if it were deed or bledde.
Of smale houndes hadde she that she fedde
With rosted flessh, or milk and wastel breed ;
But soore wepte she if any of hem were deed

---

[1] Fastidiously.   [2] Proverbial for poor French, or none at all
Morsel.   [4] Surely.   [5] Took pains to imitate courtly manners
Worthy.   [7] Bread-cake.

Or if men smoot it with a yerde[1] smerte,[2]
And al was conscience and tendre herte.   150
   Ful semyly hir wympul pynched[3] was ;
Hire nose tretys,[4] hir eyen greye as glas,
Hir mouth ful smal and ther to softe and reed,
But sikerly she hadde a fair forheed ;
It was almoost a spanne brood I trowe,
For hardily[5] she was nat undergrowe.
Ful fetys[6] was hir cloke as I was war ;
Of smal coral aboute hire arm she bar
A peire of bedes gauded al with grene,   159
And ther-on heng a brooch of gold ful sheene,
On which ther was first write a crowned A,
And after *Amor vincit omnia.*
   Another NONNE with hire hadde she
That was hire Chapeleyne,[7] and preestes thre.

   A MONK ther was a fair for the maistrie,[8]
An outridere that lovede venerie,[9]
A manly man to been an abbot able.
Ful many a deyntee hors hadde he in stable,
And whan he rood men myghte his brydel
      heere
Gynglen[10] in a whistlynge wynd als cleere,   170
And eek as loude, as dooth the chapel belle.
Ther as[11] this lord was kepere of the celle[12]
The reule of seint Maure or of seint Beneit,[13]

---

[1] Rod.   [2] Sharply.   [3] Wimple plaited.   [4] Well-proportioned.
Surely.   [6] Neat, nice.   [7] Attendant, secretary.   [8] A fair one for
the superiority   [9] Hunting.   [10] Cf.   8406.   [11] Where that.   [12] Religious house.   [13] Benedict.

By-cause that it was old and som del streit,
This ilke Monk leet olde thynges pace [1]
And heeld after the newe world the space.
He gaf nat of that text a pulled [2] hen
That seith that hunters beth nat hooly men,
Ne that a Monk whan he is recchelees [3]
Is likned til a fissh that is waterlees ;   180
This is to seyn, a Monk out of his cloystre ;
But thilke text heeld he nat worth an oystre ;
And I seyde his opinioun was good.
What, sholde he studie and make hym-selven
        wood [4]
Upon a book in cloystre alwey to poure,
Or swynken with his handes and laboure
As Austyn bit, [5] how shal the world be served?
Lat Austyn have his swynk to him reserved.
Therfore he was a prikasour [6] aright.
Grehoundes he hadde as swift as fowel in
        flight.   190
Of prikyng [7] and of huntyng for the hare
Was al his lust, for no cost wolde he spare.
I seigh [8] his sleves ypurfiled [9] at the hond
With grys, [10] and that the fyneste of a lond ;
And for to festne his hood under his chyn
He hadde of gold ywroght a ful curious pyn, —
A love knotte in the gretter ende ther was.
His heed was balled that shoon as any glas,
And eek his face as it hadde been enoynt.

[1] Pass. [2] Pilled, moulting. [3] Reckless. [4] Mad. [5] Bid. [6] Hard
ider [7] Riding. [8] Saw. [9] Trimmed. [10] Grey squirrel fur.

He was a lord ful fat and in good poynt ; 200
Hise eyen stepe [1] and rollynge in his heed,
That stemed as a forneys of a leed ; [2]
His bootes souple, his hors in greet estaat.
Now certeinly he was a fair prelaat.
He was nat pale, as a forpyned [3] goost :
A fat swan loved he best of any roost ;
His palfrey was as broun as is a berye.

A FRERE ther was, a wantowne and a merye,
A lymytour,[4] a ful solempne man,
In alle the ordres foure is noon that kan 210
So muchel of daliaunce and fair langage ;
He hadde maad ful many a mariage
Of yonge wommen at his owene cost :
Un-to his ordre he was a noble post,
And wel biloved and famulier [5] was he
With frankeleyns over al in his contree ;
And eek with worthy wommen of the toun,
For he hadde power of confessioun,
As seyde hym-selfe, moore than a curat,
For of his ordre he was licenciat. 220
Ful swetely herde he confessioun,
And plesaunt was his absolucioun.
He was an esy man to geve penaunce
Ther as he wiste to have a good pitaunce ;
For unto a povre ordre for to give
Is signe that a man is wel yshryve ;

---

[1] Fiery.   [2] Caldron.   [3] Tormented and, of course, wasted   [4] One
allowed to beg within certain limits   [5] Familiar.

For if he gaf he dorste make avaunt [1]
He wiste that a man was repentaunt :
For many a man so harde is of his herte   229
He may nat wepe al thogh hym soore smerte,
Therfore in stede of wepynge and preyeres
Men moote geve silver to the povre freres.
His typet [2] was ay farsed full of knyves
And pynnes, for to geven yonge wyves ;
And certeinly he hadde a murye note,
Wel koude he synge and pleyen on a rote : [3]
Of yeddynges [4] he baar outrely the pris ;
His nekke whit was as the flour delys, [5]
Ther to he strong was as a champioun.
He knew the tavernes well in al the toun,   240
And everich hostiler and tappestere [6]   (241 T.)
Bet [7] than a lazar or a beggestere ; [8]
For un-to swich a worthy man as he
Acorded nat, as by his facultee,
To have with sike lazars aqueyntaunce ;
It is nat honeste, it may nat avaunce
For to deelen with no swiche poraille ; [9]
But al with riche and selleres of vitaille.
And over al, ther as [10] profit sholde arise,
Curteis he was and lowely of servyse,   250
Ther nas no man nowher so vertuous.
He was the beste beggere in his hous, [11] (252 T.)

---

[1] Boast.   [2] Cowl.   [3] A kind of harp.   [4] Romantic songs
Flower-de-luce.   [6] Bar-woman.   [7] Better.   [8] Female beggar
Poor people, poor stuff.   [10] Where.   [11] Tyrwhitt inserts here the
following lines, which, though in the Hengwrt MS., are not in the
Ellesmere, Cambridge, and other good MSS. : —
And gaf a certeyn ferme for the graunt,
Noon of his bretheren cam ther in his haunt.

For thogh a wydwe hadde noght a sho,
So plesaunt was his *In principio*,[1]   (256 T.)
Yet wolde he have a ferthyng er he wente.
His purchas [2] was wel bettre than his rente,[3]
And rage he koude as it were right a whelpe ;
In love dayes [4] ther koude he muchel helpe,
For there he was nat lyk a cloystrer   259
With a thredbare cope, as is a povre scoler,
But he was lyk a maister, or a pope ;
Of double worstede was his semycope,
That rounded as a belle out of the presse.
Somwhat he lipsed for his wantownesse,
To make his Englissh sweet up-on his tonge,
And in his harpyng, whan that he hadde songe,
Hise eyen twynkled in his heed aryght
As doon the sterres in the frosty nyght.
This worthy lymytour was cleped Huberd.

A MARCHANT was ther with a forked berd,
In motlee, and hye on horse he sat ;   271
Up-on his heed a Flaundryssh bevere hat ;
His bootes clasped faire and fetisly ; [5]
Hise resons he spak ful solempnely,
Sownyge [6] alway thencrees [7] of his wynnyng.
He wolde the see were kept [8] for any thing
Bitwixe Middelburgh and Orewelle.
Wel koude he in eschaunge sheeldes [9] selle.

---

[1] End of the mass, John, i. 1. Cf. l. 8775.   [2] Perquisites.   [3] Regular income.   [4] Days appointed for settling disputes by peaceable means.   [5] Neatly.   [6] Tending to.   [7] The increase.   [8] Guarded   [9] French crowns

This worthy man ful wel his wit bisette,[1]
Ther wiste no wight that he was in dette,   280
So estatly was he of his governaunce
With his bargaynes and with his chevyssaunce.
For sothe he was a worthy man with alle
But sooth to seyn I noot [3] how men hym calle.

A CLERK ther was of Oxenford also
That un-to logyk hadde longe ygo,
And leene was his hors as is a rake,
And he nas nat right fat, I undertake,
But looked holwe and ther to sobrely ;
Ful thredbare was his overeste courtepy [4]   290
For he hadde geten hym yet no benefice,
Ne was so worldly to have office ;
For hym was levere have at his beddes heed
Twenty bookes clad in blak or reed
Of Aristotle and his philosophie,
Than robes riche or fithele [5] or gay sautrie :
But al be that he was a philosophre,
Yet hadde he but litel gold in cofre.   (300 T.)
But al that he myghte of his freendes hente [6]
On bookes and his lernynge he it spente,   300
And bisily gan for the soules preye
Of hem that gaf hym wher with to scoleye.[7]
Of studie took he moost cure and moost heede
Noght o word spak he moore than was neede,
And that was seyd in forme and reverence

Employed. [2] Agreement for borrowing. [3] Know not. [4] Up
per cloak. [5] Fiddle. [6] Get. [7] Study.

And short and quyk and ful of hy sentence.[1]
Sownynge [2] in moral vertu was his speche
And gladly wolde he lerne and gladly teche.

A SERGEANT OF THE LAWE, war and wys,
That often hadde been at the Parvys,[3]   310
Ther was also ful riche of excellence.
Discreet he was and of greet reverence;
He semed swich, hise wordes weren so wise.
Justice he was ful often in Assise,
By patente and by pleyn commissioun,
For his science and for his heigh renoun.
Of fees and robes hadde he many oon;
So greet a purchasour [4] was nowher noon.
Al was fee symple to hym in effect,
His purchasyng myghte nat been infect.[5]   320
Nowher so bisy a man as he ther nas,[6]
And yet he semed bisier than he was.
In termes hadde he [7] caas and doomes alle
That from the tyme of kyng William were
          yfalle ;
Ther-to he koude endite and make a thyng,
Ther koude no wight pynchen at [8] his writyng;
And every statut coude he pleyn [9] by rote.
He rood but hoomly in a medlee [10] cote.

[1] Meaning   [2] Tending to, or in harmony with. Cf. l. 9128   In
a note Mr. Ellis quotes from *Cassell's Magazine* for May, 1869, p.
479, a "sketch of Oxford life," there attributed to Wiclif, which is
either the original of this description of the Clerk, or a prose version
of it not by Wiclif. See *E. E. Pronunciation*, iii. 696.   [3] The por-
tico of St. Paul's, where lawyers consulted. [4] Prosecutor.   [5] Tainted
(by bribery).   [6] Ne was = was not.   [7] He knew well.   [8] Find fault
with   [9] Knew he fully.   [10] Mixed

Girt with a ceint [1] of silk with barres smale ;
Of his array telle I no lenger tale. 330

A FRANKELEYN [2] was in his compaignye.
Whit was his heed as is a dayesye,
Of his complexioun he was sangwyn.
Wel loved he by the morwe a sope in wyn ;
To lyven in delit was evere his wone, [3]
For he was Epicurus owene sone,
That heeld opinioun that pleyn delit
Was verraily felicitee parfit.
An housholdere and that a greet was he ;
Seint Julian [4] was he in his contree ; 340
His breed, his ale was alweys after oon ; [5]
A bettre envyned [6] man was nevere noon.
With oute bake mete was nevere his hous,
Of fissh and flessh, and that so plenteuous
It snewed in his hous of mete and drynke,
Of alle deyntees that men koude thynke
After the sondry sesons of the yeer, (349 T.)
So chaunged he his mete and his soper.
Ful many a fat partrich hadde he in muwe [7]
And many a breem and many a luce in
    stuwe. [8] 350
Wo was his cook but if his sauce were
Poynaunt and sharpe and redy al his geere.
His table dormant [9] in his halle alway,
Stood redy covered al the longe day.

---

[1] Belt. [2] Country gentleman. [3] Custom. [4] This saint was famous for providing good lodgings for his votaries. [5] Alike good
[6] Stored with wine. [7] Mew. [8] Fish preserve. [9] Fixed.

At sessiouns ther was he lord and sire ;
Ful ofte tyme he was knyght of the shire.
An anlaas,[1] and a gipser[2] al of silk,
Heeng at his girdel whit as morne milk ;
A shirreve hadde he been and countour.[3]
Was nowher such a worthy vavasour.[4]   360

　An HABERDASSHERE, and a CARPENTER,
A WEBBE, a DYERE, and a TAPYCER,
And they were clothed alle in o lyveree
Of a solempne and a greet fraternitee ;
Ful fressh and newe hir geere apiked[5] was ;
Hir knyves were chaped[6] noght with bras,
But al with silver, wroght ful clene and weel,
Hire girdles and hir pouches everydeel.
Wel semed ech of hem a fair burgeys
To sitten in a geldehalle, on a deys.[7]   370
Everich[8] for the wisdom that he kan[9]
Was shaply for to been an alderman.
For catel[10] hadde they ynogh and rente,
And eek hir wyves wolde it wel assente ;
And elles certeyn were they to blame.
It is ful fair to been ycleped *Madame*,
And goon to vigilies al bifore,
And have a mantel roialliche ybore.

　A COOK they hadde with hem for the nones[11]
To boille the chiknes with the marybones[12] 380

---

[1] Knife.   [2] Pouch.   [3] Auditor.   [4] Landholder.   [5] Trimmed.
Adorned.   [7] Guildhall, on a dais.   [8] Each.   [9] Knows.   [10] Chat-
els, property.   [11] For then once = for the occasion.   [12] Marrowbones

And poudre-marchant[1] tart and galyngale ;[2]
Wel koude he knowe a draughte of Londoun
    ale ;
He koude rooste and sethe and boille and frye
Maken mortreux[3] and wel bake a pye ;
But greet harm was it, as it thoughte me,
That on his shyne a mormal[4] hadde he,
For blankmanger, that made he with the beste.

  A Shipman was ther, wonynge[5] fer by weste ;
For aught I woot he was of Dertemouthe.
He rood up-on a rouncy[6] as he kouthe,   390
In a gowne of faldyng[7] to the knee.
A daggere hangynge on a laas[8] hadde he
Aboute his nekke under his arm adoun.
The hoote somer hadde maad his hewe al broun,
And certeinly he was a good felawe.
Ful many a draughte of wyn had he y-drawe
Fro Burdeuxward whil that the Chapman sleepe.
Of nyce conscience took he no keepe[9]   (400 T.)
If that he faught, and hadde the hyer hond ;
By water he sente hem hoom to every lond. 400
But of his craft to rekene wel his tydes,
His stremes and his daungers hym bisides.
His herberwe[10] and his moone, his lodemen-
    age,[11]
Ther nas noon swich from Hulle to Cartage.

---

[1] A flavoring powder. [2] Sweet cypress root. [3] A dish of which the ingredients were brayed in a mortar. [4] Cancer. [5] Dwelling [6] Hack. [7] A coarse cloth. [8] Lace. [9] Care. [10] Harbor. [11] Pilotage.

Hardy he was, and wys to undertake :
With many a tempest hadde his berd been
    shake ;
He knew alle the havenes as they were
Fron Gootlond to the Cape of Fynystere,
And every cryke [1] in Britaigne and in Spayne.
His barge ycleped was the Maudelayne.   410

   With us ther was a DOCTOUR OF PHISIK ;
In all this world ne was ther noon hym lik
To speke of phisik and of surgerye ;
For he was grounded in astronomye.
He kepte [2] his pacient a ful greet deel
In houres [3] by his magyk natureel.
Wel koude he fortunen [4] the ascendent
Of hise ymages for his pacient.
He knew the cause of everich maladye,
Were it of hoot, or cold, or moyste, or drye, 420
And where they engendred and of what humour ;
He was a verray parfit praktisour.
The cause yknowe and of his harm the roote,
Anon he gaf the sike man his boote.[5]
Ful redy hadde he hise apothecaries
To sende him drogges and his letuaries,[6]
For ech of hem made oother for to wynne,
Hir frendshipe nas nat newe to bigynne.
Wel knew he the olde Esculapius
And Deyscorides, and eek Risus,   430

---

[1] Inlet. [2] Watched. [3] Astrological hours. Cf. *House of Fame*,
iii. 1,5. [4] Knew he how to presage. [5] Remedy. [6] Electuaries
Cf. ll. 9281, 14,145.

Olde Ypocras, Haly and Galyen,
Serapion, Razis and Avycen,[1]
Averrois, Damascien and Constantyn,
Bernard and Gatesden and Gilbertyn.
Of his diete mesurable was he,
For it was of no superfluitee,
But of greet norissyng and digestible.
His studie was but litel on the Bible;
In sangwyn [2] and in pers [3] he clad was al,
Lyned with taffata [4] and with sendal.[4]   **440**
And yet he was but esy of dispence,
He kepte that he wan in pestilence.
For gold in phisik is a cordial,
Therfore he lovede gold in special.

A GOOD WIF was ther of biside BATHE,
But she was som del deef and that was scathe.
Of clooth-makyng she hadde swich an haunt [5]
She passed hem of Ypres and of Gaunt. (450 T.)
In al the parisshe wif ne was ther noon   449
That to the offrynge bifore hire sholde goon,[6]
And if ther dide, certeyn so wrooth was she,
That she was out of alle charitee.
Hir coverchiefs ful fyne weren of ground, — ⚹
I dorste swere they weyeden ten pound, —
That on a Sonday weren upon hir heed.

---

[1] Avicenna, an Arabian physician, who died in 1037. Cf. l. 9963. He is mentioned by Dante, in connection with Hippocrates and Galen, as in Limbo. *Inferno*, iv. 143, Longfellow's translation. [2] Red [3] Blue. [4] Silk stuff. [5] Custom. [6] The offering was the "sacrifice" of the Mass. Mass is a word of uncertain derivation. The Welsh *offeren* is translated both "offering" and "Mass" in the *Mabinogion*. Cf. l. 18,650.

Hir hosen weren of fyn scarlet reed
Ful streite yteyd, and shoes ful moyste **and**
    newe ;
Boold was hir face and fair and reed of hewe.
She was a worthy womman al hir lyve,   459
Housbondes at chirche dore she hadde fyve,
Withouten [1] oother compaignye in youthe, —
But ther of nedeth nat to speke as nowthe,[2] —
And thries hadde she been at Jerusalem ;
She hadde passed many a straunge strem ;
At Rome she hadde been and at Boloigne,
In Galice at Seint Jame, and at Coloigne,
She koude[3] muchel of wandrynge by the weye.
Gat-tothed[4] was she, soothly for to seye.
Up-on an amblere esily she sat,
Ywympled wel, and on hir heed an hat   470
As brood as is a bokeler or a targe ;
A foot mantel aboute hir hipes large,
And on hire feet a paire of spores sharpe.
In felaweshipe wel koude she laughe and **carpe ;**
Of remedies of love she knew per chaunce
For she koude of that art the olde daunce.[5]

A good man was ther of religioun
And was a POVRE PERSOUN [6] OF A TOUN ;
But riche he was of hooly thoght and werk ;
He was also a lerned man, a clerk,   480
That Cristes Gospel trewely wolde preche,

---

[1] Besides.   [2] Now   [3] Knew.   [4] Gap-toothed (?). Cf. l. 10,645
[5] Customs.   [6] *Persona ecclesiæ*, the church's representative.

Hise parisshens devoutly wolde he teche.
Benygne he was and wonder diligent,
And in adversitee ful pacient;
And swich he was y-preved ofte sithes.
Ful looth were hym to cursen for hise tithes,
But rather wolde he geven, out of doute,
Un-to his povre parisshens aboute,
Of his offryng and eek of his substaunce.
He koude in litel thyng have suffisaunce.   49c
Wyd was his parisshe, and houses fer a-sonder,
But he ne lafte nat for reyn ne thonder,
In siknesse nor in meschief to visite
The ferreste in his parisshe muche and lite [1]
Up-on his feet and in his hand a staf.
This noble ensample to his sheepe he gaf
That firste he wroghte and afterward he
          taughte.   (499 T.)
Out of the gospel he tho wordes caughte,
And this figure he added eek ther to,
That if gold ruste what shal iren doo ?   500
For if a preest be foul on whom we truste,
No wonder is a lewed man to ruste ;
And shame it is, if that a prest take keepe,[2]
A shiten shepherde and a clene sheepe.
Wel oghte a preest ensample for to geve
By his clennesse how that his sheepe sholde
          lyve.
He sette nat his benefice to hyre
And leet [3] his sheepe encombred in the myre,

----

[1] Great and small.   [2] Notice.   [3] Left.

And ran to Londoun un-to Saint Poules
To seken hym a chauntrie for soules;   510
Or with a bretherhed to been withholde,
But dwelleth at hoom and kepeth wel his folde,
So that the wolf ne made it nat myscarie, —
He was a shepherde, and noght a mercenarie :
And though he hooly were and vertuous,
He was nat to synful man despitous,
Ne of his speche daungerous ne digne,[1]
But in his techyng discreet and benygne,
To drawen folk to hevene by fairnesse,
By good ensample, this was his bisynesse.   520
But it were any persone obstinat,
What so he were, of heigh or lough estat,
Hym wolde he snybben [2] sharply for the
        nonys.
A bettre preest I trowe that nowher noon ys;
He waiteth after no pompe and reverence,
Ne maked him a spiced [3] conscience,
But Cristes loore, and his Apostles twelve,
He taughte, but first he folwed it hym selve.

With hym ther was a PLOWMAN, was his
        brother,   529
That hadde y-lad of dong ful many a fother,[4] —
A trewe swynkere [5] and a good was he,
Lyvynge in pees and parfit charitee.
God loved he best, with al his hoole herte

---

[1] Reserved nor haughty.   [2] Reprove.   [3] Sophisticated.   [
[4] Load.   [5] Worker

At alle tymes, thogh he gamed or smerte,[1]
And thanne his neighebore right as hym-selve.
He wolde thresshe, and ther to dyke and delve
For Cristes sake for every povre wight,
Withouten hire, if it lay in his myght.
Hise tithes payde he ful faire and wel
Bothe of his propre swynk and his catel.[2]   540
In a tabard he rood upon a mere.

   Ther was also a REVE and a MILLERE,
A SOMNOUR and a PARDONER also,
A MAUNCIPLE and my self, — ther were namo.[3]
   The MILLERE was a stout carl for the nones,
Ful byg he was of brawn and eek of bones ;
That proved wel, for over al ther he cam
At wrastlynge, he wolde have alwey the ram.[4]
He was short sholdred, brood, a thikke
        knarre,[5]   (551 T.)
Ther nas no dore that he ne wolde heve of
        harre,[6]   550
Or breke it at a rennyng with his heed.
His berd, as any sowe or fox, was reed,
And ther to brood, as though it were a spade.
Up-on the cope right of his nose he hade
A werte, and ther on stood a toft of herys,
Reed as the brustles of a sowes erys ;
His nosethirles [7] blake were and wyde ;
A swerd and a bokeler bar he by his syde ;

---

[1] Enjoyed or suffered.   [2] His own work and goods.   [3] No more
[4] Prize.   Cf. l. 6353.   [5] Knot.   [6] Hinge.   [7] Nostrils.

His mouth as greet was as a greet forneys,
He was a janglere and a goliardeys,[1]   560
And that was moost of synne and harlotries.
Wel koude he stelen corn and tollen thries,
And yet he hadde "a thombe of gold," *pardee.*[2]
A whit cote and a blew hood wered he,
A baggepipe wel koude he blowe and sowne,
And ther with al he broghte us out of towne.

A gentil MAUNCIPLE [3] was ther of a temple,
Of which achatours [4] myghte take exemple
For to be wise in byynge of vitaille ;
For wheither that he payde or took by taille [5]
Algate [6] he wayted [7] so in his achaat   571
That he was ay biforn [8] and in good staat.
Now is nat that of God a ful fair grace
That swich a lewed mannes wit shal pace [9]
The wisdom of an heepe of lerned men ?
Of maistres hadde he mo than thries ten
That weren of lawe expert and curious,
Of whiche ther weren a duszeyne in that hous
Worthy to been stywardes of rente and lond
Of any lord that is in Engelond,   580
To maken hym lyve by his propre [10] good
In honour dettelees but if he were wood,[11]
Or lyve as scarsly as hym list desire,
And able for to helpen al a shire

---

[1] Jangler and joker.   [2] Though he took toll thrice, he was honest,
as millers go.   [3] A purveyor for an inn of court.   [4] Buyers.   [5] On
trust (tally).   [6] Always.   [7] Watched.   [8] Forehanded.   [9] Surpass
[10] Own.   [11] Mad.

In any caas that myghte falle or happe,
And yet this Manciple sette hir aller cappe.[1]

   The REVE was a sclendre colerik man,
His berd was shave as ny as ever he kan ;
His heer was by his erys ful round yshorn,
His tope was doked lyk a preest biforn,   **590**
Ful longe were his legges and ful lene,
Ylyk a staf, ther was no calf y-sene.
Wel koude he kepe a gerner and a bynne,
Ther was noon auditour [2] koude of him wynne.
Wel wiste he, by the droghte and by the reyn,
The yeldynge of his seed and of his greyn.
His lordes sheepe his neet, his dayerye,
IIis swyn, his hors, his stoor,[3] and his pul-
       trye,   (600 **T.**)
Was hoolly in this reves governyng,
And by his covenant gaf the rekenyng   **600**
Syn that his lord was twenty yeer of age ;
Ther koude no man brynge hym in arrerage.
There nas baillif, ne hierde, nor oother hyne,[4]
That he ne knew his sleighte and his covyne ;
They were adrad of hym as of the deeth.
His wonyng [6] was ful faire up-on an heeth,
With grene trees yshadwed was his place.
He koude bettre than his lord purchace.
Ful riche he was a-stored pryvely,
His lord wel koude he plesen subtilly   **610**

---

[1] **Overreached** them all. Cf. l. 3143.   [2] Examiner.   [3] **Steers**
[4] **Servant.**   [5] Collusion.   [6] Dwelling.

To geve and lene [1] hym of his owene good
And have a thank, and yet a gowne and hood.
In youthe he lerned hadde a good myster,[2]
He was a wel good wrighte, a carpenter.
This Reve sat up-on a ful good stot [3]
That was al pomely [4] grey and highte Scot ;
A long surcote of pers [5] up-on he hade,
And by his syde he baar a rusty blade.
Of Northfolk was this Reve of which I telle,
Biside a toun men clepen Baldeswelle.   620
Tukked he was as is a frere aboute,
And evere he rood the hyndreste of oure route.

  A SOMONOUR was ther with us in that place
That hadde a fyr-reed cherubynnes face,
For sawcefleem [6] he was, with eyen narwe ;
As hoot he was and lecherous as a sparwe,
With scaled browes, blake and piled berd, —
Of his visage children were aferd.
Ther nas quyk-silver, lytarge, ne brymstoon,
Boras, ceruce,[7] ne oille of Tartre noon,   630
Ne oynement that wolde clense and byte,
That hym myghte helpen of the whelkes white,
Nor of the knobbes sittynge on his chekes.
Wel loved he garleek, oynons, and eek lekes,
And for to drynken strong wyn, reed as blood,
Thanne wolde he speke and crie as he were
        wood,[8]

---

[1] Lend. [2] Trade. [3] Horse. [4] Dappled. [5] Blue [6] Pimpled
White lead. [8] Mad.

And whan that he wel dronken hadde the wyn,
Than wolde he speke no word but Latyn.
A fewe termes hadde he, two or thre,
That he had lerned out of som decree, —   640
No wonder is, he herde it al the day,
And eek ye knowen wel how that a jay
Kan clepen " Watte " as wel as kan the pope.
But who so koude in oother thyng hym grope,
Thanne hadde he spent al his philosophie,
Ay, "*Questio quid juris,*" wolde he crie.
He was a gentil harlot[1] and a kynde ;
A bettre felawe sholde men noght fynde. (650 T.)
He wolde suffre for a quart of wyn
A good felawe to have his concubyn   650
A twelf monthe, and excuse hym atte[2] fulle ;
And prively a fynch eek koude he pulle,[3]
And if he foond owher[4] a good felawe,
He wolde techen him to have noon awe
In swich caas of the Ercedekenes[5] curs,
But-if a mannes soule were in his purs ;
For in his purs he sholde ypunysshed be :
" Purs is the Ercedekenes helle," seyde he.
But wel I woot he lyed right in dede,
Of cursyng oghte ech gilty man to drede,   660
For curs wol slee right as assoillyng[6] savith ;
And also war him of a *Significavit.*[7]
In daunger[8] hadde he at his owene gise[9]
The yonge girles of the diocise,

---

[1] Fellow.   [2] At the.   [3] Pull a finch = rob.   [4] Anywhere
[5] Arch-deacon's.   [6] Absolution.   [7] Warn him of a writ of excommunication.   [8] Official control.   [9] As he would wish.

And knew hir conseil, and was al hir reed.[1]
A gerland hadde he set up-on his heed,
As greet as it were for an ale-stake,
A bokeleer hadde he maad him of a cake.

    With hym ther was a gentil PARDONER
Of Rouncivale, his freend and his compeer, 670
That streight was comen fro the court of Rome.
Ful loude he soong " Com hider, love, to me !"
This Somonour bar to hym a stif burdoun,[2]
Was nevere trompe of half so greet a soun.
This Pardoner hadde heer as yelow as wex
But smothe it heeng as dooth a strike of flex ;
By ounces henge hise lokkes that he hadde,
And ther with he hise shuldres overspradde.
But thynne it lay by colpons[3] oon and oon ;
But hood, for jolitee, ne wered he noon,   680
For it was trussed up in his walet.
Hym thoughte he rood al of the newe jet,[4]
Dischevelee, save his cappe, he rood al bare.
Swiche[5] glarynge eyen hadde he as an hare,
A vernycle[6] hadde he sowed up-on his cappe ;
His walet lay biforn hym in his lappe
Bret ful[7] of pardon, comen from Rome al hoot.
A voys he hadde as smal as hath a goot ;
No berd hadde he, ne nevere sholde have,
As smothe it was as it were late shave ;   690
I trowe he were a geldyng or a mare.

---

[1] Adviser. [2] Accompaniment. Cf. 1. 4165. [3] Shreds. [4] Mode.
'Some MSS. have *get.* [5] Such. [6] A painting of the face of Christ.
Brimful.

But of his craft, fro Berwyk in to Ware
Ne was ther swich another pardoner,
For in his male [1] he hadde a pilwe-beer, [2]
Which that he seyde was oure lady veyl ;
He seyde he hadde a gobet [3] of the seyl
That Seint Peter hadde whan that he wente
Up-on the see til Jhesu Crist hym hente. [4] (700 T.)
He hadde a croys of latoun [5] ful of stones,
And in a glas he hadde pigges bones ;   700
But with thise relikes, whan that he fond
A povre person dwellynge up-on lond,
Up-on a day he gat hym moore moneye
Than that the person [6] gat in monthes tweye.
And thus with feyned flaterye and japes [7]
He made the person and the peple his apes.
But, trewely to tellen atte laste,
He was in chirche a noble ecclesiaste ;
Wel koude he rede a lessoun or a storie,
But alderbest [8] he song an Offertorie, [9]   710
For wel he wiste whan that song was songe,
He moste preche and wel affile [10] his tonge
To wynne silver, as he ful wel koude,
Therefore he song the murierly [11] and loude.
  Now have I toold you shortly in a clause
The staat, tharray, the nombre, and eek the
    cause
Why that assembled was this compaignye
In Southwerk at this gentil hostelrye,

---

[1] Bag. [2] Pillow-case. Cf. *Duchess Blanche*, l. 254. [3] Piece
Seized. [5] Brass. [6] Parson. [7] Tricks. [8] Best of all. [9] Cf
l. 9408. [10] Polish. [11] More pleasantly.

That highte the Tabard, faste by the Belle.
But now is tyme to yow for to telle   720
How that we baren us that ilke nyght,
Whan we were in that hostelrie alyght,
And after wol I telle of our viage [1]
And al the remenaunt of oure pilgrimage.

    But first, I pray yow of youre curteisye,
That ye narette it nat [2] my vileynye, [3]
Thogh that I pleynly speke in this mateere
To telle yow hir wordes and hir cheere, [4]
Ne thogh I speke hir wordes proprely,
For this ye knowen al so wel as I,   730
Who so shal telle a tale after a man,
He moote reherce as ny as evere he kan
Everich a word, if it be in his charge,
Al speke he never so rudeliche or large, [5]
Or ellis he moot telle his tale untrewe,
Or feyne thyng, or fynde wordes newe.
He may nat spare al thogh he were his brother,
He moot as wel seye o word as another.
Crist spak hym self ful brode in hooly writ
And wel ye woot no vileynye is it.   740
Eek Plato seith, who so kan hym rede,
" The wordes moote be cosyn [6] to the dede."

    Also I prey yow to forgeve it me
Al have I nat set folk in hir degree
Heere in this tale, as that they sholde stonde ;
My wit is short, ye may wel understonde.

---

[1] Journey.   [2] Ascribe it not to.   [3] Rusticity, coarseness.   [4] Appearance.   [5] Freely.   [6] Germane.   Cf. l. 18,089.   The sentiment is found in Chaucer's Boethius, book iii., prose 12, being there quoted from Plato.

Greet chiere made oure hoost us everichon,
And to the soper sette he us anon   (750 T.)
And served us with vitaille at the beste.
Strong was the wyn and wel to drynke us
      leste.   750
  A semely man OURE HOOSTE was with alle
For to han[1] been a marchal in an halle.
A large man he was with eyen stepe,[2]
A fairer burgeys was ther noon in Chepe ;[3]
Boold of his speche, and wys and well ytaught,
And of manhod hym lakkede right naught.
Eek therto he was right a myrie man,
And after soper pleyen[4] he bigan,
And spak of myrthe amonges othere thynges,
Whan that we hadde maad our rekenynges ; 760
And seyde thus : " Now, lordynges, trewely,
Ye been to me right welcome hertely ;
For by my trouthe, if that I shal nat lye,
I saugh nat this yeer so myrie a compaignye
Atones in this herberwe[5] as is now ;
Fayn wolde I doon yow myrthe, wiste I how.
And of a myrthe I am right now bythoght,
To doon yow ese, and it shal coste noght.
  " Ye goon to Canterbury, God yow speede,
The blisful martir quite yow youre meede ! 770
And wel I woot as ye goon by the weye
Ye shapen yow[6] to talen[7] and to pleye ;
For trewely confort ne myrthe is noon

[1] Not in Ellesmere MS.   [2] Bright.   [3] The Market, now called
Cheapside.   [4] To make pleasantry.   [5] Lodging-place.   [6] Plan
Tell tales.

To ride by the weye doumb as the stoon ;
And therfore wol I maken yow disport,
As I seyde erst, and doon yow som confort.
And if you liketh alle by oon assent
For to stonden at my juggement,
And for to werken as I shal yow seye,
To morwe, whan ye riden by the weye,   780
Now by my fader soule that is deed,
But if ye be myrie, I wol geve yow myn
          heed !
Hoold up youre hond withouten moore speche."
    Oure conseil was nat longe for to seche ;
Us thoughte it was noght worth to make it
          wys,[1]
And graunted hym withouten moore avys,
And bad him seye his voirdit[2] as hym leste.
    "Lordynges," quod he, " now herkneth for
          the beste,
But taak it nought, I prey yow, in desdeyn ;
This is the poynt, to speken short and pleyn, 790
That ech of yow to shorte with oure weye,
In this viage shal telle tales tweye, —
To Caunterburyward I mean it so,
And homward he shal tellen othere two, —
Of aventures that whilom han bifalle.
And which of yow that bereth hym best of alle,
That is to seyn, that telleth in this caas
Tales of best sentence[3] and moost solaas,
Shal have a soper at oure aller cost,[4]   (801 T.)

---

[1] To deliberate.   [2] Verdict.   [3] Sense.   [4] At the cost of all of us.

Heere in this place, sittynge by this post,   800
Whan that we come agayn fro Caunterbury.
And, for to make yow the moore mury,
I wol my selfe goodly with yow ryde
Right at myn owene cost, and be youre gyde,
And who so wole my juggement withseye
Shal paye al that we spenden by the weye.
And if ye vouche-sauf that it be so
Tel me anon, with-outen wordes mo,
And I wol erly shape [1] me therfore."

    This thyng was graunted, and oure othes
        swore   810
With ful glad herte, and preyden hym also
That he would vouche-sauf for to do so,
And that he wolde been oure governour,
And of our tales juge and reportour,
And sette a soper at a certeyn pris
And we wol reuled been at his devys
In heigh and lough; and thus by oon assent
We been acorded to his juggement.
And ther-up-on the wyn was fet [2] anon;
We dronken and to reste wente echon [3]   820
With-outen any lenger taryynge.

    Amorwe, whan that day gan for to sprynge,
Up roos oure Hoost and was oure aller cok, [4]
And gadrede us togidre alle in a flok,
And forth we riden, a litel moore than paas, [5]
Un-to the wateryng of Seint Thomas; [6]

---

[1] Prepare. [2] Fetched. [3] Each one. [4] Cock, or alarm, for us all
At a slow trot. [6] The second milestone on the old road to Canter
bury.

And there oure Hoost bigan his hors areste
And seyde, "Lordynges, herkneth if yow leste :
Ye woot youre foreward [1] and I it yow recorde.
If even-song and morwe-song accorde, 830
Lat se now who shal telle the firste tale.
As evere mote I drynke wyn or ale,
Who so be rebel to my juggement
Shal paye for all that by the wey is spent !
Now draweth cut, er that we ferrer twynne. [2]
He which that hath the shorteste shal bigynne.
Sire Knyght," quod he, "my mayster and my
        lord,
Now draweth cut, for that is myn accord.
Cometh neer," quod he, "my lady Prioresse,
And ye sire Clerk, lat be your shamefast-
        nesse, 840
Ne studieth noght ; ley hond to, every man."

Anon to drawen every wight bigan
And, shortly for to tellen as it was,
Were it by aventure, or sort, or cas,
The sothe is this, the cut fil to the knyght,
Of which ful blithe and glad was every wyght :
And telle he moste his tale as was resoun
By foreward and by composicioun,
As ye han herd ; what nedeth wordes mo ?
An whan this goode man saugh that it was so,
As he that wys was and obedient 851
To kepe his foreward by his free assent,

[1] Promise.   [2] Proceed.

He seyde, " Syn I shal bigynne the game,
What, welcome be the cut a Goddes name !
Now lat us ryde, and herkneth what I seye."
And with that word we ryden forth oure weye,
And he bigan with right a myrie cheere
His tale anon, and seyde in this manere. (860 T.)

TALES OF THE FIRST DAY.

Heere bigynneth The Knyghtes Tale.[1]

WHILOM, as olde stories tellen us,   (861 T.)
Ther was a duc that highte Theseus ;   860
Of Atthenes he was lord and governour,
And in his tyme swich a conquerour,
That gretter was ther noon under the sonne.
Ful many a riche contree hadde he wonne ;
That with his wysdom and his chivalrie[2]
He conquered al the regne[3] of Femenye[4]
That whilom was ycleped Scithia ;
And weddede the queene Ypolita,
And broghte hire hoom with hym in his contree

---

[1] Mr. Furnivall says with regard to the origin of this tale, which
has been styled " a translation " of the *Teseide* of Boccaccio, " Of
Chaucer's lines he has translated two hundred and seventy (less than
one eighth) from Boccaccio ; only three hundred and seventy-four
more bear a general likeness to Boccaccio ; only one hundred and
*hirty-two more a slight likeness." A few lines are taken from
Boethius, but the entire poem is an adaptation of the *Teseide*, which,
however, comprises over nine thousand lines, the treatment of the
details being very dissimilar at many points.   [2] Knightly exploits
    Kingdom.   [4] Amazons.

With muchel glorie and greet solempnytee, 870
And eek hir faire suster Emelye.
And thus with victorie and with melodye
Lete I this noble duc to Atthenes ryde
And al his hoost in armes hym bisyde.

And certes, if it nere [1] to long to heere,
I wolde have toold yow fully the manere
How wonnen was the regne of Femenye
By Theseus and by his chivalrye ; [2]
And of the grete bataille for the nones
Bitwixen Atthenes and Amazones ;   880
And how asseged [3] was Ypolita,
The faire, hardy queene of Scithia,
And of the feste that was at hir weddynge,
And of the tempest at hir hoom comynge ;
But al that thyng I moot as now forbere.
I have, God woot, a large feeld to ere, [4]
And wayke been the oxen in my plough.
The remenant of the tale is long ynough,
I wol nat letten [5] eek noon of this route.
Lat every felawe telle his tale aboute,   890
And lat se now who shal the soper wynne,
And ther I lefte I wol ageyn bigynne.

This duc of whom I make mencioun,
Whan he was come almost un-to the toun
In al his wele, [6] and in his mooste pride,
He was war, as he caste his eye aside,
Where that ther kneled in the weye   (899 T.)

---

[1] Were not. [2] Knights. [3] Besieged. [4] Plow. [5] Hinder
Opulence.

A compaignye of ladyes, tweye and tweye,
Ech after oother clad in clothes blake ;
But swich a cry and swich a wo they make 900
That in this world nys creature lyvynge
That herde swich another waymentynge: [1]
And of this cry they nolde [2] nevere stenten,
Til they the reynes of his brydel henten. [3]

  "What folk been ye, that at myn hom
      comynge
Perturben so my feste with criynge ? "
Quod Theseus. "Have ye so greet envye
Of myn honour, that thus compleyne and crye ?
Or who hath yow mysboden [4] or offended ?
And telleth me if it may been amended   910
And why that ye been clothed thus in blak ? "

  The eldeste lady of hem alle spak
Whan she hadde swowned [5] with a deedly
      cheere [6]
That it was routhe [7] for to seen and heere,
And seyde, " Lord, to whom fortune hath geven
Victorie, and as a conqueror to lyven,
Nat greveth us youre glorie and youre hon
      our,
But we biseken mercy and socour. [8]
Have mercy on oure wo and oure distresse.
Som drope of pitee thurgh thy gentillesse   920

---

[1] Wailing.   [2] Would not.   [3] Seized.   [4] Injured.   [5] Fainted.
[6] Countenance.   [7] Pity.   [8] The story of the *Seven against Thebes*
relates that it was Adrastus, one of the Seven, the one who survived
who went to ask Theseus to take vengeance on Creon, and to enforce the burial of the bodies of the heroes who had lost their lives
during the siege.

Up-on us wrecched wommen lat thou falle,
For certes, lord, ther is noon of us alle
That she nath[1] been a duchesse or a queene.
Now be we caytyves,[2] as it is wel seene :
Thanked be Fortune and hire false wheel,
That noon estat assureth to be weel.
And certes, lord, to abyden youre presence
Heere in the temple of the goddesse Clemence
We han ben waitynge al this fourtenyght ;
Now help us, lord, sith it is in thy myght.   930
   " I wrecche, which that wepe and crie thus,
Was whilom wyf to kyng Cappaneus,
That starf[3] at Thebes, — cursed be that day, —
And alle we that been in this array,
And maken al this lamentacioun.
We losten alle oure housbondes at that toun,
Whil that the seege ther aboute lay,
And yet now the olde Creon, weylaway !
That lord is now of Thebes, the citee,
Fulfild of ire and of iniquitee,   940
He for despit and for his tirannye,
To do the dede bodyes vileynye
Of alle oure lordes, whiche that been slawe,
Hath alle the bodyes on an heepe ydrawe
And wol nat suffren hem, by noon assent,
Neither to been yburyed nor ybrent,
But maketh houndes ete hem in despit."
   And with that word, with-outen moore re-
      spit,   (950 T.)

---

[1] Ne hath. Elles. MS. [2] Captives. [3] Died. He was struck by
lightning from Jove. Cf. *Troylus and Cryseyde*, v. 1509, 1517.

They fillen gruf,[1] and criden pitously,
" Have on us wrecched wommen som mercy 950
And lat oure sorwe synken in thyn herte."

This gentil duc doun from his courser sterte
With herte pitous, whan he herde hem speke.
Hym thoughte that his herte wolde breke
Whan he saugh hem, so pitous and so maat,[2]
That whilom weren of so greet estaat ;
And in his armes he hem alle up hente,[3]
And hem conforteth in ful good entente,
And swoor his ooth, as he was trewe knyght,
He wolde doon so ferforthly his myght   960
Upon the tiraunt Creon hem to wreke,
That all the peple of Grece sholde speke
How Creon was of Theseus yserved
As he that hadde his deeth ful wel deserved.
And right anoon, with-outen moore abood,
His baner he desplayeth and forth rood
To Thebesward, and al his hoost biside.
No neer[4] Atthenes wolde he go[5] ne ride,
Ne take his ese fully half a day,
But onward on his wey that nyght he lay ; 970
And sente anon Ypolita the queene,
And Emelye hir yonge suster sheene,
Un-to the toun of Atthenes to dwelle,
And forth he rit ;[6] ther is namoore to telle.

The rede statue of Mars with spere and targe
So shyneth in his white baner large,
That alle the feeldes[7] glyteren up and doun,

---

[1] **Flat.**   [2] Dejected.   [3] Seized.   [4] Nearer.   [5] Walk.   [6] **Rides**
Heraldic fields.

And by his baner born is his penoun
Of gold ful riche, in which ther was ybete [1] 979
The Mynotaur, which that he slough in Crete.

Thus rit this duc, thus rit this conquerour,
And in his hoost of chivalrie the flour,
Til that he cam to Thebes, and alighte
Faire in a feeld, ther as he thoughte fighte.
But, shortly for to speken of this thyng,
With Creon, which that was of Thebes kyng,
He faught, and slough hym manly as a knyght,
In pleyn bataille, and putte the folk to flyght,
And by assaut he wan the citee after
And rente adoun bothe wall and sparre and
          rafter,   990
And to the ladyes he restored agayn
The bones of hir housbondes that weren slayn,
To doon obsequies as was tho [2] the gyse.
But it were al to longe for to devyse
The grete clamour and the waymentynge
That the ladyes made at the brennynge
Of the bodies, and the grete honour
That Theseus, the noble conquerour, (1000 T.)
Dooth to the ladyes whan they from hym wente ;
But shortly for to telle is myn entente.   1000

Whan that this worthy duc, this Theseus,
Hath Creon slayn, and wonne Thebes thus,
Stille in that feeld he took al nyght his reste,
And dide with al the contree as hym leste.

To ransake in the taas [3] of bodyes dede,
Hem for to strepe of harneys and of **wede**,

---

[1] Limned.   [2] Then.   [3] Heap.

The pilours [1] diden bisynesse and cure
After the bataille and disconfiture.
And so bifel that in the taas they founde,
Thurgh-girt [2] with many a grevous, blody
       wounde,   1010
Two yonge knyghtes, liggynge by and by, [3]
Bothe in oon armes, [4] wroght ful richely,
Of whiche two Arcita highte that oon,
And that oother knyght highte Palamon.
Nat fully quyke, ne fully dede they were,
But by here cote-armures and by hir gere
The heraudes knewe hem best in special
As they that weren of the blood roial
Of Thebes, and of sustren two yborn.
Out of the taas the pilours han hem torn   1020
And han hem caried softe un-to the tente
Of Theseus, and ful soone he hem sente
To Atthenes to dwellen in prisoun
Perpetuelly, he nolde [5] no raunsoun.
And whan this worthy duc hath thus ydon,
He took his hoost and hoom he rood anon,
With laurer crowned as a conquerour ;
And ther he lyveth in joye and in honour
Terme of his lyve ; what nedeth wordes mo ?
And in a tour, in angwissh and in wo,   1030
This Palamon and his felawe Arcite
For everemoore, ther may no gold hem quite. [6]
   This passeth yeer by yeer and day by day,

---

[1] **Plunderers.**   [2] Pierced.   [3] Lying separately.   [4] Kind of armoi
Ne wolde = would not.   [6] Liberate.

Till it fil ones in a morwe of May
That Emelye, that fairer was to sene
Than is the lylie upon his stalke grene,
And fressher than the May with floures newe, —
For with the rose colour stroof hire hewe,
I noot[1] which was the fyner of hem two, —
Er it were day, as was hir wone[2] to do,   1040
She was arisen and al redy dight,[3]
For May wole have no slogardrie a nyght,
The sesoun priketh every gentil herte
And maketh hym out of his slepe to sterte,
And seith, " Arys, and do thyn observaunce."
This maked Emelye have remembraunce
To doon honour to May, and for to ryse.
Yclothed was she fresshe for to devyse; (1050 T.)
Hir yelow heer was broyded in a tresse
Bihynde hir bak a yerde long, I gesse ;   1050
And in the gardyn at the sonne up-riste,[4]
She walketh up and doun, and as hire liste
She gadereth floures, party white and rede,
To make a subtil gerland for hire hede,
And as an aungel, hevenysshly she soong.
   The grete tour that was so thikke and
         stroong,
Which of the castel was the chief dongeoun
(Ther as the knyghtes weren in prisoun,
Of whiche I tolde yow and tellen shal),
Was evene joynant to the gardyn wal,   1060
Ther as this Emelye hadde hir pleyynge.

---

[1] Ne wot = know not.   [2] Wont.   [3] Dressed.   [4] Uprising.

Bright was the sonne, and cleer that morwen
　　　　ynge,
And this Palamon, this woful prisoner,
As was his wone, bi leve of his gayler,
Was risen, and romed in a chambre an heigh,
In which he al the noble citee seigh,[1]
And eek the gardyn ful of braunches grene,
Ther as this fresshe Emelye the sheene
Was in hire walk and romed up and doun.
This sorweful prisoner, this Palamoun,　　1070
Goth in the chambre romynge to and fro,
And to hym-self compleynynge of his wo ;
That he was born, ful ofte he seyde, " allas ! "
And so bifel, by aventure or cas,[2]
That thurgh a wyndow, thikke of many a barre
Of iren, greet and square as any sparre,
He cast his eyen upon Emelya,
And ther with al he bleynte[3] and cride, " A ! "
As though he stongen were un-to the herte.
And with that cry Arcite anon up sterte,　　1080
And seyde, " Cosyn myn, what eyleth thee,
That art so pale and deedly on to see ?
Why cridestow ? who hath thee doon offence ?
For Goddes love, taak al in pacience
Oure prisoun, for it may noon oother be ;
Fortune hath geven us this adversitee.
Som wikke aspect or disposicioun
Of Saturne,[4] by sum constellacioun,　　1088

---

[1] Saw.　[2] Chance.　[3] Started.　[4] An unpropitious star. See Introduction, for all astrological allusions.

Hath geven us this, al though we hadde it sworn,
So stood the hevene whan that we were born ;
We moste endure . this is the short and playn."

This Palamon answerde, and seyde agayn,
"Cosyn, for sothe of this opinioun
Thow hast a veyn ymaginacioun ;
This prison caused me nat for to crye,
But I was hurt right now thurgh out myn eye
In to myn herte, that wol my bane be.
The fairnesse of that lady that I see (1100 T.)
Yond in the gardyn romen to and fro
Is cause of al my criyng and my wo.   1100
I noot wher [1] she be womman or goddesse,
But Venus is it, soothly as I gesse."
And ther with al on knees doun he fil
And seyde : "Venus, if it be thy wil
Yow in this gardyn thus to transfigure
Bifore me, sorweful, wrecche creature,
Out of this prisoun helpe that we may scapen.
And if so be my destynee be shapen,
By eterne word, to dyen in prisoun,
Of our lynage have som compassioun,   1110
That is so lowe ybroght by tirannye."

And with that word Arcite gan espye
Wher as this lady romed to and fro,
And with that sighte hir beautee hurte hym so,
That if that Palamon was wounded sore,
Arcite is hurt as moche as he, or moore ;
And with a sigh he seyde pitously :

[1] Know not whether.

"The fresshe beautee sleeth me sodeynly
Of hire that rometh in the yonder place,
And but I have hir mercy and hir grace   1120
That I may seen hire atte[1] leeste weye
I nam but deed ; ther is namoore to seye."

This Palamon, whan he tho wordes herde,
Dispitously[2] he looked and answerde,
"Wheither seistow[3] this in ernest or in pley ? "

"Nay," quod Arcite, "in ernest, by my fey !
God helpe me so, me list ful yvele pleye."

This Palamon gan knytte his browes tweye,
"It nere,"[4] quod he, "to thee no greet hon-
    our,
For to be fals, ne for to be traitour   1130
To me, that am thy cosyn and thy brother
Ysworn ful depe, and ech of us til oother,
That nevere for to dyen in the peyne,[5]
Til that deeth departe[6] shal us tweyne,
Neither of us in love to hyndre oother
Ne in noon oother cas, my leeve brother,
But that thou sholdest trewely forthren me
In every cas, as I shal forthren thee.   1138
This was thyn ooth, and myn also certeyn ;
I woot right wel thou darst it nat withseyn.
Thus artow[7] of my conseil, out of doute :[8]
And now thow woldest falsly been aboute
To love my lady, whom I love and serve,
And evere shal, til that myn herte sterve.[9]

---

[1] At the.   [2] Angrily.   [3] Sayest thou.   [4] Were not.   [5] Torture
ordeal.   [6] Separate, as formerly in the English marriage service.
[7] Art thou.   [8] Indisputably.   [9] Die.

Nay certes, false Arcite, thow shalt nat so ;
I loved hire first, and tolde thee my wo
As to my conseil, and to my brother sworn
To forthre me, as I have toold biforn. (1150 T.)
For which thou art ybounden as a knyght
To helpen me, if it lay in thy myght,   1150
Or elles artow fals, I dar wel seyn."

    This Arcite ful proudly spak ageyn ;
" Thow shalt," quod he, " be rather fals than I,
And thou art fals, I telle thee, outrely,
For *par amour* I loved hire first er thow.
What wiltow seyn ? thou wistest nat yet now
Wheither she be a womman or goddesse !
Thyn is affeccioun of hoolynesse,
And myn is love as to a creature,
For which I tolde thee myn aventure   1160
As to my cosyn and my brother sworn.
I pose [1] that thow lovedest hire biforn,
Wostow [2] nat wel the olde clerkes [3] sawe,
That *who shal geve a lovere any lawe ;*
Love is a gretter lawe, by my pan, [4]
Than may be geve of any erthely man ?
And therfore positif lawe and swich decree
Is broken al day for love in ech degree.
A man moot nedes love maugree his heed ;
He may nat flee it, thogh he sholde be deed,
Al be she mayde, or wydwe, or elles wyf ;
And eek it is nat likly al thy lyf   1172

[1] Put it.   [2] Knowest thou.   [3] See Boethius, book iii. met 12.
Brain-pan, head.

To stonden in hir grace, namoore shal I ;
For wel thou woost, thy selven verraily,
That thou and I be dampned to prisoun
Perpetuelly, us gayneth no raunsoun.
We stryven as dide the houndes for the boon,
They foughte al day, and yet hir part was noon
Ther cam a kyte, whil they weren so wrothe,
And baar awey the boon bitwixe hem bothe ;
And therfore, at the kynges court, my brother,
Ech man for hym-self, ther is noon oother.
Love, if thee list, for I love and ay shal, 1183
And soothly, leeve brother, this is al.
Heere in this prisoun moote we endure
And everich of us take his aventure."

Greet was the strif, and long, bitwix hem
tweye,
If that I hadde leyser for to seye ;
But to theffect.   It happed on a day, —
To telle it yow as shortly as I may, — 1190
A worthy duc, that highte Perotheus,
That felawe was to duc Theseus,
Syn thilke day that they were children lite,
Was come to Atthenes, his felawe to visite,
And for to pleye, as he was wont to do ;
For in this world he loved no man so,
And he loved hym als tendrely agayn.
So wel they lovede, as old bookes sayn, (1200 T.)
That whan that oon was deed, soothly to telle,
His felawe wente and soughte hym doun in
helle, — 1200

But of that storie list me nat to write.
Duc Perotheus loved wel Arcite,
And hadde hym knowe at Thebes yeer by
    yere;
And finally, at request and preyere
Of Perotheus, with-outen any raunsoun,
Duc Theseus hym leet out of prisoun
Frely to goon wher that hym liste over al,
In swich a gyse as I you tellen shal.

This was the forward,[1] pleynly for tendite,
Bitwixen Theseus and hym Arcite;   1210
That if so were that Arcite were yfounde,
Evere in his lif, by day or nyght, o stounde,[2]
In any contree of this Theseus,
And he were caught, it was acorded thus,
That with a swerd he sholde lese[3] his heed:
Ther nas noon oother remedie, ne reed,[4]
But taketh his leve and homward he him
    spedde:
Lat hym be war, his nekke lith to wedde.[5]

How greet a sorwe suffreth now Arcite!
The deeth he feeleth thurgh his herte smyte;
He wepeth, wayleth, crieth pitously;   1221
To sleen hym-self he waiteth prively.
He seyde, "Allas that day that I was born!
Now is my prisoun worse than biforn;
Now is me shape[6] eternally to dwelle,
Nat in my purgatorie, but in helle.

---

[1] Agreement. [2] One moment.   Most MSS. read, with the Elles
or stounde." [3] Lose. [4] Plan. [5] Lieth in pledge. [6] Ordained.

Allas that evere knew I Perotheus!
For elles hadde I dwelled with Theseus
Yfetered in his prisoun everemo.
Thanne hadde I been in blisse, and nat in
   wo,   1230
Oonly the sighte of hire whom that I serve, —
Though that I nevere hir grace may deserve, —
Wolde han suffised right ynough for me.
O deere cosyn Palamon," quod he,
"Thyn is the victorie of this aventure
Ful blisfully in prison maistow[1] dure, —
In prisoun? certes nay, but in paradys!
Wel hath Fortune y-turned thee the dys,
That hast the sighte of hire and I thabsence,
For possible is, syn thou hast hire presence,
And art a knyght, a worthy and an able, 1241
That som cas,[2] syn Fortune is chaungeable,
Thow maist to thy desir some tyme atteyne,
But I, that am exiled and bareyne
Of alle grace, and in so greet dispeir,
That ther nys erthe, water, fir, ne eir,
Ne creature, that of hem maked is, (1249 T.)
That may me heele, or doon confort in this.
Wel oughte I sterve in wanhope and distresse;
Farwel, my lif, my lust and my gladnesse! 1250

"Allas, why pleynen[3] folk so in commune
Of purvieaunce[4] of God, or of Fortune,
That geveth hem ful ofte in many a gyse
Wel bettre than they kan hem self devyse?

---

[1] Mayest thou. [2] Chance. [3] Complain. [4] Providence

Som man desireth for to han richesse,
That cause is of his moerdre, or greet sik·
    nesse ;
And som man wolde out of his prisoun fayn,
That in his hous is of his meynee[1] slayn.
Infinite harmes been in this mateere,
We witen nat what thing we preyen heere. 1260
We faren as he that dronke is as a mous.
A dronke man woot wel that he hath an hous,
But he noot[2] which the righte wey is thider,
And to a dronke man the wey is slider ;[3]
And certes in this world so faren we, —
We seken faste after felicitee,
But we goon wrong ful often trewely.
Thus may we seyn alle, and namely I,
That wende[4] and hadde a greet opinioun
That if I myghte escapen from prisoun, 1270
Thanne hadde I been in joye and perfit heele,[5]
That now I am exiled fro my wele.[6]
Syn that I may nat seen you, Emelye,
I nam but deed, there nys no remedye."

Upon that oother syde, Palamon,
Whan that he wiste Arcite was agon,
Swich sorwe he maketh that the grete tour
Resouned of his youlyng[7] and clamour ;
The pure[8] fettres on his shynes grete
Weren of his bittre, salte teeres wete. 1280
"Allas !" quod he, "Arcita, cosyn myn,

---

[1] Domestics, menials. [2] Knows not. [3] Slippery. [4] Supposed.
Health. [6] Wealth, weal. [7] Yelling. [8] Very.

Of al oure strif, God woot, the fruyt is thyn ;
Thow walkest now in Thebes at thy large,
And of my wo thow gevest litel charge.
Thou mayst, syn thou hast wysdom and man
        hede,
Assemblen alle the folk of oure kynrede,
And make a werre so sharpe on this citee,
That by som aventure, or som tretee,
. Thow mayst have hire to lady and to wyf
For whom that I moste nedes lese my lyf. 1290
For as by wey of possibilitee,
Sith thou art at thy large of prisoun free,
And art a lord, greet is thyn avauntage,
Moore than is myn that sterve here in a
        cage ;
For I moot wepe and wayle whil I lyve,
With al the wo that prison may me geve,
And eek with peyne that love me geveth also,
That doubleth al my torment and my wo."

  Ther with the fyr of jalousie up sterte
With-inne his brest, and hente [1] him by the
        herte   1300
So woodly,[2] that he lyk was to biholde
The boxtree, or the asshen, dede and colde.[3]

  Thanne seyde he, " O crueel gooddes that
        governe   (1305 T.)
This world with byndyng of youre word eterne
And writen in the table of atthamaunt [4]
Youre parlement and youre eterne graunt,

  [1] Seized.   [2] Madly.   [3] Cf. l. 1364.   [4] Adamant.

What is mankynde moore un-to you holde
Than is the sheepe that rouketh [1] in the folde ?
For slayn is man, right as another beest,
And dwelleth eek in prison and arreest,[2] 1310
And hath siknesse and greet adversitee,
And ofte tymes giltelees *pardee.*[3]
  " What governance is in this prescience,
That giltelees tormenteth innocence ?
And yet encresseth this al my penaunce,
That man is bounden to his observaunce
For Goddes sake to letten of [4] his wille,
Ther as a beest may al his lust fulfille ;
And whan a beest is deed he hath no peyne ,
But after his deeth man moot wepe and pleyne,
Though in this world he have care and wo, —
With-outen doute it may stonden so. 1322
The answere of this lete I to dyvynys,
But well I woot that in this world greet pyne
     ys.
Allas ! I se a serpent or a theef,
That many a trewe man hath doon mescheef,
Goon at his large, and where hym list may
     turne ;
But I moot been in prisoun thurgh Saturne,
And eek thurgh Juno, jalous and eek wood,
That hath destroyed wel ny al the blood 1330
Of Thebes with hise waste walles wyde ;
And Venus sleeth me on that oother syde
For jalousie and fere of hym Arcite."

[1] Huddleth. [2] Custody. [3] *Par dieux*, by the gods. [4] Refrain.

Now wol I stynte of Palamon a lite
And lete hym in his prisoun stille dwelle,
And of Arcita forth I wol yow telle.
    The summer [1] passeth, and the nyghtes longe
Encressen double wise the peynes stronge
Bothe of the lovere and the prisoner.
I noot which hath the wofuller mester; [2]   1340
For shortly for to seyn this Palamoun
Perpetuelly is dampned to prisoun
In cheynes and in fettres to been deed,
And Arcite is exiled upon his heed
For evere mo as out of that contree,
Ne nevere mo he shal his lady see.   (1348 T.)
    Yow [3] loveres, axe I now this questioun,
Who hath the worse, Arcite or Palamoun?
That oon may seen his lady day by day,
But in prisoun he moot dwelle alway;   1350
That oother wher hym list may ride or go,
But seen his lady shal he nevere mo.
Now demeth [4] as yow liste, ye that kan,
For I wol telle forth as I bigan.

SECOND PART.

Whan that Arcite to Thebes comen was,
Ful ofte a day he swelte [5] and seyde, "Allas!"
For seen his lady shal he nevere mo.
And, shortly to concluden al his wo,
So muche sorwe hadde nevere creature   1359

---

[1] Elles. MS. has "sonne."   [2] Necessity.   [3] Elles. MS. has
"now."   [4] Judge.   [5] Fainted.

That is or shal whil that the world may dure.
His slepe, his mete, his drynke, is hym bi-
 raft,
That lene he wexeth and drye as is a shaft ;
Hise eyen holwe, and grisly to biholde,
His hewe falow[1] and pale as asshen colde,
And solitarie he was and evere allone,
And waillynge al the nyght makynge his mone:
And if he herde song or instrument
Thanne wolde he wepe he myghte nat be stent.
So feble eek were hise spiritz and so lowe, 1369
And chaunged so that no man koude knowe
His speche nor his voys, though men it herde
And in his geere[2] for al the world he ferde,[3]
Nat oonly like the loveris maladye
Of Hereos,[4] but rather lyk manye[5]
Engendred of humour malencolik
Biforn his owene celle[6] fantastik.
And shortly turned was al up-so-doun
Bothe habit and eek disposicioun
Of hym, this woful lovere daun[7] Arcite.

What, sholde I al day of his wo endite ? —
Whan he endured hadde a yeer or two   1381
This crueel torment and this peyne and woo,
At Thebes, in his contree, as I seyde,
Up-on a nyght in sleepe as he hym leyde,
Hym thoughte how that the wynged god Mer-
 curie

---

[1] Yellow.   [2] Manner.   [3] Acted   [4] Eros=Cupid.   [5] Mania.
[6] Of the brain.   [7] Sir.

Biforn hym stood and bad hym to be murie;
His slepy yerde [1] in hond he bar uprighte,
An hat he werede upon hise heris [2] brighte.
Arrayed was this god, as I took keepe,[3]
As he was whan that Argus took his sleepe, 1390
And seyde hym thus, " To Atthenes shaltou
        wende,
Ther is thee shapen [4] of thy wo an ende."
And with that word Arcite wook and sterte, —
"Now trewely hou soore that me smerte,"
Quod he, "to Atthenes right now wol I fare,
Ne for the drede of deeth shal I nat spare,
To se my lady that I love and serve; (1399 T.)
In hire presence I recche nat to sterve."

    And with that word he caughte a greet mir-
        our   1399
And saugh that chaunged was al his colour
And saugh his visage al in another kynde;
And right anon it ran hym in his mynde
That sith his face was so disfigured
Of maladye the which he hadde endured,
He myghte wel, if that he bar hym lowe,
Lyve in Atthenes everemore unknowe,
And seen his lady wel ny day by day.
And right anon he chaunged his array
And cladde hym as a povre laborer,
And al allone, save oonly a squier   1410
That knew his privetee and al his cas,
Which was disgised povrely as he was, —

    [1] Wand, _i. e._, caduceus.   [2] Hairs.   [3] Notice.   [4] Ordained.

To Atthenes is he goon the nexte way,
And to the court he wente up-on a day
And at the gate he profreth his scrvyse
To drugge[1] and drawe, what so men wol de-
     vyse.
And, shortly of this matere for to seyn,
He fil in office with a chamberleyn
The which that dwellynge was with Emelye,
For he was wys and koude soone espye   1420
Of every servaunt which that serveth here.[2]
Wel koude he hewen wode and water bere,
For he was yong, and myghty for the nones,
And ther to he was long[3] and big of bones,
To doon that any wight kan hym devyse.
A yeer or two he was in this servyse,
Page of the chambre of Emelye the brighte,
And Philostrate he seyde that he highte.
But half so wel biloved a man as he   1429
Ne was ther nevere in court of his degree;
He was so gentil of his condicioun
That thurghout al the court was his renoun.
They seyden that it were a charitee
That Theseus wolde enhauncen his degree
And putten hym in worshipful servyse
Ther as he myghte his vertu exercise.
And thus with-inne a while his name[4] is spronge,
Bothe of hise dedes and his goode tonge,
That Theseus hath taken hym so neer,   1439

---

[1] Drudge.   [2] Her.   [3] Some MSS. have " strong."   [4] Good
same.

That of his chambre he made hym a squier,
And gaf him gold to mayntene his degree ;
And eek men broghte hym out of his con
     tree,
From yeer to yeer, ful pryvely, his rente ;
But honestly and slyly he it spente
That no man wondred how that he it hadde.
And thre yeer in this wise his lif he ladde
And bar hym so in pees, and eek in werre,
Ther was no man that Theseus hath derre.[1]
And in this blisse lete I now Arcite   (1451 T.)
And speke I wole of Palamon a lite.[2]   1450

In derknesse and horrible and strong prison
Thise seven yeer hath seten Palamon.
Forpyned, what for wo and for distresse
Who feeleth double soor and [3] hevynesse
But Palamon ? that love destreyneth so
That wood out of his wit he goth for wo ;
And eek ther to he is a prisoner
Perpetuelly, noght only for a yer.

Who koude ryme in Englyssh proprely
His martirdom ? for sothe it am nat I ;   1460
Therfore I passe as lightly as I may.

It fel that in the seventhe yer in May,
The thridde nyght, as olde bookes seyn
That al this storie tellen moore pleyn,
Were it by aventure [4] or destynee, —
As whan a thyng is shapen [5] it shal be, —
That soone after the mydnyght, Palamoun,

---

[1] **Dearer**.   [2] Little.   [3] Not in Elles. MS.   [4] Chance.   [5] Ordained

By helpyng of a freend brak his prisoun
And fleeth the citee faste as he may go,
For he hade geve his gayler drynke so   1470
Of a clarree,[1] maad of a certeyn wyn,
Of nercotikes, and opie [2] of Thebes fyn,
That al that nyght, thogh that men wolde him
    shake,
The gayler sleepe, he myghte nat awake.

   And thus he fleeth, as faste as evere he
    may,
The nyght was short and faste by the day
That nedes-cost [3] he moot him-selven hyde,
And til a grove faste ther bisyde,
With dredeful [4] foot, thanne stalketh Pala-
    moun.

For, shortly, this was his opinioun,   1480
That in that grove he wolde hym hyde al day,
And in the nyght thanne wolde he take his
    way
To Thebes-ward, his freendes for to preye
On Theseus to helpe him to werreye ; [5]
And shortly outher he wolde lese his lif
Or wynnen Emelye un-to his wyf.
This is theffect, and his entente pleyn.

   Now wol I turne to Arcite ageyn,
That litel wiste how ny that was his care,
Til that Fortune had broght him in the snare.

   The bisy larke, messager of day,   1491
Salueth in hir song the morwe gray,

[1] A mixed drink. [2] Opium [3] Of necessity. [4] Timorous. [5] Wa?

And firy Phebus riseth up so brighte
That al the orient laugheth of the lighte,
And with hise stremes dryeth in the greves [1]
The silver dropes, hangynge on the leves.
And Arcite that is in the court roial,
With Theseus, his squier principal,   (1500 T.'
Is risen, and looketh on the myrie day ;
And for to doon his observaunce to May, 1500
Remembrynge on the poynt of his desir,
He on a courser, startlynge as the fir, [2]
Is riden in to the feeldes hym to pleye,
Out of the court were it a myle or tweye ;
And to the grove of which that I yow tolde,
By aventure, his wey he gan to holde,
To maken hym a gerland of the greves,
Were it of wodebynde, or hawethorn leves,
And loude he song ageyn [3] the sonne shene :
" May, with alle thy floures and thy grene, 1510
Wel come be thou, faire, fresshe May,
In hope that I som grene gete may."
And from his courser with a lusty herte
In to a grove ful hastily he sterte,
And in a path he rometh up and doun,
Ther as by aventure this Palamoun
Was in a bussh, that no man myghte hym se,
For soore afered of his deeth was he. [4]
No thyng ne knew he that it was Arcite, —
God woot he wolde have trowed it ful lite ; 1520

---

[1] Groves.   [2] Fire.   [3] Towards.   [4] Elles. MS. reads "thanne
was he."

But sooth is seyd, gonsithen many yeres,
That feeld hath eyen, and the wode hath **eres**;
It is ful fair a man to bere hym evene,
For al day meeteth men at unset stevene.[1]
Ful litel woot Arcite of his felawe
That was so ny to herknen al his sawe,
For in the bussh he sitteth now ful stille.
Whan that Arcite hadde romed al his fille,
And songen al the roundel lustily,
In to a studie he fil al sodeynly,   1530
As doon thise loveres in hir queynte geres, —
Now in the crope,[2] now doun in the breres,
Now up, now doun, as boket in a welle.
Right as the Friday, soothly for to telle,
Now it shyneth, and[3] now it reyneth faste,
Right so kan geery[4] Venus over-caste
The hertes of hir folk; right as hir day[5]
Is gereful, right so chaungeth she array, —
Selde is the Friday al the wowke ylike.

   Whan that Arcite had songe, he gan to
      sike,[6]   1540
And sette hym doun with outen any moore:
"Allas," quod he, "that day that I was bore!
How longe, Juno, thurgh thy crueltee,
Woltow werreyen Thebes the citee?
Allas, ybroght is to confusioun   (1547 T.)
The blood roial of Cadme and Amphioun, —
Of Cadmus, which that was the firste man

---

[1] Time. [2] Top. [3] Not in Elles. MS. [4] Fickle. [5] Friday. Cf
8058. [6] Sigh.

That Thebes bulte or first the toun bigan,
And of the citee first was crouned kyng.
Of his lynage am I, and his of-spryng   1550
By verray ligne, as of the stok roial ;
And now I am so caytyf and so thral,
That he that is my mortal enemy,
I serve hym as his squier povrely.
And yet dooth Juno me wel moore shame,
For I dar noght biknowe myn owene name,
But ther as I was wont to highte Arcite,
Now highte I Philostrate, noght worth a myte.
Allas, thou felle Mars ! allas, Juno !
Thus hath youre ire oure kynrede al fordo, 1560
Save oonly me, and wrecched Palamoun,
That Theseus martireth in prisoun.
And over al this, to sleen me outrely,
Love hath his firy dart so brennyngly
Ystiked thurgh my trewe, careful herte,
That shapen was my deeth erst than my
      sherte.
Ye sleen me with youre eyen, Emelye ;
Ye been the cause wherfore that I dye.
Of al the remenant of myn oother care
Ne sette I nat the montance of a tare,   1570
So that I koude doon aught to youre ples-
      aunce."
And with that word he fil doun in a traunce
A longe tyme, and after he up sterte.
  This Palamoun, that thoughte that thurgh
      his herte

He felte a coold swerd sodeynliche glyde,
For ire he quook, no lenger wolde he byde.
And whan that he had herd Arcites tale,
As he were wood, with face deed and pale,
He stirte hym up out of the buskes thikke,
And seide, " Arcite, false traytour wikke ! 153ᵒ
Now artow hent,[1] that lovest my lady so,
For whom that I have al this peyne and wo,
And art my blood and to my conseil sworn,
As I ful ofte have seyd thee heer biforn,
And hast byjaped [2] heere duc Theseus,
And falsly chaunged hast thy name thus ;
I wol be deed, or elles thou shalt dye ;
Thou shalt nat love my lady Emelye,
But I wol love hire oonly, and namo,[3]
For I am Palamon, thy mortal foo,   1590
And though that I no wepene have in this
      place,
But out of prison am astert [4] by grace,
I drede noght, that outher thow shalt dye,
Or thow ne shalt nat loven Emelye.
Chees which thou wolt or thou shalt nat as·
      terte ! "
  This Arcite, with ful despitous herte,
Whan he hym knew, and hadde his tale herd,
As fiers as leoun pulled out his swerd, (1600 T.)
And seyde thus, " By God that sit above,
Nere [5] it that thou art sik and wood for love, 1600
And eek that thow no wepne hast in this place,

---

[1] Caught.   [2] Tricked.   [3] No other.   [4] Escaped.   [5] Ne were

Thou sholdest nevere out of this grove pace,
That thou ne sholdest dyen of myn hond,
For I defye the seurete and the bond
Which that thou seist that I have maad to
    thee.
What, verray fool, thynk wel that love is fre !
And I wol love hire mawgree [1] al thy myght.
But for as muche thou art a worthy knyght,
And wilnest to darreyne [2] hire by bataille,
Have heer my trouthe, tomorwe I wol nat
    faile,
With-oute wityng [3] of any oother wight,   1611
That heere I wol be founden as a knyght
And bryngen harneys right ynough for thee
And chese the beste and leve the worste for
    me ;
And mete and drynke this nyght wol I brynge
Ynough for thee, and clothes for thy bed-
    dynge ;
And if so be that thou my lady wynne
And sle me in this wode that I am inne,
Thou mayst wel have thy lady as for me."
  This Palamon answerde, " I graunte it thee.
And thus they been departed [4] til amorwe, 1621
Whan ech of hem had leyd his feith to borwe.[5]

  O Cupide, out of alle charitee !
O regne,[6] that wolt no felawe have with thee !

---

[1] In spite of.   [2] Contest.   [3] Knowledge.   [4] Separated
[5] Pledge.   [6] Ruler.

Ful sooth is seyd that love ne lordshipe
Wol noght, hir thankes,[1] have no felaweshipe.
Wel fynden that Arcite and Palamoun.

 Arcite is riden anon un-to the toun,
And on the morwe, er it were dayes light,
Ful prively two harneys hath he dight,[2] 163c
Bothe suffisaunt and mete to darreyne
The bataille in the feeld bitwix hem tweyne;
And on his hors, allone as he was born,
He carieth al the harneys hym biforn,
And in the grove, at tyme and place yset,
This Arcite and this Palamon ben met.
To chaungen gan the colour in hir face,
Right as the hunters in the regne [3] of Trace,
That stondeth at the gappe with a spere,
Whan hunted is the leoun and the bere, 1640
And hereth hym come russhyng in the greves [4]
And breketh bothe bowes and the leves,
And thynketh, "Heere cometh my mortal en-
  emy,
With-oute faile he moot be deed or I;
For outher I moot sleen hym at the gappe,
Or he moot sleen me if that me myshappe:"
So ferden [5] they in chaungyng of hir hewe,
As fer as everich of hem oother knewe. (1650 T.)
 Ther nas no "Good day," ne no saluyng,
But streight with-outen word or rehersyng 1650

---

[1] Willingly. Cf l 10,314. [2] Furnished. [3] Kingdom.
[4] Groves. [5] Acted

Everich of hem heelpe for to armen oother,
As frendly as he were his owene brother;
And after that, with sharpe speres stronge,
They foynen [1] ech at oother wonder longe.
Thou myghtest wene that this Palamoun,
In his fightyng were as a wood leoun,
And as a crueel tigre was Arcite:
As wilde bores gonne [2] they to smyte,
That frothen whit as foom for ire wood, [3] —
Up to the anclee foghte they in hir blood. 1660
    And in this wise I lete hem fightyng dwelle,
And forth I wole of Theseus yow telle.

    The Destinee, ministre general,
That executeth in the world over al,
The purveiaunce that God hath seyn biforn;
So strong it is that though the world had sworn
The contrarie of a thyng by ye or nay,
Yet somtyme it shal fallen on a day
That falleth nat eft [4] with-inne a thousand
        yeere.
For certeinly oure appetites heere,   1670
Be it of werre, or pees, or hate, or love,
Al is this reuled by the sighte above.
    This mene I now by myghty Theseus,
That for to hunten is so desirus,
And namely [5] at the grete hert in May,
That in his bed ther daweth hym no day
That he nys clad, and redy for to ryde

---

[1] Foin. [2] Began. [3] Mad. [4] Again. [5] Especially.

With hunte and horne, and houndes hym bi-
    syde.
For in his huntyng hath he swich delit,
That it is al his joye and appetit   1680
To been hym-self the grete hertes bane,
For after Mars he serveth now Dyane.

  Cleer was the day, as I have toold er this,
And Theseus, with alle joye and blis,
With his Ypolita, the faire queene,
And Emelye, clothed al in grene,
On huntyng be they riden roially ;
And to the grove that stood ful faste by,
In which ther was an hert, as men hym tolde,
Duc Theseus the streighte wey hath holde 1690
And to the launde¹ he rideth hym ful right, —
For thider was the hert wont have his flight, —
And over a brook, and so forth in his weye.
This duc wol han a cours at hym, or tweye,
With houndes, swiche as hym list commaunde.

  And whan this duc was come un-to the
    launde
Under the sonne he looketh, and anon,
He was war of Arcite and Palamon,   (1700 T.)
That foughten breme,² as it were bores two.
The brighte swerdes wenten to and fro   1700
So hidously, that with the leeste strook
It semed as it wolde fille an ook ;
But what they were no thyng he ne woot.
This duc his courser with his spores smoot,

¹ Champaign, hunting-ground.   ² Fiercely.

And at a stert he was bitwix hem two,
And pulled out a swerd, and cride, " Hoo !
Namoore, up-on peyne of lesynge [1] of youre
    heed.
By myghty Mars, he shal anon be deed
That smyteth any strook, that I may seen !
But telleth me what mystiers [2] men ye been,
That been so hardy for to fighten heere   1711
With-outen juge, or oother officere,
As it were in a lystes roially ? "

   This Palamon answerde hastily
And seyde, " Sire, what nedeth wordes mo ?
We have the deeth disserved bothe two.
Two woful wrecches been we, two caytyves, [3]
That been encombred of oure owene lyves,
And as thou art a rightful lord and juge
Ne geve us neither mercy ne refuge,   1720
But sle me first, for seinte [4] charitee,
But sle my felawe eek as wel as me ;
Or sle hym first, for though thow knowest it
    lite, [5]
This is thy mortal foo, this is Arcite,
That fro thy lond is banysshed on his heed,
For which he hath deserved to be deed ;
For this is he that cam un-to thy gate
And seyde that he highte Philostrate ;
Thus hath he japed [6] thee ful many a yer,
And thou hast maked hym thy chief squier ;
And this is he that loveth Emelye ;   1731

Losing.   [2] Sort of.   [3] Captives.   [4] Holy.   [5] Little.   [6] Tricked

For sith the day is come that I shal dye,
I make pleynly my confessioun
That I am thilke woful Palamoun,
That hath thy prisoun broken wikkedly.
I am thy mortal foo, and it am I
That loveth so hoote Emelye the brighte
That I wol dye present in hir sighte.
Therfore I axe deeth and my juwise ; [1]
But sle my felawe in the same wise,   1740
For bothe han we deserved to be slayn."

This worthy duc answerde anon agayn,
And seyde, " This is a short conclusioun :
Youre owene mouth, by youre confessioun,
Hath dampned yow, and I wol it recorde,
It nedeth noght to pyne [2] yow with the corde,
Ye shal be deed by myghty Mars the rede ! "

The queene anon, for verray wommanhede,
Gan for to wepe, and so dide Emelye, (1751 T.)
And alle the ladyes in the compaignye.   1750
Greet pitee was it, as it thoughte hem alle,
That evere swich a chaunce sholde falle,
For gentil men they were, of greet estaat,
And no thyng but for love was this debaat, —
And saugh hir blody woundes wyde and soore
And alle crieden, bothe lasse and moore,
" Have mercy, lord, up-on us wommen alle ! "
And on hir bare knees adoun they falle,
And wolde have kist his feet tner as he stood,
Til at the laste aslaked was his mood,   176c

---

[1] Doom.   [2] Torture.

For pitee renneth soone in gentil herte,[1]
And though he first for ire quook [2] and sterte,
He hath considered shortly in a clause
The trespas of hem bothe, and eek the cause,
And al though that his ire hir gilt accused,
Yet in his resoun he hem bothe excused,
And thus he thoghte wel that every man
Wol helpe hym-self in love, if that he kan,
And eek delivere hym-self out of prisoun ;
And eek his herte hadde compassioun   1773
Of wommen, for they wepen evere in oon ;
And in his gentil herte he thoughte anon,
And softe un-to hym-self he seyde, " Fy
Up-on a lord that wol have no mercy,
But been a leoun bothe in word and dede
To hem that been in repentaunce and drede,
As wel as to a proud despitous man
That wol maynteyne that he first bigan ;
That lord hath litel of discrecioun,
That in swich cas kan [3] no divisioun,   1780
But weyeth pride and humblesse after oon."
And shortly, whan his ire is thus agoon,
He gan to looken up with eyen lighte,
And spak thise same wordes, al on highte.[4]

" The god of love, a *benedicite*,
How myghty and how greet a lord is he !
Ageyns his myght ther gayneth none obsta-
    cles,
He may be cleped a god for hise myracles,

---

[1] Cf. l. 14,322.   [2] Quaked.   [3] Knows.   [4] In a loud voice.

For he kan maken, at his owene gyse,
Of everich herte as that hym list divyse.   1790
    "Lo heere this Arcite, and this Palamoun,
That quitly[1] weren out of my prisoun,
And myghte han lyved in Thebes roially,
And witen I am hir mortal enemy,
And that hir deth lith[2] in my myght also,
And yet hath love, maugree hir eyen two,
Y-broght hem hyder, bothe for to dye.
Now looketh, is nat that an heigh folye? (1800 T.)
    "Who may nat been a fole, but if he love?
Bihoold, for Goddes sake that sit above,   1800
Se how they blede! be they noght wel arrayed?
Thus hath hir lord, the god of love, ypayed
Hir wages and hir fees for hir servyse:
And yet they wenen for to been ful wyse
That serven love, for aught that may bifalle.
But this is yet the beste game[3] of alle,
That she, for whom they han this jolitee,
Kan hem ther fore as muche thank as me.
She woot namoore of al this hoote fare,
By God, than woot a cokkow of an hare.   1810
But all moot ben assayed, hoot and coold;
A man moot ben a fool, or yong or oold, —
I woot it by my-self ful yore agon,
For in my tyme a servant was I oon.
And therfore, syn I knowe of loves peyne,
And woot hou soore it kan a man distreyne,
As he that hath ben caught ofte in his laas,[4]

---

[1] Freely.   [2] Their death lieth.   [3] Sport.   [4] Snare.

I yow forgeve al hoolly this trespaas,
At requeste of the queene, that kneleth heere,
And eek of Emelye, my suster deere.   1820
And ye shul bothe anon un-to me swere,
That nevere mo ye shal my contree dere,[1]
Ne make werre up-on me, nyght ne day,
But been my freendes in al that ye may.
I yow forgeve this trespas every deel."

  And they him sworen his axyng, faire and
       weel,
And hym of lordshipe and of mercy preyde,
And he hem graunteth grace, and thus he
       seyde : —
" To speke of roial lynage and richesse,
Though that she were a queene or a prin-
       cesse,   1830
Ech of you bothe is worthy, doutelees,
To wedden whan tyme is, but natheless,[2] —
I speke as for my suster Emelye,
For whom ye have this strif and jalousye, —
Ye woot your self she may nat wedden two
Atones, though ye fighten everemo,
That oon of you, al be hym looth or lief,
He moote ' pipen in an yvy leef : '[3]
This is to seyn, she may nat now han bothe,
Al be ye never so jalouse ne so wrothe ;   1840
And for-thy,[4] I yow putte in this degree,
That ech of yow shal have his destynee

As hym is shape, and herkneth in what wyse ;
Lo heere your ende of that I shal devyse : —
   " My wyl is this, for plat [1] conclusioun
With-outen any repplicacioun, —
If that you liketh, take it for the beste, —
That everich of you shal goon where hym
      leste   (1850 T.)
Frely with-outen raunson or daunger ;
And this day fifty wykes, — fer ne ner,[2] — 1850
Everich of you shal brynge an hundred knyghtes
Armed for lystes up at alle rightes,
Al redy to darreyne [3] hire by bataille ;
And this bihote [4] I yow with-outen faille
Up-on my trouthe and as I am a knyght,
That wheither of yow bothe that hath myght,
This is to seyn, that wheither he or thow
May with his hundred, as I spak of now,
Sleen his contrarie, or out of lystes dryve,
Thanne shal I geve Emelya to wyve   1860
To whom that Fortune geveth so fair a grace.
Tho lystes shal I maken in this place,
And God so wisly on my soule rewe [5]
As I shal evene juge been, and trewe.
Ye shul noon oother ende with me maken
That oon of yow ne shal be deed or taken ;
And if yow thynketh this is weel ysayd,
Seyeth youre avys and holdeth you apayd.[6]
This is youre ende and youre conclusioun."

---

[1] Flat.   [2] A year hence, — no more, no less.   [3] Contend
  or.   [4] Promise.   [5] Pity.   [6] Satisfied.

Who looketh lightly now but Palamoun ?   1870
Who spryngeth up for joye but Arcite ?
Who kouthe telle, or who kouthe endite,
The joye that is maked in the place
Whan Theseus hath doon so fair a grace ?
But doun on knees wente every maner wight
And thonken hym with al hir herte and myght ;
And namely [1] the Thebans often sithe.[2]
And thus with good hope and with herte blithe
They taken hir leve, and homward goone they
ride
To Thebes with hise olde walles wyde.   1880

THIRD PART.

I trowe men wolde deme it necligence
If I forgete to tellen the dispence
Of Theseus, that gooth so bisily
To maken up the lystes roially,
That swich a noble theatre as it was
I dar wel seyn in this world there nas.
The circuit a myle was aboute,
Walled of stoon and dyched al with oute.
Round was the shape in manere of compaas,
Ful of degrees,[3] the heighte of sixty pas,   1890
That whan a man was set on o degree,
He lette [4] nat his felawe for to see.
Estward ther stood a gate of marbul whit,
Westward right swich another in the opposit.
And, shortly to concluden, swich a place

---

[1] Es₁ecially.   [2] Times.   [3] Steps.   [4] Hindered.

Was noon in erthe, as in so litel space;
For in the lond ther was no crafty man
That geometrie or *ars metrik* [1] kan,   (1900 T.)
Ne portreitour, ne kervere of ymages,
That Theseus ne gaf nem [2] mete and wages,
The theatre for to maken and devyse.   1901
And, for to doon his ryte and sacrifise,
He estward hath up-on the gate above,
In worshipe of Venus, goddesse of love,
Doon make an auter and an oratorie;
And on the westward side, [2] in memorie
Of Mars, he maked hath right swich another,
That coste largely of gold a fother. [3]
And northward, in a touret on the wal,
Of alabastre whit and reed coral,   1910
An oratorie riche for to see,
In worshipe of Dyane of chastitee
Hath Theseus doon wroght in noble wyse.

But yet hadde I forgeten to devyse
The noble kervyng and the portreitures, [4]
The shape, the contenaunce, [5] and the figures
That weren in thise oratories thre.

First, in the temple of Venus maystow se,
Wroght on the wal, ful pitous to biholde,
The broken slepes, and the sikes [6] colde,   1920
The sacred [7] teeris, and the waymentynge, [8]
The firy strokes, and the desirynge,
That loves servauntz in this lyf enduren;

[1] Arithmetic (*ars metrica*).   [2] Not in Elles. MS.   [3] Load.
Designs.   [5] Appearance.   [6] Sighs.   [7] Camb. MS. has "secret."
Wailing.

The othes that her covenantz assuren.
Plesaunce and Hope, Desir, Foolhardynesse,
Beautee and Youthe, Bauderie, Richesse,
Charmes and Force, Lesynges, Flaterye,
Despense, Bisynesse and Jalousye
That wered of yelewe gooldes[1] a gerland
And a cokkow[2] sitynge on hir hand ;   1930
Festes, instrumentz, caroles, daunces,
Lust and array, and alle the circumstaunces
Of love, whiche that I rekned have, and rekne
        shal,
By ordre weren peynted on the wal,
And mo than I kan make of mencioun ;
For soothly al the mount of Citheroun,
Ther Venus hath hir principal dwellynge,
Was shewed on the wal in portreyynge,
With al the gardyn and the lustynesse.
Nat was forgeten the porter Ydelnesse,   1940
Ne Narcisus the faire of yore agon,
Ne[3] yet the folye of kyng Salamon,
And eek the grete strengthe of Ercules,
Thenchauntementz of Medea and Circes,
Ne of Turnus with the hardy fiers corage,
The riche Cresus, kaytyf in servage. (1948 T.)

  Thus may ye seen that Wysdom ne Richesse
Beautee ne Sleighte, Strengthe, Hardynesse,
Ne may with Venus holde champartie,[4]   1949
For as hir list the world than may she gye.[5]

---

[1] Turnsols.   [2] Emblem of marital faithlessness.   [3] Elles. MS. haɪ
"and."   [4] Partnership in power.   [5] Guide.

Lo alle thise folk so caught were in hir las [1]
Til they for wo ful ofte seyde, " Allas ! "
Suffiseth heere ensamples oon or two,
And though I koude rekone a thousand mo.

The statue of Venus, glorious for to se,
Was naked, fletynge [2] in the large see,
And fro the navele doun al covered was
With wawes grene, and brighte as any glas.
A citole [3] in hir right hand hadde she,
And on hir heed, ful semely for to se,   1960
A rose gerland, fressh and wel smellynge,
Above hir heed hir dowves flikerynge.
Biforn hire stood hir sone Cupido,
Up-on his shuldres wynges hadde he two,
And blind he was, as it is often seene ;
A bowe he bar and arwes brighte and kene.

Why sholde I noght as wel eek telle yow al
The portreiture that was up-on the wal
With-inne the temple of myghty Mars the rede ?
Al peynted was the wal, in lengthe and brede,
Lyk to the estres [4] of the grisly place   1971
That highte the grete temple of Mars in Trace,
In thilke colde, frosty regioun
Ther as Mars hath his sovereyn mansioun.

First, on the wal was peynted a forest
In which ther dwelleth neither man nor best,
With knotty, knarry, bareyne trees olde
Of stubbes sharpe and hidouse to biholde,

---

[1] Snare.   [2] Floating.   [3] A stringed instrument.   [4] Interior passages.

In which ther ran a rumbel and a swough,[1]
As though a storm sholde bresten[2] every
   bough ;   1980
And dounward from an hille, under a bente,[3]
Ther stood the temple of Mars armypotente,
Wroght al of burned[4] steel, of which the entree
Was long and streit and gastly for to see ;
And ther out came a rage, and such a veze[5]
That it made all the gate for to rese.[6]
The Northren Lyght in at the dores shoon, —
For wyndowe on the wal ne was ther noon
Thurgh which men myghten any light dis-
   cerne, —
The dore was al of adamant eterne, 1990
Yclenched overthwart and endelong
With iren tough, and for to make it strong,
Every pyler the temple to sustene
Was tonne greet,[7] of iren bright and shene.
 Ther saugh I first the derke ymaginyng
Of felonye, and the compassyng ;
The crueel ire, reed as any gleede ;[8]
The pykepurs,[9] and eke the pale drede ; (2000 T.)
The smylere, with the knyfe under the cloke ;
The shepne,[10] brennynge with the blake smoke
The tresoun of the mordrynge in the bedde ;[11]
The open werre, with woundes al bi-bledde ;
Contek[12] with blody knyf, and sharpe manace
A! ful of chirkyng[13] was that sory place. 2004

---

[1] A rumble and a general, confused noise. [2] Burst. [3] Declivity
Burnished. [5] Rush of wind. [6] Quake. [7] Of the size of a tun
Live coal. [9] Pickpocket. [10] Sheep pens. [11] This refers to the
Danaïdes. [12] Contest. [13] Shrieking.

The sleere of hym self yet saugh I ther,
His herte blood hath bathed al his heer,
The nayl ydryven in the shode [1] a-nyght; [2]
The colde deeth, with mouth gapyng up right; [8]
Amyddes of the temple sat Meschaunce,
With disconfort and sory contenaunce.   2010
    Yet saugh I Woodnesse, [4] laughynge in his
       rage,
Armed compleint, out-nees, [5] and fiers outrage,
The careyne, [6] in the busk, [7] with throte ycorve,
A thousand slayn and not of qualm ystorve; [8]
The tiraunt with the pray by force yraft;
The toun destroyed, ther was no thyng laft.

    Yet saugh I brent the shippes hoppesteres; [9]
The hunte [10] strangled with the wilde beres;
The sowe freten [11] the child right in the cradel;
The cook yscalded for al his longe ladel.   2020
    Noght was forgeten by the infortune of
       Marte,
The cartere over-ryden with his carte;
Under the wheel ful lowe he lay adoun.
Ther were also of Martes divisioun,
The barbour and the bocher, and the smyth
That forgeth sharpe swerdes on his styth;
And al above, depeynted in a tour,
Saugh I Conquest [12] sittynge in greet honour
With the sharpe swerd over his heed
Hangynge by a souti' twynes threed.   2030

---

[1] Parting of the hair.   [2] Sisera.   [8] Cf. l. 8654.   [4] Anger.   Out-
cries.   [6] Corpse.   [7] Bush.   [8] Dead of disease.   [9] Dancing ships, or
opposing ships.   [10] Hunter.   [11] Devoured.   [12] Damocles(?).

Depeynted was the slaughtre of Julius,
Of grete Nero, and of Antonius, —
Al be that thilke tyme they were unborn,
Yet was hir deth depeynted ther biforn
By manasynge [1] of Mars, right by figure,[2]
So was it shewed in that portreiture
As is depeynted in the sterres [3] above
Who shal be slayn or elles deed for love ;
Suffiseth oon ensample in stories olde,
I may nat rekene hem alle though I wolde. 2040

The statue of Mars up-on a carte stood,
Armed, and looked grym as he were wood,[4]
And over his heed ther shynen two figures
Of sterres that been cleped in scriptures,
That oon Puella, that oother Rubeus.[5]
This god of armes was arrayed thus :
A wolf ther stood biforn hym at his feet
With eyen rede, and of a man he eet. (2050 T.)
With soutil pencel was depeynted this storie
In redoutynge [6] of Mars and of his glorie. 2050

Now to the temple of Dyane the chaste,
As shortly as I kan, I wol me haste
To telle yow al the descripsioun.
Depeynted been the walles up and doun
Of huntyng and of shamefast chastitee.
Ther saugh I how woful Calistopee,[7]
Whan that Diane agreved was with here,
Was turned from a womman to a bere,

---

[1] Menacing.   [2] Prefiguration.   [3] The "Six Texts" have "Ser-
res" or "Certres."   [4] Mad.   [5] Puella signified Mars "retrograde ;"
Rubeus, Mars "direct."   [6] Awe.   [7] Callisto

And after was she maad the loode-sterre ;[1]
Thus was it peynted, I kan sey[2] no ferre.[3] 2060
Hir sone[4] is eek a sterre[5] as men may see.
Ther saugh I Dane,[6] yturned til a tree, —
I mene nat the goddesse Diane,
But Penneus doughter which that highte Dane.
Ther saugh I Attheon[7] an hert ymaked,
For vengeance that he saugh Diane al naked ;
I saugh how that hise houndes have hym caught
And freeten[8] hym for that they knewe hym
        naught.

Yet peynted was a litel forther moor
How Atthalante hunted the wilde boor,   2070
And Meleagre, and many another mo,
For which Dyane wroghte hym care and wo.
Ther saugh I many another wonder storie
The whiche me list nat drawen to memorie.

This goddesse on an hert ful wel hye seet,
With smale houndes al aboute hir feet,
And undernethe hir feet she hadde a moone,
Wexynge it was, and sholde wanye soone.
In gaude grene hir statue clothed was,
With bowe in honde and arwes in a cas ; 2080
Hir eyen caste she ful lowe adoun
Ther Pluto hath his derke regioun.

A womman travaillynge was hire biforn,
But, for hir child so longe was unborn,

---

[1] This is an error, for Callisto was changed into Arctos, or the Great Bear, while the Pole-star is in the Lesser Bear. [2] Elles. MS. has "say *you.*" [3] Further. [4] Arcas. [5] Constellation (Boötes). [6] Daphne. [7] Actæon. [8] Devoured.

Ful pitously Lucyna [1] gan she calle
And seyde, "Helpe, for thou mayst best of
    alle."
Wel koude he peynten lifly,[2] that it wroghte ;
With many a floryn he the hewes boghte.

  Now been the lystes maad, and Theseus, —
That at his grete cost arrayed thus   2090
The temples, and the theatre every deel, —
Whan it was doon hym lyked wonder weel ;
But stynte I wole of Theseus a lite,
And speke of Palamon and of Arcite.

  The day approcheth of hir retournynge,
That everich sholde an hundred knyghtes
    brynge,
The bataille to darreyne,[3] as I yow tolde,
And til Atthenes, hir covenantz for to holde,
Hath everich of hem broght an hundred
    knyghtes   (2101 T.)
Wel armed for the werre at alle rightes ; 2100
And sikerly ther trowed many a man
That nevere sithen that the world bigan,
As for to speke of knyghthod of hir hond,
As fer as God hath maked see or lond,
Nas,[4] of so fewe, so noble a compaignye ;
For every wight that lovede chivalrye
And wolde, his thankes,[5] han a passant [6] name,
Hath preyed that he myghte been of that
    game ;

[1] Diana. [2] Like the life. [3] Contend. [4] Was not. [5] Willingly
Excelling.

And wel was hym that ther-to chosen was ;
For if ther fille tomorwe swich a caas,   2110
Ye knowen wel that every lusty knyght
That loveth paramours, and hath his myght,
Were it in Engelond or elles where,
They wolde, hir thankes, wilnen to be there.
To fighte for a lady, — *benedicitee !*
It were a lusty sighte for to see.

And right so ferden [1] they with Palamon.
With hym ther wenten knyghtes many on ;
Som wol ben armed in an haubergeoun,
And in bristplate and in a light gypoun ;   2120
And somme woln have a paire plates large ;
And somme woln have a Pruce sheeld or a
        targe ;
Somme woln ben armed on hir legges weel,
And have an ax, and somme a mace of steel ;
Ther is no newe gyse [2] that it nas old.
Armed were they as I have yow told
Everych after his opinioun.

Ther maistow seen comynge with Palamoun
Lygurge [3] hym-self, the grete kyng of Trace ;
Blak was his berd, and manly was his face ;
The cercles of hise eyen in his heed   2131
They gloweden bitwyxen yelow and reed,
And lik a grifphon looked he aboute,
With kempe [4] heeris on hise browes stoute ;
Hise lymes grete, hise brawnes harde and
        stronge,

---

[1] Went.   [2] Fashion.   [3] Lycurgus.   [4] Crooked, shaggy.

Hise shuldres brode, his armes rounde and
    longe,
And, as the gyse was in his contree,
Ful hye upon a chaar[1] of gold stood he
With foure white boles in the trays.[2]
In stede of cote-armure, over his harnays 2140
With nayles yelewe, and brighte as any gold,
He hadde a beres skyn, colblak for old.
His longe heer was kembd[3] bihynde his bak ;
As any ravenes fethere it shoon for blak ;
A wrethe of gold, arm greet,[4] of huge wighte,
Upon his heed set ful of stones brighte,
Of fyne rubyes and of dyamauntz ;
Aboute his chaar ther wenten white alauntz,[5]
Twenty and mo, as grete as any steer, (2151 T.)
To hunten at the leon or the deer ;   2150
And folwed hym with mosel[6] faste ybounde,
Colered[7] of gold and tourettes[8] fyled rounde.
An hundred lordes hadde he in his route,
Armed ful wel, with hertes stierne and stoute.

    With Arcite in stories as men fynde
The grete Emetreus, the kyng of Inde,
Up on a steede bay, trapped in steel,
Covered in clooth of gold, dyapred weel,
Cam ridynge lyk the god of armes, Mars.
His cote armure was of clooth of Tars   2160
Couched[9] with perles, white and rounde and
    grete ;

    Chariot.   [2] Traces.   [3] Combed.   [4] Of the size of the arm
[5] Dogs.   [6] Muzzle.   [7] Collared.   [8] Rings.   [9] Trimmed. (Literally
laid.)

His sadel was of brend [1] gold, newe ybete ;
A mantel was up on his shulder hangynge,
Brat [2] ful of rubyes rede, as fyr sparklynge ;
His crispe heer, lyk rynges was yronne,
And that was yelow, and glytered as the sonne.
His nose was heigh, his eyen bright citryn ; [3]
Hise lippes rounde, his colour was sangwyn ;
A fewe frakenes [4] in his face yspreynd, [5]
Bitwixen yelow and somdel blak ymeynd, [6] 2170
And as a leoun he his lookyng caste.
Of fyve and twenty yeer his age I caste ;
His berd was wel bigonne for to sprynge ;
His voys was as a trompe thondrynge ;
Up-on his heed he wered, of laurer grene,
A gerland, fressh and lusty for to sene.
Up-on his hand he bar for his deduyt [7]
An egle tame, as any lilye whyt.
An hundred lordes hadde he with hym there,
Al armed, save hir heddes, in al hir gere, 2180
Ful richely in alle maner thynges ;
For trusteth wel that dukes, erles, kynges,
Were gadered in this noble compaignye,
For love and for encrees of chivalrye.
Aboute this kyng ther ran on every part
Ful many a tame leoun and leopard.
And in this wise these lordes alle and some
Been on the Sonday to the citee come
Aboute pryme, [8] and in the toun alight.   2189

---

[1] Burnt.   [2] Brim.   [3] Pale yellow.   [4] Freckles.   [5] Sprinkled.
[6] Mingled.   [7] Delight.   [8] A morning hour

This Theseus, this duc, this worthy knyght
Whan he had broght hem in to his citee
And inned [1] hem, everich in his degree,
He festeth hem, and dooth so greet labour
To esen hem, and doon hem al honour,
That yet men weneth that no maner wit
Of noon estaat ne koude amenden it.

The mynstralcye, the service at the feeste,
The grete giftes to the meeste and leeste,
The riche array of Theseus paleys,   (2201 T.)
Ne who sat first, ne last up-on the deys, [2]   2200
What ladyes fairest been, or best daunsynge,
Or which of hem kan dauncen best and synge,
Ne who moost felyngly speketh of love,
What haukes sitten on the perche above,
What houndes liggen [3] in the floor adoun, —
Of al this make I now no mencioun,
Bul al theffect, that thynketh me the beste ;
Now cometh the point, and herkneth if yow
            leste.

The Sonday nyght, er day bigan to sprynge,
Whan Palamon the larke herde synge,   2210
Al though it nere nat day by houres two,
Yet song the larke, and Palamon also.
With hooly herte and with an heigh corage,
He roos to wenden on his pilgrymage
Un-to the blisful Citherea benigne, —
I mene Venus, honurable and digne, —
And in hir houre [4] he walketh forth a paas

---

[1] Housed.   [2] Dais.   [3] Lie.   [4] Monday, two hours before sunrise

Un-to the lystes ther hire temple was,
And doun he kneleth with ful humble cheer
And herte soor, and seyde in this manere : —
    " Faireste of faire, o lady myn, Venus, 2221
Doughter to Jove, and spouse of Vulcanus,
Thow gladere of the mount of Citheron,
For thilke love thow haddest to Adoon,[1]
Have pitee of my bittre teeris smerte,
And taak myn humble preyere at thyn herte.
Allas ! I ne have no langage to telle
Theffectes ne the tormentz of myn helle ;
Myn herte may myne harmes nat biwreye :
I am so confus that I kan noght seye.[2]   2230
But mercy, lady bright, that knowest weele
My thought, and seest what harmes that I feele,
Considere al this and rewe up-on my soore[3]
As wisly[4] as I shal for everemoore,
Emforth[5] my myght, thy trewe servant be,
And holden werre alwey with chastitee,
That make I myn avow, so ye me helpe,
I kepe[6] noght of armes for to yelpe.
Ne I ne axe nat tomorwe to have victorie,
Ne renoun in this cas, ne veyne glorie   2240
Of pris of armes, blowen up and doun,
But I wolde have fully possessioun
Of Emelye, and dye in thy servyse.
Fynd thow the manere, hou and in what wyse,
I recche nat, but it may bettre be   (2247 T.)
To have victorie of hem, or they of me.

[1] Adonis.   [2] Say.   [3] Grief.   [4] As truly.   [5] To the extent of.
Care

So that I have my lady in myne armes,
For though so be that Mars is god of armes,
Youre vertu is so greet in hevene above
That if yow list I shal wel have my love. 2250
　　"Thy temple wol I worshipe everemo,
And on thyn auter, where [1] I ride or go,[2]
I wol doon sacrifice and fires beete;[3]
And if ye wol nat so, my lady sweete.
Thanne preye I thee, tomorwe with a spere
That Arcita me thurgh the herte bere;
Thanne rekke I noght whan I have lost my lyf
Though that Arcita wynne hire to his wyf:
This is theffect and ende of my preyere, —
Gif me my love, thow blisful lady deere." 2260
　　Whan the orison was doon of Palamon,
His sacrifice he dide, and that anon,
Ful pitously with alle circumstaunce,
Al telle I noght as now his observaunce;
But atte laste the statue of Venus shook
And made a signe wher by that he took
That his preyere accepted was that day;
For thogh the signe shewed a delay,
Yet wiste he wel that graunted was his boone,
And with glad herte he wente hym hoom ful
　　　　soone.　　　　　　　　　　2270
　　The thridde houre [4] in-equal that Palamon
Bigan to Venus temple for to gon,
Up roos the sonne and up roos Emelye,
And to the temple of Dyane gan hye.

---

[1] Whether.　[2] Walk.　[3] Kindle.　[4] The "hour" of Diana.

Hir maydens that she thider with hire ladde
Ful redily with hem the fyr they ladde,[1]
Thencens, the clothes, and the remenant al
That to the sacrifice longen shal,
The hornes fulle of meeth [2] as was the gyse, —
Ther lakked noght to doon hir sacrifise.   2280

Smokynge the temple, ful of clothes faire,
This Emelye, with herte debonaire,
Hir body wessh with water of a welle ;[3]
But hou she dide hir ryte I dar nat telle,
But it be any thing in general,
And yet it were a game to heeren al ;
To hym that meneth wel it were no charge,[4]
But it is good a man been at his large.

Hir brighte heer was kempd,[5] untressed al,
A coroune of a grene ook cerial   2290
Up-on hir heed was set ful fair and meete ;
Two fyres on the auter gan she beete,
And dide hir thynges [6] as men may biholde
In Stace of Thebes,[7] and thise bookes olde.
Whan kyndled was the fyr, with pitous cheere,
Un-to Dyane she spak as ye may heere : —

" O chaste goddesse of the wodes grene,
To whom bothe hevene and erthe and see is
        sene,   (2300 T.)
Queene of the regne of Pluto derk and lowe,
Goddesse of maydens that myn herte hast
        knowe   2300

---

[1] Carried.   [2] Mead.   [3] Spring.   [4] Harm.   [5] Wavy.   [6] Duties
[7] The *Thebais* of Statius.

Ful many a yeer, and woost what I desire,
As keepe me fro thy vengeaunce and thyn **ire**
That Attheon aboughte [1] cruelly ;
Chaste goddesse, wel wostow that I
Desire to ben a mayden al my lyf,
Ne nevere wol I be no love, ne wyf.
I am, thow woost, yet of thy compaignye
A mayde, and love huntynge and venerye,[2]
And for to walken in the wodes wilde,   2309
And noght to ben a wyf and be with childe ;
Noght wol I knowe the compaignye of man.
Now helpe me, lady, sith ye may and kan,
For tho thre formes [3] that thou hast in thee.
And Palamon, that hath swich love to me,
And eek Arcite that loveth me so soore,
This grace I preye thee with oute moore ;
And sende love and pees bitwixe hem two,
And fro me turne awey hir hertes so
That al hire hoote love and hir desir,
And al hir bisy torment and hir fir,   2320
Be queynt or turned in another place.
And if so be thou wolt do me no grace,
And if my destynee be shapen so
That I shal nedes have oon of hem two,
As sende me hym that moost desireth me.
Bihoold, goddesse of clene chastitee,
The bittre teeres that on my chekes falle.
Syn thou art mayde, and kepere of us alle,

---

[1] Actæon atoned for.   [2] The chase.   [3] This goddess is known as
Luna, Lucina, Proserpina.

My maydenhede thou kepe and wel conserve
And whil I lyve a mayde I wol thee serve." 2330
  The fires brenne up-on the auter cleere
Whil Emelye was thus in hir preyere,
But sodeynly she saugh a sighte queynte,[1]
For right anon oon of the fyres queynte [2]
And quyked agayn, and after that, anon
That oother fyr was queynt [3] and al agon,
And as it queynte it made a whistlynge,
As doon thise wete brondes [4] in hir brennynge;
And at the brondes ende out ran anon
As it were blody dropes many oon ;   2340
For which so soore agast was Emelye
That she was wel ny mad, and gan to crye,
For she ne wiste what it signyfied,
But oonly for the feere thus hath she cried,
And weepe that it was pitee for to heere ;
And ther with al Dyane gan appeere, (2348 T.)
With bowe in honde right as an hunteresse,
And seyde, " Doghter, stynt thyn hevynesse.

  "Among the goddes hye it is affermed,
And by eterne word writen and confermed, 2350
Thou shalt ben wedded un-to oon of tho
That han for thee so muchel care and wo,
But un-to which of hem I may nat telle.
Farwel, for I ne may no lenger dwelle.
The fires whiche that on myn auter brenne
Shulle thee declare, er that thou go henne,
Thyn aventure of love, as in this cas."

---

[1] Strange.   [2] Languished.   [3] Quenched.   [4] Brands.

And with that word the arwes in the caas
Of the goddesse clateren faste and rynge,
And forth she wente and made a vanysshynge
For which this Emelye astoned was,   2361
And seyde, "What amounteth this, allas!
I putte me in thy proteccioun,
Dyane, and in thy disposicioun."
And hoom she goth anon the nexte weye.
This is theffect, ther is namoore to seye.

The nexte houre of Mars folwynge this,[1]
Arcite un-to the temple walked is
Of fierse Mars, to doon his sacrifise
With alle the rytes of his payen wyse.[2]   2370
With pitous herte and heigh devocioun
Right thus to Mars he seyde his orisoun :—

"O stronge god, that in the regnes colde
Of Trace honoured art and lord yholde,
And hast in every regne and every lond
Of armes al the brydel in thyn hond,
And hem fortunest as thee lyst devyse,
Accepte of me my pitous sacrifise.
If so be that my youthe may deserve,   2375
And that my myght be worthy for to serve
Thy godhede, that I may been oon of thyne,
Thanne preye I thee to rewe up-on my pyne.
For thilke peyne, and thilke hoote fir,
In which thou whilom brendest for desir,
Whan that thou usedeste the beautee
Of faire, yonge, fresshe Venus free,

<hr />

[1] The fourth hour of the day. [2] Pagan custom.

And haddest hire in armes at thy wille,
Al though thee ones on a tyme mysfille,
Whan Vulcanus hadde caught thee in his las,[1]
And foond thee liggynge by his wyf, — allas !
For thilke sorwe that was in thyn herte,   2391
Have routhe as wel up-on my peynes smerte.
I am yong and unkonnynge, as thow woost,
And, as I trowe, with love offended moost
That evere was any lyves[2] creature ;   (2397 T.)
For she that dooth me al this wo endure
Ne reccheth nevere wher I synke or fleete.[3]
And wel I woot er she me mercy heete [4]
I moot with strengthe wynne hire in the place,
And wel I woot withouten helpe or grace   2400
Of thee, ne may my strengthe noght availle.
Thanne helpe me, lord, tomorwe in my bataille,
For thilke fyr that whilom brente thee,
As wel as thilke fyr now brenneth me,
And do that I tomorwe have victorie.
Myn be the travaille, and thyn be the glorie.
Thy sovereyn temple wol I moost honouren
Of any place, and alwey moost labouren
In thy plesaunce, and in thy craftes stronge ;
And in thy temple I wol my baner honge, 2410
And alle the armes of my compaignye,
And evere mo, un-to that day I dye.
Eterne fir I wol biforn thee fynde :
And eek to this avow I wol me bynde.
My beerd, myn heer, that hongeth long adoun

---

[1] **Snare.**   [2] Live.   [3] Whether I sink or float   [4] Promise.

That nevere yet ne felte offensioun
Of rasour nor of shere, 1 wol thee geve,
And ben thy trewe servant whil I lyve.   2418
Now, lord, have routhe up-on my sorwes soore,
Gif me the victorie, I aske thee namoore ! "

    The preyere stynt[1] of Arcita the stronge,
The rynges on the temple dore that honge,
And eek the dores, clatereden ful faste,
Of which Arcita som what hym agaste.
The fyres brende up-on the auter brighte,
That it gan al the temple for to lighte ;
And sweete smel the ground anon up gaf,
And Arcita anon his hand up haf[2]
And moore encens in to the fyr he caste,
With othere rytes mo, and atte last   2430
The statue of Mars bigan his hauberk rynge ;
And with that soun he herde a murmurynge
Ful lowe and dym, that[3] seyde thus : "Victo-
       rie ! "
For which he gaf to Mars honour and glorie.
And thus with joye and hope wel to fare,
Arcite anon un-to his in is fare,
As fayn as fowel is of the brighte sonne.

    And right anon swich strif ther is bigonne
For thilke grauntyng in the hevene above,
Bitwixe Venus, the goddesse of love,   2440
And Mars, the stierne god armypotente,
That Juppiter was bisy it to stente ;
Til that the pale Saturnus the colde,

      [1] Ended.   [2] Heaved.   [3] Elles. MS. has " and."

That knew so manye of aventures olde,
Foond in his olde experience and art
That he ful soone hath plesed every part.[1]
As sooth is seyd, elde hath greet avantage ;
In elde is bothe wysdom and usage ; (2450 T.)
Men may the olde at-renne [2] and noght at-rede.[3]
Saturne anon, to stynten strif and drede, 2450
Al be it that it is agayn his kynde,[4]
Of al this strif he gan remedie fynde.

" My deere doghter Venus," quod Saturne,
" My cours, that hath so wyde for to turne,
Hath moore power than woot any man ;
Myn is the drenchyng [5] in the see so wan,
Myn is the prison in the derke cote,
Myn is the stranglyng and hangyng by the
        throte,
The murmure and the cherles rebellyng,
The groynynge [6] and the pryvee empoysonyng ;
I do vengeance and pleyn correccioun 2461
Whiles I dwelle in signe of the leoun ;
Myn is the ruyne of the hye halles,
The fallynge of the toures and of the walles,
Up-on the mynour or the carpenter, —
I slow Sampsoun, shakynge the piler, —
And myne be the maladyes colde,
The derke tresons and the castes [7] olde ;
My lookyng is the fader of pestilence ; 2469
Now weepe namoore, I shal doon diligence

---

[1] Party. [2] Outrun. [3] Outwit. Cf. *Troylus and Cryseyde*, iv
456. [4] Against his nature. [5] Drowning. [6] Stabbing. [7] Plots

That Palamon, that is thyn owene knyght,
Shal have his lady as thou hast him hight.[1]
Though Mars shal helpe his knyght, yet nathe-
  lees,
Bitwixe yow ther moot be som tyme pees,
Al be ye noght of o compleccioun,
That causeth al day swich divisioun.
I am thyn aiel,[2] redy at thy wille ;
Weepe now namoore, I wol thy lust fulfille."

 Now wol I stynten of the goddes above,
Of Mars, and of Venus, goddesse of love, 2480
And telle yow, as pleynly as I kan,
The grete effect[3] for which that I bygan.

FOURTH PART.

 Greet was the feeste in Atthenes that day,
And eek the lusty seson of that May
Made every wight to been in such plesaunce,
That al that Monday justen they and daunce,
And spenten it in Venus heigh servyse ;
But, by the cause that they sholde ryse
Eerly for to seen the grete fight,
Un-to hir reste wenten they at nyght. 2490
And on the morwe, whan that day gan sprynge,
Of hors and harneys noyse and claterynge
Ther was in the hostelryes al aboute,
And to the paleys rood ther many a route
Of lordes, up-on steedes and palfreys. (2497 T.
Ther maystow seen divisynge of harneys

---

 [1] Promised. [2] *A ieul*, grandfather. [3] Dénouement.

So unkouth [1] and so riche, and wroght so weel
Of goldsmythrye, of browdynge, and of steel,
The sheeldes brighte, testeres,[2] and trappures ;
Gold-hewen helmes, hauberkes, cote armures ;
Lordes in paramentz [3] on hir courseres ;   2501
Knyghtes of retenue, and eek squieres,
Nailynge the speres, and helmes bokelynge,
Giggynge [4] of sheeldes with layneres [5] lacynge ;
There, as nede is, they weren no thyng ydel.
The fomy steedes on the golden brydel
Gnawynge, and faste the armurers also,
With fyle and hamer, prikynge to and fro ;
Yemen on foyte,[6] and communes many oon,
With shorte staves thikke as they may goon ;
Pypes, trompes, nakerers,[7] clariounes,   2511
That in the bataille blowen blody sounes ;
The paleys ful of peples up and doun, —
Heere thre, ther ten, holdynge hir questioun,[8]
Dyvynynge of thise Thebane knyghtes two.
Somme seyden thus, somme seyde it shal be so,
Somme helden with hym with the blake berd,
Somme with the balled, somme with the thikke
      herd,[9]
Somme seyde he looked grymme and he wolde
      fighte,   2519
He hath a sparth [10] of twenty pound of wighte, —
Thus was the halle ful of divynynge
Longe after that the sonne gan to sprynge.

---

[1] Unknown. [2] Helms [3] Trappings. [4] Clattering. [5] Thongs
[6] Yeomen on foot. [7] Drums. [8] Debate. [9] Haired. [10] Halberd

The grete Theseus, that of his sleepe awaked
With mynstralcie and noyse that was maked,
Heeld yet the chambre of his paleys riche,
Til that the Thebane knyghtes, bothe yliche
Honured, were in to the paleys fet.[1]
Duc Theseus was at a wyndow set,
..rrayed right as he were a god in trone.
The peple preesseth thiderward ful soone 2530
Hym for to seen, and doon heigh reverence,
And eek to herkne his heste[2] and his sentence.

An heraud on a scaffold made an " Oo ! "
Til al the noyse of peple was ydo ;
And whan he saugh the noyse of peple al stille
Tho[3] shewed he the myghty dukes wille.

" The lord hath of his heih discrecioun
Considered that it were destruccioun
To gentil blood to fighten in the gyse
Of mortal bataille now in this emprise,   2540
Wherfore, to shapen that they shal nat dye,
He wolde his firste purpos modifye.

" No man ther fore, up peyne of los of lyf,
No maner shot,[4] polax, ne shorte knyf,
In to the lystes sende, ne thider brynge ;
Ne short swerd, for to steke[5] with poynt bit-
            ynge,
No man ne drawe ne bere by his syde.
Ne no man shal un-to his felawe ryde   (2550 T.)
But o cours with a sharpe ygrounde spere ;

Foyne, if hym list, on foote, hym self to were.[1]
And he that is at meschief shal be take, 2551
And noght slayn, but be broght un-to the stake
That shal ben ordeyned on either syde,
But thider he shal by force, and there abyde,

"And if so be the chieftayn be take
On outher syde, or elles sleen his make,[1]
No lenger shal the turneiynge laste.
God spede you! gooth forth, and ley on faste!
With long swerd and with maces fighteth youre
fille. 2559
Gooth now youre wey, this is the lordes will."

The voys of peple touched the hevene,
So loude cride they, with murie stevene,[2]
"God save swich a lord, that is so good,
He wilneth no destruccion of blood!"

Up goon the trompes and the melodye
And to the lystes rit the compaignye
By ordinance thurgh out the citee large,
Hanged with clooth of gold and nat with sarge.

Ful lik a lord this noble duc gan ryde,
Thise two Thebans up-on either side; 2570
And after rood the queene and Emelye,
And after that another compaignye
Of oon and oother after hir degre;
And thus they passen thurgh out the citee,
And to the lystes come they by tyme.
It nas not of the day yet fully pryme
Whan set was Theseus ful riche and hye,

[1] Guard. [2] Slay nis mate. [3] Pleasant voice

Ypolita the queene and Emelye,
And othere ladys in degrees aboute.
Un-to the seettes preesseth al the route,   2580
And westward, thurgh the gates under Marte,
Arcite, and eek the hondred of his parte,
With baner reed is entred right anon.

And in that selve moment Palamon
Is under Venus, estward in the place,
With baner whyt, and hardy chiere and face.
In al the world to seken up and doun
So evene, with outen variacioun,
Ther nere swiche compaignyes tweye ;
For ther was noon so wys that koude seye 2590
That any hadde of oother avauntage
Of worthynesse, ne of estaat, ne age,
So evene were they chosen, for to gesse,
And in two renges [1] faire they hem dresse.

Whan that hir names rad [2] were everichon,
That in hir nombre gyle were ther noon,
Tho were the gates shet and cried was loude,
"Do now youre *devoir*, yonge knyghtes proude !"

The heraudes lefte hir prikyng up and doun ;
Now ryngen trompes loude and clarioun ; 2600
Ther is namoore to seyn, but west and est,
In goon the speres ful sadly [8] in arrest ;
In gooth the sharpe spore in to the syde.
Ther seen men who kan juste and who kan
      ryde ;   (2606 т.)
Ther shyveren shaftes up-on sheeldes thikke ;

      [1] Ranks.   [2] Read.   [8] Firmly.

He feeleth thurgh the herte-spoon[1] the prikke.
Up spryngen speres twenty foot on highte ;
Out gooth the swerdes as the silver brighte ;
The helmes they to-hewen and to-shrede, 2609
Out brest the blood with stierne stremes rede ;
With myghty maces the bones they to-breste.
He, thurgh the thikkeste of the throng gan
    threste,
Ther, stomblen[2] steedes stronge, and doun
    gooth al ;
He, rolleth under foot as dooth a bal ;
He, foyneth on his feet with his tronchoun,
And he, hym hurtleth with his hors adoun ;
He, thurgh the body is hurt and sithen ytake,
Maugree his heed, and broght un-to the stake,
As forward[3] was, right ther he moste abyde.
Another lad[4] is on that oother syde. 2620
And som tyme dooth hem Theseus[5] to reste,
Hem to fresshen and drynken, if hem leste.
Ful ofte a-day han thise Thebanes two,
Togydre ymet and wroght his felawe wo ;
Unhorsed hath ech oother of hem tweye.
Ther nas no tygre in the vale of Galgopheye,[6]
Whan that hir whelpe is stole whan it is lite,[7]
So crueel on the hunte, as is Arcite
For jelous herte upon this Palamoun ;
Ne in Belmarye[8] ther nys so fel leoun 2630
That hunted is, or for his hunger wood,

---

[1] Breast-bone (nearly).   [2] Elles. MS. has "semblen."   [3] Agreement.   [4] Led.   [5] Theseus maketh them   [6] An African vale (?).
[7] Little.   [8] Cf. l. 57.

Ne of his praye desireth so the blood,
As Palamoun, to sleen his foo Arcite.
The jelous strokes on hir helmes byte ;
Out renneth blood on bothe hir sydes rede.

   Som tyme an ende ther is of every dede,
For, er the sonne un-to the reste wente,
The stronge kyng Emetreus gan hente [1]
This Palamon as he faught with Arcite,
And made his swerd depe in his flessh to byte,
And by the force of twenty is he take   2641
Unyolden,[2] and ydrawe unto the stake.
And in the rescus [3] of this Palamoun   (2645 T.)
The stronge kyng Lygurge is born adoun,
And kyng Emetreus, for al his strengthe,
Is born out of his sadel a swerdes lengthe ;
So hitte him Palamoun, er he were take ;
Bul al for noght, he was broght to the stake.
His hardy herte myghte hym helpe naught,
He moste abyde, whan that he was caught,
By force, and eek by composicioun.   2651

   Who sorweth now but woful Palamoun,
That moot namoore goon agayn to fighte ?
And whan that Theseus hadde seyn this sighte
Un-to the folk that foghten thus echon
He cryde, " Hoo ! namoore, for it is doon !
I wol be trewe juge, and no partie ; [4]
Arcite of Thebes shall have Emelie
That by his fortune hath hire faire ywonne."

   Anon ther is a noyse of peple bigonne, 2660

[1] Seize.   [2] Not yielding.   [3] Rescue.   [4] Partisan.

For joye of this, so loude and heighe with alle,
It semed that the lystes sholde falle.

What kan now faire Venus doon above?
What seith she now, what dooth this queene of
    love,
But wepeth so, for wantynge of hir wille,
Til that hir teeres in the lystes fille?
She seyde, "I am ashamed doutelees."

Saturnus seyde, "Doghter, hoold thy pees
Mars hath his wille, his knyght hath all h'
    boone,   2669
And, by myn heed, thow shalt been esed soone."

The trompes, with the loude mynstralcie,
The heraudes, that ful loude yolle and crie,
Been in hire wele,[1] for joye of daun Arcite.
But herkneth me, and stynteth now a lite,
Which a myracle ther bifel anon.

This fierse Arcite hath of his helm ydon,[2]
And on a courser, for to shewe his face,
He priketh endelong[3] the large place,
Lokynge upward up-on Emelye,
And she agayn hym caste a freendlich eye 2680
(For wommen, as to speken in comune,
Thei folwen all the favour of Fortune),[4]
And was al his, in chiere,[5] as in his herte.

Out of the ground a furie infernal sterte,
From Pluto sent, at requeste of Saturne,
For which his hors for fere gan to turne,

---

[1] Prosperity.   [2] Taken off his helm.   [3] From end to end of
These two lines are ner in the Elles. MS. [5] Countenance

And leepe aside, and foundred as he leepe,
And er that Arcite may taken keepe,[1]   2688
He pighte[2] hym on the pomel[3] of his heed,
That in the place he lay as he were deed,
His brest to-brosten with his sadel-bowe.
As blak he lay as any cole or crowe,
So was the blood yronnen in his face.
Anon he was yborn out of the place,
With herte soor, to Theseus paleys.
Tho was he korven out of his harneys,
And in a bed ybrought ful faire and blyve,[4]
For he was yet in memorie and alyve, (2700 T.)
And alwey criynge after Emelye.

　Duc Theseus with al his compaignye   2700
Is comen hoom to Atthenes his citee
With alle blisse and greet solempnitee ;
Al be it that this aventure was falle
He nolde noght disconforten hem alle, —
Men seyden eek that Arcite shal nat dye,
He shal been heeled of his maladye.

　And of another thyng they weren as fayn,
That of hem alle was ther noon yslayn,
Al were they soore yhurt, and namely oon,
That with a spere was thirled[5] his brest boon.
To othere woundes and to broken armes, 2711
Somme hadden salves and somme hadden
　charmes,
Fermacies[6] of herbes, and eek save[7]
They dronken, for they wolde hir lymes have.

---

[1] Care.　[2] Pitched.　[3] Top.　[4] Quickly.　[5] Pierced.　[6] Medicines
Sage

For which this noble duc, as he wel kan,
Conforteth and honoureth every man,
And made revel al the longe nyght
Un-to the straunge lordes as was right ;
Ne ther was holden no disconfitynge
But as a justes, or a tourneiynge ;   2720
For soothly ther was no disconfiture,
For fallyng nys nat but an aventure,
Ne to be lad by force un-to the stake
Unyolden, and with twenty knyghtes take,
O persone allone, with outen mo,
And haryed [1] forth by arme, foot and too,
And eke his steede dryven forth with staves,
With footmen, bothe yemen and eek knaves,
It nas aretted [2] hym no vileynye,
Ther may no man clepen it no [3] cowardye. 2730
   For which anon duc Theseus leet crye,
To stynten alle rancour and envye,
The gree [4] as wel of o syde as of oother,
And eyther syde ylik as ootheres brother;
And gaf hem giftes after hir degree,
And fully heeld a feeste dayes three,
And convoyed the kynges worthily
Out of his toun, a journee largely,[5]
And hoom wente every man the righte way.
Ther was namoore, but " Fare wel ! " " Have
        good day ! "   2740
Of this bataille I wol namoore endite,
But speke of Palamoun and of Arcyte.

---

[1] Taken prisoner.   [2] Counted.   [3] Not in Elles. MS.   [4] Prize.
[5] Full day's journey.

Swelleth the brest of Arcite, and the soore
Encreesseth at his herte moore and moore.
The clothered [1] blood, for any lechecraft,
Corrupteth, and is in his bouk [2] ylaft, (2748 T.)
That neither veyne-blood ne ventusynge, [3]
Ne drynke of herbes may ben his helpynge ;
The vertu [4] expulsif, or animal,
Fro thilke vertu cleped natural,   2750
Ne may the venym voyden ne expelle.
The pipes of his longes gonne to swelle,
And every lacerte [5] in his brest adoun
Is shent [6] with venym and corrupcioun.
Hym gayneth neither, for to gete his lif,
Vomyt upward, ne dounward, laxatif ;
Al is to-brosten [7] thilke regioun ;
Nature hath now no dominacioun ;
And certeinly, ther Nature wol nat wirche,
Fare wel phisik, go ber the man to chirche.
This al and som, [8] that Arcita moot dye,   2761
For which he sendeth after Emelye,
And Palamon, that was his cosyn deere.
Thanne seyde he thus as ye shal after heere :

" Naught may the woful spirit in myn herte
Declare o point of alle my sorwes smerte
To yow, my lady, that I love moost,
But I biquethe the servyce of my goost
To yow aboven every creature,
Syn that my lyf it may no lenger dure.   2770

---

[1] Clotted. [2] Body. [3] Cupping. [4] Energy. [5] Muscle. [6] Wasted
Completely burst, ruined. [8] This all said.

Allas the wo! allas, the peynes stronge,
That I for yow have suffred, and so longe!
Allas, the deeth! allas, myn Emelye!
Allas, departynge[1] of our compaignye!
Allas, myn hertes queene! allas, my wyf!
Myn hertes lady, endere of my lyf!
What is this world? what asketh men to have?
Now with his love, now in his colde grave
Allone, with outen any compaignye.
Fare wel, my swete foo, myn Emelye!   2780
And softe taak me in youre armes tweye
For love of God, and herkneth what I seye.

  " I have heer with my cosyn Palamon
Had strif and rancour many a day agon
For love of yow, and for my jalousye,
And Juppiter so wys my soule gye[2]
To speken of a servaunt proprely,
With alle circumstances trewely, —
That is to seyn, trouthe, honour, knyghthede,
Wysdom, humblesse, estaat and heigh kynrede,
Fredom, and al that longeth to that art, —
So Juppiter have of my soule part   2792
As in this world right now ne knowe I non
So worthy to ben loved as Palamon,
That serveth yow and wol doon al his lyf.
And if that evere ye shul ben a wyf, (2798 T.)
Forget nat Palamon, the gentil man," —
And with that word his speche faille gan,
And from his herte up to his brest was come

---

[1] Sundering.   So truly guide my soul.

The coold of deeth, that hadde hym overcome
And yet moore over, for in his armes two, 2801
The vital strengthe is lost and al ago.
Oonly the intellect, with outen moore
That dwelled in his herte syk and soore,
Gan faillen when the herte felte deeth,
Dusked hise eyen two and failled breeth.
But on his lady yet caste he his eye ;
His laste word was, " Mercy, Emelye ! "
His spirit chaunged hous, and wente ther,
As I cam nevere, I kan nat tellen wher.   2810
Therfore I stynte, I nam no divinistre ;
Of soules fynde I nat in this registre,
Ne me ne list thilke opinions to telle,
Of hem though that they writen wher **they**
         dwelle.
Arcite is coold, ther Mars his soule gye ;
Now wol I speken forth of Emelye.

   Shrighte Emelye, and howleth Palamon,
And Theseus his suster took anon
Swownynge, and baar hire fro the corps away.
What helpeth it to tarien forth the day   2820
To tellen how she weepe, bothe eve **and**
         morwe ?
For in swich cas wommen have swiche sorwe
Whan that hir housbonds ben from hem ago
That for the moore part they sorwen so,
Or ellis fallen in swich maladye
That at the laste certeinly they dye.

   Infinite been the sorwes and the teeres

Of olde folk, and eek of tendre yeeres,
In all the toun for deeth of this Theban ;
For hym ther wepeth bothe child and man ;
So greet a wepyng was ther noon certayn **2831**
Whan Ector was ybroght al fressh yslayn
To Troye.   Allas ! the pitee that was ther,
Cracchynge [1] of chekes, rentynge eek of heer.
" Why woldestow be deed ? " thise wommen
          crye,
" And haddest gold ynough, and Emelye."
    No man ne myghte gladen Theseus,
Savynge his olde fader Egeus,
That knew this worldes transmutacioun,
As he hadde seyn it chaungen,[2] up and doun,
Joye after wo and wo after gladnesse,   **2841**
And shewed hem ensamples and liknesse.
    " Right as ther dyed nevere man," quod he,
" That he ne lyvede in erthe in som degree,
Right so ther lyvede never man," he seyde,
" In all this world, that som tym he ne deyde ;
This world nys but a thurghfare ful of wo,
And we been pilgrymes passynge to and fro ;
Deeth is an ende of every worldes soore ; "
And over al this yet seyde he muchel moore
To this effect, ful wisely to enhorte   (2853 T.)
The peple that they sholde hem reconforte.
    Duc Theseus, with all his bisy cure,[3]   **2857**
Cast now wher that the sepulture
Of goode Arcite may best ymaked be,

---

[1] Scratching   Not in Elles. MS.   [3] Care.

And eek moost honurable in his degree ;
And at the laste he took conclusioun
That ther as first Arcite and Palamoun
Hadden for love the bataille hem bitwene,
That in that selve grove, swoote and grene,
Ther as he hadde hise amorouse desires, 286.
His compleynte, and for love hise hoote fires,
He wolde make a fyr in which the office
Funereal he myghte al accomplice ;
And leet comande anon to hakke and hewe
The okes olde, and leye hem on a rewe,[1]
In colpons,[2] wel arrayed for to brenne.
Hise officers with swifte feet they renne,
And ryden anon at his comandement.
And after this Theseus hath ysent   287c
After a beere, and it al over spradde
With clooth of gold, the richeste that he hadde ;
And of the same suyte he clad Arcite.
Up-on his hondes hadde he gloves white,
Eek on his heed a coroune of laurer grene,
And in his hond a swerd ful bright and kene.
He leyde hym, bare the visage, on the beere.
Ther-with he weepe that pitee was to heere ;
And, for the peple sholde seen hym alle,
Whan it was day he broghte hym to the halle,
That roreth of the criyng and the soun.   288ᵛ

    Tho cam this woful Theban Palamoun,
With flotery[3] berd and rugged asshy heeres,
In clothes biake, ydropped al with teeres ;

----

¹ Row.   ² Portions, logs.   ³ Flowing.

And passynge othere of wepynge, Emelye,
The rewefulleste of al the compaignye.
In as muche as the servyce sholde be
The moore noble and riche in his degree,
Duc Theseus leet forth thre steedes brynge,
That trapped were in steele al gliterynge 2890
And covered with the armes of daun Arcite.
Up-on thise steedes grete and white,
Ther sitten folk, of whiche oon baar his sheeld,
Another his spere in his hondes heeld,
The thridde baar with hym his bowe Turkeys [1]
(Of brend gold was the caas, and eek the har-
      neys),   (2898 T.)
And riden forth a paas [2] with sorweful cheere,
Toward the grove, as ye shul after heere.
The nobleste of the Grekes that ther were
Up-on hir shuldres caryeden the beere,   2900
With slake paas, and eyen rede and wete,
Thurgh out the citee by the maister [3] strete,
That sprad was al with blak and wonder hye,
Right of the same is the strete ywrye. [4]

Up-on the right hond wente olde Egeus,
And on that oother syde duc Theseus,
With vessels in hir hand of gold ful fyn
Al ful of hony, milk, and blood, and wyn :
Eek Palamon with ful greet compaignye,
And after that cam woful Emelye,   2910
With fyr in honde as was that tyme the gyse [5]
To do the office of funeral servyse.

---

[1] Turkish   [2] At a walk.   [3] Chief.   [4] Covered.   [5] Fashion.

Heigh labour, and ful greet apparaillynge,
Was at the service and the fyr makynge,
That with his grene tope the heven raughte,
And twenty fadme of brede [1] the armes
    straughte,[2]
This is to seyn the bowes weren so brode.
Of stree [3] first ther was leyd ful many a lode,
But how the fyr was maked up on highte,   2919
And eek the names that the trees highte, —
As ook, firre, birch, aspe, alder, holm, popeler,
Wylugh, elm, plane, assh, box, chasteyn,[4] lynde
    laurer,
Mapul, thorn, bech, hasel, ew, whippeltre,[5] —
How they weren feld shal nat be toold for me;
Ne hou the goddes ronnen up and doun,
Disherited of hire habitacioun,
In whiche they woneden [6] in reste and pees,
Nymphus, fawnes, and amadriades;
Ne hou the beestes and the briddes alle   2929
Fledden for fere, whan the wode was falle;
Ne how the ground agast was of the light,
That was nat wont to seen the sonne bright;
Ne how the fyr was couched [7] first with stree,
And thanne with drye stokkes, cloven a thre,
And thanne with grene wode and spicerye,
And thanne with clooth of gold, and with per·
    rye,[8]
And gerlandes, hangynge with ful many a flour,

---

[1] Fathoms broad. [2] Stretched. [3] Straw. [4] Chestnut. [5] Corne
tree. [6] Dwelt. [7] Laid. [8] Precious stones.

The mirre,[1] thencens, with al so greet odour;
Ne how Arcite lay among al this,
Ne what richesse aboute his body is,   2940
Ne how that Emelye, as was the gyse,
Putte in the fyr of funeral servyse,
Ne how she swowned whan men [2] made fyr,
Ne what she spak, ne what was hir desire,
Ne what jeweles men in the fyre caste
Whan that the fyr was greet and brente [3] faste ;
Ne how somme caste hir sheeld, and somme
            hir spere,   (2949 T.)
And of hire vestimentz, whiche that they were,
And coppes full of wyn, and milk, and blood,
In to the fyr, that brente as it were wood ; 2950
Ne how the Grekes, with an huge route,
Tries [4] riden al the place aboute
Up on the left hand, with a loud shoutynge,
And thries with hir speres claterynge,
And thries how the ladyes gonne crye,
And how that lad was homward Emelye ;
Ne how Arcite is brent to asshen colde,
Ne how that lych-wake [5] was yholde
Al thilke nyght ; ne how the Grekes pleye
The wake-pleyes ; ne kepe [6] I nat to seye 2960
Who wrastleth best naked, with oille enoynt,
Ne who that baar hym best in no disjoynt.[7]
I wol nat tellen eek how that they goon
Hoom til Atthenes, whan the pley is doon ;

Myrrh.   [2] Camb. MS. and others read " she."   [3] Burned
Thrice.   [5] Corpse-vigil.   [6] Care   [7] Difficult situation.

But shortly to the point thanne wol I wende,
And maken of my longe tale an ende.

By processe and by lengthe of certeyn yeres,
Al styntyd is the moornynge and the teres
Of Grekes, by oon general assent.
Thanne semed me ther was a parlement   2970
At Atthenes, upon certein poyntz and caas ;
Among the whiche poyntz yspoken was,
To·have with certein contrees alliaunce,
And have fully of Thebans obeissaunce.
For which this noble Theseus anon
Leet senden after gentil Palamon,
Unwist of hym what was the cause and why ;
But in hise blake clothes sorwefully
He cam at his comandement in hye.[1]
Tho sente Theseus for Emelye.   2980
Whan they were set, and hust was al the place,
And Theseus abiden hadde a space
Er any word cam fram his wise brest,
Hise eyen sette he ther as was his lest,
And with a sad visage he siked [2] stille,
And after that right thus he seyde his wille :

" The Firste Moevere of the cause above,[3]
Whan he first made the faire cheyne of love,
Greet was theffect and heigh was his entente ;
Wel wiste he why and what ther of he mente,
For with that faire cheyne of love he bond 299
The fyr, the eyr, the water and the lond,
In certeyn boundes that they may nat flee.

---

[1] **Haste.**   [2] Sighed.   [3] Cf. Boethius, *De Consolatione*, ii., met. **8**

That same Prince, and that Moevere," quod he,
" Hath stablissed in this wrecched world adoun
Certeyne dayes and duracioun
To al that is engendrid in this place,
Over the whiche day they may nat pace, —
Al mowe they yet tho dayes wel abregge,
Ther nedeth noght noon auctoritee allegge 3000
For it is preeved by experience,   (3003 T.)
But that me list declaren my sentence.[1]
Thanne may men by this ordre wel discerne
That thilke Moevere stable is and eterne.
Wel may men knowe, but it be a fool,
That every part dirryveth from his hool ;
For nature hath taken his bigynnyng
Of no partie or of cantel[2] of a thyng,
But of a thyng that parfit is and stable,
Descendynge so, til it be corrumpable.   3010
And therfore of his wise purveiaunce
He hath so wel biset his ordinaunce,
That speces of thynges and progressiouns
Shullen enduren by successiouns,
And nat cterne, with outen any lyc ;
This maystow understonde, and seen at[3] eye.

   " Loo the ook, that hath so long a norisshynge
From tyme that it first bigynneth sprynge,
And hath so long a lif as we may see,
Yet at the laste wasted is the tree.   3020
   " Considereth eek how that the harde stoon
Under oure feet, on which we trede and goon,

---

[1] Opinion.   [2] Fragment.   [3] Elles. MS. has "it."

Yit wasteth it as it lyth by the weye ;
The brode ryver somtyme wexeth dreye ;
The grete toures se we wane and wende ;[1]
Thanne may ye se that al this thyng hath ende.

" Of man and womman seen we wel also,
That nedeth in oon of thise termes two,
This is to seyn, in youthe or elles age,   3029
He moot be deed, the kyng as shal a page ;
Som in his bed, som in the depe see,
Som in the large feeld, as men may se ;
Ther helpeth noght, al goth that ilke weye :
Thanne may I seyn al this thyng moot deye.

" What maketh this but Juppiter, the kyng,
That is prince, and cause of alle thyng,
Convertynge al un-to his propre welle,[2]
From which it is dirryved, sooth to telle ?
And here agayns[3] no creature on lyve,
Of no degree, availleth for to stryve.   3040

" Thanne is it wysdom, as it thynketh me,
To maken vertu of necessitee,
And take it weel that we may not eschue
And namely that to us alle is due.
And who so gruccheth ought, he dooth folye,
And rebel is to hym that al may gye ;[4]
And certeinly a man hath moost honour,
To dyen in his excellence and flour,   (3050 T.)
Whan he is siker[5] of his goode name.
Thanne hath he doon his freend ne hym no
          shame,   3050

1 Pass away.   2 Source.   3 Against.   4 Guide.   5 Secure.

And gladder oghte his freend been of his deeth,
Whan with honour up yolden [1] is his breeth,
Than whan his name apalled [2] is for age,
For al forgeten is his vassellage. [3]
Thanne is it best, as for a worthy fame,
To dyen whan that he is best of name.

"The contrarie of al this is wilfulnesse.
Why grucchen we, why have we hevynesse
That goode Arcite, of chivalrie flour,
Departed is with duetee and honour   3060
Out of this foule prisoun of this lyf?
Why grucchen heere his cosyn and his wyf
Of his wel fare that loved hem so weel?
Kan he hem thank — Nay, God woot, never a
    deel —
That bothe his soule and eek hem self offende,
And yet they mowe hir lustes nat amende?

"What may I concluden of this longe serye,
But after wo, I rede [4] us to be merye,
And thanken Juppiter of al his grace?
And er that we departen from this place   3070
I rede that we make of sorwes two
O [5] parfit joye, lastynge everemo.
And looketh now, wher moost sorwe is her-inne,
Ther wol we first amenden and bigynne."

"Suster," quod he, "this is my fulle assent,
With all thavys heere of my parlement,
That gentil Palamon, thyn owene knyght,
That serveth yow with wille, herte, and myght,

---

[1] Yielded.   [2] Enfeebled   Valor.   [4] Advise.   [5] One.

And evere hath doon, syn that ye first hym
      knewe,   3079
That ye shul of your grace up-on hym rewe,
And taken hym for housbonde and for lord ;
Lene [1] me youre hond, for this is oure accord.
Lat se now of youre wommanly pitee ;
He is a kynges brother, sone, *pardee,*
And though he were a povre bacheler,
Syn he hath served yow so many a yeer
And had for yow so greet adversitee,
It moste been considered, leeveth [2] me,
For gentil mercy oghte to passen right." [3]
    Thanne seyde he thus to Palamon ful right :
"I trowe ther nedeth litel sermonyng   3091
To make yow assente to this thyng ;
Com neer, and taak youre lady by the hond."
Bitwixen hem was maad anon the bond
That highte matrimoigne, or mariage,
By al the conseil and the baronage ;
And thus with alle blisse and melodye
Hath Palamon ywedded Emelye,
And God, that al this wyde world hath wroght,
Sende hym his love that it deere aboght, 3100
For now is Palamon in alle wele, [4]
Lyvynge in blisse, in richesse, and in heele ;
And Emelye hym loveth so tendrely,
And he hire serveth so gentilly,
That nevere was ther no word hem bitwene
Of jalousie or any oother tene. [5]

Give. [2] **Believe.** [3] Surpass mere justice. [4] Weal. [5] Grievance

Thus endeth Palamon and Emelye, (3109 T.)
And God save al this faire compaignye. *Amen.*

*Heere folwen the wordes bitwene the Hoost and
the Millere.*

Whan that the Knyght had thus his tale
 ytoold,
In al the route ne was ther yong ne oold 3110
That he ne seyde it was a noble storie,
And worthy for to drawen to memorie,
And namely [1] the gentils everichon.
 Oure Hooste lough and swoor, " So moot **I**
 gon,
This gooth aright; unbokeled is the male ; [2]
Lat se now who shal telle another tale,
For trewely the game is wel bigonne.
Now telleth on, sire **Monk**, if that ye konne
Sumwhat to quite [3] with the Knyghtes tale."
 The Millere, that for-dronken was al pale,
So that unnethe [4] up on his hors he sat, 3121
He nolde avalen [5] neither hood ne hat,
Ne abyde no man for his curteisie,
But in Pilates voys [6] he gan to crie,
And swoor by armes, and by blood and bones,
" I kan a noble tale for the nones, (3128 T.)
With which I wol now quite the Knyghtes tale."
 Oure Hooste saugh that he was dronke of ale,

Especially.   [2] Budget.   [3] Offset.   [4] Scarcely.   [5] Doff   [6] As
Pilate spoke in the Mystery Plays.

And seyde, "Abyd, Robyn, my leeve brother,
Som bettre man shal telle us first another;
Abyde, and lat us werken thriftily."   3131
   "By Goddes soule," quod he, "that wol nat I,
For I wol speke, or elles go my wey."
   Oure Hoost answerde, "Tel on a devele wey !
Thou art a fool, thy wit is overcome."
   "Now herkneth," quod the Millere, "alle
      and some ;
But first I make a protestacioun
That I am dronke, I knowe it by my soun,
And therfore if that I mysspeke or seye,
Wyte it [1] the ale of Southwerk, I you preye ;
For I wol telle a legende and a lyf,   3141
Bothe of a carpenter and of his wyf,
How that a clerk hath set the wrightes cappe."
   The Reve answerde and seyde, "Stynt thy
      clappe !
Lat be thy lewed, dronken harlotrye ;
It is a synne, and eek a greet folye
To apeyren [3] any man, or hym defame, (3149 T.)
And eek to bryngen wyves in swich fame ;
Thou mayst ynogh of othere thynges seyn."
   This dronke Millere spak ful soone ageyn
And seyde, "Leve [4] brother Osewold,   3151
Who hath no wyf he is no cokewold,
But I sey nat therfore that thou art oon,
Ther been ful goode wyves many oon, (3156 T.)
And evere a thousand goode ageyns oon badde ;

Attribute it to.   [2] Befooled him.   Cf. l. 586.   [3] Injure.   [4] **Loved**

That knowestow wel thy self, but ' if **thou**
  madde.[1]
Why artow angry with my tale now?
I have a wyf *pardee*, as wel as thow,
Yet nolde I, for the oxen in my plogh,
Taken up-on me moore than ynogh;   3160
As demen of my-self that I were oon,
I wol bileve wel that I am noon.
An housbonde shal nat been inquisityf
Of Goddes pryvetee, nor of his wyf;
So he may fynde Goddes foysoun[2] there,
Of the remenant nedeth nat enquere." (3166 T.)

What sholde I moore seyn, but this Mill**ere**
He nolde his wordes for no man forbere,
But told his cherles tale in his manere.
Mathynketh that I shal reherce it heere,   3170
And ther-fore every gentil wight I preye,
For Goddes love, demeth[3] nat that I seye
Of yvel entente, but that I moot reherce
Hir tales alle, be they bettre or werse,
Or elles falsen som of my mateere;
And therfore, who so list it nat yheere,
Turne over the leef and chese another tale;
For he shal fynde ynowe, grete and smale,
Of storial thyng that toucheth gentillesse,
And eek moralitee, and hoolynesse, —   3180
Blameth nat me if that ye chese amys.
The Millere is a cherl, ye knowe wel this,

<hr>

[1] Maddest.   [2] Abundance.   [3] Judge.

So was the Reve, and othere manye mo,
And harlotrie [1] they tolden bothe two.
Avyseth yow, putteth me out of blame, (3185 T.)
And eek men shal nat maken ernest of game.

Heere bigynneth The Millere his Tale.

Whilom ther was dwellynge at Oxenford
A riche gnof,[2] that gestes heeld to bord,
And of his craft he was a carpenter.   (3189 T.)
With hym ther was dwellynge a povre scoler
Hadde lerned art, but al his fantasye   3191
Was turned for to lerne astrologye,
And koude a certeyn of [3] conclusiouns,
To demen [4] by interrogaciouns,
If that men asked hym in certein houres
Whan that men sholde have droghte or elles
        shoures,
Or if men asked hym what sholde bifalle
Of every thyng, I may nat rekene hem alle.
    This clerk was cleped hende [5] Nicholas.
Of deerne [6] love he koude,[7] and of solas,[8]   3200
And ther-to he was sleigh and ful privee,
And lyk a mayden meke for to see.
A chambre hadde he in that hostelrye
Allone, with-outen any compaignye,
Ful fetisly ydight,[9] with herbes swoote,
And he hym self as sweete as is the roote

---

[1] Ribaldry.   [2] Churl.   [3] Knew certain.   [4] Judge.   [5] Civil
Secret.   [7] Knew.   [8] Sport.   [9] Neatly adorned.

Of lycorys, or any cetewale.[1]
His Almageste,[2] and bookes grete and smale,
His astrelabie, longynge for [3] his art,
His augrym stones,[4] layen faire a part,   3210
On shelves couched at his beddes heed,   ·
His presse ycovered with a faldyng [5] reed,
And all above ther lay a gay sautrie,
On which he made a-nyghtes melodie
So swetely, that al the chambre rong,
And *Angelus ad Virginem*,[6] he song ;
And after that he song the " kynges noote ; "
Ful often blessed was his myrie throte,
And thus this sweete clerk his tyme spente
After his freendes fyndyng and his rente. 3220

   This carpenter hadde wedded newe a wyf,
Which that he lovede moore than his lyf ;
Of eighteteene yeer she was of age.
Jalous he was, and heeld hire narwe in cage,
For she was yong and wylde, and he was old,
And demed hym self been lik a cokewold.
He knew nat Catoun, for his wit was rude, —
That bad man sholde wedde his simylitude.
Men sholde wedden after hire estaat,
For youthe and elde is often at debaat ;   3230
But sith that he was fallen in the snare,
He moste endure, as oother folk, his care.

   Fair was this yonge wyf, and ther with al,
As any wezele, hir body gent[7] and smal.

---

[1] Valerian. [2] A work of Ptolemy. [3] Belonging to. [4] Counters
Cf. 1. 391. [6] Probably a metrical hymn (The Angel to the Virgin)
Pretty.

A ceynt [1] she werede, ybarred al of silk ;
A barmclooth [2] eek as whit as morne milk
Up-on hir lendes,[3] ful of many a goore ;
Whit was hir smok, and broyden al bifoore,
And eek bihynde, on hir coler aboute,
Of colblak silk with-inne and eek with-oute.
The tapes [4] of hir white voluper [5]   3241
Were of the same suyte of hir coler ;
Hir filet brood, of silk and set ful hye ;
And sikerly she hadde a likerous eye.
Ful smale ypulled were hire browes two,
And tho were bent, and blake as any sloo.
She was ful moore blisful on to see
Than is the newe pereionette [6] tree,
And softer than the wolle is of a wether ;
And by hir girdel heeng a purs of lether,   3250
Tasseled with grene and perled with latoun.[7]
In al this world, to seken up and doun,
There nas no man so wys that koude thenche [8]
So gay a popelote,[9] or swich a wenche.
Ful brighter was the shynyng of hir hewe
Than in the Tour the noble [10] yforged newe.

But of hir song it was as loude and yerne [11]
As any swalwe sittynge on a berne.
Ther to she koude skippe and make game,
As any kyde, or calf, folwynge his dame. 3260
Hir mouth was sweete as bragot [12] or the meeth,[13]
Or hoord of apples leyd in hey or heeth.

---

[1] Girdle.   [2] Skirt.   [3] Loins.   [4] Bands.   [5] Cap.   [6] Pear.   [7] Adorned
with brass knobs.   [8] Imagine   [9] Puppet.   [10] A coin.   [11] Brisk
[13] Drinks.

Wynsynge[1] she was, as is a joly colt ;
Long as a mast and uprighte as a bolt.
A brooch sche baar up-on hir love coler,[2]
As brood as is the boos of a bokeler ;
Hir shoes were laced on hir legges hye ;
She was a prymerole,[3] a piggesnye[4]
For any lord to leggen in his bedde,
Or yet for any good yeman to wedde.   3270
    Now, sire, and eft,[5] sire, so bifel the cas,
That on a day this hende Nicholas,
Fil with this yonge wyf to rage and pleye
Whil that hir housbonde was at Oseneye,[6]
As clerkes ben ful subtile and ful queynte,
And prively he caughte hire by the queynte,[7]
And seyde, ywis, "But if ich have my wille,
For deerne love of thee, lemman,[8] I spille ; "[9]
And heeld hire harde by the haunche bones,
And seyde, "Lemman, love me al atones, 3280
Or I wol dyen, also God me save ! "
    And she sproong, as a colt doth in the trave,[10]
And with hir heed sche wryed[11] faste awey,
And seyde, " I wol nat kisse thee, by my fey !
Why, lat be ! " quod she,[12] " lat be, Nicholas !
Or I wol crie out, ' Harrow,' and ' Allas ! '
Do wey youre handes, for your curteisye ! "
    This Nicholas gan mercy for to crye,
And spak so faire, and profred hire so faste,

---

[1] Lively. [2] Collar. [3] Primrose [4] Pig's-eye, a term of endear-
ment, — perhaps a flower. [5] Soon. [6] An abbey near Oxford
Pudenda muliebra. [8] Love. [9] Perish. [10] Travis. [11] Turned
[12] Elles. MS. has "ich."

That she hir love hym graunted atte laste, 3290
And swoor hir ooth, by Seint Thomas of Kent,
That she wol been at his comandement
Whan that she may hir leyser wel espie.
" Myn housbonde is so ful of jalousie,
That but ye wayte wel and been privee,
I woot right wel I nam but deed," quod she ;
" Ye moste been ful deerne,[1] as in this cas."
 " Nay, ther-of care thee noght," quod Nich
  olas.
" A clerk hadde litherly biset [2] his whyle
But if he koude a carpenter bigyle."   3300
And thus they been accorded and ysworn
To wayte a tyme, as I have told biforn.

 Whan Nicholas had doon thus everideel,
And thakked [3] hire aboute the lendes weel,
He kist hire sweete, and taketh his sawtrie,
And pleyeth faste, and maketh melodie.

 Thanne fil it thus, that to the paryssh chirche,
Christes owene werkes for to wirche,[4]
This goode wyf went on an haliday ;
Hir forheed shoon as bright as any day,   3310
So was it wasshen whan she leet [5] hir werk.

 Now was ther of that chirche a parissh clerk,
The which that was ycleped Absolon ;
Crul [6] was his heer and as the gold it shoon,
And strouted [7] as a fanne, large and brode,
Ful streight and evene lay his joly shode.[8]

---

[1] Secret.   [2] Lazily occupied.   [3] Slapped.   [4] Work.   [5] Stopped
Curled.   [7] Expanded.   [8] Handsome hair.

His rode [1] was reed, hise eyen greye as goos ;
With Powles wyndow corven on his shoos,
In hosen rede he wente fetisly.[2]
Yclad he was ful smal and proprely,   3320
Al in a kirtel of a lyght waget,[3]
Ful faire and thikke been the poyntes set ;
And ther up-on he hadde a gay surplys,
As whit as is the blosme up-on the rys.[4]
A myrie child he was, so God me save,
Wel koude he laten blood and clippe and shave
And maken a chartre of lond or acquitaunce.
In twenty manere koude he trippe and daunce
(After the scole of Oxenforde tho),
And with his legges casten to and fro,   3330
And pleyen songes on a small rubible ;[5]
Ther-to he song som tyme a loud quynyble,[6]
And as wel koude he pleye on his giterne.
In al the toun nas brewhous ne taverne
That he ne visited with his solas,
Ther any gaylard tappestere [7] was ;
But, sooth to seyn, he was somdel squaymous [8]
Of fartyng, and of speche daungerous.[9]

   This Absolon, that jolif was and gay,
Gooth with a sencer on the haliday,   3340
Sensynge the wyves of the parisshe faste,
And many a lovely look on hem he caste,
And namely on this carpenteris wyf.
To loke on hire hym thoughte a myrie lyf,

---

[1] Complexion.   Neatly.   [3] Blue cloth.   [4] Twig.   [5] A stringed
instrument.   [6] A part a fifth above the air.   [7] Gay bar-woman.
Scrupulous.   [9] Haughty.

She was so propre, and sweete, and likerous.
I dar wel seyn if she hadde been a mous,
And he a cat, he wold hire hente [1] anon.
This parissh clerk, this joly Absolon,
Hath in his herte swich a love longynge,
That of no wyf took he noon offrynge,   3350
For curteisie, he seyde, he wolde noon.

   The moone, whan it was nyght, ful brighte
     shoon,
And Absolon his gyterne hath ytake,
For paramours he thoghte for to wake ;
And forth he gooth, jolif and amorous,
Til he cam to the carpenteres hous
A litel after cokkes hadde ycrowe,
And dressed hym up by a shotwyndowe [2]
That was up on the carpenteris wal.
He syngeth in his voys gentil and smal :   3360
" Now, deere lady, if thy wille be,
I pray yow that ye wole thynke on me,"
Ful wel acordaunt to his gyternynge.

   This carpenter awook, and herde synge,
And spak un-to his wyf, and seyde anon,
"What, Alison, herestow nat Absolon
That chaunteth thus under oure boures [3] wal ?"
And she answerde hir housbonde ther with al,
"Yis, God woot, John, I heere it every del."

   This passeth forth ; what wol ye bet [4] than
     weel?
                           3370
Fro day to day this joly Absolon

---

[1] Seize.   [2] A bow window.   [3] Chamber's.   [4] Better.

So woweth[1] hire that hym is wo bigon ;
He waketh al the nyght and al the day,
He kembeth hise lokkes brode, and made hym
        gay,
He woweth hire by meenes[2] and brocage,[8]
And swoor he wolde been hir owene page ;
He syngeth, brokkynge[4] as a nyghtyngale ;
He sente hire pyment,[5] meeth,[6] and spiced ale,
And wafres pipyng hoot, out of the gleede,[7]
And for she was of toune[8] he profreth meede ;[9]
For som folk wol ben wonnen for richesse,
And somme for strokes, and somme for gen-
        tillesse.   3382
    Somtyme to shewe his lightnesse and mais-
        trye
He pleyeth Herodes, up-on a scaffold hye,[10]
But what availleth hym, as in this cas ?
She loveth so this hende Nicholas,
That Absolon may " blowe the bukkes horn,"[11]
He ne hadde for his labour but a scorn,
And thus she maketh Absolon hire ape
And al his ernest turneth til a jape.   3390
Ful sooth is this proverbe, it is no lye,
Men seyn right thus, " Alwey the nye slye
Maketh the ferre leeve[12] to be looth ; "
For though that Absolon be wood or wrooth,
By cause that he fer was from hire sighte,
This nye Nicholas stood in his lighte.

[1] Wooeth.   [2] Agents.   [8] Mediation.   [4] Quavering.   [5] Wine and
honey.   [6] Mead.   [7] Coals.   [8] City.   [9] Reward.   [10] In a
Mystery Play.   [11] Cf. l. 1818.   [12] More distant lover.

Now bere thee wel, thou hende Nicholas,
For Absolon may waille and synge, allas !
And so bifel it on a Saterday
This carpenter was goon til Osenay,   3400
And hende Nicholas and Alisoun
Acorded been to this conclusioun,
That Nicholas shal shapen hym a wyle
This sely,[1] jalous housbonde to bigyle ;
And, if so be the game wente aright,
She sholde slepen in his arm al nyght,
For this was his desir and hire also.
And right anon, with-outen wordes mo,
This Nicholas no lenger wolde tarie,   3409
But dooth ful softe un-to his chambre carie
Bothe mete and drynke for a day or tweye ;
And to hire housbonde bad hire for to seye,
If that he axed after Nicholas,
She sholde seye she nyste where he was ;
Of al that day she saugh hym nat with eye ;
She trowed that he was in maladye,
For for no cry hir mayde koude hym calle,
He nolde answere for thyng that myghte falle.
This passeth forth al thilke Saterday
That Nicholas stille in his chambre lay   3420
And eet and sleepe, or dide what hym leste,
Til Sonday that the sonne gooth to reste.

This sely carpenter hath greet merveyle
Of Nicholas, or what thyng myghte hym eyle,
And seyde, " I am a adrad,[2] by Seint Thomas

[1] Innocent.   [2] Afraid.

It stondeth nat aright with Nicholas.
(God shilde that he deyde sodeynly;
This world is now ful tikel[1] sikerly;[2]
I saugh to day a cors yborn to chirche,   3429
That now on Monday last I saugh hym wirche.)

    "Go up," quod he un-to his knave anoon,
"Clepe at his dore or knokke with a stoon,
Looke how it is and tel me boldely."

    This knave gooth him up ful sturdily
And at the chambre dore whil that he stood,
He cride and knokked as that he were wood, —
"What! how! what do ye, maister Nicholay?
How may ye slepen al the longe day?"

    But al for noght, he herde nat a word.
An hole he foond ful lowe up-on a bord,   3440
Ther as the cat was wont in for to crepe,
And at that hole he looked in ful depe,
And at the laste he hadde of hym a sighte.
This Nicholas sat gapyng[3] evere up-righte,
As he had kiked[4] on the newe moone.
Adoun he gooth and tolde his maister soone
In what array he saugh that ilke man.

    This carpenter to blessen hym bigan,
And seyde, "Help us, Seinte Frydeswyde!
A man woot litel what hym shal bityde;   3450
This man is falle with his astromye
in som woodnesse,[5] or in som agonye.
I thoghte ay wel how that it sholde be,

---

[1] Uncertain. [2] Surely. [3] Elles. MS. has "capyng." [4] Corpus MS., and others, have "keked," retched. [5] Madness.

Men sholde nat knowe of Goddes pryvetee.
Ye, blessed be alwey a lewed man,
That noght but oonly his bileve kan.[1]
So ferde [2] another clerk with astromye ;
He walked in the feeldes, for to prye
Up on the sterres, what ther sholde bifalle,
Til he was in a marleput [3] yfalle ;   346o
He saugh nat that.   But yet by Seint Thomas,
Me reweth soore of hende Nicholas !
He shal be rated of his studiyng,
If that I may, by Jhesus, hevene kyng !

  " Get me a staf, that I may underspore,[4]
Whil that thou, Robyn, hevest of the dore .
He shal out of his studiyng, as I gesse."
And to the chambre dore he gan hym dresse ,
His knave was a strong carl, for the noones,
And by the haspe he haaf [5] it of atones,   3470
In to the floor the dore fil anon.
This Nicholas sat ay as stille as stoon,
And evere gaped [6] upward in-to the eir.
This carpenter wende he were in despeir,
And hente hym by the sholdres myghtily
And shook hym harde and cride spitously,[7]
" What, Nicholay ! what how ! what, looke
        adoun !
Awake ! and thenk on Cristes passioun !
I crouche [8] thee from elves and fro wightes."
Ther-with the nyghtspel [9] seyde he anonrightes,

---

[1] Creed knows.   [2] Fared.   (It was Thales.)   [3] Marl pit
Spere under.   [5] Heaved.   [6] Elles. MS. has "caped."   [7] Angrily
Cross.   [9] An exorcism.

On foure halves of the hous aboute, 3481
And on the thresshfold of the dore with-oute :
　　" *Jhesu Crist and Seint Benedight*,[1]
　　Blesse this hous from every wikked wight
　　For nyghtes verye — the white Pater noster.[2]
　　Where wentestow, Seint Petres soster ? "
And atte laste this hende Nicholas
Gan for to sike soore, and seyde, " Allas !
Shal al this world be lost eftsoones now ? "
　　This carpenter answerde, " What seystow ?
What, thynk on God, as we doon, men that
　　　　swynke." [3] 3491
　　This Nicholas answerde, "Fecche me drynke ;
And after wol I speke in pryvetee
Of certeyn thyng that toucheth me and thee ;
I wol telle it noon oother man certeyn."
　　This carpenter goth doun and comth ageyn,
And broghte of myghty ale a large quart,
And whan that ech of hem had dronke his part,
This Nicholas his dore faste shette
And doun the carpenter by hym he sette. 3500
　　He seyde, " John, myn hooste, lief and deere,

---

[1] This charm is hopelessly corrupted. It may be considered a collection of unmeaning sounds.

[2] Every tenth bead on the rosary is called a Pater Noster. The charm in the text is similar to the following, quoted in the *Atlantic Monthly*, vol. v., p. 437, said to date from the time of Mary Tudor :

THE WHITE PATER NOSTER.

White Pater Noster, St. Peter's brother,
　　What hast thou in one hand ?　White-Book Leaves.
　　What hast i' th' t'other ?　Heaven Gate Keys.
Open Heaven Gates, and steike (shut) Hell Gates,
　　And let every crysom Child creep to its own mother:
　White Pater Noster, Amen

[3] **Work.**

Thou shalt up-on thy trouthe swere me heere
That to no wight thou shalt this conseil wreye,
For it is Cristes conseil that I seye ;
And if thou telle man thou art forlore,[2]
For this vengaunce thou shalt han therfore
That if thou wreye me thou shalt be wood." [3]

   " Nay, Crist forbede it for his hooly blood,"
Quod tho this sely [4] man, " I nam no labbe,[5]
Ne, though I seye, I am nat lief [6] to gabbe ;
Sey what thou wolt, I shal it nevere telle
To child ne wyf, by hym that harwed helle ! " [7]

   " Now, John," quod Nicholas, " I wol nat
       lye,   3513
I have yfounde in myn astrologye,
As I have looked in the moone bright,
That now a Monday next, at quarter nyght,
Shal falle a reyn, and that so wilde and wood,
That half so greet was nevere Noees flood.
This world," he seyde, " in lasse than an hour
Shal al be dreynt,[8] so hidous is the shour ; 3520
Thus schal mankynde drenche, and lese hir
       lyf."

   This carpenter answerde, " Allas, my wyf !
And shal she drenche ?   Allas, myn Alisoun ! '
For sorwe of this he fil almoost adoun
And seyde, " Is ther no remedie in this cas ? "

   " Why, yis, for Gode," quod hende Nicholas
" If thou wolt werken aftir loore and reed ; [9]

---

[1] Betray.   [2] Fully lost.   [3] Mad.   [4] Simple.   [5] Blab.   [6] Do
not love.   [7] Christ, who " descended into hell," and subdued it.
[8] Drowned   [9] Lore and counsel.

Thou mayst nat werken after thyn owene heed,
For thus seith Salomoun, that was ful trewe,
'Werk al by conseil and thou shalt nat rewe;'
And if thou werken wolt by good conseil, 3531
I undertake with-outen mast and seyl,
Yet shal I saven hire and thee and me.
Hastow nat herd hou saved was Noe,
Whan that oure Lord hadde warned hym bi-
        forn
That al the world with water sholde be lorn?"
    "Yis," quod this carpenter, "ful yoore ago."
    "Hastou nat herd," quod Nicholas, "also
The sorwe of Noe [1] with his felaweshipe   3539
Er that he myghte brynge his wyf to shipe?
Hym hadde be levere, I dar wel undertake,
At thilke tyme, than alle hise wetheres blake,
That she hadde had a shipe hir-self allone.
And ther-fore, woostou what is best to doone?
This asketh haste, and of an hastif thyng
Men may nat preche or maken tariyng.
    "Anon go gete us faste in to this in
A knedyng trogh, or ellis a kymelyn,[2]
For ech of us, but loke that they be large,
In whiche we mowe swymme as in a barge,
And han ther-inne vitaille suffisant   3551
But for a day, — fy on the remenant, —
The water shal aslake and goon away
Aboute pryme [3] up-on the nexte day.
But Robyn may nat wite of this, thy knave,

[1] In the Mystery Play. [2] Brewer's tub. [3] Early.

Ne eek thy mayde Gille I may nat save;
Axe nat why, for though thou aske me,
I wol nat tellen Goddes pryvetee;
Suffiseth thee, but if thy wittes madde,
To han as greet a grace as Noe hadde.   3560
Thy wyf shal I wel saven, out of doute.
Go now thy wey and speed thee heer aboute.
  "But whan thou hast for hire and thee and
     me
Ygeten us thise knedyng tubbes thre,
Thanne shaltow hange hem in the roof ful hye,
That no man of oure purveiaunce spye,
And whan thou thus hast doon as I have seyd,
And hast oure vitaille faire in hem yleyd,
And eek an ax to smyte the corde atwo   3569
Whan that the water comth, that we may go,
And broke an hole, an heigh up-on the gable,
Unto the gardynward, over the stable,
That we may frely passen forth oure way
Whan that the grete shour is goon away;
Thanne shal I swymme as myrie,[1] I undertake,
As dooth the white doke after hire drake;
Thanne wol I clepe how Alisoun, how John,
Be myrie, for the flood wol passe anon,
And thou wolt seyn, 'Hayl, maister Nicholay!
Good morwe, I se thee wel for it is day!' 3580
And thanne shul we be lordes al oure lyf
Of al the world, as Noe and his wyf.
  "But of o thyng I warne thee ful right,

---

[1] Pleasant.

Be wel avysed on that ilke nyght
That we ben entred in to shippes bord,
That noon of us ne speke nat a word,
Ne clepe,[1] ne crie, but been in his preyere,
For it is Goddes owene heeste [2] deere.
Thy wyf and thou moote hange fer atwynne,[3]
For that bitwixe yow shal be no synne,   3590
Na moore in lookyng [4] than ther shal in deede ;
This ordinance is seyd ; so God thee speede,
Tomorwe at nyght, whan folk ben alle aslepe,
In to our knedyng tubbes wol we crepe,
And sitten there, abidyng Goddes grace.
Go now thy wey, I have no lenger space
To make of this no lenger sermonyng, —
Men seyn thus, ' Sende the wise and sey no
          thyng ; '
Thou art so wys it needeth thee nat to preche,
Go save oure lyf and that I the biseche." 3600
    This sely carpenter goth forth his wey ;
Ful ofte he seith " Allas," and " Weylawey,"
And to his wyf he tolde his pryveetee,
And she was war, and knew it bet than he,
What al this queynte cast [5] was for to seye ;
But nathelees she ferde [6] as she wolde deye,
And seyde, " Allas ! go forth thy wey anon,
Help us to scape or we been lost echon !
I am thy trewe, verray, wedded wyf,   3609
Go, deere spouse, and help to save oure lyf ! "

[1] Call.   [2] Behest.   [3] Asunder.   [4] Appearance.   [5] Contrivance
[6] Behaved.

Lo which a greet thyng is affeccioun ! [1]
Men may dyen of ymaginacioun,
So depe may impressioun be take.

This sely carpenter bigynneth quake ;
Hym thynketh verraily that he may see
Noees flood, come walwynge as the see,
To drenchen Alisoun, his hony deere.
He wepeth, weyleth, maketh sory cheere ;
He siketh, with ful many a sory swogh ; [2]   3619
He gooth and geteth hym a knedyng trogh,
And after that a tubbe and a kymelyn,
And pryvely he sente hem to his in, [3]
And heng hem in the roof in pryvetee.
His owene hande made laddres thre,
To clymben by the ronges and the stalkes,
In to the tubbes, hangynge in the balkes ; [4]
And hem vitailleth, bothe trogh and tubbe,
With breed and chese and good ale in a jubbe, [5]
Suffisynge right ynogh as for a day ;
But er that he hadde maad al this array   3630
He sente his knave, and eek his wenche also,
Up on his nede to London for to go ;
And on the Monday, whan it drow to nyght.
He shette his dore with-oute candel lyght,
And dresseth alle thyng as it shal be ;
And shortly up they clomben alle thre ;
They sitten stille, wel a furlong way. [6]

---

[1] Fancy.   [2] Groan.   [3] House.   [4] Rafters.   [5] Vessel
[6] A short time.   Cf. l. 12,852.

" Now, *Pater noster*, clom,"[1] seyde Nicholay;
And " Clom," quod John, and " Clom," seyde
     Alisoun.
This carpenter seyde his devocioun,   3640
And stille he sit and biddeth[2] his preyere,
Awaitynge on the reyn, if he it heere.

The dede sleepe for wery bisynesse
Fil on this carpenter, right as I gesse
Aboute corfew tyme, or litel more;
For travaille of his goost he groneth soore,
And eft he routeth,[3] for his heed myslay.
Doun of the laddre stalketh Nicholay,
And Alisoun ful softe adoun she spedde ;
With-outen wordes mo they goon to bedde.
Ther as the carpenter is wont to lye,   3651
Ther was the revel and the melodye.
And thus lith Alison and Nicholas,
In bisynesse of myrthe and of solas,
Til that the belle of laudes gan to rynge,
And freres in the chauncel gonne synge.

  This parissh clerk, this amorous Absolon,
That is for love alwey so wo bigon,
Up-on the Monday was at Oseneye
With a compaignye, hym to disporte and pleye,
And axed up-on cas[4] a cloistrer   3661
Ful prively after John the carpenter.
And he drough hym a part out of the chirche,
And seyde, " I noot I saugh hym heere nat
     wirche

---

[1] Mum.   [2] Prayeth.   [3] Snoreth.   [4] As it were casually.

Syn Saterday ; I trow that he be went
For tymber ther our abbot hath hym sent ;
For he is wont for tymber for to go,
And dwellen at the grange [1] a day or two ;
Or elles he is at his hous certeyn ;
Where that he be I kan nat soothly seyn."

This Absolon ful joly was and light,   3671
And thoghte, " Now is tyme to [2] wake [3] al nyght,
For sikirly I saugh him nat stirynge
Aboute his dore, syn day bigan to sprynge.
So moot I thryve I shal at cokkes crowe
Ful pryvely knokke at his wyndowe
That stant ful lowe up on his boures wal.
To Alison now wol I tellen al
My love longynge ; for yet I shal nat mysse
That at the leste wey I shal hire kisse.   3680
Som maner confort shal I have, parfay.[4]
My mouth hath icched al this longe day,
That is a signe of kissyng atte leste.
Al nyght me mette,[5] eek I was at a feeste ;
Therfore I wol goon slepe an houre or tweye,
And al the nyght thanne wol I wake and pleye."

Whan that the firste cok hath crowe anon
Up rist this joly lovere Absolon,
And hym arraieth gay, at poynt devys ;[6]
But first he cheweth greyn and lycorys,   3690
To smellen sweete, er he hadde kembd his
      heer.

---

[1] The abbey farm.   [2] "To " not in Elles. MS.   [3] To watch
[4] By my faith.   [5] Dreamed.   [6] Very exactly.

Under his tonge a trewe-love [1] he beer,
For ther-by wende he to ben gracious.
He rometh to the carpenteres hous,
And stille he stant under the shot wyndowe, —
Un-to his brist it raughte,[2] it was so lowe, —
And softe he knokketh with a semy-soun :
"What do ye, hony comb, sweete Alisoun,
My faire bryd, my sweete cynamome ?
Awaketh, lemman [3] myn, and speketh to me.
Wel litel thynken ye up on my wo   3701
That for youre love I swete ther I go.
No wonder is, thogh that I swelte [4] and swete,
I moorne as dooth a lamb after the tete ;
Ywis, lemman, I have swich love longynge,
That lik a turtel trewe is my moornynge ;
I may nat ete na moore than a mayde."

"Go fro the wyndow, jakke-fool," she sayde,
"As help me God, it wol nat be, compame ; [5]
I love another, and elles I were to blame, 3710
Wel bet than thee, by Jhesu, Absolon.
Go forth thy wey, or I wol caste a ston,
And lat me slepe, a twenty devel wey ! "

"Allas," quod Absolon, "and weylawey,
That trewe love was evere so yvel biset !
Thanne kysse me, syn it may be no bet,[6]
For Jhesus love, and for the love of me."

"Wiltow thanne go thy wey ? " quod she.

"Ye certes, lemman," quod this Absolon.

---

[1] An herb.   [2] Reached.   [3] Sweetheart.   [4] Faint.   [5] Friend.
Mr. Ellis would read, "It wol nat be 'Com ba me'" ("Come fon-
dle me," alluding to some song. Cf. ll. 672, 10,475). *E. E. Pronunciation*, iii. 715.   [6] Better.

"Thanne make thee redy," quod she, "I
    come anon,"   3720
And un-to Nicholas she seyde stille,
"Now hust and thou shalt laughen al thy fille."
'This Absolon doun sette hym on his knees,
And seyde, "I am lord at alle degrees,
For after this I hope ther cometh moore.
Lemman, thy grace, and sweete bryd, thyn
    oore." [1]   (3724 T.)
    The wyndow she undoth, and that in haste,
"Have do," quod she, "com of, and speed the
    faste,
Lest that oure neighebores thee espie."   3729
    This Absolon gan wype his mouth ful drie;
Dirk was the nyght as pich, or as the cole,
And at the wyndow out she pitte hir hole,
And Absolon hym fil no bet ne wers,
But with his mouth he kiste hir naked ers
Ful savourly er he was war of this.
    Abak he stirte, and thoughte it was amys,
For wel he wiste a womman hath no berd.
He felte a thyng al rough and long yherd,[2]
And seyde, "Fy, allas, what have I do?"
    "Tehee!" quod she, and clapte the wyndow
    to,   3740
And Absolon gooth forth a sory pas.[3]
    "A berd, a berd!" quod hende Nicholas,
'By Goddes corpus,[4] this goth faire and weel."
    This sely Absolon herde every deel,

---

[1] Favor.   [2] Haired.   [3] Pace.   [4] Body

And on his lippe he gan for anger byte,
And to hym self he seyde, " I shal thee quyte."
    Who rubbeth now, who froteth now his lippes
With dust, with sond, with straw, with clooth,
        with chippes,
But Absolon?— that seith ful ofte, "Allas!
My soule bitake I un-to Sathanas,   3750
But me were levere than al this toun," quod
        he,
" Of this despit awroken [1] for to be.   (3750 T.)
Allas," quod he, " allas, I nadde [2] ybleynt." [3]
His hoote love was coold and al yqueynt ;
For fro that tyme that he hadde kiste hir
        ers,
Of paramours he sette nat a kers ;
For he was heeled of his maladie.
Full ofte paramours he gan deffie,
And weepe as dooth a child that is ybete.
A softe paas [4] he wente over the strete   3760
Un-til a smyth, men cleped daun Gerveys,
That in his forge smythed plough harneys, —
He sharpeth shaar and kultour bisily.
This Absolon knokketh al esily,
And seyde, " Undo, Gerveys, and that anon."
    " What, who artow?" " I am heere, Abso-
        lon."
' What, Absolon!   For Cristes sweete tree,
'Vhy rise ye so rathe? ey *benedicitee!*

---

[1] Avenged   [2] Elles. MS. has "ne hadde."   [3] Started aside
[4] ace

What eyleth yow? Som gay gerl, God it woot,
Hath brought yow thus up-on the viritoot;[1]
By seinte Note,[2] ye woot wel what I mene."

    This Absolon ne roghte nat a bene,   3772
Of al his pley; no word agayn he gaf;
He hadde moore tow on his distaf
Than Gerveys knew, and seyde, "Freend so deere,
That hoote kultour in the chymenee heere,
As lene[3] it me, I have ther-with to doone,
And I wol brynge it thee agayn ful soone."

    Gerveys answerde, "Certes, were it gold,
Or in a poke, nobles alle untold,   3780
Thou sholdest have, as I am trewe smyth;
Ey, Cristes foo,[4] what wol ye do ther-with?"

    "Ther of," quod Absolon, "be as be may,
I shal wel telle it thee to morwe day,"
And caughte the kultour by the colde stele.
Ful softe out at the dore he gan to stele,
And wente un-to the carpenteris wal.
He cogheth first and knokketh ther with al
Up-on the wyndowe, right as he dide er.[5]

    This Alison answerde, "Who is ther,   3790
That knokketh so? I warante it a theef."

    "Why nay," quod he, "God woot, my sweete leef,[6]
I am thyn Absolon, my deerelyng.
Of gold," quod he, "I have thee broght a ryng;

---

    [1] **Quick trot** (?).   [2] Neot.   [3] Lend.   [4] Foot.   [5] Erst.   [6] **Love.**

My mooder gaf it me, so God me save ;
Ful fyn it is, and ther-to wel ygrave ;
This wol I geve thee, if thou me kisse."

This Nicholas was risen for to pisse,
And thoughte he wolde amenden al the jape,
He sholde kisse his ers, er that he scape ;
And up the wyndowe dide he hastily,   3801
And out his ers he putteth pryvely,   (3800 T.)
Over the buttok to the haunche bon.
And ther with spak this clerk, this Absolon :
" Spek, sweete bryd, I noot nat where thou
        art."

This Nicholas anon leet fle a fart,
As greet as it had been a thonder dent,
That with the strook he was almoost yblent ;[1]
And he was redy with his iren hoot,
And Nicholas amydde ers he smoot.   3810

Of gooth the skyn, an hande brede aboute,
The hoote kultour brende so his toute ;[2]
And for the smert he wende for to dye.
As he were wood for wo he gan to crye,
" Help, water, water, help, for Goddes herte !"

This carpenter out of his slomber sterte,
And herde oon crien "water," as he were wood,
And thoughte, "Allas, now comth Nowelis
        flood !"

He sit hym up with-outen wordes mo,   3819
And with his ax he smoot the corde atwo,
And doun gooth al, ne foond neither to selle,[3]

_____

[1] **Blinded.**   [2] Hinder parts   [3] No engagement to detain him.

Ne breed ne ale, til he cam to the celle [1]
Up-on the floor, and ther aswowne he lay.

Up stirte hire Alison and Nicholay,
And criden, " Out and harrow ! " in the strete.
The neighebores bothe smale and grete
In ronnen for to gauren [2] on this man
That yet aswowne he lay, bothe pale and wan
For with the fal he brosten hadde his arm.
But stonde he moste un-to his owene harm, 3830
For whan he spak he was anon bore doun
With hende Nicholas and Alisoun.
They tolden every man that he was wood,
He was agast so of Nowelis flood
Thurgh fantasie, that of his vanytee
He hadde yboght hym knedyng tubbes thre,
And hadde hem hanged in the rove [3] above ;
And that he preyde hem, for Goddes love,
To sitten in the roof, *par compaignye.*

The folk gan laughen at his fantasye ; 3840
In to the roof they kiken [4] and they gape, [5]
And turned al his harm un-to a jape ;
For, what-so that this carpenter answerde,
It was for noght, no man his reson herde ;
With othes grete he was so sworn adoun,
That he was holde wood [6] in al the toun,
For every clerk anonright heeld with oother ;
They seyde, " The man was wood, my leeve
      broother ; "

---

[1] Cellar   [2] Gaze.   [3] Roof.   [4] Peep.   [5] Elles. MS. has " cape.
Mad.

And every wight gan laughen of this stryf.
Thus swyved [1] was this carpenteris wyf,   3850
For al his kepyng and his jalousye ;
And Absolon hath kist hir nether eye,
And Nicholas is scalded in the towte : (3851 T.)
This tale is doon, and God save al the rowte.

The Wrath of Oswald the Reve.

Whan folk hadde laughen at this nyce cas
Of Absolon and hende Nicholas,   (3854 T.)
Diverse folk diversely they seyde,
But for the moore part they loughe and pleyde ;
Ne at this tale I saugh no man hym greve,
But it were oonly Osewold the Reve.   3860
By-cause he was of carpenteris craft
A litel ire is [2] in his herte ylaft.
He gan to grucche and blamed it a lite.
    " So theek," [3] quod he, " ful wel koude I yow
        quite,
With bleryng of a proud milleres eye,[4] —
If that me liste speke of ribaudye, —
But ik [5] am oold, me list no pley for age,
Gras tyme is doon, my fodder is now for
        age ;
This white tope writeth myne olde yeris ;
Myn herte is mowled [6] also as myne heris, 3870
But [7] if I fare as dooth an openers.[8]

[1] Abused.   [2] Not in Elles. MS.   [3] So thee ich = so thrive I
Cheating a miller.   [5] I.   [6] Moulded.   [7] Except.   [8] Medlar

VOL. I.   10

That ilke fruyt is ever leng the wers
Til it be roten in mullok, or in stree.[1]
   " We olde men, I drede, so fare we,
Til we be roten kan we nat be rype.
We hoppen ay whil that the world wol pype,
For in oure wyl ther stiketh evere a nayl,
To have an hoor heed and a grene tayl,
As hath a leek ; for thogh oure myght be goon
Oure wyl desireth folie evere in oon ;   3880
For whan we may nat doon, than wol we speke,
Yet in oure asshen olde is fyr yreke.[2]
Foure gleedes[3] han we, whiche I shal devyse,
Avauntyng, liyng, anger, coveitise.
Thise foure sparkles longen[4] un-to eelde.
Oure olde lemes[5] mowe wel been unweelde,
But wyl ne shal nat faillen, that is sooth ;
And yet ik have alwey a coltes tooth,
As many a yeer as it is passed henne
Syn that my tappe of lif bigan to renne ;   3890
For sikerly whan I was bore anon
Deeth drough the tappe of lyf and leet it gon,
And ever sithe hath so the tappe yronne,
Til that almoost al empty is the tonne.
The streem of lyf now droppeth on the chymbe,[6]
The sely tonge may wel rynge and chymbe[7]
Of wrecchednesse that passed is ful yoore ;
With olde folk, save dotage, is namoore."
   Whan that oure Hoost hadde herd this ser-
    monyng,

---

[1] Rubbish or straw.   [2] Smouldering.   [3] Live coals.   [4] Belong
[5] Limbs   [6] Chimb.   [7] Chime.

He gan to speke as lordly as a kyng.   3900
He seide : "What amounteth al this wit ?
What, shul we speke alday of hooly writ ?
The devel made a Reve for to preche, (3901 T.)
And of a soutere,[1] shipman, or a leche.
Sey forth thy tale, and tarie nat the tyme, —
Lo, Depeford, and it is half wey pryme.
Lo, Grenewych, ther many a shrewe is inne,
It were al tyme thy tale to bigynne."

  "Now, sires," quod this Osewold the Reve,
" I pray yow alle that ye nat yow greve,   3910
Thogh I answere and somdeel sette his howve,[2]
For leveful [3] is, with force force of showve ; [4]
This dronke Millere hath ytoold us heer
How that bigyled was a carpenteer,
Peraventure in scorn for I am oon,
And, by youre leve, I shal him quite anoon.
Right in his cherles termes wol I speke ;
I pray to God his nekke mote breke.   3918
He kan wel in myn eye seen a stalke, (3917 T.)
But in his owene he kan nat seen a balke." [5]

Heere bigynneth The Reves Tale.[6]

At Trumpyngtoun, nat fer fro Cantebrigge,
Ther gooth a brook, and over that a brigge,

---

1 Cobbler.   2 Set his hood, *i. e.*, get the better of him.   Cf. l. 586.
3 Lawful.   4 Repel.   5 Beam.   6 The Reeve's tale is in its main
features the same as the sixth novel of the ninth day of the *Decamerone,* but it was often told in the olden time.   Two French versions,
having more details than Boccaccio gives, were printed by the Chaucer Society in 1872.

Up-on the whiche brook ther stant a melle ;
And this is verray sooth that I yow tell.
A millere was ther dwellynge many a day,
As eny pecok he was proud and gay.
Pipen he koude, and fisshe, and nettes beete,[1]
And turne coppes,[2] and wel wrastle and sheete ;[3]
And by his belt he baar a long panade,[4]   3979
And of a swerd ful trenchant was the blade.
A joly poppere [5] baar he in his pouche,
Ther was no man, for peril, dorste hym touche ;
A Sheffeld thwitel [6] baar he in his hose.
Round was his face, and camuse [7] was his nose ;
As piled [8] as an ape was his skulle ;
He was a market-betere [9] atte fulle ;
Ther dorste no wight hand up-on hym legge [10]
That he ne swoor he sholde anon abegge.[11]

A theef he was of corn and eek of mele,
And that a sly and usaunt for to stele.   3940
His name was hoote, deynous, Symkyn.[12]
A wyf he hadde, ycomen of noble kyn, —
The person [13] of the toun hir fader was, —
With hire he gaf ful many a panne of bras
For that Symkyn sholde in his blood allye.
She was yfostred in a nonnerye,
For Symkyn wolde no wyf, as he sayde,
But if she were wel ynorissed and a mayde,
To saven his estaat of yomanrye.   3949
And she was proud and peert [14] as is a pye.

---

[1] Mend. [2] Cups (in a lathe). [3] Shoot. [4] Weapon. [5] Dagger
[6] Whittle. [7] Crooked [8] Pilled. [9] Swaggerer. [10] Lay. [11] Sui
er. [12] Called in contempt "Little Simon." [13] Parson. [14] Airy

A ful fair sighte was it up-on hem two (3949 T.)
On haly dayes ; biforn hire wolde he go
With his typet ybounde about his heed ;
And she cam after in a gyte [1] of reed ;
And Symkyn hadde hosen of the same.
Ther dorste no wight clepen hire but " Dame ,"
Was noon so hardy that wente by the weye
That with hire dorste rage, or ones pleye,
But if he wolde be slayn of Symkyn,
With panade, or with knyf, or boidekyn ;   3960
For jalous folk ben perilous everemo ;
Algate they wolde hire wyves wenden so.
And eek for she was somdel smoterlich,[2]
She was as digne [3] as water in a dich,[4]
As ful of hoker,[5] and of bisemare.[6]
Hir thoughte that a lady sholde hire spare,[7]
What for hire kynrede and hir nortelrie [8]
That she hadde lerned in the nonnerie.

A doghter hadde they bitwixe hem two
Of twenty yeer, with-outen any mo,   3970
Savynge a child that was of half yeer age ;
In cradel it lay, and was a propre page.[9]
This wenche thikke and wel ygrowen was,
With kamuse nose, and eyen greye as glas ;
Buttokes brode, and brestes rounde and hye,
But right fair was hire heer, I wol nat lye.

This person of the toun, for she was feir,
In purpos was to maken hire his heir,

[1] Gown.   [2] Smutty.   [3] Repellaut.   She kept people at a dis
tance.   [5] Frowardness   [4] Abusive talk   [7] Consider.   [8] Culture
Boy.

Both of his catel and his mesuage,[1]   3979
And straunge[2] he made it of hir mariage.
His purpos was for to bistowe hire hye
In-to som worthy blood of auncetrye ;
For hooly chirches good moot been despended
On hooly chirches blood that is descended ;
Therfore he wolde his hooly blood honoure,
Though that he hooly chirche sholde devoure.

Gret sokene[3] hath this millere, out of doute,
With whete and malt of al the land aboute ;
And nameliche, ther was a greet collegge,   3989
Men clepen the Soler Halle at Cantebregge ;
Ther was hir whete and eek hir malt ygrounde ;
And on a day it happed in a stounde,[4]
Sik lay the maunciple on a maladye.
Men wenden wisly that he sholde dye,
For which this millere stal bothe mele and corn
An hundred tyme moore than biforn :
For ther biforn he stal but curteisly,
But now he was a theef outrageously ;
For which the wardeyn chidde and made fare,[5]
But ther of sette the millere nat a tare ;   4000
He craketh boost,[6] and swoor it was nat so.

Thanne were ther yonge, povre clerkes two,
That dwelten in this halle of which I seye ;
Testif[7] they were, and lusty for to pleye ;
And, oonly for hire myrthe and revelrye,
Up-on the wardeyn bisily they crye,   (4004 T.ʹ

---

[1] Messuage.   [2] Difficult.   [3] Soc, toll   [4] Moment.   [5] Proceed
ngs.   [6] Loudly boasted.   [7] Heady.

To geve hem leve, but a litel stounde,
To goon to mille and seen hir corn ygrounde,
And hardily [1] they dorste leye hir nekke,   4009
The millere shold nat stele hem half a pekke
Of corn, by sleighte, ne by force hem reve.[2]
And at the laste the wardeyn gaf hem leve.
John highte that oon, and Aleyn heet that
      oother ;
Of o toun were they born, that highte Strother,
Fer in the North, I kan nat telle where.

   This Aleyn maketh redy al his gere,
And on an hors the sak he caste anon.
Forth goth Aleyn the clerk, and also John,
With good swerd and bokeler by hir side.
John knew the wey, hem neded not [3] no gyde ;
And at the mille the sak adoun he layth.
Aleyn spak first, "Al hayl, Symond, y-fayth !
Hou fares thy faire doghter, and thy wyf ? "

   "Aleyn, welcome," quod Symkyn, "by my
      lyf!   4024
And John also, how now ? what do ye heer ? "

   "Symond," quod John, "by God, nede has
      na peer,
Hym boes [4] serve hym selne [5] 'hat has na swayn,
Or elles he is a fool as clerkes sayn.
Oure manciple, I hope [6] he will be deed,
Swa werkes ay the wanges [7] in his heed ;   4030
And forthy is I come, and eek Alayn,

---

[1] **Boldly.**   [2] Bereave.   [3] Not in Elles. MS.   [4] **Behooves.**   [5] **Self.**
Fear me. (This passage is in a Northern dialect.)   [7] **Wang-tooth**

To grynde oure corn and carie it ham agayn.
I pray yow spede us heythen [1] that ye may."
  "It shal be doon," quod Symkyn, "by my
    fay!
What wol ye doon whil that it is in hande?"
  "By God, right by the hopur wil I stande,"
Quod John, "and se how that the corn gas in
Yet saugh I nevere, by my fader kyn,
How that the hopur wagges til and fra."

  Aleyn answerde, "John, wiltow swa? [2]   4040
Thanne wil I be bynethe, by my croun!
And se how that the mele falles doun
In-to the trough, — that sal be my disport;
For John, yfaith, I may been of youre sort,
I is as ille a millere as are ye."

  This millere smyled of hir nycetee,
And thoghte, "Al this nys doon but for a wyle
They wene that no man may hem bigile;
But by my thrift yet shal I blere hir eye,
For al the sleighte in hir philosophye.   4050
The moore queynte crekes [3] that they make,
The moore wol I stele whan I take.   (4050 T.)
In stide of flour yet wol I geve hem bren;
The gretteste clerkes been noght wisest men,
As whilom to the wolf thus spak the mare, [4] —
Of al hir art ne counte I noght a tare."

  Out at the dore he gooth ful pryvely,
Whan that he saugh his tyme softely.
He looketh up and doun til he hath founde

----

[1] Hence.   [2] So   [3] Crooks   [4] The reference is to *Reynard the Fox*.

The clerkes hors ther as it stood ybounde 4060
Bihynde the mille, under a lefsel,[1]
And to the hors he goth hym faire and wel ;
He strepeth of the brydel right anon,
And whan the hors was laus,[2] he gynneth gon
Toward the fen, ther wilde mares renne, —
Forth with " Wehee ! " thurgh thikke and thurgh
       thenne. 4066

  This millere gooth agayn, no word he seyde,
But dooth his note[3] and with the clerkes pleyde,
Til that hir corn was faire and weel ygrounde ;
And whan the mele is sakked and ybounde,
This John goth out, and fynt his hors away,
And gan to crie, " Harrow ! " and, " Weylaway !
Oure hors is lorn ; Alayn, for Goddes banes [4]
Stepe on thy feet ; com out, man, al atanes !
Allas, our wardeyn has his palfrey lorn ! "
This Aleyn al forgat bothe mele and corn ;
Al was out of his mynde his housbondrie.
" What, whilk way is he geen ? " [5] he gan to crie.

  The wyf cam lepynge inward with a ren ;
She seyde, " Allas, youre hors goth to the fen
With wilde mares, as faste as he may go ; 4081
Unthank [6] come on his hand that boond hym
    so,
And he that bettre sholde han knyt the reyne ! "
  " Allas," quod John,[7] " Aleyn, for Cristes
    peyne,

Leafy shelter, bower : *Lef,* leaf, *sel,* abode. [2] Loose. [3] Need,
   [4] Bones. [5] Gore [6] No thanks. [7] Not in Elles. MS.

Lay doun thy swerd, and I wil myn alswa.
I [1] is ful wight,[2] God waat, as is a raa ; [3]
By Goddes herte ! he sal nat scape us bathe.
Why nadstow pit the capul [4] in the lathe ? [5]
Ilhayl, by God, Aleyn, thou is a fonne." [6]

This sely [7] clerkes han ful faste yronne   4090
To-ward the fen, bothe Aleyn and eek John ;
And whan the millere saugh that they were
          gon,
He half a busshel of hir flour hath take,
And bad his wyf go knede it in a cake.
He seyde, "I trowe the clerkes were aferd,
Yet kan a millere make a clerkes berd [8]
For al his art ; now lat hem goon hir weye !
Lo wher they goon ; ye lat the children pleye ;
They gete hym nat so lightly, by my croun !"

Thise sely clerkes rennen up and doun   4100
With "Keepe ! keepe ! stand ! stand ! Jossa
          warderere ! [9]   (4099 T.)
Ga whistle thou, and I shal kepe hym heere."
But shortly, til that it was verray nyght
They koude nat, though they do al hir myght,
Hir capul cacche, he ran alwey so faste,
Til in a dych they caughte hym atte laste.

Wery and weet, as beest is in the reyn,
Comth sely John, and with him comth Aleyn.
Allas !" quod John, "the day that I was
          born !   4109

---

[1] He. [2] Swift. [3] Roe. [4] Horse. [5] Stable. [6] Fool. [7] Simple.
Befool a clerk. Cf. l. 10,403. [9] Beware behind.

Now are we dryve til hethyng [1] and til scorn ;
Oure corn is stoln, men wil us fooles calle,
Bathe the wardeyn and oure felawes alle,
And namely the millere, weylaway ! "

    Thus pleyneth John, as he gooth by the way
Toward the mille, and Bayard [2] in his hond.
The millere sittynge by the fyr he fond, —
For it was nyght and forther myghte they
      noght, —
But for the love of God they hym bisoght
Of herberwe [3] and of ese as for hir peny.   4119

    The millere seyde agayn, " If ther be eny,
Swich as it is, yet shal ye have youre part ;
Myn hous is streit, but ye han lerned art,
Ye konne by argumentez make a place
A myle brood of twenty foot of space.
Lat se now if this place may suffise
Or make it rowm [4] with speche as is youre
      gise."

    " Now, Symond," seyde John, "by Seint Cut-
      berd, [5]
Ay is thou myrie, and this is faire answerd.
I have herd seyd, 'Man sal taa [6] of twa thynges,
Slyk [7] as he fyndes or taa slyk as he brynges ; '
But specially I pray thee, hoost deere,   4131
Get us som mete and drynke, and make us
      cheere,
And we wil payen trewely atte fulle ;

---

[1] Contempt.   [2] Bay horse.   [3] Lodging   [4] Roomier.   [5] Cuthbert
Take.   [7] Such.

With empty hand men may none haukes tulle ;
Loo, heere our silver, redy for to spende."

     This millere in to toun his doghter sende
For ale and breed, and rosted hem a goos,
And boond hire hors, it sholde nat goon loos,
And in his owene chambre hem made a bed,
With sheetes and with chalons [2] faire yspred,
Noght from his owene bed ten foot or twelve.
His doghter hadde a bed al by hir-selve,   4142
Right in the same chambre by and by
It mighte be no bet, and cause why ?
Ther was no rommer herberwe [3] in the place.
They soupen, and they speke hem to solace,
And drynke evere strong ale atte [4] beste.
Aboute mydnyght wente they to reste.

     Wel hath this millere vernysshed his heed ; [1]
Ful pale he was for-dronken, and nat reed. [6]
He yexeth, [7] and he speketh thurgh the nose,
As he were on the quakke or on the pose. [8] 4152
To bedde he goth, and with hym goth his wyf,
As any jay she light was and jolyf ;   (4152 T.)
So was hir joly whistle wel y-wet ;
The cradel at hir beddes feet is set,
To rokken, and to geve the child to sowke ;
And whan that dronken al was in the crowke, [9]
To bedde went the doghter right anon ;
To bedde wente Aleyn, and also John,   4160
Ther nas na moore ; hem neded no dwale. [10]

---

[1] Lure.   Cf. l. 10,457.   [2] Chalons goods.   [3] Roomier lodging.
At the.   [5] Drunk.   [6] Red.   [7] Hiccupeth.   [8] As he had an obstruction in his throat, or the rheum.   [9] Crock.   [10] A soporific.

This millere hath so wisely bibbed ale
That as an hors he snorteth in his sleepe ;
Ne of his tayl bihynde he took no keepe ;
His wyf bar him a burdon,[1] a ful strong,
Men myghte hir rowtyng heere two furlong ,
The wenche rowteth eek, *par compaignye*.
    Aleyn the clerk, that herd this melodye,
He poked John, and seyde, " Slepestow ?
Herdtow evere slyk a sang er now ?   4174
Lo, whilk a complyng is ymel[2] hem alle !
A wilde fyr up-on thair bodyes falle !
Wha herkned evere slyk a ferly[3] thyng ?
Ye, they sal have the flour of il endyng !
This lange nyght ther tydes me na reste,
But yet, nafors,[4] al sal be for the beste,
For, John," seyde he, " als evere moot I thryve,
If that I may, yon wenche wil I swyve.[5]
Som esement has lawe yshapen us ;
For, John, ther is a lawe that says thus,   4180
That gif a man in a point be ygreved,
That in another he sal be releved.
Oure corn is stoln, shortly is ne nay,
And we han had an il fit al this day ;
And syn I sal have neen[6] amendement
Agayn my los, I wil have esement.
By God sale ![7] it sal neen other bee."
    This John answerde, " Alayn, avyse thee ;
The millere is a perilous man," he seyde,

---

[1] Accompaniment. [2] What a compline (*i. e.*, even-song) is among
Marvelous. [4] No matter. [5] *Futuere*. [6] No. [7] Soul.

" And gif that he out of his sleepe abreyde,[1]
He mighte doon us bathe a vileynye."   4191
   Aleyn answerde, " I count hym nat a flye."
And up he rist, and by the wenche he crepte.
This wenche lay uprighte, and faste slepte
Til he so ny was, er she myghte espie,
That it had been to late for to crie ;
And, shortly for to seyn, they were aton.
Now pley, Aleyn, for I wol speke of John.

   This John lith stille a furlong wey[2] or two,
And to hym self he maketh routhe and wo ;
" Allas ! " quod he, " this is a wikked jape ;
Now may I seyn that I is but an ape ; (4200 T.)
Yet has my felawe som what for his harm, —
He has the milleris doghter in his arm.   4204
He auntred[3] hym, and has his nedes sped,
And I lye as a draf sek[4] in my bed ;
And when this jape is tald another day,
I sal been halde a daf, a cokenay.
I wil arise and auntre it, by my fayth ;
   Unhardy is unseely,'[5] thus men sayth."   4210
And up he roos and softely he wente
Un-to the cradel, and in his hand it hente,
And baar it softe un-to the beddes feet.

   Soone after this the wyf hir rowtyng leet,
And gan awake and wente hire out to pisse,
And cam agayn, and gan hir cradel mysse,
And groped heer and ther, but she foond noon

---

[1] Start up.   [2] A little while.   [3] Ventured.   [4] Rubbish sack
Wretched

"Allas!" quod she, "I hadde almoost mys-
    goon;
I hadde almoost goon to the clerkes bed. 4219
Ey, *benedicite!* thanne hadde I foule y-sped."
And forth she gooth til she the cradel fond ;
She gropeth alwey forther with hir hond,
And foond the bed and thoghte noght but
    good,
By cause that the cradel by it stood,
And nyste wher she was, for it was derk,
But faire and wel she creepe in-to the clerk ;
And lith ful stille and wolde han caught a
    sleepe.

With-inne a while this John the clerk up leepe,
And on this goode wyf he leith on soore ;
So myrie a fit hadde she nat ful yoore ;   4230
He priketh harde and soore as he were mad.
This joly lyf han thise two clerkes lad
Til that the thridde cok[1] bigan to synge.

    Aleyn wax wery in the dawenynge,
For he had swonken[2] al the longe nyght ;
And seyde, "Fare weel, Malyne,[3] sweete wight.
The day is come, I may no lenger byde;
But everemo, wher so I go[4] or ryde,
I is thyn awen[5] clerk, swa have I seel."[6]

    "Now, deere lemman," quod she, "go, fare-
    weel!   4240
But, er thow go, o thyng I wol thee telle ;

---

[1] An hour before day   [2] Worked   [3] Malkin, Molly.   [4] **Walk**
Own. [6] Happiness.

Whan that thou wendest homward by the
　　melle,
Right at the entree of the dore bihynde,
Thou shalt a cake of half a busshel fynde,
That was ymaked of thyn owene mele,
Which that I heelpe my fader for to stele;
And, goode lemman, God thee save and kepe!"
And with that word almoost she gan to wepe.

　　Aleyn up rist and thoughte, "Er that it
　　dawe,
I wol go crepen in by my felawe;"　　4250
And fond the cradel with his hand anon.
"By God!" thoughte he, "al wrang I have
　　mysgon;　　　　　　　　　　　(4250 T.)
Myn heed is toty[1] of my swynk to nyght,
That maketh me that I go nat aright;
I woot wel by the cradel I have mysgo;
Heere lith the millere and his wyf also."
And forth he goth, a twenty devel way,[2]
Un-to the bed ther as the millere lay.
He wende[3] have cropen by his felawe John,
And by the millere in he crepe anon,　　4260
And caughte hym by the nekke, and softe he
　　spak;
He seyde, "Thou John, thou swynesheed,
　　awak,
For Cristes saule, and heer a noble game;
For by that lord that called is seint Jame,
As I have thries in this shorte nyght

---

[1] Dizzy.　[2] Rapidly.　[3] Believed.　[4] Swine's head.

Swyved the milleres doghter bolt upright,
Whil thow hast as a coward been agast."
  "Ye, false harlot," quod the millere, "hast?
A! false traitour! false clerk!" quod he,
"Thow shalt be deed, by Goddes dignitee!
Who dorste be so boold to disparage   4271
My doghter, that is come of swich lynage?"
And by the throte bolle he caughte Alayn;
And he hente hym despitously agayn,
And on the nose he smoot hym with his fest.
Doun ran the blody streem up-on his brest,
And in the floor, with nose and mouth to-broke,
They walwe as doon two pigges in a poke;
And up they goon and doun agayn anon,
Til that the millere sporned at a stoon,   4280
And doun he fil bakward up-on his wyf,
That wiste no thyng of this nyce stryf,
For she was falle aslepe a lite [1] wight
With John the clerk, that waked hadde al
       nyght;
And with the fal out of hir sleepe she breyde.[2]
"Help, hooly croys of Bromholm," [3] she seyde,
" *In manus tuas*,[4] Lord, to thee I calle!
Awak, Symond! the feend is on us falle!
Myn herte is broken! help! I nam but deed!
Ther lyth oon up-on my wombe [5] and on myn
       heed.   4290
Helpe, Symkyn, for the false clerkes fighte!"

---

[1] Little. [2] Started [3] Bromholme was a Norfolk priory. [4] Into thy hands. [5] Belly.

This John stirte up, as soone as ever he
    myghte,
And graspeth by the walles to and fro
To fynde a staf, and she stirte up also,
And knewe the estres [1] bet than dide this John
And by the wal a staf she foond anon,
And saugh a litel shymeryng of a light,
For at an hole in shoon the moone bright;
And by that light she saugh hem bothe two,
But sikerly she nyste who was who;   4300
But as she saugh a whit thyng in hir eye,
And whan she gan the white thyng espye,
She wende the clerk hadde wered a volupeer,[2]
And with the staf she drough ay neer and neer
And wende han hit this Aleyn at the fulle;
And smoot the millere on the pyled skulle,
And doun he gooth, and cride, "Harrow! I
    dye!"   (4305 T.)
Thise clerkes beete hym weel and lete hym lye
And greythen hem [4] and tooke hir hors anon,
And eek hire mele, and on hir wey they gon,
And at the mille yet they tooke hir cake   4311
Of half a busshel flour ful wel ybake.

    Thus is the proude millere wel ybete,
And hath ylost the gryndynge of the whete,
And payed for the soper everideel
Of Aleyn and of John, that bette [5] hym weel;
His wyf is swyved, and his doghter als.

---

[1] Passages.   [2] Night-cap.   [3] Nearer and nearer.   [4] Clothed
Beat.

Lo ! swich it is a millere to be fals ;
And therfore this proverbe is seyd ful sooth,
" Hym thar nat wene wel that yvele dooth," [1]
A gylour shal hym self bigyled be, —
And God, that sitteth heighe in Trinitee, 4322
Save al this compaignye, grete and smale.
Thus have I quyt the Millere in my tale. (4322 T.)

Words of Roger, the Cook, and Harry Bailly, the Host.

The Cook of Londoun, whil that the Reve
    spak,   (4323 T.)
For joye him thoughte he clawed him on the
    bak ;
" Ha, ha ! " quod he, " for Cristes passioun
This millere hadde a sharpe conclusioun
Upon his argument of herbergage ; [2]
Wel seyde Salomon, in his langage,   4330
' Ne brynge nat every man in-to thyn hous,'
For herberwynge by nyghte is perilous.
Wel oghte a man avysed for to be
Whom that he broghte in-to his pryvetee.
I pray to God, so geve me sorwe and care,
If evere sitthe I highte Hogge [3] of Ware,
Herde I a millere bettre yset a werk.
He hadde a jape of malice in the derk ;
But God forbede that we stynte heere,

---

[1] He must not expect good who doeth evil. [2] Lodging [3] Roger, Hodge.

And therfore if ye vouche-sauf to heere   4340
A tale of me, that am a povre man,
I wol yow telle as wel as evere I kan
A litel jape that fil in oure citee."

   Oure Hoost answerde and seide, " I graunte
     it thee ;
Now telle on, Roger, looke that it be good ;
For many a pastee hastow laten blood,[1]
And many a jakke of Dovere [2] hastow soold,
That hath been twies hoot and twies coold ;
Of many a pilgrym hastow Cristes curs,
For of thy percely yet they fare the wors, 4350
That they han eten with thy stubbel goos,
For in thy shoppe is many a flye loos. (4350 T.)
Now telle on, gentil Roger by thy name,
But yet I pray thee be nat wroth for game,[3]
A man may seye ful sooth in game and pley."

   " Thou seist ful sooth," quod Roger, " by my
     fey !
But ' sooth pley quaad pley,' [4] as the Flemyng
     seith ;
And ther-fore, Herry Bailly, by thy feith,
Be thou nat wrooth, er we departen heer
Though that my tale be of an hostileer : [5]
But nathelees I wol nat telle it yit ;   4361
But er we parte, ywis, thou shalt be quit ;"
And ther with al he lough and made cheere,
And seyde his tale as ye shul after heere.

---

[1] That is, of the hart.   [2] A sea fish.   [3] Pleasantry.   [4] Earnest
pleasantry, bad pleasantry.   [5] Host

Heere bigynneth The Cookes Tale.

A prentys whilom dwelled in oure citee,
And of a craft of vitailliers was hee.   (4364 T.)
Gaillard [1] he was as goldfynch in the shawe ; [2]
Broun as a berye, a propre short felawe,
With lokkes blake ykempd ful fetisly ; [3]
Dauncen he koude so wel and jolily,   4370
That he was cleped Perkyn Revelour.
He was as ful of love and paramour
As is the hyve ful of hony sweete.
Wel was the wenche with hym myghte meete ;
At every bridale wolde he synge and hoppe,
He loved bet the taverne than the shoppe.

For whan ther any ridyng was in Chepe, [4]
Out of the shoppe thider wolde he lepe ;
Til that he hadde al the sighte yseyn,   4379
And daunced wel, he wolde nat come ageyn ;
And gadered hym a meynee [5] of his sort
To hoppe and synge and maken swich disport ;
And ther they setten stevene [6] for to meete
To pleyen at the dys in swich a streete ;
For in the toune nas ther no prentys
That fairer koude caste a paire of dys
Than Perkyn koude, and ther-to he was free
Of his dispense, in place of pryvetee.
That fond his maister wel in his chaffare ; [7]

[1] Gay   [2] Shade.   [3] Neatly.   [4] Cheapside.   [5] Following
Time.   [7] Traffic.

For often tyme he foond his box ful bare, 4390
For sikerly a prentys revelour,
That haunteth dys, riot, or paramour,
His maister shal it in his shoppe abye,[1]
Al[2] have he no part of the mynstralcye ;
For thefte and riot they been convertible,
Al konne he pleye on gyterne [3] or ribible.[4]
Revel and trouthe, as in a lowe degree,
They been ful wrothe [5] al day, as men may see.

This joly prentys with his maister bood,
Til he were ny out of his prentishood ;   4400
Al were he snybbed [6] bothe erly and late,
And somtyme lad with revel to Newegate ;
But atte laste his maister hym bithoghte,
Up-on a day whan he his papir [7] soghte,
Of a proverbe that seith this same word,
"Wel bet [8] is roten appul out of hoord,
Than that it rotie al the remenaunt." (4405 T.)
So fareth it by a riotous servaunt,
It is wel lasse harm to lete hym pace [9]
Than he shende [10] alle the servauntz in the
      place.   4410
Therfore his maister gaf hym acquitance,
And bad hym go with sorwe and with mes-
      chance ;
And thus this joly prentys hadde his leve.
Now lat him riote al the nyght or leve ;
And for ther is no theef with-oute a lowke,[11]

---

[1] Suffer.   [2] Although.   [3] Guitar.   [4] Rebec.   [5] At enmity
Snubbed, rebuked.   [7] Accounts.   [8] Better.   [9] Pass.   [10] Ruin
[11] Receiver.

That helpeth hym to wasten and to sowke,
Of that he brybe kan or borwe may,
Anon he sente his bed and his array
Un-to a compier of his owene sort   (4417 T.)
That lovede dys, and revel and disport,   4420
And hadde a wyf that heeld for contenance [1]
A shoppe, and swyved for hir sustenance [2] . . .

End of the Tales of the First Day.

TALES OF THE SECOND DAY.

The wordes of the Hoost to the compaignye.

Oure Hoost saugh wel that the brighte sonne
The ark of his artificial day hath ronne (4422 T.)
The ferthe part, and half an houre and moore,
And though he were nat depe ystert in loore,[3]
He wiste it was the eightetethe [4] day
Of Aprill that is messager to May,
And saugh wel that the shadwe of every tree
Was, as in lengthe, the same quantitee   4430
That was the body erect that caused it ;
And ther-fore by the shadwe he took his wit
That Phebus, which that shoon so clere and
          brighte,
Degrees was fyve and fourty clombe on highte ;

For appearances. [2] This tale ends thus abruptly. [3] **Advanced
in knowledge.** [4] Elles. MS. reads "eighte and twentithe."

And for that day, as in that latitude,
Jt was ten at the clokke, he gan conclude ;
And sodeynly he plighte[1] his hors aboute.

   "Lordynges," quod he, " I warne yow, at
      this route,
The fourthe party of this day is gon.
Now for the love of God and of Seint John,
Leseth[2] no tyme, as ferforth as ye may.   4441
Lordynges, the tyme wasteth nyght and day
And steleth from us, — what pryvely slepynge,
And what thurgh necligence in oure wakynge, —
As dooth the streem that turneth nevere agayn,
Descendynge fro the montaigne in to playn.

   "Wel kan Senec, and many a philosophre,
Biwaillen tyme moore than gold in cofre ;
For ' losse of catel[3] may recovered be,
But losse of tyme shendeth us,' quod he,   4450
It wol nat come agayn, with outen drede,
Namoore than wole Malkynes maydenhede,[4]
Whan she hath lost it in hir wantownesse ;
Lat us nat mowlen[5] thus in ydelnesse. (4452 T.)

   "Sire Man of Lawe," quod he, "so have ye
      blis,
Telle us a tale anon, as forward[6] is ;
Ye been submytted thurgh youre free assent
To stonden in this cas at my juggement.
Acquiteth yow now of youre biheeste,   4459
Thanne have ye do youre *devoir*[7] atte leeste."

---

[1] Pulled.   [2] Lose ye.   [3] Chattels.   [4] Maidenhood.   [5] Mould
Agreement.   [7] Duty.

" Hoost," quod he, " *depardieux*[1] ich assente.
To breke forward is nat myn entente ;
Biheste is dette, and I wole holde fayn
Al my biheste, I kan no bettre sayn,
For swich lawe as man[2] geveth another wight
He sholde hym-selven usen it by right ;
Thus wole oure text, but nathelees certeyn,
I kan right now no thrifty tale seyn,
But*[3] Chaucer, thogh he kan[4] but lewedly,
On metres and on rymyng craftily,   4470
Hath seyd hem in swich Englissh as he kan
Of olde tyme, as knoweth many a man ;
And if he have noght seyd hem, leve brother,
In o book he hath seyd hem in another ;
For he hath toold of loveris up and doun
Mo than Ovide made of mencioun
In hise Epistles, that been ful olde.
What sholde I telle hem, syn they ben tolde ?
   " In youthe he made[5] of Ceys and Alci-
         one,[6]
And sitthe hath he spoken of everichone   4480
Thise noble wyves and thise loveris eke.
Who so that wole his large volume seke,
Cleped the Seintes Legende of Cupide,[7]
Ther may he seen the large woundes wyde
Of Lucresse and of Babilan Tesbee ;
The swerd of Dido for the false Enee ;
The tree of Phillis for hire Demophon ;

---

[1] By the gods.   [2] Elles. MS. reads " a man."   [3] Elles. MS. reads
that."   [4] Knows.   [5] Wrote poetry.   [6] In the *Boke of the Duch-
ese.*   [7] *The Legende of Goode Women.*

The pleinte of Dianire[1] and of Hermyon ;
Of Adriane and of Isiphilee ;
The bareyne yle[2] stondynge in the see ;   4490
The dreynte Leandre for his fayre[3] Erro ;
The teeris of Eleyne ; and eek[3] the wo
Of Brixseyde, and of[3] the Ladomya ;
The crueltee of the queene Medea,
Thy litel children hangynge by the hals[4]
For thy Jason that was in love so fals !   ·
O Ypermystra, Penolopee, Alceste,
Youre wifhede he comendeth with the beste !

  " But certeinly no word ne writeth ne
Of thilke wikke ensample of Canacee,   4500
That loved hir owene brother synfully ;
(Of swiche cursed stories I sey fy !)   (4500 T.)
Or ellis of Tyro Appollonius,
How that the cursed kyng Antiochus
Birafte his doghter of hir maydenhede,
That is so horrible a tale for to rede,
Whan he hir threw up-on the pavement ;
And therfore he, of ful avysement,
Nolde nevere write in none of his sermons
Of swiche unkynde[5] abhomynacions,   4510
Ne I wol noon reherce, if that I may.

  "But of my tale how shall I doon this day ?
Me were looth be likned, doutelees,

---

[1] Elles. MS. reads " Diane." Deianira mourned, in her epistle to Hercules, that she (by sending him the poisoned garment given her by the Centaur) appeared to be the cause of the hero's death. See Ovid's *Epistles of the Her vines*, ep. ix., and *Metamorphoses*, book ix. Cf. l. 10,767.   [2] Naxos.   [3] Not in Elles. MS.   [4] Neck.   [5] Un atural.

To Muses that men clepe Pierides,[1] —
Methamorphosios woot what I mene, —
But nathelees, I recche noght a bene
Though I come after hym, with halvebake ;[2]
I speke in prose, and lat him rymes make."
And with that word, he with a sobre cheere
Bigan his tale, as ye shal after heere.　　4520

The Prologe of the Manne of Lawes Tale.

O hateful harm ! condicion of poverte !
With thurst, with coold, with hunger so con-
　　　　foundid ![3]　　　　　(4520 T.)
To asken help thee shameth in thyn herte ;
If thou noon aske so soore artow ywoundid,
That verray nede unwrappeth al thy wounde
　　　hid !
Maugree[4] thyn heed thou most for indigence
Or stele, or begge, or borwe thy despence !
Thow blamest Crist, and seist ful bitterly,
He mysdeparteth richesse temporal ;
Thy neighebore thou wytest[5] synfully,　　4530
And seist thou hast to lite[6] and he hath al.
"*Parfay*," seistow, "somtyme he rekene shal
Whan that his tayl shal brennen in the gleede,[7]
For he noght helpeth needfulle in hir neede."

---

[1] The daughters of Pierus are symbols of tiresome chatterers. They dared to contend with the real Muses, and, being defeated, were changed into magpies, as says Ovid, *Metamorphoses*, book v., fable 2.　[2] Crudities. The word is from the Lansdowne MS. Others have "hawebake," which has no meaning that can be determined Perplexed.　[4] Despite.　[5] Blamest.　[6] Little.　[7] Coals.

Herkne,[1] what is the sentence of the wise :
'Bet is to dyen than have indigence;"
Thy-selve neighebor wol thee despise,
If thou be povre, farwel thy reverence!
Yet of the wise man take this sentence:
"Alle dayes of povre men been wikke;"   4540
Be war therfore, er thou come to that prikke!
If thou be povre thy brother hateth thee,
And alle thy freendes fleen from thee, allas!
O riche marchauntz, ful of wele been yee,
O noble, o prudent folk, as in this cas!
Youre bagges been nat fild with *ambes as,*[2]
But with *sys cynk,*[3] that renneth for youre
   chaunce;
At Cristemasse myrie may ye daunce!
Ye seken lond and see for yowre wynnynges;
As wise folk ye knowen all thestaat   455°
Of regnes;[4] ye been fadres of tidynges
And tales, bothe of pees and of debaat.
I were right now of tales desolaat,   (4551 T.)
Nere [5] that a marchant — goon is many a
   yeere —
Me taughte a tale, which that ye shal heere.[6]

---

[1] Elles. MS. has "herke."   [2] Both aces.   Cf. *All 's Well that
Ends Well*, act ii., sc. 3, l. 84.   [3] A six-and-five throw.   Cf. l. 8273.
[4] Kingdoms.   [5] Were it not.   [6] The following story is composed of
ancient authors that frequently occur in ancient authors.   Chaucer follows
Nicholas Trivet, whose version has been published by the Chaucer
Society (1872), with a translation by Edmund Brock.   In the *Gesta
Romanorum* it is called The Tale of the Wife of Merelaus the Em-
peror

Heere begynneth The Man of Lawe his Tale.

FIRST PART.

In Surrye[1] whilom dwelte a compaignye
Of chapmen[2] riche, and therto sadde[3] and
    trewe,   (4555 ᵀ.)
That wyde-where[4] senten hir spicerye,
Clothes of gold, and satyns riche of hewe.
Hir chaffare was so thrifty and so newe   4560
That every wight hath deyntee[5] to chaffare
With hem, and eek to sellen hem hire ware.
Now fil it that the maistres of that sort
Han shapen hem to Rome for to wende,
Were it for chapmanhode, or for disport,
Noon oother message[6] wolde they thider
    sende,
But comen hem-self to Rome, this is the ende;
And in swich place as thoughte hem avantage
For hire entente, they take hir herbergage.[7]

Sojourned han thise marchantz in that toun
A certein tyme, as fil to hire plesance ;   4571
And so bifel that thexcellent renoun
Of the Emperoures[8] doghter, dame Custance,
Reported was, with every circumstance,
Un-to thise Surryen marchantz in swich wyse
Fro day to day, as I shal yow devyse.

Syria. [2] Merchants. [3] Staid. [4] Widely. [5] Pleasure. [6] Messenger. [7] Lodging [8] The emperor is said to have been Tiberius Constantine (578-582).

This was the commune voys of every man :
"Oure Emperour of Rome, God hym see !¹
A doghter hath that syn the world bigan,
To rekene as wel hir goodness as beautee,
Nas nevere swich another as is shee.   4581
I prey to God, in honour hire susteene,
And wolde she were of all Europe the queene ¡
In hire is heigh beautee with-oute pride,
Yowthe with-oute grenehede ² or folye ;
To alle hire werkes vertu is hir gyde ;
Humblesse hath slayn in hire al tirannye ;
She is mirour of alle curteisye,
Hir herte is verray chambre of hoolynesse,
Hir hand ministre of fredam for almesse." 4590
And al this voys was sooth, as God is trewe ;
But now to purpos lat us turne agayn.
Thise marchantz han doon fraught hir shippes
          newe,
And whan they han this blisful mayden sayn,
Hoom to Surrye been they went ³ ful fayn,
And doon hir nedes as they han doon yoore,
And lyven in wele, I kan sey yow namoore.
    Now fil it that thise marchantz stode in
          grace
Of hym that was the sowdan ⁴ of Surrye,
For whan they cam from any strange place
He wolde of his benigne curteisye   4601
Make hem good chiere and bisily espye
Tidynges of sondry regnes, for to leere ⁵

¹ **Preserve.** ² Childishness. ³ Turned. ⁴ Sultan. ⁵ **Learn.**

The wondres that they myghte seen or heere.
Amonges othere thynges specially,   (4603 T.)
Thise marchantz han hym toold of dame Cus-
      tance
So greet noblesse in ernest ceriously,
That this sowdan hath caught so greet plesance
To han hir figure in his remembrance,
That all his lust, and al his bisy cure,   4610
Was for to love hire while his lyf may dure.
Paraventure in thilke large book,
Which that men clipe[1] the hevene, ywriten was
With sterres,[2] whan that he his birthe took,
That he for love sholde han his deeth, allas !
For in the sterres, clerer than is glas,
Is written, God woot, who-so koude it rede,
The deeth of every man, withouten drede.
In sterres many a wynter ther biforn
Was writen the deeth of Ector, Achilles,   4620
Of Pompei, Julius, er they were born,
The strif of Thebes, and of Ercules,
Of Sampson, Turnus, and of Socrates
The deeth ; but mennes wittes ben so dulle
That no wight kan wel rede it atte fulle.

This sowdan for his privee conseil sente,
And, shortly of this matiere for to pace,[3]
He hath to hem declared his entente,
And seyde hem, certein but he myghte have
      grace
To han Custance with-inne a litel space,   4630

---

[1] Call.   [2] His fortune was written in the stars.   [3] Pass.

He nas but deed, and charged hem in hye
To shapen for his lyf som remedye.

Diverse men diverse thynges seyden,
They argumenten, casten up and doun ;
Many a subtil resoun forth they leyden ;
They speken of magyk and abusioun ; [1]
But finally, as in conclusioun,
They kan nat seen in that noon avantage,
Ne in noon oother wey, save mariage.

Thanne sawe they ther-inne swich difficultee,
By wey of reson, for to speke al playn,   4641
By-cause that ther was swich diversitee
Bitwene hir bothe lawes, that they sayn,
They trowe that no cristene prince wolde fayn
Wedden his child under oure lawes sweete,
That us were taught by Mahoun,[2] oure prophete

And he answerde, " Rather than I lese
Custance, I wol be cristned, doutelees ;
I moot been hires, I may noon oother chese.[3]
I prey yow hoold youre argumentz in pees ;
Saveth my lyf, and beth noght recchelees, 4651
To geten hire that hath my lyf in cure ; (4650 T.)
For in this wo I may nat longe endure."

What nedeth gretter dilatacioun ? [4]
I seye, by tretys and embassadrie,
And by the popes mediacioun,
And al the chirche, and al the chivalrie,
That in destruccioun of maumettrie,[5]
And in encrees of Cristes lawe deere,

---

[1] Abuse.   [2] This is an anachronism, for Mohammed was a smal
child at this time   [3] Choose.   [4] Enlargement.   [5] Image worship.

They been acorded, so as ye shal heere,   4660
How that the sowdan and his baronage,
And alle hise liges, sholde ycristned be,
And he shal han Custance in mariage,
And certein gold, I noot what quantitee ;
And heer to founden sufficient suretee
This same accord was sworn on eyther syde.
Now, faire Custance, almyghty God thee gyde !
    Now wolde som men waiten, as I gesse,
That I sholde tellen al the purveiance
That themperoure, of his grete noblesse,   4670
Hath shapen [1] for his doghter, dame Custance.
Wel may men knowen that so greet ordinance
May no man tellen in a litel clause,
As was arrayed for so heigh a cause.
Bisshopes been shapen with hire for to wende,
Lordes, ladies, knyghtes of renoun,
And oother folk ynogh, this is the ende ;
And notified is thurgh-out the toun
That every wight, with greet devocioun,
Sholde preyen Crist, that he this mariage 4680
Receyve in gree [2] and spede this viage.[3]
    The day is comen of hir departynge —
I seye, the woful day fatal is come,
That ther may be no lenger tariynge,
But forthward they hem dressen alle and some.
Custance, that was with sorwe al overcome,
Ful pale arist, and dresseth hire to wende,
For wel she seeth ther is noon oother ende.

---

[1] Prepared.   [2] Favor.   [3] Voyage.

Allas ! what wonder is it thogh she wepte,
That shal be sent to strange nacioun,   4690
Fro freendes that so tendrely hire kepte,
And to be bounden under subjeccioun
Of oon she knoweth nat his condicioun ?
Housbondes been alle goode and han ben
        yoore ;
That knowen wyves, I dar say yow na moore.

    " Fader," she seyde, " thy wrecched child,
        Custance,
Thy yonge doghter, fostred up so softe,
And ye, my mooder, my soverayn plesance,
Over alle thyng, out-taken [1] Crist on lofte,[2]
Custance, youre child, hire recomandeth ofte
Un-to your grace ; for I shal to Surrye,   4701
Ne shal I nevere seen yow moore with eye.

Allas ! un-to the barbre nacioun   (4701 T.)
I moste goon, syn that it is youre wille ;
But Crist, that starf [3] for our savacioun
So geve me grace hise heestes to fulfille ;
I, wrecche womman, no fors [4] though I spille ! [5]
Wommen are born to thraldom and penance
And to been under mannes governance."

    I trowe at Troye, whan Pirrus [6] brak the wal
Or [7] Ilion brende, — at Thebes the citee, —

___

[1] Except. [2] High. [3] Died. [4] Matter. [5] Perish. [6] Neoptole-
mus, the valorous son of Achilles, who entered Troy through the
broken wall, in the wooden horse, before the city was burned. He
killed Priam, sacrificed Polyxena, and married Andromache. Called
also Pyrrhus, especially in the *Geste Hystoriale* of the Destruction
of Troy (E. E. Text Society, 1874), book xxix. Cf. Ovid, *Heroïdes*
viii. ; *Ars Amatoria*, i. ; *Metamorphoses*, xiii. [7] Ere. In this line
Elles. MS. omits " at," which is in the Cambridge MS.

Nat[1] Rome, for the harm thurgh Hanybal,
That Romayns hath venquysshed tymes thre,
Nas herd swich tendre wepyng for pitee,   4714
As in the chambre was for hire departynge;
But forth she moot, wher so she wepe or synge.

O firste moevyng, crueel firmament,
With thy diurnal sweigh that crowdest ay,
And hurlest al from Est til Occident,
That naturelly wolde holde another way;   4720
Thy crowdyng set the hevene in swich array
At the bigynnyng of this fiers viage,
That crueel Mars hath slayn this mariage!
Infortunat ascendent[2] tortuous,
Of which the lord is helplees, falle, allas,
Out of his angle[2] in to the derkeste hous.[2]
O Mars, O Atazir,[3] as in this cas!
O fieble Moone, unhappy been thy paas!
Thou knyttest thee ther thou art nat receyved,
Ther thou were weel, fro thennes artow weyved.[4]
Imprudent emperour of Rome, allas!   4731
Was ther no philosophre in al thy toun?
Is no tyme bet than oother in swich cas?
Of viage is ther noon eleccioun,
Namely to folk of heigh condicioun,
Noght whan a roote[5] is of a burthe yknowe?
Allas! we been to lewed or to slowe!

To ship is come this woful, faire mayde,
Solempnely, with every circumstance.

---

[1] Nor at (ne at).   [2] Astrological terms.   [3] Evil influence.
[4] Turned aside.   [5] A radix from which celestial calculations are
made.

"Now Jhesu Crist be with yow alle," she
    sayde.   4740
Ther nys namoore, but "Farwel, faire Cus-
    tance!"
She peyneth hire to make good contenance;
And forth I lete hire saille in this manere,
And turne I wole agayn to my matere.

    The mooder of the sowdan, welle [1] of vices,
Espied hath hir sones pleyn entente,
How he wol lete [2] hise olde sacrifices;
And right anon she for hir conseil sente,   4748
And they been come to knowe what she mente;
And whan assembled was this folk in feere, [3]
She sette hire doun and seyde as ye shal heere.

    "Lordes," she seyde, "ye knowen everichon,
How that my sone in point is for to lete
The hooly lawes of oure Alkaron, [4]   (4752 T.)
Geven by Goddes message [5] Makomete;
But oon avow to grete God I heete, [6]
The lyf shal rather out of my body sterte,
Than Makometes lawe out of myn herte!
What sholde us tyden [7] of this newe lawe,
But thraldom to our bodies and penance, 4760
And afterward in helle to be drawe,
For we reneyed [8] Mahoun oure creance? [9]
But, lordes, wol ye maken assurance
As I shal seyn, assentynge to my loore,
And I shal make us sauf for everemoore."

---

[1] Source.   [2] Stop.   [3] Company.   [4] Alcoran.   [5] Messenger
Promise.   [7] Betide.   [8] Denied.   [9] Faith.

They sworen, and assenten every man
To lyve with hire, and dye, and by hire stonde,
And everich, in the beste wise he kan,
To strengthen hire shal alle hise frendes fonde.[1]
And she hath this emprise ytake on honde 4770
Which ye shal heren that I shal devyse ;
And to hem alle she spak right in this wyse :
    " We shul first feyne us cristendom [2] to
        take, —
Coold water shal nat greve us but a lite, —
And I shal swiche a feeste and revel make,
That as I trowe I shal the sowdan quite ;[3]
For thogh his wyf be cristned never so white
She shal have nede to wasshe awey the rede,[4]
Thogh she a font-ful water with hire lede ! "
    O sowdanesse, roote of iniquitee ! 4780
Virago thou, Semyrame the secounde,
O serpent, under femynynytee,
Lik to the serpent depe in helle ybounde !
O feyned womman, al that may confounde
Vertu and innocence thurgh thy malice
Is bred in thee, as nest of every vice !
O Sathan, envious syn thilke day
That thou were chaced from oure heritage,
Wel knowestow to wommen the olde way !
Thou madest Eva brynge us in servage, 4790
Thou wolt fordoon this cristen mariage.
Thyn instrument so, weylawey the while !
Makestow of wommen whan thou wolt bigile.

---

[1] Try.   [2] Accept baptism   [3] Quit.   [4] Red.

This sowdanesse, whom I thus blame and
    warye,[1]
Leet prively hire conseil goon hire way.
What sholde I in this tale lenger tarye ?
She rydeth to the sowdan on a day,
And seyde hym that she wolde reneye hir lay,
And cristendom of preestes handes fonge,[8]
Repentynge hire she hethen was so longe ; 4800
Bisechynge hym to doon hire that honour,
That she moste han the cristen folk to feeste, —
"To plesen hem, I wol do my labour." (4801 T.)
The sowdan seith, "I wol doon at youre
    heeste ;"
And knelynge, thanketh hire of that requeste ;
So glad he was he nyste what to seye.
She kiste hir sone, and hoome she gooth hir
    weye.

SECOND PART.

Arryved been this cristen folk to londe
In Surrye, with a greet solempne route ;   4809
And hastifliche this sowdan sente his sonde [4]
First to his mooder, and all the regne [5] aboute,
And seyde his wyf was comen, oute of doute,
And preyde hire for to ryde agayn [6] the queene
The honour of his regne to susteene.
Greet was the prees,[7] and riche was tharray
Of Surryens and Romayns met yfeere.[8]

---

[1] Abuse.   [2] Deny her law.   [3] Receive.   [4] Message.   [5] **Kingdom**
[6] **Towards.**   [7] Press.   [8] In company.

The mooder of the sowdan, riche and gay,
Recyveth hire with al so glad a cheere [1]
As any mooder myghte hir doghter deere,
And to the nexte citee ther bisyde,   4820
A softe paas [2] solempnely they ryde.
Noght trowe I the triumphe of Julius, —
Of which that Lucan maketh swich a boost, —
Was roialler or moore curius,
Than was thassemblee of this blisful hoost;
Bute [3] this scorpioun, this wikked goost,
The sowdanesse, for all hire flaterynge,
Caste [4] under this fui mortally to stynge.
The sowdan comth hymself soone after this
So roially, that wonder is to telle,   4830
And welcometh hire with alle joye and blis;
And thus in murthe and joye I lete hem dwelle;
The fruyt of this matiere is that I telle.
Whan tyme cam men thoughte it for the beste,
The revel stynte and men goon to hir reste.

    The tyme cam this olde sowdanesse
Ordeyned hath this feeste of which I tolde,
And to the feeste cristen folk hem dresse
In general, ye, bothe yonge and olde.   4839
Heere may men feeste and roialtee biholde,
And deyntees mo than I kan yow devyse,
But all to deere they boghte it, er they ryse.

    O sodeyn wo! that evere art successour

---

[1] Countenance.   [2] Slow pace.   [3] Elles. MS. has "but," but the
final *e* in the text is supported by O. E. (the word being *butan*.
ute) and by the Corpus and Petworth MSS., which add the tag in-
dicative of a final *e*, in this place.   [4] Planned.

To worldly blisse spreynd [1] with bitternesse !
The ende of the joye of oure worldly labour !
Wo occupieth the fyn [2] of oure gladnesse.
Herke this conseil, for thy sikernesse, [3]
Up-on thy glade day have in thy mynde
The unwar wo or harm that comth bihynde.
For soothly for to tellen, at o word,   4850
The sowdan and the cristen everichone
Been al tohewe, and stiked at the bord,
But [4] it were oonly dame Custance allone.
This olde sowdanesse, cursed krone ! (4852 T.)
Hath with hir freendes doon this cursed dede,
For she hir-self wolde all the contree lede.
Ne was Surryen noon, that was converted,
That of the conseil of the sowdan woot,
That he nas al tohewe er he asterted, [5]
And Custance han they take anon foot-hoot [6]
And in a ship all steerelees, God woot,   4861
They han hir set and biddeth hire lerne saille
Out of Surrye, agaynward to Ytaille.
A certein tresor that she with hire ladde, [7]
And, sooth to seyn, vitaille greet plentee,
They han hire geven, and clothes eek she
          hadde,
And forth she sailleth in the salte see !
    O my Custance, ful of benignytee,
O emperours yonge doghter deere,   4869
He that is lord of fortune be thy steere ! [8]

She blesseth hire, and with ful pitous voys,
Un-to the croys of Crist thus seyde she :
" O clccre, O weleful [1] auter, hooly croys,
Reed [2] of the Lambes blood, ful of pitee,
That wesshe the world fro the olde iniqui-
    tee,
Me fro the feend and fro his clawes kepe,
That day that I shal drenchen [3] in the depe !
Victorious tree, proteccioun of trewe,
That oonly worthy were for to bere   4879
The Kyng of Hevene with his woundes newe,
The white Lamb that hurt was with the spere ;
Flemere [4] of feendes out of hym and here,
On which thy lymes feithfully extenden,
Me helpe, and gif me myght my lyf tamen-
    den." [5]

Yeres and dayes fleteth this creature
Thurghout the See of Grece un-to the Strayte
Of Marrok,[6] as it was hire aventure.
On many a sory meel now may she bayte ;[7]
After hir deeth ful often may she wayte,
Er that the wilde wawes [8] wol hire dryve   4890
Un-to the place ther she shal arryve.

Men myghten asken why she was nat slayn
Eek at the feeste, who myghte hir body save ?
And I answere to that demande agayn,
Who saved Danyel in the horrible cave,
Ther every wight save he, maister and knave,

---

[1] Elles. MS. has " woful."   [2] Red.   [3] Drown.   [4] Banisher
To amend.   [6] Gibraltar (Morocco).   [7] Feed.   [8] Waves.

Was with the leoun frete,[1] er he asterte?[2]
No wight but God, that he bar in his herte.
God liste to shewe his wonderful myracle
In hire, for we sholde seen his myghty werkis.
Crist, which that is to every harm triacle,[3]   4901
By certeine meenes ofte, as knowen clerkis,
Dooth thyng for certein ende that ful derk is
To mannes wit, that for oure ignorance
Ne konne noght knowe his prudent purvei-
    ance.   (4903 T.)
Now sith she was nat at the feeste yslawe,
Who kepte hire fro the drenchyng in the see?
Who kepte Jonas in the fisshes mawe,
Til he was spouted up at Nynyvee?   4909
Wel may men knowe it was no wight but He
That kepte peple Ebrayk from hir drench-
    ynge,
With drye feet thurgh-out the see passynge.
Who bad the foure spirites of tempest,
That power han tanoyen lond and see,
Bothe north and south, and also west and est,
Anoyeth neither see, ne land, ne tree?[4]
Soothly the comandour of that was He
That fro the tempest ay this womman kepte
As wel when she wook as whan she slepte.
Where myghte this womman mete and drynke
    have,   4920
Thre yeer and moore? how lasteth hire vit-
    aille?

---

[1] **Devoured.**   [2] Escaped.   [3] Remedy.   [4] See Revelation vii. 1-3

Who fedde the Egypcien Marie [1] in the cave,
Or in desert? No wight but Crist, *sanz faille*.
Fyve thousand folk it was as greet mervaille
With loves fyve, and fisshes two, to feede.
God sente his foyson [2] at hir grete neede.
She dryveth forth in-to oure occian,
Thurgh-out oure wilde see, til atte laste   4928
Under an hoold,[3] that nem pnen [4] I ne kan,
Fer in Northumberlond the wawe hire caste,
And in the sond [5] hir ship stiked so faste
That thennes woide it noght of al a tyde.[6]
The wyl of Crist was that she sholde abyde.
The constable of the castel doun is fare
To seen this wrak, and al the ship he soghte,
And foond this wery womman, ful of care ;
He foond also the tresor that she broghte.
In hir langage mercy she bisoghte,
The lyf out of hire body for to twynne,[7]   4939
Hire to delivere of wo that she was inne.
A maner Latyn corrupt was hir speche,
But algates ther-by was she understonde.
The constable, whan hym lyst no lenger
      seche,[8]
This woful womman broghte he to the londe ,
She kneleth doun and thanketh Goddes sonde ;
But what she was she wolde no man seye
For foul ne fair, thogh that she sholde deye.

---

[1] Mary of Egypt is said to have been miraculously sustained, in the Wilderness beyond the Jordan, forty-eight years. She is one of the penitents who intercede for the soul of Margaret in Goethe's *Faust*, Second Part, act v., sc. 7.   [2] Plenty.   [3] A fortification. **Name**.   [5] Sand.   [6] Time   [7] Separate.   [8] Search.   [9] Decree.

She seyde she was so mazed in the see
That she forgat hir mynde, by hir trouthe.
The constable hath of hire so greet pitee, 4950
And eke his wyf, that they wepen for routhe.
She was so diligent, with-outen slouthe, (4950 T.)
To serve and plese everich in that place,
That alle hir loven that looken in hir face.
This constable and dame Hermengyld, his
          wyf,
Were payens,[1] and that contree every-where ;
But Hermengyld loved hire right as hir lyf,
And Custance hath so longe sojourned there,
In orisons with many a bitter teere,   4959
Til Jhesu hath converted, thurgh his grace,
Dame Hermengyld, constablesse of that place.
In al that lond no cristen dorste route,[2]
Alle cristen folk been fled fro that contree,
Thurgh payens, that conquereden al aboute
The plages[3] of the North by land and see.
To Walys fledde the cristyanytee
Of olde Britons dwellynge in this ile ;
Ther was hir refut for the meene while.
But yet nere[4] cristene Britons so exiled   4969
That ther nere somme, that in hir privetee
Honoured Crist, and hethen folk bigiled ;
And ny the castel swiche ther dwelten three.
That oon of hem was blynd and myghte nat
          see,
But it were with thilke eyen of his mynde,

---
[1] Pagans.   [2] Assemble, come.   [3] Regions.   [4] Were not.

With whiche men seen whan that they ben
    blynde.
  Bright was the sonne, as in that someres
    day,
For which the constable and his wyf also,
And Custance, han ytake the righte way
Toward the see, a furlong wey or two,
To pleyen and to romen to and fro;   4980
And in hir walk this blynde man they mette,
Croked and oold, with eyen faste yshete.
" In name of Crist," cride this olde Britoun,
"Dame Hermengyld, gif me my sighte agayn!"
This lady weex affrayed of the soun,
Lest that hir housbonde, shortly for to sayn,
Wolde hire for Jhesu Cristes love han slayn;
Til Custance made hire boold, and bad hire
       wirche [1]   4988
The wyl of Crist as doghter of his chirche.
The constable weex abasshed of that sight,
And seyde, "What amounteth all this fare!"
Custance answerde, "Sire, it is Cristes myght
That helpeth folk out of the feendes snare:"
And so ferforth she gan oure lay [2] declare,
That she the constable, er that it were eve,
Converteth, and on Crist maketh hym bileve.
This constable was no-thyng lord of this place
Of which I speke, ther he Custance fond,
But kepte it strongly, many wyntres space,
Under Alla,[3] kyng of al Northhumbrelond,

---

[1] Work   [2] Law.   [3] He ruled from A. D. 560 to A. D. 588

That was ful wys and worthy of his hond, 5001
Agayn the Scottes, as men may wel heere ;
But turne I wole agayn to my mateere. (5001 T.)
   Sathan, that evere us waiteth to bigile,
Saugh of Custance al hire perfeccioun,
And caste anon how he myghte quite hir while,
And made a yong knyght, that dwelte in that
    toun,
Love hire so hoote, of foul affeccioun,
That verraily hym thoughte he sholde spille [1]
But he of hire myghte ones have his wille. 5010
He woweth [2] hire, but it availleth noght,
She wolde do no synne by no weye,
And for despit he compassed in his thoght
To maken hire on shameful deeth to deye.
He wayteth [3] whan the constable was aweye
And pryvely up-on a nyght he crepte
In Hermengyldes chambre whil she slepte.
Wery, for-waked, in hire orisouns,
Slepeth Custance, and Hermengyld also.
This knyght, thurgh Sathanas temptaciouns,
All softely is to the bed ygo,   5021
And kitte [4] the throte of Hermengyld atwo,
And leyde the blody knyf by dame Custance,
And wente his wey, ther God geve hym mes
    chance !
Soone after cometh this constable hoom agayn
And eek Alla, that kyng was of that lond,
And saugh his wyf despitously yslayn,

    [1] Perish.   [2] Wooeth.   [3] Watcheth.   [4] Cut.

For which ful ofte he weepe and wroong his
    hond,
And in the bed the blody knyf he fond
By dame Custance; allas! what myghte she
    seye?   5030
For verray wo, hir wit was al aweye.
To kyng Alla was toold al this meschance
And eek the tyme, and where, and in what
    wise;
That in a ship was founden dame Custance,
As heer biforn that ye han herd devyse.
The kynges herte of pitee gan agryse,[1]
Whan he saugh so benigne a creature
Falle in disese, and in mysaventure:
For as the lomb toward his deeth is broght,
So stant this innocent bifore the kyng.   5040
This false knyght, that hath this tresoun wroght,
Berth hire on hond[2] that she hath doon thys
    thyng;
But nathelees, ther was greet moornyng
Among the peple, and seyn[3] they kan nat gesse
That she had doon so greet a wikkednesse:
For they han seyn[4] hire evere so vertuous,
And lovynge Hermengyld right as hir lyf.
Of this baar witnesse everich in that hous, 5048
Save he that Hermengyld slow with his knyf.
This gentil kyng hath caught a greet motyf
Of this witnesse, and thoghte he wolde enquere
Depper in this, a trouthe for to lere.[5] (5050 T.)

---

[1] Shudder   [2] Accuseth.   [3] Say.   [4] Seen.   [5] Learn.

Allas ! Custance, thou hast no champioun,
Ne fighte kanstow noght, so weylaway !
But he that starf [1] for our redempcioun,
And boond Sathan,— and yet lith ther he lay,—
So be thy stronge champion this day ;
For, but if Crist open myracle kithe,[2]
Withouten gilt, thou shalt be slayn as swithe.[3]
She sit hire doun on knees and thus she sayde
"Immortal God that savedest Susanne   5061
Fro fals blame, and thou merciful mayde,
Mary I meene, doghter to Seint Anne,
Bifore whos child angeles synge Osanne,
If I be giltlees of this felonye
My socour be, or ellis shal I dye ! "

Have ye nat seyn som tyme a pale face
Among a prees, of hym that hath be lad
Toward his deeth, wher as hym gat no grace ?
And swich a colour in his face hath had,   5070
Men myghte knowe his face that was bistad,[4]
Amonges alle the faces in that route ;
So stant Custance, and looketh hire aboute.

O queenes, lyvynge in prosperitee !
Duchesses, and ladyes everichone !
Haveth som routhe on hire adversitee.
An emperoures doghter stant allone ;
She hath no wight to whom to make hir mone !
O blood roial, that stondest in this drede,
Fer been [5] thy freendes at thy grete nede ! 5080
This Alla, kyng, hath swich compassioun,

1 Died.   2 Show.   3 Quickly.   4 Bestead.   5 Are.

As gentil herte is fulfild of pitee,
That from hise eyen ran the water doun.
" Now hastıly do tecche a book," quod he,
" And if this knyght wol sweren how that she
This womman slow, yet wol we us avyse
Whom that we wole that shal been our jus-
       tise."
A Briton book written with Evaungiles
Was fet,[1] and on this book he swoor anoon
She gilty was, and in the meene whiles   5090
An hand hym smoot upon the nekke boon,
That doun he fil atones as a stoon ;
And bothe hise eyen broste [2] out of his face
In sighte of every body in that place !

    A voys was herd in general audience
And seyde, " Thou hast desclaundred, giltlees,
The doghter of hooly chirche in heigh presence ;
Thus hastou doon, and yet holde I my pees ! "
Of this mervaille agast was al the prees ;
As mazed folk they stoden everichone,   5100
For drede of wreche,[3] save Custance allone.

    Greet was the drede, and eek the repentance,
Of hem that hadden wronge suspecioun
Upon this sely,[4] innocent Custance ; (5102 T.)
And for this miracle, in conclusioun,
And by Custances mediacioun,
The kyng, and many another in that place,
Converted was, — thanked be Cristes grace !
    This false knyght was slayn for his untrouthe

    [1] Fetched.   [2] Burst   [3] Vengeance.   [4] Simple.

By juggement of Alla, hastifly ;   5110
And yet Custance hadde of his deeth greet
    routhe ;
And after this Jhesus, of his mercy,
Made Alla wedden, ful solempnely,
This hooly mayden, that is so bright and
    sheene;
And thus hath Crist ymaad Custance a queene.

  But who was woful — if I shal nat lye —
Of this weddyng but Donegild and na mo,
The kynges mooder, ful of tirannye ?
Hir thoughte hir cursed herte brast atwo, —
She wolde noght hir sone had do so.   5120
Hir thoughte a despit that he sholde take
So strange a creature un-to his make.[1]

  Me list nat of the chaf, or of the stree,[2]
Maken so long a tale as of the corn.
What sholde I tellen of the roialtee
At mariage, or which cours goth biforn,
Who bloweth in the trumpe, or in an horn ?
The fruyt of every tale is for to seye,
They ete, and drynke, and daunce, and synge
    and pleye.

They goon to bedde, as it was skile[3] and right,
For thogh that wyves be ful hooly thynges,
They moste take in pacience at nyght   5132
Swiche manere necessaries as been plesynges
To folk that han ywedded hem with rynges,
And leye a lite hir hoolynesse aside,

       [1] Mate.   [2] Straw.   [3] Reasonable.

As for the tyme, — it may no bet bitide.
On hire he gat a knave [1] childe anon,
And to a bisshop, and his constable eke,
He took his wyf to kepe whan he is gon
To Scotlondward his foomen for to seke. 5140
   Now faire Custance, that is so humble and
      meke,
So longe is goon with childe, til that stille
She halt hire chambre abidyng Cristes wille.
The tyme is come a knave child she beer, —
Mauricius at the fontstoon they hym calle.
This constable dooth [2] forth come a messageer,
And wroot un-to his kyng, that cleped was Alle,
How that this blisful tidyng is bifalle,
And othere tidynges spedeful for to seye. 5149
He taketh the lettre and forth he gooth his
     weye.
   This messager, to doon his avantage,
Un-to the kynges mooder rideth swithe, (5150 T.)
And salueth hire ful faire in his langage :
  Madame," quod he, "ye may be glad and
     blithe
Ard thanketh God an hundred thousand sithe,
My lady queene hath child with-outen doute
To joye and blisse to al this regne aboute.
Lo, heere the lettres seled of this thyng,
That I moot bere with al the haste I may.
If ye wol aught un-to youre sone the kyng, 5160
I am youre servant bothe nyght and day."

        [1] Man   [2] Maketh.

Donegild answerde, " As now, at this tyme, nay ,
But heere al nyght I wol thou take thy reste.
To-morwe wol I seye thee what me leste."

   This messager drank sadly[1] ale and wyn,
And stolen were hise lettres pryvely,
Out of his box whil he sleep as a swyn,
And countrefeted was ful subtilly
Another lettre, wroght ful synfully,
Un-to the kyng direct, of this mateere,   5170
Fro his constable, as ye shal after heere.

The lettre spak, the queene delivered was
Of so horrible a feendly creature,
That in the castel noon so hardy was
That any while dorste ther endure.
The mooder was an elf, by aventure,[2]
Ycomen by charmes, or by sorcerie,
And everich hateth hir compaignye.

   Wo was this kyng whan he this lettre had
     sayn,
But to no wight he tolde his sorwes soore,
But of his owene hand he wroot agayn :   5181
" Wel-come the sonde[3] of Crist for everemoore,
To me that am now lerned in his loore !
Lord, wel-come be thy lust and thy plesaunce
My lust I putte al in thyn ordinaunce.
Kepeth this child, al be it foul or feir,
And eek my wyf un-to myn hoom-comynge ;
Crist whan hym list may sende me an heir
Moore agreable than this to my likynge."

---

[1] Steadily, continuously.   [2] Perchance.   [3] Thing sent.

This lettre he seleth, pryvely wepynge,   5190
Which to the messager was take soone,
And forth he gooth ; ther is na moore to doone.

  O messager, fulfild of dronkenesse !
Strong is thy breeth, thy lymes faltren ay,
And thou biwreyest [1] alle secreenesse.
Thy mynde is lorn, thou janglest as a jay ;
Thy face is turned in a newe array !
Ther dronkenesse regneth in any route, [2]
Ther is no conseil hyd, with-outen doute.

  O Donegild ! I ne have noon Englissh digne
Un-to thy malice and thy tirannye,   5201
And therfore to the feend I thee resigne,
Lat hym enditen of thy traitorie !   (5201 T.)
Fy, mannysh, fy, — O nay, by God, I lye, —
Fy, *feendlych* spirit, for I dar wel telle,
Thogh thou heere walke, thy spirit is in helle.

  This messager comth fro the kyng agayn,
And at the kynges moodres court he lighte ;
And she was of this messager ful fayn,   5209
And plesed hym, in al that ever she myghte.
He drank, and wel his girdel underpighte ; [3]
He slepeth, and he snoreth in his gyse
All nyghte, til the sonne gan aryse.
Eft [4] were hise lettres stolen everychon,
And countrefeted lettres in this wyse :
" The king comandeth his constable anon,
Up peyne of hangyng, and on heigh juyse, [5]
That he ne sholde suffren, in no wyse,

---

[1] Betrayest. [2] Body. Stuffed. [4] Again [5] Judgment.

Custance in-with his reawme [1] for tabyde
Thre dayes and o quarter of a tyde ;   5220
But in the same ship as he hire fond,
Hire, and hir yonge sone, and al hir geere
He sholde putte, and croude hire fro the lond,
And chargen hire she never eft coome theere ! "
O my Custance, wel may thy goost have feere,
And slepynge in thy dreem been in penance,
Whan Donegild cast al this ordinance.

This messager on morwe, whan he wook,
Un-to the castel halt the nexte [2] way,
And to the constable he the lettre took ;   5230
And whan that he this pitous lettre say,
Ful ofte he seyde, " Allas ! and weylaway !
Lord Crist," quod he, " how may this world
          endure ?
So ful of synne is many a creature !

" O myghty God, if that it be thy wille,
Sith thou art rightful juge, how may it be
That thou wolt suffren innocentz to spille,[3]
And wikked folk regnen in prosperitee ?
O goode Custance ! Allas, so wo is me,
That I moot be thy tormentour or deye   5240
On shames deeth, ther is noon oother weye."

Wepen bothe yonge and olde in al that
          place,
Whan that the kyng this cursed lettre sente,
And Custance, with a deedly pale face,
The ferthe day toward the ship she wente ;

          Kingdom, French *royaume*.   [2] Nearest.   [3] Perish.

But nathelees she taketh in good entente
The wyl of Crist, and knelynge on the stronde,
She seyde, " Lord, ay wel-come be thy sonde ;[1]
He that me kepte fro the false blame,
While I was on the lond amonges yow,   5250
He kan me kepe from harm, and eek fro
    shame,
In salte see, al thogh I se noght how. (5250 T.)
As strong as evere he was he is yet now.
In hym triste I, and in his mooder deere, —
That is to me my seyl,[2] and eek my steere."[3]
Hir litel child lay wepyng in hir arm,
And knelynge, pitously to hym she seyde,[4]
" Pees, litel sone, I wol do thee noon harm ! "
With that hir kerchef[5] of hir heed she breyde,[6]
And over hise litel eyen she it leyde,   5260
And in hir arm she lulleth it ful faste,
And in-to hevene hire eyen up she caste.

   " Mooder," quod she, " and mayde, bright
    Marie,
Sooth is that thurgh wommanes eggement[7]
Man-kynde was lorn, and damned ay to dye,
For which thy child was on a croys yrent, —
Thy blisful eyen sawe al his torment, —
Thanne is ther no comparison bitwene
Thy wo and any wo man may sustene.   5269
Thow sawe thy child yslayn bifore thyne eyen,
And yet now lyveth my litel[8] child, *parfay !*

---

[1] Thing sent. [2] Sail. [3] Guide. [4] Cf. l. 12,891, etc. [5] Elles. MS
has "coverchief." [6] Drew. [7] Instigation. [8] Not in Elles. MS.

Now, lady bright, to whom alle woful cryen, —
Thow glorie of wommanhede, thow faire May,
Thow haven of refut,[1] brighte sterre of day, —
Rewe on [2] my child, that of thy gentillesse
Ruest on every reweful in distresse.

"O litel child, allas! what is thy gilt,
That nevere wroghtest synne as yet, *pardee ?*
Why wil thyn harde fader han thee spilt ? [3]
O mercy, deere constable," quod she,   5280
"As lat my litel child dwelle heer with thee ;
And if thou darst nat saven hym for blame,
Yet kys hym ones in his fadres name ! "
Ther with she looked bakward to the londe,
And seyde, "Fare-wel, housbonde routhelees ! '
And up she rist, and walketh doun the stronde
Toward the ship, — hir folweth al the prees, —
And evere she preyeth hire child to hold his
        pees ;
And taketh hir leve, and with an hooly en-
        tente,
She blissed [4] hire and in-to ship she wente.

Vitailled was the ship, it is no drede,   5291
Habundantly for hire ful longe space ;
And othere necessaries that sholde nede
She hadde ynogh, heryed [5] be Goddes grace !
For wynd and weder, almyghty God purchace ! [6]
And brynge hire hoom, I kan no bettre seye ;
But in the see she dryveth forth hir weye.

[1] Refuge.   [2] Pity.   [3] Destroyed.   [4] Crossed.   [5] Praised.   [6] Pro-
vid.

THIRD PART.

Alla the kyng comth hoom soone after this
Un-to his castel of the which I tolde,
And asketh where his wyf and his child is?
The constable gan aboute his herte colde [1] 5301
And pleynly al the manere he hym tolde,
As ye han herd, — I kan telle it no bettre, —
And sheweth the kyng his seele and his lettre;
And seyde, " Lord, as ye comanded me,
Up peyne of deeth, so have I doon certein."
This messager tormented was til he   (5305 T.)
Moste biknowe,[2] and tellen plat and pleyn,
Fro nyght to nyght in what place he had leyn;
And thus by wit and sobtil enquerynge   5310
Ymagined was by whom this harm gan
        sprynge.

The hand was knowe that the lettre wroot,
And all the venym of this cursed dede;
But in what wise certeinly I noot.
Theffect is this, that Alla, out of drede,[3]
His mooder slow, — that may men pleynly
        rede, —
For that she traitoure was to hire ligeance.
Thus endeth olde Donegild with meschance.

The sorwe that this Alla nyght and day
Maketh for his wyf, and for his child also,
Ther is no tonge that it telle may;   5321

[1] To grow cold.   [2] Must make known.   [3] You may be sure

But now wol I un-to Custance go,
That fleteth in the see in peyne and wo
Fyve yeer and moore, as liked Cristes sonde,[1]
Er that hir ship approched un-to the londe.

Under an hethen castel atte laste, —
Of which the name I in my text noght fynde, —
Custance, and eek hir child, the see up caste.
Almyghty God, that saved al mankynde,
Have on Custance and on hir child som
     mynde,   5330
That fallen is in hethen hand eft soon
In point to spille,[2] as I shal telle yow soone.

Doun fro the castel comth ther many a wight,
To gauren[3] on this ship, and on Custance;
But, shortly, from the castel on a nyght,
The lordes styward, — God geve him mes-
     chance! —
A theef, that hadde reneyed oure creance,[4]
Came in-to the ship allone, and seyde he sholde
Hir lemman[5] be, wher-so she wolde or nolde.

Wo was this wrecched womman tho bigon;[6]
Hir childe cride, and she cride pitously; 5341
But blisful Marie heelp hire right anon,
For with hir struglyng wel and myghtily,
The theef fil over bord al sodeynly,
And in the see he dreynte[7] for vengeance;
And thus hath Crist unwemmed[8] kept Cus-
     tance!

---

[1] Decree. [2] Perish. [3] Gaze. [4] Denied our faith. [5] Paramour
[6] Wobegone = surrounded with woe. [7] Drowned. [8] Unspotted.

O foule lust of luxurie, lo, thyn ende !
Nat oonly that thou feyntest mannes mynde,
But verraily thou wolt his body shende.[1] 5349
Thende of thy werk, or of thy lustes blynde,
Is compleynyng. Hou many oon may men
    fynde
That noght for werk som tyme, but for then-
    tente (5350 T.)
To doon this synne, been outher slayn or
    shente.

How may this wayke[2] womman han this
    strengthe
Hire to defende agayn this renegat ?
    O Golias, unmeasurable of lengthe,
Hou myghte David make thee so maat?[3]
So yong and of armure so desolaat,
Hou dorste he looke up-on thy dredful face ?
Wel may men seen it nas but Goddes grace.

    Who gaf Judith corage or hardynesse 5361
To sleen hym Oloferne in his tente,
And to deliveren out of wrecchednesse
The peple of God ? I seye for this entente,
That right as God spirit of vigour sente
To hem, and saved hem out of meschance,
So sente he myght and vigour to Custance.

    Forth gooth hir ship thurgh out the narwe
    mouth
Of Jubaltare and Septe,[4] dryvynge aiway,
Som tyme West and som tyme North and South,

---

[1] Ruin. [2] Weak [3] Struck dead. [4] Opposite Gibraltar.

And som tyme Est, ful many a wery day,　5371
Til Cristes mooder — blessed be she ay ! —
Hath shapen, thurgh hir endelees goodnesse,
To make an ende of al hir hevynesse.

　　Now lat us stynte of Custance but a throwe,[1]
And speke we of the Romayn emperour,
That out of Surrye hath by lettres knowe
The slaughtre of cristen folk, and dishonour
Doon to his doghter by a fals traytour, —
I mene the cursed wikked sowdanesse,　5380
That at the feeste leet sleen both moore and
　　　lesse ;
For which this emperour hath sent anon
His senatour with roial ordinance,
And othere lordes, God woot many oon,
On Surryens to taken heigh vengeance.
They brennen, sleen, and brynge hem to mes-
　　　chance
Ful many a day, but, shortly, this is thende,
Homward to Rome they shapen hem to wende.

　　This senatour repaireth with victorie
To Rome-ward, saillynge ful roially,　5390
And mette the ship dryvynge, as seith the sto-
　　　rie,
In which Custance sit ful pitously.
No thyng ne [2] knew he what she was, ne why
She was in swich array ; ne she nyl seye [3]
Of hire estaate, thogh she sholde deye.
He bryngeth hire to Rome. and to his wyf

　　　　　[1] While.　[2] Not in Elles. MS.　[3] Tell.

He gaf hire, and hir yonge sone also ;
And with the senatour she ladde hir lyf.
Thus kan oure lady bryngen out of wo
Woful Custance and many another mo ;   5400
And longe tyme dwelled she in that place
In hooly werkes evere, as was hir grace.
The senatoures wyf hir aunte was,   (5401 T.)
But for all that she knew hire never the moore
I wol no lenger tarien in this cas,
But to kyng Alla, which I spake of yoore,
That wepeth for his wyf and siketh [1] soore,
I wol retourne, and lete I wol Custance
Under the senatoures governance.

   Kyng Alla, which that hadde his mooder
      slayn,   5410
Up-on a day fil in swich repentance,
That, if I shortly tellen shal and playn,
To Rome he comth to receyven his penance,
And putte hym in the popes ordinance,
In heigh and logh ; and Jhesu Crist bisoghte
Forgeve his wikked werkes that he wroghte.

   The fame anon thurgh-out the toun is born,
How Alla, kyng, shal comen on pilgrymage,
By herbergeours [2] that wenten hym biforn,
For which the senatour, as was usage,   5420
Rood hym agayns,[3] and many of his lynage,
As wel to shewen his heighe magnificence,
As to doon any kyng a reverence.

   Greet cheere dooth this noble senatour

---

[1] Sigheth.   [2] Providers of lodgings, harbingers.   [3] Towards.

To kyng Alla, and he to hym also ;
Everich of hem dooth oother greet honour ;
And so bifel that in[1] a day or two
This senatour is to kyng Alla go
To feste, and, shortly, if I shal nat lye,
Custances sone wente in his compaignye. 5430
 Som men wolde seyn at requeste of Cus-
  tance
This senatour hath lad this child to feeste, —
I may nat tellen every circumstance ;
Be as be may, ther was he at the leeste ;
But sooth is this, that at his moodres heeste
Biforn Alla, durynge the metes space,[2]
The child stood, lookynge in the kynges face.
 This Alla kyng hath of this child greet won-
  der,
And to the senatour he seyde anon,
" Whos is that faire child, that stondeth yon-
  der ? "   5440
" I noot," quod he, " by God and by Seint
  John !
A mooder he hath, but fader hath he noon,
That I of woot ; " but shortly, in a stounde[3]
He tolde Alla how that this child was founde ;
" But God woot," quod this senatour also,
" So vertuous a lyvere in my lyf
Ne saugh I nevere as she, ne herde of mo,
Of worldly wommen, mayde ne of wyf ;
I dar wel seyn hir hadde levere a knyf

---

[1] Elles. MS. has "in with." [2] Between courses. [3] Short space.

Thurgh out hir brest, than ben a womman
    wikke ; 5450
There is no man koude brynge hire to that
    prikke." [1]
Now was this child as lyke un-to Custance
As possible is a creature to be. (5451 T.)
This Alla hath the face in remembrance
Of dame Custance, and ther-on mused he,
If that the childes mooder were aught [2] she
That is his wyf, and pryvely he sighte,[3]
And spedde hym fro the table that he myghte.
"*Parfay !*" thoghte he, "fantome [4] is in myn
    heed !
I oghte deme of skilful [5] juggement, 5460
That in the salte see my wyf is deed ;"
And afterward he made his argument,
"What woot I, if that Crist have hyder ysent
My wyf by see, as wel as he hire sente
To my contree fro thennes that she wente ? "
And after noon, hoom with the senatour
Goth Alla, for to seen this wonder chaunce.
This senatour dooth Alla greet honour,
And hastifly he sente after Custaunce ; 5469
But trusteth [6] weel hire liste nat to daunce,
Whan that she wiste wherfore was that sonde ;[7]
Unnethe [8] up-on hir feet she myghte stonde.

Whan Alla saugh his wyf, faire he hire grette,
And weep, that it was routhe for to see ;

---

[1] Point.   [2] At all.   [3] Sighed.   [4] Fancy.   [5] Reasonable.
[6] Trust ye.   [7] Summons.   [8] Scarcely.

For at the firste look he on hire sette,
He knew wel verraily that it was she,
And she for sorwe as doumb stant as a tree ;
So was hir herte shet in hir distresse
When she remembred his unkyndenesse.
Twyes she swowned in his owene sighte.   5480
He weep, and hym excuseth pitously :
"Now God," quod he, "and hise halwes
    brighte,
So wisly on my soul as have mercy,
That of youre harm as giltelees am I,
As is Maurice my sone, so lyk your face ;
Elles the feend me fecche out of this place ! "
    Long was the sobbyng and the bitter peyne,
Er that hir woful hertes myghte cesse ;
Greet was the pitee for to heere hem pleyne,
Thurgh whiche pleintes gan hir wo encresse.
I pray yow all my labour to relesse,   5491
I may nat tell hir wo un-til to morwe,
I am so wery for to speke of sorwe.
But finally, whan that the sothe [2] is wist,
That Alla giltelees was of hir wo,
I trowe an hundred tymes been they kist ;
And swich a blisse is ther bitwix hem two,
That, save the joye that lasteth everemo,
Ther is noon lyk that any creature
Hath seyn, or shal, whil that the world may
    dure.   5500
Tho preyde she hir housbonde, mekely,

---

[1] Saints.   [2] Truth.

In relief of hir longe pitous pyne,   (5500 T.)
That he wolde preye hir fader specially,
That of his magestee he wolde enclyne
To vouche-sauf som day with hym to dyne.
She preyde hym eek he wolde by no weye
Un-to hir fader no word of hire seye.

    Som men wold seyn how that the child Mau-
       rice
Dooth this message un-to the emperour,
But, as I gesse, Alla was nat so nyce [1]   5510
To hym, that was of so sovereyn honour
As he that is of cristen folk the flour,
Sente any child ; but it is bet to deeme
He wente hym-self, and so it may well seeme.

    This emperour hath graunted gentilly
To come to dyner, as he hym bisoughte,
And wel rede [2] I, he looked bisily
Up-on this child, and on his doghter thoghte.
Alla goth to his in, and as him oghte,
Arrayed for this feste in every wise,   5520
As ferforth as his konnyng may suffise.

    The morwe cam, and Alla gan hym dresse,[3]
And eek his wyf, this emperour to meete ;
And forth they ryde in joye and in gladnesse ;
And whan she saugh hir fader in the strete
She lighte doun and falleth hym to feete ;
" Fader," quod she, " youre yonge child, Cus-
       tance,
Is now ful clene out of youre remembrance.

       [1] Simple.   [2] I assure you.   [3] Prepare.

l am youre doghter Custance," quod she,
"That whilom ye han sent un-to Surrye. 553c
It am I, fader, that in the salte see
Was put allone, and dampned for to dye.
Now, goode fader, mercy, I yow crye !
Sende me namoore un-to noon hethenesse,
but thonketh my lord heere of his kyndenesse.'

Who kan the pitous joye tellen al
Bitwixe hem thre, syn they been thus ymette ?
But of my tale make an ende I shal, —
The day [1] goth faste, I wol no lenger lette.
This glade folk to dyner they hem sette. 554c
In joye and blisse at mete I lete hem dwelle,
A thousand foold wel moore than I kan telle.

This child Maurice was sithen [2] emperour
Maad by the pope and lyved cristenly.
To Cristes chirche he dide greet honour ;
But I lete all his storie passen by ;
Of Custance is my tale specially.
In the olde Romane Geestes [3] may men fynde
Maurices lyf, I bere it noght in mynde.

This kyng Alla, whan his tyme say [4] 5550
With his Custance, his hooly wyf so sweete,
To Engelond been they come the righte way,
Wher as they lyve in joye and in quiete ;
But litel while it iasteth, I yow heete.[5] (5552 T.
Joye of this world for tyme wol nat abyde,
Fro day to nyght it changeth as the tyde.

---

[1] Of the pilgrimage to Canterbury. [2] Afterwards. [3] *Gesta Romanorum.* [4] Saw. [5] Promise.

Who lyved evere in swich delit o day
That hym ne moeved outher conscience,
Or ire, or talent,[1] or som kynnes affray,[2]
Envye, or pride, or passion, or offence?   5560
I ne seye but for this ende this sentence,
That litel while in joye, or in plesance,
Lasteth the blisse of Alla with Custance;
For Deeth, that taketh of heigh and logh his
    rente,
Whan passed was a yeer, evene as I gesse,
Out of this world this kyng Alla he hente,[3]
For whom Custance hath ful greet hevynesse.
Now lat us praye to God his soule blesse !
And dame Custance, finally to seye,
Toward the toun of Rome goth hir weye.   5570

  To Rome is come this hooly creature,
And fyndeth hire freendes hoole and sounde.
Now is she scaped al hire aventure,
And whan that she hir fader hath yfounde,
Doun on hir knees falleth she to grounde;
Wepynge for tendrenesse in herte blithe,
She heryeth [4] God an hundred thousand sithe.

  In vertu and hooly almus dede
They lyven alle, and nevere asonder wende.
Till deeth departed [5] hem this lyf they lede, 5580
And fareth now weel, my tale is at an ende.
Now Jhesu Crist, that of his myght may sende
Joye after wo, governe us in his grace,
And kepe us alle that been in this place.
    Amen.   (5582 T.)

[1] Desire.   [2] Kind of fear.   [3] Seized.   [4] Praiseth   [5] Separated.

Words of the Host, the Parson, and the Shipman.

Oure Hoste upon his stirupes stode anon,
And seyde, "Good men, herkeneth, ever₋hon !
This was a thrifty tale for the nones ! (12,905 T.)
Sir Parish Prest," quod he, "for Goddes bones,
Tell us a tale, as was thy forward[1] yore ;
I se wel that ye lerned men in lore   5590
Can moche good, by Goddes dignitee ! "

The Persone him answerde, "*Benedicite !*
What eyleth the man so sinfully to swere ? "

Our Hoste answerde, "O Jankyn, be ye
       there ?
I smelle a Loller[2] in the wind," quod he.
"Ho ! good men," quod our Hoste, "herkneth
       me,
Abydeth, for Goddes digne passioun,
For we shul han a predicacioun ;
This Loller here wol prechen us somwhat."

"Nay, by my fader soule ! that shal he nat ! '
Seyde the Shipman ; "here shal he nat preche ;
He shal no gospel glosen here, ne teche. 5602
We leven[3] alle in the grete God," quod he,
"He wolde sowen som difficulte,
Or sprengen[4] cokkel in our clene corn ;
And therfore, Hoste, I warne the biforn,
My joly body shal a tale telle,
And I shal clynken yow so mery a belle

---

[1] Agreement.   [2] Lollard.   [3] Believe.   [4] Sprinkle.

That I shal wakyn al this companye ;
But it shal nat ben of philosophye,   5610
Ne of phisyk, ne termes queint of lawe ;
There is but litel Latin in my mawe."

Heere bigynneth The Shipmannes Tale.[1]

A marchant whilom dwelled at Seint Denys,[2]
That riche was, for which men helde hym
    wys ;   (12,932 T.)
A wyf he hadde of excellent beautee,
And compaignable and revelous was she,
Which is a thyng that causeth more dispence
Than worth is al the chiere and reverence
That men hem doon at festes and at daunces.
Swiche salutaciouns and contenaunces   5620
Passen as dooth a shadwe up-on the wal,
But wo is hym that payen moot for al !
" The sely housbonde algate [3] he moste paye ;
He moot us clothe and he moot us arraye,
Al for his owene worship richely,
In which array we daunce jolily.
And if that he noght may, par aventure,
Or ellis list no swich dispence endure,
But thynketh it is wasted and ylost, (12,947 T.)
Thanne moot another payen for oure cost,
Or lene [4] us gold, and that is perilous."   5631
    This noble marchaunt heeld a worthy hous,

---

[1] A story, the plot of which is tne same as that of this one, is
briefly related, with different accessories, by Boccaccio, being the first
novel of the eighth day.   [2] A suburb of Paris.   [3] Always.   [4] Lend

For which he hadde alday so greet **repair**
For his largesse, and for his wyf was fair,
That wonder is; but herkneth to my tale.

Amonges alle hise gestes grete and smale
Ther was a monk, a fair man and a boold, —
I trowe of thritty wynter he was oold, —
That evere in oon was comynge to that place.
This yonge monk, that was so fair of face, 564c
Aqueynted was so with the goode man
Sith that hir firste knoweliche bigan,
That in his hous as famulier was he
As is possible any freend to be.

And for as muchel as this goode man
And eek this monk, of which that I bigan,
Were bothe two yborn in o village,
The monk hym claymeth as for cosynage;[1]
And he agayn he seith nat ones nay,
But was as glad ther-of as fowel of day; 565c
For to his herte it was a greet plesaunce.
Thus been they knyt with eterne alliaunce,
And ech of hem gan oother for tassure
Of bretherhede whil that hir lyf may dure.

Free was Daun John, and namely[2] of dis-
pence,
As in that hous, and ful of diligence
To doon plesaunce; and also greet costage
He noght forgat to geve the leeste page
In al the hous, but after hir degree. 5659
He gaf the lord and sitthe al his meynee,[3]

---

[1] Relationship. [2] Especially. [3] Afterwards all his household.

Whan that he cam, som manere honest thyng,
For which they were as glad of his comyng
As fowel is fayn whan that the sonne up·riseth ;
Na moore of this as now, for it suffiseth.

But so bifel this marchant on a day
Shoop [1] hym to make redy his array
Toward the toun of Brugges for to fare,
To byen there a porcioun of ware ;
For which he hath to Parys sent anon
A messager, and preyed hath Daun John 5670
That he sholde come to Seint Denys, to pleye
With hym and with his wyf a day or tweye,
Er he to Brugges wente, in alle wise.

This noble monk, of which I yow devyse,
Hath of his abbot as hym list licence, —
By cause he was a man of heigh prudence,
And eek an officer, — out for to ryde
To seen hir graunges and hire bernes wyde,
And un-to Seint Denys he comth anon.   5679
Who was so welcome as my lord Daun John,
" Oure deere cosyn, ful of curteisye " ?
With hym broghte he a jubbe of malvesye [2]
And eek another, ful of fyn vernage,[3]
And volatyl,[4] as ay was his usage,   (13,002 T.)
And thus I lete hem drynke and pleye,
This marchant and this monk, a day or tweye.

The thridde day this marchant up ariseth,
And on hise nedes sadly [5] hym avyseth,

---

[1] Prepared.   [2] Jug of a sort of wine.   [3] A white wine.   Cf. l.
14,143   [4] Fowls.   [5] Seriously.

And up in-to his countour-hous gooth he,
To rekene with hym self, as [1] wel may be, 5690
Of thilke yeer, how that it with hym stood,
And how that he despended hadde his good,
And if that he encressed were or noon.
Hise bookes and hise bagges many oon
He leith biforn hym on his countyng-bord.
Ful riche was his tresor and his hord,
For which ful faste his countour dore he shette,
And eek he nolde that no man sholde hym lette
Of hise accountes, for the meene tyme ;
And thus he sit til it was passed pryme.   5700

Daun John was rysen in the morwe also
And in the gardyn walketh to and fro
And hath hise thynges [2] seyd ful curteisly.

This goode wyf cam walkynge pryvely
In to the gardyn, there he walketh softe,
And hym saleweth, as she hath doon ofte.
A mayde child cam in hire compaignye,
Which as hir list she may governe and gye, [3]
For yet under the yerde [4] was the mayde. 5709
" O deere cosyn myn, Daun John," she sayde,
" What eyleth yow, so rathe [5] for to ryse ? "

" Nece," quod he, " it oghte ynough suffise
Fyve houres for to slepe up-on a nyght,
But it were for an old appalled [6] wight,
As been thise wedded men that lye and dare, [7]
As, in a fourme, sit a wery hare

[1] Not in Elles. MS.   [2] Devotions.   [3] Guide.   [4] Rod, i. e., under control.   [5] Early.   [6] Enfeebled.   [7] Stare.

Were al forstraught with houndes grete and
    smale ;
But, deere nece, why be ye so pale ?
I trowe certes that oure goode man
Hath yow laboured sith the nyght bigan,   5720
That yow were nede to resten hastily ;"
And with that word he lough ful murily
And of his owene thought he wax al reed.[1]

This faire wyf gan for to shake hir heed,
And seyde thus : " Ye, God woot al," quod she,
"Nay, nay, cosyn myn, it stant nat so with
    me,
For by that God that gaf me soule and lyf,
In al the reawme of France is ther no wyf
That lasse [2] lust hath to that sory pleye ;
For I may synge allas ! and weylawey !   5730
That I was born ; but to no wight," quod she,
" Dar I nat telle how that it stant with me ;
Wherfore I thynke out of this land to wende,
Or elles of my-self to make an ende, (13,052 T.)
So ful am I of drede and eek of care."

This monk bigan up-on this wyf to stare,
And seyde, " Allas, my nece, God forbede
That ye, for any sorwe or any drede,
Fordo [3] youre-self ; but tel me of youre grief ;
Paraventure I yow may in youre meschief 5740
Conseille or helpe ; and therfore telleth me
All youre anoy, for it shal been secree ;
For on my porthors [4] I make an ooth

---

[1] Red   [2] Less.   [3] Ruin.   [4] Breviary.

That nevere in my lyf, for lief ne looth,
Ne shal I of no conseil yow biwreye."
   " The same agayn to yow," quod she, " I
      seye,
By God and by this porthors I yow swere,
Though men me wolde al in-to pieces tere,
Ne shal I nevere, for to goon to helle,
Biwreye a word of thyng that ye me telle, 5750
Nat for no cosynage ne alliance,
But verraily for love and affiance."
Thus been they sworn, and heer-upon they
      kiste,
And ech of hem tolde oother what hem liste.
   "Cosyn," quod she, "if that I hadde a
      space,
As I have noon, and namely in this place,
Thanne wolde I telle a legende of my lyf,
What I have suffred sith I was a wyf
With myn housbonde, al be he of youre kyn."
   " Nay," quod this monk, " by God, and by
      Seint Martyn !   5760
He is na moore cosyn un-to me
Than in this lief that hangeth on the tree.
I clepe hym so, by Seint Denys of Fraunce !
To have the moore cause of aqueyntaunce
Of yow, which I have loved specially,
Aboven alle wommen sikerly.
This swere I yow on my professioun.
Telleth youre grief lest that he come adoun,
And hasteth yow, and gooth youre wey anon.

"My deere love," quod she, "O my Daun
     John,   5770
Ful lief were me this conseil for to hyde,
But out it moot, I may namoore abyde !
Myn housbonde is to me the worste man
That evere was sith that the world bigan,
But sith I am a wyf, it sit[1] nat me
To tellen no wight of oure privetee,
Neither a bedde ne in noon oother place,
God shilde I sholde it tellen for his grace !
A wyf ne shal nat seyn of hir housbonde
But al honour, as I kan understonde,   5780
Save un-to yow, thus muche I tellen shal ;
As helpe me God, he is noght worth at al
In no degree the value of a flye ;   (13,101 T.)
But yet me greveth moost his nygardye.
And wel ye woot that wommen naturelly
Desiren thynges sixe, as wel as I :
They wolde that hir housbondes sholde be
Hardy and wise, and riche, and ther-to free,
And buxom[2] to his wyf, and fressh abedde ;
But by that ilke Lord that for us bledde, 5790
For his honour my-self for to arraye,
A Sonday next, I moste nedes paye
An hundred frankes, or ellis I am lorn ;[3]
Yet were me levere that I were unborn
Than me were doon a sclaundre or vileynye ;
And if myn housbonde eek it myghte espye
I nere but lost, and therfore I yow preye,

---

[1] Becomes.   [2] Yielding.   [3] Lost

Lene me this somme, or ellis moot I deye.
Daun John, I seye, lene me thise hundred
    frankes ;
Pardee, I wol nat faille yow my thankes, 5800
If that yow list to doon that I yow praye,
For at a certeyn day I wol yow paye,
And doon to yow what plesance and service
That I may doon, right as yow list devise,
And but I do, God take on me vengeance
As foul as evere hadde Genyloun[1] of France!'

   This gentil monk answerde in this manere :
" Now trewely, myn owene lady deere,
I have," quod he, " on yow so greet a routhe,
That I yow swere, and plighte yow my trouthe,
That whan youre housbonde is to Flaundres
    fare   5811
I wol delyvere yow out of this care ;
For I wol brynge yow an hundred frankes ;"
And with that word he caughte hire by the
    flankes
And hire embraceth harde and kiste hire ofte.
" Gooth now youre wey," quod he, " all stille
    and softe,
And lat us dyne as soone as that ye may,
For by my chilyndre[2] it is pryme[3] of day.
Gooth now, and beeth as trewe as I shal be."

   " Now elles God forbede, sire," quod she ;
And forth she gooth as jolif as a pye, 5821

---

[1] Who betrayed Roland at Roncesvalles. Cf. l. 8839   [2] Cylin
cal, portable sundial.   [3] Nine o'clock in the morning.

And bad the cookes that they sholde hem hye,[1]
So that men myghte dyne [2] and that anon.
Up to hir housbonde is this wyf ygon,
And knokketh at his countour boldely.

"Who is [3] ther?" quod he. "Peter! it am 1,"
Quod she ; " what, sire, how longe wol ye faste ?
How longe tyme wol ye rekene and caste
Youre sommes, and youre bookes, and youre
　　　thynges ?　　　　　　　　　　5829
The devel have part on alle swiche rekenynges !
Ye have ynough, *pardee*, of Goddes sonde ; [4]
Com doun to-day, and lat youre bagges stonde.
Ne be ye nat ashamed that Daun John
Shal fasting al this day alenge [5] goon ? (13,152 T.)
What ! [3] lat us heere a messe, and go we dyne !"

"Wyf," quod this man, "litel kanstow devyne
The curious bisynesse that we have ;
For of us chapmen, — al so God me save,
And by that lord that clepid is Seint Yve,[6] —
Scarsly amonges twelve, ten shuln thryve, 5840
Continuelly lastynge un-to oure age.
We may wel make chiere and good visage,
And dryve forth the world as it may be,
And kepen oure estaat in pryvetee
Til we be deed ; or elles that we pleye
A pilgrymage, or goon out of the weye ;[7]
And therfore have I greet necessitee
Up-on this queynte world-tavyse [8] me,

---

[1] Hasten.　[2] Take the first meal.　[3] Not in Elles. MS.　[4] Sending
Comfortless.　[6] A priest of Bretagne.　[7] Of creditors.　[8] To advise

For, everemoore we moote stonde in drede
Of hap and fortune in oure chapmanhede. 5850
  "To Flaundres wol I go to morwe at day,
And come agayn as soone as evere I may,
For which, my deere wyf, I thee biseke
As be to every wight buxom and meke,
And for to kepe oure good be curious,
And honestly governe wel oure hous.
Thou hast ynough in every maner wise,
That to a thrifty houshold may suffise ;
Thee lakketh noon array ne no vitaille,
Of silver in thy purs shaltow nat faille." 5860
And with that word his countour dore he shette,
And doun he gooth, no lenger wolde he lette ;
But hastily a messe was ther seyd,
And spedily the tables were yleyd,
And to the dyner faste they hem spedde,
And richely this monk the chapman fedde.[1]
  At after dyner Daun John sobrely
This chapman took a-part and prively
He seyde hym thus : "Cosyn, it standeth so
That, wel I se, to Brugges wol ye go. 5870
God and Seint Austyn spede yow and gyde !
I prey yow, cosyn, wisely that ye ryde ;
Governeth yow also of youre diete
Atemprely, and namely [2] in this hete.
Bitwix us two nedeth no strange fare ;
Fare wel, cosyn, God shilde yow fro care !
And if that any thyng, by day or nyght,

[1] Cf. l. 5684. [2] Especially.

If it lye in my power and my myght
That ye me wol comande in any wyse
It shal be doon right as ye wol devyse.   5880
   "O thyng, er that ye goon, if it may be :
I wolde prey yow for to lene me   (13,200 T.)
An hundred frankes for a wyke or tweye,
For certein beestes that I moste beye
To stoore with a place that is oures, —
God helpe me so, I wolde it were youres !
I shal nat faille surely at my day,
Nat for a thousand frankes a mile way ![1]
But lat this thyng be secree, I yow preye, 5889
For yet to-nyght thise beestes moot I beye ;
And fare now wel, myn owene cosyn deere,
Graunt mercy [2] of youre cost and of youre
       cheere !"
   This noble marchant gentilly anon
Answerde and seyde, "O cosyn myn, Daun
      John,
Now sikerly this is a smal requeste,
My gold is youres whan that it yow leste,
And nat oonly my gold, but my chaffare ; [3]
Take what yow list, God shilde [4] that ye spare !
   "But o thyng is, ye knowe it wel ynogh,
Of chapmen, that hir moneie is hir plogh ; 5900
We may creaunce [5] whil we have a name,
But goldlees for to be, it is no game ;
Paye it agayn whan it lith in youre ese ;
After my myght ful fayn wolde I yow plese."

---

[1] Compare the expressions "a furlong way;" "a long way."
[2] Many thanks.   [3] Goods.   [4] Forbid.   [5] Get on trust.

Thise hundred frankes he fette [1] hym forth
    anon
And prively he took hem to Daun John ;
No wight in al this world wiste of this loone,
Savynge this marchant and Daun John alloone.
They drynke, and speke, and rome a while and
    pleye,
Til that Daun John rideth to his abbeye. 5910
   The morwe cam and forth this marchant
     rideth
To Flaundres-ward, — his prentys wel hym
    gydeth, —
Til he cam in to Brugges murily.
Now gooth this marchant faste and bisily
Aboute his nede, and byeth and creaunceth ;
He neither pleyeth at dees, ne daunceth,
But as a marchant, shortly for to telle,
He lad [2] his lyf, and there I lete hym dwelle.

   The Sonday next this marchant was agon,
To Seint Denys ycomen is Daun John, 5920
With crowne and berde all fressh and newe
    y-shave.
In al the hous ther nas so litel a knave, [3]
Ne no wight elles, that he nas ful fayn
For that my lord Daun John was come agayn ;
And shortly, right to the point for to gon,
This faire wyf accorded with Daun John
That for thise hundred frankes he sholde a.
    nyght

---

[1] Fetched.　[2] Elles. MS. has "let."　[3] Boy servant.

Have hire in hise armes bolt upright,
And this acord parfourned was in dede.
In myrthe al nyght a bisy lyf they lede   593c
Til it was day, that Daun John wente his way,
And bad the meynee,[1] Fare wel, have good
      day ;   (13,250 T.)
For noon of hem, ne no wight in the toun,
Hath of Daun John right no suspecioun ;
And forth he rydeth hoom to his abbeye,
Or where hym list ; namoore of hym I seye.
    This marchant, whan that ended was the
      faire,
To Seint Denys he gan for to repaire,
And with his wyf he maketh feeste and cheere,
And telleth hire that chaffare is so deere 5940
That nedes moste he make a chevyssaunce,[2]
For he was bounden in a reconyssaunce,
To paye twenty thousand sheeld [3] anon ;
For which this marchant is to Parys gon,
To borwe of certeine freendes that he hadde
A certeyn frankes [4] and somme with him he
      ladde ; [5]
And whan that he was come in to the toun,
For greet chiertee,[6] and greet affectioun,
Un to Daun John he gooth hym first to pleye, —
Nat for to axe or borwe of hym moneye, —
But for to wite and seen of his welfare,   5951
And for to tellen hym of his chaffare,

---

[1] Menials. [2] Loan. [3] Crowns. [4] A certain sum of francs
Took. [6] Tenderness.

As freendes doon whan they been met yfeere.[1]
Daun John hym maketh feeste and murye
    cheere,
And he hym tolde agayn, ful specially,
How he hadde wel yboght and graciously, —
Thanked be God ! — al hool his marchandise
Save that he moste,[2] in alle maner wise,
Maken a chevyssaunce as for his beste,   5959
And thanne he sholde been in joye and reste.

    Daun John answerde, " Certes I am fayn,
That ye in heele ar comen hom agayn,
And if that I were riche, as have I blisse,
Of twenty thousand sheeld shold ye nat mysse,
For ye so kyndely this oother day
Lente me gold, and as I kan and may
I thanke yow, by God and by Seint Jame !
But nathelees I took un-to oure dame,
Youre wyf, at hom, the same gold ageyn   5969
Upon youre bench, she woot it wel certeyn,
By certeyn tokenes that I kan yow telle.
Now by youre leve I may no lenger dwelle ;
Oure abbot wole out of this toun anon
And in his compaignye moot I goon.
Grete wel oure dame, myn owene nece sweete,
And fare wel, deere cosyn, til we meete ! "

    This marchant, which that was ful war and
    wys,
Creanced hath and payd eek in Parys
To certeyn Lumbardes[3] redy in hir hond   5979

---

[1] In company.   [2] Must.   [3] Lenders of money.

The somme of gold, and hadde of hem his
  bond ;   (13,298 T.)
And hoom he gooth, murie as a popynjay,[1]
For wel he knew he stood in swich array
That nedes moste he wynne in that viage [2]
A thousand frankes aboven al his costage.

 His wyf ful redy mette hym atte gate,
As she was wont of oold usage algate,
And al that nyght in myrthe they bisette,[8]
For he was riche and cleerly out of dette.
Whan it was day this marchant gan embrace
His wyf al newe, and kiste hire on hir face,
And up he gooth and maketh it ful tough.[4] 5991
  " Namoore," quod she, "by God, ye have
   ynough ! "
And wantownely agayn with hym she pleyde ;
Til atte laste thus [5] this marchant seyde :
" By God," quod he, " I am a li:el wrooth
With yow, my wyf, al-though it were me looth ;
And woot ye why ?   By God, as that I gesse
That ye han maad a manere straungenesse
Bitwixen me and my cosyn daun John, —
Ye sholde han warned me, er I had gon, 6000
That he yow hadde an hundred frankes payed,
By redy tokene, — and heeld hym yvele apayed [6]
For that I to hym spak of chevyssaunce ;
Me semed so as by his contenaunce ;
But nathelees, by God, oure hevene kyng,

<hr>

[1] Elles. MS. has "papeiay."   [2] Journev   [8] Employ.   [4] Took
ʌ. ns about it.   [5] Not in Elles. MS.   [6] Dispieased.

I thoughte nat to axen hym no thyng.
I prey thee, wyf, as do namoore so ;
Telle me alwey, er that I fro thee go,
If any dettour hath in myn absence
Ypayed thee, lest thurgh thy necligence   6010
I myghte hym axe a thing that he hath payed.'

  This wyf was nat afered nor affrayed,
But boldely she seyde, and that anon,
" Marie, I deffie the false monk, Daun John !
I kepe nat of hise tokenes never a deel !
He took me certeyn gold, that woot I weel.
What, yvel thedam [1] on his monkes snowte !
For, God it woot, I wende withouten doute
That he hadde geve it me bycause of yow, 6019
To doon ther-with myn honour and my prow, [2]
For cosynage, and eek for beele cheere [3]
That he hath had ful ofte tymes heere ;
But sith I se I stonde in this disjoynt,
I wol answere yow shortly to the poynt.

  " Ye han mo slakkere dettours than am I,
For I wol paye yow wel and redily
Fro day to day, and if so be I faille,
I am youre wyf, score it up-on my taille,
And I shal paye as soone as ever I may ;
For by my trouthe, I have on myn array, 6030
And nat on wast, bistowed every deel ;
And for I have bistowed it so weel (13,350 T.)
For youre honour, for Goddes sake, I seye,
As be r at wrooth, but lat us laughe and pleye

---

[1] Evil success.   [2] Profit.   [3] Good cheer

Ye shal my joly body have to wedde ; [1]
By God ! I wol nat paye yow but a-bedde.
Forgyve it me, myn owene spouse deere,
Turne hiderward, and maketh bettre cheere !"

This marchant saugh ther was no remedie,
And for to chide it nere but greet folie,   6040
Sith that the thyng may nat amended be.
" Now, wyf," he seyde, "and I forgeve it thee,
But by thy lyf ne be namoore so large ; [2]
Keepe bet oure good that geve I thee in
        charge."   (13,362 T.)
Thus endeth now [8] my tale, and God us sende
Taillynge ynough un-to oure lyves ende. *Amen.*

Bihoold the murie wordes of the Hoost to the
Shipman, and to the lady Prioresse.

" Wel seyd ! by *corpus dominus*," quod our
        Hoost ,   (13,365 T.)
" Now longe moote thou saille by the cost, [4]
Sire gentil maister, gentil maryneer !
God geve this monk a thousand last [5] quade [6]
        yeer !   6050
A ha, felawes, beth ware of swiche a jape !
The monk putte in the mannes hood an ape, [7]
And in his wyves eek, by Seint Austyn !
Draweth no monkes moore un-to youre in.

" But now passe over, and lat us seke aboute,

---

[1] Pledge.   [2] Free.   [8] Not in Elles. MS.   [4] Coast.   [5] Loads of
Bad   Cf. l. 4357.   [7] Made a fool of.   Cf. ll. 3389, 7984.

Who shal now telle first of al this route
Another tale;" and with that word he sayde,
As curteisly as it had ben a mayde,
" My lady Prioresse, by youre leve,
So that I wiste I sholde yow nat greve,   6060
I wolde demen that ye tellen sholde
A tale next, if so were that ye wolde.
Now wol ye vouche sauf, my lady deere ?"

"Gladly," quod she, and seyde as ye shal
heere.

The Prologe of the Prioresses Tale.

" O Lord, oure Lord, thy name how merveil-
lous   (13,383 T.)
Is in this large world ysprad," quod she ;
" For noght oonly thy laude precious
Parfourned is by men of dignitee,
But by the mouth of children thy bountee [1]
Parfourned is ; for on the brest soukynge 6070
Somtyme shewen they thyn heriynge.[2]
Wherfore, in laude as I best kan or may,
Of thee, and of the white [3] lylye flour,
Which that the bar and is a mayde alway,
To telle a storie I wol do my labour ;
Nat that I may encreessen hir honour.
For she hir-self is honour and the roote
Of bountee, next hir sone, and soules boote [4]
O mooder mayde ! O mayde mooder fre !

---

[1] Goodness.   [2] Praise.   [3] Not in Elles. MS.   [4] Cure.

O bussh unbrent,[1] brennynge in Moyses sighte !
That ravysedest [2] doun fro the Deitee,　6081
Thurgh thyn humblesse, the goost that in tha-
　　　lighte ; [3]　　　　　　　　　(13,400 T.)
Of whos vertu, whan he, thyn herte lighte,
Conceyved was, the Fadres sapience,
Helpe me to telle it in thy reverence !
Lady, thy bountee, thy magnificence,[4]
Thy vertu, and thy grete humylitee,
Ther may no tonge expresse in no science ;
For somtyme, lady, er men praye to thee,
Thou goost biforn of thy benygnytee,　6090
And getest us thurgh lyght of thy preyere,
To gyden us un-to thy Sone so deere.
My konnyng is so wayk, O blisful queene,
For to declare thy grete worthynesse,
That I ne may the weighte nat susteene ;
But as a child of twelf monthe oold or lesse,
That kan unnethes [5] any word expresse,
Right so fare I, and therfore I yow preye,
Gydeth my song that I shal of yow seye."

Heere bigynneth The Prioresses Tale.

Ther was in Asye, in a greet citee,　6100
Amonges cristene folk, a Jewerye,
Sustened by a lord of that contree
For foule usure, and lucre of vileynye,[6]

---

[1] Unburned. Cf. *A B C*, l. 90.　[2] Didst transport.　[3] Thee
.fighted.　[4] Cf. l. 16,450, etc.　[5] Scarcely.　[6] Filthy lucre.

Hateful to Crist and to his compaignye ;
And thurgh the strete men myghte ride or
  wende,
For it was free, and open at eyther ende.
A litel scole of cristen folk ther stood
Doun at the ferther ende, in which ther were
Children an heepe, ycomen of cristen blood,
That lerned in that scole yeer by yere   6110
Swich manere doctrine as men used there, —
This is to seyn, to syngen, and to rede,
As smale children doon in hire childhede.
Among thise children was a wydwes sone,
A litel clergeoun,[1] seven yeer of age,
That day by day to scole was his wone ;[2]
And eek also, where as he saugh thymage
Of Cristes mooder, he hadde in usage,
As hym was taught, to knele adoun and seye
His *Ave Marie*, as he goth by the weye.   6120
Thus hath this wydwe hir litel sone ytaught
Oure blisful lady, Cristes mooder deere,
To worshipe ay, and he forgate it naught,
For sely[3] child wol alday[4] soone leere, —
But ay whan I remembre on this mateere,
Seint Nicholas stant evere in my presence,
For he so yong to Crist dide reverence.

 This litel child his litel book lernynge.
As he sat in the scole at his prymer,
He *Alma redemptoris*[5] herde synge,   6130

---

[1] Chorister boy. [2] Wont. [3] Good. [4] Always. [5] A hymn: "O
Nursing Mother of the Redeemer."

As children lerned hire anthiphoner;[1]
And, as he dorste, he drough hym ner and
    ner,[2]   (13,450 T.)
And herkned ay the wordes and the noote,
Til he the firste vers koude[3] al by rote.
Noght wiste he what this Latyn was to seye,
For he so yong and tendre was of age ;
But on a day his felawe gan he preye
Texpounden hym this song in his langage,
Or telle him why this song was in usage ;
This preyde he hym to construe and declare
Ful often time upon hise knowes[4] bare.   6141

    His felawe, which that elder was than he,
Answerde hym thus : "This song I have herd
    seye
Was maked of oure blisful lady free,
Hire to salue, and eek hire for to preye
To been oure help and socour whan we deye ;
I kan na moore expounde in this mateere,
I lerne song, I kan but smal grammeere."

    "And is this song maked in reverence
Of Cristes mooder ?" seyde this innocent. 6150
"Now certes, I wol do my diligence
To konne it al er Cristemasse is went,
Though that I for my prymer shal be shent,[5]
And shal be beten thries in an houre,
I wol it konne oure lady for to honoure !"

    His felawe taughte hym homward prively

---

[1] Anthem book.   [2] Nearer and nearer.   [3] Knew.   [4] Knees.
Scolded.

Fro day to day, til he koude [1] it by rote,
And thanne he song it wel and boldely
Fro word to word, acordynge with the note.
Twies a day it passed thurgh his throte,   616c
To scoleward and homward whan he wente;
On Cristes mooder set was his entente.

As I have seyd, thurgh-out the Jewerie
This litel child, as he cam to and fro,
Ful murily wolde he synge and crie
O *Alma redemptoris* evere-mo.
The swetnesse hath [2] his herte perced so
Of Cristes mooder, that to hire to preye
He kan nat stynte of syngyng by the weye.

Oure firste foo, the serpent Sathanas,   6170
That hath in Jewes herte his waspes nest,
Up swal,[3] and seide, "O Hebrayk peple, allas!
Is this to yow a thyng that is honest
That swich a boy shal walken as hym lest
In youre despit, and synge of swich sentence,
Which is agayn youre lawes reverence?"

Fro thennes forth the Jewes han conspired
This innocent out of this world to chace.
An homycide ther-to han they hyred,
That in an aleye hadde a privee place;   6180
And as the child gan forby for to pace,
This cursed Jew hym hente [4] and heeld hym
              faste,   (13,500 T.)
And kitte his throte, and in a pit hym caste.

[1] Knew.   [2] Not in Elles. MS.   [3] Swelled up.   [4] Seized.

I seye that in a wardrobe [1] they hym threwe
Where as thise Jewes purgen hire entraille.
  O cursed folk of Herodes al newe !
What may youre yvel entente yow availle ?
Mordre wol out certeyn, it wol nat faille,
And namely, ther [2] thonour of God shal sprede
The blood out-crieth on youre cursed dede.

  O martir, sowded [3] to virginitee !   6191
Now maystow syngen, folwynge evere in oon
The white Lamb celestial, quod she,
Of which the grete Evaungelist, Seint John,
In Pathmos wroot, which seith that they that
        goon
Biforn this Lamb, and synge a song al newe,
That nevere fleshly wommen they ne knewe.

  This povre wydwe awaiteth al that nyght
After hir litel child, but he cam noght,
For which, as soone as it was dayes lyght, 6200
With face pale of drede and bisy thoght,
She hath at scole and elles-where hym soght ;
Til finally she gan so fer espie
That he last seyn was in the Jewerie.
With moodres pitee in hir brest enclosed
She gooth, as she were half out of hir mynde,
To every place where she hath supposed
By liklihede hir litel child to fynde ;
And evere on Cristes mooder, meeke and kynde,
She cride, and atte laste thus she wroghte,
Among the cursed Jewes she hym soghte. 6211

        [1] Privy.   [2] Where.   [3] Joined.

She frayneth [1] and she preyeth pitously,
To every Jew that dwelte in thilke place,
To telle hire if hir child wente oght forby.
They seyde " Nay," but Jhesu of his grace
Gaf in hir thoght inwith a litel space,
That in that place after hir sone she cryde,
Where he was casten in a pit bisyde.

O grete God that parfournest [2] thy laude
By mouth of innocentz, lo, heere thy myght !
This gemme of chastite, this emeraude,   6221
And eek of martirdom the ruby bright,
Ther he, with throte ykorven,[3] lay upright,
He *Alma redemptoris* gan to synge
So loude, that all the place gan to rynge !

The cristene folk that thurgh the strete wente
In coomen, for to wondren on [4] this thyng ;
And hastily they for the provost sente.
He cam anon, with outen tariyng,   (13,547 T.)
And herieth [5] Crist that is of hevene kyng,
And eek his mooder, honour of mankynde,
And after that the Jewes leet he bynde.   6232

This child, with pitous lamentacioun,
Up taken was, syngynge his song alway ;
And with honour of greet processioun
They carien hym un-to the nexte abbay.
His mooder swownynge [6] by his beere lay ;
Unnethe myghte the peple that was theere
This newe Rachel brynge fro his beere.

---

[1] Asketh.   [2] Performest.   [3] Cut.   [4] Elles. MS. has " wondre up
on "   [5] Praiseth.   [6] Swooning.

With torment, and with shameful deeth
     echon,   6240
This provost dooth the Jewes for to sterve,[1]
That of this mordre wiste, and that anon ;
He nolde no swich cursednesse observe,[2]—
" Yvele shal have that yvele wol deserve," —
Therfore with wilde hors he dide hem drawe,
And after that he heng hem by the lawe.

   Up-on his beere ay lith this innocent
Biforn the chief auter, whil masse laste,
And after that the abbot with his covent 6249
Han sped hem for to burien hym ful faste ;
And when they hooly water on hym caste,
Yet spak this child whan spreynd[3] was hooly
     water
And song, *O Alma redemptoris mater !*

   This abbot, which that was an hooly man,
As monkes been, or elles oghte be,
This yonge child to conjure he bigan,
And seyde, " O deere child, I halse[4] thee,
In vertu of the hooly Trinitee,
Tel me what is thy cause for to synge, 6259
Sith that thy throte is kut to my semynge ? "[5]

   " My throte is kut un-to my nekke boon,"
Seyde this child, " and as by wey of kynde[6]
I sholde have dyed, ye, longe tyme agon ;
But Jhesu Crist, as ye in bookes fynde,
Wil that his glorie laste and be in mynde,

   Die. [2] Countenance. [3] Sprinkled. [4] Clasp around the neck,
i. e., entreat. [5] As appears to me. [6] Nature.

And, for the worship of his mooder deere,
Yet may I synge *O Alma* loude and cleere.

"This welle [1] of mercy, Cristes mooder sweete,
I loved alwey, as after my konnynge,
And whan that I my lyf sholde forlete,[2]   627c
To me she cam, and bad me for to synge
This anthem verraily in my deyynge,
As ye han herd, and whan that I hadde songe
Me thoughte she leyde a greyn up-on my
   tonge :
Wherfore I synge, and synge I moot certeyn
In honour of that blisful mayden free,
Til fro my tonge of-taken is the greyn ;
And afterward thus seyde she to me,
' My litel child, now wol I fecche thee
Whan that the greyn is fro thy tonge ytake ;
Be nat agast, I wol thee nat forsake.' "   6281

 This hooly monk, this abbot, hym meene I,
His tonge out caughte and took a-wey the
   greyn,   (13,601 T.)
And he gaf up the goost ful softely.
And whan this abbot hadde this wonder seyn,
Hise salte teeris trikled doun as reyn,
And gruf [3] he fil, al plat up-on the grounde,
And stille he lay as he had ben [4] ybounde.
The covent eek lay on the pavement   6289
Wepynge, and heryen Cristes mooder deere,
And after that they ryse and forth been went,
And tooken awey this martir from his beere ;

  1 Source.   **2** Yield up.   **3** Prostrate.   **4** Elles. MS. has " leyn."

And in a temple of marbul stones cleere,
Enclosen they his litel body sweete :
Ther he is now, God leve [1] us for to meete !

O yonge Hugh of Lyncoln,[2] slayn also
With cursed Jewes, as it is notable,
For it is but a litel while ago,
Preye eek for us, we synful folk unstable,
That of his mercy God, so merciable,   6300
On us his grete mercy multiplie   (13,619 T.)
For reverence of his mooder, Marie.   *Amen.*

Bihoold the murye wordes of the Hoost to Chaucer.

Whan seyd was al this miracle, every man
As sobre was that wonder was to se, (13,622 T.)
Til that oure Hoost japen tho [3] bigan,
And thanne at erst he looked up-on me,
And seyde thus : " What man artow ? " quod he ;
" Thou lookest as thou woldest fynde an hare ;
For evere up-on the ground I se thee stare.
Approche neer, and looke up murily.   6310
Now war yow, sires, and lat this man have place ;
He in the waast is shape as wel as I ;
This were a popet in an arm tenbrace [4]
For any womman smal, and fair of face.

---

[1] Grant.   [2] The story of Hugh of Lincoln is dated 1255.   **A story** like the tale of the Prioress, entitled *Alphonsus of Lincoln,* was printed by the Chaucer Society in 1875   It is dated 1459, however { Elles. MS. has "to."   [4] To embrace.

He semeth elvyssh by his contenaunce,
For un-to no wight dooth he daliaunce.
Sey now somwhat, syn oother folk han sayd ;
Telle us a tale of myrthe, and that anon."

"Hoost," quod I, "ne beth nat yvele apayd,
For oother tale certes kan I noon,   6320
But of a rym I lerned longe agoon."

"Ye, that is good," quod he, "now shul we
    heere
Som deyntee thyng, me thynketh by his
    cheere ! "

Heere bigynneth Chaucers Tale of Thopas.[1]

THE FIRST FIT.

Listeth, lordes, in good entent,   (13,642 T.)
And I wol telle verrayment
Of myrthe and of solas ;
Al of a knyght was fair and gent[2]
In bataille and in tourneyment,
His name was sire Thopas.

Yborn he was in fer contree,   6330
In Flaundres al biyonde the see,
At Poperyng,[3] in the place ;   (13,650 T.)
His fader was a man ful free,
And lord he was of that contree,
As it was Goddes grace.

---

[1] This laughable burlesque is full of phrases suggestive of the absurd metrical romances it is intended to satirize by imitation and exaggeration. [2] Gentle. [3] A parish twenty-six miles from Ostend

Sire Thopas wax a doghty swayn ;
Whit was his face as payndemayn,[1]
Hise lippes rede as rose ;
His rode [2] is lyk scarlet in grayn,[3]
And I yow telle in good certayn 6340
He hadde a semely nose.

His heer, his berd, was lyk saffroun,
That to his girdel raughte [4] adoun ;
Hise shoon of cordewane.
Of Brugges were his hosen broun,
His robe was of syklatoun [5]
That coste many a jane.[6]

He koude hunte at wilde deer,
And ride an haukyng for river [7]
With grey goshauk on honde ; 6350
Ther-to he was a good archeer ;
Of wrastlyng was ther noon his peer,
Ther any ram [8] shal stonde.

Ful many a mayde bright in bour [9]
They moorne for hym, *paramour*,
Whan hem were bet to slepe ;
But he was chaast, and no lechour,
And sweete as is the brembul flour
That bereth the rede hepe.[10]

And so bifel up-on a day 6360
For sothe, as I yow telle may
Sire Thopas wolde out ride ;

---

[1] Bread of our Lord, the very finest. [2] Complexion. [3] Dyed with cochineal. Cf. l. 9071. [4] Reached. [5] A costly cloth [6] Coin of Genoa. [7] River fowl. Cf. l. 10,926. [8] The usual prize at a wrestling-match. Cf. l. 548. [9] Chamber. [10] Fruit of the dog rose.

He worth[1] upon his steede gray,
And in his hand a launcegay,
A long swerd by his side.

He priketh thurgh a fair forest
Ther-inne is many a wilde best,
Ye, bothe bukke and hare ;
And as he priketh north and est
I telle it yow hym hadde almest   **6370**
Bitidde[2] a sory care.

Ther spryngen herbes grete and smale,
The lycorys and cetewale[3]
And many a clowe-gylofre,[4]
And notemuge to putte in ale,
Wheither it be moyste or stale,
Or for to leye in cofre.

The briddes synge, it is no nay,
The sparhauk and the papejay,
That joye it was to heere.   **6380**
The thrustelcok made eek hir lay,
The wodedowve[5] up-on the spray . (13,700 T.)
She sang ful loude and cleere.

Sire Thopas fil in love-longynge
Al whan he herde the thrustel synge,
And pryked[6] as he were wood ;
His faire steede in his prikynge
So swatte that men myghte him wrynge,
His sydes were al blood.

Sire Thopas eek so wery was   **6390**

---

1 **Was**.   2 Happened.   3 Valerian.   4 Clove.   5 **Wood dove**
Rode hard, by spurring his steed.

For prikyng, on the softe gras, —
So fiers was his corage, —
That doun he leyde him in that plas
To make his steede som solas,
And gaf hym good forage.

" O seinte Marie, *benedicite !*
What eyleth this love at me
To bynde me so soore ?
Me dremed al this nyght, *pardee*,
An Elf-queene shal my lemman be   6400
And slepe under my goore.[1]
An Elf-queene wol I love, ywis,
For in this world no womman is
Worthy to be my make [2]
            In towne.
Alle othere wommen I forsake,
And to an Elf-queene I me take
By dale and eek by downe."

In-to his sadel he clamb anon,
And priketh over stile and stoon   6410
An Elf-queene for tespye ;
Til he so longe hadde riden and goon
That he foond in a pryve woon [3]
The contree of Fairye
            So wilde ;
For in that contree was ther noon
That to him dorste ryde or goon,[4]
Neither wyf ne childe ;
Til that ther cam a greet geaunt,

[1] Garment. [2] Mate. [3] Resort. [4] This line not in Elles. MS.

His name was sire Olifaunt,[1]   6420
A perilous man of dede.
He seyde, " Child, by Termagaunt ![2]
But if thou prike out of myn haunt,
Anon I sle thy steede
          · With mace !
Heere is the queene of Fairye,
With harpe, and pipe, and symphonye,
Dwellynge in this place."

   The child seyde, " Al so moote I thee ![3]
Tomorwe wol I meete with thee   6430
Whan I have myn armoure.
And yet I hope, *par ma fay*,[4]   (13,750 T.)
That thou shalt with this launcegay
Abyen it ful sowre ;
          Thy mawe
Shal I percen, if I may,
Er it be fully pryme of day,[5]
For heere thow shalt be slawe."

   Sire Thopas drow abak ful faste ;
This geant at hym stones caste   6440
Out of a fel staf-slynge ;
But faire escapeth sire Thopas ;
And al it was thurgh Goddes gras,
And thurgh his fair berynge.

   Yet listeth, lordes, to my tale
Murier than the nightyngale,
For now[6] I wol yow rowne[7]

---

[1] Elephant.   [2] An imaginary idol.   [3] Thrive.   [4] By my faith.
Nine A. M.   [6] Not in Elles. MS.   [7] Whisper.

How sir Thopas, with sydes smale,
Prikyng over hill and dale
Is comen agayn to towne.   6450
His murie men comanded he
To make hym bothe game and glee,
For nedes moste he fighte
With a geaunt, with hevedes [1] three,
For *paramour* and jolitee
Of oon that shoon ful brighte.
" Do come," he seyde, " my mynstrales,
And geestours for to tellen tales,
Anon in myn armynge ;
Of romances that been roiales   6460
Of Popes and of Cardinales
And eek of love-likynge."

      They sette hym first the sweete wyn
And mede eek in a mazelyn,[2]
And roial spicerye ;
And gyngebreed that was ful fyn,
And lycorys, and eek comyn,
With sugre that is so trye.[3]
He dide next his white leere [4]
Of clooth of lake, fyn and cleere,   6470
A breech and eek a sherte ;
And next his sherte an aketoun,[5]
And over that an haubergeoun
For percynge of his herte ;
And over that a fyn hawberk,
Was al ywroght of Jewes werk,

---

[1] Heads.   [2] Cup.   [3] Refined.   [4] Skin.   [5] Leathern coat.

Ful strong it was of plate ;
And over that his cote armour,
As whit as is a lilye flour,
In which he wol debate.[1]   6480
His sheeld was al of gold so reed,
And ther-inne was a bores heed,
A charbocle bisyde ;   (13,800 T.)
And there he swoor, on ale and breed,
How that the geaunt shal be deed,
" Bityde what bityde ! "
Hise jambeux were of quyrboilly,[2]
His swerdes shethe of yvory,
His helm of laton [3] bright ;
His sadel was of rewel [4] boon ;   6490
His brydel as the sonne shoon,
Or as the moone light.
His spere it was of fyn ciprees,[5]
That bodeth werre, and no thyng pees,
The heed ful sharpe ygrounde ;
His steede was al dappull-gray,
It gooth an ambil in the way
Ful softely and rounde
          In londe.

Loo, lordes myne, heere is a Fit ;   6500
If ye wol any moore of it
To telle it wol I fonde.[6]

---

[1] Strive.   [2] Stiff leather that had been soaked in hot water.
[3] Brass.   [4] Rounded (?).   [5] Cypress-wood.   [6] Try.

THE SECOND FIT.

Now holde youre mouth, *par charitee,*
Bothe knyght and lady free,
And herkneth to my spelle ;
Of batailles and of chivalry,
And of ladyes love-drury,[1]
Anon I wol yow telle.

Men speken of romances of prys,[2] —
Of Hornchild, and of Ypotys,　　　6510
Of Beves and of sir Gy,
Of sir Lybeux and *Pleyn-damour ;*
But sir Thopas he bereth the flour
Of roial chivalry !
His goode steede al he bistrood,
And forth upon his wey he rood,
As sparcle out of the bronde ;
Up on his creest he bar a tour,
And ther inne stiked a lilie flour, —
God shilde his cors fro shonde ![3]　　6520
And for he was a knyght auntrous,[4]
He nolde slepen in noon hous,
But liggen[5] in his hoode ;
His brighte helm was his wonger,[6]
And by hym baiteth his dextrer[7]
Of herbes fyne and goode ;
Hym self drank water of the well,[8]

---

[1] Courtship.　[2] Prize.　[3] Harm.　[4] Adventurous.　[5] Lie
Pillow.　[7] War-horse.　[8] Spring.

As dide the knyght sire Percyvell,
So worthy under wede ;[1]
Til on a day ——   (13,846 T.)

*Heere the Hoost stynteth Chaucer of his Tale of
Thopas.*

" Na moore of this, for Goddes dignitee ! "
Quod oure Hoost, "for thou makest me   6532
So wery of thy verray lewednesse [2]   (13,849 T.)
That, also wisly God my soule blesse,
Min eres aken of thy drasty [3] speche.
Now swich a rym the devel I biteche ! [4]
This may wel be rym dogerel," quod he.

" Why so ? " quod I ; " why wiltow lette me
Moore of my tale than another man,
Syn that it is the beste ryme [5] I kan ? "   6540

" By God," quod he, " for pleynly at a word,
Thy drasty rymyng is nat worth a toord ;
Thou doost noght elles but despendest tyme ;
Sire, at o word, thou shalt no lenger ryme.
Lat se wher thou kanst tellen aught in geeste,[6]
Or telle in prose somwhat, at the leeste,
In which ther be som murthe, or som doc-
       tryne."

" Gladly," quod I, " by Goddes sweete pyne !
I wol yow telle a litel thyng in prose
That oghte liken yow, as I suppose,   6550

' Arms.   [2] Foolish talk.   [3] Filthy.   [4] Hand over to.   [5] Elles
MS. has " tale."   [6] Like the *Gesta Romanorum*, for example

Or elles, certes, ye been to daungerous.[1]
It is a moral tale vertuous,
Al be it told [2] somtyme in sondry wyse [3]
Of sundry folk, as I shal yow devyse.

  "As thus ; ye woot that every Evaungelist
That telleth us the peyne of Jhesu Crist
Ne seith nat alle thyng as his felawe dooth ;
But nathelees hir sentence is al sooth,
And alle acorden as in hire sentence,[4]
Al be ther in hir tellyng difference ;   6560
For somme of hem seyn moore, and somme
        seyn lesse,
Whan they his pitous passioun expresse, —
I meene of Marke, Mathew, Luc and John, —
But doutelees hir sentence is all oon.

  "Therfore, lordynges alle, I yow biseche
If that ye thynke I varie as in my speche,
As thus, though that I telle som-what moore
Of proverbes, than ye han herd bifoore
Comprehended in this litel tretys heere,
To enforce with theffect of my mateere ;   6570
And though I nat the same wordes seye,
As ye han herd, yet to yow alle I preye,
Blameth me nat, for as in my sentence
Ye shul not fynden moche difference [5]
Fro the sentence of this tretys lyte [6] (13,891 T.)
After the which this murye tale I write ;

---

[1] Fastidious.   [2] Elles. MS. has "take"   [3] This is a reference to
the fact that the following tale is not a literal translation from the
Latin of Albertano of Brescia.   [4] Sense.   [5] Elles. MS. has " shul
re nowher fynden difference."   [6] Little.

And therfore herkneth what that I shal seye,
And lat me tellen al my tale,[1] I preye." 6578

Heere bigynneth Chaucer's Tale of Melibee.

A yong man called Melibeus, myghty and
riche, bigat up on his wyf, that called was Prudence, a doghter whieh that called was Sophie.

[6580 [2]] Upon a day bifel, that he for his desport is went in to the feeldes, hym to pleye;
his wyf and eek his doghter hath he left inwith
his hous, of which the dores weren fast yshette.
Thre of hise olde foes han it espyed, and setten
laddres to the walles of his hous, and by wyndowes been entred, and betten his wyf, and
wounded his doghter with fyve mortal woundes
in fyve sondry places, — this is to seyn, in hir
feet, in hire handes, in hir erys, in hir nose,
and in hire mouth, — and leften hire for deed,
and wenten awey.

Whan Melibeus retourned was in to his hous
and saugh al this meschief, he, lyk a mad man,
rentynge his clothes, gan to wepe and crie.

Prudence, his wyf, as ferforth as she dorste,
bisoghte hym of his wepyng for to stynte; but
nat for-thy[3] he gan to crie and wepen evere
enger the moore.

---

[1] Chaucer's original in this case was the *Liber Consolationis et
Consilii*, of Albertano of Brescia, a free French translation of whicu,
said to be by Jean de Meung, was used by the poet. The Latin was
issued by the Chaucer Society in 1873. [2] Every tenth break made
by Tyrwhitt, and followed in the Six-Text edition, is numbered
here. [3] Therefore.

This noble wyf Prudence remembred hire upon the sentence of Ovide, in his book that cleped is The Remedie of Love, where as he seith, "He is a fool that destourbeth the mooder to wepen in the deeth of hire child, til she have wept hir fille, as for a certein tyme, [6590] and thanne shal man doon his diligence with amyable wordes hire to reconforte, and preyen hire of hir wepyng for to stynte." For which resoun this noble wyf Prudence suffred hir housbonde for to wepe and crie as for a certein space; and whan she saugh hir tyme, she seyde hym in this wise : "Allas, my lord," quod she, "why make ye youre self for to be lyk a fool ! For sothe it aperteneth nat to a wys man to maken swiche a sorwe. Youre doghter with the grace of God shal warisshe[1] and escape ; and, al were it so that she right now were deed, ye ne oughte nat, as for hir deeth, youre self to destroye. Senek seith, 'The wise man shal nat take to greet discon-fort for the deeth of his children, but, certes, he sholde suffren it in pacience as wel as he abideth the deeth of his owene propre per-sone.' "

This Melibeus answerde anon, and seyde, What man," quod he, "sholde of his wepyng stente that hath so greet a cause for to wepe ? Jhesu Crist, oure Lord, hym self wepte for the deeth of Lazarus hys freend."

[1] Recover

[6600] Prudence answerde, " Certes, wel I woot attempree [1] wepyng is no thyng deffended [2] to hym that sorweful is amonges folk in sorwe, but it is rather graunted hym to wepe.

" The Apostle Paul un-to the Romayns writeth, 'Man shal rejoyse with hem that maken joye, and wepen with swich folk as wepen;' but though attempree wepyng be ygraunted, outrageous wepyng certes is deffended. Mesure of wepyng sholde be considered, after the loore that techeth us Senek : 'Whan that thy frend is deed,' quod he, 'lat nat thyne eyen to moyste been of teeris, ne to muche drye ; although the teeris come to thyne eyen, lat hem nat falle, and whan thou hast for-goon [3] thy freend, do diligence to gete another freend, and this is moore wysdom than for to wepe for thy freend which that thou hast lorn, for therinne is no boote ;' and therfore, if ye governe yow by sapience, put awey sorwe out of youre herte. Remembre yow that Jhesus Syrak seith, 'A man that is joyous, and glad in herte, it hym conserveth florissynge in his age, but soothly sorweful herte maketh hise bones drye.' He seith eek thus, that sorwe in herte sleeth ful many a man. Salomon seith that 'right as motthes in the shepes flees [4] anoyeth to the clothes, and the smale wormes to the tree, right [6610] so anoyeth sorwe to the herte ;' wherfore

---

[1] Temperate. [2] Forbidden. [3] Lost. [4] Sheep's fleece.

us oghte as wel in the deeth of oure children as in the losse of oure [1] goodes temporels have pacience.

"Remembre yow up on the pacient Job. Whan he hadde lost his children and his temporeel substance, and in his body endured and receyved ful many a grevous tribulacion, yet seyde he thus : 'Oure Lord [has given it to me ; our Lord [2]] hath biraft it me ; right as oure Lord hath wold, right so it is doon ; blessed be the name of oure Lord ! ' "

To thise foreseide thynges answerde Melibeus un-to his wyf Prudence : " Alle thy wordes," quod he, " been sothe, and therwith profitable, but trewely myn herte is troubled with this sorwe so grevously that I noot what to doone."

"Lat calle," quod Prudence, "thy trewe freendes alle, and thy lynage whiche that been wise. Telleth youre cas and herkneth what they seye in conseillyng, and yow governe after hire sentence. Salomon seith, ' Werk alle thy thynges by conseil, and thou shalt never repente.' "

Thanne by the conseil of his wyf Prudence this Melibeus leet callen a greet congregacioun of folk, as surgiens, phisiciens, olde folk and yonge, and somme of hise olde enemys reconsiled, as by hir semblaunt, to his love and in to

---

[1] Elles. MS. has "othere." [2] From the French. Not in Elles MS.

his grace, and ther-with-al ther coomen somme of hise neighebores that diden hym reverence moore for drede than for love, as it happeth ofte. Ther coomen also ful many subtille flatereres, and wise advocatz, lerned in the lawe.

[6620] And whan this folk togidre assembled weren, this Melibeus in sorweful wise shewed hem his cas, and by the manere of his speche it semed wel that in herte he baar a crueel ire, redy to doon vengeance up-on hise foes, and sodeynly desired that the werre sholde bigynne, but nathelees, yet axed he hire conseil upon this matiere.

A surgien, by licence and assent of swiche as weren wise, up roos and to Melibeus seyde as ye may heere : " Sire," quod he, " as to us surgiens aperteneth that we do to every wight the beste that we kan, where as we been withholde,[1] and to oure pacientz that we do no damage ; wherfore it happeth many tyme and ofte that whan twey men han everich wounded oother, oon same surgien heeleth hem bothe : wherfore un-to oure art it is nat pertinent to norice werre, ne parties to supporte. But certes, as to the warisshynge [2] of youre doghter, al be it so that she perilously be wounded, we shullen do so ententif bisynesse fro day to nyght that with the grace of God she shal be hool and sound as soone as is possible."

[1] Retained.   [2] Curing.

Almoost right in the same wise the phisiciens answerden, save that they seyden a fewe woordes moore ; that right as maladies been cured by hir contraries, right so shul men warisshe werre by vengeaunce.

[6630] Hise neighebores ful of envye, hise feyned freendes that semeden reconsiled, and hise flatereres maden semblant of wepyng, and empeireden [1] and agreggeden [2] muchel of this matiere, in preisynge greetly Melibee, of myght, of power, of richesse, and of freendes, despisynge the power of hise adversaries, and seiden outrely that he anon sholde wreken hym on hise foes, and bigynne werre.

Up roos thanne an advocat that was wys, by leve and by conseil of othere that were wise, and seide, "Lordynges, the nede for which we been assembled in this place is a ful hevy thyng, and an heigh matiere, by cause of the wrong and of the wikkednesse that hath be doon, and eek by resoun of the grete damages hat in tyme comynge been possible to fallen lor this same cause, and eek by resoun of the grete richesse and power of the parties bothe, for the whiche resouns it were a ful greet peril to erren in this matiere ; wherfore, Melibeus, this is oure sentence : we conseille yow aboven alle thyng, that right anon thou do thy diligence in kepynge of thy propre persone in

---

[1] Impaired. [2] Aggravated.

swich a wise that thou wante [1] noon espie, ne
wacche, thy persone for to save ; and after
that we conseille that in thyn hous thou sette
sufficeant garnisoun, so that they may as wel
[6640] thy body as thyn hous defende ; but
certes, for to moeve werre, or sodeynly for to
doon vengeaunce, we may nat demen [2] in so
litel tyme that it were profitable. Wherfore
we axen leyser and espace [3] to have deliberacioun in this cas to deme, for the commune
proverbe seith thus : ' He that soone deemeth,
soone shal repente ; ' and eek men seyn that
thilke juge is wys that soone understondeth a
matiere and juggeth by leyser ; for, al be it so
that alle tariyng be anoyful, algates it is nat to
repreve in gevynge of juggement, ne in vengeance takyng, whan it is sufficeant and resonable ; and that shewed oure Lord Jhesu Crist
by ensample, for whan that the womman that
was taken in avowtrie [4] was broght in his presence to knowen what sholde be doon with hire
persone, — al be it so that he wiste wel hym
self what that he wolde answere, — yet ne
wolde he nat answere sodeynly, but he wolde
have deliberacioun, and in the ground he
wroot twies ; and by thise causes we axen de-
iberacioun, and we shal thanne, by the grace
of God, conseille thee thyng that shal be profit
able."

[1] Lack.　[2] Judge.　[3] Leisure and time.　[4] Adultery.

Up stirten thanne the yonge folk atones, and the mooste partie of that compaignye scorned the wise olde men, and bigonnen to make noyse, and seyden that "Right so as whil that iren is hoot men sholden smyte, right so men sholde wreken hir wronges while that they been fresshe and newe ;" and with loud voys they criden, "Werre ! werre !"

Up roos tho oon of thise olde wise,[1] and with his hand made contenaunce that men sholde holden hem stille, and geven hym audience

[6650] "Lordynges," quod he, "ther is ful many a man that crieth 'Werre! werre !' that woot ful litel what werre amounteth. Werre at his bigynnyng hath so greet an entryng and so large, that every wight may entre whan hym liketh and lightly fynde werre ; but certes, what ende that shal ther-of bifalle it is nat light[2] to knowe ; for soothly, whan that werre is ones bigonne ther is ful many a child unborn of his mooder that shal sterve yong by cause of that ilke werre, or elles lyve in sorwe, and dye in wrecchednesse ; and ther fore, er that any werre bigynne, men moste have greet conseil and greet deliberacioun."

And whan this olde man wende[3] to enforcen his tale by resons, wel ny alle atones bigonne they to rise fore to breken[4] his tale, and beden hym ful ofte hise wordes for to abregge ; for

---

[1] Wise men. [2] Easy. [3] Thought. [4] Break off.

soothly, he that precheth to hem that listen nat heeren [1] hise wordes, his sermon hem anoi- eth ; for Jhesus Syrak seith, that "musik in wepynge is anoyous thyng ;" this is to seyn, as muche availleth to speken bifore folk to whiche his speche anoyeth, as it is to synge biforn hym that wepeth. And this wise man saugh that hym wanted audience, and al shamefast he sette hym doun agayn ; for Salomon seith, "Ther as thou ne mayst have noon audience, enforce thee nat to speke."

[6660] "I see wel," quod this wise man, "that the commune proverbe is sooth, 'That good conseil wanteth whan it is moost nede.'"

Yet hadde this Melibeus in his conseil many folk that prively in his eere conseilled hym cer- teyn thyng, and conseilled hym the contrarie in general audience.

Whan Melibeus hadde herd that the gretteste partie of his conseil weren accorded [2] that he sholde maken werre, anoon, he consented to hir conseillyng and fully affermed hire sen- tence.

Thanne dame Prudence, whan that she saugh how that hir housbonde shoope hym for to wreken hym on hise foes, and to bigynne werre, she in ful humble wise, whan she saugh hir tyme, seide to hym thise wordes.

"My lord," quod she, "I yow biseche, as

---

[1] Care not to hear.   [2] Agreed.

hertely as I dar and kan, ne haste yow nat to
faste, and for alle gerdons, as geveth me audience ; for Piers Alfonce seith, 'Who so that
dooth to that oother good or harm, haste thee
nat to quiten it ; for in this wise thy freend
wole abyde,[1] and thyn enemy shal the lenger
lyve in drede.' The proverbe seith, 'He hasteth wel that wisely kan abyde,[2] and in wikked
haste is no profit.' "

This Melibee answerde un-to his wyf Prudence, "I purpose nat," quod he, "to werke by
thy conseil, for many causes and resouns ; for
certes, every wight wolde holde me thanne a
fool. This is to seyn, if I, for thy conseillyng,
wolde chaungen thynges that been ordeyned
and affermed by so manye wyse.[3] Secound-
ly, I seye that alle wommen been wikke, and
noon good of hem alle; for, 'Of a thousand
men,' seith Salomon, 'I foond a good man, but
certes, of alle wommen, good womman foond I
[6670] nevere ;' and also, certes, if I governed
me by thy conseil, it sholde seme that I hadde
geve to thee over me the maistrie, and God for
bede that it so weere ! for Jhesus Syrak seith,
that if the wyf have maistrie she is contrarious
to hir housbonde ; and Salomon seith, 'Nevere
in thy lyf, to thy wyf, ne to thy child, ne to thy
freend, ne geve no power over thy self, for
bettre it were that thy children aske of thy

[1] Remain. [2] Wait. [3] Wise men.

persone thynges that hem nedeth than thou be
thy self in the handes of thy children ;' and if
I wolde werke by thy conseillyng, certes, my
conseillyng moste som tyme be secree til it
were tyme that it moste be knowe and this ne
may noght be [for it is written, 'The janglerie of women can hide thyngis that they wot
nought ;' furthermore, the philosophre saith,
' In wikke conseyl women venquysse men ;' and
for these reasons I ought not to make use of thy
counsel [1]."

Whanne dame Prudence, ful debonairly and
with greet pacience, hadde herd al that hir
housbonde liked for to seye, thanne axed she
of hym licence for to speke, and seyde in this
wise : " My lord," quod she, " as to youre firste
resoun, certes it may lightly been answered ;
for I seye that it is no folie to chaunge conseil
whan the thyng is chaunged, or elles whan the
thyng semeth ootherweyes than it was biforn ;
and mooreover, I seye that though ye han
sworn and bihight to perfourne youre emprise,[2]
and nathelees ye weyve to perfourne thilke
same emprise by juste cause, men sholde nat
seyn therfore that ye were a lier ne forsworn,
for the book seith that the wise man maketh
no lesyng whan he turneth his corage to the
[6680] bettre, and al be it so that youre emprise

---

[1] This passage is not in Elles. MS., but as it is necessary for the
argument, it is supplied from the Cambridge MS., which follows the
Livre de Melibée, and the Latin.   [2] Enterprise.

ɒe establissed and ordeyned by greet multitude
of folk, yet thar ye nat accomplice thilke ordinaunce but yow like ; for the trouthe of
thynges and the profit been rather founden in
fewe folk that been wise and ful of resoun,
than by greet multitude of folk ther every man
crieth and clatereth what that hym liketh ,
soothly, swich multitude is nat honeste.

"As to the seconde resoun, where-as ye seyn
that alle wommen been wikke ; save youre
grace, certes ye despisen alle wommen in this
wyse [and 'he that al despiseth al displeseth,'
as seith the book [1]] ; and Senec seith, that who
so wole have sapience shal no man despise,
but he shal gladly techen the science that he
kan with-outen presumpcioun or pride, and
swiche thynges as he nought ne kan he shal
nat been ashamed to lerne hem and enquere of
lasse folk than hym self ; and, sire, that ther
hath been many a good womman may lightly
be preved, for certes, sire, oure Lord Jhesu
Crist wolde nevere have descended to be born
of a womman, if alle wommen hadden ben
wikke ; and after that, for the grete bountee
that is in wommen, oure Lord Jhesu Crist,
whan he was risen fro deeth to lyve, appeered
rather to a woman than to hise Apostles ;
and though that Salomon seith that he ne foond
nevere womman good, it folweth nat therfore

---

[1] Not in Elles. MS. ; supplied hom the Hengwrt MS.

that alle womman ben wikke, for though that
he ne foond no good womman, certes, ful many
another man hath founden many a womman ful
[6690] good and trewe ; or elles, per aventure,
the entente of Salomon was this, that, as in sovereyn bounte,[1] he foond no womman ; that is to
seyn that ther is no wight that hath sovereyn
bountee, save God allone,[2] — as he hym self
recordeth in hys evaungelie, — for ther nys no
creature so good that hym ne wanteth somwhat
of the perfeccioun of God, that is his maker.

"Youre thridde resoun is this, — ye seyn if ye
governe yow by my conseil it sholde seme that
ye hadde geve me the maistrie and the lordshipe over youre persone. Sire, save youre
grace, it is nat so, for if it were so that no man
sholde be conseilled but oonly of hem that hadden lordshipe and maistrie of his persone, men
wolden nat be conseilled so ofte, for soothly
thilke man that asketh conseil of a purpos, yet
hath he free choys wheither he wole werke by
that conseil or noon.

"And as to youre fourthe resoun ; ther ye
seyn that the janglerie of wommen hath hyd
thynges that they wiste noght, as who seith that
a womman kan nat hyde that she woot, sire,
thise wordes been understonde of wommen
that been jangleresses and wikked, of whiche
wommen men seyn that thre thynges dryven a

---

[1] Perfect goodness. [2] Cf. l. 14,626

man out of his hous, — that is to seyn, smoke,
droppyng of reyn, and wikked wyves; and
swiche wommen seith Salomon, that it were
bettre dwelle in desert than with a womman
[6700] that is riotous, and, sire, by youre leve,
that am nat I; for ye haan ful ofte assayed
my grete silence and my gret pacience, and
eek how wel that I kan hyde and hele [1] thynges
that men oghte secreely to hyde.

"And soothly, as to youre fifthe resoun,
where as ye seyn that in wikked conseil wommen venquisshe men, God woot thilke resoun
stant heere in no stede;[2] for, understoond now,
ye asken conseil to do wikkednesse, and if ye
wole werken wikkednesse, and youre wif re-
streyneth thilke wikked purpos and overcometh
yow by resoun and by good conseil, certes
youre wyf oghte rather to be preised than
yblamed. Thus sholde ye understonde the
philosophre that seith, 'In wikked conseil wommen venquisshen hir housbondes.'

"And ther as ye blamen alle wommen and
hir resouns, I shal shewe yow by manye ensamples, that many a womman hath ben ful
good, and yet been, and hir conseils ful hool-
some and profitable. Eek som men han seyd
that the conseillynge of wommen is outher to
deere, or elles to litel of pris;[3] but, al be it so
that ful many a womman is badde and hir con-

---

[1] Conceal. [2] Is of no weight. [3] Worth

seil vile and noght worth, yet han men founde
ful many a good womman [1] and ful discrete and
wise in conseillynge.

[6710] " Loo, Jacob, by good conseil of his
mooder Rebekka, wan the benysoun of Yssak
his fader, and the lordshipe over alle hise bretheren : Judith, by hire good conseil, delivered
the citee of Bethulie, in which she dwelled, out
of the handes of Olofernus, that hadde it biseged and wolde have al-destroyed it : Abygail
delivered Nabal hir housbonde fro David the
kyng that wolde have slayn hym, and apaysed
the ire of the kyng by hir wit and by hir good
conseillyng : Hester enhaunced greetly by hir
good conseil the peple of God in the regne of
Assuerus the kyng : and the same bountee [2] in
good conseillyng of many a good womman may
men telle, and moore over, whan oure Lord
hadde creat Adam oure forme [3] fader, he seyde
in this wise : ' It is nat good to been a man
alloone, make we to hym an helpe semblable
to hym self.'

" Heere may ye se that if that wommen were
nat goode and hir conseils goode and profitable, oure Lord God of hevene wolde nevere
han wroght hem, ne called hem 'help' of man,
but rather confusioun of man.   And ther seyde
ɔones a clerk in two vers, 'What is bettre than
Gold ? Jaspre.   What is bettre than Jaspre

---

[1] Cf. l. 14,616.   [2] Goodness (Fr. *bonté*).   [3] First

6720] Wisedoom. And what is better than Wisedoom? Womman. And what is bettre than a good Womman? No thyng.' And, sire, by manye of othre resouns may ye seen that manye wommen been goode, and hir conseils goode and profitable, and therfore, sire, if ye wol triste to my conseil, I shal restoore yow youre doghter hool and sound, and eek I wol do to yow so muche that ye shul have honour in this cause."

Whan Melibee hadde herd the wordes of his wyf Prudence, he seyde thus : " I see wel that the word of Salomon is sooth. He seith that wordes that been spoken discreetly, by ordinaunce, been honycombes, for they geven swetnesse to the soule and hoolsomnesse to the body ; and, wyf, by-cause of thy sweete wordes, and eek for I have assayed and preved thy grete sapience and thy grete trouthe, I wol governe me by thy conseil in alle thyng."

"Now, sire," quod dame Prudence, "and syn ye vouche sauf to been governed by my conseil, I wol enforme yow how ye shul governe youre self in chesynge of youre conseillours. Ye shul first in alle youre werkes mekely biseken to the heighe God that he wol be youre conseillour, and shapeth yow to swich entente that he geve yow conseil and confort, as taughte [6730] Thobie his sone : 'At alle tymes thou shalt blesse God and praye hym to dresse thy

weyes, and looke that alle thy conseils been in
hym for everemoore.' Seint Jame eek seith.
'If any of yow have nede of sapience, axe it
of God.' And afterward, thanne shul ye taken
conseil of youre self and examyne wel youre
thoghtes of swich thyng as yow thynketh that
is best for youre profit, and thanne shul ye
dryve fro youre herte thre thynges that been
contrariouse to good conseil, — that is to seyn,
ire, coveitise, and hastifnesse.

"First, he that axeth conseil of hym-self,
certes he moste been with-outen ire, for manye
causes. The firste is this : he that hath greet ire
and wratthe in hym self, he weneth alwey that
he may do thyng that he may nat do. And sec-
oundely, he that is irous and wrooth, he ne may
nat wel deme,[1] and he that may nat wel deme,
may nat wel conseille. The thridde is this, that
he that is irous and wrooth, as seith Senec, ne
[6740] may nat speke but he blame thynges,
and with hise viciouse wordes he stireth oother
.olk to angre and to ire. And eek, sire, ye
moste dryve coveitise [2] out of youre herte, for
the Apostle seith that coveitise is roote of alle
harmes ; and trust wel that a coveitous man ne
kan noght deme, ne thynke, but oonly to fulfille the ende of his coveitise, and certes, that
ne may nevere been accompliced, for evere the
moore habundaunce that he hath of richesse

---

[1] Judge. [2] Covetousness.

the moore he desireth. And, sire, ye moste
also dryve out of youre herte hastifnesse, for
certes, ye ne may nat deeme for the beste a
sodeyn thought that falleth in youre herte, but
ye moste avyse yow on it ful ofte, for as ye
herde biforn, the commune proverbe is this,
that 'he that soone deemeth, soone repenteth.'
Sire, ye ne be nat alwey in lyke disposicioun,
for certes som thyng that somtyme semeth to
yow that it is good for to do, another tyme it
semeth to yow the contrarie.

[6750] "Whan ye han taken conseil of youre
self and han deemed by good deliberacion swich
thyng as you list best, thanne rede [1] I yow that
ye kepe it secree.   Biwrey nat youre conseil to
no persone, but if so be that ye wenen sikerly [2]
that thurgh youre biwreyyng youre condicioun
shal be to yow the moore profitable ; for Jhesus
Syrak seith, 'Neither to thy foo, ne to thy frend,
discovere nat thy secree, ne thy folie, for they
wol geve yow audience and lookynge to sup-
portacioun in thy presence, and scorne thee in
thyn absence.'   Another clerk seith, that scarsly
shaltou fynden any persone that may kepe conseil sikerly.

"The book seith, 'Whil that thou kepest thy
conseil in thyn herte, thou kepest it in thy
prisoun, and whan thou biwreyest thy conseil
to any wight he holdeth thee in his snare ;'

[1] Advise.   [2] Believe sure y.

and therfore yow is bettre to hyde youre conseil in youre herte than praye hem to whom ye
han biwreyed youre conseil that he wole kepen
it cloos and stille ; for Seneca seith, ' If so be
that thou ne mayst nat thyn owene conseil
hyde, how darstou prayen any oother wight thy
conseil sikerly [1] to kepe ? '

[6760] "But nathelees, if thou wene sikerly
that the biwreiyng of thy conseil to a persone
wol make thy condicioun to stonden in the bettre plyt, thanne shaltou tellen hym thy conseil
in this wise: first, thou shalt make no semblant wheither thee were levere pees or werre,
or this or that, ne shewe hym nat thy wille and
thyn entente, — for trust wel, that comenli thise
conseillours been flatereres, namely the conseillours of grete lordes, for they enforcen
hem alwey rather to speken plesante wordes,
enclynynge to the lordes lust, than wordes that
been trewe or profitable ; and therfore men
seyn, that the riche man hath seeld [3] good conseil, but if he have it of hym self.

"And after that thou shalt considere thy
freendes and thyne enemys ; and as touchynge
thy freendes thou shalt considere wiche of hem
that been moost feithful and moost wise, and
oldest, and most approved in conseillyng, and
of hem shalt thou aske thy conseil as the caas
requireth.

---

[1] Surely.   [2] Force.   [3] Seldom.

"I seye that first ye shul clepe to youre con-
[6770] seil youre freendes that been trewe, for
Salomon seith that 'Right as the herte of a
man deliteth in savour that is soote, right so
the conseil of trewe freendes geveth swetenesse
to the soule;' he seith also, 'Ther may no thyng
be likned to the trewe freend, for certes gold
ne silver beth nat so muche worth as the goode
wyl of a trewe freend;' and eek, he seith that
'A trewe freend is a strong deffense; who so
that hym fyndeth, certes, he fyndeth a greet
tresour.'

"Thanne shul ye eek considere if that youre
trewe freendes been discrete and wise, for the
book seith, 'Axe alwey thy conseil of hem that
been wise;' and by this same resoun shul ye
clepen to youre conseil of youre freendes that
been of age, swiche as han seyn and been expert in manye thynges, and been approved in
conseillynges; for the book seith that in the olde
men is the sapience, and in longe tyme the
prudence; and Tullius seith, that grete thynges
ne been nat ay accompliced by strengthe, ne
by delivernesse [1] of body, but by good conseil,
by auctoritee [2] of persones, and by science; [3]
the whiche thre thynges ne been nat fieble by
age, but certes, they enforcen and encreescen
day by day.   And thanne shul ye kepe this for
a general reule; first, shul ye clepen to youre

---

[1] Agility   [2] Authority.   [3] Knowledge.

conseil a fewe of youre freendes that been es-
peciale; for Salomon seith, 'Manye freendes
have thou, but among a thousand, chese [1] thee
oon to be thy conseillour, for, al be it so that
[6780] thou first ne telle thy conseil but to a
fewe, thou mayst afterward telle it to mo folk if
it be nede.' But looke alwey that thy conseillours have thilke thre condiciouns that I have
seyd bifore, that is to seyn, that they be trewe,
wise, and of oold experience. And werke nat
alwey in every nede by oon counseillour allone,
for somtyme bihooveth it to been conseilled
by manye, for Salomon seith, 'Salvacioun of
thynges is where as ther been manye conseillours.'

"Now, sith I have toold yow of which folk ye
sholde been counseilled, now wol I teche yow
which conseil ye oghte to eschewe. First, ye
shul eschue the conseillyng of fooles, for Salomon seith, 'Taak no conseil of a fool, for he
ne kan noght conseille but after his owene lust
and his affeccioun.' The book seith that the
propretee [2] of a fool is this, 'He troweth lightly
harm of every wight, and lightly troweth alle
bountee [3] in hym self.' Thou shalt eek eschue
the conseillyng of flatereres, swiche as enforcen
hem rather to preise youre persone by flaterye,
than for to telle yow the sooth-fastnesse of
thynges.

[1] Choose   [2] Peculiar trait.   [3] Goodness.

" Wherfore Tullius seith, ' Amonges alle the pestilences that been in freendshipe the gretteste is flaterie ; ' and therfore is it moore nede that thou eschue and drede flatereres than any oother peple. The book seith, ' Thou shalt rather drede and flee fro the sweete wordes of flaterynge preiseres than fro the egre [1] wordes [6790] of thy freend that seith thee thy sothes.' Salomon seith that ' The wordes of a flaterere is a snare to chacche with innocentz.' [2] He seith also that ' He that speketh to his freend wordes of swetnesse and of plesaunce, setteth a net biforn his feet to cacche hym ; ' and ther fore, seith Tullius, ' Enclyne nat thyne eres to flatereres, ne taaketh no conseil of the wordes of flaterye ; ' and Caton seith, ' Avyse thee wel, and eschue the wordes of swetnesse and of plesaunce.'

" And eek thou shalt eschue the conseillyng of thyne olde enemys that been reconsiled. The book seith that no wight retourneth saufly in-to the grace of his olde enemy ; and Isope [3] seith, ' Ne trust nat to hem to whiche thou has, had som tyme werre or enemytee, ne telle hem nat thy conseil ; ' and Seneca telleth the cause why : ' It may nat be,' seith he, ' that where greet fyr hath longe tyme endured, that ther ne dwelleth som vapour of warmnesse ; ' and therfore seith Salomon, ' In thyn olde foo trust

[1] Eager. [2] Catch innocents with. [3] Æsop.

nevere ;' for sikerly though thyn enemy be reconsiled and maketh thee chiere of humylitee,
and lowteth [1] to thee with his heed, ne trust
[6800] hym nevere; for certes, he maketh thilke
feyned humilitee moore for his profit than for
any love of thy persone, by-cause that he
deemeth to have victorie over thy persone by
swich feyned contenance, the which victorie he
myghte nat wynne by strif or werre. And
Peter Alfonce seith, ' Make no felawshipe with
thyne olde enemys, for if thou do hem bountee
they wol perverten it in to wikkednesse.'

"And eek thou most eschue the conseillyng
of hem that been thy servantz and beren thee
greet reverence, for peraventure they doon it
moore for drede than for love. And therfore
seith a philosophre in this wise: ' Ther is no
wight parfitly trewe to hym that he to soore
dredeth;' and Tullius seith, ' Ther nys no
myght so greet of any emperour that longe
may endure, but if he have moore love of the
peple than for-drede.' [2]

"Thou shalt also eschue the conseiling of folk
that been dronkelewe,[3] for they kan no conseil
hyde, for Salomon seith, ' Ther is no privetee
ther as regneth dronkenesse.' Ye shul also
han in suspect the conseillyng of swich folk as
conseille yow a thyng prively and conseille
yow the contrarie openly ; for Cassidorie seith

Boweth.   [2] Great dread.   [3] Drunken

that 'It is a manere sleighte [1] to hyndre, whan he sheweth to doon a thyng openly and werketh prively the contrarie.'

"Thou shalt also have in suspect the conseillyng of wikked folk, for the book seith, 'The conseillyng of wikked folk is alwey ful [6810] of fraude;' and David seith, 'Blisful is that man that hath nat folwed the conseilyng of shrewes.' [2] Thou shalt also eschue the conseillyng of yong folk, for hir conseil is nat rype.

"Now, sire, sith I have shewed yow of which folk ye shul take youre conseil, and of which folk ye shul folwe the conseil, now wol I teche yow how ye shal examyne youre conseil, after the doctrine of Tullius.

"In the examynynge thanne of youre conseillour ye shul considere manye thynges. Alderfirst [3] thou shalt considere, that in thilke thyng that thou purposest and upon what thyng thou wolt have conseil, that verray trouthe be seyd and conserved; this is to seyn, telle trewely hy tale, for he that seith fals may nat wel be conseilled in that cas of which he lieth.

"And after this thou shalt considere the thynges that acorden [4] to that thou purposest for to do by thy conseillours if resoun accorde therto, and eek if thy myght may atteine therto : and if the moore part and the bettre part of thy conseillours acorde ther-to or noon.

Sort of cunning. [2] Wicked men, shrews [3] First of all. [4] Agree

Thanne shaltou considere what thyng shal folwe after hir conseillyng, as hate, pees, werre, grace, profit, or damage, and manye othere [6820] thynges. Thanne, of alle thise thynges, thou shalt chese the beste, and weyve[1] alle othere thynges. Thanne shaltow considere of what roote is engendred the matiere of thy conseil, and what fruyt it may conserve and engendre. Thou shalt eek considere alle thise causes fro whennes they been sprongen.

"And whan ye han examyned youre conseil as I have seyd, and which partie is the bettre and moore profitable, and hast approved it by manye wise folk, and olde, thanne shaltou considere if thou mayst parfourne it and maken of it a good ende; for certes, resoun wol nat that any man sholde bigynne a thyng, but if he myghte parfourne it as hym oghte, ne no wight sholde take up on hym so hevy a charge that he myghte nat bere it; for the proverbe seith, 'He that to muche embraceth, distreyneth[2] litel;' and Catoun seith, 'Assay to do swich thyng as thou hast power to doon, lest that the charge oppresse thee so soore that thee bihov- eth to weyve thyng that thou hast bigonne.' And, if so be that thou be in doute wheither thou mayst parfourne a thing or noon, chese [6830] rather to suffre than bigynne. And Piers Alphonce seith, 'If thou hast myght to

---

[1] Forsake. [2] Keepeth.

doon a thyng of which thou most repente thee, it is bettre "nay" than "ye;"'[1] this is to seyn, that thee is bettre holde thy tonge stille than for to speke.

"Thanne may ye understonde by strenger resons that if thou hast power to parfourne a werk of which thou shalt repente, thanne is it bettre that thou suffre than bigynne. Wel seyn they that defenden[2] every wight to assaye any thyng of which he is in doute wheither he may parfourne it or noon. And after, whan ye han examyned youre conseil, as I have seyd biforn, and knowen wel that ye may parfourne youre emprise, conferme it thanne sadly[3] til it be at an ende.

"Now is it resoun and tyme that I shewe yow whanne and wherfore that ye may chaunge youre conseillours with-outen youre repreve.[4] Soothly a man may chaungen his purpos and his conseil if the cause cesseth, or whan a newe caas bitydeth;[5] for the lawe seith that upon thynges that newely bityden bihoveth newe conseil; and Senec seith, 'If thy conseil is comen to the eeris of thyn enemy, chaunge thy conseil.' Thou mayst also chaunge thy conseil if so be that thou mayst fynde that by errour, or by oother cause, harm or damage may bi-[6840] tyde. Also if thy conseil be dishonest, or ellis cometh of dishoneste cause, chaunge thy

---

Nay than yea.   [2] Forbid.   [3] Surely   [4] Censure.   [5] Comes to pass

conseil, for the lawes seyn that alle bihestes that been dishoneste been of no value, and eek if so be that it be inpossible or may nat goodly be parfourned or kept.

"And take this for a general reule, that every conseil that is affermed so strongly that it may nat be chaunged for no condicioun that may bityde, I seye that thilke conseil is wikked."

This Melibeus, whanne he hadde herd the doctrine of his wyf, dame Prudence, answerde in this wyse: "Dame," quod he, "as yet in to this tyme ye han wel and covenablely [1] taught me as in general how I shal governe me in the chesynge and in the withholdynge of my con-seillours, but now wolde I fayn that ye wolde condescende in especial, and telle me how liketh yow, or what semeth yow by oure con-seillours that we han chosen in oure present nede."

"My lord," quod she, "I biseke yow in al humblesse that ye wol nat wilfully replie agayn my resouns, ne distempre youre herte, thogh I speke thyng that yow displese, for God woot that as in myn entente I speke it for youre [6850] beste, for youre honour, and for youre profite eke; and soothly I hope that youre be-nyngnytee wol taken it in pacience. Trusteth me wel," quod she, "that youre conseil as in this caas ne sholde nat, as to speke properly

[1] Suitably.

be called a conseillyng, but a mocioun or a moevyng of folye, in which conseil ye han erred in many a sondry wise.

" First and forward ye han erred in thassemblynge of youre conseillours ; for ye sholde first have cleped a fewe folk to youre conseil, and after ye myghte han shewed it to mo folk, if it hadde been nede ; but certes, ye han sodeynly cleped to youre conseil a greet multitude of peple ful chargeant[1] and ful anoyous for to heere. Also, ye han erred, for there as ye sholden oonly have cleped to youre conseil youre trewe frendes olde and wise, ye han ycleped straunge folk, and yong folk, false flatereres and enemys reconsiled, and folk that doon yow reverence withouten love. And eek also ye have erred for ye han broght with yow to youre conseil ire, coveitise, and hastifnesse ; the whiche thre thinges been contrariouse to [6860] every conseil honeste and profitable,[2] the whiche thre ye han nat anientissed[3] or destroyed hem, neither in youre self ne in youre conseillours, as yow oghte. Ye han erred also, for ye han shewed to youre conseillours youre talent[4] and youre affeccioun[5] to make werre anon, and for to do vengeance. They han espied by youre wordes to what thyng ye been enclyned, and therfore han they rather con-

---

[1] Burdensome.   [2] A French construction, giving evidence that Chaucer had the French version before him.   [3] Annihilated (Fr *anéantissé*)   [4] Desire.,   [5] Inclination.

seilled yow to youre talent than to youre profit.

"Ye han erred also, for it semeth that it suffiseth to han been conseilled by thise conseillours oonly, and with litel avys,[1] where-as in so greet and so heigh a nede it hadde been necessarie mo conseillours and moore deliberacioun to parfourne youre emprise.[2]

"Ye han erred also, for ye han nat examyned youre conseil in the forseyde manere, ne in due manere as the caas requireth. Ye han erred also, for ye han nat maked no divisioun bitwixe youre conseillours, this is to seyn, bitwixen youre trewe freendes and youre feyned conseillours ; ne ye han nat knowe the wil of youre trewe freendes, olde and wise, but ye han cast alle hire wordes in an *hochepot*,[3] and enclyned youre herte to the moore partie and to the gretter nombre, and there been ye conde- [6870] scended.[4] And, sith ye woot wel that men shal alwey fynde a gretter nombre of fooles than of wise men, and therfore the conseils that been at congregaciouns and multitudes of folk, there as men take moore reward [5] to the nombre than to the sapience of persones, ye se wel that in swiche conseillynges fooles han the maistrie."

Melibeus answerde agayn, and seyde, "I

---

[1] Advice. [2] Enterprise. [3] Hodge-podge. The word is French [4] Submitted. [5] Regard.

graunte wel that I have erred, but there as thou
hast toold me heerbiforn that he nys nat to
blame that chaungeth hise conseillours in certein caas, and for certeine juste causes, I am
al redy to chaunge my conseillours right as
thow wolt devyse. The proverbe seith, that
for to do synne is mannyssh, but certes, for to
persevere longe in synne is werk of the devel."

To this sentence answereth anon dame Prudence and seyde, "Examineth," quod she,
" youre conseil and lat us see the whiche of hem
han spoken most resonablely, and taught yow
best conseil ; and for as muche as that the ex-
amynacioun is necessarie, lat us bigynne at the
surgiens and at the phisiciens that first speeken
[6880] in this matiere. I sey yow that the surgiens and phisiciens han seyd yow in youre con
seil discreetly as hem oughte, and in hir speche
seyd ful wisely that to the office of hem aperteneth to doon to every wight honour and profit,
and no wight for to anoye,[1] and in hir craft to
doon greet diligence un-to the cure of hem
whiche that they han in hir governaunce. And,
sire, right as they han answered wisely and discreetly, right so rede [2] I that they been heighly
and sovereynly gerdoned [3] for hir noble speche,
and eek, for they sholde do the moore ententif
bisynesse in the curacioun of youre doghter
deere ; for, al be it so that they been youre

---

[1] Harm.   [2] Counsel.   [3] Rewarded.

freendes, therfore shal ye nat suffren that they serve yow for noght, but ye oghte the rather gerdone hem and shewe hem youre largesse.

"And as touchynge the proposicioun which that the phisiciens encreesceden [1] in this caas; this is to seyn, that in maladies that oon con-[6890] trarie is warisshed [2] by another contra-rie; I wolde fayn knowe hou ye understonde this text, and what is youre sentence." [3]

"Certes," quod Melibeus, "I understonde it in this wise: that right as they han doon me a contrarie, right so sholde I doon hem anoth-er; for right as they han venged hem on me and doon me wrong, right so shal I venge me upon hem, and doon hem wrong, and thanne have I cured oon contrarie by another."

"Lo, lo," quod dame Prudence, "how light-ly [4] is every man enclined to his owene desir and to his owene plesaunce! Certes," quod she, "the wordes of the phisiciens ne sholde nat han been understonden in thys wise, for certes, wikkednesse is nat contrarie to wikked-nesse, ne vengeance to vengeaunce, ne wrong to wrong, but they been semblable; and ther-fore, o vengeaunce is nat warisshed by another vengeaunce, ne o wroong by another wroong, but everich of hem encreesceth and aggreggeth oother.

[6900] "But certes, the wordes of the phis-

---

[1] Amplified.   [2] Cured.   [3] Opinion.   [4] Easily.

ciens sholde been understonden in this wise ;
for good and wikkednesse been two contraries,
and pees and werre, vengeaunce and suffraunce,
discord and accord, and manye othere thynges ;
but certes, wikkednesse shal be warisshed by
goodnesse, discord by accord, werre by pees,
and so forth of othere thynges ; and heer-to
accordeth Seint Paul the Apostle in manye
places.

"He seith, 'Ne yeldeth nat harm for harm,
ne wikked speche for wikked speche ; but do
wel to hym that dooth thee harm, and blesse
hym that seith to thee harm.' And in manye
othere places he amonesteth [1] pees and accord.

"But now wol I speke to yow of the conseil
which that was geven to yow by the men of
lawe, and the wise folk, that seyden alle by
oon accord, as ye han herd bifore, that over
alle thynges ye sholde doon youre diligence to
kepen youre persone and to warnestoore [2] youre
⌐6910⌐ hous ; and seyden also, that in this caas
yow oghten for to werken ful avysely and with
greet deliberacioun.   And, sire, as to the firste
point that toucheth to the kepyng of youre persone, ye shul understonde that he that hath
werre shal everemoore mekely and devoutly
preyen, biforn alle thynges, that Jhesus Crist
of his grete mercy wol han hym in his proteccioun and been his sovereyn helpyng at his

---

[1] Admonishes.   [2] Fortify

nede, for certes, in this world ther is no wight that may be conseilled ne kept sufficeantly withouten the kepyng of oure Lord Jhesu Crist.

"To this sentence [1] accordeth the prophete David, that seith, 'If God ne kepe the citee, in ydel waketh he that it kepeth.' Now, sire, thannes hul ye committe the kepyng of youre persone to youre trewe freendes that been approved and knowe, and of hem shul ye axen helpe, youre persone for to kepe, for Catoun seith, 'If thou hast nede of help, axe it of thy freendes, for ther nys noon so good a phisicien as thy trewe freend.'

[6920] "And after this, thanne shul ye kepe yow fro alle straunge folk, and fro lyeres, and have alwey in suspect hire compaignye, for Piers Alfonce seith, 'Ne taak no compaignye by the weye of straunge men, but if so be that thou have knowe hym of a lenger tyme. And if so be, that he be falle in-to thy compaignye, paraventure, withouten thyn assent, enquere thanne as subtilly as thou mayst of his conversacioun, and of his lyf bifore, and feyne thy wey, — seye that thou goost thider as thou wolt nat go, — and if he bereth a spere, hoold thee on the right syde, and if he bere a swerd, hoold thee on his lift syde.' And after this thanne shul ye kepe yow wisely from all swich manere peple as I have seyd bifore, and hem and hir consei eschewe.

[1] Sentiment.

" And after this, thanne shul ye kepe yow in
swich manere that for any presumpcioun of
youre strengthe, that ye ne dispise nat ne
acounte nat the myght of youre adversarie so
litel that ye lete [1] the kepyng of youre persone
for youre presumpcioun, for every wys man
dredeth his enemy, and Salomon seith, ' Wele-
[6930] ful [2] is he that of alle hath drede, for
certes, he that thurgh the hardynesse of his
herte and thurgh the hardynesse of hym self
hath to greet presumpcioun, hym shal yvel bityde.'   Thanne shul ye everemoore countre-
wayte [8] embusshementz and alle espiaille.[4]   For
Senec seith, that the wise man he dredeth
harmes escheweth harmes, ne he ne falleth in-to
perils that perils escheweth.   And, al be it so,
that it seme that thou art in siker [5] place, yet
shaltow alwey do thy diligence in kepynge of
thy persone ; this is to seyn, ne be nat necligent
to kepe thy persone, nat oonly for thy gretteste enemys, but for thy leeste enemy.   [Senek
seith, ' A man that is wel avysed, he dredeth
his leste enemye.' [6]]   Ovyde seith that the litel
wesele wol slee the grete bole and the wilde
hert.   And the book seith, ' A litel thorn may
prikke a greet kyng ful soore, and an hound
wol holde the wilde boor.'

" But nathelees, I sey nat thou shalt be

---

[1] Omit, hinder. [2] Happy   [8] Watch against.   [4] Spying.   [5] Secure.   [6] Not in Elles. MS.

cowaid, that thou doute [1] ther wher as is no
[6940] drede. The book seith that somme folk
han greet lust to deceyve, but yet they dreden
hem to be deceyved. Yet shaltou drede to
been empoisoned, and kepe yow from the compaignye of scorneres, for the book seith, ' With
scorneres make no compaignye, but flee hire
wordes as venym.'

"Now as to the seconde point ; where as
youre wise conseillours conseilled yow to warnestoore [2] youre hous with gret diligence, I wolde
fayn knowe how that ye understonde thilke
wordes, and what is youre sentence."

Melibeus answerde and seyde, "Certes, I
understande it in this wise : That I shal warnestoore myn hous with toures, swiche as han
castelles, and othere manere edifices, and armure and artelries,[3] by whiche thynges I may
my persone and myn hous so kepen and deffenden, that myne enemys shul been in drede
myn hous for to approche."

To this sentence [4] answerde anon Prudence.
"Warnestooryng," quod she, "of heighe toures
and of grete edifices [appertains sometimes to
pride. Towers and great buildings are made [5]]
with grete costages and with greet travaille, and
whan that they been accompliced yet be they nat
worth a stree,[6] but if they be defended by trewe

---

[1] Fear.   [2] Fortify.   [3] Artillery. The word is not in the Latin
original.   [4] Opinion.   [5] This passage is not in Elles. MS., but is
supplied from the French.   [6] Straw.

freendes that been olde and wise. And understoond wel that the gretteste and strongeste
garnyson that a riche man may have, as wel to
[6950] kepen his persone as hise goodes, is that
he be biloved amonges hys subgetz and with
hise neighebores ; for thus seith Tullius, that
ther is a manere garnysoun that no man may
venquysse ne disconfite, and that is a lord to
be biloved of hise citezeins and of his peple.

"Now, sire, as to the thridde point, where
as youre olde and wise conseillours seyden that
yow ne oghte nat sodeynly ne hastily proceden
in this nede, but that yow oghte purveyen and
apparaillen [1] yow in this caas with greet diligence and greet deliberacioun, trewely, I trowe
that they seyden right wisely and right sooth,
for Tullius seith, 'In every nede er thou bigynne it, apparaille thee with greet diligence.'
Thanne seye I that in vengeance takyng, in
werre, in bataille, and in warnestooryng, er
thow bigynne, I rede [2] that thou apparaille thee
ther to and do it with greet deliberacioun, for
Tullius seith, 'The longe apparaillyng biforn
[6960] the bataille maketh short victorie,' and
Cassidorus seith, 'The garnyson is stronger
whan it is longe tyme avysed.'

"But now lat us speken of the conseil that
was accorded by youre neighebores, swiche as
doon yow reverence withouten love, youre olde

[1] Prepare. [2] Advise.

enemys reconsiled, youre flatereres, that conseilled yow certeyne thynges prively, and openly
conseilleden yow the contrarie, the yonge folk
also, that conseilleden yow to venge yow, and
make werre anon. And certes, sire, as I have
seyd biforn, ye han greetly erred to han cleped
swich manere folk to youre conseil, which conseillours been ynogh repreved by the resouns
aforeseyd.

"But nathelees, lat us now descende to the
special. Ye shuln first procede after the doctrine of Tullius. Certes, the trouthe of this
matiere, or of this conseil, nedeth nat diligently
enquere, for it is wel wist whiche they been
that han doon to yow this trespas and vileynye,
[6970] and how manye trespassours and in what
manere they han to yow doon al this wrong
and all this vileynye. And after this thanne
shul ye examyne the seconde condicioun which
that the same Tullius addeth in this matiere;
for Tullius put a thyng which that he clepeth
consentynge, this is to seyn, who been they,
and how manye [and whiche been they[1]],
that consenten to thy conseil, in thy wilfulnesse to doon hastif vengeance. And lat us
considere also who been they, and how manye
been they, and whiche been they, that consenteden to youre adversaries. And certes, as to
the firste poynt, it is wel knowen whiche folk

[1] Not in Elles. MS

been they that consenteden to youre hastif wilfulnesse, for trewely, alle tho[1] that conseilleden
yow to maken sodeyn werre ne been nat youre
freendes.

"Lat us now considere whiche been they that
ye holde so greetly youre freendes as to youre
persone ; for al be it so that ye be myghty and
riche, certes, ye ne been nat but allone, for
certes, ye ne han no child but a doghter, ne
[6980] ye ne han bretheren, ne cosyns germayns,
ne noon oother neigh kynrede, wherfore[2] that
youre enemys for drede sholde stinte to plede
with yow, or to destroye youre persone. Ye
knowen also that youre richesses mooten been
dispended in diverse parties, and whan that
every wight hath his part, they ne wollen taken
but litel reward[3] to venge thy deeth ; but thyne
enemys been thre, and they han manie children, bretheren, cosyns, and oother ny kynrede,
and though so were that thou haddest slayn of
hem two or thre, yet dwellen[4] ther ynowe to
wreken hir deeth, and to sle thy persone. And
though so be that youre kynrede be moore
siker and stedefast than the kyn of youre adversarie, yet nathelees, youre kynrede nys but a
.er kynrede, they been but litel syb[5] to yow, and
the kyn of youre enemys been ny syb to hem,
and certes, as in that hir condicioun is bet than
youres.

[1] Those.   [2] That is, for fear of whom.   [3] Regard.   [4] Remain.   [5] Kin.

"Thanne lat us considere also of the consei!
!yng of hem that conseilleden yow to taker
sodeyn vengeaunce, wheither it accorde to re-
[6990] soun. And certes, ye knowe wel, nay for
as by right and resoun, ther may no man taken
vengeance on no wight but the juge that hath
the jurisdiccioun of it, whan it is graunted
hym to take thilke [1] vengeance hastily or attemprely [2] as the lawe requireth. And yet
moore over of thilke word that Tullius clepeth
'consentynge,' thou shalt considere if thv
myght and thy power may consenten and suffise to thy wilfulnesse, and to thy conseillours.
And certes, thou mayst wel seyn that nay ; for
sikerly, as for to speke proprely, we may do no
thyng, but oonly swich thyng as we may doon
rightfully, and certes, rightfully ne mowe ye
take no vengeance, as of youre propre auctoritee.

"Thanne mowe ye seen that youre power ne
consenteth nat, ne accordeth nat, with youre
wilfulnesse.

"Lat us now examyne the thridde point, that
[7000] Tullius clepeth 'consequent.' Thou shalt
understonde that the vengeance that thou purposest for to take is the consequent, and ther-
of folweth another vengeaunce, peril and werre
and othere damages with-oute nombre, of
whiche we be nat war, as at this tyme. And

The same.   [2] Moderately.

as touchynge the fourthe point, that Tullius
clepeth 'engendrynge,' thou shalt considere
that this wrong which that is doon to thee is
engendred of the hate of thyne enemys, and of
the vengeance takynge upon that wolde engendre another vengeance, and muchel sorwe and
wastynge of richesses, as I seyde.

"Now, sire, as to the point that Tullius
clepeth 'causes,' which that is the laste point.
Thou shalt understonde that the wrong that
thou hast receyved hath certeine causes, whiche
that clerkes clepen *Oriens* and *Efficiens*, and
Causa longinqua and *Causa propinqua*, this is
to seyn, the fer cause and the ny cause. The
fer cause is Almyghty God, that is cause of
alle thynges ; the neer cause is thy thre enemys.
[7010] The cause accidental was hate, the cause
material been the fyve woundes of thy doghter.
The cause formal is the manere of hir werkynge that broghten laddres and cloumben in
at thy wyndowes ; the cause final was for to
sle thy doghter. It letted nat in as muche as
in hem was.

"But for to speken of the fer cause, as to
what ende they shul come, or what shal finally
bityde of hem in this caas, ne kan I nat deme
but by conjectynge and by supposynge. For
we shul suppose that they shul come to a
wikked ende by-cause that the book of de-
rees seith, 'Seelden, or with greet peyne, been

causes broght to good ende whanne they been baddely bigonne.'

"Now, sire, if men wolde axe me why that God suffred men to do yow this vileynye, certes, I kan nat wel answere, as for no sooth-fastnesse, for thapostle seith that the sciences [1] and the juggementz of oure Lord God Al-myghty been ful depe, — ther may no man com-[7020] prehende ne serchen hem suffisantly. Nathelees, by certeyne presumpciouns and con-jectynges, I holde and bileeve, that God, which that is ful of justice and of rightwisnesse, hath suffred this bityde by juste cause, resonable.

"Thy name is Melibee, this is to seyn, 'a man that drynketh hony.' Thou hast ydronke so muchel hony of sweete temporeel richesses, and delices [2] and honours of this world, that thou art dronken, and hast forgeten Jhesu Crist, thy creatour ; thou ne hast nat doon to hym swich honour and reverence as thee oughte, ne thou ne hast nat wel ytaken kepe [3] to the wordes of Ovide, that seith, 'Under the hony of the goodes of the body is hyd the venym that sleeth the soule ;' and Salomon seith, 'If thou hast founden hony, ete of it that suffiseth, for if thou ete of it out of mesure, thou shalt [7030] spewe, and be nedy and povre ;' and per-aventure, Crist hath thee in despit, and hath turned awey fro thee his face and hise eeris of

---

[1] Knowledge.   [2] Delicacies.   [3] Care.

misericorde,[1] and also he hath suffred that thou
hast been punysshed in the manere that thow
hast ytrespassed. Thou hast doon synne agayn
oure Lord Crist, for certes, the thre enemys
of mankynde, — that is to seyn, the flessh, the
feend and the world, — thou hast suffred hem
entre in to thyn herte wilfully by the wyndowes
of thy body, and hast nat defended thy self suffisantly agayns hire assautes, and hire tempta
ciouns, so that they han wounded thy soule in
five places ; this is to seyn, the deedly synnes
that been entred in-to thyn herte by thy five
wittes. And in the same manere oure Lord
Crist hath wold [2] and suffred that thy thre enemys been entred in-to thyn hous by the wyndowes, and han ywounded thy doghter in the
foreseyde manere."

   "Certes," quod Melibee, "I se wel that ye
enforce yow muchel by wordes to overcome me
in swich manere that I shal nat venge me of
7040] myne enemys, shewynge me the perils
and the yveles that myghten falle of this vengeance ; but who-so wolde considere in alle venge-
ances the perils and yveles that myghte sewe [3]
of vengeance takynge, a man wolde nevere take
vengeance ; and that were harm, for by the
vengeance takynge been the wikked men dis-
severed fro the goode men, and they that han
wyl to do wikkednesse restreyne hir wikked

<hr>

[1] Pity.   [2] Willed.   [3] Follow.

purpos whan they seen the punyssynge and chastisynge of the trespassours."

[And to this answered dame Prudence, "Certes," said she, " I grant you that from vengeance come many evils and many benefits, and yet vengeance belongeth not to a lay person but only to the judges, and to those who have jurisdiction over evil-doers.[1]]

"And yet seye I moore, that right as a singuler [2] persone synneth in takynge vengeance of another man, right so synneth the juge if he do no vengeance of hem that it han disserved ; for Senec seith thus : That maister, he seith, is [7050] good that proveth [3] shrewes.[4] And, as Cassidore seith, ' A man dredeth to do outrages whan he woot and knoweth that it displeseth to the juges and sovereyns.' Another seith, ' The juge that dredeth to do right maketh men shrewes,' and Seint Paule the Apostle seith in his Epistle, whan he writeth un-to the Romayns, that ' The juges beren nat the spere [5] with-outen cause, but they beren it to punysse the shrewes and mysdoeres, and to defende the goode men.' If ye wol thanne take vengeance of youre enemys, ye shul retourne, or have youre recours to the juge that hath the jurisdiccion up-on hem, and he shal punysse hem as the lawe axeth and requireth."

---

[1] Not in Elles. MS. Supplied from the French, collated with the Latin. [2] Lay, private. [3] Trieth. [4] Wicked men. [5] St. Pau and the Latin original have "sword."

" A ! " quod Melibee, " this vengeance liketh [1]
me no thyng.   I bithenke me now, and take
heede how Fortune hath norissed me fro my
childhede, and hath holpen me to passe many
a stroong paas.   Now wol I assayen hire, trow-
ynge with Goddes helpe that she shal helpe
me my shame for to venge."

" Certes," quod Prudence, " if ye wol werke
by my conseil ye shul nat assaye [2] Fortune by
[7060] no wey, ne ye shul nat lene or bowe un-to
hire after the word of Senec, for thynges that
been folily doon and that been in hope of Fortune shullen nevere come to good ende.   And,
as the same Senec seith, ' The moore cleer and
the moore shynyng that Fortune is, the moore
brotil [3] and the sonner broken she is ; trusteth
nat in hire, for she nys nat stidefaste, ne stable,
for whan thow trowest to be moost seur and
siker of hire helpe, she wol faille thee and deceyve thee.'   And where as ye seyn that Fortune hath norissed yow fro youre childhede, I
seye, that in so muchel shul ye the lasse truste
in hire and in hir wit ; for Senec seith, ' What
man that is norissed by Fortune she maketh
hym a greet fool.'   Now thanne, syn ye desire
and axe vengeance, and the vengeance that is
doon after the lawe and bifore the juge ne liketh
yow nat, and the vengeance that is doon in hope
[7070] of Fortune is perilous and uncertein,

[1] Pleaseth.   [2] Try.   [3] Brittle.

thanne have ye noon oother remedie, but for to
have youre recours unto the sovereyn juge that
vengeth alle vileynyes and wronges, and he shal
venge yow after that hym self witnesseth, where
as he seith, ' Leveth the vengeance to me, and
I shal do it.' "

Melibee answerde, " If I ne venge me nat
of the vileynye that men han doon to me, I
sompne[1] or warne hem that han doon to me
that vileynye, and alle othere, to do me another
vileynye, for it is writen, ' If thou take no vengeance of an oold vileynye, thou sompnest thyne
adversaries to do thee a newe vileynye.'   And
also for my suffrance men wolden do to me so
muchel vileynye that I myghte neither bere it
ne susteene, and so sholde I been put and
holden over lowe, for men seyn, ' In muchel suf-
frynge shul manye thynges falle un-to thee
whiche thou shalt nat mowe[2] suffre.' "

" Certes," quod Prudence, " I graunte yow
that over muchel suffraunce nys nat good, but
[7080] yet ne folweth it nat ther-of that every
persone to whom men doon vileynye take of it
vengeance, for that aperteneth and longeth[3] al
oonly to the juges, for they shul venge the
vileynyes and injuries ; and ther-fore tho two
auctoritees that ye han seyd above been oonly
understonden in the juges, for whan they suf-
tren over muchel the wronges and the vileynyes

---

[1] Summon.　[2] Be able to.　[3] Belongeth.

to be doon withouten punysshynge, they sompne nat a man al oonly for to do newe wronges, but they comanden it.   Also a wys man seith that the juge that correcteth nat the synnere comandeth and biddeth hym do synne ; and the juges and sovereyns myghten in hir land so muchel suffre of the shrewes and mysdoeres, that they sholden, by swich suffrance, by proces of tyme wexen of swich power and myght that they sholden putte out the juges and the sovereyns from hir places, and atte laste maken hem lesen [1] hire lordshipes.

" But lat us now putte [2] that ye have leve to [7090] venge yow.   I seye ye been nat of myght and power as now to venge yow, for if ye wole maken comparisoun un-to the myght of youre adversaries, ye shul fynde in manye thynges that I have shewed yow er this that hire condicioun is bettre than youres ; and therfore seye I that it is good as now that ye suffre and be pacient.

" Forthermoore, ye knowen wel that after the comune sawe, it is a woodnesse [3] a man to stryve with a stranger, or a moore myghty man than he is hym self ; and for to stryve with a man of evene strengthe, that is to seyn, with as stronge a man as he, it is peril ; and for to stryve with a weyker [4] man, it is folie ; and therfore sholde a man flee stryvynge as muche' as

---

[1] Lose.   [2] Put it, suppose.   [3] Madness.   [4] Weaker.

he myghte; for Salomon seith, 'It is a greet worshipe to a man to kepen hym fro noyse and stryf.' And if it so bifalle or happe that a man of gretter myght and strengthe than thou art do thee grevaunce, studie and bisye thee rather to stille the same grevaunce, than for to [7100] venge thee, for Senec seith, that 'He putteth hym in greet peril that stryveth with a gretter man than he is hym self;' and Catoun seith, 'If a man of hyer estaat or degree, or moore myghty than thou, do thee anoy[1] or grevaunce, suffre hym, for he that oones hath greved thee, another tyme may releeve thee and helpe.'

"Yet sette I caas[2] ye have bothe myght and licence for to venge yow, I seye that ther be ful manye thynges that shul restreyne yow of vengeance takynge, and make yow for to en-clyne to suffre and for to han pacience in the thynges that han been doon to yow. First and foreward, if ye wole considere the defautes that been in youre owene persone, for whiche defautes God hath suffred yow have this tribu-lacioun, as I have seyd yow heer biforn; for the poete seith, that we oghte paciently taken the tribulacions that comen to us whan we thynken and consideren that we han disserved to have hem; and Seint Gregorie seith, that whan a man considereth wel the nombre of hise

[1] Harm. [2] Suppose I a case in which.

[7110] defautes and of his synnes, the peynes and the tribulaciouns that he suffreth semen the lesse un-to hym ; and in as muche as hym thynketh hise synnes moore hevy and grevous, in so muche semeth his peyne the lighter, and the esier un-to hym.

"Also ye owen [1] to enclyne and bowe youre herte to take the pacience of oure Lord Jhesu Crist, as seith Seint Peter in hise Epistles : 'Jhesu Crist,' he seith, 'hath suffred for us and geven ensample to every man to folwe and sewe [2] hym, for he dide nevere synne, ne nevere cam ther a vileynous word out of his mouth ; whan men cursed hym he cursed hem noght, and whan men betten [3] hym he manaced [4] hem noght.' Also the grete pacience which the seintes that been in paradys han had in tribulaciouns that they han ysuffred with-outen hir desert or gilt oghte muchel stiren yow to pacience. Forthermoore, ye sholde enforce yow [7120] to have pacience, consideryge that the tribulaciouns of this world but litel while endure, and soone passed been and goone, and the joye that a man seketh to have by pacience in tribulaciouns is perdurable [5] after that : the Apostle seith in his Epistle, 'The joye of God,' he seith, 'is perdurable,' that is to seyn, evere lastynge.

"Also trowe and bileveth stedefastly that he

[1] Ought. [2] Pursue. [3] Beat.   Menaced [5] Very durable.

nys nat wel ynorissed, ne wel ytaught, that kan
nat have pacience, or wol nat receyve pacience ,
for Salomon seith that the doctrine and the wit
of a man is knowen by pacience. And in another place he seith that he that is pacient
governeth hym by greet prudence. And the
same Salomon seith, 'The angry and wrathful
man maketh noyses,[1] and the pacient man
atempreth[2] hem and stilleth.' He seith also,
' It is moore worth to be pacient, than for to
be right strong,' and he that may have the
lordshipe of his owene herte is moore to preyse
than he that by his force or strengthe taketh
grete citees ; and therfore seith Seint Jame in
his Epistle, that pacience is a greet vertu of
perfeccioun."

[7130] "Certes," quod Melibee, " I graunte
yow, dame Prudence, that pacience is a greet
vertu of perfeccioun, but every man may nat
have the perfeccioun that ye seken, ne I nam
nat of the nombre of right parfite men, for myn
herte may nevere been in pees un-to the tyme
it be venged ; and al be it so that it was greet
peril to myne enemys to do me a vileynye in
takynge vengeance up-on me, yet tooken they
noon heede of the peril, but fulfilleden hir
wikked wyl, and hir corage ;[3] and therfore, me
thynketh, men oghten nat repreve me, though
I putte me in a litel peril for to venge me

---

[1] Quarrels. [2] Moderateth. [3] Inclination.

and though I do a greet excesse, that is to
seyn, that I venge oon outrage by another."

" A ! " quod dame Prudence, "ye seyn youre
wyl and as yow liketh, but in no caas of the
world a man sholde nat doon outrage, ne ex-
[7140] cesse, for to vengen hym, for Cassidore
seith that as yvele dooth he that vengeth hym
by outrage as he that dooth the outrage ; and
therfore, ye shul venge yow after the ordre of
right, that is to seyn, by the lawe, and noght by
excesse ne by outrage. And also, if ye wol
venge yow of the outrage of youre adversaries
in oother manere than right comandeth, ye
synnen, and therfore seith Senec, that a man
shal nevere vengen shrewednesse [1] by shrewednesse. And if ye seye that right axeth a man
to defenden violence by violence, and fightyng
by fightyng, certes, ye seye sooth, whan the
defense is doon anon with-outen intervalle or
with-outen tariyng or delay, for to deffenden
hym and nat for to vengen hym. And it bihoveth that a man putte swich attemperance [2]
in his deffense that men have no cause ne matiere [3] to repreven hym that deffendeth hym of
excesse and outrage, for ellis were it agayn resoun. *Pardee* ye knowen wel that ye maken
no deffense as now for to deffende yow, but for
[7150] to venge yow, and so sheweth it that ye
han no wyl to do youre dede attemprely, and

[1] **Wickedness.**   [2] **Moderation.**   [3] Occasion (Fr *matière*)

therfore me thynketh that pacience is good,
for Salomon seith that he that is nat pacient
shal have greet harm."

"Certes," quod Melibee, "I graunte yow
that whan a man is inpacient and wrooth, of
that that toucheth hym noght and that aperteneth nat un-to hym, though it harme hym, it
is no wonder, for the lawe seith that he is cou-
pable [1] that entremetteth [2] or medleth with
swych thyng as aperteneth nat un-to hym.
And Salomon seith, that he that entremetteth
hym of the noyse or strif of another man is
lyk to hym that taketh an hound by the eris;
for right as he that taketh a straunge hound by
the eris is outherwhile [3] biten with the hound,
right in the same wise is it resoun that he have
harm that by his inpacience medleth hym of
the noyse of another man where-as it aperteneth nat un-to hym. But ye knowen wel that
this dede, that is to seyn, my grief and my disese,[4] toucheth me right ny, and therfore, though
I be wrooth and inpacient, it is no merveille;
and, savynge youre grace, I kan nat seen that
it myghte greetly harme me though I tooke
[7160] vengeaunce, for I am richer and moore
myghty than myne enemys been. And wel
knowen ye that by moneye and by havynge
grete possessions been alle the thynges of this
world governed; and Salomon seith, that alle
thynges obeyen to moneye.

[1] Culpable   [2] Intermeddleth.   [3] At times   [4] Discomfort.

Whan Prudence hadde herd hir housbonde avanten hym of his richesse and of his moneye, dispreisynge the power of hise adversaries, she spak, and seyde in this wise: "Certes, deere sire, I graunte yow that ye been riche and myghty, and that the richesses been goode to hem that han wel ygeten hem and wel konne usen hem; for, right as the body of a man may nat lyven with-oute the soule, namoore may it lyve with-outen temporeel goodes; and for richesses may a man gete hym grete freendes. And therfore seith Pamphilles,[1] 'If a netherdes doghter,' seith he, 'be riche, she may chesen of a thousand men [which she wol take to her housebonde'[2]], for of a thousand men oon wol [7170] nat forsaken hire ne refusen hire. And this Pamphilles seith also, 'If thow be right happy, that is to seyn, if thou be right riche, thou shalt fynde a greet nombre of felawes and freendes; and if thy fortune change that thou wexe povre, farewel freendshipe and felawe-shipe, for thou shalt be al alloone with-outen any compaignye, but if it be the compaignye of povre folk.' And yet seith this Pamphilles moreover, that they that been thralle and bonde of lynage shullen been maad worthy and noble by the richesses; and right so as by richesses ther comen manye goodes, right so by poverte come ther manye harmes and yveles, for greet

---

[1] Cf. l. 15,886. [2] Not in Elles. MS From Hengwrt MS.

poverte constreyneth a man to do manye yveles,
and therfore clepeth Cassidore poverte the
mooder of ruyne, — that is to seyn, the mooder of overthrowynge or fallynge doun. And
therfore seith Piers Alfonce, ' Oon of the gretteste adversitees of this world is whan a free
man by kynde [1] or by burthe is constreyned by
poverte to eten the almesse of his enemy ;' and
[7180] the same seith Innocent in oon of hise
bookes ; he seith that sorweful and myshappy
is the condicioun of a povre beggere, for if he
axe nat his mete he dyeth for hunger, and if
he axe, he dyeth for shame, and algates [2] necessitee constreyneth hym to axe. And therfore
seith Salomon that bet it is to dye than for to
have swich poverte. And as the same Salomon seith, ' Bettre it is to dye of bitter deeth
than for to lyven in swich wise.' By thise resons that I have seid un-to yow, and by manye
othere resons that I koude seye, I graunte yow
that richesses been goode to hem that geten
hem wel and to hem that wel usen tho richesses. And therfore wol I shewe yow hou ye
shul have yow, and how ye shul bere yow in
gaderynge of richesses, and in what manere ye
shul usen hem.

" First, ye shul geten hem with-outen greet
desir, by good leyser, sokyngly, [3] and nat over
nastily ; for a man that is to desirynge to gete

---

[1] Nature. [2] Notwithstanding. [3] Suckingly, gently.

richesses abaundoneth hym first to thefte, and
[7190] to alle other yveles ; and therfore seith
Salomon, ' He that hasteth hym to bisily to
wexe riche shal be noon innocent.' He seith
also, that the richesse that hastily cometh to
a man soone and lightly[1] gooth and passeth fro
a man ; but that richesse that cometh litel and
litel wexeth alwey and multiplieth. And, sire,
ye shul geten richesses by youre wit and by
youre travaille un-to youre profit, and that
with-outen wrong or harm doynge to any oother
persone, for the lawe seith that ther maketh
no man himselven riche if he do harm to another wight : this is to seyn, that nature deffendeth[2] and forbedeth by right that no man
make hym-self riche un-to the harm of another
persone. And Tullius seith that no sorwe, ne
no drede of deeth, ne no thyng that may falle
un-to a man, is so muchel agayns nature as a
man to encressen his owene profit to the harm
of another man. And though the grete men
and the myghty men geten richesses moore
[7200] lightly than thou, yet shaltou nat been
ydel ne slow to do thy profit, for thou shalt in
alle wise flee ydelnesse ; for Salomon seith that
ydelnesse techeth a man to do manye yveles.
And the same Salomon seith that he that trav-
ailleth and bisieth hym to tilien his land shal
eten breed, but he that is ydel and casteth hym

---

[1] Easily. [2] Prohibiteth.

to no bisynesse ne occupacioun shal falle in-to
poverte, and dye for hunger. And he that is
ydel and slow kan nevere fynde covenable [1]
tyme for to doon his profit ; for ther is a versi-
fiour seith that the ydel man excuseth hym in
wynter by cause of the grete coold, and in
somer by enchesoun [2] of the heete. For thise
causes seith Caton, ' Waketh and enclyneth nat
yow over muchel for to slepe, for over muchel
reste norisseth and causeth manye vices.' And
therfore seith Seint Jerome, ' Dooth somme
goodes, that the devel, which is oure enemy,
ne fynde yow nat unocupied, for the devel ne
taketh nat lightly un-to his werkynge swiche as
he fyndeth occupied in goode werkes.'

"Thanne thus in getynge richesses ye mosten
[7210] flee ydelnesse ; and afterward ye shul use
the richesses whiche ye have geten by youre
wit and by youre travaille, in swich a manere
that men holde nat yow to scars, ne to spar-
ynge, ne to fool large, [3] — that is to seyn, over
large a spendere ; for right as men blamen an
avaricious man by cause of his scarsetee [4] and
chyngerie, [5] in the same wise is he to blame that
spendeth over largely. And therfore seith Caton, ' Use,' he seith, ' thy richesses that thou
hast geten in swich a manere that men have no
matiere ne cause to calle thee neither wrecche

---

[1] Convenient.　[2] Occasion.　[3] Too extravagant.　[4] Penuriousness
Niggardness (Fr. *chiche*).　Cf. l. 13,524.

ne chynche ;[1] for it is a greet shame to a man
to have a povere herte and a riche purs.' He
seith also, ' The goodes that thou hast ygeten,
use hem by mesure, that is to seyn, spende
hem mesurably ; for they that folily [2] wasten
and despenden the goodes that they han, whan
they han namoore propre [3] of hir owene they
shapen hem to take the goodes of another man.'

[7220] " I seye thanne that ye shul fleen avarice, usynge youre richesses in swich manere
that men seye nat that youre richesses been
yburyed, but that ye have hem in youre myght
and in youre weeldynge ; [4] for a wys man repreveth [5] the avaricious man and seith thus in
two vers : ' Wherto and why burieth a man hise
goodes by his grete avarice, and knoweth wel
that nedes moste he dye, for deeth is the ende
of every man, as in this present lyf ; and for
what cause or enchesoun [6] joyneth he hym or
knytteth he hym so faste un-to hise goodes
that alle hise wittes mowen nat disseveren hym
or departen [7] hym from hise goodes ; and knoweth wel, or oghte knowe, that whan he is deed
he shal no thyng bere with hym out of this
world ? ' And ther-fore seith Seint Augustyn,
that the avaricious man is likned un-to helle,
[7230] that the moore it swelweth [8] the moore
desir it hath to swelwe and devoure. And as

---

[1] Villain nor churl. [2] Foolishly. [3] Property. [4] Power. [5] Re-
proveth. [6] Occasion. [7] Separate. [8] Swalloweth.

wel as ye wolde eschewe to be called an avari
cious man or chynche, as wel sholde ye kepe
yow and governe yow in swich a wise that men
calle yow nat fool-large.[1] Therfore seith Tullius, 'The goodes,' he seith, 'of thyn hous ne
sholde nat been hyd, ne kept so cloos but that
they myghte been opened by pitee and debonairetee,'[2] — that is to seyn, to geven part to
hem that han greet nede, — 'ne thy goodes
shullen nat been so opene to been every mannes
goodes.'

   " Afterward, in getynge of youre richesses and
in usynge hem, ye shul alwey have thre thynges
in youre herte, that is to seyn, oure Lord God,
conscience, and good name. First, ye shul
have God in youre herte, and for no richesse ye
shullen do no thyng which may in any manere
displese God, that is youre creatour and mak-
[7240] ere ; for after the word of Salomon, 'It
is bettre to have a litel good with the love of
God, than to have muchel good and tresour
and lese[3] the love of his Lord God.' And the
prophete seith that bettre it is to been a good
man and have litel good and tresour, than to
been holden a shrewe, and have grete richesses. And yet seye I ferthermoore, that ye
sholde alwey doon youre bisynesse to gete yow
richesses, so that ye gete hem with good con
science, and thapostle seith that ther nys thyng

---

[1] Foolishly liberal.   [2] Kindliness.   [3] Lose.

in this world of which we sholden have so greet joye as whan oure conscience bereth us good witnesse ; and the wise man seith, 'The substance of a man is ful good whan synne is nat in mannes conscience.'

"Afterward, in getynge of youre richesses and in usynge of hem, yow moste have greet bisynesse and greet diligence that youre goode [7250] name be alwey kept and conserved, for Salomon seith that bettre it is and moore it availleth a man to have a good name than for to have grete richesses. And therfore he seith in another place, 'Do greet diligence,' seith Salomon, 'in kepyng of thy freend and of thy goode name, for it shal lenger abide with thee than any tresour, be it never so precious.' And certes, he sholde nat be called a gentil man that after God and good conscience, alle thynges left, ne dooth his diligence and bisynesse to kepen his good name. And Cassidore seith that it is signe of gentil herte whan a man loveth and desireth to han a good name. And therfore seith Seint Augustyn, that ther been two thynges that arn necessarie and nedefulle, and that is, good conscience and good loos ;[1] that is to seyn, good conscience to thyn owene persone inward, and good loos for thy neighebore outward. And he that trusteth hym so muchel in his gooode conscience that he

[1] Fame (Latin, *laus*, good repute).

displeseth and setteth at noght his goode name
or loos, and rekketh noght though he kepe nat
his goode name, nys but a crueel cherl.

[7260] " Sire, now have I shewed yow how ye
shul do in getynge richesses, and how ye shullen usen hem, and I se wel that for the trust
that ye han in youre richesses ye wole moeve
werre and bataille. I conseille yow that ye
bigynne no werre in trust of youre richesses,
for they ne suffisen noght werres to mayntene.
And therfore seith a philosophre, ' That man
that desireth and wole algates[1] han werre shal
nevere have suffisaunce, for the richer that he
is, the gretter despenses moste he make if he
wole have worshipe and victorie.' And Salomon seith that the gretter richesses that a man
hath, the mo despendours he hath. And, deere
sire, al be it so that for youre richesses ye
mowe have muchel folk, yet bihoveth it nat,
ne it is nat good to bigynne werre where as ye
mowe in oother manere have pees un-to youre
worshipe and profit. For the victories of batailles that been in this world lyen nat in greet
nombre or multitude of the peple, ne in the
vertu[2] of man, but it lith in the wyl and in the
hand of oure Lord God Almyghty.

[7270] " And therfore Judas Machabeus,
which was Goddes knyght, whan he sholde fighte
agayn his adversarie that hadde a greet nombre

---

[1] Always. [2] Valor.

and a gretter multitude of folk and strenger
than was this peple of Machabee, yet he re-
conforted his litel compaignye, and seyde right
in this wise: 'Als lightly,'[1] quod he, 'may oure
Lord God Almyghty geve victorie to a fewe
folk as to many folk, for the victorie of a ba-
taile comth nat by the grete nombre of peple,
but it come from oure Lord God of hevene.'

"And, deere sire, for as muchel as ther is no
man certein if he be worthy that God geve hym
victorie [no more than he is sure whether he is
worthy of the love of God [2]] or naught. After
that Salomon seith, 'Therfore every man sholde
greetly drede werres to bigynne;' and by cause
that in batailles fallen manye perils, and happeth outher while that as soone is the grete
[7280] man slayn as the litel man; and as it is
writen in the Seconde book of Kynges, 'The
dedes of batailles been aventurouse and no
thyng certeyne, for as lightly is oon hurt with
a spere as another;' and for ther is gret peril
in werre, therfore sholde a man flee and eschue
werre, in as muchel as a man may goodly, for
Salomon seith, 'He that loveth peril shal falle
in peril.'"

After that dame Prudence hadde spoken in
this manere, Melibee answerde and seyde, "I
see wel, dame Prudence, that by youre faire
wordes, and by youre resouns that ye han

---

[1] Easily.   Not in Elles. MS.   Supplied from the French.

shewed me, that the werre liketh yow no thyng,
but I have nat yet herd youre conseil how I
shal do in this nede."

"Certes," quod she, "I conseille yow that
ye accorde with youre adversaries and that ye
have pees with hem; for Seint Jame seith, in
hise Epistles, that by concord and pees the
smale richesses wexen grete, and by debaat
and discord the grete richesses fallen doun :
[7290] and ye knowen wel that oon of the gretteste and moost sovereyn thyng that is in this
world is unytee and pees.   And therfore seyde
oure Lord Jhesu Crist to hise Apostles in this
wise, ' Wel happy and blessed been they that
loven and purchacen pees, for they been called
children of God.' "

"A !" quod Melibee, "now se I wel that ye
loven nat myn honour ne my worshipe.   Ye
knowen wel that myne adversaries han bigonnen this debaat and bryge [1] by hire outrage,
and ye se wel that they ne requeren ne preyen
me nat of pees, ne they asken nat to be reconsiled.   Wol ye thanne that I go and meke me
and obeye me to hem and crie hem mercy?
For sothe that were nat my worshipe ; [2] for
right as men seyn that over greet hoomlynesse
engendreth dispreisynge, so fareth it by to
greet humylitee or mekenesse."

---

[1] Contention (French, *brigue*, intrigue; Italian, *briga*, quarrel).
Honor.

Thanne bigan dame Prudence to maken sem-
[7300] blant[1] of wratthe, and seyde, " Certes,
sire, sauf youre grace, I love youre honour and
youre profit as I do myn owene, and evere
have doon ; ne ye, ne noon oother, syen[2] nevere
the contrarie ! And yit if I hadde seyd that ye
sholde han purchaced the pees and the recon-
siliacioun, I ne hadde nat muchel mystaken
me, ne seyd amys, for the wise man seith, ' The
dissensioun bigynneth by another man and
the reconsilyng by-gynneth by thy self ; ' and
the prophete seith, ' Flee shrewednesse and do
goodnesse, seke pees and folwe it, as muchel
as in thee is.' Yet seye I nat that ye shul
rather pursue to youre adversaries for pees
than they shuln to yow ; for I knowe wel that
ye been so hard-herted that ye wol do no thyng
for me ; and Salomon seith, ' He that hath over
hard an herte atte laste he shal myshappe and
mystyde.' "[3]

Whanne Melibee hadde herd dame Prudence maken semblant of wratthe, he seyde
[7310] in this wise : " Dame, I prey yow that
ye be nat displesed of thynges that I seye, for
ye knowe wel that I am angry and wrooth, and
that is no wonder, and they that been wrothe
witen nat wel what they don ne what they seyn ;
therfore the prophete seith that troubled eyen
han no cleer sighte. But seyeth and conseil

---

[1] Appearance.   [2] Saw.   [3] Have misfortune.

eth me as yow liketh, for I am redy to do right as ye wol desire, and if ye repreve me of my folye I am the moore holden to love yow and preyse yow, for Salomon seith that he that repreveth hym that dooth folye he shal fynde gretter grace than he that deceyveth hym by sweete wordes."

Thanne seide dame Prudence, "I make no semblant of wratthe ne anger but for youre grete profit, for Salomon seith, ' He is moore worth that repreveth or chideth a fool for his folye, shewynge hym semblant of wratthe, than [7320] he that supporteth hym and preyseth hym in his mysdoynge, and laugheth at his folye.' And this same Salomon seith afterward that by the sorweful visage of a man, that is to seyn, by the sory and hevy contenaunce of a man, the fool correcteth and amendeth hym self."

Thanne seyde Melibee, "I shal nat konne[1] unswere to so manye faire resouns as ye putten to me and shewen ; seyeth shortly youre wyl and youre conseil, and I am al redy to fulfille and parfourne it."

Thanne dame Prudence discovered[2] al hir wyl to hym, and seyde, "I conseille yow," quod she, "aboven alle thynges, that ye make pees bitwene God and yow, and beth reconsiled un-to hym and to his grace ; for as I have seyd yow heer biforn, God hath suffred yow to

---

[1] Be able to.   [2] Expressed.

have this tribulacioun and disese[1] for youre
synnes, and if ye do as I sey yow, God wol
[7330] sende youre adversaries un-to yow and
maken hem fallen at youre feet redy to do youre
wyl and youre comandementz ; for Salomon
seith, ' Whan the condicioun of man is plesaunt
and likynge to God, he chaungeth the hertes of
the mannes adversaries and constreyneth hem
to biseken hym of pees and of grace.' And I
prey yow, lat me speke with youre adversaries
in privee place, for they shul nat knowe that it
be of youre wyl or youre assent, and thanne,
whan I knowe hir wil and hire entente, I may
conseille yow the moore seurely."

"Dame," quod Melibee, "dooth youre wil
and youre likynge, for I putte me hoolly in
youre disposicioun and ordinaunce."

Thanne dame Prudence, whan she saugh the
goode wyl of hir housbonde, delibered[2] and
took avys in hir self, thinkinge how she myghte
brynge this nede un-to a good conclusioun and
[7340] to a good ende. And whan she saugh
hir tyme she sente for thise adversaries to come
un-to hire in to a pryvee place, and shewed
wisely un-to hem the grete goodes that comen
of pees, and the grete harmes and perils that
been in werre, and seyde to hem in a goodly
manere hou that hem oughten have greet repentaunce of the injurie and wrong that they

---

[1] Trouble.   [2] Deliberated.

hadden doon to Melibee, hir lord, and to hire, and to hire doghter.

And whan they herden the goodliche wordes of dame Prudence, they weren so supprised and ravysshed, and hadden so greet joye of hire, that wonder was to telle. "A! lady," quod they, "ye han shewed un-to us the blessynge of swetnesse after the sawe [1] of David the prophete, for the reconsilynge which we been nat worthy to have in no manere, but we oghte requeren it with greet contricioun and humyli-[7350] tee, ye, of youre grete goodnesse, have presented unto us. Now se we wel that the science and the konnynge [2] of Salomon is ful trewe, for he seith that sweete wordes multiplien and encreesen freendes, and maken shrewes to be debonaire and meeke.

"Certes," quod they, "we putten oure dede and al oure matere and cause al hoolly in youre goode wyl, and been redy to obeye to the speche and comandement of my lord Melibee. And therfore, deere and benygne lady, we preien yow and biseke yow as mekely as we konne and mowen, [3] that it lyke [4] un-to youre grete goodnesse to fulfillen in dede youre goodliche wordes, for we consideren and knowechen [5] that we han offended and greved my lord Melibee out of mesure, so ferforth that we be

[1] Saying, maxim. [2] Knowledge and the wisdom. [3] May, are able Please. [5] Acknowledge.

nat of power to maken hise amendes, and therfore we oblige and bynden us and oure freendes
to doon al his wyl and hise comandementz.
[7360] But peraventure he hath swich hevynesse
and swich wratthe to us ward by cause of oure
offense, that he wole enjoyne us swich a peyne
as we mowe nat bere ne susteene, and therfore,
noble lady, we biseke to youre wommanly pitee
to taken swich avysement in this nede that we
ne oure freendes be nat desherited ne destroyed
thurgh oure folye."

"Certes," quod Prudence, "it is an hard
thyng and right perilous that a man putte hym
al outrely[1] in the arbitracioun and juggement,
and in the myght and power of hise enemys,
for Salomon seith, 'Leeveth[2] me, and geveth
credence to that I shal seyn; I seye,' quod
he, 'ye peple, folk and governours of hooly
chirche, to thy sone, to thy wyf, to thy freend,
ne to thy broother, ne geve thou nevere myght
ne maistrie of thy body whil thou lyvest.'

"Now sithen he deffendeth[3] that man shal
nat geven to his broother, ne to his freend, the
[7370] myght of his body, by strenger resoun he
deffendeth and forbedeth a man to geven hym
self to his enemy. And nathelees I conseille
you that ye mystruste nat my lord, for I woot
wel and knowe verraily that he is debonaire[4]
and meeke, large,[5] curteys, and no thyng desir·

[1] **Utterly.**   [2] Believe.   [3] Forbiddetn.   [4] Mild.   [5] Generous.

ous, ne coveitous of good ne richesse ; for ther
nys no thyng in this world that he desireth
save oonly worshipe and honour. Forthermoore I knowe wel and am right seur that he
shal no thyng doon in this nede with-outen my
conseil, and I shal so werken in this cause
that, by grace of oure Lord God, ye shul been
reconsiled un-to us."

Thanne seyden they with o voys, "Worshipful lady, we putten us and oure goodes al fully
in youre wil and disposicioun, and been redy
to comen what day that it like un-to youre noblesse to lymyte us or assigne us, for to maken
oure obligacioun and boond as strong as it
[7380] liketh un-to youre goodnesse, that we
mowe fulfille the wille of yow and of my lord
Melibee."

Whan dame Prudence hadde herd the an-
sweres of thise men, she bad hem goon agayn
prively, and she retourned to hir lord Melibee,
and tolde hym how she foond hise adversaries
ful repentant, knowelechynge ful lowely hir
synnes and trespas, and how they were redy to
suffren all peyne, requirynge and preiynge hym
of mercy and pitee.

Thanne seyde Melibee, "He is wel worthy
to have pardoun and forgifnesse of his synne
that excuseth nat his synne, but knowelecheth
it and repenteth hym, axinge indulgence. For
Senec seith, 'Ther is the remissioun and forgif

nesse, where as confessioun is, for confessioun
is neighebore to innocence' [and he saith in
another place that he that hath shame of his
synne, and knowelecheth it, is worthi remys-
sioun[1]]; and therfore I assente and conforme
[7390] me to have pees; but it is good that we
do it nat with-outen the assent and wyl of oure
freendes."

Thanne was Prudence right glad and joyeful,
and seyde, "Certes, sire," quod she, "ye han
wel and goodly answered, for right as by the
conseil, assent and helpe of youre freendes, ye
han been stired to venge yow and maken werre,
right so with-outen hire conseil shul ye nat ac-
corden yow, ne have pees with youre adversaries; for the lawe seith, 'Ther nys no thyng
so good by wey of kynde[2] as a thyng to been
unbounde by hym that it was ybounde.'"

And thanne dame Prudence, with-outen delay or tariynge, sente anon hire messages[3] for
hire kyn and for hire olde freendes, whiche
that were trewe and wyse, and tolde hem by
ordre, in the presence of Melibee, al this mateere as it is aboven expressed and declared,
and preyden that they wolde geven hire avys
and conseil what best were to doon in this
nede. And whan Melibees freendes hadde
taken hire avys and deliberacioun of the for-
[7400] seide mateere, and hadden examyned

---

[1] Not in Elles. MS.   [2] Nature.   [3] Messengers.   Cf. l 4566.

it by greet bisynesse and greet diligence, they
gave ful conseil for to have pees and reste, and
that Melibee sholde receyve with good herte
hise adversaries to forgifnesse and mercy.

And whan dame Prudence hadde herd the
assent of hir lord Melibee, and the conseil of
hise freendes accorde with hire wille and hire
entencioun, she was wonderly glad in hire herte,
and seyde, " Ther is an old proverbe," quod
she, " seith that the goodnesse that thou mayst
do this day, do it, and abide nat, ne delaye it
nat til to morwe.   And therfore I conseille
that ye sende youre messages, swiche as been
discrete and wise, un-to youre adversaries, tell-
[7410] ynge hem on youre bihalve, that if they
wole trete of pees and of accord, that they
shape hem,[1] with-outen delay or tariyng, to
comen un-to us." Which thyng parfourned
was in dede ; and whanne thise trespassours
and repentynge folk of hire folies, — that is to
seyn, the adversaries of Melibee, — hadden herd
what thise messagers seyden un-to hem, they
weren right glad and joyeful, and answereden
ful mekely and benignely, yeldynge graces and
thankynges to hir lord Melibee and to al his
compaignye, and shopen[2] hem with-outen delay
to go with the messagers, and obeye to the
comandement of hir lord Melibee.

And right anon they tooken hire wey to the

[1] Prepare.   [2] Prepared

court of Melibee, and tooken with hem somme
of hire trewe freendes to maken feith for hem
[7420] and for to been hire borwes,[1] and whan
they were comen to the presence of Melibee,
he seyde hem thise wordes : "It standeth thus,"
quod Melibee, " and sooth it is, that ye, causelees and with-outen skile[2] and resoun, han
doon grete injuries and wronges to me and to
my wyf Prudence, and to my doghter also ; for
ye han entred in to myn hous by violence, and
have doon swich outrage that alle men knowen
wel that ye have disserved the deeth, and therfore wol I knowe and wite of yow wheither ye
wol putte the punyssement and the chastisynge and the vengeance of this outrage in the
wyl of me and of my wyf Prudence, or ye wol
nat ? "

Thanne the wiseste of hem thre answerde
for hem alle, and seyde, " Sire," quod he, " we
knowen wel that we been unworthy to comen
un-to the court of so greet a lord, and so wor-
[7430] thy as ye been, for we han so greetly
mystaken[3] us, and han offended and agilt[4] in
swich a wise agayn youre heigh lordshipe that
trewely we han disserved the deeth ; but yet
for the grete goodnesse and debonairetee that
al the world witnesseth in youre persone, we
submytten us to the excellence and benignitee
of youre gracious lordshipe, and been redy to

1 Pledges.   2 Cause.   3 Erred.   4 Sinned.

obeie to alle youre comandementz, bisekynge yow that of youre merciable pitee ye wol considere oure grete repentaunce and lough [1] submyssioun, and graunten us forgevenesse of oure outrageous trespas and offense; for wel we knowe that youre liberal grace and mercy strecchen hem ferther in-to goodnesse than doon oure outrageouse giltes and trespas in-to wikkednesse; al be it that cursedly and dampnablely we han agilt agayn youre heigh lordshipe."

Thanne Melibee took hem up fro the ground [7440] ful benignely, and receyved hire obligaciouns and hir boondes by hire othes up-on hire plegges and borwes,[2] and assigned hem a certeyn day to retourne un-to his court, for to accepte and receyve the sentence and juggement that Melibee wolde comande to be doon on hem by the causes aforeseyd; whiche thynges ordeyned, every man retourned to his hous.

And whan that dame Prudence saugh hir tyme, she freyned [3] and axed hir lord Melibee what vengeance he thoughte to taken of hise adversaries.

To which Melibee answerde and seyde, "Certes," quod he, "I thynke and purpose me fully to desherite hem of al that evere they han, and for to putte hem in exil for evere."

"Certes," quod dame Prudence, "this were

[1] Low. [2] Pledges and securities. [3] Questioned.

a crueel sentence and muchel agayn resoun ;
for ye been riche ynough and han no nede of
[7450] oother mennes good, and ye myghte
lightly in this wise gete yow a coveitous name,
which is a vicious thyng and oghte been es-
chued of every good man ; for after the sawe
of the word of the Apostle, ' Coveitise is roote
of alle harmes.'   And therfore it were bettre
for yow to lese so muchel good of youre owene
than for to taken of hir good in this manere ;
for bettre it is to lesen with worshipe,[1] than it
is to wynne with vileynye and shame ; and
everi man oghte to doon his diligence and his
bisynesse to geten hym a good name.   And
yet shal he nat oonly bisie hym in kepynge of
his good name, but he shal also enforcen hym
alwey to do som thyng by which he may re-
novelle [2] his good name ; for it is writen ' that
the olde good loos [3] and good name of a man
is soone goon and passed whan it is nat newed
ne renovelled.'

"And as touchynge that ye seyn ye wole ex-
[7460] ile youre adversaries, that thynketh me
muchel agayn resoun, and out of mesure, considered the power that they han geve yow up-on
hem self.   And it is writen 'hat he is worthy
to lesen his privilege that mysuseth the myght
and the power that is geven hym.   And I sette
cas,[4] ye myghte enjoyne hem that peyne by

1 Honor.   2 Renew.   3 Praise.   4 Put the case.

right and by lawe, which I trowe ye mowe nat do. I seye ye mighte nat putten it to execucioun per-aventure, and thanne were it likly to retourne to the werre as it was biforn ; and therfore if ye wole that men do yow obeisance, ye moste deemen [1] moore curteisly, this is to seyn, ye moste geven moore esy sentences and juggementz. For it is writen that he that moost curteisly comandeth, to hym men moost [7470] obeyen. And therfore I prey yow that in this necessitee and in this nede ye caste yow [2] to overcome youre herte. For Senec seith that he that overcometh his herte overcometh twies ; and Tullius seith, ' Ther is no thyng so comendable in a greet lord as whan he is debonaire and meeke, and appeseth lightly.' [3] And I prey yow that ye wole forbere now to do vengeance in swich a manere, that youre goode name may be kept and conserved, and that men mowe have cause and mateere to preyse yow of pitee and of mercy, and that ye have no cause to repente yow of thyng that ye doon ; for Senec seith, ' He overcometh in an yvel manere that repenteth hym of his victorie.' Wherfore, I pray yow, lat mercy been in youre mynde and [7480] in youre herte, to theffect and entente that God Almyghty have mercy on yow in his laste juggement ; for Seint Jame seith in his Epistle, ' Juggement with-outen mercy shal be

---

[1] Judge. [2] Endeavor. [3] Is easily pacified.

doon to hym that hath no mercy of another wight!'"

Whanne Melibee hadde herd the grete skiles[1] and resouns of dame Prudence, and hire wise informaciouns and techynges, his herte gan enclyne to the wil of his wif, considerynge hir trewe entente, and conformed hym anon and assented fully to werken after hir conseil, and thonked God, of whom procedeth al vertu[2] and alle goodnesse, that hym sente a wyf of so greet discrecioun.

And whan the day cam that hise adversaries sholde appieren in his presence, he spak un-to hem ful goodly, and seyde in this wyse: "Al be it so that of youre pride and presumpcioun and folie, and of youre necligence and unkonnynge,[3] ye have mysborn[4] yow and tres-[7490] passed un-to me; yet, for as muche as I see and biholde youre grete humylitee, and that ye been sory and repentant of youre giltes, it constreyneth me to doon yow grace and mercy. Therfore I receyve yow to my grace and forgeve yow outrely alle the offenses, injuries and wronges that ye have doon agayn me and myne, to this effect and to this ende, that God of his endelees mercy wole at the tyme of oure diynge forgeven us oure giltes that we han trespassed to hym in this wrecched world; for doutelees if we be sory and repent-

[1] Arguments. [2] Power Ignorance. [4] Misconducted.

ant of the synnes and giltes whiche we han
trespassed in the sighte of oure Lord God, he
is so free and so merciable that he wole for-
[7500] geven us oure giltes, and bryngen us to
his blisse that nevere hath ende." *Amen.*

The murye wordes of the Hoost to the Monk.

Whan ended was my tale of Melibee,
And of Prudence and hire benignytee,
Oure Hoost seyde, " As I am feithful man,
And by that precious *corpus* Madrian,[1]
I hadde levere than a barel ale   (13,899 T.)
That good lief,[2] my wyf, hadde herd this tale!
For [3] she nys no thyng of swich pacience
As was this Melibeus wyf Prudence.
By Goddes bones ! whan I bete my knaves,
She bryngeth me forth the grete clobbed staves
And crieth, ' Slee the dogges everichoon, 7511
And brek hem, bothe bak and every boon ! '
   " And if that any neighebore of myne
Wol nat in chirche to my wyf enclyne,[4]
Or be so hardy to hire to trespace,
Whan she comth home she rampeth [5] in my
        face,
And crieth, ' False coward ! wrek [6] thy wyf !
By *corpus* bones ! I wol have thy knyf,
And thou shalt have my distaf and go spynne !

---

[1] St. Mathurin.   [2] Love.   Corpus MS. has " leef," and Petworth
'love "   [3] Not in Elles. MS.   [4] Bow.   [5] Rageth.   [6] Avenge.

Fro day to nyght, right thus she wol bigynne, —
' Allas ! ' she seith, ' that evere I was shape
To wedden a milksope or a coward ape   7522
That wol been overlad [1] with every wight !
Thou darst nat stonden by thy wyves right !'

   "This is my lif, but if that I wol fighte ;
And out at dore anon I moot me dighte,
Or elles I am but lost, but if that I
Be lik a wilde leoun, fool-hardy.
I woot wel she wol do [2] me slee som day
Som neighebore, and thanne go my way ; 7530
For I am perilous with knyf in honde ;
Al be it that I dar hire nat withstonde,
For she is byg in armes, by my feith,
That shal he fynde that hire mysdooth **or**
    seith.
But lat us passe awey fro this mateere.

   "My lord the Monk," quod he, "be myrie of
    cheere,
For ye shul telle a tale trewely.
Loo, Rouechestre [3] stant heer faste by !
Ryde forth, myn owene lord, brek **nat oure**
    game,
But by my trouthe I knowe nat youre name,[4] —
Wher [5] shal I calle yow, my lord daun John, 7541
Or daun Thomas, or elles daun Albon ?
Of what hous be ye, by youre fader kyn ?
I vowe to God, thou hast a ful fair skyn !

---

[1] Put uoon. [2] Cause. [3] The MSS. have " Rouchestre." The read-
ere adopted is suggested by Skeat. [4] Cf. l. 8404. [5] Whether.

It is a gentil pasture ther thow goost ;
Thou art nat lyk a penant,[1] or a goost.
Upon my feith, thou art som officer,
Som worthy sexteyn, or som celerer,
For by my fader soule, as to my doom[2]
Thou art a maister, whan thou art at hoom ;
No povre cloystrer, ne no novys,   755I
But a governour, both[3] wily and wys,
And therwith-al of brawnes and of bones,
A wel-farynge persone, for the nones.
I pray to God, geve hym confusioun (13,949 T.)
That first thee broghte un-to religioun.[4]
Thou woldest han been a tredefowel aright,
Haddestow as greet a leeve as thou hast myght ·
To parfourne al thy lust in engendrure
Thou haddest bigeten ful many a creature.
Allas ! why werestow so wyd a cope ?   756I
God geve me sorwe ! but and I were a pope,
Nat oonly thou, but every myghty man,
Though he were shorn ful hye upon his pan,[5]
Sholde have a wyf, — for al the world is lorn ;
Religioun hath take up al the corn (13,960 T.)
Of tredyng, and we borel[6] men been shrympes ;[7]
Of fieble trees ther comen wrecched ympes.[8]
This maketh that oure heires beth so sklendre
And feble that they may nat wel engendre ;[9]
This maketh that oure wyves wole assaye 757I
Religious folk, for ye mowe bettre paye

---

[1] Penitent.   [2] Judgment.   [3] Not in Elles. MS.   [4] A religious
order.   [5] Head.   [6] Laymen.   [7] Dwarfs.   [8] Scions.   [9] Lines 7569
7570 are not in Elles. MS.

Of Venus paiementz than mowe we. (13,967 T.)
God woot, no Lussheburghes[1] payen ye!
But be nat wrooth, my lord, for that I pleye,
Ful ofte, ' in game a sooth,' I have herd seye ! "

This worthy Monk took al in pacience
And seyde, " I wol doon al my diligence,
As fer as sowneth in-to honestee,[2]
To telle yow a tale, or two, or three ;   7580
And if yow list to herkne hyderward,
I wol yow seyn the lyf of Seint Edward,
Or ellis, first, tragedies wol I telle,
Of whiche I have an hundred in my celle.[3]

"Tragedie[4] is to seyn a certeyn storie,
As olde bookes maken us memorie,
Of hym that stood in greet prosperitee
And is yfallen out of heigh degree
In to myserie, and endeth wrecchedly ;
And they ben versified communely   7590
Of six feet, which men clepen exametron.
In prose eek been endited many oon,
And eek in meetre in many a sondry wyse ;
Lo, this declaryng oghte ynogh suffise.
Now herkneth, if yow liketh for to heere ;
But first, I yow biseeke in this mateere,
Though I by ordre telle nat thise thynges
Be it of popes, emperours, or kynges,
After hir ages as men writen fynde,
But tellen hem, som bifore and som bihynde,

Base coins.   Elles. MS. has "lussheburgh."   [2] Consists with
propriety.   [3] Religious house. Or, probably, "celle fantastik." Cf
l. 1376.   [4] Cf. l. 8373, and Boethius, bk. ii., pr. 2.

As it now comth un-to my remembraunce, 7601
Have me excused of min ignoraunce."

*Heere bigynneth The Monkes Tale, de Casibus
Virorum Illustrium.*[1]

I wol biwaille, in manere of tragedie,
The harm[2] of hem that stoode in heigh de-
     gree,   (13,998 T.)
And fillen so that ther nas no remedie
To brynge hem out of hir adversitee ;
For certein, whan that Fortune list to flee,
Ther may no man the cours of hire withholde.
Lat no man truste on blynd prosperitee ; 7609
Be war by[3] thise ensamples trewe and olde.

   At LUCIFER, — though he an angel were,
And nat a man, — at hym wol I bigynne,
For though Fortune may noon angel dere,[4]
From heigh degree yet fel he for his synne
Doun in-to helle, where he yet is inne.
O Lucifer ! brightest of angels alle,
Now artow Sathanas that mayst nat twynne[5]
Out of miserie in which that thou art falle.

   Loo ADAM, in the feeld of Damyssene.
With Goddes owene fynger wroght was he, 7620
And nat bigeten of mannes sperme unclene,

---

[1] *De Casibus Virorum Illustrium* is the title of one of the works
of Boccaccio, which began with Adam and ended with King John of
France, who was captured by the English in 1356. It was translated into Italian, Spanish, French, and English. The Monk's instances are compiled from that and various other sources. [2] Dis-
aster. [3] Elles. MS. has "of." [4] Harm. [5] Separate, depart.

And welte [1] all paradys savynge o tree.
Hadde nevere worldly man so heigh degree
As Adam, til he for mysgovernaunce
Was dryven out of hys hye prosperitee
To labour, and to helle, and to meschaunce.

Loo SAMPSON, which that was annunciat
By angel, longe er his nativitee,
And was to God Almyghty consecrat,
And stood in noblesse whil he myghte see.
Was nevere swich another as was hee,   7631
To speke of strengthe, and ther-with hardy-
          nesse ;
But to hise wyves toolde he his secree,
Thurgh which he slow hym self for wrecched-
          nesse.

Sampson, this noble almyghty champioun,
With-outen wepene save his handes tweye,
He slow and al to-rente [2] the leoun,
Toward his weddyng walkynge by the weye.
His false wyf koude hym so plese and preye
Til she his conseil knew ; and she untrewe 7640
Un-to hise foos his conseil gan biwreye,
And hym forsook, and took another newe.
Thre hundred foxes took Sampson for ire,
And alle hir tayles he togydre bond,
And sette the foxes tayles alle on fire,
For he on every tayl had knyt a brond ;
And they brende [3] alle the cornes in that lond,
And alle hire olyveres, and vynes eke.   7648

---

[1] Ruled (wieldeɑ).   [2] Completely rent.   [3] Burned.

A thousand men he slow eek with his hond,
And hadde no wepene but an asses cheke.
Whan they were slayn so thursted hym that he
Was wel ny lorn, for which he gan to preye
That God wolde on his peyne han som pitee,
And sende hym drynke, or elles moste he deye
And of this asses cheke, that was dreye,
Out of a wang-tooth [1] sprang anon a welle,
Of which he drank ynow,[2] shortly to seye ;
Thus heelpe hym God, as *Judicum* [3] can telle.
By verray force at Gazan, on a nyght,
Maugree Philistiens of that citee,   (14,054 T.)
The gates of the toun he hath up-plyght,   7661
And on his bak ycaryed hem hath hee
Hye on an hille, that men myghte hem see.

O noble, almyghty Sampson, lief and deere,
Had thou nat toold to wommen thy secree,
In all this world ne hadde been thy peere !
This Sampson nevere ciser [4] drank, ne wyn,
Ne on his heed cam rasour noon, ne sheere,
By precept of the messager divyn ;
For alle hise strengthes in hise heeres weere ;
And fully twenty wynter, yeer by yeere,   7671
He hadde of Israel the governaunce ;
But soone shal he wepe many a teere,
For wommen shal hym bryngen to meschaunce

Un-to his lemman [5] Dalida he tolde
That in hise heeris al his strengthe lay,

---

[1] Jaw-tooth.   [2] Enough.   Elles. MS. has "anon."   [3] The book
of Judges.   [4] Strong drink (Lat. *sicera*).   [5] Sweetheart.

And falsly to hise foomen she hym solde ;
And slepynge in hir barm [1] up-on a day   7678
She made to clippe or shere hise heres away,
And made hise foomen al his craft espyen ;
And whan that they hym foond in this array,
They bounde hym faste and putten out hise
        eyen.
But er his heer were clipped or yshave,
Ther was no boond with which men myghte
        him bynde ;
But now is he in prison in a cave,[2]
Where as they made hym at the queerne [3]
        grynde.

O noble Sampson, strongest of mankynde !
O whilom juge, in glorie and in richesse ! 7688
Now maystow wepen with thyne eyen blynde,
Sith thou fro wele art falle in wrecchednesse.

    The ende of this caytyf was as I shal seye ;
Hise foomen made a feeste up-on a day,
And made hym as a fool biforn hem pleye ;
And this was in a temple of greet array ;
But atte laste he made a foul affray ; [4]
For he the pilers shook and made hem falle,
And doun fil temple and al, and ther it lay ;
And slow hym self, and eek his foomen alle :
This is to seyn, the prynces everichoon ;
And eek thre thousand bodyes were ther slayn
With fallynge of the grete temple of stoon.
Of Sampson now wol I na moore sayn ;   7702

[1] Lap.   [2] Cellar, vault   [3] Mill   [4] Terror.

Beth war by this ensample oold and playn
That no men telle hir conseil til hir wyves
Of swich thyng as they wolde han secree fayn,
If that it touche hir lymes or hir lyves. (14,100 T.)

Off HERCULES, the sovereyn conquerour,
Syngen hise werkes, laude, and heigh renoun ;
For in his tyme of strengthe he was the flour.
He slow, and rafte the skyn of the leoun ; 7710
He of Centauros leyde the boost [1] adoun ;
He Arpies slow, the crueel bryddes felle ;
He golden apples refte of the dragoun ;
He drow out Cerberus, the hound of helle ;
He slow the crueel tyrant Busirus,
And made his hors to frete [2] hym flessh and
        boon ;
He slow the firy serpent [3] venymus ;
Of Acheloys hornes two he brak oon ;
And he slow Cacus in a cave of stoon ;
He slow the geant Antheus the stronge ; 7720
He slow the grisly boor, and that anon ;
And bar the hevene on his nekke longe. [4]
Was nevere wight sith that this world bigan,
That slow so manye monstres as dide he ;
Thurgh-out this wyde world his name ran, —
What for his strengthe and for his heigh boun
        tee, [5] —
And every reawme [6] wente he for to see.
He was so stroong that no man myghte hym
        lette ;

[1] Boast.   [2] Eat.   [3] The Hydra.   [4] Long time.   [5] Great goodness
Kingdom.

At bothe the worldes endes, seith Trophee,[1]
In stide of boundes he a pileer[2] sette.   7730
    A lemman hadde this noble champioun
That highte Dianira, fressh as May ;
And as thise clerkes maken mentioun,
She hath hym sent a sherte, fressh and gay.
Allas, this sherte — allas, and weylaway ! —
Evenymed was so subtilly with-alle,
That er that he had wered it half a day,
It made his flessh al from hise bones falle ;
But nathelees somme clerkes hire excusen
By oon that highte Nessus, that it maked. 7740
Be as be may, I wol hire noght accusen ;
But on his bak this sherte he wered al naked
Til that his flessh was for the venym blaked ;
And whan he saugh noon oother remedye,
In hoote coles he hath hym-selven raked ;
For with no venym deigned hym to dye.
    Thus starf this worthy, myghty Hercules.
Lo ! who may truste on Fortune any throwe ?[8]
For hym that folweth al this world of prees,[4]
Er he be war, is ofte yleyd ful lowe.   7750
Ful wys is he that kan hym selven knowe !
Beth war, for whan that Fortune list to glose,[5]
Thanne wayteth she her man to overthrowe
By swich a wey as he wolde leest suppose.
    The myghty trone, the precious tresor,
The glorious ceptre, and roial magestee

---

[1] An unknown auther.   [2] The Pillars of Hercules, at Gibraltar.
[3] While   [4] Crowd.   [7] Flatter.

That hadde the kyng NABUGODONOSOR,
With tonge unnethe [1] may discryved bee.
He twyes wan Jerusalem the citee ; (14,153 T.)
The vessel [2] of the temple he with hym ladde. [3]
At Babiloigne was his sovereyn see, [4]   7761
In which his glorie and his delit he hadde.

The faireste children of the blood roial
Of Israel he leet do gelde anoon,
And maked ech of hem to been his thral.
Amonges othere Daniel was oon,
That was the wiseste child of everychon,
For he the dremes of the kyng expowned,
Where as in Chaldeye clerk ne was ther noon,
That wiste to what fyn [5] hise dremes sowned. [6]
This proude kyng leet maken a statue of gold,
Sixty cubites long and sevene in brede,   7772
The which ymage, bothe [7] yonge and oold
Comanded he [8] to loute, [9] and have in drede,
Or in a fourneys ful of flambes rede
He shal be brent that wolde noght obeye ;
But nevere wolde assente to that dede
Daniel, ne hise yonge felawes tweye.
This kyng of kynges proud was and elaat ;
He wende that God that sit in magestee   7780
Ne myghte hym nat bireve of his estaat ;
But sodeynly he loste his dignytee
And lyk a beest hym semed for to bee ;
And eet hey as an oxe, and lay ther-oute

---

[1] Scarcely.   [2] Plate.   [3] Carried.   [4] Seat.   [5] End.   [6] Tended
Elles. MS. has "he bothe."   [8] Not in Elles. MS.   [9] Bow.

In reyn ; with wilde beestes walked hee
Til certein tyme was ycome aboute ;
And lik an egles fetheres wex his heres ; [1]
Hise nayles lik a briddes clawes weere ;
Til God relessed hym a certeyn yeres,
And gaf hym wit, and thanne with many a
     teere   7790
He thanked God, and evere his lyf in feere
Was he to doon amys, or moore trespace ;
And, til that tyme he leyd was on his beere,
He knew that God was ful of myght and grace.

  His sone, which that highte BALTHASAR,
That heeld the regne after his fader day,
He by his fader koude noght be war ; [2]
For proud he was of herte and of array,
And eek an ydolastre he was ay.
His hye estaat assured hym in pryde ;   7800
But Fortune caste hyme doun and ther he lay,
And sodeynly his regne gan divide.

  A feeste he made un-to hise lordes alle,
Upon a tyme, and bad hem blithe bee ;
And thanne hise officeres gan he calle, —
" Gooth, bryngeth forth the vessels," tho [3] quod
     he,   (14,200 T.)
" Whiche that my fader in his prosperitee
Out of the temple of Jerusalem birafte,
And to our hye goddes thanke we
Of honour that oure eldres with us lafte." 7810
Hys wyf, hise lordes, and hise concubynes

---

[1] Hairs [2] Ware. [3] Then not in MSS

Ay dronken, whil hire appetites laste,
Out of thise noble vessels sondry wynes;
And on a wal this kyng hise eyen caste,
And saugh an hand armlees that wroot ful **fast**
For feere of which he quook, and siked [1] soore.
This hand, that Balthasar so soore agaste,
Wroot *Mane, techel, phares,* and na moore.
In al that land magicien was noon
That koude expounde what this lettre **mente**;
But Daniel expowned it anon,   7821
And seyde, "King, God to thy fader sente
Glorie and honour, regne, tresour, rente,
And he was proud, and no-thyng God ne dradde,
And therfore God greet wreche [2] up-on hym
              sente,
And hym birafte the regne that he hadde;
He was out-cast of mannes compaignye;
With asses was his habitacioun,
And eet hey as a beest in weet and drye,
Til that he knew, by grace and by resoun, 7830
That God of hevene hath domynacioun
Over every regne and every creature;
And thanne hadde God of hym compassioun,
And hym restored his regne and his figure.
Eek thou that art his sone art proud also,
And knowest alle thise thynges verraily,
And art rebel to God and art his foo;
Thou drank eek of hise vessels boldely;
Thy wyf eek, and thy wenches, synfully

----

[1] Sighed.   [2] Vengeance.

Dronke of the same vessels sondry wynys, 7840
And heryest[1] false goddes cursedly;
Therfore to thee yshapen[2] ful greet pyne[3] ys.
This hand was sent from God, that on the wal
Wroot, ' *Mane, techel, phares,*' truste me, —
Thy regne is doon, thou weyest noght at al,
Dyvyded is thy regne, and it shal be
To Medes and to Perses geve," quod he.
And thilke same nyght this kyng was slawe,
And Darius occupieth his degree,   7849
Thogh he therto hadde neither right ne lawe.

Lordynges, ensample heer-by may ye take,
How that in lordshipe is no sikernesse;[4]
For whan Fortune wole a man forsake,
She bereth awey his regne and his richesse,
And eek his freendes, bothe moore and lesse,
For what man that hath freendes thurgh For-
        tune   (14,250 T.)
Mishape wol maken hem enemys, as I gesse;
This proverbe is ful sooth and ful commune.

CENOBIA, of Palymerie queene,[5] —
As writen Persiens of hir noblesse, —   7860
So worthy was in armes, and so keene,
That no wight passed hire in hardynesse,
Ne in lynage, nor in oother gentillesse.
Of kynges blood of Perce[6] is she descended;
I seye nat that she hadde moost fairnesse,
But of hire shape she myghte nat been amended.

---

[1] Praisest.   [2] Ordained.   [3] Pain.   [4] Surety.   [5] This story is mainly from Boccaccio's *De Claris Mulieribus.*   [6] Persia.

From hire childhede I fynde that she fledde [1]
Office of wommen, and to wode she went,
And many a wilde hertes blood she shedde
With arwes brode that she to hem sente ; 7870
She was so swift that she anon hem hente, [2]
And whan that she was elder she wolde kille
Leouns, leopardes, and beres al to-rente,
And in hir armes weelde hem at hir wille.
She dorste wilde beestes dennes seke,
And rennen [3] in the montaignes al the nyght,
And slepen under the bussh ; and she koude
        eke
Wrastlen, by verray force and verray myght,
With any yong man, were he never so wight. [4]
Ther myghte no thyng in hir armes stonde. 7880
She kepte hir maydenhod from every wight ;
To no man deigned hire for to be bonde ;
But atte laste hir freendes han hire maried
To Onedake, [5] a prynce of that contree ;
Al were it so that she hem longe taried.
And ye shul understonde how that he
Hadde swiche fantasies as hadde she ;
But nathelees, whan they were knyt infeere, [6]
They lyved in joye and in felicitee,   7889
For ech of hem hadde oother lief and deere,
Save o thyng, that she wolde nevere assente
By no wey that he sholde by hire lye
But ones, for it was hir pleyn entente

---

[1] Eschewed. [3] Caught. [3] Run. [4] Active. [5] Odenathus. [6] In
company.

To have a child the world to multiplye ;
And also soone as that she myghte espye
That she was nat with childe with that dede,
Thanne wolde she suffre hym doon his fantasye
Eft soone, and nat but oones, out of drede ; [1]
And if she were with childe at thilke cast,
Na moore sholde he pleyen thilke game,   7900
Til fully fourty dayes weren past ;
Thanne wolde she ones suffre hym do the same.
Al were this Onedake wilde or tame
He gat na moore of hire, for thus she seyde,
It was to wyves lecherie and shame,
In oother caas, if that men with hem pleyde.
Two sones by Onedake hadde she,   (14,301 T.)
The whiche she kepte in vertu and lettrure ; [2]
But now un-to our tale turne we.

I seye so worshipful a creature,   7910
And wys ther-with, and large [3] with mesure,
So penyble in the werre, and curteis eke,
Ne moore labour myghte in werre endure
Was noon, though al this world men sholde [4]
          seke.
Hir riche array ne myghte nat be told,
As wel in vessel [5] as in hire clothyng.
She was al clad in perree [6] and in gold,
And eek she lafte [7] noght, for noon huntyr.g,
To have of sondry tonges ful knowyng,
Whan that she leyser hadde ; and for to entende [8]

---

[1] Depend upon it.   [2] Letters.   [3] Generous.   [4] Elles. MS. has
wolde "   [5] Plate.   [6] Jewels.   [7] Omitted.   Apply herself.

To lerne bookes was al hire likyng,   792
How she in vertu myghte hir lyf dispende.

And, shortly of this proces [1] for to trete,
So doghty was hir housbonde and eek she,
That they conquered manye regnes grete
In the Orient, with many a faire citee
Apertenaunt un-to the magestee
Of Rome, and with strong hond held hem ful
            faste,
Ne nevere myghte hir foo-men doon [2] hem flee,
Ay, whil that Onedakes dayes laste.   7930
Hir batailles, who so list hem for to rede, —
Agayn Sapor the kyng and othere mo,
And how that [3] al this proces fil [4] in dede,
Why she conquered, and what title had [5] therto,
And after of hir meschief and hire wo,
How that she was biseged and ytake, —
Lat hym un-to my maister Petrak go,
That writ ynough of this, I undertake.

Whan Onedake was deed she myghtily
The regnes [6] heeld, and with hire propre [7] hond
Agayn hir foos she faught so cruelly   7941
That ther nas kyng, ne prynce, in al that lond
That he nas glad if he that grace fond,
That she ne wolde up-on his lond werreye.[8]
With hire they maden alliance by bond
To been in pees, and lete hire ride and pleye.
The emperour of Rome, Claudius,

---

[1] Story.   [2] Make.   [3] Not in Elles. MS.   [4] Fell out.   [5] Not in
Elles. MS.   [6] Kingdoms.   [7] Own.   [8] Make war

Ne hym bifore, the Romayn Galien,
Ne dorste nevere been so corageous
Ne noon Ermyn,[1] ne noon Egipcien,   7950
Ne Surrien, ne noon Arabyen,
With-inne the feelde that dorste with hire fighte
Lest that she wolde hem with hir handes slen,[2]
Or with hir meignee[3] putten hem to flighte.
In kynges habit wente hir sones two,
As heires of hir fadres regnes alle,   (14,350 T.)
And Hermanno and Thymalao
Hir names were, as Persiens hem calle;
But ay Fortune hath in hire hony galle:
This myghty queene may no while endure.
Fortune out of hir regne made hire falle   7961
To wrecchednesse and to mysaventure.
Aurelian, whan that the governaunce
Of Rome cam in-to hise handes tweye,
He shoope up-on this queene to doon venge-
      aunce;
And with hise legions he took his weye
Toward Cenobie, and, shortly for to seye,
He made hire flee and atte last hire hente,[4]
And fettred hire, and eek hire children tweye,
And wan the land, and hoom to Rome he
      wente.   7970
Amonges othere thynges that he wan
Hir chaar, that was with gold wroght and perree,[5]
This grete Romayn, this Aurelian,
Hath with hym lad, for that men sholde it see

---

[1] Armenian.   [2] Slay.   [3] Retainers.   [4] Seized.   [5] Precious stones.

Biforen his triumphe walketh shee
With gilte [1] cheynes on hire nekke hangynge.
Coroned [2] was she after hir degree,
And ful of perree charged [3] hire clothynge.
Allas, Fortune ! she that whilom was (14,373 T.)
Dredeful to kynges and to emperoures,   798ᴏ
Now gaureth [4] al the peple on hire, allas !
And she that helmed was in starke stoures,[5]
And wan by force townes stronge, and toures,
Shal on hir heed now were a vitremyte ; [6]
And she that bar the ceptre ful of floures
Shal bere a distaf hire costes for to quyte.[7]

O noble, o worthy PETRO,[8] glorie of Spayne
Whom Fortune heeld so hye in magestee, 7988
Wel oghten men thy pitous deeth complayne !
Out of thy land thy brother made thee flee,
And after, at a seege, by subtiltee,   (14,689 T.)
Thou were bitraysed and lad un-to his tente,
Where as he with his owene hand slow thee,
Succedynge in thy regne and in thy rente.
The feeld of snow with thegle [9] of blak therinne
Caught him [10] with the lymerod coloured as the
          gleede,[11]
He brew this cursednesse and al this synne.
The " wikked-nest " [12] was werker of this nede,

---

[1] Gilded.   [2] Crowned.   [3] Loaded.   [4] Gaze   [5] Stout contests.
Wear a glass hood, *i. e.*, be deluded.   Cf. ll. 3389, 6052 ; also *Troy-
us and Cryseyde*, ii. 867.   Suggested by Skeat.   [7] To make a living.   [8] Peter the Cruel was the father of Constance, who became
the wife of John of Gaunt.   [9] The eagle.   [10] Not in Elles. MS
[11] These two lines describe the arms of Bertrand du Guesclin. Lyme
od, lime twig ; gleede, live coal.   [12] Old Fr. *mau*, bad, *ni*, nest
uiver de Mauny.

Noght Charles-Olyvver,[1] that took ay heede
Of trouthe and honour, but of Armorike   8000
Genylon-Olyver,[2] corrupt for meede, (14,699 T.)
Broghte this worthy kyng in swiche a brike.[3]

O worthy PETRO, kyng of Cipre [4] also,
That Alisandre wan by heigh maistrie,
Ful many an hethen wroghtestow ful wo,
Of which thyne owene liges hadde envie,
And for no thyng but for thy chivalrie
They in thy bed han slayn thee by the morwe.
Thus kan Fortune hir wheel governe and gye,[5]
And out of joye brynge men to sorwe.   8010

Of Melan, grete BARNABO VISCOUNTE,
God of delit, and scourge of Lumbardye,
Why sholde I nat thyn infortune acounte,
Sith in estaat thow cloumbe were so hye ?
Thy brother sone, that was thy double allye,
For he thy nevew was, and sone-in-lawe,
With-inne his prisoun made thee to dye, —
But why, ne how, noot [6] I that thou were slawe.[7]

Of the erl HUGELYN OF PYZE the langour
Ther may no tonge telle for pitee ;   8020
But litel out of Pize stant a tour,
In whiche tour in prisoun put was he,
And with hym been hise litel children thre ;
The eldeste scarsly fyf yeer was of age.
Allas, Fortune ! it was greet crueltee

---

[1] Charlemagne's Oliver.   [2] Oliver, like Genelon. Cf. l. 5806.
Breach   [4] Pierre de Lusignan.   Cf. l. 51.   [5] Guide.   [6] Know I
not.   [7] This occurred in 1385, and is the latest event mentioned
incidentally in the *Canterbury Tales*.

Swiche briddes for to putte in swiche a cage !
Dampned was he to dyen in that prisoun,
For Roger, which that bisshope was of Pize,
Hadde on hym maad a fals suggestioun [1]
Thurgh which the peple gan upon hym rise
And putten hym to prisoun in swich wise   8031
As ye han herd, and mete and drynke he hadde
So smal, that wel [2] unnethe [3] it may suffise,
And therwith-al it was ful povre and badde.

    And on a day bifil that in that hour
Whan that his mete wont was to be broght,
The gayler shette the dores of the tour.
He herde it wel, but he ne [4] spak right noght,
And in his herte anon ther fil a thoght   8039
That they for hunger wolde doon hym dyen.
"Allas !" quod he, "allas, that I was wroght!"
Ther-with the teeris fillen from hise eyen.
His yonge sone, that thre yeer was of age,
Un-to hym seyde, "Fader, why do ye wepe ?
Whanne wol the gayler bryngen oure potage ;
Is ther no morsel breed that ye do kepe ?
I am so hungry that I may nat slepe ;
Now wolde God that I myghte slepen evere !
Thanne sholde nat hunger in my wombe [5] crepe ;
Ther is no thyng but breed that me were
        levere."   8050
    Thus day by day this child bigan to crye,
Til in his fadres barm [6] adoun it lay, (14,750 T.)

---

[1] Information not under oath.   [2] Not in Elles. MS.   [3] Scarcely
Inserted by Skeat.   [5] Belly.   [6] Lap.

And seyde, " Fare-wel, fader, I moot dye ! "
And kiste his fader, and dyde the same day ;
And whan the woful fader deed it say,[1]
For wo hise armes two he gan to byte,
And seyde, " Allas, Fortune ! and weylaway !
Thy false wheel my wo al may I wyte ! "[2]
Hise children wende[3] that it for hunger was
That he hise armes gnow,[4] and nat for wo ,
And seyde, " Fader, do nat so, allas !   8061
But rather ete the flessh up-on us two ;
Oure flessh thou gaf us,[5] take oure flessh us
          fro,
And ete ynogh," — right thus they to hym seyde,
And after that, with-inne a day or two,
They leyde hem in his lappe adoun and deyde.
Hym-self, despeired, eek for hunger starf ;[6]
Thus ended is this myghty erl of Pize ;
From heigh estaat Fortune awey hym carf.[7]
Of this tragedie it oghte ynough suffise.   8070
Who so wol here it in a lenger wise,
Redeth the grete poete of Ytaille   (14,770 T.)
That highte Dant, for he kan al devyse
Fro point to point, — nat o word wol he faille.[8]

   Al though that NERO were as[5] vicious
As any feend that lith in helle adoun,
Yet he, as telleth us Swetonius,   (14,383 T.)
This wyde world hadde in subjeccioun
Bothe est and west, south[9] and septemtrioun ;[10]

---

[1] Saw it dead.   [2] Impute .o.   [3] Thought.   [4] Gnawed.   [5] Not
n Elles. MS.   [6] Died.   [7] Cut.   [8] The *Inferno*, xxxiii. 13.   [9] The
MSS. have " north."   [10] North.

Of rubies, saphires, and of peerles white, 808c
Were alle hise clothes brouded up and doun ;
For he in gemmes greetly gan delite.
Moore delicaat, moore pompous of array,
Moore proud, was nevere emperour than he ;
That ilke clooth that he hadde wered o day,
After that tyme he nolde it nevere see.
Nettes of gold threed hadde he greet plentee
To fisshe in Tybre, whan hym liste pleye.
Hise lustes were al lawe in his decree,
For Fortune, as his freend, hym wolde obeye.
He Rome brende [1] for his delicasie ; [2]   8091
The senatours he slow up-on a day; (14,398 T.)
To heere how men wolde wepe and crie ;
And slow his brother, and by his suster lay.
His mooder made he in pitous array,
For he hire wombe slitte, to biholde
Where he conceyved was, so, weilaway !
That he so litel of his mooder tolde. [3]
No teere out of hise eyen for that sighte
Ne cam, but seyde, " A fair womman was she ! '
Greet wonder is how that he koude or myghte
Be domesman [4] of hire dede beautee ;   8102
The wyn to bryngen hym comanded he,
And drank anon, — noon oother wo he made.
Whan myght is joyned un-to crueltee,
Allas, to depe wol the venym wade !
    In yowthe a maister hadde this emperour,
To teche hym lettrure [5] and curteisye, —

---

[1] Burned.   [2] Delight.   [3] Counted.   [4] Judge.   [5] Letters.

For of moralitee [1] he was the flour,
As in his tyme, but if bookes lye ;   8110
And whil this maister hadde of hym maistrye,
He maked hym so konnyng [2] and so sowple,[8]
That longe tyme it was er tirannye,
Or any vice, dorste on hym uncowple.[4]
This Seneca, of which that I devyse,
By cause that [5] Nero hadde of hym swich drede,
For he fro vices wolde hym ay [5] chastise
Discreetly, as by word, and nat by dede ;
"Sire," wolde he seyn, "an emperour moot nede
Be vertuous and hate tirannye ; "   8120
For which he in a bath made hym to blede
On bothe hise armes, til he moste dye.
This Nero hadde eek of acustumaunce
In youthe agayns his maister for to ryse,
Which afterward hym thoughte a greet grev-
        aunce ;
Therfore he made hym dyen in this wise ;
But nathelees this Seneca the wise
Chees in a bath to dye in this manere
Rather than han any oother tormentise ;
And thus hath Nero slayn his maister deere.
Now fil it so that Fortune liste no lenger 8131
The hye pryde of Nero to cherice,
For though that he were strong yet was she
        strenger ;
She thoughte thus : "By God, I am to nyce,[6]

---

[1] Manners (Latin, *mos*, fashion)   [2] Wise.   [8] Not obstinate
Attack.   [5] Not in Elles. MS.   Foolish.

To sette a man that is fulfild of vice
In heigh degree, and emperour hym calle.
By God! out of his sete I wol hym trice;[1]
Whan he leest weneth sonnest shal he falle!"

    The peple roos up-on hym on a nyght
For his defaute, and whan he it espied,   8140
Out of hise dores anon he hath hym dight
Allone, and, ther he wende han ben allied,[2]
He knokked faste, and ay the moore he cried
The fastere shette they the dores alle; (14,450 r.)
Tho wiste he weel he hadde hymself mysgy'd,[3]
And wente his wey, no lenger dorste he calle.
The peple cride and rombled up and doun
That with his erys herde he how they seyde,
"Where is this false tiraunt, this Neroun?"
For fere almoost out of his wit he breyde,[4]
And to hise goddes pitously he preyde   8151
For socour, but it myghte nat bityde.
For drede of this, hym thoughte that he deyde,
And ran in-to a garden hym to hyde;
And in this gardyn foond he cherles tweye
That seten by a fyr, ful[5] greet and reed;
And to thise cherles two he gan to preye
To sleen hym, and to girden of[6] his heed,
That to his body, whan that he were deed,
Were no despit ydoon for his defame.   8160
Hym self he slow, he koude[7] no bettre reed,[8]
Of which Fortune lough, and hadde a game[9]

---

[1] Thrust.   [2] Thought he had allies.   [3] This line from Camb
MS; not in Elles.   [4] Started.   [5] Not in Elles. MS.   [6] Strike off
Knew.   [8] Advice.   [9] Jest.

Was nevere capitayn under a kyng
That regnes mo putte in subjeccioun,
Ne strenger was in feeld of alle thyng,
As in his tyme, ne gretter of renoun,
Ne moore pompous in heigh presumpcioun,
Than OLOFERNE, which that [1] Fortune ay kiste
So likerously, and ladde hym up and doun,
Til that his heed was of, er that he wiste. 8170
Nat oonly that this world hadde hym in awe
For lesynge [2] of richesse or libertee,
But he [1] made every man reneyen [3] his lawe.
"Nabugodonosor was god," seyde hee,
"Noon oother god ne sholde adoured bee."
Agayns his heeste no wight dorst trespace
Save in Bethulia, a strong citee
Where Eliachim a preest was of that place.
But taak kepe [4] of the deeth of Oloferne :
Amydde his hoost he dronke lay a nyght, 8180
With-inne his tente, large as is a berne,
And yet, for al his pompe and al his myght,
Judith, a womman, as he lay upright
Slepynge, his heed of smoot, and from his tente
Ful pryvely she stal from every wight,
And with his heed un-to hir toun she wente.

What nedeth it of kyng ANTHIOCHUS
To telle his hye roial magestee,
His hye pride, hise werkes venymus ?
For swich another was ther noon as he.   8190
Rede which that he was in Machabee,

---

[1] Not in Elles MS.   [2] Fear of Losing.   [3] Deny.   [4] Notice.

And rede the proude wordes that he seyde,
And why he fil fro heigh prosperitee,
And in an hill how wrecchedly he deyde.
Fortune hym hadde enhaunced so in pride
That verraily he wende he myghte attayne
Unto the sterres up-on every syde ; (14,503 T.)
And in balance weyen ech montayne ;
And alle the floodes of the see restrayne ; 8199
And Goddes peple hadde he moost in hate ;
IIem wolde he sleen in torment and in payne,
Wenynge that God ne myghte his pride abate.
And for that Nichanore and Thymothee,
Of Jewes weren venquysshed myghtily,
Un-to the Jewes swich an hate hadde he
That he bad greithen [1] his chaar [2] ful hastily,
And swoor, and seyde ful despitously
Un-to Jerusalem he wolde eft soone,
To wreken his ire on it ful cruelly ;
But of his purpos he was let ful soone.   8210
God for his manace hym so soore smoot
With invisible wounde, ay incurable,
That in his guttes carf [3] it so and boot, [4]
That hise peynes weren importable ;
And certeinly the wreche was resonable, [5]
For many a mannes guttes dide he peyne ;
But from his purpos cursed and dampnabie
For all his smert he wolde hym nat restreyne ;
But bad anon apparaillen his hoost, —
And, sodeynly, er he was of it war,   8220

[1] Make ready. [2] Chariot. [3] Cut. [4] Bit. [5] Vengeance was jus'

God daunted al his pride and all his boost ; [1]
For he so soore fil out of his char,
That it hise lemes and his skyn to-tar, [2]
So that he neyther myghte go ne ryde,
But in a chayer men aboute hym bar
Al for-brused, bothe bak and syde.
The wreche [3] of God hym smoot so cruelly,
That thurgh his body wikked wormes crepte,
And ther-with-al he stank so [4] horriblely
That noon of al his meynee [5] that hym kepte,
Wheither so he a-wook or ellis slepte,   8231
Ne myghte noght for stynk of hym endure.
In this meschief he wayled and eek wepte,
And knew God lord of every creature.
To all his hoost and to hym self also
Ful wlatsom [6] was the stynk of his careyne ; [7]
No man ne myghte hym bere to ne fro ;
And in this stynk and this horrible peyne,
He starf [8] ful wrecchedly in a monteyne.   8239
Thus hath this robbour and this homycide,
That many a man made to wepe and pleyne,
Swich gerdoun [9] as bilongeth un-to pryde.

The storie of ALISAUNDRE is so commune.
That every wight that hath discrecioun
Hath herd somwhat or al of his fortune.
This wyde world, as in conclusioun, (14,552 T.)
He wan by strengthe, or for his hye renoun
They weren glad for pees un-to hym sende.

[1] Boast.   [2] Lacerated.   [3] Vengeance.   [4] Not in Elles. MS.
[Attendants.   [6] Loathsome.   [7] Carrion.   [8] Died.   [9] Reward.

The pride of man and beest he leyde adoun
Wher so he cam un-to the worldes ende. 8250
Comparisoun myghte nevere yet been maked
Bitwixen hym and another conquerour ;
For al this world for drede of hym hath quaked,
He was of knighthod and of fredom flour,
Fortune hym made the heir of hire honour
Save wyn and wommen no thyng [1] mighte
            aswage
His hye entente in armes and labour,
So was he ful of leonyn corage.
What preys [2] were it to hym though I yow tolde
Of Darius, and an hundred thousand mo, 8260
Of kynges, princes, erles, dukes bolde,
Whiche he conquered and broghte hem in-to
            wo ?
I seye, as fer as man may ryde or go, [3]
The world was his, — what sholde I moore de-
            vyse ?
For though I writ or tolde yow everemo
Of his knyghthode, it myghte nat suffise.
Twelf yeer he regned, as seith Machabee.
Philippes sone of Macidoyne he was,
That first was kyng in Grece the contree.

    O worthy, gentil Alisandre, allas !   8270
That evere sholde fallen swich a cas !
Empoysoned of thyn owene folk thou weere ;
Thy *sys* [4] Fortune hath turned in-to *aas*, [5]

---

[1] Elles. MS. has "man." [2] Elles. MS. has "pris." [3] Walk
Six. [5] Ace. Cf. ll. 4546, 4547.

And yet for thee ne weepe she never a teere !
Who shal me geven teeris to compleyne
The deeth of gentillesse and of franchise,[1]
That al the world weelded in his demeyne ?[2]
And yet hym thoughte it myghte nat suffise,
So ful was his corage of heigh emprise.
Allas ! who shal me helpe to endite   8280
False Fortune, and poyson to despise,
The whiche two of al this wo I wyte ?[3]

By wisedom, manhede, and by greet [4] laboul
From humble bed to roial magestee
Up roos he, JULIUS the conquerour,
That wan al thoccident, by land and see,
By strengthe of hand, or elles by tretee,
And un-to Rome made hem tributarie ;
And sitthe [5] of Rome the emperour was he
Til that Fortune weex his adversarie.   8290
O myghty Cesar ! that in Thessalie
Agayn Pompeus, fader thyn in lawe,
That of thorient [6] hadde all the chivalrie
As fer as that the day bigynneth dawe,
Thou thurgh thy knyghthod hast hem take and
       slawe,   (14,601 T.)
Save fewe folk that with Pompeus fledde,
Thurgh which thou puttest al thorient in awe, —
Thanke Fortune, that so wel thee spedde !

But now a litel while I wol biwaille
This Pompeus, this noble governour   8300

---

[1] Frankness.   [2] Domain.   [3] Blame.   [4] Not in **Elles. MS**
Afterwards.   [6] Elles. MS. has " the Orient."

Of Rome, which that fleigh [1] at this bataille.
I seye, oon of hise men, a fals traitour,
His heed of smoot, to wynnen hym favour
Of Julius, and hym the heed he broghte.
Allas, Pompeye, of thorient conquerour,
That Fortune un-to swich a fyn [2] thee broghte
To Rome agayn repaireth Julius
With his triumphe, [3] lauriat ful hye ;
But on a tyme Brutus and [4] Cassius,
That evere hadde of his hye estaat envye,
Ful prively had [5] maad conspiracye   8311
Agayns this Julius in subtil wise,
And caste the place in which he sholde dye
With boydekyns, [6] as I shal yow devyse.

   This Julius to the Capitolie wente
Upon a day, as he was wont to goon,
And in the Capitolie anon hym hente [7]
This false Brutus, and hise othere foon, [8]
And stiked hym with boydekyns anoon
With many a wounde, and thus they lete hym
       lye ;   8320
But nevere gronte [9] he at no strook but oon,
Or elles at two, but if his storie lye.
So manly was this Julius of herte,
And so wel lovede estaatly honestee,
That though hise deedly woundes soore smerte,
His mantel over his hypes caste he
For no man sholde seen his privetee ;

[1] Fled.   [2] End.   [3] Cf. l. 4822.   [4] Not in Elles. MS.   [5] Elles
MS. reads "hath."   [6] Daggers.   Cf. *Hamlet*, act iii., sc. 1, l. 76
Seized.   [8] Foes.   [9] Groaned.

And as he lay of diyng in a traunce,
And wiste verraily that deed was hee,
Of honestee [1] yet hadde he remembraunce.
Lucan, to thee this storie I recomende.   8331
And to Swetoun, and to Valerius also,
That of this storie writen word and ende,[2]
How that to thise grete conqueroures two
Fortune was first freend and sitthe foo.
No man ne truste up-on hire favour longe,
But have hire in awayt [3] for evere moo ;
Witnesse on alle thise conquerouers stronge.

   This riche CRESUS, whilom kyng of Lyde,
Of which Cresus [4] Cirus soore hym dradde,
Yet was he caught amyddes al his pryde   8341
And to be brent men to the fyr hym ladde ;
But swich a reyn doun fro the welkne [5] shadde,
That slow [6] the fyr and made hym to escape ;
But to be war, no grace yet he hadde, (14,651 T.)
Til Fortune on the galwes made hym gape.
Whanne he escaped was he kan nat stente
For to bigynne a newe werre agayn.   8348
He wende wel [7] for that Fortune hym sente
Swich hape that he escaped thurgh the rayn,
That of hise foos he myghte nat be slayn ;
And eek a swevene [8] up-on a nyght he mette,[9]
Of which he was so proud, and eek so fayn,
That in vengeance he al his herte sette.

---

[1] Decency.   [2] Dr. Hicks would read " ord and end," beginning
and end.   Cf. *Troylus and Cryseyde*, ii. 1495, iii. 702, and v. 1683.
The expression is not uncommon.   [3] Watch her.   [4] Cf. l. 8750.
[5] Welkin.   [6] Extinguished.   [7] Fully believed.   [8] Dream.   [9] Dreamed

Up-on a tree he was, as that hym thoughte,
Ther Juppiter hym wesshe, bothe bak and syde,
And Phebus eek a fair towaille hym broughte
To dryen hym with, and therfore wex his pryde ;
And to his doghter, that stood hym bisyde,
Which that he knew in heigh science habounde,[1]
He bad hire telle hym what it signyfyde,   8361
And she his dreem bigan right thus expounde :
" The tree," quod she, " the galwes is to meene ;
And Juppiter bitokneth snow and reyn,
And Phebus with his towaille so clene,
Tho been the sonne-bemes for to seyn ;
Thou shalt anhanged be, fader, certeyn, —
Reyn shal thee wasshe and sonne shal thee
       drye ;"   8368
Thus warned she [2] hym ful plat and ful pleyn,
His doghter which that called was Phanye.
An-hanged was Cresus, the proude kyng ;
His roial trone myghte hym nat availle.

Tragedie [3] *is* [2] *noon oother maner thyng ;*
Ne kan in syngyng crie ne biwaille   (14,680 T.)
But for [2] *that Fortune alwey wole assaille*
With unwar strook the regnes [4] *that been proude ;*
For whan men trusteth hire, thanne wol she faille,
And covere hire brighte face with a clowde. 8378

---

[1] Great knowledge to abound.   [2] Not in Elles. MS.   [3] Cf. l.
7585, and Boethius.   [4] Kingdoms.
NOTE. — The reader will notice by Tyrwhitt's numbers that he
did not arrange the Monk's examples as in the text. The references
in the conversation that follows prove that the series should end as
above. Tyrwhitt arranged the last examples thus : Zenobia, Nero,
Holofernes, Antiochus, Alexander, Julius Cæsar, Crœsus, Peter of
Spain, Peter of Cyprus, Barnabo, and Ugolino of Pisa.

The Knight and the Host complain of this Tale.

"Hoo!" quod the Knyght, "good sire, na-
    moore of this!   (14,773 T.)
That ye han seyd is right ynough, ywis,   8380
And muchel moore; for litel hevynesse
Is right ynough to muche folk, I gesse.
I seye for me it is a greet disese [1]
Where as men han been in greet welthe and ese
To heeren of hire sodeyn fal, allas!
And the contrarie is joye and greet solas,
As whan a man hath ben in povre estaat,
And clymbeth up, and wexeth fortunat,
And there abideth in prosperitee;   8389
Swich thyng is gladsom, as it thynketh me,
And of swich thyng were goodly for to telle."
   "Ye," quod oure Hoost, "by Seint Poules
    belle!
Ye seye right sooth; this Monk he clappeth
    lowde;
He spak how 'Fortune covered with a
    clowde,' [2] —
I noot [3] nevere what, — and als of a 'tragedie'
Right now ye herde, and, *pardee*, 'no remedie' [4]
It is for to 'biwaille,' [5] ne compleyne
That that is doon; and als,[6] it is a peyne,
As ye han seyd, to heere of hevynesse.

---

[1] Discomfort.   [2] Cf. l. 8378.   [3] Know not.   [4] Cf. l. 7605.   [5] Cf.
l. 8374.   [6] Also.

Sire Monk, namoore of this, so God yow blesse !
Youre tale anoyeth all this compaignye ;   8401
Swich talkyng is nat worth a boterflye,
For ther-inne is ther no desport ne game.
Wherfore, sire Monk, daun Piers [1] by youre
       name,   (14,798 T.)
I pray yow hertely, telle us somwhat elles,
For sikerly nere [2] clynkyng of youre belles, [3]
That on youre bridel hange on every syde,
By hevene kyng, that for us alle dyde !
I sholde er this han fallen doun for sleepe,
Al-thogh the slough had never been so deepe ;
Thanne hadde youre tale al be toold in veyn,
For certeinly, as that thise clerkes seyn,   8412
Where as a man may have noon audience,
Noght helpeth it to tellen his sentence ;
And wel I woot the substance is in me,
If any thyng shal wel reported be.
Sir, sey somwhat of huntyng, I yow preye."

   "Nay !" quod this Monk, "I have no lust
    to pleye ;
Now lat another telle, as I have toold."

   Thanne spak oure Hoost with rude speche
    and boold,   8420
And seyde un-to the Nonnes Preest anon,
' Com neer, thou preest, com hyder, thou sir
   John.
Telle us swich thyng as may oure hertes glade ,

---

[1] Cf. l. 7540.   The Host has now learned the Monk's name.
Were it not for the.   [3] Cf. l. 170.

Be blithe, though thou ryde up-on a jade.
What thogh thyn hors be bothe foule and lene?
If he wol serve thee, rekke nat a bene;
Looke that thyn herte be murie everemo."
   "Yis, sir," quod he, "yis, Hoost, so moot I
     go,   (14,822 T.)
But I be myrie, ywis I wol be blamed."
And right anon his tale he hath attamed,[1] 8430
And thus he seyde un-to us everichon,
This sweete preest, this goodly man, sir John.[2]

*Heere bigynneth The Nonnes Preestes Tale of the
Cok and Hen, — Chauntecleer and Pertelote.*

  A povre wydwe, somdel stape [3] in age,
Was whilom dwellyng in a narwe cotage
Beside a greve,[4] stondynge in a dale. (14,829 T.)
This wydwe, of which I telle yow my tale,
Syn thilke day that she was last a wyf,
In pacience ladde a ful symple lyf,
For litel was hir catel [5] and hir rente.[6]   8439
By housbondrie of swich as God hire sente
She foond [7] hir self, and eek hire doghtren two.
Thre large sowes hadde she, and namo;
Three keen [8] and eek a sheep that highte Malle.
Ful sooty [9] was hir bour,[10] and eek hire halle,

---

[1] Begun.   [2] The tale of the Cock and the Fox is found in the French *Roman du Renart*, where it was enlarged from a series of Æsop's fables, translated by Marie de France from the English of King Alfred. Chaucer's version is more picturesque and true to life than the earlier ones. [3] Advanced, stept. Cf. l. 13,850. [4] Grove. [5] Wealth. [6] Income. [7] Supplied. [8] Kine. [9] Foul. [10] Chamber

In which she eet ful many a sklendre meel;
Of poynaunt sauce hir neded never a deel.
No deyntee morsel passed thurgh hir throte,
Hir diete was accordant to hir cote;[1]
Repleccioun ne made hire nevere sik,
Attempree diete was al hir phisik,   8450
And exercise, and hertes suffisaunce.
The goute lette hire no-thyng[2] for to daunce,
Napoplexie shente[3] nat hir heed;
No wyn ne drank she, neither whit ne reed;
Hir bord was served moost with whit and
        blak, —
Milk and broun breed, — in which she foond
        no lak;   (14,850 т.)
Seynd[4] bacoun and somtyme an ey[5] or tweye,
For she was, as it were, a maner deye.[6]

    A yeerd she hadde, enclosed al aboute
With stikkes, and a drye dych with-oute,   8460
In which she hadde a cok, heet Chauntecleer.
In al the land of crowyng nas his peer.
His voys was murier than the murie orgon
On messe[7] dayes that in the chirche gon;
Wel sikerer[8] was his crowyng in his logge[9]
Than is a clokke,[10] or an abbey orlogge.[11]
By nature he knew[12] eche ascencioun
Of the equynoxial in thilke toun;
For whan degrees fiftene weren ascended,
Thanne crew he that it myghte nat been
        amended.   8470

---

[1] Cottage. [2] Hindered her not at all. [3] Hurt. [4] Broiled. [5] Egg
Female farm servant, or dairy-woman. [7] Mass. [8] Surer. [9] Lodge
[10] Bell or clock. [11] Time-keeper. [12] Elles. MS. has "crew."

His coomb was redder than the fyn coral,
And batailled as it were a castel wal ;
His byle [1] was blak, and as the jeet [2] it **shoon** ;
Lyk asure were hise legges and his toon ;
Hise nayles whiter than the lylye flour,
And lyk the burned [3] gold was his colour.

This gentil cok hadde in his governaunce
Sevene hennes for to doon al his plesaunce,
Whiche were hise sustres and his paramours,
And wonder lyk to hym, as of colours ;   8480
Of whiche the faireste hewed on hir throte
Was cleped faire damoysele Pertelote.
Curteys she was, discreet and debonaire,
And compaignable, and bar hyr-self so faire
Syn thilke day that she was seven nyght oold,
That trewely she hath the herte in hoold
Of Chauntecleer, loken in every lith ; [4]
He loved hire so that wel was hym therwith ;
But swiche a joye was it to here hem synge, —
Whan   that   the   brighte   sonne   bigan   to
          sprynge, —   8490
In sweete accord, "My lief is faren in londe ;" [5]
For thilke tyme, [6] as I have understonde,
Beestes and briddes koude speke and synge.

And so bifel, that in the dawenynge,
As Chauntecleer among hise wyves alle
Sat on his perche, that was in the halle,
And next hym sat this faire Pertelote,

---

[1] Bill.   [2] Jet.   [3] Some MSS. have " burnished."   [4] Locked in
every limb.   [5] My love is gone away.   At that time

This Chauntecleer gan gronen in his throte
As man that in his dreem is drecched [1] soore.

   And whan that Pertelote thus herde hym
      roore,   8500
She was agast, and seyde, " O herte deere !
What eyleth yow, to grone in this manere ?
Ye been a verray sleper ; fy, for shame ! "

   And he answerde and seyde thus : " Madame,
I pray yow that ye take it nat agrief ; [2]
By God, me thoughte I was in swich meschief
Right now, that yet myn herte is soore afright.
Now God," quod he, " my swevene recche [3]
      aright,   (14,902 T.)
And kepe my body out of foul prisoun ;
Me mette [4] how that I romed up and doun 8510
With-inne our yeerd, wheer as I saugh a beest
Was lyk an hound, and wolde han maad areest [5]
Up-on my body, and han had me deed.
His colour was bitwixe yelow and reed,
And tipped was his tayl, and bothe hise eeris,
With blak, unlyk the remenant of hise heeris ;
His snowte smal, with glowynge eyen tweye.
Yet of his look for feere almoost I deye ;
This caused me my gronyng douteles." 8519

   " Avoy ! " quod she, " fy on yow, hertelees !
Allas ! " quod she, " for by that God above !
Now han ye lost myn herte and al my love.
I kan nat love a coward, by my feith !
For certes, what so any womman seith,

<hr>

[1] Troubled.   [2] Amiss.   [3] Dream fall out.   [4] Dreamed.   [5] Seizure

We alle desiren, if it myghte bee,
To han housbondes hardy, wise, and free,
And secree, and no nygard, ne no fool,
Ne hym that is agast of every tool,[1]
Ne noon avauntour,[2] by that God above !
How dorste ye seyn, for shame, un-to youre love
That any thyng myghte make yow aferd ? 8531
Have ye no mannes herte, and han a berd ?

   " Allas ! and konne ye been agast of sweve-
      nys ?
No thyng, God woot, but vanitee in swevene is.
Swevenes engendren of replecciouns,
And ofte of fume, and of complecciouns
Whan humours been to habundant in a wight.

   " Certes this dreem, which ye han met[3] to-
      nyght,
Cometh of the[4] greet superfluytee
Of youre rede colera,[5] *pardee*,   8540
Which causeth folk to dreden in hir dremes
Of arwes, and of fyre with rede lemes,[6]
Of grete beestes that they wol hem byte,
Of contekes[7] and of whelpes, grete and lyte ;
Right as the humour of malencolie
Causeth ful many a man in sleepe to crie,
For feere of blake beres, or boles[8] blake,
Or elles blake develes wole hem take.
Of othere humours koude I telle also
That werken many a man in sleepe ful wo ;

Weapon. ² Braggart.   Dreamed.   Not in Elles. MS. ⁵ Bile.
Gleams. ⁷ Struggles. ⁵ Bulls.

But I wol passe as lightly as I kan.   8551
Lo, Catoun, which that was so wys a man,
Seyde he nat thus, 'Ne do no fors[1] of dremes'
    "Now, sire," quod she, "whan ye flee fro
        the bemes,
For Goddes love, as taak som laxatyf.
Up peril of my soule, and of my lyf, (14,950 T.)
I conseille yow the beste, I wol nat lye,
That bothe of colere [2] and of malencolye
Ye purge yow, and, for ye shal nat tarie,
Though in this toun is noon apothecarie, 8560
I shal my-self to herbes techen yow
That shul been for youre hele, and for youre
        prow ;[3]
And in oure yeerd tho herbes shal I fynde,
The whiche han of hire propretee by kynde [4]
To purge yow, bynethe and eek above.
Forget nat this, for Goddes owene love !
Ye been ful coleryk of compleccioun.
Ware [5] the sonne in his ascencioun
Ne fynde yow nat repleet of humours hoote ;
And if it do, I dar wel leye a grote   8570
That ye shul have a fevere terciane,
Or an agu, that may be youre bane.
A day or two ye shul have digestyves
Of wormes, er ye take youre laxatyves
Of lawriol, centaure [6] and fumetere,[7]
Or elles of ellebor that groweth there,

---

[1] Account nothing.   [2] Choler.   [3] Profit.   [4] Property by that
nature.   [5] Beware.   [6] Century.   [7] Fumitory.

Of katapuce [1] or of gaitrys [2] beryis,
Of herbe yve growyng in oure yeerd ther mery is,[3]
Pekke hem up right as they growe and ete hem
    yn ;
Be myrie, housbonde, for youre fader kyn ! 8580
Dredeth no dreem ; I kan sey yow namoore."
    "Madame," quod he, "*graunt mercy* of youre
    loore,
But nathelees, as touchyng daun Catoun,
That hath of wysdom swich a greet renoun,
Though that he bad no dremes for to drede,
By God, men may in olde bookes rede
Of many a man, moore of auctorite
Than evere Caton was, so moot I thee ! [4]
That al the revers seyn of this sentence,
And han wel founden by experience   8590
That dremes been significaciouns
As wel of joye as tribulaciouns
That folk enduren in this lif present.
Ther nedeth make of this noon argument,
The verray preeve sheweth it in dede.
    "Oon of the gretteste auctours that men
    rede [5]
Seith thus, that whilom two felawes wente
On pilgrimage in a ful good entente,
And happed so they coomen in a toun,
Wher as ther was swich congregacioun   8600
Of peple, and eek so streit [6] of herbergage,[7]

---

[1] Spurge. [2] Dogwood. [3] That pleasant. [4] Thrive. [5] Cicero
De Divinatione, pt. i. [6] Restricted [7] Lodging.

That they ne founde as muche as o cotage
In which they bothe myghte logged bee ;
Wherfore they mosten of necessitee, (14,998 T.)
As for that nyght, departen compaignye ;
And ech of hem gooth to his hostelrye,
And took his loggyng as it wolde falle.
That oon of hem was logged in a stalle
Fer in a yeerd, with oxen of the plough ;
That oother man was logged wel ynough, 8610
As was his aventure, or his fortune,
That us governeth alle as in commune.

    " And so bifel that longe er it were day,
This man mette in his bed, ther as he lay,
How that his felawe gan up-on hym calle,
And seyde, ' Allas ! for in an oxes stalle
This nyght I shal be mordred ther I lye ;
Now helpe me, deere brother, or I dye ;
In alle haste com to me ! ' he sayde.   8619
    " This man out of his sleepe for feere
        abrayde ;
But whan that he was wakened of his sleepe,
He turned hym and took of it no keepe ;
Hym thoughte his dreem nas but a vanitee.
Thus twies in his slepyng dremed hee,
And atte thridde tyme yet his felawe
Cam as hym thoughte, and seide, ' I am now
        slawe !
Bihoold my bloody woundes, depe and wyde ;
Arys up erly in the morwe tyde,
And at the west gate of the toun,' quod he,

' A carte ful of donge ther shaltow se,   8630
In which my body is hid ful prively ;
Do thilke carte arresten boldely ;
My gold caused my mordre, sooth to sayn.'
And tolde hym every point how he was slayn,
With a ful pitous face pale of hewe ;
And truste wel his dreem he foond ful trewe ;
For on the morwe, as soone as it was day,
To his felawes in he took the way,
And whan that he cam to this oxes stalle,
After his felawe he bigan to calle.   8640
    " The hostiler answerde hym anon
And seyde, ' Sire, your felawe is agon ;
As soone as day he wente out of the toun.'
    " This man gan fallen in suspecioun, —
Remembrynge on hise dremes, that he mette, —
And forth he gooth, no lenger wolde he lette,
Un-to the westgate of the toun, and fond
A dong carte, as it were to donge lond,
That was arrayed in that same wise
As ye han herd the dede man devyse ;   8650
And with an hardy herte he gan to crye
Vengeance and justice of this felonye.
' My felawe mordred is this same nyght,
And in this carte heere he lith gapyng upright[1]
I crye out on the ministres,' quod he, (15,049 T.)
    That sholden kepe and reulen this citee ;
Harrow ! allas ! heere lith my felawe slayn !
What sholde I moore un-to this tale sayn ?

[1] Cf   2008.

The peple out sterte and caste the cart to
      grounde,   • 8659
And in the myddel of the dong they founde
The dede man, that mordred was al newe.

    " O blisful God, that art so just and trewe!
Lo, howe that thou biwreyest mordre alway!
Mordre wol out, that se we day by day;
Mordre is so wlatsom,[1] and abhomynable
To God, that is so just and resonable,
That he ne wol nat suffre it heled[2] be,
Though it abyde a yeer, or two, or thre;
Mordre wol out, this my conclusioun.
And right anon, ministres of that toun   8670
Han hent the carter, and so soore hym pyned,
And eek the hostiler so soore engyned,[3]
That they biknewe[4] hire wikkednesse anon,
And were an-hanged by the nekke bon.

    " Heere may men seen that dremes been to
      drede;
And certes, in the same book I rede,
Right in the nexte chapitre after this, —
I gabbe nat, so have I joye or blis, —

    " Two men that wolde han passed over see
For certeyn cause in-to a fer contree,   8680
If that the wynd ne hadde been contrarie,
That made hem in a citee for to tarie
That stood ful myrie upon an haven syde;
But on a day, agayn the even tyde,
The wynd gan chaunge, and blew right as hem
      leste.

---

[1] Loathsome.   [2] Hidden.   [3] Tortured.   [4] Confessed

Jolif and glad they wente un-to hir reste,
And casten hem ful erly for to saille.

"But [1] to that o man fil a greet mervaille :
That oon of hem in slepyng as he lay,   8685
Hym mette a wonder dreem agayn the day :
Him thoughte a man stood by his beddes syde
And hym comanded that he sholde abyde,
And seyde hym thus : ' If thou tomorwe wende.
Thou shalt be dreynt,[2] my tale is at an ende.

"He wook, and tolde his felawe what he
      mette,
And preyde hym his viage for [3] to lette ;
As for that day, he preyde hym to byde.

"His felawe, that lay by his beddes syde ;
Gan for to laughe, and scorned him ful faste ;
'No dreem,' quod he, 'may so myn herte agaste,
That I wol lette for to do my thynges ;   8701
I sette nat a straw by thy dremynges,
For swevenes been but vanytees and japes ;
Men dreme al day of owles or of apes,
And of many a maze ther-with-al ;   (15,099 T.)
Men dreme of thyng that nevere was ne shal ;
But sith I see that thou wolt heere abyde,
And thus forslewthen [4] wilfully thy tyde,   8708
God woot it reweth me, and have good day !'
And thus he took his leve, and wente his way ;
But er that he hadde half his cours yseyled,
Noot I [5] nat why, ne what myschaunce it eyled,

---

[1] Elles. MS. has "but herkneth."   [2] Drowned.   [3] Not in Elles.
MS.   [4] Lose by sloth.   [5] I know not

But casuelly [1] the shippes botme rente,
And shipe and man under the water wente
In sighte of othere shippes it bisyde
That with hem seyled at the same tyde !
And therfore, faire Pertelote so deere,
By swiche ensamples olde yet maistow leere, [2]
That no man sholde been to recchelees
Of dremes, for I seye thee doutelees,   8720
That many a dreem ful soore is for to drede.

    " Lo, in the lyf of Seint Kenelm I rede,
That was Kenulphus sone, the noble kyng
Of Mercenrike, [3] how Kenelm mette a thyng.
A lite er he was mordred, on a day
His mordre in his avysioun he say. [4]
His norice [5] hym expowned every deel
His swevene, and bad hym for to kepe [6] hym
        weel
For traisoun ; but he nas but seven yeer oold,
And therfore litel tale hath he toold   8730
Of any dreem, so hooly is his herte.
By God, I hadde levere than my sherte
That ye hadde rad his legende as have I.
Dame Pertelote, I sey yow trewely,
Macrobeus, [7] that writ the avisioun
In Affrike of the worthy Cipioun,
Affermeth dremes, and seith that they been
Warnynge of thynges that men after seen ;
And forther-moore, I pray yow looketh wel

---

[1] Accidentally.   [2] Mayest thou learn.   [3] Mercia.   [4] Saw.   [5] Nurse
[6] Guard.   [7] Cf. *The Parlement of Foules*, l. 31.

In the Olde Testament of Daniel, 8740
If he heeld dremes any vanitee.

    " Reed eek of Joseph, and ther shul ye see
Wher [1] dremes be somtyme, — I sey nat alle, —
Warnynge of thynges that shul after falle.

    " Looke of Egipte the kyng, daun Pharao,
His baker and his butiller also,
Wher they ne felte noon effect in dremes.
Who-so wol seken actes of sondry remes [2]
May rede of dremes many a wonder thyng.

    " Lo, Cresus, which that was of Lyde kyng, [3]
Mette he nat that he sat up-on a tree, 8751
Which signified he sholde anhanged bee?

    " Lo heere [4] Adromacha, Ectores wyf,
That day that Ector sholde lese his lyf,
She dremed on the same nyght biforn,
How that the lyf of Ector sholde be lorne,
If thilke day he wente in-to bataille ; (15,151 T.)
She warned hym, but it myghte nat availle ;
He wente for to fighte natheles,
And [5] he was slayn anon of Achilles ; [6] 8760
But thilke tale is al to longe to telle,
And eek it is ny day, I may nat dwelle ;
Shortly I seye, as for conclusioun,
That I shal han of this avisioun
Adversitee ; and I seye forthermoor,
That I ne telle of laxatyves no stoor,
For they been venymes, I woot it weel ;
I hem diffye, I love hem never a deel !

---

[1] Whether.   [2] Realms.   [3] Cf. l 8340.   [4] Her.   [5] Elles. MS
has " but."   [6] See the *Geste Hystoriale* of the Destruction of Troy,
book xxi. ; and Dares Phrygius.

"Now let us speke of myrthe, and stynte a
  this ;
Madame Pertelote, so have I blis,   8770
Of o thyng God hath sent me large grace ;
For whan I se the beautee of youre face
Ye been so scarlet reed aboute youre eyen,
It maketh al my drede for to dyen,
For, al-so siker as *In principio*,[1]
Mulier est hominis confusio,[2] —
Madame, the sentence [3] of this Latyn is,
'Womman is mannes joye, and al his blis ;'
For whan I feele a-nyght your softe syde,
Al be it that I may nat on yow ryde   8780
For that oure perche is maad so narwe, al-
  las !
I am so ful of joye and of solas,
That I diffye bothe swevene and dreem : "
And with that word he fly doun fro the beem,
For it was day, and eke hise hennes alle ;
And with a " chuk " he gan hem for to calle,
For he hadde founde a corn lay in the yerd.
Real [4] he was, he was namoore aferd,
And fethered Pertelote twenty tyme,
And trad as ofte er that [5] it was pryme.   8790
He looketh as it were a grym leoun,
And on hise toos he rometh up and doun ;
Hym deigned nat to sette his foot to grounde
He chukketh whan he hath a corn yfounde,

[1] " In the beginning."   Cf. l. 254.   [2] Woman is man's confusior
Sense.   [4] Regal.   [5] Not in Elles. MS.

And to hym rennen thanne hise wyves alle.
Thus roial as a prince is in an halle,
Leve I this Chauntecleer in his pasture,
And after wol I telle his aventure.

Whan that the monthe in which the world
      bigan,
That highte March, whan God first maked man,
Was compleet, and passed were also,   8801
Syn March bigan, thritty dayes and two,
Bifel that Chauntecleer in al his pryde,
Hise sevene wyves walkynge by his syde,
Caste up hise eyen to the brighte sonne
That in the signe of Taurus hadde yronne
Twenty degrees and oon, and som-what moore,
And knew by kynde,[1] and by noon oother loore,
That it was pryme, and crew with blisful
      stevene.[2]   (15,203 T.)
"The sonne," he seyde, " is clomben up on
      hevene   8810
Fourty degrees and oon, and moore ywis.[3]
Madame Pertelote, my worldes blis,
Herkneth thise blisful briddes how they synge,
And se the fresshe floures how they sprynge ;
Ful is myn herte of revel and solas ! "
But sodeynly hym fil a sorweful cas ;
For evere the latter ende of joy is wo.
God woot that worldly joye is soone ago,
And if a rethor[4] koude faire endite,
He in a cronycle saufly myghte it write,   8820

---

[1] **Nature.** Cf. l. 8467.   [2] **Voice**   Truly.   [4] **Rhetorician.**

As for a sovereyn notabilitee.
Now every wys man, lat him herkne **me** ;
This storie is al so trewe, I undertake,
As is the book of Launcelot de Lake
That wommen holde in ful greet reverence.
Now wol I come agayn to my sentence.

A colfox,[1] ful of sly iniquitee,
That in the grove hadde wonned[2] yeres three,
By heigh ymaginacioun forn-cast,[3]   8829
The same nyght thurgh-out the hegges brast
In-to the yerd ther Chauntecleer the faire
Was wont, and eek hise wyves, to repaire ;
And in a bed of wortes stille he lay,
Til it was passed undren[4] of the day,
Waitynge his tyme on Chauntecleer to falle ;
As gladly doon thise homycides alle
That in await liggen[5] to mordre men.

O false mordrour lurkynge in thy den !
O newe Scariot, newe Genyloun ![6]
False dissynulour, O Greek Synoun,[7]   8840
That broghtest Troye al outrely to sorwe !
O Chauntecleer, acursed be that morwe
That thou in-to that yerd flaugh fro the bemes !
Thou were ful wel ywarned by thy dremes
That thilke day was perilous to thee ;
But what that God forwoot moot nedes bee,
After the opinioun of certein clerkis.
Witnesse on hym that any parfit clerk is,

---

[1] Crafty fox.   [2] Dwelt.   [3] Pre-ordained by high intelligence.   Cf
8846.   [4] Forenoon.   [5] Lie.   [6] Cf. l. 5806.   [7] Sinon advised the
Trojans to take the wooden horse into Troy.   Cf. l. 14,985.

That in scole is greet altercacioun
In this mateere, and greet disputisoun,   8850
And hath been of an hundred thousand men ;
But I ne kan nat bulte it to the bren,[1]
As kan the hooly doctour Augustyn,
Or Boece,[2] or the bisshope Bradwardyn,
Wheither that Goddes worthy forwityng
Streyneth [3] me nedefully to doon a thyng, —
Nedely clepe I symple necessitee, — (15,251 T.)
Or elles if free choys be graunted me
To do that same thyng, or do it noght,
Though God forwoot it er that it was wroght ;
Or if his wityng streyneth never a deel,   8861
But by necessitee condicioneel.
I wil nat han to do of swich mateere,
My tale is of a cok, as ye may heere,
That took his conseil of his wyf with sorwe
To walken in the yerd upon that morwe
That he hadde met [4] that dreem that I of tolde.

   Wommennes conseils been ful ofte colde ;
Wommannes conseil broghte us first to wo
And made Adam fro [5] Paradys to go   8870
Ther as he was ful myrie and wel at ese ;
But for I noot [6] to whom it myght displese.
If I conseil of wommen wolde blame,
Passe over, for I seye it in my game.
Rede auctours where they trete of swich mat-
    eere,

---

[1] Sift it to the bran.   [2] Boethius.   [3] Constraineth.   [4] Dreamed.
[5] Elles. MS. has " out of."   [6] Because I know not.

And what they seyn of wommen ye may
     heere ;
Thise been the cokkes wordes, and nat myne,
I kan noon harm of no womman divyne !

    Faire in the soond,[1] to bathe hire myrily,
Lith Pertelote, and alle hire sustres by,   8880
Agayn [2] the sonne, and Chauntecleer so free
Soong murier than the mermayde in the see ;
For *Phisiologus* [3] seith sikerly,
How that they syngen wel and myrily.

    And so bifel that as he cast his eye
Among the wortes, on a boterflye,
He was war of this fox that lay ful lowe.
No-thyng ne liste hym thanne for to crowe,
But cride anon, "Cok, cok !" and up he sterte,
As man that was affrayed in his herte, — 8890
For natureelly a beest desireth flee
Fro his contrarie, if he may it see,
Though he never erst hadde seyn it with his
    eye.   (15,287 T.)

    This Chauntecleer, whan he gan hym espye,
He wolde han fled, but that the fox anon
Seyde, "Gentil sire, allas ! wher wol ye gon ?
Be ye affrayed of me that am youre freend ?
Now, certes, I were worse than a feend,
If I to yow wolde harm or vileynye.
I am nat come your conseil for tespye,   8900
But trewely the cause of my comynge
Was oonly for to herkne how that ye synge ;

---

[1] Sand.   [2] Towards.   [3] A mediæval work on natural history

For trewely, ye have as myrie a stevene [1]
As any aungel hath [2] that is in hevene.
Ther-with ye han in musyk moore feelynge
Than hadde Boece,[3] or any that kan synge.
My lord youre fader, — God his soule blesse !
And eek youre mooder, of hire gentillesse,
Han in myn hous ybeen to my greet ese, 8909
And certes, sire, ful fayn wolde I yow plese.
But for men speke of syngyng, I wol seye,[4] —
So moote I brouke [5] wel myne eyen tweye, —
Save yow, herde I nevere man yet synge
As dide youre fader in the morwenynge.
Certes, it was of herte, al that he song ;
And for to make his voys the moore strong,
He wolde so peyne hym that with bothe hise
   eyen   (15,311 T.)
He moste wynke, so loude he wolde cryen ;
And stonden on his tiptoon ther-with al,
And strecche fortn his nekke, long and smal ;
And eek he was of swich discrecioun 8921
That ther nas no man in no regioun
That hym in song or wisedom myghte passe.
I have wel rad, in ' Daun Burnel the Asse,' [6]
Among hise vers, how that ther was a cok
For that a preestes sone gaf hym a knok
Up-on his leg whil he was yong and nyce,
He made hym for to lese his benefice ;
But certeyn, ther nys no comparisoun

---

[1] Voice. [2] Not in Elles. MS   [3] Boethius wrote on music.   [4] Ellen
MS has " yow seye."   [5] Enjoy.   [6] A satirical poem in Latin.

Bitwixe the wisedom and discrecioun   8930
Of youre fader and of his subtiltee.
Now syngeth, sire, for seinte [1] charitee ;
Lat se, konne ye youre fader countrefete."
This Chauntecleer hise wynges gan to bete,
As man that koude his traysoun nat espie,
So was he ravysshed with his flaterie.

Allas, ye lordes, many a fals flatour
Is in youre courtes, and many a losengeour,[2]
That plesen yow wel moore, by my feith,
Than he that soothfastnesse un-to yow seith, —
Redeth Ecclesiaste [3] of flaterye, —   8941
Beth war, ye lordes, of hir trecherye.

This Chauntecleer stood hye up-on his toos
Strecchynge his nekke, and heeld hise eyen
        cloos,
And gan to crowe loude for the nones,
And daun Russell,[4] the fox, stirte up atones,
And by the gargat [5] hente Chauntecleer,
And on his bak toward the wode hym beer ;
For yet ne was ther no man that hym sewed.[6]

O destinee, that mayst nat been eschewed !
Allas, that Chauntecleer fleigh fro the bemes !
Allas, his wyf ne roghte nat of dremes !   8952
And on a Friday fil al this meschaunce.

O Venus, that art goddesse of plesaunce,
Syn that thy servant was this Chauntecleer,
And in thy servyce dide al his poweer,

---

[1] Holy.   [2] Liar.   [3] Ecclesiastes.   [4] So called from his russe
color.   [5] Throat.   [6] Followed.

Moore for delit than world to multiplye,
Why woltestow suffre hym on thy day [1] to dye?
　O Gaufred,[2] deere maister soverayn,　　8959
That, whan thy worthy kyng Richard was slayn
With shot, compleynedest his deeth so soere!
Why ne hadde I now thy sentence, and thy
　　　　loore,　　　　　　　(15,356 T.)
The Friday for to chide, as diden ye? —
For on a Friday, soothly, slayn was he.
Thanne wolde I shewe yow how that I koude
　　　pleyne
For Chauntecleres drede, and for his peyne.

　Certes, swich cry, ne lamentacioun,
Was nevere of ladyes maad whan Ylioun
Was wonne, and Pirrus, with his streite swerd,
Whan he hadde hent kyng Priam by the berd,
And slayn hym, — as seith us *Eneydos*, — 8971
As maden alle the hennes in the clos,
Whan they had seyn of Chauntecleer the sighte.
But sovereynly [3] dame Pertelote shrighte,
Ful louder than dide Hasdrubales wyf,
Whan that hir housbonde hadde lost his lyf,
And that the Romayns hadde brend Cartage, —
She was so ful of torment and of rage,
That wilfully in-to the fyr she sterte,
And brende hir-selven with a stedefast herte.

　O woful hennes, right so criden ye,　　8981
As, whan that Nero brende the citee

---

[1] Cf. l. 1537.　[2] It is Geoffrey de Vinsauf (*temp.* Richard I.) whom Chaucer ridicules here.　[3] Elles. MS. has "sodeynlv."

Of Rome, cryden senatours wyves,
For that hir husbondes losten alle hir lyves
With-outen gilt, — this Nero hath hem slayn.
Now turne I wole to my tale agayn.

This sely wydwe, and eek hir doghtres two,
Herden thise hennes crie and maken wo,
And out at dores stirten they anon,
And syen the fox toward the grove gon,   8990
And bar up-on his bak the cok away,
And cryden out, "Harrow! and weylaway!
Ha! ha! the fox!" and after hym they ran,
And eek with staves many another man ;
Ran Colle, oure dogge, and Talbot, and Gerland
And Malkyn, with a dystaf in hir hand ;
Ran cow and calf, and eek [1] the verray hogges,
For [2] fered for berkynge of the dogges,
And shoutyng of the men and wommen eek ;
They ronne so hem thoughte hir herte breek.
They yolleden, as feendes doon in helle ;   9001
The dokes cryden, as men wolde hem quelle ;
The gees, for feere, flowen over the trees ;
Out of the hyve cam the swarm of bees ;
So hydous was the noyse, *a benedicitee!*
Certes, he Jakke Straw, and his meynee, [4]
Ne made nevere shoutes half so shrille,
Whan that they wolden any Flemyng kille,
As thilke day was maad up-on the fox.   9009
Of bras they broghten bemes, [5] and of box,

---

[1] Not in Elles. MS.   [2] Elles. MS. has "so fered."   [3] Kil
Followers.   [5] Horns, trumpets.   Cf. *Parlement of Foules*, 178.

Of horn, of boon, in whiche they blewe and
   powped,   (15,405 T.)
And ther-with-al they skriked and they howped;[1]
It semed as that hevene sholde falle.

 Now, goode men, I pray yow herkneth alle;
Lo, how Fortune turneth sodeynly
The hope and pryde of hir enemy!
This cok, that lay upon the foxes bak,
In al his drede un-to the fox he spak,
And seyde, "Sire, if that I were as ye,
Yet wolde I seyn, as wys God helpe me, 9020
'Turneth agayn, ye proude cherles alle!
A verray pestilence up-on yow falle;
Now am I come un-to the wodes syde,
Maugree youre heed, the cok shal heere abyde;
I wol hym ete in feith, and that anon!'"

 The fox answerde, "In feith it shal be don;"
And as he spak that word, al sodeynly
This cok brak from his mouth delyverly,[2]
And heighe up-on a tree he fleigh anon; 9029
And whan the fox saugh that he was ygon, —

 "Allas!" quod he, "O Chauntecleer, allas!
I have to yow," quod he, "ydoon trespas,
In as muche as I maked yow aferd,
Whan I yow hente and broght out of the [3] yerd;
But, sire, I dide it of no wikke entente.
Com doun, and I shal telle yow what I mente;
I shal seye sooth to yow, God help me so!"

  Nay thanne," quod he, "I shrewe us bothe
   two,

And first I shrewe my self, bothe blood **and**
      bones,
If thou bigyle me any ofter than ones.   9040
Thou shalt na moore, thurgh thy flaterye,
Do [1] me to synge, and wynke with myn eye,
For he that wynketh, whan he sholde see,
Al wilfully, God lat him nevere thee ! " [2]
    "Nay," quod the fox, "but God geve hym
      meschaunce,
That is so undiscreet of governaunce
That jangleth whan he sholde holde his pees.'
    Lo, swich it is for to be recchelees,
And necligent, and truste on flaterye.
But ye that holden this tale a folye, —   9050
As of a fox, or of a cok and hen, —
Taketh the moralite, goode men ;
For Seint Paul seith that al that writen is,
To oure doctrine it is ywrite ywis ; (15,448 T.)
Taketh the fruyt and lat the chaf be stille.
Now, goode God, if that it be thy wille,
As seith my lord, so make us alle goode men,
And brynge us to his heighe blisse ! *Amen.*

Words of the Host to the Nun's Priest. [3]

  "Sire Nonnes Preest," oure Hooste seide
    anon,
"I-blessed be thy breche and every stone !

---

[1] **Cause.** [2] Thrive. [3] These lines are from Camb. **Univ. MS**
Dd 4, 24. Not in Elles. MS.

This was a murie tale of Chaunticleer ,   9061
But, by my trouthe, if thou were seculer,
Thou woldest ben a tredefoul aright ;
For if thou have corage, as thou hast might,
The were nede of hennes, as I wene,
Ye, mo than sevene tymes seventene !
Se, which braunes hath this gentil preest,
So gret a nekke, and swich a large breest !
He loketh as a sparhawke with hise eyen ;
Him nedeth nat his colour for to dyghen   9070
With Brasile, ne with greyn [1] of Portyngale.
Now, sire, faire falle yow for youre tale."
And after that, he with ful merie chere
Seide un-to another as ye shuln heere.

End of the Tales of the Second Day.[2]

TALES OF THE THIRD DAY.

Heere folweth The Phisiciens Tale

Ther was, as telleth Titus Livius,[3] (11,935 T.)
A knyght that called was Virginius,
Fulfild of honour and of worthynesse,
And strong of freendes and of greet richesse.

---

[1] Cf.1. 6339. [2] See preliminary chapter for remarks on the conject-
ural arrangement of the Tales. [3] Livy was the original author of
his tale, but it is clear that he is not copied by Chaucer. Other versions were extant, in French and English ; the one in the *Romaunt
of the Rose* has more resemblance to the one in the text than the
others. It is also in Gower's *Confessio Amantis*

This knyght a doghter hadde by his wyf, —
No children hadde he mo in al his lyf.   9080
Fair was this mayde in excellent beautee
Aboven every wight that man may see ;
For Nature hath with sovereyn diligence
Yformed hire in so greet excellence,
As though she wolde seyn, "Lo, I, Nature,
Thus kan I forme, and peynte a creature,
Whan that me list, — who kan me countrefete ?
Pigmalion ? Noght, though he ay forge and bete,
Or grave, or peynte ; for I dar wel seyn
Apelles, Zanzis [1] sholde werche in veyn,   9090
Outher to grave, or peynte, or forge, or bete,
If they presumed me to countrefete. (11,952 T.)
For He that is the Formere principal
Hath maked me his vicaire-general
To forme and peynten erthely creaturis
Right as me list, and ech thyng in my cure is
Under the moone that may wane and waxe ;
And for my werk right no thyng wol I axe ;
My lord and I been ful of oon accord.
I made hire to the worshipe of my lord ;   9100
So do I alle myne othere creatures,
What colour that they han, or what figures."
Thus semeth me that Nature wolde seye.

This mayde of age twelve yeer was and tweye
In which that Nature hadde swich delit ;
For, right as she kan peynte a lilie whit,

---

[1] Other MSS. have "Zephirus," but see *Troylus*, iv. 414, where
Zanzis is again mentioned.

And reed[1] a rose, right with swich peynture
She peynted hath this noble creature
Er she were born up-on hir lymes fre,
Where as by right swiche colours sholde be ;
And Phebus dyed hath hire treses grete   9111
Lyk to the stremes of his burned heete ;
And if that excellent was hire beautee,
A thousand foold moore vertuous was she.
In hire ne lakked no condicioun
That is to preyse, as by discrecioun.
As wel in goost, as body, chast was she,
For which she floured in virginitee
With alle humylitee and abstinence,
With alle attemperaunce and pacience,   9120
With mesure eek of beryng and array.
Discreet she was in answeryng alway,
Though she were wise as Pallas, dar I seyn ;
Hir facound[2] eek, ful wommanly and pleyn ;
No countrefeted termes hadde she
To seme wys ; but after hir degree
She spak, and alle hire wordes moore and lesse
Sownynge[3] in vertu and in gentillesse ;
Shamefast she was, in maydens shamefastnesse,
Constant in herte, and evere in bisynesse 9130
To dryve hire out of ydel slogardye.
Bacus[4] hadde of hire mouth right no maistrie,
For wyn and youtne dooth Venus encresse ;
As man in fyr wol wasten oille or greesse.
And of hir owene vertu unconstreyned

---

[1] Make red.   [2] Speech.   [3] Tending to. Cf. . 307.   [4] Bacchus

She hath ful ofte tyme syk hire feyned,
For that she wolde fleen the compaignye
Where likly was to treten of folye, —
As is at feestes, revels, and at daunces,
That been occasions of daliaunces.   9140
Swich thyng maken children for to be
To soone rype and boold, as men may se,
Which is ful perilous, and hath been yoore,
For al to soone may they lerne loore (12,004 r.)
Of booldnesse, whan she woxen is a wyf.

    And ye maistresses, in youre olde lyf,
That lordes doghtres han in governaunce,
Ne taketh of my wordes no displesaunce ;
Thenketh that ye been set in governynges
Of lordes doghtres, oonly for two thynges :
Outher for ye han kept youre honestee,   9151
Or elles ye han falle in freletee,
And knowen wel ynough the olde daunce,
And han forsaken fully swich meschaunce
For everemo, therfore for Cristes sake
To teche hem vertu looke that ye ne slake.

    A theef of venysoun, that hath forlaft
His likerousnesse and al his olde craft,
Kan kepe a forest best of any man ;
Now kepeth wel, for if ye wolde ye kan ;   9160
Looke wel that ye un-to no vice assente,
Lest ye be dampned for youre wikke entente ;
For who so dooth a traitour is certeyn ;
And taketh kepe of that that I shal seyn ;
Of alle tresons, sovereyn pestilence
Is whan a wight bitrayseth innocence.

Ye fadres and ye moodres eek, also,
Though ye han children, be it oon or two,
Youre is the charge of al hir surveiaunce 9169
Whil that they been under youre governaunce ;
Beth war, if by ensample of youre lyvynge,
Or by youre necligence in chastisynge,
That they perisse ; for I dar wel seye,
If that they doon, ye shul it deere abeye.
Under a shepherde softe and necligent
The wolf hath many a sheepe and lamb to-rent.
Suffiseth oon ensample now as heere,
For I moot turne agayne to my matere.[1]

This mayde, of which I wol this tale expresse,
So kepte hir self hir neded no maistresse ; 9180
For in hir lyvyng maydens myghten rede,
As in a book, every good word or dede
That longeth to a mayden vertuous,
She was so prudent and so bounteuous ;
For which the fame out sprong on every syde,
Bothe of hir beautee and hir bountee [2] wyde,
That thurgh that land they preised hire echone
That loved vertu, save Envye allone,
That sory is of oother mennes wele,
And glad is of his sorwe and his unheele ; [3]
The doctour [4] maketh this descripcioun.   9191

This mayde up-on a day wente in the toun
Toward a temple, with hire mooder deere,
As is of yonge maydens the manere.

[1] Lines 9177, 9178 are not in Elles. MS.   [2] Goodness.   [3] Misfortune.   [4] St. Augustine. Cf. Parson's Tale, l. 18,175.

Now was ther thanne a justice in that toun,
That governour was of that regioun, (12,056 T.)
And so bifel this juge hise eyen caste
Up-on this mayde, avysynge [1] her [2] ful faste
As she cam forby, ther as this juge stood.
Anon his herte chaunged and his mood,   9200
So was he caught with beautee of this mayde,
And to hym-self ful pryvely he sayde,
" This mayde shal be myn, for any man ! "
   Anon the feend in-to his herte ran,
And taughte hym sodeynly that he by slyghte
The mayden to his purpos wynne myghte ;
For certes, by no force, ne by no meede, [3]
Hym thoughte, he was nat able for to speede,
For she was strong of freendes, and eek she
Confermed was in swich soverayn bountee,
That wel he wiste he myghte hire nevere wynne
As for to maken hire with hir body synne ;
For which, by greet deliberacioun   9213
He sente after a cherl [4] was in the toun,
Which that he knew for subtil and for boold.
This juge un-to this cherl his tale hath toold
In secree wise, and made hym to ensure
He sholde telle it to no creature,
And if he dide he sholde lese [5] his heed.
Whan that assented was this cursed reed [6] 9220
Glad was this juge, and maked him greet
         cheere,
And gaf hym giftes, preciouse and deere.

[1] Observing. [2] Elles. MS. has " hym." [3] Bribery. [4] Some MSS
have "clerk." [5] Lose. [6] Counsel.

Whan shapen was al hire conspiracie,
Fro point to point, how that his lecherie
Parfourned sholde been ful subtilly,
As ye shul heere it after openly,
Hoom gooth the cherl that highte Claudius.
This false juge that highte Apius, —
So was his name, for this is no fable,
But knowen for historial thyng notable ;   9230
The sentence of it sooth is, out of doute, —
This false juge gooth now faste aboute
To hasten his delit al that he may ;
And so bifel soone after on a day,
This false juge, as telleth us the storie,
As he was wont, sat in his consistorie,[1]
And gaf his doomes up-on sondry cas,
This false cherl cam forth, a ful greet pas,[2]
And seyde, " Lord, if that it be youre wille,
As dooth me right up-on this pitous bille, 9240
In which I pleyne [3] up-on Virginius ;
And if that he wol seyn it is nat thus,
I wol it preeve, and fynde good witnesse
That sooth is that my bille wol expresse."

The juge answerde, " Of this in his absence
I may nat geve diffynytyve sentence ; (12,106 T.)
Lat do hym calle, and I wol gladly heere ;
Thou shalt have al right and no wrong heere."

Virginius cam to wite the juges wille,
And right anon was rad this cursed bille ; 9250
The sentence of it was as ye shul heere : —

---

[1] Court of justice   [2] Rapidly.   [3] Complain.

To yow, my lord, sire Apius so deere,
Sheweth youre povre servant Claudius,
How that a knyght called Virginius,
Agayns the lawe, agayn al equitee,
Holdeth expres agayn the wyl of me
My servant, which that is my thral by right,
Which fro my hous was stole up-on a nyght,
Whil that she was ful yong; this wol I preeve
By witnesse, lord, so that it nat yow greeve.
She nys his doghter, nat what so he seye;   9261
Wherfore to yow, my lord, the juge, I preye,
Yeld me my thral, if that it be youre wille.
Lo, this was al the sentence of his bille.

Virginius gan up-on the cherl biholde,
But hastily, er he his tale tolde,
And wolde have preeved it, as sholde a knyght,
And eek by witnessyng of many a wight,
That it was fals that seyde his adversarie;
This cursed juge wolde no thyng tarie,   9270
Ne heere a word moore of Virginius,
But gaf his juggement, and seyde thus:—

"I deeme anon this cherl his servant have;
Thou shalt no lenger in thyn hous hir save.
Go, bryng hire forth, and put hire in oure
      warde.
The cherl shal have his thral; this I awarde."

And whan this worthy knyght, Virginius,
Thurgh sentence of this justice Apius
Moste by force his deere doghter geven
Un-to the juge, in lecherie to lyven,   9280

He gooth hym hoom and sette him in his halle,
And leet anon his deere doghter calle,
And with a face deed as asshen colde,
Upon hir humble face he gan biholde
With fadres pitee stikynge thurgh his herte,
Al wolde he from his purpos nat converte.

"Doghter," quod he, "Virginia by thy name,
Ther been two weyes, outher deeth or shame,
That thou most suffre ; allas! that I was bore!
For nevere thou deservedest wherfore   9290
To dyen with a swerd, or with a knyf.
O deere doghter, endere of my lyf,
Which I have fostred up with swich plesaunce
That thou were nevere out of my remem-
       braunce ;   (12,154 T.)
O doghter, which that art my laste wo,
And in my lyf my laste joye also ;
O gemme of chastitee ! in pacience
Take thou thy deeth, for this is my sentence.
For love, and nat for hate, thou most be deed;
My pitous hand moot smyten of thyn heed !
Allas ! that evere Apius the say !   9301
Thus hath he falsly jugged the to day ;"
And tolde hire al the cas, as ye bifore
Han herd, nat nedeth for to telle it moore.

"O mercy, deere fader ! " quod this mayde,
And with that word she both hir armes layde
About his nekke, as she was wont to do ;
The teeris bruste out of hir eyen two,
And seyde, "Goode fader, shal I dye ?
Is ther no grace, is ther no remedye ? "   9310

"No, certes, deere doghter myn," quod he.

"Thanne gif me leyser, fader myn," quod she
"My deeth for to compleyne a litel space,
For *pardee* Jepte gaf his doghter grace
For to compleyne, er he hir slow, allas!
And God it woot, no thyng was hir trespas,
But for she ran hir fader for to see,
To welcome hym with greet solempnitee."
And with that word she fil aswowne anon,
And after, whan hir swowning is agon,   9320
She riseth up, and to hir fader sayde,
"Blissed be God, that I shal dye a mayde;
Gif me my deeth, er that I have a shame;
Dooth with youre child youre wyl, a Goddes
      name!"

And with that word she preyed hym ful ofte
That with his swerd he wolde smyte softe;
And with that word aswowne doun she fil.
Hir fader, with ful sorweful herte and wil,
Hir heed of smoot, and by the tope it hente,
And to the juge he gan it to presente,   9330
As he sat yet in doom in consistorie;
And whan the juge it saugh, as seith the storie,
He bad to take hym and anhange hym faste;
But right anon a thousand peple in thraste,
To save the knyght, for routhe and for pitee,
For knowen was the false iniquitee.
The peple anon hath suspect of this thyng,
By manere of the cherles chalangyng,
That it was by the assent of Apius;

They wisten wel that he was lecherus,   9340
For which un-to this Apius they gon,
And caste hym in a prisoun right anon,
Ther as he slow hym self ; and Claudius,
That servant was un-to this Apius,
And demed for to hange upon a tree ;
But that Virginius, of his pitee,   (12,206 T.)
So preyde for hym that he was exiled,
And elles, certes, he had been bigyled.
The remenant were anhanged, moore and lesse,
That were consentant of this cursednesse. 9350
   Heere men may seen how synne hath his
     merite.[1]
Beth war, for no man woot whom God wol smyte,
In no degree ; ne in which manere wyse
The worm of conscience may agryse [2]
Of wikked lyf, though it so pryvee be
That no man woot ther-of but God and he ;
For be he lewed [3] man, or ellis lered,[4]
He noot how soone that he shal been afered ; [5]
Therfore, I rede yow, this conseil take,   9359
Forsaketh synne, er synne yow forsake.[6] (12,220 T.)

The wordes of the Hoost to the Phisicien and the
Pardoner.

   Oure Hooste gan to swere as he were wood ;
"Harrow !" quod he, "by nayles,[7] and by
blood !   (12,222 T.)

---

[1] Reward. [2] Make shudder. [3] Ignorant. [4] Learned. [5] Frightened. [6] Cf. l. 18,336. [7] Nails of the cross.

This was a fals cherl and a fals justise!
As shameful deeth as herte may devyse
Come to thise juges,[1] and hire advocatz!
Algate[2] this sely mayde is slayn, allas!
Allas! to deere boughte she beautee!
Wherfore I seye al day, as men may see,
That giftes of Fortune and of Nature
Been cause of deeth to many a creature.   9370
Hire beautee was hire deth, I dar wel sayn;
Allas! so pitously as she was slayn![3]
Of bothe giftes that I speke of now
Men han ful ofte moore for harm than prow.[4]

    "But trewely, myn owene maister deere,
This is a pitous tale for to heere;
But nathelees, passe over, is no fors,[5]
I pray to God so save thy gentil cors,
And eek thyne urynals, and thy jurdones,[6]
Thyn Ypocras,[7] and eek thy Galiones,[7]   9380
And every boyste[8] ful of thy letuarie;[9]
God blesse hem, and oure lady Seint Marie!
So moot I theen,[10] thou art a propre man,
And lyk a prelat, by Seint Ronyan!
Seyde I nat wel, I kan nat speke in terme?[11]
But wel I woot thou doost[12] myn herte to erme[13]
That I almoost have caught a cardynacle.[14]
By *corpus* bones! but I have triacle,[15]

---

¹ Elles. MS. has "false juges." ² However. ³ Lines 9371, 9372
not in Elles. MS. ⁴ Profit. ⁵ Consequence. ⁶ Jordens. ⁷ Bev-
erages named after Hippocrates and Galen. ⁸ Box. ⁹ Electuary
Cf. l. 426. ¹⁰ Thrive. ¹¹ Elaborately. ¹² Causest. ¹³ Grieve
¹⁴ Heartache. ¹⁵ Remedy; properly, *Theriaca Andromachi*, a
compound remedy and antidote, invented by Andromachus the
Elder, physician to Nero, containing the dried flesh of vipers, and
many other ingredients.

Or elles a draughte of moyste and corny ale,
Or but I heere anon a myrie tale,   939ᵃ
Myn herte is lost, for pitee of this mayde.
Thou *beel amy*,[1] thou Pardoner," he sayde,
" Telle us som myrthe, or japes, right anon ! "
    " It shal be doon," quod he, " by Seint Ron-
            yon !   (12,254 T.)
But first," quod he, " heere at this ale stake [2]
I wol bothe drynke and eten of a cake."

    And right anon the gentils gonne to crye,
" Nay ! lat hym telle us of no ribaudye ;
Telle us som moral thyng, that we may leere [3]
Som wit, and thanne wol we gladly heere."
    " I graunte, ywis," quod he, " but I moot
            thynke   9401
Up-on som honeste thyng, while that I drynke."

*Heere folweth The Preamble of the Pardoners
Tale.*

    " Lordynges," quod he, " in chirches whan I
            preche,   (12,263 T.)
I peyne me to han an hauteyn [4] speche,
And rynge it out as round as gooth a belle,
For I kan [5] al by rote that I telle.
My theme is alwey oon, and evere was, —
Radix malorum est Cupiditas.[6]
    " First, I pronounce whennes that I come,

---

[1] Good friend.   [2] From which the " bush " was suspended, at the
ale house.   Cf. l. 667.   [3] Learn   [4] Lofty.   [5] Know.   [6] Avarice is
the root of evils.   Cf. l. 710.

And thanne my bulles shewe I alle and some ;
Oure lige lordes [1] seel on my patente,   9411
That shewe I first, my body to warente,
That no man be so boold, ne preest ne clerk,
Me to destourbe of Cristes hooly werk ;
And after that thanne telle I forth my tales,
Bulles of popes and of cardynales,
Of patriarkes and bishoppes I shewe,
And in Latyn I speke a wordes fewe
To saffron with [2] my predicacioun,
And for to stire hem to devocioun ;   9420
Thanne shewe I forth my longe cristal stones
Ycrammed ful of cloutes and of bones, —
Relikes been they, as wenen they echoon ;
Thanne have I in latoun [3] a sholder boon [4]
Which that was of an hooly Jewes sheepe.

   " ' Goode men,' I seye, ' taak of my wordes
      keepe, —
If that this boon be wasshe in any welle,
If cow, or calf, or sheepe, or oxe swelle
That any worm hath ete, or worm ystonge,
Taak water of that welle and wassh his tonge,
And it is hool anon ; and forthermoor   9431
Of pokkes, and of scabbe, and every soor,
Shal every sheepe be hool that of this welle
Drynketh a draughte.   Taak kepe eek what I
      telle.

   " ' If that the goode man that the beestes
      oweth [5]

---

[1] The Pope's.   [2] To spice or color my sermon with.   [3] Brass
Cf. l. 18,846.   [5] Owneth.

Wol every wyke,[1] er that the cok hym croweth,
Fastynge, drinke of this welle a draughte,
As thilke hooly Jew oure eldres taughte,
Hise beestes and his stoor shal multiplie.

  " 'And, sires, also it heeleth jalousie,   9440
For though a man be falle in jalous rage,
Lat maken with this water his potage,
And nevere shal he moore his wyf mystriste,
Though he the soothe of hir defaute wiste, —
Al had she taken preestes [2] two or thre.
Heere is a miteyn eek, that ye may se ;
He that his hand wol putte in this mitayn,
He shal have multipliyng of his grayn,
Whan he hath sowen, be it whete or otes,
So that he offre [3] pens, or elles grotes.   9450

  " 'Goode men and wommen, o thyng warne
     I yow,   (12,311 T.)
If any wight be in this chirche now
That hath doon synne horrible that he
Dar nat for shame of it yshryven be,
Or any womman, be she yong or old,
That hath ymaked hir housbonde cokewold,
Swich folk shal have no power ne no grace
To offren to my relikes in this place ;
And who-so fyndeth hym out of swich fame
They wol come up and offre on Goddes name,
And I assoille [4] hem by the auctoritee   9461
Which that by bulle ygraunted was to me.'

---

  [1] Week.   [2] Not pardoners, of course. but secular clerics.   [3] Contribute.   [4] Absolve.

" By this gaude have I wonne, yeer by yeer,
An hundred mark sith I was Pardoner.
I stonde lyk a clerk in my pulpet,
And whan the lewed [1] peple is doun yset,
I preche so as ye han herd bifoore,
And telle an hundred false japes moore ;
Thanne peyne I me to strecche forth the nekke
And est and west up-on the peple I bekke,
As dooth a dowve, sittynge on a berne ;   9471
Myne handes and my tonge goon so yerne,[2]
That it is joye to se my bisynesse.
Of avarice and of swich cursednesse
Is al my prechyng, for to make hem free
To geven hir pens, and namely [3] un-to me ;
For myn entente is nat but for to wynne,
And no thyng for correccioun of synne.
I rekke nevere whan that they been beryed,
Though that hir soules 'goon a blakeberyed ; ' [4]
For certes many a predicacioun   9481
Comth ofte tyme of yvel entencioun ;
Som for plesaunce of folk and flaterye,
To been avaunced by ypocrisye ;
And som for veyne glorie, and som for hate,
For whan I dar noon oother weyes debate,
Thanne wol I stynge hym with my tonge
        smerte
In prechyng, so that he shal nat asterte [5]
To been defamed falsly, if that he

[1] Lay, ignorant.   [2] Briskly.   [3] Especially.   [4] Where it may be
For construction, cf. ll. 10,396, 16,356.   [5] Escape

Hath trespased to my bretheren or to me ;
For though I telle noght his propre name, 9491
Men shal wel knowe that it is the same,
By signes, and by othere circumstances.
Thus quyte [1] I folk that doon us displesances ;
Thus spitte I out my venym under hewe
Of hoolynesse, to semen hooly and trewe.

" But, shortly, myn entente I wol devyse, —
I preche of no thyng but for coveityse ;
Therfore my theme is yet and evere was,
Radix malorum est Cupiditas.   (12,360 T.)
Thus kan I preche agayn that same vice 9501
Which that I use, and that is avarice ;
But though my-self be gilty in that synne
Yet kan I maken oother folk to twynne [2]
From avarice, and soore to repente ;
But that is nat my principal entente, —
I preche no thyng but for coveitise.
Of this mateere it oghte ynogh suffise.

"Thanne telle I hem ensamples many oon
Of olde stories longe tyme agoon, —   9510
For lewed peple loven tales olde, —
Swiche thynges kan they wel reporte and
        holde.
What ! trowe ye the whiles I may preche,
And wynne gold and silver for I teche,
That I wol lyve in poverte wilfully ?
Nay, nay, I thoghte it nevere, trewely,
For I wol preche and begge in sondry landes ;

----

[1] Requite, pay.   [2] Separate.

I wol nat do no labour with myne handes,
Ne make baskettes [1] and lyve therby,
By cause I wol nat beggen ydelly.   9520
I wol noon of the Apostles countrefete,
I wol have moneie, wolle, chese and whete.
Al were it geven of the povereste page,
Or of the povereste wydwe in a village,
Al sholde hir children sterve [2] for famyne.
Nay, I wol drynke licour of the vyne,
And have a joly wenche in every toun ;
But herkneth, lordynges, in conclusioun.

" Youre likyng is that I shal telle a tale.
Now have I dronke a draughte of corny ale,
By God, I hope I shal yow telle a thyng   9531
That shal by resoun been at youre likyng ;
For though my-self be a ful vicious man,
A moral tale yet I yow telle kan,
Which I am wont to preche for to wynne.
Now hoold youre pees, my tale I wol bigynne."

Heere bigynneth The Pardoners Tale.

In Flaundres whilom was a compaignye
Of yonge folk, that haunteden [4] folye,
As riot, hasard, stywes and tavernes,
Where as with harpes, lutes and gyternes,[5]

---

[1] As Egyptian monks once did.   [2] Die.   [3] Three stories similar
to that of the Pardoner were reprinted by the Chaucer Society in
1875 : *Christ and his Disciples*, from the *Cento Novelle Antiche*
The Hermit, Death, and the Robbers, from another edition of the
same ; and *The Treasure in the Tiber*, from Morlinus.   [4] Fre
quented.   [5] Guitars.

They daunce and pleyen at dees,[1] bothe day
    and nyght, 9541
And eten also, and drynken over hir myght,
Thurgh which they doon the devel sacrifise
With-inne that develes temple, in cursed wise,
By superfluytee abhomynable. (12,405 T.)
Hir othes been so grete and so dampnable
That it is grisly[2] for to heere hem swere ;
Oure blissed Lordes body[3] they to-tere ;
Hem thoughte that Jewes rente hym noght
    ynough,
And ech of hem at otheres synne lough ; 9550
And right anon thanne comen tombesteres[4]
Fetys[5] and smale, and yonge frutesteres,[6]
Syngeres with harpes, baudes, wafereres,[7] —
Whiche been the verray develes officeres, —
To kyndle and blowe the fyr of lecherye
That is annexed un-to glotonye.
The Hooly Writ take I to my witnesse
That luxurie is in wyn and dronkenesse.

    Lo, how that dronken Looth unkyndely[8]
Lay by hise doghtres two unwityngly ; 9560
So dronke he was he nyste[9] what he wroghte.

    Herodes, — who so wel the stories soghte, —
Whan he of wyn was repleet at his feeste,
Right at his owene table, he gaf his heeste[10]
To sleen the Baptist John, ful giltelees.

---

[1] Dice. [2] Frightful. [3] For such oatns, cf. ll. 6047, 9362, 9388, 9725, 9728, and 18,835. [4] Women tumblers. [5] Nice, graceful. [6] Women selling fruit. [7] Women selling wafers. [8] Unnaturaily. [9] Knew not. [10] Command.

Seneca seith a good word, doutelees ;[1]
He seith he kan no difference fynde
Bitwix a man that is out of his mynde
And a man which that is dronkelewe,
But that woodnesse, fallen in a shrewe,   9570
Persevereth lenger than dooth dronkenesse.
O glotonye, ful of cursednesse ;
O cause first of oure confusioun ;
O original of oure dampnacioun ;
Til Crist hadde boght us with his blood agayn !
    Lo, how deere, shortly for to sayn,
Aboght[2] was thilke cursed vileynye ;
Corrupt was al this world for glotonye !
Adam oure fader, and his wyf also,
Fro Paradys to labour and to wo   9580
Were dryven for that vice, it is no drede,[3]—
For whil that Adam fasted, as I rede,[4]
He was in Paradys, and whan that he
Eet of the fruyt deffended,[5] on the tree,
Anon he was out cast to wo and peyne.
O glotonye, on thee wel oghte us pleyne !
    O, wiste a man how manye maladyes
Folwen of excesse and of glotonyes,
He wolde been the moore mesurable
Of his diete, sittynge at his table !   9590
Allas ! the shorte throte, the tendre mouth,
Maketh that est and west, and north and south
In erthe, in eir, in water, man to swynke[6]

---

[1] In faith.   [2] Atoned for.   [3] Without doubt.   [4] In *Hieronymus
contra Jovinianum* (St. Jerome).   [5] Forbidden.   [6] Work.

To gete a glotoun deyntee mete and drynke !
Of this matiere, O Paul, wel kanstow trete !
" Mete un-to wombe,[1] and wombe eek un-to
     mete,   (12,456 T.)
Shal God destroyen bothe," as Paulus seith.
Allas ! a foul thyng is it, by my feith,
To seye this word, and fouler is the dede
Whan man so drynketh of the white and rede,[2]
That of his throte he maketh his pryvee, 9601
Thurgh thilke cursed superfluitee.

   The Apostel wepyng seith ful pitously,
" Ther walken manye of whiche yow toold
     have I,
I seye it now wepyng with pitous voys,
That they[3] been enemys of Cristes croys,
Of whiche the ende is deeth, wombe is hir god."
O wombe ! O bely ! O stynkyng cod !
Fulfilled of donge and of corrupcioun !
At either ende of thee foul is the soun ; 9610
How greet labour and cost is thee to fynde ![4]
Thise cookes, how they stampe, and streyne,
     and grynde,
And turnen substaunce in-to accident,
To fulfillen al thy likerous talent ![5]
Out of the harde bones knokke they
The mary, for they caste noght a-wey
That may go thurgh the golet[6] softe and swoote.
Of spicerie, of leef, and bark, and roote,

---

[1] Belly.   [2] Wines.   [3] Elles. MS. has "ther," for " that they."
[4] Supply. [5] Fastidious disposition. [6] Gullet.

Shal been his sauce ymaked by delit,
To make hym yet a newer appetit;   9620
But certes he that haunteth [1] swiche delices
Is deed whil that he lyveth in tho vices.

A lecherous thyng is wyn, and dronkenesse
Is ful of stryvyng and of wrecchednesse.
O dronke man ! disfigured is thy face,
Sour is thy breeth, foul artow to embrace,
And thurgh thy dronke nose semeth the soun,
As though thou seydest ay, " Sampsoun ! Samp-
     soun ! "
And yet, God woot, Sampsoun drank nevere
     no wyn.
Thou fallest as it were a styked swyn,   9630
Thy tonge is lost and al thyn honeste cure ;
For dronkenesse is verray sepulture
Of mannes wit and his discrecioun,
In whom that drynke hath dominacioun ;
He kan no conseil kepe, it is no drede.
Now kepe yow fro the white and fro the rede,
And namely fro the white wyn of Lepe
That is to selle in Fysshstrete, or in Chepe.[2]
This wyn of Spaigne crepeth subtilly
In othere wynes growynge faste by, (12,500 T.)
Of which ther ryseth swich fumositee,   9641
That whan a man hath dronken draughtes thre
And weneth [3] that he be at hoom in Chepe,
He is in Spaigne right at the toune of Lepe, —
Nat at the Rochele, ne at Burdeux-toun, —

----

[1] Frequently indulges in.   [2] Cheapside.   [3] Thinketh.

And thanne wol he seye, " Sampsoun, Samp-
    soun ! "

But herkneth, lordes, o word, I yow preye,
That alle the sovereyn actes dar I seye
Of victories in the Olde Testament,
Thurgh verray [1] God that is omnipotent, 9650
Were doon in abstinence and in preyere ;
Looketh the Bible and ther ye may it leere.

Looke, Attilla, the grete conquerour,
Deyde in his sleepe, with shame and dishonour
Bledynge ay at his nose in dronkenesse.
A capitayn sholde lyve in sobrenesse ;
And over al this avyseth yow right wel
What was comaunded un-to Lamwel, —
Nat Samuel, but Lamwel seye I ;
Redeth the Bible, and fynde it expresly 9660
Of wyn gevyng, to hem that han justise.
Namoore of this, for it may wel suffise.

And now I have spoken of glotonye,
Now wol I yow deffenden [2] hasardrye.
Hasard is verray mooder of lesynges,[3]
And of deceite, and cursed forswerynges ;
Blaspheme of Crist, manslaughtre, and wast
    also
Of catel, and of tyme, and forthermo
It is repreeve [4] and contrarie of honour
For to ben holde a commune hasardour ; 9670
And ever the hyer he is of estaat,
The moore is he holden desolaat.

---

[1] True [2] Denounce. [3] Lyings. [4] Reproved

If that a prynce useth hasardrye
In alle governaunce and policye,
He is, as by commune opinioun,
Yholde the lasse in reputacioun.

    Stilbon,[1] that was a wys embassadour,
Was sent to Corynthe in ful greet honour
Fro Lacidomye to maken hire alliaunce ;
And whan he cam, hym happede *par chaunce*,
That alle the gretteste that were of that lond
Pleyynge atte hasard he hem fond ;   9682
For which, as soone as it myghte be,
He stal hym hoom agayn to his contree,
And seyde, "Ther wol I nat lese my name,
Ne I[2] wol nat take on me so greet defame,
Yow for to allie un-to none hasardours ;
Sendeth othere wise embassadours,
For, by my trouthe, me were levere dye,
Than I yow sholde to hasardours allye ; 9690
For ye that been so glorious in honours,
Shul nat allyen yow with hasardours
As by my wyl, ne as by my tretee !" (12,553 T.'
This wise philosophre thus seyde hee.

    Looke eek that to the kyng Demetrius,
The kyng of Parthes, as the book seith us,
Sente him a paire of dees [3] of gold, in scorn,
For he hadde used hasard ther-biforn ;
For which he heeld his glorie or his renoun
At no value or reputacioun.   9700
Lordes may fynden oother maner pley
Honeste ynough to dryve the day awey.

---

[1] Probably Chilon.   [2] Pronounced " ny."   [3] Dice.

Now wol I speke of othes false and grete
A word or two, as olde bookes trete.
Gret sweryng is a thyng abhominable,
And fals sweryng is yet moore reprevable.
The heighe God forbad sweryng at al, —
Witnesse on Mathew, but in special
Of sweryng seith the hooly Jeremye,
" Thou shalt seye sooth thyne othes, and nat
      lye   9710
And swere in doom, and eek in rightwisnesse ; "
But ydel sweryng is a cursednesse.
Bihoold and se, that in the firste table
Of heighe Goddes heestes, honurable,
Hou that the seconde heeste of hym is this :
" Take nat my name in ydel, or amys ; "
Lo, rather he forbedeth swich sweryng
Than homycide, or any cursed thyng ;
I seye that as by ordre, thus it stondeth.   9719
This knowen, that hise heestes understondeth,
How that the seconde heeste of God is that ;
And forther over, I wol thee telle al plat
That vengeance shal nat parten from his hous
That of hise othes is to outrageous, —
" By Goddes precious herte," and " By his
      nayles,"
And " By the blood of Crist that is in Hayles,"[1]
" Sevene is my chaunce, and thyn is *cynk* and
      treye,"
By Goddes armes, if thou falsly pleye,

[1] The Abbey of Hailes.

This daggere shal thurgh-out thyn herte go ! "
This fruyt cometh of the bicched bones [1] two,
Forsweryng, ire, falsnesse, homycide.   9731
Now for the love of Crist that for us dyde,
Lete [2] youre othes, bothe grete and smale.
But, sires, now wol I telle forth my tale.

Thise riotoures thre, of whiche I telle,
Longe erst er prime rong of any belle,
Were set hem in a taverne to drynke ;
And as they sat they herde a belle clynke
Biforn a cors, was caried to his grave.
That oon of hem gan callen to his knave : 9740
" Go bet," [3] quod he, " and axe redily
What cors is this that passeth heer forby,
And looke that thou reporte his name weel."

" Sire," quod this boy, " it nedeth neveradeel,
It was me toold er ye cam heer two houres ;
He was, *pardee*, an old felawe of youres,
And sodeynly he was yslayn to-nyght, (12,607 T.)
For-dronke,[4] as he sat on his bench upright ;
Ther cam a privee theef, men clepeth Deeth,
That in this contree al the peple sleeth,   9750
And with his spere he smoot his herte atwo,
And wente his wey with-outen wordes mo.
He hath a thousand slayn this pestilence,
And, maister, er ye come in his presence,
Me thynketh that it were necessarie
For to be war of swich an adversarie ;
Beth redy for to meete hym everemoore ;
Thus taughte me my dame ; I sey namoore."

---

[1] Dice.   [2] Stint.   [3] Better, *i. e.*, faster.   [4] Very drunk.

" By Seinte Marie ! " seyde this taverner,
' The child seith sooth, for he hath slayn this
      yeer   9760
Henne [1] over a mile, with-inne a greet village,
Bothe man and womman, child, and hyne,[2] and
      page ;
I trowe his habitacioun be there ;
To been avysed greet wysdom it were,
Er that he dide a man a dishonour."

" Ye, Goddes armes ! " quod this riotour,
" Is it swich peril with hym for to meete ?
I shal hym seke by wey, and eek by strete ;
I make avow to Goddes digne [3] bones !
Herkneth, felawes, we thre been al ones, 9770
Lat ech of us holde up his hand til oother,
And ech of us bicomen otheres brother,
And we wol sleen this false traytour, Deeth ;
He shal be slayn which that so manye sleeth,
By Goddes dignitee, er it be nyght ! "

Togidres han thise thre hir trouthes plight
To lyve and dyen ech of hem for oother,
As though he were his owene ybore brother ;
And up they stirte, al [4] dronken in this rage ;
And forth they goon towardes that village 9780
Of which the taverner hadde spoke biforn ;
And many a grisly ooth thanne han they sworn ;
And Cristes blessed body they to-rente, —
Deeth shal be deed, if that they may hym hente.
Whan they han goon nat fully half a mile,

---

[1] Hence.   [2] Servant.   [3] Worthy.   [4] Elles. MS. has "and"

Right as they wolde han troden over a stile,
An oold man and a povre with hem mette ;
This olde man ful mekely hem grette,
And seyde thus : " Now, lordes, God yow see ! '
    The proudeste of thise riotours three   9790
Answerde agayn, " What, carl with sory grace,
Why artow al forwrapped, save thy face ?
Why lyvestow so longe in so greet age ? "
    This olde man gan looke in his visage,
And seyde thus : " For I ne kan nat fynde
A man, though that I walked in to Ynde,
Neither in citee, nor in no village,   (12,657 T.)
That wolde chaunge his youthe for myn age ;
And therfore moot I han myn age stille,
As longe tyme as it is Goddes wille.   9800
Ne Deeth, allas ! ne wol nat han my lyf ;
Thus walke I, lyk a restelees kaityf,[1]
And on the ground, which is my moodres gate,
I knokke with my staf bothe erly and late,
And seye, ' Leeve mooder, leet me in !
Lo, how I vanysshe, flessh and blood and skyn ;
Allas ! whan shul my bones been at reste ?
Mooder, with yow wolde I chaunge my cheste[2]
That in my chambre longe tyme hath be,
Ye, for an heyre-clowt to wrappe me ! '   9810
But yet to me she wol nat do that grace,
For which ful pale and welked[3] is my face ;
But, sires, to yow it is no curteisye
To speken to an old man vileynye,

---

[1] Captive, wretch.   [2] Money-box, locker.   [3] Furrowed.

But he trespasse in word, or elles in dede.
In Hooly Writ ye may your self wel rede,
Agayns an oold man hoor upon his heed,
Ye sholde arise ; wherfore I geve yow reed,[1]
Ne dooth un-to an oold man noon harm now,
Namoore than that ye wolde men did to yow
In age, if that ye so longe abyde.   982ı
And God be with yow where ye go[2] or ryde ;
I moote go thider as I have to go."

   "Nay, olde cherl, by God, thou shalt nai
      so ! "
Seyde this oother hasardour anon ;
"Thou partest nat so lightly, by Seint John !
Thou spak right now of thilke traytour, Deeth
That in this contree alle oure freendes sleeth ;
Have heer my trouthe, as thou art his espye,
Telle where he is, or thou shalt it abye,[3]   983ơ
By God and by the hooly sacrement !
For soothly, thou art oon of his assent
To sleen us yonge folk, thou false theef ! "

   "Now, sires," quod he, "if that ye be so leef
To fynde Deeth, turne up this croked wey,
For in that grove I lafte hym, by my fey,
Under a tree, and there he wole abyde ;
Noght for youre boost he wole him no thyng
      hyde.   9838
Se ye that ook ? Right there ye shal hym fynde.
God save yow that boghte agayn mankynde,
And yow amende ! " thus seyde this olde man ;

---

[1] Advice. [2] Wherever ye walk. [3] Pay for it.

And everich of thise riotours ran   (12,702 T.)
Til he cam to that tree, and ther they founde,
Of floryns fyne of gold ycoyned rounde,
Wel ny an eighte busshels, as hem thoughte.
No lenger thanne after Deeth they soughte,
But ech of hem so glad was of that sighte,
For that the floryns been so faire and brighte,
That doun they sette hem by this precious
        hoord.
The worste of hem he spak the firste word.

    " Bretheren," quod he, " taak kepe what I
        seye ;   9851
My wit is greet, though that I bourde [1] and
        pleye.
This tresor hath Fortune un-to us geven
In myrthe and joliftee oure lyf to lyven,
And lightly as it comth so wol we spende.
Ey, Goddes precious dignitee ! who wende [2]
To-day, that we sholde han so fair a grace ?
But myghte this gold be caried fro this place
Hoom to myn hous, or elles un-to youres, —
For wel ye woot that al this gold is oures, —
Thanne were we in heigh felicitee.   9861
But trewely, by daye it may nat bee ,
Men wolde seyn that we were theves stronge,
And for oure owene tresor doon us honge.
This tresor moste ycaried be by nyghte,
As wisely and as slyly as it myghte.
Wherfore, I rede [3] that cut among us alle

---

[1] Jest.   [2] Thought.   [3] Advise.

Be drawe, and lat se wher the cut wol falle;
And he that hath the cut with herte blithe
Shal renne to the[1] towne, and that ful swithe,[4]
And brynge us breed and wyn ful prively,
And two of us shul kepen subtilly   9872
This tresor wel; and if he wol nat tarie,
Whan it is nyght we wol this tresor carie
By oon assent where as us thynketh best."
That oon of hem the cut broghte in his fest,[8]
And bad hym drawe and looke where it wol
          falle;
And it fil on the yongeste of hem alle,
And forth toward the toun he wente anon;
And al so soone as that he was gon,   988c
That oon of hem spak thus un-to that oother:
"Thow knowest wel thou art my sworne brother:
Thy profit wol I telle thee anon;
Thou woost wel that oure felawe is agon,
And heere is gold, and that ful greet plentee,
That shal departed been among us thre;
But nathelees, if I kan shape it so
That it departed were among us two,
Hadde I nat doon a freendes torn to thee?"
    That oother answerde, "I noot hou that may
          be;   989c
He woot how that the gold is with us tweye;
What shal we doon, what shal we to hym
          seye?"
    "Shal it be conseil?"[4] seyde the firste
    shrewe,[5]

Not in Elles. MS.   [2] Quickly   [8] Fist.   [4] Secret.   [5] Rascal.

" And I shal tellen in a wordes fewe (12,754 T.)
What we shal doon, and bryngen it wel aboute.'
    " I graunte," quod that oother, " out of doute,
That by my trouthe I shal thee nat biwreye."
    " Now," quod the firste, " thou woost wel we
        be tweye,
And two of us shul strenger be than oon. 9899
Looke, whan that he is set, and [1] right anoon
Arys, as though thou woldest with hym pleye,
And I shal ryve [2] hym thurgh the sydes tweye
Whil that thou strogelest with hym as in game,
And with thy daggere looke thou do the same,
And thanne shal al this gold departed [3] be,
My deere freend, bitwixen me and thee.
Thanne may we bothe oure lustes all fulfille,
And pleye at dees right at oure owene wille."
And thus acorded been thise shrewes tweye,
To sleen the thridde, as ye han herd me seye.
    This yongeste, which that wente un-to the
        toun,   9911
Ful ofte in herte he rolleth up and doun
The beautee of thise floryns newe and brighte;
" O Lord," quod he, " if so were that I myghte
Have al this tresor to my self allone,
Ther is no man that lyveth under the trone
Of God, that sholde lyve so murye as I ! "
And atte laste the feend, oure enemy,
Putte in his thought that he sholde poyson
        beye,

----

[1] Elles. MS. has "that."   [2] Pierce.   [3] Divided.

With which he myghte sleen hise felawes
    tweye ;   9920
For why ? The feend foond hym in swich lyv-
    ynge,
That he hadde leve hem to sorwe brynge,
For this was outrely his fulle entente
To sleen hem bothe and nevere to repente.
And forth he gooth, no lenger wolde he
    tarie,
Into the toun, un-to a pothecarie,
And preyde hym that he hym wolde selle
Som poysoun, that he myghte hise rattes
    quelle ; [1]
And eek ther was a polcat in his hawe, [2] 9929
That, as he seyde, his capouns hadde yslawe,
And fayn he wolde wreke hym, if he myghte,
On vermyn, that destroyed hem [3] by nyghte.
    The pothecarie answerde, " And thou shalt
    have
A thyng that, al so God my soule save !
In al this world ther nis no creature,
That ete or dronke hath of this confiture,
Noght but the montance of a corn of whete,
That he ne shal his lif anon forlete ;
Ye, sterve he shal, and that in lasse while
Than thou wolt goon a paas [4] nat but a mile,
This poysoun is so strong and violent." 9941
    This cursed man hath in his hond yhent

[1] Kill.   [2] Farmyard.   [3] Elles. MS. has " hym ; " but the refer-
ance appears to be to the " capouns," rather than to the man.   [4] To
go is to walk ; to " goon a paas," to walk at an ordinary pace.

This poysoun in a box, and sith [1] he ran
In-to the nexte strete un-to a man,   (12,804 T.)
And borwed of hym large botels thre,
And in the two his poyson poured he ;
The thridde he kepte clene for his owene
        drynke,
For al the nyght he shoope hym for to swynke
In cariynge of the gold out of that place ;
And whan this riotour with sory grace   9950
Hadde filled with wyn his grete botels thre,
To hise felawes agayn repaireth he.

    What nedeth it to sermone of it moore?
For right so as they hadde cast his deeth bi·
        foore,
Right so they han hym slayn, and that anon,
And whan that this was doon thus spak that
        oon :
" Now lat us sitte and drynke, and make us
        merie,
And afterward we wol his body berie ; "
And with that word it happed hym, *par cas*, [3]
To take the botel ther the poysoun was,   9960
And drank and gaf his felawe drynke also,
For which anon they storven [4] bothe two.

    But certes, I suppose that Avycen [5]
Wroot nevere in no Canon, ne in no fen,
Mo wonder signes of empoisonyng
Than hadde thise wrecches two, er hir endyng

---

[1] Then.   [2] Planned to work.   [3] By chance.   [4] Died.   [5] Avicenna, Arabian physician, author of *Canon Medicinæ*, the parts o
which were called "fens."   Cf. l. 432

Thus ended been thise homycides two,
And eek the false empoysonere also.
   O cursed synne ful of alle cursednesse!
O traytours homycide! O wikkednesse!   9970
O glotonye, luxurie, and hasardrye!
Thou blasphemour of Crist with vileynye,
And othes grete, of usage and of pride!
Allas! mankynde, how may it bitide
That to thy Creatour which that the wroghte,
And with his precious herte-blood thee boghte,
Thou art so fals and so unkynde, allas!

   Now, goode men, God forgeve yow **youre**
      trespas,
And ware yow fro the synne of avarice.
Myn hooly pardoun may yow alle warice,[1]
So that ye offre nobles, or sterlynges,[2]   9981
Or elles silver broches, spoones, rynges.
Boweth youre heed under this hooly bulle!
Com up, ye wyves, offreth of youre wolle!
Youre names I entre heer in my rolle anon;
In-to the blisse of hevene shul ye gon;
I yow assoille[3] by myn heigh power, —
Yow that wol offre, — as clene and eek as cleer
As ye were born; and lo, sires, thus I preche,
And Jhesu Crist, that is oure soules leche,[4]
So graunte yow his pardoun to receyve,   9991
For that is best, I wol yow nat deceyve.

   [1] Heal. [2] Sterling money, pence. [3] Absolve. [4] Physician.
   VOL. I.   27

Words of the Pardoner, the Host and the Knight.

" But, sires, o word forgat I in my tale ;
I have relikes and pardoun in my male [1]
As faire as any man in Engelond,   (12,855 T.)
Whiche were me geven by the popes hond.
If any of yow wole of devocioun
Offren, and han myn absolucioun,
Com forth anon, and kneleth heere adoun,
And mekely receyveth my pardoun ;   10,000
Or elles taketh pardoun as ye wende,
Al newe and fressh at every miles ende, —
So that ye offren alwey newe and newe
Nobles or pens whiche that be goode and trewe.
It is an honour to everich that is heer
That ye mowe have a suffisant Pardoneer
Tassoille yow in contree as ye ryde,
For aventures [2] whiche that may bityde.
Paraventure ther may fallen oon or two
Doun of his hors and breke his nekke atwo ;
Looke which a seuretee is it to yow alle, 10,011
That I am in youre felaweshipe yfalle,
That may assoille yow, bothe moore and lasse,
Whan that the soule shal fro the body passe.
I rede that oure Hoost heere shal bigynne,
For he is moost envoluped in synne !
Com forth, sire Hoost, and offre first anon,

[1] Bag.   [2] Accidents.   [3] Great and small.

And thou shalt kisse my relikes everychon, —
Ye, for a grote ! Unbokele anon thy purs."
   " Nay, nay," quod he, "thanne have I Cristes
      curs !   10,020
Lat be," quod he, " it shal nat be, so theech ; [1]
Thou woldest make me kisse thyn olde breech,
And swere it were a relyk of a seint,
Though it were with thy fundement depeint ; [2]
But, by the croys which that Seint Eleyne fond',
I wolde I hadde thy coillons [3] in myn hond
In stide of relikes, or of seintuarie.
Lat kutte hem of, I wol with thee hem carie,
They shul be shryned in an hogges toord."
   This Pardoner answerde nat a word ; 10,030
So wrooth he was no word ne wolde he seye.
   " Now," quod oure Hoost, " I wol no lenger
      pleye   (12,892 T.)
With thee, ne with noon oother angry man."
But right anon the worthy Knyght bigan, —
Whan that he saugh that al the peple lough, —
   " Namoore of this, for it is right ynough !
Sire Pardoner, be glad and myrie of cheere ;
And ye, sir Hoost, that been to me so deere,
I prey yow that ye kisse the Pardoner ; 10,039
And Pardoner, I prey thee drawe thee neer,
And as we diden, lat us laughe and pleye."
Anon they kiste and ryden forth hir weye.

   [1] Thrive I.   [2] Painted   [3] Testicles.

The Preamble of the Wyves Tale of Bathe.

Experience, though noon auctoritee (5583 T.)
Were in this world, were right ynogh to me
To speke of wo that is in mariage ;
For, lordynges, sith I twelf yeer was of age, —
Ythonked be God, that is eterne on lyve !
Housbondes at chirche dore I have had fyve ;
For I so ofte have ywedded bee ;
And alle were worthy men in hir degree. 10,050
But me was toold certeyn, nat longe agoon is,
That sith that Crist ne wente nevere but onis
To weddyng in the Cane of Galilee,
That by the same ensample taughte [1] he me
That I ne sholde wedded be but ones.
Herkne, eek, which a sharpe worde for the
    nones,
Beside a welle Jhesus, God and man,
Spak in repreeve of the Samaritan :
" Thou hast yhad fyve housbondes," quod he,
" And that man the which that hath now thee
Is noght thyn housbonde ; " thus seyde he cer
    teyn.   10,061
What that he mente ther by, I kan nat seyn ;
But that I axe why that the fifthe man
Was noon housbonde to the Samaritan ?
How manye myghte she have in mariage ?
Yet herde I nevere tellen in myn age (5606 T.

---

[1] **Elles.** MS. has " thoughte," and omits " that " and " he "

Upon this nombre diffinicioun.
Men may devyne, and glosen up and doun,
But wel I woot, expres, with-oute lye,
God bad us for to wexe and multiplye. 10,070
That gentil text kan I wel understonde ;
Eek wel I woot he seyde myn housbonde
Sholde lete [1] fader and mooder, and take **me** ;
But of no nombre mencioun made he,
Of bigamye,[2] or of octogamye ;
Why sholde men speke of it vileynye.

Lo, heere the wise kyng daun Salomon ;
I trowe he hadde wyves mo than oon ;
As, wolde God, it were leveful un-to me
To be refresshed half so ofte as he ! 10,080
Which [3] gifte of God hadde he for alle hise
    wyvys !
No man hath swich that in this world alyve **is.**
God woot this noble kyng, as to my wit,
The firste nyght had many a myrie fit
With ech of hem, so wel was hym on lyve.

Yblessed be God, that I have wedded fyve !
Welcome the sixte, whan that evere he shal,
For sothe I wol nat kepe me chaast in al.
Whan myn housbonde is fro the world ygon,
Som cristen man shal wedde me anon ; 10,090
For thanne, thapostle seith, I am free
To wedde, a Goddes half,[4] where it liketh
    me.
He seith to be wedded is no synne, —

---

[1] Leave. [2] Marrying twice [3] What a. [4] "In the Lord"

" Bet is it [1] tó be wedded than to brynne." [2]
What rekketh me thogh folk seye vileynye
Of shrewed Lameth, and his [3] bigamye ?
I woot wel Abraham was an hooly man,
And Jacob eek, as ferforth as I kan,
And ech of hem hadde wyves mo than two,
And many another man also.   10,100
Whanne saugh ye evere in any manere age
That hye God defended [4] mariage
By expres word ? I pray you telleth me ;
Or where comanded he virginitee ?
I woot as wel as ye, it is no drede, [5]
Whan thapostel speketh of maydenhede,
He seyde that precept ther-of hadde he noon.
Men may conseille a womman to been oon,
But conseillyng is nat comandement.
He putte it in oure owene juggement ;   10,110
For hadde God comanded maydenhede
Thanne hadde he dampned [6] weddyng with the
            dede ;   (5652 T.)
And certein, if ther were no seed y-sowe,
Virginitee, wher-of thanne sholde it growe ?
Poul ne dorste nat comanden, atte leeste,
A thyng of which his maister gaf noon heeste.
The dart [7] is set up of virginitee,
Cacche who so may, who renneth best lat see !

   But this word is nat taken of every wight,
But ther as God lust gyve it of his myght.

---

[1] Not in Elles. MS.   [2] Burn.   [3] Elles. MS. has " of "   [4] For-
bade.   [5] In faith.   [6] Condemned.   [7] Prize.

I woot wel the Apostel was a mayde,   10,121
But nathelees, thogh that he wroot and sayde
He wolde that every wight were swich as he,
Al nys but conseil to virginitee ;
And for to been a wyf he gaf me leve
Of indulgence, so it is no repreve
To wedde me if that my make [1] dye,
With outen excepcioun of bigamye,
Al were it good no womman for to touche, —
He mente as in his bed or in his couche ;
For peril is bothe fyr and tow tassemble ;
Ye knowe what this ensample may resemble.
This is al and som, that virginitee   10,133
Moore profiteth than weddyng in freletee ; [2]
Freeltee clepe [3] I, but if that he and she
Wolde lede al hir lyf in chastitee.

  I graunte it wel I have noon envie
Thogh maydenhede preferre [4] bigamye ;
Hem liketh to be clene body and goost.
Of myn estaat I nyl nat make no boost, 10,140
For wel ye knowe a lord in his houshold
He nath nat every vessel al of gold ;
Somme been of tree, and doon hir lord servyse.
God clepeth folk to hym in sondry wyse,
And everich hath of God a propre gifte, —
Som this, som that, as hym liketh to shifte.

  Virginitee is greet perfeccioun,
And continence eek, with devocioun ;
But Crist, that of perfeccioun is welle, [5]

  [1] Mate.   [2] Frailty.   [3] Call.   [4] Be superior to.   [5] Source.

Bad nat every wight he sholde go selle   10,15c
All that he hadde, and gyve it to the poore,
And in swich wise folwe hym and his foore.[1]
He spak to hem that wolde lyve parfitly,
And, lordynges, by youre leve, that am **nat I.**
I wol bistowe the flour of myn age
In the actes and in fruyt of mariage.

   Telle me also, to what conclusioun
Were membres ymaad of generacioun,
And for what profit was a wight ywroght?
Trusteth right wel, they were nat maad for
             noght.   10,160
Glose who so wole, and seye bothe up and doun,
That they were maad for purgacioun
Of uryne bothe, and thynges smale,   (5703 T.)
And eek to knowe a femele from a male,
And for noon oother cause, — sey ye no?
The experience woot wel it is noght so;
So that the clerkes be nat with me wrothe,
I sey, yis, that they beth maked for bothe;
This is to seye, for office, and for ese   10,169
Of engendrure, ther we nat God displese.
Why sholde men elles in hir bookes sette
That a man shal yelde to his wyf hire dette?
Now wher-with sholde he make his paiement,
If he ne used his sely[2] instrument?
Thanne were they maad up-on a creature,
To purge uryne and for engendrure.

---

[1] Conduct (faring, going). Cf. l. 11,977.   [2] Harmless (Ge
selig, happy).

But I seye noght that every wight is holde,
That hath swich harneys as I of tolde,
To goon and usen hem in engendrure, —
They shul nat take of chastitee no cure. 10,180
Crist was a mayde and shaped as a man,
And many a seint sith that [1] the world bigan,
Yet lyved they evere in parfit chastitee.
I nyl nat envye no virginitee,
Lat hem be breed of pured whete seed,
And lat us wyves hoten [2] barly breed,
And yet with barly breed Mark telle kan
Oure Lord refresshed many a man.

In swich estaat as God hath cleped us
I wol persevere, I nam nat precius ; [3] 10,190
In wyfhode I wol use myn instrument
As frely as my Makere hath it sent.
If I be daungerous,[4] God geve me sorwe ;
Myn housbonde shal it have bothe eve and
      morwe,
Whan that hym list com forth and paye his
      dette.
An housbonde I wol have, I nyl nat lette,
Which shal be bothe my dettour and my thral,
And have his tribulacioun with al
Up-on his flessh, whil that I am his wyf.
I have the power durynge al my lyf   10,200
Up-on his propre body, and noght he.
Right thus the Apostel tolde it un-to me,
And bad oure housbondes for to love us weel ;
Al this sentence me liketh every deel.

[1] Not in Elles. MS. [2] Be called. [3] Fastidious. [4] Sparing.

Behold the words of the Pardoner to the Wife of Bath.

Up stirte the Pardoner, and that anon ;
" Now, dame," quod he, " by God and by **Seint**
    John !
Ye been a noble prechour in this cas.
I was aboute to wedde a wyf, allas !
What, sholde I bye[1] it on my flessh so deere ?
Yet hadde I levere wedde no wyf to-yeere ! "[2]
    " Abyde," quod she, " my tale is nat bi-
        gonne.   10,211
Nay, thou shalt drynken of another tonne
Er that I go, shal savoure wors than ale ;
And whan that I have toold forth my tale
Of tribulacioun in[3] mariage,   (5755 T.)
Of which I am expert in al myn age, —
This to seyn, my self have been the whippe, —
Than maystow chese wheither thou wolte sippe
Of that tonne that I shal abroche.[4]
Be war of it, er thou to ny approche,   10,220
For I shal tell ensamples mo than ten,
' Who so that nyl be war by othere men,
By hym shul othere men corrected be ;'[5]
The same wordes writeth Protholomee ;
Rede it in his Almageste and take it there."
    " Dame, I wolde praye, if youre wyl it were,'
Seyde this Pardoner, " as ye bigan

---

[1] Suffer.   [2] This year.   [3] Elles MS. has " that is in."   [4] Tap

Telle forth youre tale ; spareth for no man,
And teche us yonge men of youre praktike."
    " Gladly, sires, sith it may yow like ;   10,230
But yet I praye to al this compaignye,
If that I speke after my fantasye,
As taketh not agrief [1] of [2] that I seye,
For myn entente is nought [2] but for to pleye."

Bihoold how this goode Wyf served hir hous-
bondes.

    Now, sire, now wol I telle forth my tale.
As evere moote I drynken wyn or ale
I shal seye sooth of housbondes that I hadde,
As thre of hem were goode, and two were
        badde.
The thre were goode men and riche, and olde ;
Unnethe myghte they the statut holde   10,240
In which that they were bounden un-to me ;
Ye woot wel what I meene of this, *pardee !*
As help me God, I laughe whan I thynke
How pitously a-nyght I made hem swynke !
And, by my fey, I tolde [3] of it no stoor ;
They had me geven hir gold and hir tresoor,
Me neded nat do lenger diligence
To wynne hir love, or doon hem reverence ;
They loved me so wel, by God above,
That I ne tolde no deyntee [4] of hir love ! 10,250
A wys womman wol sette hire evere in oon

---

[1] **Amiss.**   [2] Not in Elles. MS.   [3] Counted.   [4] Set no value on.

To gete hire love ther as she hath noon ;
But sith I hadde hem hoolly in myn hond,
And sith they hadde me geven all hir lond,
What sholde I taken heede hem for to plese,
But it were for my profit and myn ese ?
I sette hem so a werke, by my fey,
That many a nyght they songen " weilawey ! "
The bacoun was nat fet [1] for hem, I trowe,
That som men han in Essexe at Dunmowe.[2]
I governed hem so wel after my lawe,   10,261
That ech of hem was ful blisful and fawe [3]
To brynge me gaye thynges fro the fayre ;
They were ful glad whan I spak to hem faire,
For, God it woot, I chidde hem spitously.

  Now herkneth hou I baar me proprely,
Ye wise wyves that kan understonde. (5807 T.)
  Thus shul ye speke, and beren hem on
      honde,
For half so boldely kan ther no man
Swere and lye as a womman kan.   10,270
I sey nat this by wyves that been wyse,
But if it be whan they hem mysavyse.
A wys wyf shal,[4] if that she kan [5] hir good,
Bere hym on honde that [4] the cow is wood,[6]
And take witnesse of hir owene mayde
Of hir assent ; but herkneth how I sayde.

  " Sire, olde kaynard,[7] is this thyn array ?

---

[1] Fetched. [2] Happy married couples have claimed the flitch as
ately as 1838, 1851, 1855, and 1876. [3] Fain. [4] Not in Elles. MS
[5] Know. [6] Face him down with the false assertion that the cow is
mad. The allusion appears to be to some story. [7] Rascal.

Why is my neighebores wyf so gay?
She is honoured over al ther she gooth;
I sitte at hoom, I have no thrifty clooth. 10,280
What dostow at my neighebores hous?
Is she so fair? artow so amorous?
What rowne [1] ye with oure mayde?   *Benedicite!*
Sire, olde lecchour, lat thy japes be!
And if I have a gossib or a freend,
With-outen gilt thou chidest as a feend,
If that I walke or pleye un-to his hous.
Thou comest hoom as dronken as a mous
And prechest on thy bench with yvel preef: [2]
Thou seist to me it is a greet meschief   10,290
To wedde a povre womman for costage;
And if she be riche and of heigh parage, [3]
Thanne seistow it is a tormentrie
To soffren hire pride and hire malencolie;
And if that she be faire, thou verray knave,
Thou seyst that every holour [4] wol hire have;
She may no while in chastitee abyde
That is assailled up-on eche syde.

    " Thou seyst som folk desiren us for richesse,
Somme for oure shape, somme for oure fair-
         nesse,   10,300
And som for she kan synge and daunce,
And som for gentillesse, and som for daliaunce,
Som for hir handes, and hir armes smale, —
Thus goth al to the devel by thy tale!
Thou seyst men may nat kepe a castel wal,
It may so longe assailled been over al.

    [1] Whisper.   [2] Proof.   [3] Kindred.   [4] Rake.

" And if that she be foul, thou seist that she
Coveiteth every man that she may se,
For as a spaynel she wol on hym lepe,   10,309
Til that she fynde som man hire to chepe ;[1]
Ne noon so grey a goos gooth in the lake,
As, seistow, wol been with-oute make ;
And seyst it is an hard thyng for to welde[2]
A thyng that no man wole, his thankes,[3] helde.[4]
Thus seistow, lorel,[5] whan thow goost to bedde,
And that no wys man nedeth for to wedde,
Ne no man that entendeth un-to hevene.
With wilde thonder dynt and firy levene[6]
Moote thy welked[7] nekke be to-broke ! (5859 T.)

" Thow seyst that droppyng houses, and eek
    smoke,   10,320
And chidyng wyves, maken men to flee
Out of hir owene houses, *a benedicitee !*
What eyleth swich an old man for to chide ?

" Thow seyst that we wyves wol oure vices
    hide
Til we be fast, and thanne we wol hem shewe, —
Wel may that be a proverbe of a shrewe.

" Thou seist that oxen, asses, hors, and
    houndes,
They been assayd at diverse stoundes ;[8]
Basyns, lavoures, er that men hem bye,
Spoones and stooles, and al swich housbondrye
And so been pottes, clothes, and array ; 10,331

---

[1] Buy, market.   [2] Govern.   [3] Willingly. Cf. l. 1626.   [4] **Hold**
Scamp. [6] Lightning.   [7] Dried up.   [8] Times.

But folk of wyves maken noon assay
Til they be wedded, — olde dotard shrewe !
Thanne, seistow, we wol oure vices shewe.

"Thou seist also that it displeseth me
But if that thou wolt preyse my beautee,
And but thou poure [1] alwey up-on my face,
And clepe me 'faire dame' in every place ;
And but thou make a feeste on thilke day
That I was born, and make me fressh and gay;
And but thou do to my norice honour,   10,341
And to my chambrere with-inne my bour, [2]
And to my fadres folk and hise allyes, —
Thus seistow, olde barel-ful of lyes !

"And yet of oure apprentice Janekyn,
For his crispe heer, shynynge as gold so fyn,
And for he squiereth [3] me bothe up and doun,
Yet hastow caught a fals suspicioun, —
I wol hym noght, thogh thou were deed to-
        morwe !

"But tel me, why hydestow with sorwe 10,350
The keyes of thy cheste, awey fro me ?
It is my good, as wel as thyn, *pardee !*
What ! wenestow make an ydiot of oure dame ?
Now, by that lord that called is Seint Jame,
Thou shalt nat bothe, thogh thou were wood,
Be maister of my body and of my good ;
That oon thou shalt forgo, maugree thyne eyen !
What nedeth thee of me to enquere or spyen ?
I trowe thou woldest loke [4] me in thy chiste ;

---

[1] Pore, gaze. [2] Chamber. [3] Escort-th. [4] Lock.

Thou sholdest seye, 'Wyf, go wher thee liste ;
Taak youre disport, I wol leve [1] no talys ;
I knowe yow for a trewe wyf, dame Alys.'
We love no man that taketh kepe, or charge,
Wher that we goon ; we wol ben at our large.

   "Of alle men yblessed moot he be,   10,365
The wise astrologien, Daun Protholome,
That seith this proverbe in his Almageste,
'Of alle men his wysdom is the hyeste (5908 T.)
That rekketh nevere who hath the world in
     honde.'
By this proverbe thou shalt understonde,
Have thou ynogh, what thar thee recche [2] or
     care   10,371
How myrily that othere folkes fare ?
For certeyn, olde dotard, by youre leve,
Ye shul have queynte [3] right ynogh at eve.
He is to greet a nygard that wolde werne [4]
A man to lighte his candle at his lanterne.
He shal have never the lasse light, *pardee !*
Have thou ynogh, thee thar nat pleyne [5] thee.

   "Thou seyst also, that if we make us gay
With clothyng, and with precious array, 10,380
That it is peril of oure chastitee ;   .
And yet with sorwe thou most enforce thee,
And seye thise wordes in the Apostles name :
'In habit maad with chastitee and shame,
Ye wommen shul apparaille yow,' quod he,
'And noght in tressed heer, and gay perree,[6]

---

[1] Believe.   [2] Reck.   [3] Cf. l. 3276.   [4] Warn, ward off.   [5] Complain.   [6] Jewels.

As perles, ne with gold, ne clothes riche.'
After thy text, ne after thy rubriche,
I wol nat wirche as muchel as a gnat.

  " Thou seydest this, that I was lyk a cat ;
For who so wolde senge a cattes skyn, 10,391
Thanne wolde the cat wel dwellen in his in ;[1]
And if the cattes skyn be slyk and gay,
She wol nat dwelle in house half a day ;
But forth she wole, er any day be dawed,[2]
To shewe hir skyn, and goon a caterwawed ;[3]
This is to seye, if I be gay, sire shrewe,
I wol renne out my borel[4] for to shewe.

  " Sire, olde fool, what eyleth thee to spyen ?
Thogh thou preye Argus with hise hundred
    eyen   10,400
To be my wardecors,[5] as he kan best,
In feith, he shal nat kepe me but me lest ;
Yet koude I make his berd,[6] so moot I thee !

  " Thou seydest eek, that ther been thynges
    thre
The whiche thynges troublen al this erthe,
And that no wighte may endure the ferthe.
O leeve sire shrewe, Jhesu shorte thy lyf !
Yet prechestow and seyst an hateful wyf
Yrekened is for oon of thise meschances.
Been ther none othere maner[7] resemblances
That ye may likne youre parables to, 10,411
But if a sely[8] wyf be oon of tho ?

---

[1] Lodging. [2] Dawned. [3] Caterwauling. [4] Clothes. [5] Body
guard. [6] Befool him. Cf. l. 4096. Not in Elles. MS. [8] Harmless

" Thou liknest eek [1] wommenes love to helle.
To bareyne lond, ther water may nat dwelle ;
Thou liknest it also to wilde fyr,   (5955 T.)
The moore it brenneth the moore it hath desir
To consumen every thyng that brent wole be ;
Thou seyst, right as wormes shende a tree,
Right so a wyf destroyeth hire housbond ;
This knowe they that been to wyves bonde."

Lordynges, right thus as ye have under-
          stonde   10,421
Baar I stifly myne olde housbondes [2] on honde,
That thus they seyden in hir dronkenesse ;
And al was fals, but that I took witnesse
On Janekyn, and on my nece also.
O Lord, the peyne I dide hem and the wo !
Ful giltelees, by Goddes sweete pyne !
For as an hors I koude byte and whyne ;
I koude pleyne, thogh I were in the gilt,
Or elles often tyme hadde I been spilt.[3] 10,430
"Who so that [1] cometh first to mille first grynt ;"
I pleyned first, so was oure werre y-stynt ;
They were ful glad to excusen hem blyve
Of thyng of which they nevere agilte [4] hir lyve.

Of wenches wolde I beren hym on honde, [6]
Whan that for syk unnethes [5] myghte he stonde ;
Yet tikled it his herte, for that he
Wende that I hadde of hym so greet chiertee ! [7]
I swoor that al my walkynge out by nyghte

---

[1] Not in Elles. MS.   [2] Cf. l. 10,239.   [3] Ruined.   [4] Were guilt·
of.   [5] Scarcely.   [6] Falsely accuse.   Cf. l. 5042.   [7] Tenderness.

Was for tespye wenches that he dighte.[1] 10,440
Under that colour hadde I many a myrthe,
For al swich thyng was geven us in oure
      byrthe, —
Deceite, wepyng, spynnyng, God hath geve
To wommen kyndely [2] whil that they may lyve ;
And thus of o thyng I avaunte me,
Atte ende I hadde the bettre in ech degree, —
By sleighte, or force, or by som maner thyng,
As by continueel murmure or grucchyng.
Namely [3] abedde hadden they meschaunce ;
Ther wolde I chide and do hem no plesaunce ,
I wolde no lenger in the bed abyde,   10,451
If that I felte his arm over my syde,
Til he had maad his raunsoun un-to me ;
Thanne wolde I suffre hym do his nycetee ;
And ther-fore every man this tale I telle, —
Wynne who so may, for al is for to selle ;
With empty hand men may none haukes lure.[4]
For wynnyng [5] wolde I al his lust endure
And make me a feyned appetit,   10,459
And yet in bacoun hadde I nevere delit ;
That made me that evere I wolde hem chide ;
For thogh the pope hadde seten hem biside
I wolde nat spare hem at hir owene bord,
For, by my trouthe, I quitte hem word for word.
As helpe me verray God omnipotent, (6005 T.)
Though I right now sholde make my testa-
      ment,

[1] **Decked.** [2] By ature. [3] Especially. [4] Cf. l. 4134. [5] Profit.

I ne owe hem nat a word that it nys quit.
I broghte it so aboute by my wit
That they moste geve it up as for the beste,
Or elles hadde we nevere been in rest ;   10,470
For thogh he looked as a wood leoun,
Yet sholde he faille of his conclusioun.

   Thanne wolde I seye, "Goode lief,[1] taak
      keepe, —
How mekely looketh Wilkyn, oure sheepe !
Com neer, my spouse, lat me ba[2] thy cheke ;
Ye sholde been al pacient and meke,
And han a sweete, spiced[3] conscience,
Sith ye so preche of Jobes pacience.
Suffreth alwey, syn ye so wel kan preche,
And, but ye do, certein we shal yow teche
That it is fair to have a wyf in pees.   10,481
Oon of us two moste bowen, doutelees,
And sith a man is moore resonable
Than womman is, ye moste been suffrable.
What eyleth yow to grucche thus and grone ?
Is it for ye wolde have my queynte allone ?
Wy, taak it al ! lo, have it every deel !
Peter ! I shrewe yow, but ye love it weel ;
For if I wolde selle my *bele chose*,
I koude walke as fressh as is a rose ;   10,490
But I wol kepe it for youre owene tooth.
Ye be to blame, by God ! I sey yow sooth."
Swicne manere wordes hadde we on honde.

   Now wol I speken of my fourthe housbonde.

---

[1] Love. [2] Kiss. [3] Scrupulous. Cf. l. 526

My fourthe housbonde was a revelour;
This is to seyn, he hadde a paramour;
And I was yong and ful of ragerye,
Stibourne and strong and joly as a pye.
Wel koude I daunce to an harpe smale,
And synge, ywis, as any nyghtyngale,   10,500
Whan I had dronke a draughte of sweete wyn.

  Metellius,[1] the foule cherl, the swyn!
That with a staf birafte his wyf hire lyf,
For she drank wyn; thogh I hadde been his
    wyf
He sholde nat han daunted me fro drynke!
And after wyn on Venus moste I thynke,
For al so siker as cold engendreth hayl,
A likerous mouth moste han a likerous tayl.
In wommen vinolent is no defence, —
This knowen lecchours by experience.   10,510

  But, Lord Crist! whan that it remembreth me
Up-on my yowthe, and on my jolitee,   (6052 T.)
It tikleth me aboute myn herte roote!
Un-to this day it dooth myn herte boote
That I have had my world as in my tyme.
But Age, allas! that al wole envenyme,
Hath me biraft my beautee and my pith, —
Lat go, fare wel, the devel go therwith!
The flour is goon, ther is namoore to telle,
The bren, as I best kan, now moste I selle;
But yet to be right myrie wol I fonde.[2]   10,521

  Now wol I tellen of my fourthe housbonde.

<hr>

[1] The margin of the Elles. MS refers to Valerius Maximus.   [2] Try.

I seye I hadde in herte greet despit
That he of any oother had delit ;
But he was quit, by God, and by Seint Joce ![1]
I made hym of the same wode [2] a croce.
Nat of my body in no foul manere,
But certeinly I made folk swich cheere,
That in his owene grece I made hym frye
For angre, and for verray jalousye.   10,530
By God, in erthe I was his purgatorie,
For which I hope his soule be in glorie !
For God it woot, he sat ful ofte and song
Whan that his shoo ful bitterly hym wrong.[3]
Ther was no wight save God and he that wiste
In many wise how soore I hym twiste.
He deyde whan I cam fro Jerusalem,
And lith ygrave under the roode [4] beem.
Al is his tombe noght so curyus
As was the sepulcre of hym Daryus,   10,540
Which that Appelles wroghte subtilly ;
It nys but wast to burye hym preciously.
Lat hym fare wel, God geve his soule reste,
He is now in his grave and in his cheste !
    Now of my fifthe housbonde wol I telle.
God lete hise soule nevere come in helle !
And yet was he to me the mooste shrewe ;
That feele I on my ribbes al by rewe,[5]
And evere shal, un-to myn endyng day ; 10,549
But in oure bed he was ful fressh and gay ;

---

[1] Judocus. [2] That is, of jealousy. [3] An allusion to the Roman who
divorced his wife for some fault not apparent. He said the wearer
knows where his shoe pinches. Cf. l. 13,889. [4] Cross. [5] Row

And ther-with-al so wel koude he me glose,
Whan that he wolde han my *bele chose*,
That thogh he hadde me bet on every bon,[1]
He koude wynne agayn my love anon.
I trowe I loved hym beste for that he
Was of his love daungerous [2] to me.
We wommen han, if that I shal nat lye,
In this matere a queynte fantasye ;
Wayte ! what thyng we may nat lightly have
Ther after wol we crie al day and crave. 10,560
Forbede us thyng, and that desiren we ;
Preesse on us faste and thanne wol we fle.
With daunger oute [3] we al oure chaffare ;
Greet prees [4] at market maketh deere ware,
And to greet cheepe [5] is holde at litel prys ;
This knoweth every womman that is wys.

My fifthe housbonde, God his soule blesse !
Which that I took for love, and no richesse,
He som tyme was a clerk of Oxenford, (6109 T.)
And hadde left scole and wente at hom to
        bord   10,570
With my gossib,[6] dwellynge in oure toun ;
God have hir soule, hir name was Alisoun.
She knew my herte, and eek my privetee,
Bet than oure parisshe preest, as moot I thee.[7]
To hire biwreyed I my conseil al,
For hadde myn housbonde pissed on a wal,
Or doon a thyng that sholde han cost his lyf,

---

[1] Beaten on every bone.   [2] Sparing.   [3] Give out.   [4] Demand
Market, supply.   [6] Godmother sponsor.   (*Sib*, kin.)   [7] Thrive.

To hire, and to another worthy wyf,
And to my nece, which that I loved weel,
I wolde han toold his conseil every deel ;
And so I dide ful often, God it woot,   10,581
That made his face ful often reed and hoot
For verray shame, and blamed hym self for he
Had toold to me so greet a pryvetee.

    And so bifel that ones in a lente,
So often tymes I to my gossyb, wente, —
For evere yet I loved to be gay,
And for to walke in March, Averill and May,
Fro hous to hous to heere sondry talys, —
That Jankyn clerk, and my gossyb, dame Alys
And I my self in-to the feeldes wente.   10,591
Myn housbonde was at London al the lente ;
I hadde the bettre leyser for to pleye,
And for to se, and eek for to be seye [1]
Of lusty folk.   What wiste I wher my grace [2]
Was shapen for to be, or in what place ?
Therfore I made my visitaciouns
To vigilies and to processiouns,
To prechyng eek, and to thise pilgrimages,
To pleyes of myracles, and to mariages, 10,600
And wered upon [3] my gaye scarlet gytes. [4]
Thise wormes, ne thise motthes, ne thise mytes
Upon my peril frete [5] hem never a deel.
And wostow why ? For they were used weel.

    Now wol I tellen forth what happed me.
I seye that in the feeldes walked we

---

[1] Seen. [2] Favor. [3] Upon me. [4] Gowns. [5] Did eat.

Till trewely we hadde swich daliance,
This clerk and I, that of my purveiance [1]
I spak to hym, and seyde hym how that he,
If I were wydwe, sholde wedde me ;   10,610
For certeinly, — I sey for no bobance,[2] —
Yet was I nevere with-outen purveiance
Of mariage, nof [3] othere thynges eek.
I holde a mouses herte nat worth a leek
That hath but oon hole for to sterte to,
And if that faille thanne is al ydo.   (6156 T.)
    I bar hym on honde he hadde enchanted
        me, —
My dame taughte me that soutiltee, —
And eek I seyde, I mette of hym al nyght,
He wolde han slayn me as I lay up right, 10,620
And al my bed was ful of verray blood ;
But yet I hope that he shal do me good,
For blood bitokeneth gold, as me was taught ;
And al was fals, I dremed of it right naught,
But I folwed ay my dames loore,
As wel of this as of othere thynges moore.
    But now, sire, — lat me se, — what I shal
        seyn ?
A ha ! by God, I have my tale ageyn.
    Whan that my fourthe housbonde was on
        beere
I weepte algate and made sory cheere, 10,630
As wyves mooten, for it is usage,
And with my coverchief [4] covered my visage ;

---

[1] Prudence. [2] Boast.   Nor of [4] Pronounced kerchef.

But, for that I was purveyed of a make,[1]
I wepte but smal, and that I undertake !
 To chirche was myn housbonde boin a
  morwe
With neighebores, that for hym maden sorwe,
And Jankyn, oure clerk, was oon of tho.
As help me God, whan that I saugh hym go
After the beere, me thoughte he hadde a paire
Of legges and of feet so clene and faire, 10,640
Thal al myn herte I gaf un-to his hoold.
He was, I trowe, a twenty wynter oold,
And I was fourty, if I shal seye sooth ;
But yet I hadde alwey a coltes tooth.
Gat-tothed[2] I was, and that bicam me weel,
I hadde the prente of seint Venus seel.
As help me God, I was a lusty oon,
And faire and riche, and yong, and wel bigon,[3]
And trewely, as myne housbondes tolde me,
I hadde the beste *quonyam*[4] myghte be ; 10,650
For certes, I am al Venerien
In feelynge, and myn herte is Marcien ;
Venus me gaf my lust, my likerousnesse,
And Mars gaf me my sturdy hardynesse.
Myn ascendent was Taur and Mars ther-inne
Allas ! allas ! that evere love was synne !
I folwed ay myn inclinacioun
By vertu of my constellacioun,
That made me I koude noght withdrawe
My chambre of Venus from a good felawe.

  [1] Mate [2] Cf. l 468. [3] In a good way. [4] Cf. l. 10,374.

Yet have I Martes mark up-on my face, 10,661
And also in another, privee, place,
For God so wys be my savacioun,
I ne loved nevere by no discrecioun,
But evere folwed myn appetit, —   (6205 T.)
Al were he short, or long, or blak, or whit ;
I took no kepe, so that he liked me,
How poore he was, ne eek of what degree.

What sholde I seye, but at the monthes ende
This joly clerk, Jankyn, that was so hende,[1]
Hath wedded me with greet solempnytee,
And to hym gaf I all the lond and fee, 10,672
That evere was me geven ther-bifoore ;
But afterward repented me ful soore.
He nolde suffre nothyng of my list ;
By God, he smoot me ones, on the lyst,[2]
For that I rente out of his book a leef,
That of the strook myn ere wax al deef.
Stibourne I was as is a leonesse,
And of my tonge a verray jangleresse ; 10,680
And walke I wolde, as I had doon biforn,
From hous to hous, al-though he had it sworn ;
For which he often tymes wolde preche,
And me of olde Romayn geestes teche ;   ·
How he, Symplicius Gallus,[3] lefte his wyf,
And hire forsok for terme of al his lyf,
Noght but for open-heveded [4] he hir say [5]
Lokynge out at his dore upon a day.   10,688

---

[1] Civil. [2] Fillet. Cf. l. 3243. Camb. MS. has " with hyse fyst
The margin again refers to Valerius. [4] Bare-headed. [5] Saw.

Another Romayn [1] tolde he me by name
That, for his wyf was at a someres game
With-outen his wityng, he forsook hire eke ;
And thanne wolde he up-on his Bible seke
That ilke proverbe of Ecclesiaste,
Where he comandeth, and forbedeth faste,[2]
Man shal nat suffre his wyf go roule [3] aboute.
Thanne wolde he seye right thus, with-outen
      doute :

Who so that buyldeth his hous al of salwes,[4]
And priketh his blynde hors over the falwes,[5]
And suffreth his wyf to go seken halwes,[6]
Is worthy to been hanged on the galwes ; 10,700
But al for noght, I sette noght an hawe
Of his proverbes nof [7] his olde sawe ;
Ne I wolde nat of hym corrected be.
I hate hym that my vices telleth me,
And so doo mo, God woot, of us than I.
This made hym with me wood al outrely ;
I nolde noght forbere hym in no cas.

Now wol I seye yow sooth, by Seint Thomas !
Why that I rente out of his book a leef, 10,709
For which he smoot me so that I was deef.
He hadde a book that gladly nyght and day
For his desport he wolde rede alway.
He cleped it "Valerie" [8] and "Theofraste,"[9]
At whiche book he lough alwey ful faste :

---

[1] Sempronius Sophus   [2] Positively.   [3] Ramble   [4] Oziers
Fallow lands   [6] Shrines. Cf. l. 10,599.   [7] Ne of.   [8] *Epistola*
Valerii ad Rufinum, De non Ducenda Uxore, by Walter May
Liber Aureolus Theophrasti, De Nuptiis. Cf. l. 13,630.

And eek ther was som tyme a clerk at Rome,
A cardinal, that highte Seint Jerome, (6256 T.)
That made a book agayn Jovinian,[1]
In whiche book eek ther was Tertulan,[2]
Crisippus,[3] Trotula,[4] and Helowys,[5]
That was abbesse nat fer fro Parys ;   10,720
And eek the Parables of Salomon,
Ovides Art,[6] and bookes many on ;
And alle thise were bounden in o volume ;
And every nyght and day was his custume,
Whan he hadde leyser and vacacioun
From oother worldly occupacioun,
To reden on this book of wikked wyves.
He knew of hem mo legendes and lyves
Than been of goode wyves in the Bible ;
For, trusteth wel, it is an impossible   10,730
That any clerk wol speke good of wyves, —
But if it be of hooly Seintes lyves, —
Ne noon oother womman never the mo.
Who peynted the leoun ? Telle me who.[7]
By God ! if wommen hadde writen stories,
As clerkes han with-inne hire oratories,
They wolde han writen of men moore wikked·
        nesse
Than all the mark[8] of Adam may redresse.
The children of Mercurie and Venus

---

[1] *Liber adversus Jovinianum*, in which the two works above mentioned are quoted. [2] Tertullian wrote, in *De Cultu Feminarum*, on the folly of woman's over-much dressing. [3] Perhaps the Stoic A medical writer. [5] Letters of Héloise to Abelard. [6] *Art of Love*. Perhaps Chaucer, in the now lost *Boke of the Leon*, for which he asks pardon in the Parson's Tale, 19,330. [8] Image, *i. e.*, sons.

Been in hir wirkyng ful contrarius ;   10,740
Mercurie loveth wysdam and science,
And Venus loveth ryot and dispence ;
And for hire diverse disposicioun
Each falleth in otheres exaltacioun ;
And thus, God woot, Mercurie is desolat
In Pisces, wher Venus is exaltat ;
And Venus falleth ther Mercurie is reysed ;
Therefore no womman of no clerk is preysed.
The clerk whan he is oold, and may noght do
Of Venus werkes worth his olde sho,   10,750
Thanne sit he doun and writ in his dotage
That wommen kan nat kepe hir mariage.

But now to purpos why I tolde thee
That I was beten for a book, *pardee.*
Up-on a nyght Jankyn that was oure sire
Redde on his book, as he sat by the fire,
Of Eva first, that for hir wikkednesse
Was al mankynde broght to wrecchednesse ;
For whiche Crist hym self was slayn,   10,759
That boghte us with his herte blood agayn.
Lo, heere expres of womman may ye fynde,
That womman was the los of al mankynde.

Tho redde he me how Sampson loste hise
    heres ;   (6303 T.)
Slepynge, his lemman kitte it with hir sheres ;
Thurgh which tresoun loste he bothe hise eyen

Tho redde he me, if that I shal nat lyen,
Of Hercules and of his Dianyre,
That caused hym to sette hymself afyre.

No thyng forgat he the sorwe and wo
That Socrates hadde with hise wyves two ;
How Xantippa caste pisse up-on his heed.
This sely man sat stille as he were deed ; 10,772
He wiped his heed, namoore dorste he seyn
But, " Er that thonder stynte comth a reyn ! "

Of Phasifpha, that was the queene of Crete,
For shrewednesse hym thoughte the tale swete.
Fy ! speke namoore ; it is a grisly thyng,
Of hire horrible lust and hir likyng !

Of Clitermystra, for hire lecherye
That falsly made hire housbonde for to dye ;
He redde it with ful good devocioun. 10,781

He tolde me eek for what occasioun
Amphiorax at Thebes loste his lyf ;
Myn housbonde hadde a legende of his wyf.

Eriphilem, that for an ouche of gold
Hath prively un-to the Grekes told
Wher that hir housbonde hidde hym in a place,
For which he hadde at Thebes sory grace.

Of Lyma tolde he me, and of Lucye ; 10,789
They bothe made hir housbondes for to dye, —
That oon for love, that oother was for hate.
Lyma hir housbonde up-on an even late
Empoysoned hath for that she was his fo ;
Lucia likerous loved hire housbonde so,
That, for he sholde alwey up-on hire thynke,
She gaf hym swich a manere love drynke
That he was deed, er it were by the morwe ;
And thus algates housbondes han sorw.

Thanne tolde he me how oon Latumyus
Compleyned un-to his felawe Arrius   10,800
That in his gardyn growed swich a tree,
On which he seyde how that hise wyves thre
Hanged hem self for herte despitus.

"O leeve brother," quod this Arrius,
"Gif me a plante of thilke blissed tree,
And in my gardyn planted it shal be!"

Of latter date of wyves hath he red,
That somme han slayn hir housbondes in hir
            bed,   10,808
And lete hir lecchour dighte hire al the nyght,
Whan that the corps lay in the floor up-right;
And somme han dryve nayles in hir brayn
Whil that they slepte, and thus they han hem
            slayn.   (6352 T.)
Somme han hem geve poysoun in hire drynke;
He spak moore harm than herte may bithynke;
And ther-with-al he knew of mo proverbes,
Than in this world ther growen gras or herbes.
"Bet is," quod he, "thyn habitacioun
Be with a leoun or a foul dragoun,   10,818
Than with a womman usynge for to chyde."
"Bet is," quod he, "hye in the roof abyde,
Than with an angry wyf doun in the hous."
They been so wikked and contrarious,
They haten that hir housbondes loven ay.
He seyde a womman cast hir shame away
Whan she cast of hir smok; and forther mo,
A fair womman, but she be chaast also,

Is lyk a gold ryng in a sowes nose.
Who wolde leeve,[1] or who wolde suppose,
The wo that in myn herte was, and pyne?
   And whan I saugh he wolde nevere fyne[2]
To reden on this cursed book al nyght, 10,831
Al sodeynly thre leves have I plyght[3]
Out of his book, right as he radde, and eke
I with my fest so took hym on the cheke,
That in oure fyr he fil bakward adoun ;
And he up stirte as dooth a wood leoun,
And with his fest he smoot me on the heed,
That in the floor I lay as I were deed ;
And whan he saugh how stille that I lay,
He was agast and wolde han fled his way,
Til atte laste out of my swogh I breyde. 10,841
" O hastow slayn me, false theef ? " I seyde ;
" And for my land thus hastow mordred me ?
Er I be deed, yet wol I kisse thee."
   And neer he cam, and kneled faire adoun,
And seyde, " Deere suster Alisoun !
As help me God, I shal thee nevere smyte.
That I have doon it is thy self to wyte ;[4]
Forgeve it me, and that I thee biseke ;" 10,849
And yet, eft-soones, I hitte hym on the cheke,
And seyde, " Theef ! thus muchel am I wreke
Now wol I dye, I may no lenger speke."
But atte laste, with muchel care and wo,
We fille acorded by us selven two.
He gaf me al the bridel in myn hond,

---

[1] Believe.   [2] End.   [3] Plucked.   [4] Blame.

To han the governance of hous and lond,
And of his tonge, and his hond also,
And made hym brenne his book anon right
    tho ;
And whan that I hadde geten un-to me
By maistrie al the soveraynetee, —   10,860
And that he seyde, " Myn owene trewe wyf,
Do as thee lust to terme of al thy lyf ;
Keepe thyn honour, and keepe eek myn es-
    taat," —   (6403 T.)
After that day we hadden never debaat.
God helpe me so, I was to hym as kynde
As any wyf from Denmark un-to Ynde,
And also trewe, and so was he to me.
I prey to God, that sit in magestee,
So blesse his soule for his mercy deere.
Now wol I seye my tale, if ye wol heere. 10,870

*Biholde the wordes bitwene the Somonour ana
the Frere.*

The Frere lough whan he hadde herd al
    this ;
" Now, dame," quod he, " so have I joye or
    blis,
This is a long preamble of a tale."
And whan the Somonour herde the Frere gaie,[1]
" Lo," quod the Somonour, " Goddes armes
    two !   (6415 T.)

---

[1] Chuckle, or yell.

A frere wol entremette[1] him evere-mo.
Lo, goode men, a flye, and eek a frere,
Wol falle in every dyssh and mateere.
What spekestow of 'preambulacioun'?[2]
What? amble, or trotte, or pees, or go sit
    doun! 10,880
Thou lettest oure disport in this manere."
   "Ye, woltow so, sire Somonour?" quod the
    Frere;
" Now, by my feith! I shal, er that I go,
Telle of a somonour swich a tale or two
That alle the folk shal laughen in this place."
   "Now elles, Frere, I bishrewe thy face!"
Quod this Somonour, "and I bishrewe me
But if I telle tales, two or thre,
Of freres, er I come to Sidyngborne,[3]
That I shal make thyn herte for to morne,
For wel I woot thy pacience is gon." 10,891
   Oure Hoost cride, "Pees! and that anon;"
And seyde, "Lat the womman telle hire tale;
Ye fare as folk that dronken were of ale.
Do, dame, telle forth youre tale, and that is
    best."
   "Al redy, sire," quod she, "right as yow
    lest;
If I have licence of this worthy Frere." 10,897
   "Yis, dame," quod he, "tel forth, and I
    wol heere." (6438 T.)

---

[1] Interpose. [2] He had just neard the word "preamble." [3] Forty miles from London, where the Pilgrims are supposed to ha;e halted for dinner on the third day, after the Summoner's Tale. Cf. l. 12,336.

The Wife of Bath's Tale.

In tholde dayes of the Kyng Arthour,
Of which that Britons speken greet honour,
All was this land fulfild of fairye.   10,901
The elf queene with hir joly compaignye
Daunced ful ofte in many a grene mede.
This was the olde opinion as I rede, —
I speke of manye hundred yeres ago, —
But now kan no man se none elves mo,
For now the grete charitee and prayeres
Of lymytours, and othere hooly freres,
That serchen every lond and every streem,
As thikke as motes in the sonne beem, —
Blessynge halles, chambres, kichenes, boures
Citees, burghes, castels, hye toures,   10,912
Thropes,[1] bernes, shipnes,[2] dayeryes, —
This maketh that ther been no fairyes ;
For ther as wont to walken was an elf, (6455 T.)
Ther walketh now the lymytour hym self,
In undermeles[3] and in morwenynges,
And seyth his matyns and his hooly thynges
As he gooth in his lymytacioun.
Wommen may go saufly up and doun ; 10,920
In every bussh or under every tree,
Ther is noon oother incubus but he,
And he ne wol doon hem non[4] dishonour.

---

[1] Thorps, hamlets. [2] Sheep-folds. [3] Dinner time. [4] The Elles.
MS and in fact most of the others have "but," which can hardly
be correct. It is probably a mistaken repetition, by the scrivener, of
the same word in the previous line.

And so bifel that this kynge, Arthour,
Hadde in hous a lusty bacheler
That on a day cam ridynge fro ryver,[1]
And happed that allone as he was born,
He saugh a mayde walkynge hym biforn,
Of whiche mayde, anon, maugree hir heed,
By verray force birafte hire maydenhed ;[2]
For which oppressioun was swich clamour,
And swich pursute [3] un-to the kyng Arthour,
That dampned was this knyght for to be deed
By cours of lawe, and sholde han lost his
    heed, —   10,934
Paraventure [4] swich was the statut tho,[5] —
But that the queene and othere ladyes mo,
So longe preyden the kyng of grace,
Til he his lyf hym graunted in the place,
And gaf hym to the queene al at hir wille
To chese wheither she wolde hym save or
    spille.[6]   10,940
    The queene thanketh the kyng with al hir
        myght,
And after this thus spak she to the knyght,
Whan that she saugh hir tyme up-on a day :
" Thou standest yet," quod she, " in swich ar-
    ray,
That of thy lyf yet hastow no suretee.
I grante thee lyf, if thou kanst tellen me
What thyng is it that wommen moost desiren, —

---

[1] Hawking for water-fowl. Cf. l. 6349   [2] Maidenhood.   [3] Pros-
ecution.   [4] By chance.   [5] Then.   [6] Destroy.

Be war, and keepe thy nekke-boon from iren, —
And if thou kanst nat tellen it anon,
Yet shal I geve thee leve for to gon   10,950
A twelf-month and a day to seche and leere [1]
An answere suffisant in this mateere ;
And suretee wol I han er that thou pace,
Thy body for to yelden in this place."

   Wo was this knyght, and sorwefully he sik-
     eth ; [2]
But what ? [3] he may nat do al as hym liketh,
And at the laste he chees hym for to wende,
And come agayn right at the yeres ende,
With swich answere as God wolde hym purveye,
And taketh his leve, and wendeth forth his
     weye.   10,960

   He seketh every hous and every place
Where as he hopeth for to fynde grace
To lerne what thyng wommen loven moost ;
But he ne koude arryven in no coost (6504 T.)
Wher as he myghte fynde in this mateere
Two creatures accordynge in feere. [4]

   Somme seyde wommen loven best richesse,
Somme seyde honour, somme seyde jolynesse,
Somme riche array, somme seyden lust abedd,
And ofte tyme to be wydwe and wedde. 10,970
Somme seyde that oure hertes been moost esed
Whan that we been yflatered and yplesed.

   He gooth ful ny the sothe, I wol nat lye, —
A man shal wynne us best with flaterye ;

    [1] Learn.   [2] Sigheth.   [3] From the Hengwrt MS.   [4] Together.

And with attendance and with bisynesse,
Been we ylymed, bothe moore and lesse.[1]

And somme seyn that we loven best
For to be free, and do right as us lest,
And that no man repreve us of oure vice,
But seye that we be wise and no thyng nyce ;[2]
For trewely ther is noon of us alle,   10,981
If any wight wol clawe us on the galle,[3]
That we nel kike,[4] for he seith us sooth.
Assay, and he shal fynde it, that so dooth,
For, be we never so vicious with-inne,
We wol been holden wise and clene of synne.

And somme seyn that greet delit han we
For to been holden stable and eke secree,
And in o purpos stedefastly to dwelle,
And nat biwreye thyng that men us telle ;
But that tale is nat worth a rake-stele.[5]   10,991
Pardee, we wommen konne no thyng hele ;[6]
Witnesse on Myda, — wol ye heere the tale ?

Ovyde, amonges othere thynges smale,
Seyde Myda hadde under his longe heres,
Growynge up-on his heed, two asses eres,
The whiche vice[7] he hydde as he best myghte,
Ful subtilly, from every mannes sighte,
That save his wyf ther wiste of it namo.
He loved hire moost, and triste hire also ;
He preyde hire that to no creature   11,001
She sholde tellen of his disfigure.

---

[1] Great and small. [2] Silly, ignorant (Fr. *nice*, Lat. *nescius*)
[4] Touch a sore spot. Kick. [5] Rakestale. [6] Hide. [7] Blemish

She swoor him nay, for al this world to
    wynne,
She nolde do that vileynye or synne,
To make hir housbonde han so foul a name.
She nolde nat telle it for hir owene shame;
But nathelees, hir thoughte that she dyde,
That she so longe sholde a conseil hyde;
Hir thoughte it swal[1] so soore aboute hir herte,
That nedely som word hire moste asterte;
And sith she dorste telle it to no man,   11,011
Doun to a mareys [2] faste by she ran.   (6552 T.)
Til she came there her herte was a-fyre,
And as a bitore [3] "bombleth" in the myre
She leyde hir mouth un-to the water doun :
"Biwreye me nat, thou water, with thy soun,"
Quod she, "to thee I telle it and namo, —
Myn housbonde hath longe asses erys two.
Now is myn herte all hool, now it is oute,   11,019
I myghte no lenger kepe it, out of doute." [4]
Heere may ye se, thogh we a tyme abyde,
Yet, out it moot, we kan no conseil hyde.
The remenant of the tale if ye wol heere,
Redeth Ovyde, and ther ye may it leere.

This knyght, of which my tale is specially,
Whan that he saugh he myghte nat come
    therby,
That is to seye, what wommen love moost,
With-inne his brest ful sorweful was the goost
But hoom he gooth, he myghte nat sojourne,

---

[1] Swelled.   [2] Marsh.   [3] Bittern.   [4] In faith.

The day was come that homward moste he
  tourne,   11,030
And in his wey it happed hym to ryde
In al this care, under a forest syde,
Wher as he saugh up-on a daunce go
Of ladyes foure and twenty, and yet mo ;
Toward the which daunce he drow ful yerne,[1]
In hope that som wysdom sholde he lerne ;
But certeinly, er he came fully there,
Vanysshed was this daunce, he nyste where.
No creature saugh he that bar lyf,   11,039
Save on the grene he saugh sittynge a wyf ;
A fouler wight ther may no man devyse.
Agayn the knyght this olde wyf gan ryse,
And seyde, "Sire knyght, heer forth ne lith no
  wey ;
Tel me what that ye seken, by youre fey ![2]
Paraventure it may the bettre be,
Thise olde folk kan [3] muchel thyng," quod she.
 "My leeve mooder," quod this knyght, "cer-
  teyn
I nam but deed but if that I kan seyn
What thyng it is that wommen moost desire :
Koude ye me wisse I wolde wel quite [4] youre
  hire."   11,050
 "Plight me thy trouthe heere in myn hand,"
  quod she,
'The nexte thyng that I requere thee
Thou shalt it do, if it lye in thy myght,
And I wol telle it yow, er it be nyght."

---

[1] Quickly. [2] Faith. [3] Know. [4] Requite

"Have heer my trouthe," quod the knyght,
    "I graunte!"
    Thanne quod she, "I dar me wel avaunte [1]
Thy lyf is sauf, for I wol stonde therby;
Up-on my lyf, the queene wol seye as I.
Lat se, which is the proudeste of hem alle
That wereth on a coverchief or a calle,[2] 11,060
That dar seye 'nay' of that I shal thee teche.
Lat us go forth with-outen lenger speche."
Tho rowned [3] she a pistel [4] in his ere,
And bad hym to be glad and have no fere.

    Whan they be comen to the court, this
        knyght   (6605 T.)
Seyde he had holde his day as he hadde hight
And redy was his answere, as he sayde.
Ful many a noble wyf, and many a mayde,
And many a wydwe, for that they been wise,
The queene hir-selfe sittynge as justise, 11,070
Assembled been, his answere for to heere;
And afterward this knyght was bode appeere.

    To every wight comanded was silence,
And that the knyght sholde telle in audience
What thyng that worldly wommen loven best.
This knyght ne stood nat stille as doth a best,
But to his questioun anon answerde,
With manly voys, that al the court it herde.

    "My lige lady, generally," quod he,
'Wommen desiren have sovereynetee,   11,080
As wel over hir housbond, as hir love,

    [1] Boast.   [2] Cap.   [3] Then whispered.   [4] Epistle, i. e., a few words.

And for to been in maistrie hym above.
This is youre mooste desir, thogh ye me kille.
Dooth as yow list, I am at youre wille."
    In al the court ne was ther wyf, ne mayde,
Ne wydwe, that contraried that he sayde,
But seyden he was worthy han his lyf ;
And with that word up stirte the olde wyf,
Which that the knyght saugh sittynge in the
      grene ;
"Mercy!" quod she, "my sovereyn lady
      queene !   11,090
Er that youre court departe,[1] do me right ;
I taughte this answere un-to the knyght,
For which he plighte me his trouthe there,
The firste thyng I wolde hym requere,
He wolde it do, if it lay in his myght.
Bifore the court thanne, preye I thee, sir
      knyght,"
Quod she, "that thou me take un-to thy wyf,
For wel thou woost that I have kept thy lyf.
If I sey fals, sey 'nay,' up-on thy fey !"
    This knyght answerde, "Allas, and weyla-
      wey !   11,100
I woot right wel that swich was my biheste.
For Goddes love, as chees a newe requeste !
Taak al my good, and lat my body go."
    "Nay, thanne," quod she, "I shrewe us
      bothe two !
For thogh that I be foul, and [2] oold, and poore,

---

[1] Separate.   [2] Not in Elles. MS.

I nolde, for al the metal, ne for oore
That under erthe is grave,[1] or lith above,
But if thy wyf I were, and eek thy love ! "
　　" My 'love' ! " quod he, " nay, my dampna
　　　　cioun !
Allas ! that any of my nacioun　　　11,115
Sholde evere so foule disparaged be ! "
But al for noght, thende is this, that he
Constreyned was, he nedes moste hire wedde,
And taketh his olde wyf, and gooth to bedde.

　　Now wolden som men seye, paraventure,
That for my necligence I do no cure　(6656 **T.**)
To tellen yow the joye and al tharray,
That at the feeste was that ilke day ;
To which thyng shortly answeren I shal ;
I seye, ther nas no joye ne feeste at al. 11,120
Ther nas but hevynesse, and muche sorwe,
For prively he wedded hire on morwe,
And al day after hidde hym as an owle,
So wo was hym, his wyf looked so foule.

　　Greet was the wo ₊the knyght hadde in his
　　　　thoght,
Whan he was with his wyf abedde ybroght.
He walweth,[2] and he turneth to and fro ;
His olde wyf lay smylynge everemo,
And seyde, " O deere housbonde, *benedicitee !*
Fareth every knyght thus with his wyf, as ye ?
Is this the lawe of kyng Arthures hous ? 11,131
Is every knyght of his so dangerous ?[3]

---

[1] Buried.　[2] Tumbleth about.　[3] Distant.

I am youre owene love, and youre wyf ;
I am she which that saved hath youre lyf,
And certes, I dide [1] yow nevere unright.
Why fare ye thus with me, this firste nyght ?
Ye faren lyk a man had lost his wit ;
What is my gilt ? For Goddes love tel it,
And it shal been amended, if I may."

   "Amended !" quod this knyght, "allas ! nay,
       nay !   11,140
It wol nat been amended nevere mo,
Thou art so loothly, and so oold also,
And ther-to comen of so lough a kynde,
That litel wonder is thogh I walwe and wynde.
So, wolde God ! myn herte wolde breste !"
   "Is this," quod she, "the cause of youre
      unreste ?"
   "Ye, certeinly," quod he, "no wonder is."
   "Now, sire," quod she, "I koude amende al
      this,
If that me liste, er it were dayes thre ;
So, wel ye myghte bere yow un-to me.   11,150
   "But for ye speken of swich gentillesse
As is descended out of old richesse,
That therfore sholden ye be gentil men,
Swich arrogance is nat worth an hen.
Looke, who that is moost vertuous alway,
Pryvee and apert, [3] and moost entendeth ay
To do the gentil dedes that he kan,

---

[1] From the Cambridge MS. The Elles. MS. has "yet ne did I."
Tumble and turn.   [3] In private and public.

Taak hym for the grettest gentil man.
Crist, wole we clayme of hym oure gentillesse,[1]
Nat of oure eldres for hire old richesse ; 11,160
For, thogh they geve us al hir heritage, —
For which we clayme to been of heigh par-
　　　age,[2] —
Yet may they nat biquethe for no thyng,
To noon of us, hir vertuous lyvyng,　(6704 T.)
That made hem gentil men ycalled be,
And bad us folwen hem in swich degree.

　"Wel kan the wise poete of Florence, 11,167
That highte Dant, speken in this sentence, —
Lo, in swich maner rym is Dantes tale,[3] —
　Ful selde up riseth by his branches smale
Prowesse of man, for God of his goodnesse
Wole that of hym we clayme oure gentillesse ;
For of oure eldres may we no thyng clayme,
But temporel thyng that man may hurte and
　　　mayme.'

　"Eek every wight woot this as wel as I,
If gentillesse were planted natureelly,
Un-to a certeyn lynage doun the lyne,
Pryvee nor apert, thanne wolde they nevere
　　　fyne[4]
To doon of gentillesse the faire office ;
They myghte do no vileynye or vice.　11,18c

　"Taak fyr and ber it in the derkeste hous,
Bitwix this and the mount of Kaukasous,

---

[1] Cf Chaucer's ballad, *Gentilnesse*.　[2] Family.　[3] Cf. Longfe-
ow's Dante, *Purgatorio*, vii. 121, and note.　[4] Stint.

And lat men shette the dores and go thenne,[1]
Yet wole the fyr as faire lye and brenne
As twenty thousand men myghte it biholde ;
His office natureel ay wol it holde,
Up peril of my lyf, til that it dye.

"Heere may ye se wel how that genterye
Is nat annexed to possessioun,[2]
Sith folk ne doon hir operacioun   11,190
Alwey, as dooth the fyr, lo, in his kynde ;
For, God it woot, men may wel often fynde
A lordes sone do shame and vileynye ;
And he that wole han pris [3] of his gentrye,
For he was boren of a gentil hous,
And hadde hise eldres noble and vertuous,
And nel hym selven do no gentil dedis,
Ne folwen his gentil auncestre that deed is,
He nys nat gentil, be he duc or erl ;
For vileyns synful dedes make a cherl ; 11,200
For gentillesse nys but renomee [4]
Of thyne auncestres, for hire heigh bountee,[5]
Which is a strange [6] thyng to thy persone.
Thy gentillesse cometh fro God allone ;
Thanne comth oure verray gentillesse of grace,
It was no thyng biquethe us with oure place.

"Thenketh hou noble, as seith Valerius,
Was thilke Tullius Hostillius,
That out of poverte roos to heigh noblesse.
Redeth Senek, and redeth eek Boece,   11,210

---

[1] Thence.   [2] Property.   [3] Praise.   [4] Renown.   [5] Goodness
Foreign.

Ther shul ye seen expres, that no drede is, [1]
That he is gentil that dooth gentil dedis ;
And therfore, leeve housbonde, I thus con-
    clude ;
Al were it that myne auncestres weren rude,
Yet may the hye God, and so hope I, (6755 T.)
Grante me grace to lyven vertuously ;
Thanne am I gentil, whan that I bigynne
To lyven vertuously and weyve synne.

  "And ther as ye of poverte me repreeve,
The hye God, on whom that we bileeve, 11,220
In wilful poverte chees to lyve his lyf,
And certes, every man, mayden, or wyf,
May understonde that Jhesus, hevene kyng,
Ne wolde nat chesen vicious lyvyng.
Glad poverte is an honeste thyng, certeyn ;
This wole Senec and othere clerkes seyn ;
Who so that halt hym payd of [2] his poverte,
I holde hym riche, al hadde he nat a sherte ;
He that coveiteth is a povere wight,   11,229
For he wolde han that is nat in his myght ;
But he that noght hath, ne coveiteth have,
Is riche, al-though ye holde hym but a knave.

  "Verray poverte, it syngeth proprely ;
Juvenal seith of poverte, myrily, [3]
' The povre man, whan he goth by the weye,
Bifore the theves he may synge and pleye.'
Poverte is hateful good, and as I gesse
A ful greet bryngere-out of bisynesse,

----

[1] In faith.   [2] Content in.   [3] Pleasantly.

A greet amendere eek of sapience,
To hym that taketh it in pacience.   11,240
Poverte is this, al-though it seme alenge [1]
Possessioun that no wignt wol chalenge,
Poverte ful ofte, whan a man is lowe,
Maketh his God, and eek hym-self, to knowe.[2]
Poverte a spectacle [3] is, as thynketh me,
Thurgh which he may hise verray [4] freendes see,
And therfore, sire, syn that I noght yow greve,
Of my poverte namoore ye me repreve.

  "Now, sire, of elde [5] ye repreve me ;
And certes, sire, thogh noon auctoritee   11,250
Were in no book, ye gentils of honour
Seyn that men sholde an oold wight doon fa-
        vour,[6]
And clepe hym fader, for youre gentillesse,
And auctours [7] shal I fynden, as I gesse.

  "Now, ther ye seye that I am foul and old,
Than drede you noght to been a cokewold ;
For filthe and eelde, al so moot I thee ! [8]
Been grete wardeyns up-on chastitee :
But nathelees, syn I knowe youre delit,
I shal fulfille youre worldly appetit.   11,260
  "Chese now," quod she, "oon of thise
        thynges tweye :
To han me foul and old til that I deye,
And be to yow a trewe, humble wyf,
And nevere yow displese in al my lyf ;

[1] Sad.   [2] To be known.   [3] Mirror, glass.   [4] True.   [5] Age.
[6] Respect.   [7] Authorities.   [8] Thrive.

Or elles ye wol han me yong and fair, (6805 т.)
And take youre aventure of the repair [1]
That shal be to youre hous by cause of me,
Or in som oother place may wel be ;
Now chese your selven, wheither that yow
     liketh."   11,269
  This knyght avyseth hym [2] and sore siketh ;
But atte laste he seyde in this manere :
" My lady and my love, and wyf so deere,
I put me in youre wise governance ;
Cheseth youre self which may be moost ple-
     sance,
And moost honour to yow and me also ;
I do no fors [3] the wheither of the two,
For as yow liketh it suffiseth me."
    " Thanne have I gete of yow maistrie," quod
     she,
" Syn I may chese, and governe as me lest ? "
    " Ye, certes, wyf," quod he, " I holde it best.'
    " Kys me," quod she, " we be no lenger
     wrothe,   11,281
For, by my trouthe, I wol be to yow bothe, —
This is to seyn, ye, bothe fair and good.
I prey to God that I moote sterven wood, [4]
But I to yow be al so good and trewe,
As evere was wyf syn that the world was newe
And but I be tomorn as fair to seene
As any lady, emperice, or queene,   11,288
That is bitwixe the est and eke the west,

    [1] Resorting.   [2] Considereth.   [3] Care not.   [4] Die mad.

Dooth with my lyf and deth right as yow lest.
Cast up the curtyn, — looke, how that it is."

And whan the knyght saugh verraily al this,
That she so fair was, and so yong ther-to,
For joye he hente hire in hise armes two,
His herte bathed in a bath of blisse;
A thousand tyme arewe,[1] he gan hire kisse,
And she obeyed hym in every thyng
That myghte doon hym plesance or likyng.

And thus they lyve un-to hir lyves ende
In parfit joye; and Jhesu Crist us sende 11,300
Housbondes meeke, yonge, fressh a-bedde,
And grace toverbyde [2] hem that we wedde,
And eek, I praye Jhesu, shorte hir lyves
That nat wol be governed by hir wyves; (6844 T.)
And olde and angry nygardes of dispence,
God sende hem soone verray pestilence!

The words of the Friar Limitour and the Summoner.

This worthy Lymytour, this noble Frere,
He made alway a maner louryng chiere
Upon the Somonour, but for honestee [3] 11,309
No vileyns [4] word as yet to hym spak he;
But atte laste he seyde un-to the Wyf, (6851 T.)
"Dame," quod he, "God geve yow right good
        lyf!
Ye han heer touched, al so moot I thee!

[1] A-row.   [2] Outlive.   [3] Politeness.   [4] Impolite.

In scole matere greet difficultee.
Ye han seyd muche thyng right wel, I seye ;
But, dame, heere as we ryde by the weye
Us nedeth nat to speken but of game,
And lete auctoritees,[1] on Goddes name,
To prechyng, and to scole of clergye,
And if it lyke to this compaignye   11,326
I wol yow of a somonour telle a game.
Pardee, ye may wel knowe by the name
That of a somonour may no good be sayd.
I praye that noon of you be yvele apayd,[2] —
A somonour is a rennere up and doun
With mandementz [3] for fornicacioun,
And is y-bet [4] at every townes ende."

   Oure Hoost tho spak, " A, sire, ye sholde **be**
      hende [5]
And curteys, as a man of youre estaat,
In compaignye ; we wol have no debaat ! 11,33c
Telleth youre tale, and lat the Somonour be."

   "Nay," quod the Somonour, " lat hym seye
      to me
What so hym list, — whan it comth to my lot,
By God ! I shal hym quiten every grot !
I shal hym tellen which a greet honour
It is to be a flaterynge lymytour ;
And of many another manere cryme,
Which nedeth nat rehercen for this tyme,
And his office I shal hym telle ywis.' [6]

[1] Leave Scripture texts.   [2] Offended.   [3] Citations.   [4] Beate
[5] Civil.   [6] Truly.

Oure Hoost answerde, "Pees! namoore of
    this!"   11,340
And after this he seyde un-to the Frere,
"Tel forth youre tale,[1] leeve maister deere."

Heere bigynneth The Freres Tale.

Whilom ther was dwellynge in my contree
An erchedekene, a man of heigh degree,
That boldely dide execucioun   (6885 T.)
In punysshynge of fornicacioun,
Of wicchecraft, and eek of bawderye,
Of diffamacioun and avowtrye,[2]
Of chirche-reves,[3] and of testamentz,
Of contractes, and eek of lakke[4] of sacra-
    mentz,   11,350
Of usure, and of symonye also,
But certes, lecchours dide he grettest wo;
They sholde syngen if that they were hent;
And smale tytheres weren foule yshent;[5]
If any persone wolde up-on hem pleyne
Ther myghte asterte[6] hym no pecunyal peyne.
For smale tithes, and smal offrynge,
He made the peple pitously to synge,
For er the bisshope caughte hem with his hook,
They were in the erchedeknes book;   11,360

---

[1] The Friar's Tale is based upon one included in a mediæval collection made in the form of the *Gesta Romanorum*, but it was
probably old then. Two similar Latin stories were printed by the
Chaucer Society in 1872: *Narratio de quodam Senescallo Sceleroso*,
and *De Advocato et Diabolo*. [2] Adultery. [3] Church wardens
Neglect. [5] Oppressed [6] Escape.

And thanne hadde he, thurgh his jurisdicci
  oun,
Power to doon on hem correccioun.
He hadde a somonour redy to his hond ;
A slyer boye was noon in Engelond ;
For subtilly he hadde his espiaille (6905 T.)
That taughte hym wher hym myghte aught[1]
  availle.[2]
He koude spare of lecchours oon or two,
To techen hym[3] to foure and twenty mo ;
For thogh this somonour wood was as an hare,
To telle his harlotrye I wol nat spare, 11,370
For we been out of his correccioun,
They han of us no jurisdiccioun,[4]
Ne nevere shullen, terme of hir lyves.

 "Peter ! so been wommen of the styves,"[5]
Quod the Somonour, "yput out of my cure ! "

 " Pees ! with myschance and with mysaven
  ture ! "

Thus seyde our Hoost, " and lat hym telle his
  tale.

Now telleth forth, thogh that the Somonour
  gale,[6]

Ne spareth nat, myn owene maister deere."

 This false theef, this somonour, quod the
  Frere, 11,380
Hadde alwey bawdes redy to his hond,
As any hauk to lure in Engelond,

---

[1] Not in Elles. MS. [2] Fall. [3] Point out to him [4] Friars (of
whom the speaker was one) were responsible to the Pope, directly
Stews were exempt from ecclesiastical jurisdiction. [6] Yell.

That tolde hym al the secree that they knewe,
For hire acqueyntance was nat come of newe ;
They weren hise approwours [1] prively.
He took hym self a greet profit therby ;
His maister knew nat alwey what he wan.
With-outen mandement, a lewed man
He koude somne,[2] on peyne of Cristes curs,
And they were glade for to fille his purs, 11,390
And make hym grete feestes atte nale ; [3]
And right as Judas hadde purses smale,
And was a theef, right swich a theef was he.
His maister hadde but half his duetee.
He was, if I shal geven hym his laude,
A theef, and eek a somnour, and a baude.
He hadde eek wenches at his retenue
That wheither that sir Robert,[4] or sir Huwe,[4]
Or Jakke, or Rauf, or who so that it were
That lay by hem, they tolde it in his ere. 11,400

    Thus was the wenche and he of oon assent,
And he wolde fecche a feyned mandement,[5]
And somne hem to the chapitre bothe two,
And pile [6] the man, and lete the wenche go.
    Thanne wolde he seye, " Freend, I shal for
        thy sake
Do striken hire out of oure lettres blake,
Thee thar namoore as in this cas travaille,[7]
I am thy freend, ther I thee may availle."
    Certeyn he knew of briberyes mo

Informers.   [2] Summon.   [3] Ale-house.   [4] Secular clergy
[5] Forged citation. [6] Plunder. [7] Sin thus no more.

Than possible is to telle in yeres two;   11,410
For in this world nys dogge for the bowe
That kan an hurt deer from an hool yknowe
Bet than this somnour knew a sly lecchour,
Or an avowtier, or a paramour ;
And, for that was the fruyt of al his rente,
Therfore on it he sette al his entente. (6956 T.)
    And so bifel that ones on a day
This somnour, — evere waityng on his pray,
For to somne an old wydwe, a ribibe,[1]
Feynynge a cause, for he wolde brybe, —
Happed that he saugh bifore hym ryde   11,421
A gay yeman under a forest syde.
A bowe he bar, and arwes brighte and kene ;
He hadde up-on a courtepy[2] of grene,
An hat up-on his heed with frenges blake.
    " Sire," quod this somnour, " hayl ! and wel
      atake ! "
    " Wel-come ! " quod he, " and every good
      felawe.
Wher rydestow, under this grene-wode shawe,"[3]
Seyde this yeman ; " wiltow fer to day ? "
    This somnour hym answerde and seyde,
      " Nay,   11,430
Heere faste by," quod he, " is myn entente
To ryden, for to reysen up a rente
That longeth to my lordes duetee."
    " Artow thanne a bailly ? "   " Ye," quod
      he, —

---

[1] Dry, and shrill of voice. Cf. l. 3331.   [2] Short cloak.   [3] Shade.

He dorste nat for verray filthe and shame
Seye that he was a somonour, for the name.

"*Depardieux!*" quod this yeman, "deere
  broother!
Thou art a bailly, and I am another.
I am unknowen as in this contree ;   11,439
Of thyn aqueyntance I wolde praye thee,
And eek of bretherhede, if that yow leste ;
I have gold and silver in my cheste ;
If that thee happe to comen in oure shire
Al shal be thyn, right as thou wolt desire."

"*Grantmercy!*" quod this somonour, "by
  my feith ! "
Everych in ootheres hand his trouthe leith,
For to be sworn bretheren til they deye ;
In daliance they ryden forth hir weye.

This somonour that was as ful of jangles
As ful of venym been thise waryangles,[1] 11,450
And evere enqueryng up-on every thyng ;
"Brother," quod he, "where is now youre
  dwellyng,
Another day if that I sholde yow seche ? "
This yeman hym answerde, in softe speche :
"Brother," quod he, "fer in the north[2] con-
  tree,
Where as I hope som tyme I shal thee see.
Er we departe I shal thee so wel wisse
That of myn hous ne shaltow nevere mysse."

---

[1] A spiteful bird. [2] Cf. *Paradise Lost*, v. 755; Isaiah xiv. 13,
.4; and *Piers Plowman*, B. Text, i. 118. The arch-fiend is associated with the North, as a place of discomfort.

"Now, brother," quod this somonour, "I
    yow preye,
Teche me whil that we ryden by the weye,
Syn that ye been a baillif as am I,   11,461
Som subtiltee, and tel me feithfully
In myn office how I may mooste wynne,
And spareth nat for conscience ne synne,
But as my brother tel me how do ye." (7005 T.)

    "Now, by my trouthe, brother deere," seyde
        he,
" As I shal tellen thee a feithful tale,
My wages been ful streite and ful smale ;
My lord is hard to me and daungerous,[1]
And myn office is ful laborous ;   11,470
And therfore by extorcions I lyve ;
For sothe, I take all that men wol me geve,
Algate by sleyghte, or by violence.
Fro yeer to yeer I wynne al my dispence ;
I kan no bettre telle, feithfully."

    "Now certes," quod this somonour, "so
        fare I ;
I spare nat to taken, God it woot,
But if it be to hevy or to hoot,
What I may gete in conseil prively ;
No maner conscience of that have I ;   11,480
Nere[2] myn extorcioun I myghte nat lyven,
Nor of swiche japes wol I nat be shryven.
Stomak, ne conscience, ne knowe I noon :
I shrewe[3] thise shrifte-fadres everychoon !

---

[1] Imperious.   [2] But for.   [3] Curse.

Wel be we met, by God and by Seint Jame !
But, leeve brother, tel me thanne thy name,"
Quod this somonour ; in this meene while
This yeman gan a litel for to smyle.

 " Brother," quod he, " wiltow that I thee
  telle ?
I am a feend ; my dwellyng is in helle, 11,490
And heere I ryde aboute my purchasyng,[1]
To wite wher[2] men wolde me geven any-thyng.
My purchas[3] is theffect[4] of al my rente.[5]
Looke how thou rydest for the same entente.
To wynne good,[6] thou rekkest nevere how ;
Right so fare I, for ryde I wolde right now
Un-to the worldes ende for a preye."

 " A ! " quod this somonour, " *benedicite !* what
  sey ye ?
I wende[7] ye were a yeman trewely.
Ye han a mannes shape as wel as I,   11,500
Han ye a figure thanne determinat
In helle, ther ye been in youre estat ? "

 " Nay, certeinly," quod he, " ther have we
  noon,
But whan us liketh we kan take us oon,
Or elles make yow seme[8] we been shape
Som tyme lyk a man, or lyk an ape ;
Or lyk an angel kan I ryde or go.
It is no wonder thyng thogh it be so ;
A lowsy jogelour kan deceyve thee,   11,509
And *pardee !* yet kan I moore craft than he."

  Pursuits.   [2] Whether.   [3] Perquisites.   [4] Sum.   [5] Income
Goods.   [7] Thought.   [8] It appear to you

"Why," quod the somonour, "ryde ye thanne
    or goon
In sondry shape, and nat alwey in oon ? "
   "For we," quod he, "wol us swiche formes
    make   (7053 T.)
As moost able [1] is oure preyes for to take."
   "What maketh yow to han al this labour ? "
   "Ful many a cause, leeve sire somonour,"
Seyde this feend ; "but alle thyng hath tyme ;
The day is short, and it is passed pryme,
And yet ne wan I no-thyng in this day ;
I wol entende to wynnen if I may,   11,520
And nat entende our [2] wittes to declare ;
For, brother myn, thy wit is al to bare
To understonde, al-thogh I tolde hem thee ;
But for thou axest why labouren we, —
For som tyme we been Goddes instrumentz,
And meenes to doon hise comandementz
Whan that hym list up-on his creatures,
In divers art and in diverse figures.
With-outen hym we have no myght, certayn,
If that hym list to stonden ther agayn.[3]   11,530
And som tyme at oure prayere han we leve
Oonly the body and nat the soule greve ;
Witnesse on Job, whom that we diden wo ;
And som tyme han we myght of bothe two,
This is to seyn, of soule and body eke ;
And somtyme be we suffred for to seke [4]

---

[1] Handy (Fr. *habile*).   [2] Elles MS. has "hir."   [3] Against
Essay.

Up-on a man and doon his soule unreste,
And nat his body, and al is for the beste.
Whan he withstandeth oure temptacioun
It is the [1] cause of his savacioun, —   11,540
Al be it that it was nat oure entente
He sholde be sauf, but that we wolde nym
   hente,[2] —
And som tyme be we servant un-to man,
As to the erche bisshope, Seint Dunstan ;
And to the Apostles servant eek was I."
  "Yet tel me," quod the somonour, "feith-
   fully,
Make ye yow newe bodies thus alway
Of elementz ? "   The feend answerde, " Nay,
Som tyme we feyne, and som tyme we aryse
With dede bodyes, in ful sondry wyse,   11,550
And speke as renably [3] and faire and wel,
As to the Phitonissa dide Samuel ;
And yet wol som men seye it was nat he.
I do no fors [4] of youre dyvynytee,
But o thyng warne I thee, I wol nat jape,
Thou wolt algates [5] wite how we been shape,
Thou shalt herafterwardes, my brother deere,
Come there thee nedeth nat of me to leere,[6]
For thou shalt by thyn owene experience
Konne in a chayer rede [7] of this sentence
Bet than Virgile while he was on lyve, 11,561
Or Dant also ; now lat us ryde blyve,[8]

---

[1] Not in Elles. MS.   [2] Seize.   [3] Reasonably.   [4] I care not for
Notwithstanding (thy " divinity").   [6] Learn.   [7] Know enough to
lecture in a professor's chair   [5] Quickly.

For I wole holde compaignye with thee
Til it be so that thou forsake me."

   "Nay," quod this somonour, "that shal nat
       bityde!   (7105 T.)
I am a yeman knowen is ful wyde;
My trouthe wol I holde as in this cas;
For though thou were the devel, Sathanas,
My trouthe wol I holde to my brother,
As I am sworn, and ech of us til oother, 11,570
For to be trewe brother in this cas;
And bothe we goon abouten oure purchas.
Taak thou thy part, what that men wol thee geve,
And I shal myn, — thus may we bothe lyve, —
And if that any of us have moore than oother,
Lat hym be trewe and parte it with his brother."

   "I graunte," quod the devel, "by my fey!"
And with that word they ryden forth hir wey,
And right at the entryng of the townes ende
To which this somonour shoope[1] hym for to
       wende,   11,580
They saugh a cart that charged was with hey,
Which that a cartere droof forth in his wey.
Deepe was the wey, for which the carte stood:
The cartere smoot and cryde as he were wood,
"Hayt, Brok![2] hayt, Scot![3] what spare ye for
       the stones!
The feend," quod he, "yow fecche body and
       bones,
As ferforthly as evere were ye foled!

---

[1] Planned.   [2] Badger, gray.   [3] Cf. l. 616.

So muche wo as I have with you tholed ! [1]
The devel have al, bothe hors and cart and
      hey ! "

   This somonour seyde, " Heere shal we have
      a pley ; "   11,590
And neer the feend he drough as noght ne were
Ful prively, and rowned [2] in his ere,
" Herkne, my brother ! herkne, by thy feith !
Herestow nat how that the cartere seith ?
Hent [3] it anon, for he hath geve it thee,
Bothe hey and cart and eek hise caples [4] thre."

   " Nay," quod the devel, " God woot, never a
      deel.
It is nat his entente, trust thou me weel ;
Axe hym thy self, if thou nat trowest me,
Or elles stynt a while, and thou shalt see."

   This cartere thakketh his hors up-on the
      croupe,   11,601
And they bigonne drawen and to stoupe.
" Heyt ! now," quod he, " ther Jhesu Crist yow
      blesse !
And al his handwerk bothe moore and lesse,
That was wel twight,[5] myn owene lyard [6] boy !
I pray to God to save thee ! and Seint Loy ! [7]
Now is my cart out of the slow, *pardee !* "

   " Lo, brother," quod the feend, " what tolde
      I thee ?
Heere may ye se, myn owene deere brother,

---

[1] Suffered. [2] Whispered. [3] Seize.   Nags. [5] Twisted. [6] Gray
St. Eligius patron of smiths.

The carl spak oon, but he thoghte another.
Lat us go forth abouten oure viage ;   11,611
Heere wynne I no thyng up-on cariage."

Whan that they coomen som-what out of
    towne
This somonour to his brother gan to rowne :
" Brother," quod he, " heere woneth an old re-
        bekke [1]   (7155 T.)
That hadde almoost as lief to lese hire nekke,
As for to geve a peny of hir good.
I wole han twelf pens though that she be wood,
Or I wol sompne hire un-to oure office,
And yet, God woot, of hire knowe I no vice ;
But, for thou kanst nat, as in this contree, 11,621
Wynne thy cost, taak heer ensample of me."

This somonour clappeth at the wydwes gate :
" Com out," quod he, "thou olde virytrate ! [2]
I trowe thou hast som frere or preest with
    thee."

"Who clappeth ? " seyde this wyf, " *benedi-
    citee !*

God save you, sire ! what is youre sweete
    wille ? "

" I have," quod he, " of somonce a bille ;
Up-on peyne of cursyng [3] looke that thou be
Tomorn bifore the erchedeknes knee,   11,630
Tanswere to the court of certeyn thynges."

" Now, Lord," quod she, " Crist Jhesu, kyng
    of kynges,

---

[1] Cf. ll. 3331, 11,419.   [2] Old trot (?).   [3] Excommunication.

So wisly helpe me, as I ne may !
I have been syk, and that ful many a day ;
I may nat go [1] so fer," quod she, " ne ryde,
But I be deed, so priketh it in my syde.
May I nat axe a libel, sire somonour,
And answere there by my procuratour
To swich thyng as men wole apposen [2] me ? "
   " Yis," quod this somonour, "pay anon —
       lat se —   11,640
Twelf pens to me and I wol thee acquite.
I shal no profit han ther-by but lite,
My maister hath the profit, and nat I.
Com of, and lat me ryden hastily ;
Gif me twelf pens, I may no lenger tarye ! "
   " Twelf pens ! " quod she, "now lady Seinte
       Marie !
So wisly help me God out of care and synne,
This wyde world thogh that I sholde wynne,
Ne have I nat twelf pens with-inne myn hoold ;
Ye knowen wel that I am povre and oold.
Kithe [8] youre almesse on me, povre wrecche."
   " Nay, thanne," quod he, " the foule feend
       me fecche,   ·   11,652
If I thexcusen thongh thou shul be spilt ! " [4]
   " Allas ! " quod she, "God woot I have no
       gilt."
   " Pay me ! " quod he, " or by the sweete
       Seinte Anne,
As I wol bere awey thy newe panne

[1] Walk.   [2] Question.   [8] Show.   [4] Ruined.
VOL. I.   3¹

For dette which that thou owest me of old, —
Whan that thou madest thyn housbonde coke-
     wold
I payde at hoom for thy correccioun."   11,659
  "Thou lixt !" quod she, "by my savacioun
Ne was I nevere er now, wydwe ne wyf,
Somoned un-to youre court in al my lyf !
Ne nevere I nas but of my body trewe.
Un-to the devel, blak and rough of hewe,
Geve I thy body and my panne also !" (7205 T.)
  And whan the devel herde hire cursen so
Up-on hir knees, he seyde in this manere :
"Now, Mabely, myn owene moder deere,
Is this youre wyl in ernest that ye seye ?"
  "The devel," quod she, "so fecche hym er
     he deye, —   11,670
And panne and al, but he wol hym repente !"
  "Nay, olde Stot ! that is nat myn entente,"
Quod this somonour, "for to repente me
For any thyng that I have had of thee ;
I wolde I hadde thy smok and every clooth."
  "Now, brother," quod the devil, "be nat
     wrooth :
Thy body and this panne been myne by right ;
Thou shalt with me to helle yet to-nyght,
Where thou shalt knowen of oure privetee
Moore than a maister of dyvynytee." [1]   11,680
And with that word this foule feend hym hente.
Body and soule he with the devel wente

     [1] Cf. l. 11,554.   [2] Seized

Where as that somonours han hir heritage ;
And God, that made after his ymage
Mankynde, save and gyde us alle and some,
And leve thise somonours goode men bicome !
   Lordynges, I koude han toold you, quod this
     Frere,
Hadde I had leyser for this Somnour heere,
After the text of Criste, Poul, and John,
And of oure othere doctours many oon, 11,690
Swiche peynes that youre herte myghte agryse,[1]
Al be it so no tonge may it devyse ;
Thogh that I myghte a thousand wynter telle
The peynes of thilke cursed hous of helle ;
But for to kepe us fro that cursed place
Waketh[2] and preyeth[2] Jhesu for his grace,
So kepe us fro the temptour Sathanas.
Herketh[2] this word, beth[2] war, as in this cas.
" The leoun sit in his awayt alway
To sle the innocent, if that he may."   11,700
Disposeth[2] ay youre hertes to withstonde
The feend that yow wolde make thral and
     bonde ;
He may nat tempte yow over youre myght,
For Crist wol be youre champion and knyght ;
And prayeth[2] that thise somonours hem re-
     pente   (7245 T.)
Of hir mysdedes, er that the feend hem hente !

---

[1] Affright.   [2] Imperative mode.

The words of the Wood Somonour.

This Somonour in his styropes hye stood.
Up-on this Frere his herte was so wood,[1]
That lyk an aspen-leef he quook for ire.
    " Lordynges," quod he, " but o thyng I de
       sire, —   11,710
I yow biseke that of youre curteisye, (7251 T.)
Syn ye han herd this false Frere lye,
As suffereth me I may my tale telle.
    " This Frere bosteth that he knoweth helle,
And God it woot, that it is litel wonder ;
Freres and feendes been but lyte [2] a-sonder ;
For, *pardee !* ye han ofte tyme herd telle
How that a frere ravysshed was to helle
In spirit ones by a visioun ;   11,719
And as an angel ladde hym up and doun
To shewen hym the peynes that ther were,
In al the place saugh he nat a frere.
Of oother folk he saugh ynowe [3] in wo.
Un-to this angel spak the frere tho :
    " ' Now, sire,' quod he, ' han freres swich a
       grace
That noon of hem shal come to this place ? '
    " ' Yis,' quod this angel, ' many a millioun ,
And un-to Sathanas he ladde hym doun,
And now hath Sathanas, seith he, a tayl,
Brodder than of a carryk [4] is the sayl.   11,730

    [1] Angry.   [2] Little.   [3] Enough.   [4] Ship.

Hold up thy tayl, thou Sathanas,' quod he,
' Shewe forth thyn ers, and lat the frere se
Where is the nest of freres in this place ; '
And er than half a furlong wey of space,
Right so as bees out swarmen from an hyve
Out of the develes ers ther gonne dryve
Twenty thousand freres in a route,
And thurgh-out helle swarmeden aboute,
And comen agayn as faste as they may gon,
And in his ers they crepten everychon ;   11,740
He clapte his tayl agayn and lay ful stille.
This frere, whan he hadde looked al his fille
Upon the tormentz of this sory place,
His spirit God restored of his grace
Un-to his body agayn, and he awook ;
But natheles, for fere yet he quook,
So was the develes ers ay in his mynde ;
That is his heritage of verray kynde.[1] (7288 T.)
God save yow alle, save this cursed Frere !
My prologe wol I ende in this manere." [2]   11,750

Heere bigynneth The Somonour his Tale.

Lordynges, ther is in Yorkshire, as I gesse,
A mersshe contree called Holdernesse, (7292 T.)
In which ther wente a lymytour aboute
To preche, and eek to begge, it is no doute.

---

[1] Nature.   [2] The Summoner's story resembles one entitled, in
the version of M. Legrand d'Aussy, *La Vescie du Curé*, by Jacques
de Baisieux, intended as a burlesque upon the cupidity of the
friars.

And so bifel that on a day this frere
Hadde preched at a chirche in his manere,
And specially, aboven every thyng,
Excited he the peple in his prechyng
To trentals,[1] and to geve for Goddes sake,
Wher-with men myghte hooly houses make,
Ther as [2] divine servyce is honoured,   11,761
Nat ther as it is wasted and devoured,
Ne ther it nedeth nat for to be geve,   (7303 T.)
As to possessioners [3] that mowen lyve,
Thanked be God! in wele and habundaunce.
" Trentals," seyde he, " deliveren fro penaunce
Hir freendes soules, as wel olde as yonge ;
Ye, whan that they been hastily ysonge,
Nat for to holde a preest joly and gay,
He syngeth nat but o masse in a day.   11,770
Delivereth out," quod he, " anon, the soules !
Ful hard it is, with flesshhook or with oules [4]
To been yclawed, or to brenne, or bake ;
Now spede yow hastily for Cristes sake."
And whan this frere had seyd al his entente
With *qui cum patre*,[5] forth his wey he wente.
   Whan folk in chirche had geve him what
      hem lest,
He went his wey, no lenger wolde he reste.
With scrippe and tipped staf, ytukked hye,
In every hous he gan to poure and prye, 11,780
And beggeth mele, and chese, or elles corn.

---

[1] Thirty masses recited for the dead. [2] Where. [3] Monks and
parish priests owning property. [4] Awls. [5] Who with the Father
-- words still used at the close of sermons.

His felawe hadde a stafe tipped with horn,
A peyre of tables [1] al of yvory,
And a poyntel [2] polysshed fetisly, [3]
And wroote the names alwey as he stood
Of alle folk that gaf hym any good,
Asaunces [4] that he wolde for hem prey.
"Gif us [5] a busshel whete, malt or reye,
A Goddes kechyl, [6] or a trype [7] of chese,
Or elles what yow lyst, we may nat cheese ;
A Goddes halfpeny, [8] or a masse peny,   11,791
Or gif us of youre brawn, if ye have eny ;
A dagoun [9] of youre blanket, leeve dame,
Oure suster deere, lo heere I write youre
        name, —
Bacoun, or beef, or swich thyng as ye fynde."
(A sturdy harlot wente ay hem bihynde,
That was hir hostes-man, [10] and bar a sak,
And what men gaf hem leyde it on his bak.)
And whan that he was out at dore anon,
He planed awey the names everichon   11,800
That he biforn had writen in his tables.
He served hem with nyfles [11] and with fables.

  "Nay ! ther thou lixt, thou Somonour ! " quod
        the Frere.

  "Pees ! " quod oure Hoost, "for Cristes
        mooder deere ;
Tel forth thy tale and spare it nat at al."

---

[1] Tablets.   [2] Pencil.   [3] Neatly.   [4] As if.   [5] Elles. MS. has
"hym."   [6] A cake from God.   [7] Morsel.   [8] A ha'penny, God's
gift.   [9] Slip.   [10] He was in charge of guests at the monastery.
[11] Trifles.

"So thryve I," quod this Somonour, "so ᴵ
 shal !"

So longe he wente hous by hous til he
Cam til an hous ther he was wont to be
Refresshed moore than in an hundred placis ;
Syk lay the goode man whos the place is ;
Bedrede up-on a couche lowe he lay. 11,811

 "*Deus hic !*"[1] quod he, "O Thomas, freend,
 good day !"
Seyde this frere, curteisly and softe.
"Thomas," quod he, "God yelde yow !"[2] ful
 ofte (7354 ᵀ·)
Have I up-on this bench faren ful weel ;
Heere have I eten many a myrie meel ;"
And fro the bench he droof awey the cat,
And leyde adoun his potente [3] and his hat,
And eek his scrippe, and sette hym softe adoun.
His felawe was go walked in-to toun, 11,820
Forth with his knave in-to that hostelrye
Where as he shoope [4] hym thilke nyght to lye.

 "O deere maister," quod this sike man,
"How han ye fare sith that March bigan ?
I saugh yow noght this fourtnyght or moore."

 "God woot," quod he, "laboured I have ful
 soore,
And specially for thy savacioun
Have I seyd many a precious orisoun ;
And for oure othere freendes, God hem blesse ⸮
I have to day been at youre chirche at messe

---

[1] God be here! [2] God bless you for it ! [3] Staff. [4] Planned.

And seyd a sermoun after my symple wit,
Nat al after the text of hooly writ,   11,832
For it is hard to yow, as I suppose,
And therfore wol I teche yow al the glose.[1]
Glosynge is a glorious thyng certeyn,
For lettre sleeth, so as thise clerkes seyn.
There have I taught hem to be charitable,
And spende hir good ther it is resonable ;
And there I saugh oure dame, — a, where is
          she ? "   11,839
  " Yond, in the yerd, I trowe that she be,"
Seyde this man, " and she wol come anon."
  " Ey, maister, wel com be ye, by Seint
          John ! "
Seyde this wyf ; " how fare ye, hertely ? "
  The frere ariseth up ful curteisly
And hire embraceth in his armes narwe,
And kiste hire sweete, and chirteth[2] as a
          sparwe
With his lyppes : " Dame," quod he, " right
          weel,
As he that is youre servant every deel.
Thanked be God, that yow gaf soule and lyf,
Yet saugh I nat this day so fair a wyf   11,850
In al the chirche, God so save me ! "
  " Ye, God amende defautes, sire," quod she,
" Algates wel come be ye, by my fey ! "
  " *Graunt mercy*,[3] dame, this have I founde
          alwey,

----

[1] Interpretation.   [2] Chirpeth.   [3] Many thanks.

But of youre grete goodnesse, by youre leve,
I wolde prey yow that ye nat yow greve,
I wole with Thomas speke a litel throwe ; [1]
Thise curatz been ful necligent and slowe
To grope [2] tendrely a conscience.
In shrift, in prechyng is my diligence,   11,860
And studie in Petres wordes and in Poules.
I walke, and fisshe cristen mennes soules,
To yelden Jhesu Crist his propre rente.
To sprede his word is set al myn entente."

   " Now, by youre leve, O deere sire," quod
        she,   (7405 T.)
" Chideth him weel, for, seinte Trinitee !
He is as angry as a pissemyre,
Though that he have al that he kan desire,
Though I him wrye [3] a-nyght and make hym
        warm,   11,869
And on hym leye my leg, outher myn arm,
He groneth lyk oure boor, lith in oure sty.
Oother desport ryght noon of hym have I,
I may nat plese hym in no maner cas."

   " O Thomas, je vous dy, [4] Thomas ! Thomas !
This maketh [5] the feend, this moste ben
        amended ;
Ire is a thyng that hye God defended,
And ther-of wol I speke a word or two."

   " Now, maister," quod the wyf, " er that
        go,
What, wol ye dyne ? I wol go ther-aboute."

Little while.   [2] Search.   [3] Cover.   [4] I tell you.   [5] Doeth.

"Now, dame," quod he, "*je vous dy sanz
doute*,[1]   11,880
Have I nat of a capoun but the lyvere,
And of youre softe breed nat but a shyvere,
And after that a rosted pigges heed, —
But that I nolde no beest for me were deed, —
Thanne hadde I with yow hoomly suffisaunce,
I am a man of litel sustenaunce.
My spirit hath his fostryng in the Bible,
The body is ay so redy and penyble [2]
To wake,[3] that my stomak is destroyed ;
I prey yow, dame, ye be nat anoyed   11,890
Though I so freendly yow my conseil shewe.
By God, I wolde nat telle it but a fewe ! "

"Now, sire," quod she, " but o word er I go :
My child is deed with-inne thise wykes two,
Soone after that ye wente out of this toun."

"His deeth saugh I by revelacioun,"
Seith this frere, "at hoom in oure dortour.[4]
I dar wel seyn that er that half an hour
After his deeth, I saugh hym born to blisse
In myn avisioun, so God me wisse !   11,900
So dide our sexteyn and oure fermerer,[5]
That han been trewe freres fifty yeer, —
They may now, God be thanked of his loone !
Maken hir jubilee, and walke allone.
And up I roos, and al oure covent eke,
With many a teare triklyng on my cheke,

---

[1] I tell you, in faith !   [2] Assiduous.   [3] Watch.   [4] Dormitory
Director of the infirmary

Withouten noyse, or claterynge of belles,
Te deum was oure song and no thyng elles ;
Save that to Crist I seyde an orisoun,
Thankynge hym of his revelacioun ;   11,910
For, sire and dame, trusteth me right weel,
Oure orisons been wel moore effectueel,
And moore we seen of Cristes secree thynges,
Than burel [1] folk al though they weren kynges
We lyve in poverte and in abstinence, (7455 T.)
And burell folk in richesse and despence
Of mete and drynke, and in hir foul delit.
We han this worldes lust al in despit.
Lazar and Dives lyveden diversly   11,919
And diverse gerdoun [2] hadden they ther-by.
Who so wol preye he moot faste and be clene,
And fatte his soule and make his body lene.
We fare as seith thapostle ; clooth and foode
Suffisen us, though they be nat ful goode ;
The clennesse [3] and the fastynge of us freres
Maketh that Crist accepteth oure preyeres.

" Lo, Moyses fourty dayes and fourty nyght
Fasted, er that the heighe God of myght
Spak with hym in the mount of Synay.
With empty wombe,[4] fastynge many a day,
Receyved he the lawe that was writen   11,931
With Goddes fynger ; and Elye,[5] wel ye witen,
In mount Oreb, er he hadde any speche
With hye God, that is oure lyves leche,[6]
He fasted longe, and was in contemplaunce.

Lay.   [2] Reward.   [3] Purity   [4] Stomach   [5] Elijah   [6] Physician

" Aaron, that hadde the temple in govern-
     aunce,
And eek the [1] othere preestes everichon,
In-to the temple whan they sholde gon
To preye for the peple, and do servyse,
They nolden drynken in no maner wyse   11,940
No drynke which that myghte hem dronke make;
But there, in abstinence preye and wake,
Lest that they deyden, — taak heede what I
     seye, —
But they be sobre that for the peple preye,
War [2] that! — I seye namoore, — for it suffiseth.
Oure Lord Jhesu, as hooly writ devyseth,
Gaf us ensample of fastynge and preyeres ;
Therfore we mendynantz,[3] we sely freres,
Been wedded to poverte and continence,
To charite, humblesse, and abstinence,   11,950
To persecucioun for rightwisnesse,
To wepynge, misericorde [4] and clennesse ;
And therfore may ye se that oure preyeres, —
I speke of us, we mendynantz, we freres, —
Been to the hye God moore acceptable
Than youres with youre feestes at the table.
Fro Paradys first, if I shal nat lye,
Was man out chaced for his glotonye,
And chaast was man in Paradys certeyn.

   " But herkne, Thomas, what I shal the [5] seyn
I ne have no text of it, as I suppose,   11,961
But I shal fynde it in a maner glose,[6]

- Elles. MS. has "that."   [2] Note.   [3] Mendicants.   [4] Pity   [5] Not
a Elles. MS.   [6] Kind of exposition.

That specially oure sweete Lord Jhesu
Spak this by[1] freres whan he seyde thus :
  " ' Blessed be they that povere in spirit
       been,' —   (7505 T.)
And so forth al the gospel may ye seen
Wher[2] it be likker oure professioun,
Or hirs that swymmen in possessioun, —
Fy on hire pompe and hire glotonye !
And for hir lewednesse, I hem diffye !   11,970
  " Me thynketh they been lyk Jovinyan,[3]
Fat as a whale, and walkynge as a swan,
Al vinolent as botel in the spence.[4]
Hir preyere is of ful greet reverence
Whan they for soules seye the Psalm of Davit, —
Lo, but they seye, *cor meum eructavit,*[5] —
Who folweth Cristes gospel, and his foore,[6]
But we that humble been and chaast and
      poore,
Werkeris of Goddes word, not auditours ?
Therfore, right as an hauk up at a sours   11,980
Up springeth in-to their,[7] right so prayeres
Of charitable and chaste, bisy freres
Maken hir sours[8] to Goddes eres two.
Thomas, Thomas, so moote I ryde or go, —
And by that lord that clepid is Seint Yve !
Nere[9] thou oure brother sholdestou nat thryve !
In our chapitre praye we day and nyght

---

[1] Of.   [2] Whether.   [3] A fabulous emperor of Rome.   [4] Store-room.   [5] Ps. xiv. 1. There is a pun in the word *eructavit ;* English eructate.   [6] Conduct, walk. Cf. l. 10,152.   [7] The air.   [8] Ascent   [9] Wert thou not.

To Crist that he thee sende heele [1] and myght
Thy body for to weelden,[2] hastily."
   "God woot," quod he, "no thyng ther-of
     feele I!   11,990
As help me Crist, as in a fewe yeres
I han spent up-on diverse manere freres
Ful many a pound, yet fare I never the bet.
Certeyn my good I have almoost biset,[3] —
Farwel my gold, for it is al ago!"
   The frere answerde, "O Thomas, dostow so?
What nedeth yow diverse freres seche?
What nedeth hym that hath a parfit leche
To sechen othere leches in the toun?
Youre inconstance is youre confusioun. 12,000
Holde ye thanne me, or elles oure covent,
To praye for yow been insufficient?
Thomas, that jape nys nat worth a myte;
Youre maladye is for we han to lyte.[4]
A! gif that covent half a quarter otes!
A! gif that covent foure and twenty grotes!
A! gif that frere a peny, and lat hym go!
Nay, nay, Thomas, it may no thyng be so!
What is a ferthyng worth parted in twelve?
Lo ech thyng that is oned [5] in it selve 12,010
Is moore strong than whan it is to-scatered.
Thomas, of me thou shalt nat been yflatered;
Thou woldest han oure labour al for noght;
The hye God, that al this world hath wroght,
Seith that the werkman worthy is his hyre.

[1] Health. [2] Use. [3] Spent. [4] Little. [5] United.

Thomas, noght of youre tresor I desire, (7556 T.)
As for my self, but that al oure covent
To preye for yow is ay so diligent,
And for to buylden Cristes owene chirche.
Thomas, if ye wol lernen for to wirche   12,020
Of buyldynge up of chirches, may ye fynde
If it be good in Thomas lyf of Inde.[1]
Ye lye heere ful of anguish and [2] of ire,
With which the devel set youre herte afyre,
And chiden heere the sely innocent
Youre wyf, that is so meke and pacient ;
And therfore, Thomas, trowe me if thee leste,
Ne stryve nat with thy wyf, as for thy beste,
And ber this word awey now, by thy feith,
Touchynge this thyng, lo what the wise man[3]
      seith :   12,030
' With-inne thyn hous ne be thou no leoun ;
To thy subgitz do noon oppressioun,
Ne make thyne aqueyntances nat for to flee.'
And, Thomas, yet eft-soones I charge thee,
Be war from hire that in thy bosom slepeth,
Be war fro the serpent that so slily crepeth
Under the gras and styngeth subtilly ;
Be war, my sone, and herkne paciently,
That twenty thousand men han lost hir lyves
For stryvyng with hir lemmans and hir wyves.
Now sith ye han so hooly, meke a wyf   12,041
What nedeth yow, Thomas, to maken stryf ?

---

[1] The Apostle, who is said to have builded churches in India.
Elles. MS. has " anger," omitting " and." [3] Not in Elles. MS.

Ther nys, ywys, no serpent so cruel
Whan man tret on his tayl, ne half so fel
As womman is, whan she hath caught an ire ;
Vengeance is thanne al that they desire.
Ire is a synne, oon of the grete of sevene,
Abhomynable un-to the God of hevene,
And to hym self it is destruccioun.
This every lewed viker, or persoun,   12,050
Kan seye, how ire engendreth homycide.
Ire is in sooth executour of pryde.
I koude of ire seye so muche sorwe
My tale sholde laste til tomorwe ;
And therfore preye I God, bothe day and
          nyght,
An irous man God sende hym litel myght.
It is greet harme and eek greet pitee
To sette an irous man in heigh degree.

     "Whilom ther was an irous potestat,
As seith Senek,[1] that durynge his estaat 12,060
Up-on a day out ryden knyghtes two ;
And as Fortune wolde that it were so (7602 T.)
That oon of hem cam hoom, that oother noght.
Anon the knyght bifore the juge is broght,
That seyde thus : ' Thou hast thy felawe slayn,
For which I deme thee to the deeth certayn ; '
And to another knyght comanded he,
' Go lede hym to the deeth, I charge thee ! '
And happed as they wente by the weye,
Toward the place ther he sholde deye,   12,070

---

[1] This story is told of " Eraclius " in the *Gesta Romanorum.*

The knyght cam which men wenden had be
    deed.
Thanne thoughte they it was the beste reed,[1]
To lede hem bothe to the juge agayn.
They seiden, 'Lord, the knyght ne hath nat
    slayn
His felawe ; heere he standeth hool alyve.'
'Ye shul be deed,' quod he, 'so moot I thryve!
That is to seyn, bothe oon, and two, and thre.'
And to the firste knyght right thus spak he :
'I dampned thee, thou most algate be deed ;
And thou, also, most nedes lese thyn heed,
For thou art cause why thy felawe deyth ;'
And to the thridde knyght right thus he seith :
'Thou hast nat doon that I comanded thee ;'
And thus he dide doon sleen hem alle thre.

  "Irous Cambises was eek dronkelewe 12,085
And ay delited hym to been a shrewe ;
And so bifel a lord of his meynee,[2]
That loved vertuous moralitee,
Seyde on a day bitwene hem two right thus :

  "'A lord is lost if he be vicius,   12,090
And dronkenesse is eek a foul record
Of any man, and namely [3] in a lord.
Ther is ful many an eye, and many an ere,
Awaityng on a lord, and he noot [4] where.
For Goddes love drynk moore attemprely !
Wyn maketh man to lesen [5] wrecchedly
His mynde and hise lymes everichon.'

---

    [1] Counsel. [2] Retinue. [3] Especially. [4] Knows not. [5] Lose.

" ' The revers shaltou se,' quod he anon,
' And preeve it by thyn owene experience,
That wyn ne dooth to folk no swich offence.
Ther is no wyn bireveth me my myght   12,101
Of hand, ne foot, ne of nyne eyen sight ; '
And for despit he drank ful muchel moore
An hondred part than he hadde doon [1] bifoore ;
And right anon, this irous, cursed wrecche
Leet this knyghtes sone anon [1] bifore hym
    fecche,
Comandynge hym he sholde bifore hym stonde ;
And sodeynly he took his bowe in honde,
And up the streng he pulled to his ere,   12,109
And with an arwe he slow the child right
    there.
' Now, wheither have I a siker hand or noon ? '
Quod he ; ' is al my myght and mynde agon?
Hath wyn bireft me myne eyen sight ? '
What sholde I telle thanswere of the knyght ?
His sone was slayn, ther is namoore to seye.
Beth war, therfore, with lordes how ye pleye.
Syngeth *Placebo*,[2] — and I shal if I kan ;
But if it be un-to a povre man.   (7658 T.)
To a povre man men sholde hise vices telle,
But nat to a lord, thogh he sholde go to helle.

" Lo, irous Cirus, thilke Percien,   12,121
How he destroyed the ryver of Gysen,[3]
For that an hors of his was dreynt ther-inne,
Whan that he wente Babiloigne to wynne.

---

[1] Not in Elles. MS. [2] Be complaisant. Cf. l. 18,860. [3] Gyndes

He made that the ryver was so smal
That wommen myghte wade it over al.

Lo, what seyde he [1] that so wel teche kan:
'Ne be no felawe to an irous man,   12,128
Ne with no wood man walke by the weye,
Lest thee repente,' — ther is namoore to seye.

"Now, Thomas, leeve brother, lef thyn ire,
Thou shalt me fynde as just as is a squyre;
Hoold nat the develes knyf ay at thyn herte,
Thyn angre dooth thee al to soore smerte,
But shewe to me al thy confessioun."

"Nay," quod the sike man, "by Seint Sy-
        moun!
I have be shryven this day at my curat; [2]
I have hym toold hoolly al myn estat.
Nedeth namoore to speken of it, seith he,
But if me list, of myn humylitee."   12,140

"Gif me thanne of thy gold, to make oure
        cloystre,"
Quod he, "for many a muscle and many an
        oystre,
Whan othere men han ben ful wel at eyse,
Hath been oure foode, our cloystre for to reyse; [3]
And yet, God woot, unnethe the fundement [4]
I'ai fourned is, ne of our pavement
Nys nat a tyl yet with-inne oure wones, [5] —
By God, we owen fourty pound for stones!

"Now help, Thomas! for hym [6] that harwed
        helle,

----

[1] Solomon.   [2] Cf. l. 19,253.   [3] They had economized in food
[4] Scarcely the foundation.   [5] Dwelling.   [6] Jesus.

For elles moste we oure bookes selle ;   12,150
And if ye lakke oure predicacioun [1]
Thanne goth the world al to destruccioun.
For who so wolde us fro this world bireve,
So God me save, Thomas, by youre leve,
He wolde bireve out of this world the sonne ;
For who kan teche, and werchen, as we konne?
And that is nat of litel tyme," quod he,
" But syn that Elie [2] was, or Elise,[3]
Han freres been, — that fynde I of record,
In charitee ythanked be oure Lord !   12,160
Now, Thomas, helpe for seinte [4] charitee ! "
And doun anon he sette hym on his knee.

   This sike man wax wel ny wood for ire ;
He wolde that the frere had been on fire
With his false dissymulacioun.   (7705 T)

   " Swich thyng as is in my possessioun,"
Quod he, " that may I geven, and noon oother.
Ye sey me thus, ' that I am youre brother ' ? "

   " Ye, certes," quod the frere, " trusteth weel,
I took oure dame oure lettre and oure seel."

   " Now wel," quod he, " and som what shal I
       geve   12,171
Un-to youre hooly covent whil I lyve,
And in thyn hand thou shalt it have anon,
On this condicioun, and oother noon ;
That thou departe [5] it so, my leeve brother,
That every frere have also muche as oother ;

---

[1] Preaching. [2] Elles. MS. has " Ennok." [3] The friars claimed Elijah and Elisha. [4] Holy. [5] Divide.

This shaltou swere on thy professioun,
With-outen fraude or cavillacioun."

  "I swere it," quod this frere, "by my feith !
And ther-with-al his hand in his he leith, —
"Lo heer my feith, in me shal be no lak."

  "Now thanne put in thyn hand doun by my
     bak,"   12,182
Seyde this man, " and grope wel bihynde ;
Bynethe my buttok ther shaltow fynde
A thyng that I have hyd in pryvetee."

  "A !" thoghte this frere, "this shal go with
    me ! "
And doun his hand he launcheth to the clifte,
In hope for to fynde there a gifte ;
And whan this sike man felte this frere
Aboute his tuwel [1] grope there and heere,
Amydde his hand he leet the frere a fart ;
Ther nys no capul [2] drawynge in a cart   12,192
That myghte have lete a fart of swich a soun.

  The frere up stirte, as dooth a wood leoun, —
"A ! fals cherl," quod he, "for Goddes bones !
This hastow for despit doon for the nones ;
Thou shalt abye [3] this fart, if that I may ! "

  His meynee,[4] whiche that herden this affray,
Cam lepynge in, and chaced out the frere ;
And forth he gooth with a ful angry cheere,
And fette [5] his felawe, ther as lay his stoor.
He looked as it were a wilde boor, —   12,202
He grynte with his teeth, so was he wrooth ;

---

[1] Tuel.   [2] Horse.   [3] Pay for.   [4] Servants.   [5] Fetched.

A sturdy paas doun to the lordes court he
    gooth,
Wher as woned[1] a man of greet honour,
To whom that he was alwey confessour;
This worthy man was lord of that village.
This frere cam as he were in a rage,   12,208
Where as this lord sat etyng at his bord;
Unnethes[2] myghte the frere speke a word,
Til atte laste he seyde, " God yow see ! "

    This lord bigan to looke and seide, " Bene-
      dicitee !   (7752 T)
What, frere John, what maner world is this?
I trowe som maner thyng ther is amys;
Ye looken as the wode were ful of thevys;
Sit doun anon, and tel me what youre grief is,
And it shal been amended if that I may."

    " I have," quod he, " had a despit this day,
God yelde yow ! adoun in youre village,
That in this world is noon so povre a page,
That he nolde have abhomynacioun   12,221
Of that I have receyved in youre toun;
And yet nè greveth me no thyng so soore,
As that this olde cherl, with lokkes hoore,
Blasphemed hath oure hooly covent eke."

    " Now, maister," quod this lord, " I yow bi-
      seke " —

    " No ' maister,' sire," [3] quod he, " but servi-
      tour,
Thogh I have had in scole swich honour,

        [1] Dwelt.   [2] Scarcely.   Not in Elles. MS.

God liketh nat that ' Raby ' men us calle,
Neither in market ne in youre large halle."

 " No fors," quod he, " but tel me al youre
   grief."   12,231

 " Sire," quod this frere,[1] " an odious meschief
This day bityd is to myn ordre and me ;
And so *par consequens* in ech degree
Of hooly chirche ; God amende it soone ! "

 " Sire," quod the lord, " ye woot what is to
   doone ;

Distempre yow noght, ye be my confessour ;
Ye been the salt of the erthe and the savour ;
For Goddes love youre pacience ye holde ;
Tel me youre grief ; " and he anon hym tolde,
As ye han herd biforn, ye woot wel what.

 The lady of the hous al stille sat 12,242
Til she had herde what the frere sayde ;
" Ey ! Goddes mooder," quod she, — " blisful
   mayde !
Is ther oght elles ? Telle me feithfully."

 " Madame," quod he, " how thynke ye here-
   by ? "

 " How that me thynketh ? " quod she ; " so
   God me speede !
I seye, a cherle hath doon a cherles dede.
What shold I seye ? God lat hym nevere thee,[2]
His sike heed is ful of vanytee ; 12,250
I holde hym in a manere frenesye."

 " Madame," quod he, " by God I shal nat lye

---

[1] " This frere " not in Elles. MS., which has " he." [2] Thrive

But I on oother wise may be awreke,[1]
I shal disclaundre hym, over al ther I speke, —
This false blasphemour that charged me
To parte[2] that wol nat departed be, —
To every man yliche, with meschaunce!"

The lord sat stille, as he were in a traunce,
And in his herte he rolled up and doun 12,259
"How hadde the cherl this ymaginacioun,
To shewe swich a probleme to the frere?
Nevere erst er now herd I of swich mateere;
I trowe the devel putte it in his mynde.
In ars-metrike shal ther no man fynde,
Biforn this day of swich a questioun. (7805 T.)
Certes, it was a shrewed[3] conclusioun,
That every man sholde have yliche his part,
As of the soun or savour of a fart.
O vile proude cherl! I shrewe his face!
Lo, sires," quod the lord, with harde grace,
"Who evere herd of swich a thyng er now?
'To every man ylike,' — tel me how? 12,272
It is an inpossible, it may nat be.
Ey, nyce cherl? God lete thee nevere thee!
The rumblynge of a fart, and every soun,
Nis but of eir reverberacioun,
And evere it wasteth, litel and litel awey.
Ther is no man kan demen,[4] by my fey!
If that it were departed equally.
What, lo, my cherl, lo, yet how shrewedly,

Elles. MS. has "but I on him oother weyes be wreke." [2] Divide
Cursed malicious. [4] Judge.

Un-to my confessour to day he spak ;   12,281
I holde hym certeyn a demonyak.
Now ete youre mete, and lat the cherl go pleye.
Lat hym go honge hymself a devel weye ! "

*The wordes of the lordes Squier and his kerv-
ere for departynge of the fart on twelve.*

Now stood the lordes Squier at the bord
That karf his mete, and herde word by word
Of alle thynges whiche that I have sayd ;
' My lord," quod he, " beth nat yvele apayd ;[1]
I koude telle for a gowne-clooth
To yow, sire frere, so ye be nat wrooth, 12,290
How that this fart evene delt shal be
Among youre covent, if it lyked me."
    " Tel," quod the lord, " and thou shalt have
        anon
A gowne-clooth, by God, and by Seint John ! "
    " My lord," quod he, " whan that the weder
        is fair,
With-outen wynd, or perturbynge of air,
Lat brynge a cartewheel in-to this halle, —
But looke that it have his spokes alle, —
Twelve spokes hath a cartwheel comunly ;
And bryng me thanne twelf freres, — woot ye
        why ?   12,300
For thritten [2] is a covent, as I gesse ;
The confessour heere, for his worthynesse,

----

[1] Dissatisfied.   [2] Elles. MS. has " twelve."

Shal parfourne up [1] the nombre of his covent.
Thanne shal they knele doun, by oon assent,
And to every spokes ende, in this manere,
Ful sadly [2] leye his nose shal a frere.
Youre noble confessour there, God hym save !
Shal holde his nose upright under the nave.[3]
Thanne shal this cherl, with bely stif, and toght [4]
As any tabour, been hyder ybroght,   12,310
And sette hym on the wheel right of this cart,
Upon the nave, and make hym lete a fart,
And ye shul seen, up peril of my lyf,
By preeve which that is demonstratif,
That equally the soun of it wol wende, (7855 T.)
And eke the stynk, un-to the spokes ende, —
Save that this worthy man, youre confessour,
By-cause he is a man of greet honour,
Shal have the firste fruyt, as resoun is.
As yet the noble usage of freres is   12,320
The worthy men of hem shul first be served, —
And certeinly, he hath it weel disserved,
He hath to day taught us so muchel good
With prechyng in the pulpit ther he stood,
That I may vouche-sauf, I sey for me,
He hadde the firste smel of fartes three,
And so wolde al the covent hardily,
He bereth hym so faire and hoolily."

 The lord, the lady, and alle men save the
  frere,
Seyden that Jankyn spak in this matere 12,330

---

[1] Complete.   [2] Firmly.   [3] The centre of the wheel.   [4] Taut.

As wel as Euclude, or Protholomee,
Touchynge this cherl ; they seyden subtiltee
And heigh wit made hym speken as he **spak** ;
He nys no fool, ne no demonyak ;
And Jankyn hath ywonne a newe gowne.
My tale is doon, — we been almoost at **towne.**

Halt for Dinner, at Sittingbourne.

Heere folweth The Prologe of the Clerkes Tale of
Oxenford.

" Sire   Clerk   of   Oxenford,"   oure   Hooste
        sayde,   (7877 T.)
" Ye ryde as coy and stille as dooth a mayde
Were newe spoused, sittynge at the bord ;
This day ne herde I of youre tonge a word.
I trowe ye studie aboute som sophyme ; 12,341
But Salomon seith ' every thyng hath tyme.'

  " For Goddes sake ! as beth of bettre cheere !
It is no tyme for to studien heere ;
Telle us som myrie tale, by youre fey !
For what man that is entred in a pley,
He nedes moot unto the pley assente ;
But precheth nat, as freres doon in lente,
To make us for oure olde synnes wepe,
Ne that thy tale make us nat to slepe.   12,350

  " Telle us som murie thyng of aventures, —
Youre termes, youre colours, and youre figures
Keepe hem in stoor til so be that ye endite

Heigh style, as whan that men to kynges write ;
Speketh so pleyn at this tyme, we yow preye,
That we may understonde what ye seye."
    This worthy clerk benignely answerde,
" Hoost," quod he, " I am under youre yerde,[1]
Ye han of us, as now, the governance,
And therfore wol I do yow obeisance   12,360
As fer as resoun axeth hardily.[2]
I wol yow telle a tale which that I
Lerned at Padwe of a worthy clerk,
As preved by his wordes and his werk ;
He is now deed and nayled in his cheste,
I prey to God so geve his soule reste ! (7906 T.)
    " Fraunceys Petrak, the lauriat poete,
Highte this clerk whos rethorike sweete
Enlumyned al Ytaille of poetrie, —
As Lynyan [3] dide of philosophie,   12,370
Or lawe, or oother art particuler, —
But deeth, that wol nat suffre us [4] dwellen heer,
But as it were a twynklyng of an eye,
Hem bothe hath slayn, and alle shul we dye.
But forth to tellen of this worthy man
That taughte me this tale, as I bigan,
I seye that first with heigh stile he enditeth,
Er he the body of his tale writeth,
A prohemye, in the which discryveth he
Pemond,[5] and of Saluces [6] the contree ;   12,380
And speketh of Apennyn, the hilles hye

---

[1] Orders (literally, *rod*).   [2] Certainly.   [3] John of Lignano
Not in Elles. MS.   [5] Piedmont.   [6] Saluzzo.

That been the boundes of West **Lumbardye,**
And of Mount Vesulus [1] in special,
Where as the Poo out of a welle smal
Taketh his firste spryngyng and his sours,
That estward ay encresseth in his cours
To Emeleward,[2] to Ferrare and Venyse, —
The which a longe thyng were to devyse,
And trewely, as to my juggement,
Me thynketh it a thyng impertinent,   12,390
Save that he wole convoyen his mateere ;[3]
But this his tale [4] which that ye may heere."

Heere bigynneth The Tale of the Clerk of Oxen-
ford.

FIRST PART.

Ther is, at the West syde of Ytaille,
Doun at the roote of Vesulus the colde,
A lusty playne, habundant of vitaille,
Where many a tour and toun thou mayst bi-
        holde
That founded were in tyme of fadres olde,
And many another delitable sighte,
And Saluces this noble contree highte.

---

[1] Monte Viso; Virgil's "pine-clad Vesulus." (Æneid, x. 708.)
[2] Towards the Æmilian road in Northern Italy.   [3] Give the information.   [4] The story was an old one, that Boccaccio had inserted
in the *Decamerone*, as a happy conclusion of the series. Petrarch
learned it by heart to repeat it to his friends, and he may have told
it to Chaucer. In 1373, he made a Latin version for the benefit of
those who did not read Italian, and this is the one that Chaucer fol
owed.

A markys whilom lord was of that lond, 12,400
As were hise worthy eldres hym bifore,
And obeisant and redy to his hond
Were alle hise liges, bothe lasse and moore.
Thus in delit he lyveth, and hath doon yoore,
Biloved and drad, thurgh favour of Fortune,
Bothe of hise lordes and of his commune.[1]
Therwith he was, to speke as of lynage,
The gentilleste yborn of Lumbardye ;
A faire persone, and strong, and yong of age,
And ful of honour and of curteisye ;   12,410
Discreet ynogh his contree for to gye,[2] —
Save in somme thynges that he was to blame, —
And Walter was this yonge lordes name.

  I blame him thus, that he considereth noght
In tyme comynge what hym myghte bityde ;
But in his lust present was al his thoght,
As for to hauke and hunte on every syde,
Wel ny alle othere cures leet he slyde ;[3]
And eek he nolde, and that was worst of alle,
Wedde no wyf for noght that may bifalle. 12,420
Oonly that point his peple bar so soore (7961 T.)
That flokmeele[4] on a day they to hym wente,
And oon of hem that wisest was of loore, —
Or elles that the lord best wolde assente
That he sholde telle hym what his peple mente,
Or elles koude he showe wel swich mateere, —
He to the markys seyde as ye shul heere :

---

[1] Commons.   [2] Guide.   [3] An " Americanism."   [4] Together, the opposite of piecemeal.

"O noble markys, youre humanitee
Asseureth us and geveth us [1] hardinesse
As ofte as tyme is of necessitee   12,430
That we to yow mowe telle oure hevynesse.
Accepteth, lord, now for youre gentillesse,
That we with pitous herte un-to yow pleyne,
And lat youre eres nat my voys desdeyne,
Al [2] have I noght to doone in this mateere
Moore than another man hath in this place,
Yet for as muche as ye, my lord so deere,
Han alwey shewed me favour and grace,
I dar the bettre aske of yow a space
Of audience, to shewen oure requeste,   12,440
And ye, my lord, to doon right as yow leste ;
For certes, lord, so wel us liketh yow
And al youre werk, and evere han doon, that **we**
Ne koude nat us-self devysen how
We myghte lyven in moore felicitee,
Save o thyng, lord, if it youre wille be,
That for to been a wedded man yow leste,
Thanne were youre peple in sovereyn **hertes**
        reste.
Boweth youre nekke under that blisful yok
Of soveraynetee, noght of servyse,   12,450
Which that men clepeth spousaille or wedlok,
And thenketh, lord, among youre thoghtes wyse,
How that oure dayes passe in sondry wyse,
For thogh we slepe, or wake, or rome, or ryde
Ay fleeth the tyme, it nyl no man abyde ;

---

[1] Elles. MS. has "to geve us."   [2] Although

And thogh youre grene youthe floure as yit,
In crepeth age alwey, as stille as stoon,
And Deeth manaceth every age and smyt
In ech estaat, for ther escapeth noon ;
And al so certein as we knowe echoon   12,460
That we shul deye, as uncerteyn we alle
Been of that day whan deeth shal on us falle.

  " Accepteth thanne of us the trewe entente
That nevere yet refuseden thyn heeste,[1]
And we wol, lord, if that ye wole assente,
Chese yow a wyf in a short tyme atte leeste,
Born of the gentilleste and of the meeste[2]
Of al this land, so that it oghte seme   (8008 T.)
Honour to God and yow, as we kan deeme.
Delivere us out of al this bisy drede,   12,470
And taak a wyf, for hye Goddes sake,
For if it so bifelle, as God forbede !
That thurgh youre deeth youre lyne sholde
      slake,
And that a straunge successour sholde take
Youre heritage, O, wo, were us alyve !
Wherfore we pray you hastily to wyve."

  Hir meeke preyere, and hir pitous cheere,
Made the markys herte han pitee.
"Ye wol," quod he, " myn owene peple deere,
To that I nevere erst thoughte streyne[3] me.
I me rejoysed of my libertee,   12,481
That seelde tyme is founde in mariage ;
Ther I was free, I moot been in servage ;

---

[1] Bidding. [2] Most, *i. e.*, highest. [3] Constrain.

But nathelees, I se youre trewe entente,
And trust upon youre wit, and have doon **ay ;**
Wherfore, of my free wyl, I wole assente
To wedde me as soone as evere I may.
But ther as ye han profred me this day
To chese me a wyf, I yow relesse   12,489
That choys, and prey you of that profre cesse,
For, God it woot, that children ofte been
Unlyk hir worthy eldres hem bifore ;
Bountee [1] comth al of God, nat of the streen [2]
Of which they been engendred and ybore.
I truste in Goddes bontee,[1] and therfore
My mariage, and myn estaat and reste,
I hym bitake,[3] — he may doon as hym leste.
Lat me allone in chesynge of my wyf.
That charge up-on my bak I wole endure ;
But I yow preye, and charge up-on youre lyf,
That [4] what wyf that I take, ye me assure 12,501
To worshipe hire, whil that hir lyf may dure,
In word and werk, bothe heere and every-
          wheere,
As she an emperoures doghter weere ;
And forthermoore, this shal ye swere, that ye
Agayn my choys shul neither grucche ne stryve ;
For sith I shal forgoon my libertee   (8047 T.)
At youre requeste, as evere moot I thryve !
Ther as myn herte is set, ther wol I wyve ;
And, but ye wole assente in this manere, 12,51c
I prey yow speketh namoore of this matere."

---

[1] Goodness.   [2] Strain, stock.   [3] Commit.   [4] Not in Elles. MS.

With hertely wyl they sworen and assenten ;
To al this thyng, ther seyde no wight nay ;
Bisekynge hym of grace, er that they wenten,
That he wolde graunten hem a certein day
Of his spousaille, as soone as evere he may ;
For yet alwey the peple som what dredde
Lest that this markys no wyf wolde wedde.

He graunted hem a day, swich as hym leste,
On which he wolde be wedded sikerly,   12,520
And seyde he dide al this at hir requeste ;
And they, with humble entente, buxomly,[1]
Knelynge up-on hir knees ful reverently,
Hym thonken alle ; and thus they han an ende
Of hire entente, and hoom agayn they wende.

And heer up-on he to hise officeres
Comaundeth for the feste to purveye ;
And to hise privee knyghtes and squieres
Swich charge gaf as hym liste on hem leye ;
And they to his comandement obeye,   12,530
And ech of hem dooth al his diligence
To doon un-to the feeste reverence.

SECOND PART.

Noght fer fro thilke paleys honurable
Ther as this markys shoope his mariage,
There stood a throop,[2] of site delitable,
In which that povre folk of that village
Hadden hir beestes and hir herbergage,[3]

---

[1] Bowingly, obediently.   [2] Thorpe, hamlet.   [3] Lodging.

And of hire labour tooke hir sustenance,
After that the erthe gaf hem habundance.
Amonges thise povre folk ther dwelte **a man**
Which that was holden povrest of hem alle, —
But hye God som tyme senden kan   12,542
His grace in-to a litel oxes stalle ;
Janicula, men of that throope hym calle ;
A doghter hadde he fair ynogh to sighte,
And Grisildis this yonge mayden highte.

But for to speke of vertuous beautee [1]
Thanne was she oon the faireste under sonne,
For povreliche yfostred up was she ;
No likerous lust was thurgh hire herte yronne,
Wel ofter of the welle than of the tonne 12,551
She drank, and for she wolde vertu plese
She knew wel labour, but noon ydel ese.
But thogh this mayde tendre were of age,
Yet in the brest of hire virginitee
Ther was enclosed rype and sad [2] corage,
And in greet reverence and charitee
Hir olde, povre fader fostred shee ;
A fewe sheepe, spynnynge, on feeld she kepte,
She wolde noght been ydel til she slepte. 12,560
And whan she homward cam she wolde brynge
Wortes, or othere herbes, tymes ofte,
The whiche she shredde and seeth for hir lyv·
       ynge,
And made hir bed ful harde and no thyng
       softe ;   (8104 T.)

---

[1] Elles. MS. has "bountee."   [2] Established, firm.

And ay she kepte hir fadres lyf on-lofte [1]
With everich obeisaunce and diligence
That child may doon to fadres reverence.
Up-on Grisilde, this povre creature,
Ful ofte sithe this markys caste his eye
As he on huntyng rood *paraventure;*   12,570
And whan it fil that he myghte hire espye
He noght with wantowne lookyng of folye
Hise eyen caste on hire, but in sad [2] wyse
Up-on hir chiere [3] he gan hym ofte avyse,
Commendynge in his herte hir wommanhede,
And eek hir vertu, passynge any wight
Of so yong age, as wel in chiere as dede ;
For thogh the peple hadde no greet insight
In vertu, he considered ful right   12,579
Hir bountee, and disposed that he wolde
Wedde hire oonly, if evere he wedde sholde.

The day of weddyng cam, but no wight kan
Telle what womman that it sholde be ;
For which merveille wondred many a man,
And seyden, whan they were in privetee,
" Wol nat oure lord yet leve his vanytee ?
Wol he nat wedde ? allas ! allas ! the while !
Why wole he thus hym-self and us bigile ? "

But nathelees this markys hath doon make,
Of gemmes set in gold and in asure,   12,590
Brooches and rynges, for Grisildis sake ;
And of hir clothyng took he the mesure
By a mayde lyke to hire stature,

---

[1] Supported her father's life.   [2] Grave.   [3] Appearance.

And eek of othere ornementes alle
That un-to swich a weddyng sholde falle.
  The time of undren of the same day
Approcheth, that this weddyng sholde be,
And al the paleys put was in array,
Bothe halle and chambres, ech in his degree ;
Houses of office stuffed with plentee,   12,600
Ther maystow seen of deynteuous vitaille
That may be founde as fer as last Ytaille.
This roial markys richely arrayed,
Lordes and ladyes in his compaignye,
The whiche that to the feeste weren yprayed,
And of his retenue the bachelrye,[1]
With many a soun of sondry melodye,
Un-to the village of the which I tolde,
In this array the righte wey han holde.
  Grisilde of this, God woot, ful innocent
That for hire shapen was al this array,   12,611
To fecchen water at a welle is went,   (8152 T.)
And comth hoom as soone as ever she may ;
For wel she hadde herd seyd that thilke day
The markys sholde wedde, and if she myghte
She wolde fayn han seyn [2] som of that sighte.
She thoghte, "I wole with othere maydens
        stonde,
That been my felawes, in oure dore and se
The markysesse, and therfore wol I fonde [8]
To doon at hoom as soone as it may be   12,620
The labour which that longeth un-to me ;

---

[1] Young knights.   [2] Seen.   [8] Try.

And thanne I may at leyser hire biholde
If she this wey un-to the castel holde."
And as she wolde over hir thresshfold gon
The markys cam, and gan hire for to calle;
And she set doun hir water pot anon
Biside the thresshfold in an oxes stalle,
And doun up-on hir knes she gan to falle,
And with sad contenance kneleth stille
Til she had herd what was the lordes will.
This thoghtful markys spak un-to this mayde
Ful sobrely, and seyde in this manere : 12,632
"Where is youre fader, O Grisildis?" he sayde;
And she with reverence, in humble cheere,
Answerde, "Lord, he is al redy heere;"
And in she gooth with-outen lenger lette,
And to the markys she hir fader fette.
He by the hand thanne took this olde man,
And seyde thus, whan he hym hadde asyde,
"Janicula, I neither may ne kan   12,640
Lenger the plesance of myn herte hyde.
If that thou vouche-sauf what-so bityde,
Thy doghter wol I take er that I wende
As for my wyf un-to hir lyves ende.
Thou lovest me, I woot it wel certeyn,
And art my feithful lige man ybore,
And all that liketh me, I dar wel seyn.
It liketh thee, and specially therfore,
Tel me that poynt that I have seyd bifore,
If that thou wolt un-to that purpos drawe,
To take me as for thy sone in lawe."   12,651

This sodeyn cas [1] this man astonyed so
That reed he wax abayst, and al quakyng
He stood ; unnethes [2] seyde he wordes mo,
But oonly thus : " Lord," quod he, " my willynge
Is as ye wole, ne ageyns youre likynge
I wol no thyng, ye be my lord so deere ;
Right as yow lust governeth this mateere."

" Yet wol I," quod this markys softely,
" That in thy chambre, I, and thou, and she,
Have a collacioun, [3] and wostow why ?   12,661
For I wol axe if it hire wille be   (8202 T.)
To be my wyf, and reule hire after me ;
And al this shal be doon in thy presence,
I wol noght speke out of thyn audience."

And in the chambre whil they were aboute
Hir tretys, which as ye shal after heere,
The peple cam un-to the hous with-oute,
And wondred hem in how honeste manere,
And tentifly, [4] she kepte hir fader deere ; 12,670
But outrely [5] Grisildis wondre myghte,
For nevere erst ne saugh she swich a sighte.
No wonder is thogh that [6] she were astoned
To seen so greet a gest come in that place ;
She nevere was to swiche gestes woned, [7]
For which she looked with ful pale face.
But, shortly forth this tale for to chace,
Thise arn the wordes that the markys sayde
To this benigne, verray, [8] feithful mayde :

---

[1] Hap.   [2] Scarcely.   [3] Conference.   [4] Attentively.   [5] Utterly
[6] Not in Elles. MS.   [7] Accustomed.   [8] True.

"Grisilde," he seyde, "ye shal wel under-
  stonde   12,680
It liketh to youre fader and to me
That I yow wedde ; and eek it may so stonde,
As I suppose ye wol that it so be ;
But thise demandes axe I first," quod he,
" That sith it shal be doon in hastif wyse,
Wol ye assente or elles yow avyse ?
I seye this, be ye redy with good herte
To al my lust, and that I frely may 12,688
As me best thynketh do yow laughe or smerte,
And nevere ye to grucche it nyght ne day ?
And eek whan I sey 'ye' ne sey nat 'nay,'
Neither by word, ne frownyng contenance ?
Swere this, and heere I swere yow alliance."

 Wondrynge up-on this word, quakynge for
  drede,
She seyde, " Lord, undigne and unworthy
Am I to thilke honour that ye me beede ;
But as ye wole youre self, right so wol I,
And heere I swere that nevere willyngly
In werk, ne thoght, I nyl yow disobeye, 12,699
For to be deed, though me were looth to deye !"

 " This is ynogh, Grisilde myn," quod he,
And forth he gooth with a ful sobre cheere
Out at the dore, and after that cam she,
And to the peple he seyde in this manere :
" This is my wyf," quod he. " that standeth
  heere ;
Honoureth hire, and loveth hire, I preye,
Who-so me loveth ; ther is namoore to seye."

And for that no thyng of hir olde geere
She sholde brynge in to his hous, he bad
That wommen sholde dispoillen hire right
      theere ;   12,710
Of which thise ladyes were nat right glad
To handle hir clothes wher-inne she was clad ;
But nathelees this mayde, bright of hewe,
Fro foot to heed they clothed han al newe.
Hir heris han they kembd, that lay untressed
Ful rudely, and with hir fyngres smale (8256 T.)
A corone on hire heed they han ydressed,
And sette hire ful of nowches [1] grete and smale.
Of hire array what sholde I make a tale ? 12,719
Unnethe [2] the peple hire knew for hire fairnesse,
Whan she translated was in swich richesse.

This markys hath hire spoused with a ryng,
Broght for the same cause, and thanne hire sette
Up-on an hors snow-whit and wel amblyng,
And to his paleys er he lenger lette
With joyful peple that hire ladde and mette,
Convoyed hire, and thus the day they spende
In revel til the sonne gan descende ;
And, shortly forth this tale for to chace,
I seye that to this newe markysesse   12,730
God hath swich favour sent hire of his grace,
That it ne semed nat by liklynesse
That she was born and fed in rudenesse,
As in a cote, or in an oxe stalle,
But norissed in an emperoures halle.

To every wight she woxen is so deere

---

[1] Jewels. [2] Scarcely.

And worshipful, that folk ther she was bore,
And from hire birthe knewe hire yeer by yeere,
Unnethe trowed they, but dorste han swore
That[1] to Janicle of which I spak bifore 12,740
She doghter nere,[2] for as by conjecture,
Hem thoughte she was another creature ;
For though that evere vertuous was she,
She was encressed in swich excellence
Of thewes[3] goode yset in heigh bountee,
And so discreet and fair of eloquence,
So benigne, and so digne of reverence,
And koude so the peples herte embrace,
That ech hire lovede that looked on hir face.

Noght oonly of Saluces in the toun 12,750
Publiced was the bountee[4] of hir name.
But eek biside in many a regioun,
If oon seide wel, another seyde the same.
So spradde of hire heighe bountee the name
That men and wommen, as wel yonge as olde,
Goon to Saluce upon hire to bihold.
Thus Walter lowely — nay, but roially —
Wedded with fortunat honestetee,
In Goddes pees lyveth ful esily 12,759
At hoom, and outward[5] grace ynogh had he ;
And for he saugh that under lowe[6] degree
Was ofte vertu hid, the peple hym heelde
A prudent man, and that is seyn ful seelde.

Nat oonly this Grisildis thurgh hir wit

---

[1] Elles. MS. has "that she." [2] Ne were. [3] Traits. [4] Goodness
Elles. MS. has "beautee ' [5] Abroad. [6] Elles. MS. has "heigh."

Koude al the feet [1] of wyfly homlynesse,[2]
But eek whan that the cas required it (8306 T.)
The commune profit koude she redresse ;
Ther nas discord, rancour, ne hevynesse,
In al that land, that she ne koude apese,
And wisely brynge hem alle in reste and ese.
Though that hire housbonde absent were, anon
If gentil men or othere of hire contree   12,772
Were wrothe, she wolde bryngen hem aton ;[3]
So wise and rype wordes hadde she,
And juggementz of so greet equitee,
That she from hevene sent was, as men wende,
Peple to save and every wrong tamende.

    Nat longe tyme after that this Grisild
Was wedded, she a doghter hath ybore,
Al had hire levere have born a knave [4] child.
Glad was this markys and the folk therfore,
For though a mayde child coome al bifore,
She may un-to a knave [4] child atteyne,   12,783
By liklihede, syn she nys nat bareyne.

THIRD PART.

    Ther fil, as it bifalleth tymes mo,
Whan that this child had souked but a throwe,[4]
This markys in his herte longeth so
To tempte his wyf hir sadnesse [6] for to knowe,
That he ne myghte out of his herte throwe

Feat (performance).   [2] Elles. MS. has "humblenesse."   [3] A
 [4] Elles. MS. has "man."   [5] Short time.   [6] Firmness.

This merveillous desir his wyf tassaye ; 12,790
Nedelees, God woot, he thoghte hire for taf-
    fraye.
He hadde assaved hire ynogh bifore,
And foond hire evere good, — what neded it
Hire for to tempte, and alwey moore and
    moore ?
Though som men preise it for a subtil wit,
But as for me, I seye that yvele it sit
To assaye a wyf whan that it is no nede,
And putten hire in angwyssh and in drede.
For which this markys wroghte in this manere ;
He cam allone a nyght ther as she lay 12,800
With stierne face and with ful trouble cheere,
And seyde thus : "Grisilde," quod he, "that
    day
That I yow took out of youre povere array
And putte yow in estaat of heigh noblesse, —
Ye have nat that forgeten, as I gesse ?
I seye, Grisilde, this present dignitee
In which that I have put yow, as I trowe,
Maketh yow nat forgetful for to be 12,808
That I yow took in povre estaat ful lowe,
For any wele ye moot youre selven knowe ;
Taak heede of every word that I yow seye,
Ther is no wight that hereth it but we tweye.
Ye woot youre self wel how that ye cam heere
In to this hous, it is nat longe ago, (8354 T.)
And though to me that ye be lief and deere,
Un-to my gentils ye be no thyng so ;

They seyn, to hem it is greet shame and wo
For to be subgetz, and been in servage,
To thee, that born art of a smal village;
And namely [1] sith thy doghter was ybore,
Thise wordes han they spoken, doutelees;
But I desire, as I have doon bifore,   12,822
To lyve my lyf with hem in reste and pees;
I may nat in this caas be recchelees,
I moot doon with thy doghter for the beste,
Nat as I wolde, but as my peple leste;
And yet, God woot, this is ful looth to me;
But nathelees, with oute youre wityng
I wol nat doon, but this wol I," quod he,
" That ye to me assente, as in this thyng.   12,830
Shewe now youre pacience in youre werkyng,
That ye me highte and swore in youre village,
That day that maked was oure mariage."

    Whan she had herd al this she noght ameved,
Neither in word, or chiere, or countenaunce,
For as it semed she was nat agreved.
She seyde, " Lord, al lyth in youre plesaunce;
My child and I, with hertely obeisaunce,
Been youres al, and ye mowe save or spille [3]
Youre owene thyng; werketh after youre wille.
Ther may no thyng, God so my soule save!
Liken [4] to yow that may displese me;   12,842
Ne I ne desire no thyng for to have,
Ne drede for to leese save oonly yee;
This wyl is in myn herte, and ay shal be.

---

[1] Especially.   [2] Changed not.   [3] Destroy.   [4] Please.

No lengthe of tyme, or deeth, may this deface,
Ne chaunge my corage [1] to another place."
  Glad was this markys of hire answeryng,
But yet he feyned as he were nat so ;
Al drery was his cheere and his lookyng, 12,850
Whan that he sholde out of the chambre go.
Soone after this, a furlong wey [2] or two,
He prively hath toold al his entent
Un-to a man, and to his wyf hym sente.
A maner sergeant was this privee man,
The which that feithful ofte he founden hadde
In thynges grete, and eek swich folk wel kan
Doon execucioun on thynges badde ;
The lord knew wel that he hym loved and
       dradde :   12,859
And whan this sergeant wiste his [3] lordes wille,
In-to the chambre he stalked hym ful stille.
  " Madame," he seyde, "ye moote [4] forgeve it
    me,
Though I do thyng to which I am constreyned ;
Ye been so wys, that ful wel knowe ye
That lordes heestes mowe [5] nat been yfeyned : [6]
They mowe wel been biwailled and compleyned,
But men moote nede un-to hire lust obeye,
And so wol I ; ther is namoore to seye. (8408 T.)
This child I am comanded for to take," —
And spak namoore but out the child he hente [7]
Despitously, and gan a cheere make   12,871

---

[1] Inclination.   [2] A little while. Cf. i. 3637.   [3] Elles. MS. has "the." [4] Must. [5] May. [6] Evaded. [7] Snatched.

As though he wolde han slayn it er he wente.
Grisildis moot al suffren and consente ;
And as a lamb she sitteth meke and stille,
And leet this crueel sergeant doon his wille.

   Suspecious was the diffame [1] of this man,
Suspect his face, suspect his word also,
Suspect the tyme in which he this bigan ;
Allas, hir doghter that she loved so,   12,879
She wende he wolde han slawen it right tho ;
But nathelees she neither weepe ne syked,[2]
Consentynge hire to that the markys lyked ;
But atte laste to speken she bigan,
And mekely she to the sergeant preyde,
So as he was a worthy gentil man,
That she moste kisse hire child er that it deyde
And in hir barm [3] this litel child she leyde
With ful sad face, and gan the child to kisse,
And lulled it, and after gan it blisse ;
And thus she seyde in hire benigne voys, 12,890
"Fare weel, my child,[4] I shal thee nevere see !
But sith I thee have marked with the croys,
Of thilke Fader blessed moote he be,
That for us deyde up on a croys of tree.
Thy soule, litel child, I hym bitake,[5]
For this nyght shaltow dyen for my sake."

   I trowe that to a norice [6] in this cas
It had been hard this reuthe [7] for to se ;
Wel myghte a mooder thanne han cryd, allas !

---

[1] Bad name. [2] Sighed. [3] Lap. [4] Cf. l. 5258, etc. [5] Commend
to him. [6] Nurse. [7] Pitiful sight.

But nathelees, so sad and stidefast was she,
That she endured al adversitee,   12,901
And to the sergeant mekely she sayde,
" Have heer agayn youre litel yonge mayde ;
Gooth now," quod she, " and dooth my lordes
          heeste ;
And o thyng wol I prey yow of youre grace,
That, but my lord forbad yow, atte leeste
Burieth this litel body in som place
That beestes ne no briddes it to-race ; " [1]
But he no word wol to that purpos seye, 12,909
But took the child and wente upon his weye.

This sergeant cam un-to his lord ageyn,
And of Grisildis wordes and hire cheere
He tolde hym point for point, in short and
          pleyn,   (8453 T.)
And hym presenteth with his doghter deere.
Somwhat this lord hath routhe in his manere,
But nathelees his purpos heeld he stille,
As lordes doon whan they wol han hir wille ;
And bad his sergeant that he pryvely
Sholde this child ful [2] softe wynde and wrappe
With alle circumstances, tendrely,   12,920
And carie it in a cofre, or in a lappe ;
But, up-on peyne his heed of for to swappe, [3]
That no man sholde knowe of his entente,
Ne whenne [4] he cam [2] ne whider that he wente ;
But at Boloigne to his suster deere,
That thilke tyme of Panik was countesse,

[1] Tear to pieces. [2] Not in Elles. MS. [3] Strike. [4] Whence.

He sholde it take, and shewe hire this mateere,
Bisekynge hire to doon hire bisynesse
This child to fostre in alle gentillesse ; 12,929
And whos child that it was he bad hir [1] hyde
From every wight for oght that may bityde.

　　The sergeant gooth, and hath fulfild this
　　　thyng ;
But to this markys now retourne we,
For now gooth he ful faste ymaginyng
If by his wyves cheere he myghte se
Or by hire word aperceyve that she
Were chaunged ; but he nevere hire koude fynde
But evere in oon ylike sad and kynde, [2]
As glad, as humble, as bisy in servyse,
And eek in love, as she was wont to be, 12,940
Was she to hym in every maner wyse ;
Ne of hir doghter noght a word spak she.
Noon accident for noon adversitee [3]
Was seyn in hire, ne nevere hir doghter name
Ne nempned [4] she, in ernest nor in game.

FOURTH PART.

　　In this estaat ther passed been foure yeer
Er she with childe was ; but, as God wolde,
A knave child she bar by this Walter,
Ful gracious and fair for to biholde ;
And whan that folk it to his fader tolde, 12,950

---

[1] Elles. MS. has "hym." [2] Constant and natural. [3] No accidental token of adversity. [4] Named.

Nat oonly he, but al his contree, merye
Was for this child, and God they thanke and
    herye.[1]
Whan it was two yeer old, and fro the brest
Departed of his norice, on a day
This markys caughte yet another lest [2]
To tempte his wyf yet ofter, if he may.
O, nedelees was she tempted in assay !
But wedded men ne knowe no mesure
Whan that they fynde a pacient creature !

  "Wyf," quod this markys, "ye han herd er
    this   12,960
My peple sikly berth oure mariage,
And namely [3] sith my sone yborn is,   (8502 T.)
Now is it worse than evere in al oure age.
The murmure sleeth [4] myn herte and my corage ;
For to myne eres comth the voys so smerte
That it wel ny destroyed hath myn herte.

  "Now sey they thus : 'Whan Walter is agon
Thanne shal the blood of Janicle succede,
And been oure lord, for oother have we noon ;'
Swiche wordes seith my peple, out of drede,[5]
Wel oughte I of swich murmur taken heede,
For certeinly I drede swich sentence,[6]   12,972
Though they nat pleyn speke in myn audience.
I wolde lyve in pees, if that I myghte,
Wherfore I am disposed outrely,[7]
As I his suster servede by nyghte,

---

[1] Praise.   [2] Desire.   [3] Especially   [4] Slayeth.   [5] In faith
[6] Expression of opinion.   [7] Fully.

Right so thenke I to serve hym pryvely.
This warne I yow, that ye nat sodeynly
Out of youre-self for no wo sholde outreye,[1] —
Beth pacient, and ther of I yow preye." 12,980
  " I have," quod she, " seyd thus, and evere
    shal,
I wol no thyng, ne nyl[2] no thyng certayn,
But as yow list ; naught greveth me at al
Though that my doughter and my sone be
    slayn
At youre comandement ; this is to sayn,
I have noght had no part of children tweyne,
But first siknesse and after wo and peyne.
Ye been oure lord, dooth with youre owene
    thyng
Right as yow list, — axeth no reed[3] at me,
For as I lefte at hoom al my clothyng   12,990
Whan I first cam to yow, right so," quod she,
" Lefte I my wyl, and al my libertee,
And took youre clothyng ; wherfore I yow
    preye,
Dooth youre plesaunce, I wol youre lust obeye.
And certes, if I hadde prescience
Youre wyl to knowe er ye youre lust me tolde,
I wolde it doon with-outen necligence ;
But now I woot[4] youre lust and what ye wolde,
Al youre plesance ferme and stable I holde ;
For wiste I that my deeth wolde do yow ese,
Right gladly wolde I dyen yow to plese ; 13,001

<hr>

[1] Rave.   [2] Dislike.   [3] Counsel.   [4] Know.

Deth may noght make no comparisoun
Un-to youre love ; " and whan this markys say [1]
The constance of his wyf, he caste adoun
Hise eyen two, and wondreth that she may
In pacience suffre al this array ; [2]
And forth he goth with drery contenance,
But to his herte it was ful greet plesance.

   This ugly sergeant, in the same wyse
That he hire doghter caughte, right so he,
Or worse, if men worse kan devyse,   13,011
Hath hent hire sone that ful was of beautee.
And evere in oon so pacient was she (8553 T.)
That she no chiere maade of hevynesse,
But kiste hir sone, and after gan it blesse ;
Save this : she preyde hym, that if he myghte,
Hir litel sone he wolde in erthe grave,
His tendre lymes, delicaat to sighte,
Fro foweles and fro beestes for to save ;
But she noon answere of hym myghte have ;
He wente his wey, as hym no-thyng ne roghte,
But to Boloigne he tendrely it broghte. 13,022

   This markys wondred evere lenger the moore
Up-on hir pacience, and if that he
Ne hadde soothly knowen ther bifoore
That parfitly hir children loved she,
He wolde have wend that of som subtiltee,
And of malice, or for crueel corage, [4]
That she hadde suffred this with sad visage ;
but wel he knew, that next hym-self, certayn

     [1] Saw.   [2] Ordinance.   [3] Recked   [4] Inclination.

She loved hir children best in every wyse.
But now of wommen wolde I axen fayn 13,032
If thise assayes myghte nat suffise?
What koude a sturdy housbonde moore devyse
To preeve hire wyfhod, or hir stedefastnesse,
And he continuynge evere in sturdinesse?
But ther been folk of swich condicioun
That whan they have a certein purpos take,
They kan nat stynte of hire entencioun,
But right as they were bounden to that stake
They wol nat of that firste purpos slake.
Right so this markys fulliche hath purposed
To tempte his wyf as he was first disposed.
He waiteth,[1] if by word or contenance, 13,044
That she to hym was changed of corage;
But nevere koude he fynde variance;
She was ay oon in herte and in visage,
And ay the forther that she was in age
The moore trewe, if that it were possible,
She was to hym in love, and moore penyble;[2]
For which it semed thus that of hem two
Ther nas but o wyl, for as Walter leste,
The same lust was hire plesance also; 13,053
And, God be thanked, al fil for the beste.
She shewed wel,[3] for no worldly unreste
A wyf, as of hir self, no thing ne sholde
Wille in effect, but as hir housbonde wolde.

  The sclaundre[4] of Walter ofte and wyde
       spradde,

[1] Watcheth.   [2] Painstaking.   [3] Made it clear that.   [4] Ill repute.

That of a crueel herte he wikkedly,   13,059
For [1] he a povre womman wedded hadde,
Hath mordred bothe his children prively.
Swich murmure was among hem comunly.
No wonder is, for to the peples ere
Ther cam no word but that they mordred were;
For which, where-as his peple ther bifore
Hadde loved hym wel, tne sclaundre of his
     diffame   (8606 T.)
Made hem that they hym hatede therfore.

   To been a mordrere is an hateful name,
But nathelees, for ernest ne for game,
He of his crueel purpos nolde stente;   13,070
To tempte his wyf was set al his entente.

   Whan that his doghter twelf yeer was of age
He to the court of Rome, in subtil wyse
Enformed of his wyl, sente his message,[2]
Comaundynge hem swiche bulles to devyse
As to his crueel purpos may suffyse,
How that the pope, as for his peples reste,
Bad hym to wedde another if hym leste.
I seye, he bad they sholde countrefete
The popes bulles, makynge mencioun   13,080
That he hath leve his firste wyf to lete,[3]
As by the popes dispensacioun,
To stynte rancour and dissencioun
Bitwixe his peple and hym; thus seyde the
     bulle,
The which they han publiced atte fulle.

         [1] Because.   [2] Messenger.   [3] Leave.

The rude peple, as it no wonder is,
Wenden [1] ful wel that it hadde be right so ;
But whan thise tidynges cam to Grisildis
I deeme that hire herte was ful wo ;
But she — ylike sad [2] for everemo —   13,090
Disposed was, this humble creature,
The adversitee of Fortune al tendure,
Abidynge evere his lust and his plesance
To whom that she was geven herte and al,
As to hire verray worldly suffisance.

But, shortly if this storie I tellen shal,
This markys writen hath in special
A lettre, in which he sheweth his entente,
And secreely he to Boloigne it sente.
To the erl of Panyk, which that hadde tho [3]
Wedded his suster, preyde he specially 13,101
To bryngen hoom agayn hise children two
In honurable estaat al openly ;
But o thyng he hym preyde outrely,
That he to no wight, though men wolde en-
          quere,
Sholde nat telle whos children that they were
But seye, the mayden sholde ywedded be
Un-to the markys of Saluce anon.

And as this erl was preyd, so dide he ;
For at day set he on his wey is goon   13,110
Toward Saluce, and lordes may oon
In riche array, this mayden for to gyde,
Hir yonge brother ridynge hire bisyde.

---

[1] Thought.   [2] Constant.   [3] Then.

Arrayed was toward hir mariage   (8654 T.)
This fresshe mayde ful of gemmes cleere.
Hir brother, which that seven yeer was of age,
Arrayed eek ful fressh in his manere ;
And thus in greet noblesse and with glad cheere,
Toward Saluces shapynge hir journey,
Fro day to day they ryden in hir wey.   13,120

FIFTH PART.

Among al this, after his wikke usage,
This markys, yet his wyf to tempte moore,
To the outtreste preeve of hir corage,
Fully to han experience and loore
If that she were as stidefast as bifoore,
He on a day, in open audience,
Ful boistously hath seyd hire this sentence :
" Certes, Grisilde, I hadde ynogh plesance
To han yow to my wyf for youre goodnesse
As for youre trouthe and for youre obeisance,
Noght for youre lynage, ne for youre richesse :
But now knowe I in verray soothfastnesse
That in greet lordshipe, if I wel avyse,   13,133
Ther is greet servitute, in sondry wyse.
I may nat doon as every plowman may, —
My peple me constreyneth for to take
Another wyf, and crien day by day.
And eek the pope, rancour for to slake,
Consenteth it, that dar I undertake ;
And treweliche thus muche I wol yow seye,

My newe wyf is comynge by the weye.   13,141
Be strong of herte, and voyde anon hir place,
And thilke dowere that ye broghten me,
Taak it agayn, I graunte it of my grace.
Retourneth to youre fadres hous," quod he
" No man may alwey han prosperitee.
With evene herte I rede [1] yow tendure
This strook of Fortune or of aventure."
And she answerde agayn in pacience :
" My lord," quod she, " I woot and wiste alway
How that bitwixen youre magnificence   13,151
And my poverte no wight kan ne may
Maken comparisoun, it is no nay ;
I ne heeld me nevere digne in no manere
To be youre wyf, no, ne youre chambrere ;
And in this hous ther ye me lady maade,
The heighe God take I for my witnesse,
And also wysly [2] he my soule glaade !
I nevere heeld me lady, ne maistresse,
But humble servant to youre worthynesse, 13,160
And evere shal, whil that my lyf may dure,
Aboven every wordly creature.
That ye so longe of youre benignitee
Han holden me in honour and nobleye,
Where as I was noght worthy for to [3] bee,
That thonke I God, and yow, to whom I preye
Foryelde it yow ; ther is namoore to seye :
Un-to my fader gladly wol I wende   (8708 T.)
And with hym dwelle un-to my lyves ende ;

---

[1] Counsel.   [2] Truly.   [3] " For to" not in Elles. MS.

Ther I was fostred of a child ful smal. 13,170
Til I be deed my lyf ther wol I lede,
A wydwe clene, in body, herte and al;
For sith I gaf to yow my maydenhede,
And am youre trewe wyf, it is no drede,
God shilde swich a lordes wyf to take
Another man to housbonde or to make;[1]
And of youre newe wyf God of his grace
So graunte yow wele[2] and prosperitee;
For I wol gladly yelden hire my place,
In which that I was blisful wont to bee, 13,180
For sith it liketh yow, my lord," quod shee,
"That whilom weren al myn hertes reste,
That I shal goon, I wol goon whan yow leste.
But ther as ye me profre swich dowaire
As I first broghte, it is wel in my mynde
It were my wrecched clothes, no thyng faire,
The whiche to me were hard now for to fynde.

"O goode God, how gentil and how kynde
Ye semed by youre speche and youre visage
The day that maked was oure mariage! 13,190
But sooth is seyd, algate[3] I fynde it trewe,
For in effect it preeved is on me,
Love is noght oold as whan that it is newe!
But certes, lord, for noon adversitee
To dyen in the cas, it shal nat bee
That evere in word or werk I shal repente
That I yow gaf myn herte in hool entente.
My lord, ye woot that in my fadres place

[1] Mate. [2] Wealth, *i. e.*, well-being. [3] Always.

Ye dide me streepe out of my povre weede,[1]
And richely me cladden of youre grace. 13,200
To yow broghte I noght elles, out of drede,
But feith and nakednesse and maydenhede ;
And heere agayn my clothyng I restoore,
And eek my weddyng ryng, for everemore.
The remenant of youre jueles redy be
In with youre chambre, dar I saufly sayn.
Naked out of my fadres hous," quod she,
" I cam and naked moot I turne agayn ;
Al youre plesance wol I folwen fayn ;
But yet I hope it be nat youre entente   13,210
That I smoklees out of youre paleys wente.
Ye koude nat doon so dishoneste [2] a thyng
That thilke wombe [3] in which youre children
          leye   (8753 T.)
Sholde biforn the peple in my walkyng
Be seyn al bare, wherfore I yow preye,
Lat me nat lyk a worm go by the weye.
Remembre yow, myn owene lord, so deere,
I was youre wyf though I unworthy weere ;
Wherfore in gerdoun [4] of my maydenhede
Which that I broghte, and noght agayn 1
          bere,   13,220
As voucheth sauf to geve me to my meede [4]
But swich a smok as I was wont to were,
That I ther-with may wrye [5] the wombe of here
That was youre wyf ; and heer take I my leeve
Of yow, myn owene lord, lest I yow greve."

---

[1] Garment.   [2] Disreputable.   [3] Belly.   [4] Reward.   [5] Cover.

' The smok," quod he, " that thou hast on **thy**
    bak,
Lat it be stille, and bere ıt forth with thee."
But wel unnethes [1] thilke word he spak,
But wente his wey, for routhe and for pitee.

Biforn the folk hir-selven strepeth she, **13,230**
And in hir smok, with heed and foot al bare,
Toward hir fader hous forth is she fare.[2]
The folk hire folwe wepynge in hir weye,
And Fortune ay they cursen as they goon ;
But she fro wepyng kepte hire eyen dreye,
Ne in this tyme word ne spak she noon.

Hir fader, that this tidynge herde anoon,
Curseth the day and tyme that nature
Shoope hym to been a lyves creature ;
For out of doute this olde povre man   **13,240**
Was evere in suspect of hir mariage ;
For evere he demed, sith that it bigan,
That whan the lord fulfild hadde his corage,[3]
Hym wolde thynke it were a disparage
To his estaat, so lowe for talighte,
And voyden hire as soone as ever he myghte.
Agayns [4] his doghter hastiliche goth he,
For he by noyse of folk knew hire comynge,
And with hire olde coote as it myghte be,
He covered hire ful sorwefully wepynge ;
But on hire body myghte he it nat brynge,
For rude was the clooth and moore of age
By dayes fele [5] than at hire mariage.   **13,253**

---

[1] Scarcely.   [2] Gone.   [3] Desire.   [4] Towards.   [5] Many

Thus with hire fader, for a certeyn space,
Dwelleth this flour of wyfly pacience,
That neither by hire wordes ne hire face,
Biforn the folk, ne eek in hire [1] absence,
Ne shewed she that hire was doon offence ;
Ne of hire heighe estaat no remembraunce
Ne hadde she, as by hire contenaunce.   13,260
No wonder is, for in hire grete estaat,
Hire goost was evere in pleyn humylitee ;
No tendre mouth, noon herte delicaat,[2]
No pompe, no semblant of roialtee ;
But ful of pacient benyngnytee,   (8805 r.)
Discreet and pridelees, ay honurable,
And to hire housbonde evere meke and stable.

Men speke of Job, and moost for his hum-
          blesse,   13,268
As clerkes, whan hem list, konne wel endite,
Namely [3] of men, but as in soothfastnesse,
Though clerkes preise wommen but a lite,
Ther kan no man in humblesse hym acquite
As womman kan, ne kan been half so trewe
As wommen been, but it be falle of newe.[4]

SIXTH PART.

Fro Boloigne is this erl of Panyk come,
Of which the fame up sprang to moore and
          lesse,[5]

---

[1] Their.   [2] Fastidious.   [3] Especially.   [4] Unless some case has
occurred very lately.   [5] Great and small.

And in the peples eres, alle and some,
Was kouth eek that a newe markysesse
He with hym broghte, in swich pompe and
    richesse,
That nevere was ther seyn with mannes eye
So noble array in al West Lumbardye.   13,281
  The markys, which that shoope and knew al
    this,
Er that this erl was come, sente his message [1]
For thilke sely, povre Grisildis;
And she with humble herte and glad visage,
Nat with no swollen thoght in hire corage,
Cam at his heste, and on hire knees hire sette,
And reverently and wisely she hym grette.
"Grisilde," quod he, "my wyl is outrely
This mayden that shal wedded been to me
Received be to-morwe as roially   13,291
As it possible is in myn hous for [2] to be,
And eek that every wight in his degree
Have his estaat in sittyng and servyse
And heigh plesaunce as I kan best devyse.
I have no wommen suffisaunt, certayn,
The chambres for tarraye in ordinaunce
After my lust, and therfore wolde I fayn
That thyn were al swich manere governaunce,
Thou knowest eek of old al my plesaunce;
Thogh thyn array be badde and yvel biseye, [3]
Do thou thy devoir [4] at the leeste weye."
  "Nat oonly, lord, that I am glad," quod she,

---

[1] Messenger.   [2] Not in Elles. MS.   [3] Provided.   [4] Duty.

" To doon youre lust, but I desire also   13,304
Yow for to serve and plese in my degree
With-outen feyntyng, and shal everemo ;
Ne nevere for no wele, ne no wo,
Ne shal the goost with-inne myn herte stente
To love yow best, with al my trewe entente."
And with that word she gan the hous to
        dighte,
And tables for to sette and beddes make,
And peyned hire to doon al that she myghte,
Preyynge the chambreres for Goddes sake
To hasten hem, and faste swepe and shake ;
And she the mooste servysable of alle   13,315
Hath every chambre arrayed and his halle.

Abouten undren gan this erl alighte (8857 T.)
That with him broghte thise noble children
        tweye,
For which the peple ran to seen the sighte
Of hire array so richely biseye ;   13,320
And thanne at erst amonges hem they seye,
That Walter was no fool, thogh that hym leste
To chaunge his wyf, for it was for the beste ;
For she is fairer, as they deemen alle,
Than is Grisilde, and moore tendre of age,
And fairer fruyt bitwene hem sholde falle,
And moore plesant, for hire heigh lynage ;
Hir brother eek so faire was of visage
That hem to seen the peple hath caught ple-
        saunce,   13,329
Commendynge now the markys governaunce. —

"O stormy peple! unsad,[1] and evere untrewe!
Ay undiscreet, and chaungynge as a vane,
Delitynge evere in rumbul[2] that is newe;
For lyk the moone, ay wexe ye and wane!
Ay ful of clappyng[3] deere ynogh a-jane![4]
Youre doom is fals, youre constance yvele
        preeveth,
A ful greet fool is he that on yow leeveth."[5]
Thus seyden sadde[6] folk in that citee
Whan that the peple gazed up and doun, —
For they were glad right for the noveltee
To han a newe lady of hir toun.   13,341
Namoore of this make I now mencioun,
But to Grisilde agayn wol I me dresse,
And telle hir constance and hir bisynesse. —

    Ful bisy was Grisilde in every thyng
That to the feeste was apertinent;
Right noght was she abayst[7] of hire clothyng,
Thogh it were rude and somdeel eek to-rent,
But with glad cheere to the gate is she went[8]
With oother folk to greete the markysesse,
And after that dooth forth hire bisynesse. 13,351
With so glad chiere hise gestes she receyveth,
And so konnyngly,[9] everich in his degree,
That no defaute no man aperceyveth,
But ay they wondren what she myghte bee
That in so povre array was for to see,
And koude swich honour and reverence,

---

[1] Unstable, inconstant.   [2] Rumor.   [3] Empty talk.   [4] A small coin of Genoa. Cf. l. 6347.   [5] Believeth.   [6] Discreet.   [7] Abashed.   [8] Gone.   [9] Understandingly.

And worthily they preisen hire prudence.
In al this meene-while she ne stente   13,359
This mayde, and eek hir brother, to commende
With al hir herte, in ful benyngne entente,
So wel that no man koude hir pris [1] amende ;
But atte laste whan that thise lordes wende
To sitten doun to mete, he gan to calle
Grisilde, as she was bisy in his halle. (8905 T.)
" Grisilde," quod he, as it were in his pley,
" How liketh [2] thee my wyf, and hire beautee ? "
" Right wel," quod she, " my lord, for in good
          fey
A fairer saugh I nevere noon than she ;
I prey to God geve hire prosperitee ;   13,370
And so hope I that he wol to yow sende
Plesance ynogh un-to youre lyves ende.
O thyng biseke I yow, and warne also,
That ye ne prikke with no tormentynge
This tendre mayden, as ye han doon mo ; [3]
For she is fostred in hire nourssynge
Moore tendrely, and to my supposynge,
She koude nat adversitee endure
As koude a povre fostred creature."
And whan this Walter saugh hire pacience,
Hir glad chiere, and no malice at al,   13,381
And he so ofte had doon to hire offence
And she ay sad [4] and constant as a wal,
Continuynge evere hire innocence overal,
This sturdy markys gan his herte dresse

----

[1] Praise.   [2] Pleaseth.   [3] Another, somebody else.   [4] Stable.

To 1ewen [1] up-on hire wyfly stedfastnesse.
"This is ynogh, Grisilde myn," quod he,
"Be now namoore agast, ne yvele apayed; [2]
I have thy feith and thy benyngnytee
As wel as evere womman was, assayed, 13,390
In greet estaat and povreliche arrayed.
Now knowe I, goode wyf, thy stedfastnesse;"
And hire in armes took, and gan hire kesse.
And she for wonder took of it no keepe, [3]
She herde nat what thyng he to hire seyde,
She ferde, as she had stert out of a sleepe,
Til she out of hire mazednesse abreyde. [4]
"Grisilde," quod he, "by God that for us
      deyde,
Thou art my wyf, ne noon oother I have,
Ne nevere hadde, as God my soul save! 13,400
This is thy doghter, which thou hast supposed
To be my wyf, — that oother feithfully
Shal be myn heir, as I have ay purposed;
Thou bare hym in thy body trewely;
At Boloigne have I kept hem prively.
Taak hem agayn, for now maystow nat seye
That thou hast lorn noon [5] of thy children
      tweye;
And folk that ootherweys han seyd of me,
I warne hem wel that I have doon this deede
For no malice, ne for no crueltee, 13,410
But for tassaye in thee thy wommanheede,
And nat to sleen my children, God forbeede!

Pity. [2] Dispieased [3] Heed. [4] Awoke. [5] Not one.

But for to kepe hem pryvely and stille
Til I thy purpos knewe and al thy wille."
Whan she this herde, aswowne doun she falleth
For pitous joye, and after hire swownynge
She bothe hire yonge children un-to hire calleth,
And in hire armes, pitously wepynge,   (8958 T.)
Embraceth hem, and tendrely kissynge,
Ful lyk a mooder, with hire salte teeres 13,420
She bathed bothe hire visage and hire heeres.
O which a pitous thyng it was to se
Hir swownyng, and hire humble voys to heere !
" *Graunt mercy*,[1] lord ! that thanke I yow,"
        quod she,
" That ye han saved me my children deere.
Now rekke I nevere [2] to been deed right heere,
Sith I stonde in youre love and in youre grace.
No fors of [3] deeth, ne whan my spirit pace ! [4]
O tendre, O deere, O yonge children myne !
Youre woful mooder wende stedfastly   13,430
That crueel houndes, or som foul vermyne,
Hadde eten yow ; but God, of his mercy,
And youre benyngne fader, tendrely
Hath doon yow kept " — and in that same
        stounde [5]
Al sodeynly she swapte [6] adoun to grounde ;
And in hire swough so sadly [7] holdeth she
Hire children two, whan she gan hem tembrace,
That with greet sleighte, and greet difficultee
The children from hire arm they goone arrace.[8]

<hr />

[1] Great thanks. [2] I reck not. [3] No matter for. [4] Pass. [5] Moment. [6] Swooped. [7] Firmly. [8] Tear.

O many a teere on many a pitous face 13,440
Doun ran of hem that stooden hire bisyde ;
Unnethe [1] abouten hire myghte they abyde !
Walter hire gladeth, and hire sorwe slaketh ;
She riseth up abaysed [2] from hire traunce,
And every wight hire joye and feeste maketh,
Til she hath caught agayn hire contenaunce.
Walter hire dooth so feithfully plesaunce
That it was deyntee for to seen the cheere
Bitwixe hem two, now they been met yfeere.[3]
Thise ladyes, whan that they hir tyme saye,
Han taken hire and in-to chambre gon, 13,451
And strepen hire out of hire rude array,
And in a clooth of gold that brighte shoon,
With a coroune of many a riche stoon
Up-on hire heed, they in-to halle hire broghte,
And ther she was honured as hire oghte.
Thus hath this pitous day a blisful ende,
For every man and womman dooth his myght
This day in murthe and revel to dispende,
Til on the welkne shoon the sterres lyght ;
For more solempne in every mannes syght
This feste was, and gretter of costage,[4] 13,462
Than was the revel of hire mariage.

Ful many a yeer in heigh prosperitee
Lyven thise two in concord and in reste,
And richely his doghter maryed he   (9006 T.)
Un-to a lord, oon of the worthieste
Of al Ytaille ; and thanne in pees and reste

---

[1] Scarcely.   [2] Abashed.   [3] Together.   [4] Expense.

His wyves fader in his court he kepeth,
Til that the soule out of his body crepeth.
His sone succedeth in his heritage   13,471
In reste and pees after his fader day,
And fortunat was eek in mariage ;
Al putte he nat his wyf in greet assay.
This world is nat so strong, it is no nay,
As it hath been of olde tymes yoore ;
And herkneth what this auctour seith ther-
      foore.

    This storie is seyd, nat for that wyves sholde
Folwen Grisilde as in humylitee,
For it were inportable,[1] though they wolde, —
But for that every wight in his degree   13,481
Sholde be constant in adversitee
As was Grisilde, therfore this [2] Petrak writeth
This storie, which with heigh stile he endit-
      eth ;
For sith a womman was so pacient
Un-to a mortal man, wel moore us oghte
Receyven al in gree [3] that God us sent,
For, greet skile [4] is, he preeve that he wroghte.
But he ne tempteth no man that he boghte,
As seith Seint Jame, if ye his pistel rede.
He preeveth folk al day, it is no drede,   13,491
And suffreth us, as for oure exercise,
With sharpe scourges of adversitee
Ful ofte to be bete in sondry wise,

---

[1] Unbearable.   [2] Not in Elles. MS.   [3] Favor.   [4] Reason.

Nat for to know oure wyl, for certes he,
Er we were born, knew al [1] oure freletee ;
And for oure beste is al his governaunce ;
Lat us thanne lyve in vertuous suffraunce.[2]

But o word, lordynges, herkneth, er I go :
It were ful hard to fynde now a dayes   13,500
In al a toun Grisildis thre or two,
For if that they were put to swiche assayes,
The gold of hem hath now so badde alayes [3]
With bras, that thogh the coyne be fair at eye
It wolde rather breste [4] atwo than plye ; [5]
For which heere, for the Wyves love of Bathe, —
Whos lyf and al hire secte [6] God mayntene
In heigh maistrie, and elles were it scathe, —
I wol with lusty herte, fressh and grene,
Seyn yow a song to glade yow I wene ; 13,510
And lat us stynte of ernestful matere :
Herkneth my song that seith in this manere.

Lenvoy de Chaucer.

Grisilde is deed, and eek hire pacience,
And bothe atones buryed in Ytaille ;
For which I crie in open audience,   (9055 r.)
No wedded man so hardy be tassaille
His wyves pacience in hope to fynde
Grisildis, for in certein he shal faille !

---

[1] Nc' in Elles. MS.   [2] The paraphrase of the Latin of Petrarch
ends he e.   [3] Alloys.   [4] Burst.   [5] Bend.   [6] Suite.

O noble wyves, ful of heigh prudence,
Lat noon humylitee youre tonge naill,　13,520
Ne lat no clerk have cause or diligence
To write of yow a storie of swich mervaille
As of Grisildis pacient and kynde,
Lest *Chichivache*[1] yow swelwe in hire entraille !
Folweth Ekko, that holdeth no silence,
But evere answereth at the countretaille.[2]
Beth nat bidaffed[3] for youre innocence,
But sharply taak on yow the governaille.[4]
Emprenteth wel this lessoun in youre mynde
For commune profit sith it may availle.　13,53c
Ye archiwyves[5] stondeth at defense,
Syn ye be strong as is a greet camaille,[6]
Ne suffreth nat that men yow doon offense ;
And sklendre wyves, fieble, as in bataille,
Beth egre as is a tygre yond in Ynde ;
Ay clappeth as a mille, I yow consaille ;
Ne dreed hem nat, doth hem no reverence,
For though thyn housbonde armed be in maille,
The arwes of thy crabbed eloquence
Shal perce his brest, and eek his aventaille.[7]
In jalousie I rede eek thou hym bynde,　13,541
And thou shalt make hym couche as dooth a
　　　quaille.
If thou be fair, ther folk been in presence
Shewe thou thy visage and thyn apparaille ;

---

[1] *Chiche*, stingy, *vache*, cow, apparently corrupted from *chiche
face*, one whose stingy character is written in his face.　A fabulous
beast of mediæval literature that fed on patient wives.　Cf. l. 7212
and *Romaunt of the Rose*, l. 5591.　[2] Counter tally, *i. e.*, in return.
[3] Befooled.　[4] Helm.　[5] Ruling wives.　[6] Camel.　[7] Ventail, helmet

If thou be foul, be fre of thy dispence,
To gete thee freendes, ay do thy travaille ;
Be ay of chiere, as light as leef on lynde,[1]
And lat hym care and wepe, and wryng **and**
      waille !   (9088 **T.)**

The Prologe of the Marchantes Tale.

"Wepyng and waylyng, care and oother
      sorwe   (9089 **T.)**
I knowe ynogh, on even and a morwe," 13,550
Quod the Marchant, " and so doon othere **mo**
That wedded been, I trowe that it be so ;
For wel I woot it fareth so with me.
I have a wyf, the worste that may be,
For thogh the feend to hire ycoupled were,
She wolde hym overmacche, I dar wel swere.
What sholde I yow reherce in special
Hir hye malice ? She is a shrewe at al.
Ther is a long and large difference
Bitwix Grisildis grete pacience,   13,560
And of my wyf the passyng crueltee ;
Were I unbounden, al so moot I thee ![2]
I wolde nevere eft comen in the snare.[3]
We wedded men lyve in sorwe and care.
Assaye who so wole and he shal fynde (9105 **T.)**
I scye sooth, by Seint Thomas of Ynde !
As for the moore part, I sey nat alle ;
God shilde that it sholde so bifalle !

---

[1] Linden tree. [2] Thrive. [3] Cf. Chaucer's lines To Bukton.

"A! good sire Hoost! I have ywedded bee
Thise monthes two, and moore nat, *pardee!*
And yet I trowe he that al his lyve   13,571
Wyflees hath been, though that men wolde him
    ryve
Un-to the herte, ne koude in no manere
Tellen so muchel sorwe as I now heere
Koude tellen of my wyves cursednesse!"

   "Now," quod our Hoost, "Marchant, so **God**
    yow blesse!
Syn ye so muchel knowen of that art,
Ful hertely I pray yow telle us part."

   "Gladly," quod he, "but of myn owene
    soore,
For soory herte, I telle may namoore."   13,580

Heere bigynneth The Marchantes Tale.

Whilom ther was dwellynge in Lumbardye
A worthy knyght that born was of Pavye,
In which he lyved in greet prosperitee;
And sixty yeer a wyflees man was hee,
And folwed ay his bodily delyt   (9125 T.)
On wommen ther as was his appetyt,
As doon thise fooles that been seculeer;[1]
And whan that he was passed sixty yeer,
Were it for hoolynesse or for dotage   13,589
I kan nat seye, but swich a greet corage[2]

---

[1] The Merchant being himself "seculeer," this must be considered
as a sly expression of ironical respect for the clerics present.   [2] Inclination.

Hadde this knyght to been a wedded man
That day and nyght he dooth al that he kan
Tespien where he myghte wedded be ;
Preyinge oure Lord to granten him that he
Mighte ones knowe of thilke blisful lyf
That is bitwixe an housbonde and his wyf,
And for to lyve under that hooly boond
With which that first God man and womman
        bond.
" Noon oother lyf," seyde he, " is worth a bene,
For wedlok is so esy, and so clene,[1]   13,600
That in this world it is a paradys ; "
Thus seyde this olde knyght that was so wys.

  And certeinly, as sooth as God is kyng,
To take a wyf it is a glorious thyng,
And namely [2] whan a man is oold and hoor, —
Thanne is a wyf the fruyt of his tresor,[3] —
Thanne sholde he take a yong wyf and a feir,
On which he myghte engendren hym an heir,
And lede his lyf in joye and in solas ;
Where as thise bacheleris synge, " Allas ! "
Whan that they fynden any adversitee   13,611
In love, which nys but childyssh vanytee ;
And trewely it sit wel [4] to be so   (9153 T.)
That bacheleris have often peyne and wo ;
On brotel [5] ground they buylde, and brotelnesse
They fynde whan they wene sikernesse.[6]
They lyve but as a bryd, or as a beest,
In libertee and under noon arreest ; [7]

  [1] Pure.   [2] Especially.   [3] Bought with his money!   [4] Is appro
priate.   [5] Insecure.   [6] Suppose security.   [7] Restraint.

Ther as a wedded man, in his estaat,
Lyveth a lyf blisful and ordinaat,   13,620
Under this yok of mariage ybounde.
Wel may his herte in joye and blisse habounde,
For who kan be so buxom [1] as a wyf?
Who is so trewe and eek so ententyf
To kepe hym, syk and hool, as is his make? [2]
For wele or wo she wole hym nat forsake;
She nys nat wery hym to love and serve
Thogh that he lye bedrede til he sterve. [3]
     And yet somme clerkes seyn it nys nat so,
Of whiche he, Theofraste, [4] is oon of tho. 13,630
What force [5] though Theofraste liste lye?
"Ne take no wyf," quod he, "for housbondrye,
As for to spare in houshold thy dispence;
A trewe servant dooth moore diligence
Thy good to kepe, than thyn owene wyf,
For she wol clayme half part al hir lyf;
And if that [6] thou be syk, so God me save!
Thy verray freendes or a trewe knave
Wol kepe thee bet than she that waiteth ay
After thy good, and hath doon many a day;
And if thou take a wyf un-to thyn hoold, [7]
Ful lightly maystow been a cokewold." 13,642
This sentence, and an hundred thynges worse,
Writeth this man, ther God his bones corse!
But take no kepe of al swich vanytee;
Deffieth Theofraste and herke me.   (9184 T.)

---

[1] Compliant (*bugan*, to bend).   [2] Mate.   [3] Die.   [4] Cf. l. 13,713
Matter.   [6] Not in Elles. MS.   [7] Abode.

A wyf is Goddes gifte verraily ;
Alle othere manere giftes hardily,
As londes, rentes, pasture, or commune,
Or moebles,[1] alle been giftes of Fortune 13,650
That passen as a shadwe upon a wal ;
But dredelees, if pleynly speke I shal,
A wyf wol laste and in thyn hous endure,
Wel lenger than thee list, *paraventure.*

Mariage is a ful greet sacrement ;
He which that hath no wyf I holde hym shent ,
He lvveth helplees and al desolat, —
I speke of folk in seculer estaat ;   13,658
And herke why, I sey nat this for noght,
That womman is for mannes helpe ywroght.
The hye God whan he hadde Adam maked,
And saugh him al allone, bely naked, (9200 T.)
God of his grete goodnesse seyde than,
" Lat us now make an helpe un-to this man,
Lyk to hym self ; " and thanne he made him Eve.
Heere may ye se, and heer-by may ye preve,
That wyf is mannes helpe and his confort,
His Paradys terrestre, and his disport ;
So buxom and so vertuous is she,
They moste nedes lyve in unitee.   13,670
O flessh they been, and o flessh, as I gesse,
Hath but oon herte in wele [3] and in distresse.

A wyf ! a ! Seinte Marie, *benedicite,*
How myghte a man han any adversitee
That hath a wyf ?   Certes, I kan nat seye.

---

[1] Furniture, movables.   [2] Ruined.   [3] Wealth, *i. e.,* prosperity

The blisse which that is bitwixe hem **tweye** [1]
Ther may no tonge telle or herte thynke.
If he be povre she helpeth hym to swynke,[2]
She kepeth his good and wasteth never a deel
Al that hire housbonde lust hire liketh weel ;
She seith not ones, " nay," whan he seith, " ye."
" Do this," seith he ; " Al redy, sire," seith she.

　O blisful ordre of wedlok precious !   13,683
Thou art so murye,[3] and eek so vertuous,
And so commended and appreved eek,
That every man that halt hym worth a leek
Up-on his bare knees oughte al his lyf
Thanken his God that hym hath sent a wyf ;
Or elles preye to God hym for to sende
A wyf, to laste un-to his lyves ende ;   13,690
For thanne his lyf is set in sikernesse ;
He may nat be deceyved, as I gesse,
So that he werke after his wyves reede.[4] (9231 T.)
Thanne may he boldely kepen up his heed,
They been so trewe, and ther with al so wyse ;
For which, if thou wolt werken as the wyse,
Do alwey so as wommen wol thee reede.[5]

　Lo, how that Jacob, as thise clerkes rede,
By good conseil of his mooder Rebekke,
Boonde the kydes skyn aboute his nekke, 13,700
Thurgh which his fadres benysoun he wan.

　Lo Judith, as the storie telle [6] kan, (9240 T.)
By wys conseil she Goddes peple kepte,
And slow hym Olofernus whil he slepte.

---

[1] Cf. l. 15,581.   [2] Work.   [3] Pleasant.   [4] Advice.   [5] Lines 13,694–
13,697 are not in Elles. MS.   [6] Elles. MS. has "eek telle."

Lo Abigayl, by good conseil how she
Saved hir housbonde, Nabal, whan that he
Sholde han be slayn ; and looke Ester also,
By good conseil delyvered out of wo
The peple of God, and made hym Mardochee
Of Assuere enhaunced for to be.   13,710
    Ther nys no thyng in gree superlatyf,
As seith Senek, above an humble wyf.[1] (9250 T.)
    Suffre thy wyves tonge, as Catoun [2] bit,
She shal comande, and thou shalt suffren it,
And yet she wole obeye of curteisye ;
A wyf is kepere of thyn housbondrye.
Wel may the sike man biwaille and wepe,
Ther as ther nys no wyf the hous to kepe.
I warne thee if wisely thou wolt wirche, 13,719
Love wel thy wyf, as Crist loved his chirche.
If thou lovest thy self thou lovest thy wyf.
No man hateth his flessh, but in his lyf
He fostreth it, and therfore bidde I thee
Cherisse thy wyf, or thou shalt nevere thee.[3]
Housbonde and wyf, what so men jape or pleye,
Of worldly folk holden the siker [4] weye ;
They been so knyt ther may noon harm bityde,
And namely [5] upon the wyves syde ;
For which this Januarie, of whom I tolde,
Considered hath inwith [6] hise dayes olde 13,730
The lusty lyf, the vertuous quyete,
That is in mariage hony sweete ;

---

[1] Cf. l. 6720. [2] Dionysius Cato was the *nom de guerre* of a me
ʒiæval compiler. His work was translated by Caxton. [3] **Thrive**
[4] **Sure** [5] Especially. [6] Within.

And for hise freendes on a day he sente,
To tellen hem theffect of his entente.

 With face sad his tale he hath hem toold.
He seyde, " Freendes, I am hoor and oold,
And almoost, God woot, on my pittes [1] brynke
Up-on the soule somwhat moste I thynke,
I have my body folily despended ;
Blessed be God ! that it shal been amended,
For I wol be certeyn a wedded man, 13,741
And that anoon, in al the haste I kan.
Un-to som mayde, fair and tendre of age,
I prey yow shapeth for my mariage
Al sodeynly, for I wol nat abyde,
And I wol fonde [2] tespien on my syde
To whom I may be wedded hastily ;
But for as muche as ye been mo than I,
Ye shullen rather [3] swich a thyng espyen
Than I, and where me best were to allyen.
But o thyng warne I yow, my freendes deere,
I wol noon oold wyf han in no manere. 13,752
She shal nat passe twenty yeer certayn,
Oold fissh and yonge flessh wolde I have fayn.
Bet is," quod he, " a pyk than a pykerel,
And bet than olde boef is the tendre veel.
I wol no womman thritty yeer of age, —
It is but benestraw and greet forage ;
And eek this olde wydwes, God it woot, 13,759
They konne so muchel craft on Wades boot,[4]

---

[1] Grave's.   [2] Try.   [3] Sooner.   [4] Wade was a Scandinavian hero tamed for craft. His boot was called Guingelot. Cf. *Troylus ana Cryseyde*, iii. 614.

So muchel broken harm whan that hem leste,
That with hem sholde I nevere lyve in reste;
For sondry scoles maken sotile clerkis. (9301 T.)
Womman of manye scoles half a clerk is;
But certeynly a yonge thyng may men gye,[1]
Right as men may warm wex with handes plye.[2]
Wherfore I sey yow pleynly in a clause,
I wol noon oolde wyf han for this cause;
For if so were that I hadde swich myschaunce
That I in hire ne koude han no plesaunce,
Thanne sholde I lede my lyf in avoutrye,[3] 13,771
And go streight to the devel whan I dye;
Ne children sholde I none up-on hire geten;
Yet were me levere houndes had me eten,
Than that myn heritage sholde falle
In straunge hand, and this I telle yow alle.
I dote [4] nat; I woot the cause why
Men sholde wedde, and forthermoore woot I
Ther speketh many a man of mariage, 13,779
That woot namoore of it than woot my page.
For whiche causes man sholde take a wyf:
Siththe he may nat lyven chaast his lyf,
Take hym a wyf with greet devocioun,
By cause of leveful [5] procreacioun
Of children, to thonour of God above,
And nat oonly for *paramour* or love;
And for they sholde leccherye eschue,
And yelde hir dettes whan that they ben due;
Or for that ech of hem sholde helpen oother

---

[1] Guide. [2] Mould. [3] Adultery. [4] Doat. [5] Lawful.

In meschief, as a suster shal the brother, 13,79c
And lyve in chastitee ful holily ;
But, sires, by youre leve, that am nat I,
For, God be thanked, I dar make avaunt,
I feele my lymes stark and suffisaunt
To do al that a man bilongeth to ;
I woot my selven best what I may do.
Though I be hoor I fare as dooth a tree
That blosmeth, er that fruyt ywoxen bee ;
And blosmy tree nys neither drye ne deed.
I feele me nowhere hoor but on myn heed ;
Myn herte and alle my lymes been as grene
As laurer thurgh the yeer is for to sene ; 13,80a
And syn that ye han herd al myn entente,
I prey yow to my wyl ye wole assente."

    Diverse men diversely hym tolde
Of mariage manye ensamples olde.
Somme blamed it, somme preysed it certeyn,
But atte laste, shortly for to seyn,
As al day falleth altercacioun
Bitwixen freendes in disputisoun,   13,810
Ther fil a stryf bitwixe hise bretheren two,
Of whiche that oon was cleped Placebo, (9350 T.)
Justinus soothly called was that oother.

    Placebo seyde, " O Januarie brother,
Ful litel nede hadde ye, my lord so deere,
Conseil to axe of any that is heere,
But that ye been so ful of sapience
That yow ne liketh for youre heighe prudence
To weyven fro the word of Salomon.

This word seyde he un-to us everychon, 13,820
'Wirk alle thyng by conseil,' thus seyde he,
'And thanne shaltow nat repente thee ;'
But though that Salomon spak swich a word,
Myn owene deere brother, and my lord,
So wysly God my soule brynge at reste,
I holde youre owene conseil is the beste ;
For, brother myn, of me taak this motyf,
I have now been a court man al my lyf,
And, God it woot, though I unworthy be,
I have stonden in ful greet degree   13,830
Abouten lordes of ful heigh estaat ;
Yet hadde I nevere with noon of hem debaat ;
I nevere hem contraried trewely.
I woot wel that my lord kan[1] moore than I ;
What that he seith I holde it ferme and stable ;
I seye the same, or elles thyng semblable.
A ful greet fool is any conseilloui,
That serveth any lord of heigh honour,
That dar presume, or elles thenken it,
That his conseil sholde passe his lordes wit.[2]
Nay, lordes been no fooles, by my fay ! 13,841
Ye han youre selven seyed heer to day
So heigh sentence, so holily and weel,
That I consente and conferme everydeel
Youre wordes alle, and youre opinioun.
By God, ther nys no man in al this toun,
Ne in Ytaille, that koude bet han sayd.
Crist halt hym of this conseil wel[3] apayd ;[4]

----

[1] Knows. [2] Knowledge. [3] Elles. MS. has " ful wel." [4] Satisfied

And trewely it is an heigh corage
Of any man that stapen [1] is in age   13,85c
To take a yong wyf ; by my fader kyn,
Youre herte hangeth on a joly pyn !
Dooth now in this matiere right as yow leste,
For, finally, I holde it for the beste."

    Justinus, that ay stille sat and herde,
Right in this wise [2] to Placebo answerde :
" Now, brother myn, be pacient I preye,
Syn ye han seyd, and herkneth what I seye.

    " Senek among hise othere wordes wyse
Seith that a man oghte hym right wel avyse
To whom he geveth his lond or his catel ; [3]
And syn I oghte avyse me right wel   13,862
To whom I geve my good awey fro me,
Wel muchel moore I oghte avysed be (9402 T.)
To whom I geve my body for alwey.
I warne yow wel, it is no childes pley
To take a wyf with-oute avysement.
Men moste enquere, this is myn assent,
Wher [4] she be wys, or sobre, or dronkelewe,
Or proud, or elles ootherweys a shrewe,   13,87c
A chidestere, or wastour of thy good,
Or riche, or poore, or elles mannyssh wood ; [5]
Al be it so that no man fynden shal
Noon in this world that trotteth hool in al,
Ne man ne beest, which as men koude devyse ;
But nathelees it oghte ynough suffise

---

[1] Advanced, stept.   Cf. l. 8433.   [2] Elles. MS. reads " wise he.
[3] Goods.   [4] Whether.   [5] Madly attracted to men.

With any wyf, if so were that she hadde
Mo goode thewes [1] than hire vices badde ;
And al this axeth leyser for tenquere, —
For, God it woot, I have wept many a teere
Ful pryvely, syn I have had a wyf.   13,881
Preyse who so wole a wedded mannes lyf,
Certein I fynde in it but cost and care,
And observances of alle blisses bare ;
And yet, God woot, my neighebores aboute,
And namely [2] of wommen many a route,
Seyn that I have the mooste stedefast wyf,
And eek the mekeste oon that bereth lyf ;
But I woot best where wryngeth me my sho. [8]
Ye mowe, for me, right as yow liketh do.
Avyseth yow, ye been a man of age,   13,891
How that ye entren in-to mariage,
And namely with a yong wyf and a fair.
By hym that made water, erthe, and air,
The yongeste man that is in al this route
Is bisy ynough to bryngen it aboute
To han his wyf allone ; trusteth me,
Ye shul nat plesen hire fully yeres thre, —
This is to seyn, to doon hire ful plesaunce.
A wyf axeth ful many an observaunce.   13,900
I prey yow that ye be nat yvele apayd." [4]

   "Wel," quod this Januarie, " and hastow
        ysayd ?
Straw for thy Senek, and for thy proverbes !
I counte nat a panyer ful of herbes

---

[1] Traits.   [2] Especially.   [8] Cf. l. 10,534.   [4] Displeased.

Of scole termes ; wyser men than thow,
As thou hast herd, assenteden right now
To my purpos.   Placebo, what sey ye ? "

    " I seye it is a cursed man," quod he,
" That letteth [1] matrimoigne sikerly ! "
And with that word they rysen sodeynly,
And been assented fully that he sholde   13,911
Be wedded whanne hym list and where he
        wolde.   (9450 T.)

    Heigh fantasye and curious bisynesse
Fro day to day gan in the soule impresse [2]
Of Januarie, aboute his mariage.
Many fair shape and many a fair visage
Ther passeth thurgh his herte nyght by nyght,
As who so tooke a mirour polisshed bryght
And sette it in a commune market-place ;
Thanne sholde he se ful many a figure pace [3]
By his mirour ; and in the same wyse   13,921
Gan Januarie inwith his thoght devyse
Of maydens whiche that dwellen hym bisyde.
He wiste nat wher that he myghte abyde, [4]
For, if that oon have beaute in hir face,
Another stant so in the peples grace
For hire sadnesse [5] and hire benyngnytee,
That of the peple grettest voys hath she ;
And somme were riche, and hadden badde
        name ;
But nathelees, bitwixe ernest and game, 13,930
He atte laste apoynted hym on oon,

    Hindereth.   [2] Crowd.   [3] Pass.   [4] Settle.   [5] Gravity.

And leet alle othere from his herte goon,
And chees hire of his owene auctoritee ;
For love is blynd al day, and may nat see.
And whan that he was in his bed ybroght
He purtreyed in his herte and in his thoght
Hir fresshe beautee, and hir age tendre,
Hir myddel smal, hire armes longe and sklen-
    dre,
Hir wise governaunce, hir gentillesse,   13,939
Hir wommanly berynge, and hire sadnesse.

And whan that he on hire was condescended
Hym thoughte his choys myghte nat ben
    amended ;
For whan that he hym self concluded hadde,
Hym thoughte ech oother mannes wit so badde
That inpossible it were to repplye
Agayn his choys, — this was his fantasye.

Hise freendes sente he to, at his instaunce,
And preyed hem to doon hym that plesaunce,
That hastily they wolden to hym come ; 13,949
He wolde abregge hir labour alle and some,
Nedeth namoore for hym to go [1] ne ryde,
He was apoynted ther he wolde abyde.

Placebo cam, and eek hise freendes soone,
And alderfirst he bad hem alle a boone [2]
That noon of hem none argumentes make
Agayn the purpos which that he hath take,
Which purpos was plesant to God, seyde he,
And verray ground of his prosperitee.

---

[1] Walk.   [2] A request, boon.

He seyde, ther was a mayden in the toun,
Which that of beautee hadde greet renoun,
Al were it so she were of smal degree,   13,961
Suffiseth hym hir yowthe, and hir beautee ;
Which mayde, he seyde, he wolde han to his
      wyf,   (9501 T.)
To lede in ese and hoolynesse his lyf ;
And thanked God that he myghte han hire al,
That no wighte his blisse parten [1] shal ;
And preyde hem to laboure in this nede
And shapen that he faille nat to spede ; [2]
For thanne he seyde his spirit was at ese.
" Thanne is," quod he, " no thyng may me dis-
      plese,   13,970
Save o thyng priketh in my conscience,
The which I wol reherce in youre presence.

" I have," quod he, " herd seyd ful yoore ago
Ther may no man han parfite blisses two, —
This is to seye, in erthe and eek in hevene, —
For though he kepe hym fro the synnes sevene
And eek from every branche of thilke tree,
Yet is ther so parfit felicitee
And so greet ese and lust in mariage,
That evere I am agast now in myn age,   13,982
That I shal lede now so myrie a lyf,
So delicat,[3] with-outen wo and stryf,
That I shal have myn hevene in erthe heere,
For sith that verray hevene is boght so deere
With tribulacioun and greet penaunce,

---

[1] Divide, share.   [2] Prosper.   [3] Luxurious.

How sholde I thanne that lyve in swich ple-
    saunce,
As alle wedded men doon with hire wyvys,
Come to the blisse ther Crist eterne on lyve
    ys?
This is my drede, and ye my bretheren tweye,
Assoilleth [1] me this questioun, I preye." 13,990
    Justinus, which that hated his folye,
Answerde anon right in his japerye; [2]
And for he wolde his longe tale abregge,
He wolde noon auctoritee allegge,
But seyde, "Sire, so ther be noon obstacle
Oother than this, God of his hygh myracle,
And of his mercy, [3] may so for yow wirche
That er ye have youre right of hooly chirche,
Ye may repente of wedded mannes lyf,
In which ye seyn ther is no wo ne stryf;
And elles, God forbede, but he sente   14,001
A wedded man hym grace to repente
Wel ofte rather than a sengle man;
And therfore, sire, — the beste reed I kan, [4] —
Dispeire yow noght, but have in youre memorie,
Paraunter [5] she may be youre purgatorie;
She may be Goddes meene, [6] and Goddes
    whippe!
Thanne shal youre soule up to hevene skippe
Swifter than dooth an arwe out of the bowe.
I hope to God her-after shul ye knowe   14,010

---

[1] Solve. [2] Mockery. [3] Elles. MS. has "hygh mercy." [4] Advice
I know. [5] Peradventure. [6] Means.

That ther nys no so greet felicitee
In mariage, ne nevere mo shal bee,   (9550 T.
That yow shal lette of youre savacioun,
So that ye use, as skile [1] is and resoun,
The lustes of youre wyf attemprely,
And that ye plese hire nat to amorously,
And that ye kepe yow eek from oother synne.
My tale is doon, for my witte is thynne ;
Beth nat agast her-of, my brother deere,
But lat us waden out of this mateere.   14,020
The Wyf of Bathe, if ye han understonde,
Of mariage which ye have on honde
Declared hath ful wel in litel space.[2]
Fareth now wel, God have yow in his grace."

   And with this word this Justyn and his
      brother
Han take hir leve, and ech of hem of oother ;
For whan they saughe that it moste be,
They wroghten so, by sly and wys tretee,[3]
That she this mayden, which that Mayus
      highte,
As hastily as evere that she myghte   14,030
Shal wedded be un-to this Januarie.
I trowe it were to longe yow to tarie,
If I yow tolde of every scrit and bond
By which that she was feffed [4] in his lond,
Or for to herknen of hir riche array.
But finally ycomen is the day

---

[1] Judgment, discrimination.   [2] Justinus had not been a hearer
of the Wife's Tale, however.   [3] Diplomacy.   [4] Enfeoffed.

That to the chirche bothe be they went
For to receyve the hooly sacrement.
Forth comth the preest with stole aboute his
    nekke,
And bad hire "be lyk to Sarra and Rebekke"
In wysdom and in trouthe of mariage,   14,041
And seyde hir orisons as is usage,
And croucheth [1] hem and bad God sholde hem
    blesse,
And made al siker [2] ynogh with hoolynesse.

  Thus been they wedded with solempnitee,
And at the feeste sitteth he and she,
With othere worthy folk, up on the deys.[3]
Al ful of joye and blisse is the paleys,
And ful of instrumentz, and of vitaille
The moste deynteuous of all Ytaille.   14,050
Biforn hem stoode swich [4] instrumentz of soun
That Orpheus, ne of Thebes Amphioun,
Ne maden nevere swich a melodye.

  At every cours thanne cam loud mynstralcye
That nevere tromped Joab for to heere,
Nor he Theodomas [5] yet half so cleere
At Thebes, whan the citee was in doute.
Bacus the wyn hem skynketh [6] al aboute,
And Venus laugheth up-on every wight, —
For Januarie was bicome hir knyght, — 14,060
And wolde bothe assayen his corage
In libertee, and eek in mariage ;   (9600 T.)

---

[1] Crosseth. [2] Sure. [3] Dais. [4] Elles. MS. reads "stooden in strumentz of swich." [5] A famed trumpeter. [6] Poureth.

And with hire fyrbrond in hire hand aboute
Daunceth biforn the bryde and al the route ;
And certeinly I dar right wel seyn this
Ymeneus,[1] that god of weddyng is,
Saugh nevere his lyf so myrie a wedded man.
Hoold thou thy pees, thou poete Marcian,[2] —
That writest us that ilke weddyng murie
Of hire Philologie and hym Mercurie,   14,070
And of the songes that the Muses songe, —
To smal is bothe thy penne and eek thy tonge,
For to descryven of this mariage,
Whan tendre youthe hath wedded stoupyng
        age ;
Ther is swich myrthe that it may nat be writen.
Assayeth it youre self, thanne may ye witen
If that I lye or noon in this matiere.

    Mayus, that sit with so benyngne a chiere,
Hire to biholde it semed fairye.
Queene Ester looked nevere with swich an eye
On Assuer, so meke a look hath she.   14,081
I may yow nat devyse al hir beautee,
But thus muche of hire beautee telle I may,
That she was lyk the brighte morwe of May
Fulfild of alle beautee and plesaunce.

    This Januarie is ravysshed in a traunce
At every tyme he looked on hir face ;
But in his herte he gan hire to manace [3]
That he that nyght in armes wolde hire streyne
Harder than evere Parys dide Eleyne ;   14,090

----

[1] Hymen.   [2] An African poet.   [3] Threaten.

But nathelees yet hadde he greet pitee
That thilke nyght offenden hire moste he,
And thoughte, "Allas! O tendre creature!
Now wolde God ye myghte wel endure
Al my corage,[1] it is so sharpe and keene!
I am agast ye shul it nat susteene;
But God forbede that I dide al my myght.
Now wolde God that it were woxen nyght,
And that the nyght wolde lasten everemo.
I wolde that al this peple were ago!" 14,100
And finally he dooth al his labour,
As he best myghte, savynge his honour,
To haste hem fro the mete in subtil wyse.

The tyme cam that resoun was to ryse,
And after that men daunce and drynken faste,
And spices al aboute the hous they caste,
And ful of joye and blisse is every man, —
All but a squyer highte Damyan, (9646 T.)
Which carf biforn the knyght ful many a
    day.
He was so ravysshed on his lady May 14,110
That for the verray peyne he was ny wood.[2]
Almoost he swelte and swowned ther he stood,
So soore hath Venus hurt hym with hire brond
As that she bar it daunsynge in hire hond,
And to his bed he wente [3] hym hastily.
Namoore of hym at this tyme speke I,
But there I lete hym wepe ynogh and pleyne
Til fresshe May wol rewen [4] on his peyne.

     [1] Passion. [2] Mad. [3] Turned. [4] Show pity

O perilous fyr that in the bedstraw bredeth i
O famulier foo, that his servyce bedeth ! [1] 14,120
O servant traytour, false, hoomly hewe, [2]
Lyk to the naddre in bosom sly, untrewe,
God shilde us alle from youre aqueyntance !
O Januarie, dronken in plesance
In mariage, se how thy Damyan,
Thyn owene squier and thy borne man,
Entendeth for to do thee vileynye !
God graunte thee thyn hoomly fo tespye,
For in this world nys worse pestilence
Than hoomly foo al day in thy presence ! 14,130

Parfourned hath the sonne his ark diurne,
No lenger may the body of hym sojurne
On thorisonte, as in that latitude.
Night with his mantel, that is derk and rude,
Gan oversprede the hemysperie aboute,
For which departed is this lusty route
Fro Januarie, with thank on every syde.
Hoom to hir houses lustily they ryde,
Where as they doon hir thynges as hem leste,
And whan they sye hir tyme goon to reste.
Soone after that this hastif Januarie   14,141
Wolde go to bedde, he wolde no lenger tarye.
He drynketh ypocras, clarree and vernage, [3]
Of spices hoote, tencreessen his corage ;
And many a letuarie [4] hath he ful fyn

1 Proffereth.   2 Familiar servant (O. E. *hiwe*, domestic servant)
Hot drinks often taken at bed-time.   4 Electuary.   Cf. l. 426.

Swiche as the monk, Daun Constantyn,[1]
Hath writen in his book, *De Coitu,*
To eten hem alle, he nas no thyng eschu ;[2]
And to hise privee freendes thus seyde he :
" For Goddes love, as soone as it may be,
Lat voyden al this hous in curteys wyse ;" 14,151
And they han doon right as he wol devyse.
Men drynken and the travers [3] drawe anon ;
The bryde was broght a-bedde as stille as stoon,
And whan the bed was with the preest yblessed,
Out of the chambre hath every wight hym
        dressed ;
And Januarie hath faste in armes take
His fresshe May, his paradys, his make.
He lulleth hire, he kisseth hire ful ofte,
With thilke brustles of his berd unsofte, 14,160
Lyk to the skyn of houndfyssh,[4] sharpe as brere ;
For he was shave al newe in his manere.
He rubbeth hire aboute hir tendre face (9701 T.)
And seyde thus, " Allas ! I moot trespace
To yow, my spouse, and yow greetly offende,
Er tyme come that I wil doun descende ;
But nathelees, considereth this," quod he,
" Ther nys no werkman, what so evere he be,
That may bothe werke wel and hastily.
This wol be doon at leyser parfitly, 14,170
It is no fors [5] how longe that we pleye ;
In trewe wedlok wedded be we tweye,

---

[1] A mediæval writer on medicine   [2] Disinclined.   [3] Curtains
[4] Dog-fish, a kind of shark   [5] Consequence.

And blessed be the yok that we been inne !
For in oure actes we mowe do no synne.
A man may do no synne with his wyf,
Ne hurte hym-selven with his owene knyf ; [1]
For we han leve to pleye us, by the lawe."

   Thus laboureth he til that the day gan dawe,
And thanne he taketh a sope in fyne clarree,
And upright in his bed thanne sitteth he ; 14,180
And after that he sang ful loude and cleere,
And kiste his wyf, and made wantowne cheere.
He was al coltissh, ful of ragerye,
And ful of jargon [2] as a flekked pye. [3]
The slakke skyn aboute his nekke shaketh
Whil that he sang, so chaunteth he and craketh ;
But God woot what that May thoughte in hire
      herte
Whan she hym saugh up sittynge in his sherte,
In his nyght cappe, and with his nekke lene !
She preyseth nat his pleyyng worth a bene.

   Thanne seide he thus, " My reste wol I take ;
Now day is come, I may no lenger wake ; "
And doun he leyde his heed and sleepe til
      pryme.   14,193
And afterward, whan that he saugh his tyme,
Up ryseth Januarie, but fresshe May
Heeld hire chambre un-to the fourthe day,
As usage is of wyves, for the beste ;
For every labour som tyme moot han reste,

---

[1] The Parson does not believe this. Cf. l. 19,102.   [2] Gabble
[3] Spotted magpie.

Or elles longe may he nat endure;
This is to seyn, no lyves creature,   14,200
Be it of fyssh, or bryd, or beest, or man.

Now wol I speke of woful Damyan,
That langwissheth for love, as ye shul heere;
Therfore I speke to hym in this manere.

I seye, O sely Damyan, allas!
Andswere [1] to my demaunde as in this cas.
How shaltow to thy lady, fresshe May,
Telle thy wo?   She wole alwey seye nay.
Eek if thou speke, she wol thy wo biwreye.
God be thyn helpe, I kan no bettre seye. 14,210

This sike Damyan in Venus fyr
So brenneth, that he dyeth for desyr;   (9750 T.)
For which he putte his lyf in aventure.
No lenger myghte he in this wise endure,
But prively a penner [2] gan he borwe,
And in a lettre wroot he al his sorwe, —
In manere of a compleynte or a lay, —
Un-to his faire, fresshe lady May;
And in a purs of sylk neng on his sherte,
He hath it put and leyde it at his herte. 14,220
The moone, that at noon was thilke day
That Januarie hath wedded fresshe May,
In two of Tawr, [3] was in to Cancre glyden
So longe hath Mayus in hir chambre byden,
As custume is un-to thise nobles alle.

[1] Answer (O. E. *andswerian*) [2] Pen-case. [3] The sign Taurus.

A bryde shal nat eten in the halle
Til dayes foure or thre dayes atte leeste
Ypassed been, thanne lat hire go to feeste.
The fourthe day compleet fro noon to noon,
Whan that the heighe masse was ydoon, 14,230
In halle sit this Januarie and May,
As fressh as is the brighte someres day ;
And so bifel, how that this goode man
Remembred hym upon this Damyan,
And seyde, " Seynte Marie ! how may this be
That Damyan entendeth [1] nat to me ?
Is he ay syk ? or how may this bityde ? "
Hise squieres, whiche that stooden ther bisyde,
Excused hym by cause of his siknesse, 14,239
Which letted hym to doon his bisynesse, —
Noon oother cause myghte make hym tarye.

" That me forthynketh," [2] quod this Januarie,
" He is a gentil squier, by my trouthe !
If that he deyde, it were harm and routhe ;
He is as wys, discreet, and as secree,
As any man I woot of his degree ;
And ther-to manly and eek servysable,
And for to been a thrifty man right able ;
But after mete, as soone as evere I may,
I wol my self visite hym, and eek May, 14,250
To doon hym al the confort that I kan ; "
And for that word hym blessed every man,
That of his bountee and his gentillesse
He wolde so conforten in siknesse

----

[1] Attendeth. [2] Vexeth.

His squier, for it was a gentil dede.
" Dame," quod this Januarie, " taak good hede
At after mete [1] ye with youre wommen alle,
Whan ye han been in chambre out of this
    halle,
That alle ye go se this Damyan.
Dooth hym disport, he is a gentil man, 14,260
And telleth hym that I wol hym visite,
Have I no thyng but rested me a lite ; (9800 T.)
And spede yow faste, for I wole abyde
Til that ye slepe faste by my syde ; "
And with that word he gan to hym to calle
A squier, that was marchal of his halle,
And tolde hym certeyn thynges, what he wolde.
  This fresshe May hath streight hir wey
    yholde,
With alle hir wommen, un-to Damyan.
Doun by his beddes syde sit she than, 14,270
Confortynge hym as goodly as she may.
This Damyan, whan that his tyme he say,[2]
In secree wise, his purs and eek his bille,
In which that he ywriten hadde his wille,
Hath put in to hire hand, with-outen moore,[3]
Save that he siketh wonder depe and soore,
And softely to hire right thus seyde he :
" Mercy ! and that ye nat discovere me,
For I am deed, if that this thyng be kyd." [4]
This purs hath she inwith hir bosom hyd,
And wente hire wey. — ye gete namoore of me,

[1] Elles. MS. has " noon." [2] Saw [3] More ado. [4] Known.

But un-to Januarie ycomen is she   14,282
That on his beddes syde sit ful softe.
He taketh hire and kisseth hire ful ofte,
And leyde hym doun to slepe, and that anon.
She feyned hire as that she moste gon
Ther as ye woot that every wight moot neede ;
And whan she of this bille hath taken heede,
She rente it al to cloutes atte laste,
And in the pryvee softely it caste.   14,290
  Who studieth now, but faire, fresshe May ?
Adoun by olde Januarie she lay,
That sleepe til that the coughe hath hym
          awaked.
Anon he preyde hire strepen hire al naked,
He wolde of hire, he seyde, han som plesaunce ;
And seyde hir clothes dide hym encombraunce.
And she obeyeth, be hire lief or looth ;
But, lest ye precious [1] folk be with me wrooth,
How that he wroghte I dar nat to yow telle,
Or wheither that hire thoughte it paradys or
          helle ;   14,300
But heere I lete hem, werken in hir wyse,
Til evensong rong, and that they moste aryse.
  Were it by destynee, or by aventure,[2]
Were it by influence, or by nature,
Or constellacioun, that in swich estaat
The hevene stood, that tyme fortunaat
Was, for to putte a bille [3] of Venus werkes
(For alle thyng hath tyme, as seyn thise clerkes)

---

[1] Fastidious.   Chance. [3] Billet.

To any womman for to gete hire love,
I kan nat seye ; but grete God above   14,310
That knoweth that noon act is causelees,
He deme [1] of al, for I wole holde my pees ;
But sooth is this, how that this fresshe May
Hath take swich impressioun that day
For pitee of this sike Damyan,   (9853 T.)
That from hire herte she ne dryve kan
The remembrance for to doon hym ese.
" Certeyn," thoghte she, " whom that this thyng
      displese
I rekke noght, for heere I hym assure
To love hym best of any creature,   14,320
Though he namoore hadde than his sherte."
Lo, pitee renneth soone in gentil herte ! [2]

   Heere may ye se how excellent franchise [3]
In wommen is whan they hem narwe avyse. [4]
Som tyrant is, as ther be many oon,
That hath an herte as hard as any stoon,
Which wolde han lat hym storven in the place,
Wel rather than han graunted hym hire grace ;
And hem rejoysen in hire crueel pryde,
And rekke nat to been an homycide.   14,330
   This gentil May, fulfilled of pitee,
Right of hire hand a lettre made she,
In which she graunteth hym hire verray grace
Ther lakketh noght oonly but day and place
Wher that she myghte un-to his lust suffise,
For it shal be right as he wole devyse ;

   [1] Judge.   [2] Cf. l. 1761.   [3] Generosity.   [4] Carefully consider.

And whan she saugh hir tyme, up on a day,
To visite this Damyan gooth May,
And sotilly this lettre doun she threste [1]
Under his pilwe, rede it if hym leste.   14,340
She taketh hym by the hand and harde hym
      twiste,
So secrely that no wight of it wiste,
And bad hym been al hool; and forth she [1]
      wente
To Januarie, whan that he for hire [2] sente.

 Up riseth Damyan the nexte morwe;
Al passed was his siknesse and his sorwe.
He kembeth hym, he proyneth [3] hym and
      pyketh, [4]
He dooth al that his lady lust and lyketh;
And eek to Januarie he gooth as lowe
As evere dide a dogge for the bowe.   14,350
He is so plesant un-to every man, —
For craft is al, who so that do it kan, —
That every wight is fayn to speke hym good,
And fully in his lady grace he stood.
Thus lete I Damyan aboute his nede,
And in my tale forth I wol procede.

 Somme clerkes holden that felicitee [5]
Stant in delit, and therfore certeyn he,
This noble Januarie with al his myght,
In honeste wyse, as longeth [6] to a knyght,
Shoope hym to lyve ful deliciously.   14,361

---

[1] Thrust.   [2] Elles. MS. reads "he" and "hym."   [3] Pruneth.
Trimmeth.   [5] Supreme felicity, *summum bonum*.   [6] Belongeth

His housynge, his array, as honestly (9900 **T.**)
To his degree was maked, as a kynges.
Amonges othere of hise honeste thynges
He made a gardyn walled al with stoon.
So fair a gardyn woot I nowher noon,
For out of doute, I verraily suppose
That he that wroot the Romance of the Rose
Ne koude of it the beautee wel devyse ;
Ne Priapus ne myghte nat suffise,   14,370
Though he be god of gardyns, for to telle
The beautee of the gardyn, and the welle
That stood under a laurer, alwey grene.
Ful ofte tyme he Pluto, and his queene
Proserpina, and al hire fairye,
Disporten hem and maken melodye
Aboute that welle, and daunced as men tolde.

   This noble knyght, this Januarie the olde,
Swich deyntee hath in it to walke and pleye
That he wol no wight suffren bere the keye,
Save he hym self, for of the smale wyket
He baar alwey of silver a clyket,[1]   14,382
With which whan that hym leste he it un-
      shette,
And whan he wolde paye his wyf hir dette
In somer sesoun, thider wolde he go,
And May his wyf, and no wight but they two,
And thynges whiche that were nat doon a
      bedde
He in the gardyn parfourned hem and spedde ;[2]

----

[1] Latch-key   Dispatched.

And in this wyse many a murye [1] day
Lyved this Januarie and fresshe May ;   14,390
But worldly joye may nat alwey dure
To Januarie, ne to no creature.

  O sodeyn hape ! O thou Fortune instable !
Lyk to the scorpion so deceyvable
That flaterest with thyn heed whan thou woli
    stynge ;
Thy tayl is deeth, thurgh thyn envenymynge !
O brotil [2] joye ! O sweete venym queynte !
O monstre, that so subtilly kanst peynte
Thy giftes, under hewe of stidefastnesse,
That thou deceyvest bothe moore and lesse,
Why hastow Januarie thus deceyved   14,401
That haddest hym for thy ful freend receyved ?
And now thou hast biraft hym bothe hise
    eyen,
For sorwe of which desireth he to dyen.

  Allas ! this noble Januarie free,
Amydde his lust and his prosperitee,
Is woxen blynd, and that al sodeynly !
He wepeth and he wayleth pitously
And ther with al the fyr of jalousie —
Lest that his wyf sholde falle in som [3] folye —
So brente his herte, that he wolde fayn   14,411
That som man bothe hym and hire had slayn ;
For neither after his deeth nor in his lyf,

      [1] Pleasant.   [2] Fragile.   [3] Elles MS. has " swich."

Ne wolde he that she were love ne wyf, (9952 **T.**)
But evere lyve as wydwe in clothes blake,
Soul [1] as the turtle that lost hath hire **make**.

But atte laste, after a monthe or tweye,
His sorwe gan aswage, sooth to seye,
For whan he wiste it may noon oother be
He paciently took his adversitee,   14,420
Save, out of doute, he may nat forgoon [2]
That he nas jalous everemoore in oon.
Which jalousye it was so outrageous,
That neither in halle nyn [3] noon oother **hous,**
Nyn noon oother place neverthemo,
He nolde suffre hire for to ryde or go, [4]
But if that he had hond on hire alway ;
For which ful ofte wepeth fresshe May,
That loveth Damyan so benyngnely
That she moot outher dyen sodeynly   14,430
Or elles she moot han hym as hir leste ;
She wayteth whan hir herte wolde breste.

Up on that oother syde Damyan
Bicomen is the sorwefulleste man
That evere was, for neither nyght ne day
Ne myghte he speke a word to fresshe **May,**
As to his purpos, of no swich mateere,
But if that Januarie moste it heere,
That hadde an hand up-on hire everemo ;
But nathelees, by writyng to and fro,   14,440
And privee signes, wiste he what she mente,
And she knew eek the fyn of his entente.

          [1] Sole. [2] Pass over. [3] Ne in. [4] Walk.

O Januarie ! what myghte it thee availle
Thogh thou myghtest se as fer as shippes saille ?
For also [1] good is blynd deceyved be
As to be deceyved whan a man may se.

Lo Argus, which that hadde an hondred eyen,
For al that evere he koude poure or pryen,
Yet was he blent,[2] and God woot so been mo
That wenen wisly that it be nat so ;   14,450
" Passe-over is an ese," [3] — I sey namoore.

This fresshe May, that I spak of so yoore,[4]
In warm wex hath emprented the clyket
That Januarie bar of the smale wyket,
By which in-to his gardyn ofte he wente ;
And Damyan, that knew al hire entente,
The cliket countrefeted pryvely.
Ther nys namoore to seye ; but hastily
Som wonder by this clyket shal bityde,
Which ye shul heeren, if ye wole abyde. 14,460

O noble Ovyde ! ful sooth seystou, God woot,
What sleighte is it, thogh it be long and hoot,
That he nyl fynde it out in som manere.
By Piramus and Tesbee may men leere,[5]
Thogh they were kept ful longe streite overal,
They been accorded, rownynge [6] thurgh a wal,
Ther no wight koude han founde out swich a
            sleighte.   (10,005 T.)

---

[1] Elles. MS. has "as."   [2] Blinded.   [3] It is a comfort to overlook
Lately.   [5] Learn.   [6] Whispering.

But now to purpos, — er that dayes eighte
Were passed er the monthe of Juyn [1] bifille,
That Januarie hath caught so greet a wille,
Thurgh eggyng of his wyf, hym for to pleye
In his gardyn, and no wight but they tweye,
That in a morwe un-to this May seith he,
" Rys up, my wyf, my love, my lady free !
The turtle voys is herd, my dowve sweete,
The wynter is goon with his reynes weete ;
Com forth now with thyne eyen columbyn !
How fairer been thy brestes than is wyn !
The gardyn is enclosed al aboute ;   14,479
Com forth, my white spouse ! out of doute
Thou hast me wounded in myn herte, O wyf !
No spot of thee ne knew I al my lyf ;
Come forth, and lat us taken som disport ;
I chees thee for my wyf and my confort ! "
Swiche olde lewed wordes used he.

On Damyan a signe made she
That he sholde go biforn with his cliket.
This Damyan thanne hath opened the wyket
And in he stirte, and that in swich manere
That no wight myght it se neither yheere,
And stille he sit under a bussh anon.   14,491

This Januarie, as blynd as is a stoon,
With Mayus in his hand and no wight mo,
In-to his fresshe gardyn is ago,
And clapte to the wyket sodeynly.

---

[1] Elles. MS. reads " Juyl " (July, Fr. *Juillet*), though Mr. Skeat,
following Mr. Brae, says that the word should be *Juin*, June.

"Now, wyf," quod he, "heere nys but thou
    and I,
That art the creature that I best love ;
For, by that Lord that sit in hevene above,
Levere ich hadde to dyen on a knyf,
Than thee offende, trewe, deere wyf.   14,500
For Goddes sake, thenk how I thee chees
Noght for no coveitise doutelees,
But oonly for the love I had to thee,
And though that I be oold and may nat see,
Beth to me trewe, and I shal telle yow why.
Thre thynges, certes, shal ye wynne ther by ;
First, love of Crist, and to youre self honour,
And al myn heritage, toun and tour ;
I geve it yow, maketh chartres [1] as yow leste.
This shal be doon tomorwe er sonne reste,
So wisly God my soule brynge in blisse ! 14,511
I prey yow first in covenat ye me kisse,
And though that I be jalous, wyte [2] me noght.
Ye been so depe enprented in my thoght
That whan that [3] I considere youre beautee
And ther with al the unlikly elde of me,
I may nat, certes, though I sholde dye,
Forbere to been out of youre compaignye
For verray love, this is with outen doute.
Now kys me, wyf, and lat us rome aboute."

    This fresshe May, whan she thise wordes
        herde,   14,521
Benyngnely to Januarie answerde ; (10,060 T.)

---

[1] Make deeds. [2] Blame. [3] Not in Elles. MS.

But first and forward, she bigan to wepe ;
" I have," quod she, " a soule for to kepe
As wel as ye, and also myn honour ;
And of my wyfhod, thilke tendre flour
Which that I have assured in youre hond
Whan that the preest to yow my body bond ;
Wherfore I wole answere in this manere,
By the leve of yow, my lord so deere ;   14,530
I prey to God that nevere dawe the day
That I ne sterve[1] as foule as womman may,
If evere I do un-to my kyn that shame,
Or elles I empeyre[2] so my name,
That I be fals ; and if I do that lakke,[3]
Do strepe me, and put me in a sakke,
And in the nexte ryver do me drenche,[4] —
I am a gentil womman and no wenche ! 14,538
Why speke ye thus ?   But men been evere un-
        trewe,
And wommen have repreve[5] of yow ay newe.
Ye han noon oother contenance, I leeve,[6]
But speke to us of untrust and repreeve."
And with that word she saugh wher Damyan
Sat in the bussh, and coughen she bigan,
And with hir fynger signes made she
That Damyan sholde clymbe up-on a tree
That charged was with fruyt, and up he wente ;
For verraily he knew al hire entente,
And every signe that she koude make   14,549
Wel bet than Januarie, hir owene make ;

Die.   [2] Impair.   [3] Fault   [4] Drown   [5] Blame.   [6] Believe.

For in a lettre she hadde toold hym al
Of this matere, how he werchen shal ;
And thus I lete hym sitte up-on the pyrie,[1]
And Januarie and May romynge myrie.

Bright was the day, and blew the firmament
Phebus hath of gold hise stremes doun ysent
To gladen every flour with his warmnesse.
He was that tyme in Geminis, as I gesse,
But litel fro his declynacioun
Of Cancer, Jovis exaltacioun ;   14,560
And so bifel, that brighte morwe tyde,
That in that gardyn, in the ferther syde,
Pluto that is the [2] kyng of fairye,   (10,101 T.)
And many a lady in his compaignye,
Folwynge his wyf, the queene Proserpyne,
Ech after oother right as ony [3] lyne,
Whil that she gadered floures in the mede, —
'n Claudyan [4] ye may the stories rede, —
And in hise grisely carte he hire sette.   14,569
This kyng of fairye thanne adoun hym sette
Up-on a bench of turves, fressh and grene,
And right anon thus seyde he to his queene :

"My wyf," quod he, "ther may no wight
          seye nay,
Thexperience so preveth every day

---

[1] Pear tree. The "pear tree story" is of very ancient, probably
Eastern origin. It is included in the *Comœdia Lydiæ*; in the Fa-
bles of Adolphus (*circ.* 1315); in an appendix to the Fables of Æsop
circ. 1430), translated by Caxton in 1483; and it was recounted by
Boccaccio (seventh day, ninth novel) and by La Fontaine, though
somewhat varying in its names and incidental features.   [2] Not in
Elles. MS.   [3] Elles. MS. reads "a."   [4] Claudianus, *De Rapta
Proserpinæ*. Cf. *House of Fame*, iii. 419.

The tresons whiche that wommen doon to man.
Ten hondred thousand stories [1] tellen I kan
Notable of youre untrouthe and brotilnesse. [2]
O Salomon! wys, and richest of richesse,
Fulfild of sapience and of worldly glorie,
Ful worthy been thy wordes to memorie 14,580
To every wight that wit and reson kan! [3]
Thus preiseth he yet the bountee [4] of man :
'Amonges a thousand men yet foond I oon,
But of wommen alle foond I noon.'
    "Thus seith the kyng that knoweth youre
        wikkednesse,
And Jhesus *filius* Syrak, as I gesse,
Ne speketh of yow but seelde reverence.
A wylde fyr and corrupt pestilence,
So falle up-on youre bodyes yet to nyght!
Ne se ye nat this honurable knyght?   14,590
By-cause, allas! that he is blynd and old
His owene man shal make hym cokewold.
Lo, heere he sit, the lechour, in the tree!
Now wol I graunten of my magestee
Un-to this olde, blynde, worthy knyght,
That he shal have ageyn hise eyen syght,
Whan that his wyf wold doon hym vileynye.
Thanne shal he knowen al hire harlotrye
Bothe in repreve of hire and othere mo." 14,599
    " Ye shal? " quod Proserpyne ; " wol ye so ?
Now by my moodres sires [5] soule! I swere

Omitted from the MSS.   [2] Frailty.   [3] Knows.   [4] Goodness
Saturn was the sire of Ceres the mother of Proserpine

That I shal geven hire suffisant answere,
And alle wommen after, for hir sake,
That though they be in any gilt ytake,
With face boold they shulle hem self excuse,
And bere hem doun that wolden hem accuse ;
For lakke of answere noon of hem shal dyen.
Al hadde man seyn a thyng with bothe hise
   eyen,   (10,146 T.)
Yit shul we wommen visage it hardily,
And wepe, and swere, and chide [1] subtilly,
So that ye men shul been as lewed [2] as gees.
What rekketh me of youre auctoritees ? 14,612
 " I woot wel that this Jew, this Salomon,
Foond of us wommen fooles many oon,
But though that he ne foond no good womman,
Yet hath ther founde many another man [3]
Wommen ful trewe, ful goode and vertuous ;
Witnesse on hem that dwelle in Cristes hous ;
With martirdom they preved hire constance.
The Romayn Geestes [4] eek make remembrance
Of many a verray trewe wyf also ;   14,621
But, sire, ne be nat wrooth, — al be it so
Though that he seyde he foond no good wom-
   man ;
I prey yow take the sentence [5] of the man,
He mente thus, that in sovereyn bontee
Nis noon but God that sit in Trinitee, [6]
Ey, for verray God that nys but oon !

---

[1] Elles. MS. reads " visage it." [2] Ignorant. [3] Cf. l. 6709. [4] *Gesta Romanorum.* [5] Sense. [6] Cf. l. 6692.

What make ye so muche of Salomon?
What though he made a temple, Goddes hous?
What though he were riche and glorious?
So made he eek a temple of false goddis.
How myghte he do a thyng that moore for-
       bode [1] is?   · 14,632
Pardee! as faire as ye his name emplastre
He was a lecchour and an ydolastre,
And in his elde he verray God forsook;
And if God ne hadde, as seith the book,
Yspared for his fadres sake, he sholde
Have lost his regne [2] rather [3] than he wolde.
I sette right noght of al the vileynye
That ye of wommen write [4] a boterflye! 14,640
I am a womman, nedes moot I speke,
Or elles swelle til myn herte breke;
For sithen he seyde that we been jangleresses,
As evere hool I moote brouke [5] my tresses!
I shal nat spare for no curteisye
To speke hym harm that wolde us vileynye!" [6]
    "Dame," quod this Pluto, "be no lenger
       wrooth,
I geve it up! but sith I swoor myn ooth
That I wolde graunten hym his sighte ageyn,
My word shal stonde, I warne yow certeyn.
I am a kyng, it sit [7] me noght to lye!" 14,651
    "And I," quod she, "a queene of fairye!
Hir answere shal she have, I undertake.

---

[1] Forbidden. [2] Kingdom. [3] Sooner. [4] Pluto had not been writing, however. [5] Use, enjoy. [6] A remarkable speech and strange "auc'oritees" to come from Pluto's queen! [7] Becomes.

Lat us namoore wordes heer-of make,
For sothe I wol no lenger yow contrarie."

   Now lat us turne agayn to Januarie,
That in the gardyn with his faire May
Syngeth ful murier than the papejay : [1]
"Yow love I best, and shal, and oother noon.'
So longe aboute the aleyes is he goon   14,660
Til he was come agayns [2] thilke pyrie
Where as this Damyan sitteth ful myrie
Anheigh among the fresshe leves grene.

   This fresshe May, that is so bright and
      sheene,   (10,202 T.)
Gan for to syke and seyde, "Allas, my syde !
Now, sire," quod she, "for aught that may bi-
      tyde,
I moste han of the peres that I see,
Or I moot dye, so soore longeth me
To eten of the smale peres grene.   14,669
Help, for hir love that is of hevene queene !
I telle yow wel a womman in my plit
May han to fruyt so greet an appetit
That she may dyen but she of it have."

   "Allas !" quod he, "that I ne had heer a
      knave [3]
That koude clymbe ! Allas, allas !" quod he,
"That I am blynd !" "Ye, sire, no fors," quod
      she ;
" But wolde ye vouche-sauf, for Goddes sake,
The pyrie inwith youre armes for to take, —

---

[1] Popinjay, parrot (Italian, *pappagallo*). [2] Opposite. [3] Boy.

For wel I woot that ye mystruste me, —
Thanne sholde I clymbe wel ynogh," quod
     she,   14,680
" So I my foot myghte sette upon youre bak."

  " Certes," quod he, " ther-on shal be no lak,
Mighte I yow helpen with myn herte blood ! "
He stoupeth doun, and on his bak she stood,
And caughte hire by a twiste,[1] and up she
     gooth, —
Ladyes, I prey yow that ye be nat wrooth,
I kan nat glose,[2] I am a rude man, —
And sodeynly anon this Damyan
Gan pullen up the smok, and in he throng.

  And whan that Pluto saugh this grete wrong,
To Januarie he gaf agayn his sighte,   14,691
And made hym se as wel as evere he myghte ;
And whan that he hadde caught his sighte
     agayn,
Ne was ther nevere man of thyng so fayn ;[3]
But on his wyf his thoght was everemo.
Up to the tree he caste hise eyen two,
And saugh that Damyan his wyf had dressed
In swich manere it may nat been expressed,
But if I wolde speke uncurteisly ;
And up he gaf a roryng and a cry,   14,700
As dooth the mooder whan the child shal
     dye .
"Out ! helpe ! allas ! harrow ! " he gan to crye ;
" O stronge lady, stoore,[4] what dostow ? "

---

[1] Twig.   [2] Use specious terms.   [3] Glad.   [4] Rude

And she answerde, " Sire, what eyleth yow?
Have pacience and resoun in youre mynde.
I have yow holpe on bothe youre eyen
      blynde, —
Up peril of my soule, I shal nat lyen, —
As me was taught to heele with [1] youre eyen.
Was no thyng bet to make yow to see
Than strugle with a man up-on a tree.   14,710
God woot, I dide it in ful good entente."

   " Strugle," quod he, " ye, algate in it wente !
God geve yow bothe on shames deth to dyen !
He swyved thee, I saugh it with myne eyen,
And elles be I hanged by the hals ! " [2]

   " Thanne is," quod she, " my medicyne fals,
For certeinly, if that ye myghte se,   (10,255 T.)
Ye wolde nat seyn this wordes un-to me ;
Ye han som glymsyng, and no parfit sighte."

   " I se," quod he, " as wel as evere I myghte,
Thonked be God ! with bothe myne eyen two,
And, by my trouthe, me thoughte he dide thee
     so."   14,722

   " Ye maze, maze, goode sire," quod she ;
" This thank have I for I have maad yow see.
Allas ! " quod she, " that evere I was so kynde."

   " Now, dame," quod he, " lat al passe out of
     mynde.
Com doun, my lief, and if I have myssayd,
God helpe me so, as I am yvele apayd.[3]
But, by my fader soule ! I wende han seyn [4]

---

[1] " To heele with " means to heal.   [2] Neck.   [3] Displeased.   [4] Seen

How that this Damyan hadde by thee leyn,
And that thy smok hadde leyn up-on his brest."
   "Ye, sire," quod she, "ye may wene as yow
       lest,   14,732
But, sire, a man that waketh out of his sleepe,
He may nat sodeynly wel taken keepe
Up on a thyng, ne seen it parfitly,
Til that he be adawed [1] verraily.
Right so a man that longe hath blynd ybe,
Ne may nat sodeynly so wel yse,
First whan his sighte is newe come ageyn,
As he that hath a day or two yseyn.   14,740
Til that youre sighte ysatled [2] be a while,
Ther may ful many a sighte yow bigile.
Beth war, I prey yow, for, by hevene kyng,
Ful many a man weneth to seen a thyng,
And it is al another than it semeth.
He that mysconceyveth, he mysdemeth," —
And with that word she leepe doun fro the
       tree.
   This Januarie, who is glad but he?
He kisseth hire and clippeth [3] hire ful ofte,
And on hire wombe [4] he stroketh hire ful softe;
And to his palays hoom he hath hire lad.[5]
Now, goode men, I praye yow be glad. 14,752
Thus endeth heere my tale of Januarie.
God blesse us, and his mooder Seinte Marie !

---

[1] Awakened   [2] Confirmed   [3] Embraceth.   [4] Belly   [5] Led.

The Host's words to the Squire.

"Ey, Goddes mercy," seyde oure Hoost tho,[1]
" Now swich a wyf, I pray God kepe me fro!
Lo, whiche sleightes and subtiltees
In wommen been! for ay as bisy as bees
Been they, us sely [2] men for to deceyve ;
And from a sooth evere wol they weyve.[3]   14,760
By this Marchauntes tale it preveth weel ;
But doutelees, as trewe as any steel (10,300 T.)
I have a wyf, though that she povre be ;
But of hir tonge a labbyng [4] shrewe is she ;
And yet she hath an heepe of vices mo,
Ther-of no fors, lat alle swiche thynges go ;
But wyte ye what?   In conseil be it seyd,
Me reweth soore I am un-to hire teyd ;
For, and I sholde rekenen every vice [5]
Which that she hath, ywis I were to nyce ;
And cause why,[6] it sholde reported be,   14,771
And toold to hire of somme of this meynee,
Of whom it nedeth nat for to declare
(Syn wommen konnen outen [7] swich chaffare [8])
And eek my wit suffiseth nat ther to
To tellen al, wherfore my tale is do."

End of the Tales of the Third Day.

----

[1] Then.   [2] Innocent.   [3] Stray   [4] Blabbing.   [5] Fault.   [6] Now
teemed a vulgarism.   [7] Express   Cf. l. 10,563.   [8] Gossip.

Paul Elder
& Company

San Francisco

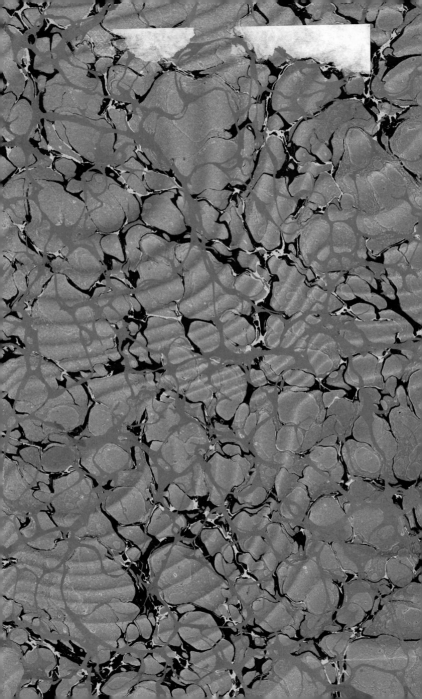